WATER
AND
POWER

WATER
AND
POWER :

The Conflict over Los Angeles' Water Supply in the Owens Valley

WILLIAM L. KAHRL

University of California
Press · BERKELEY ·
LOS ANGELES · LONDON

Cartography by Migel Abalos, Los Angeles
Department of Water and Power

University of California Press
Berkeley and Los Angeles, California

University of California Press, Ltd.
London, England

Printed in the United States of America

1 2 3 4 5 6 7 8 9

Library of Congress Cataloging in Publication Data

Kahrl, William L.
    Water and power.

    Bibliography: p.
    Includes index.
    1. Los Angeles (Calif.)—Water-supply.
2. Water-supply—California—Owens Valley.   I. Title.
HD4464.L7K33 1982ᴠ   333.91'009794'9   81-7428 √
ISBN 0-520-04431-2   AACR2

Contents

He who lets himself in for politics, that is,
for power and force as means, contracts with
diabolical powers and for his action it is *not*
true that good can follow only from good
and evil only from evil, but that often the
opposite is true. Anyone who fails to see this
is, indeed, a political infant.

Max Weber

Preface

I was brought up to love a good story, and I suspect that is what first attracted me to the history of this controversy. It is a story of ideals in conflict, rich with incidents of great daring, deceit, achievement, betrayal, and faith. Despite the fact that it spans more than three-quarters of a century and boasts a cast of characters ranging from Teddy Roosevelt and the American Legion to Clarence Darrow and the Wobblies, it possesses a remarkable degree of consistency, both in the personalities involved and the objectives they pursued. As the first major water project in the West and one of the largest public works ever undertaken by a municipality, the story of Los Angeles' aqueduct forms an important and illuminating chapter in the history of urbanization, the growth of the western states, the development of the American engineering profession, and the organization of the federal reclamation service. And because the record of these events has become so potent a symbol for both the advocates and opponents of public resource development, it is a story which yields particular insight into the potential benefits and dangers inherent in the public ownership of natural resources and the evolving concept of environmental protection as an element of public policy.

Above all, it is essentially a story of California—perhaps the most essential—because it deals with water. More than the discovery of gold and oil, the construction of the railroad and freeway systems, and the rise of the film and aerospace industries, the development of water has shaped the patterns of settlement within California and laid the basis for the modern prosperity of the nation's richest and most populous state. No problems for the future hold so great a potential for changing the quality of life in California as the current controversies over water policy. And as the oldest and most enduring of California's water wars, no controversy has exercised as great an influence over the evolution of that policy as the conflict in the Owens Valley. In the story of the aqueduct, therefore, we confront not only the foundation of the modern metropolis of Los Angeles but the origins as well of California as we know it today.

Although the Owens Valley conflict is a familiar topic in almost any capsule history of the state, the historiography, and hence the public understanding of these events, have been shaped in large part by the controversy itself. Only two books have attempted to treat the original conflict as a whole, and each was written to promote particular interests in a continuing debate. Willie Arthur Chalfant's *Story of Inyo* was written by a resident of the valley and a leader of the resistance to Los Angeles during the 1920s as a depiction of "the rape of the valley." Chalfant's treatment and attitude recur without significant variation in a host of subsequent histories of Southern California, and it is his perception which has informed most of the fictional accounts of the conflict that have appeared as novels and films. In 1950, however, Remi Nadeau published *The Water Seekers* to counter what he regarded as "wild charges and inaccurate history" in the popular condemnation of the city's actions. In striving to correct this imbalance, Nadeau constructed an elaborate apologia for Los Angeles as part of his own series of popular historical tributes to the developers of the South Coast.

As a result, two distinct versions of the controversy have emerged. Critics of the city's policies present Los Angeles as the conscienceless destroyer of one of California's prime agricultural regions. To develop their aqueduct, the city's water officials first stole the valley's water rights by bribing federal reclamation officials and then bullied Los Angeles' voters into funding the project by secretly diverting the municipal water supply into the sewers in order to create the illusion of a drought. Only later, in this version of the story, is it discovered that the aqueduct has been designed to benefit not the city but a cabal of wealthy financiers who have been plotting to divert the waters of the Owens Valley to their own otherwise worthless lands. Faced with the city's oppression, the valley residents meanwhile band together in a valiant effort to win back their freedom. But they are ultimately crushed by Los Angeles' superior wealth and power.

Alternatively, Nadeau and the official publications of the Los Angeles Department of Water and Power present the conflict in terms of the heroic advance of civilization. Driven by a critical water shortage, Los Angeles turns to the barren wastes of the Owens Valley, where it appears that a sufficient new water supply can be found to save the city from impending disaster. The federal government, recognizing that the water can be put to more productive use by Los Angeles than it ever could in the Owens Valley, gives its blessing to this monumental undertaking. But despite the city's generous determination to pay fully for every water right it secures, the valley residents choose to ignore the manifold benefits that construction of the aqueduct has brought to their economy. Instead, the ranchers revert to lawlessness and destruction in a campaign of terrorism devised and directed by unscrupulous speculators whose manipulations ultimately destroy the valley.

Neither account is accurate, although both have contributed vitally to the interplay of legend, myth, and political manipulation that has driven the controversy throughout this century. The respective biases of Chalfant and Nadeau encouraged them to leave out large parts of the story, and neither attempted to deal with the evolution of the conflict since 1930. Perhaps most important, neither Chalfant nor Nadeau made any substantial use of the extensive public records available on the subject. Chalfant, for example, drew the substance of his account from his experience as a valley newspaper publisher. His view is fixed on his own community, and he consequently pays scant attention to events in Los Angeles. Nadeau, in contrast, relied heavily upon interviews with former officials of the Los Angeles Department of Water and Power. But because he seems never to have verified the accuracy of their accounts, names, dates, and sometimes whole elements of the city's water programs become scrambled or lost altogether in his rendering.

These problems possess more than a merely pedantic significance for the later scholars and commentators who have tried, with indifferent success, to thread together these disparate, contradictory, and incomplete reports. For the Owens Valley today is one area where the past is a vital part of the present. Within the past ten years, Los Angeles has built a second aqueduct which it proposes to fill through a greatly expanded pumping program which many valley residents fear will cause irrevocable environmental damage. The long-dormant conflict has consequently flared up once again, the bombing of the aqueduct has been renewed, and the public memory of Los Angeles' actions in the Owens Valley in the early part of this century has suddenly assumed a critical relevance in shaping the valley's response to the city's latest initiatives. Suggestions are now being made that California's laws of equitable water use, first adopted to protect other regions of the state from the fate of the Owens Valley, should now be applied retroactively to preserve the valley itself. And all of this has come about at a time when California as a whole, for the first time in its history, is struggling to develop some means of controlling the continued depletion of its principal groundwater reservoirs. It appears, therefore, that the problems of the Owens Valley may lie once again at the center of yet another critical juncture in the development of California's water laws.

It is not the purpose of this work to propose a specific format for the settlement of the city's current difficulties with the valley, to resolve the environmental questions associated with Los Angeles' proposed groundwater pumping program, or to promote any cause associated with the developing situation in the Owens Valley. But by performing the essential historical task of separating what happened from what did not, and by distinguishing in this way the choices which have been made from those which have yet to be decided, it is my hope that this effort will help to establish that common basis for understanding which is essential for the debate over specific issues to proceed most effectively. This book, then, is scarcely the last word on the Owens Valley conflict: the final chapter, after all, has yet to be written.

The story that has emerged here is at once very different and more troubling than the conventional treatments of the conflict as a simplistic political morality play. Any attempt to deal with so controversial a subject, however, is almost certain to spark controversy itself. For that reason, with the exception of a small collection of private letters, I have chosen to construct the work entirely from published documents and other materials available to the general public, anchoring the narrative in sources the reader can consult to trace the line of my argument on any point with which he or she may disagree. In addition, the work as a whole has been reviewed for technical accuracy by officials of the Los Angeles Department of Water and Power, although the department is in no way responsible for the content of this study or the conclusions I have drawn from it.

I have benefited immeasurably as well from the long hours many participants in the current controversy have devoted to enhancing my understanding of the documents, issues, and personalities involved. In this connection, I should like to thank Moe Jacobson, Emilie Martin, Antonio Rossman, and, most particularly, Duane Georgeson and Mary W. Gorman. I should also like to offer a personal tribute to Donald D. Stark, special counsel to the Department of Water and Power, whose untimely death while this book was in preparation has deprived everyone concerned with water problems in California of the insight that comes from a generous spirit which is more concerned with the equity than with the limits of the law.

This project was conducted under the auspices of a Rockefeller Foundation Fellowship in Environmental Affairs. I am deeply grateful to the current and former officials of the foundation for their support, particularly R. W. Richardson, Jr., Joel Colton, Gary Toenniessen, D. Lydia Bronte, and Robert Fischelis. But the work might never have begun without the early encouragement of J. S. Holliday, James V. Hurst, Robert Kelley, and William K. Muir. I am grateful as well to the California Historical Society, which has given permission to reprint certain passages of this book which earlier appeared as a series of articles in the *California Historical Quarterly*. The finished work would be much less than it is without the brilliant and painstaking assistance of Renée M. Jaussaud at the National Archives, Jay Ector at the Inyo County Free Library, and Mary Deane at the Water Resources Center Archives of the University of California. And I might never have finished at all but for the forbearance of JeanAnne M. Kelley and Lynn Boller, who typed the manuscript, and my wife Kathleen, who has lived with it far too long.

WILLIAM L. KAHRL
Sacramento, 1980

CHAPTER ONE

Organizing
for Development

The history of California in the twentieth century
is the story of a state inventing itself with water. The principal
centers of urban settlement and industrial and agricultural production in California today were in large part arid wastelands
and malarial bogs in their natural condition. The modern prosperity of the state has consequently been founded upon a massive
rearrangement of the natural environment through public water
development. The largest of these artificial water systems operate
today principally for the benefit of agriculture in California's
interior valleys. The impetus for water development on this scale,
however, originated not on the farms but in the cities and the
particular problems they faced as a consequence of growing up in
a state that developed backward and in the wrong direction.

The early settlement of California followed traditional lines
of civilization. People lived where there was sufficient water to
sustain them, and towns and villages grew up along the river
courses which provided the means of life and commerce. But the
new Californians who began to arrive with the discovery of gold
in 1849 did not bring families to open up the land. Their skills
were in trade and merchant shipping, and when the mines played
out they returned to the port cities along the coast. At the same
time as the great wheat empires were flourishing in the Sacra-

mento and San Joaquin valleys during the last decades of the nineteenth century, the proportionate size of California's rural population was steadily shrinking.[1] For the nation as a whole, the central event distinguishing the nineteenth and twentieth centuries was the gradual transition from a predominantly rural to an urban society. But in California, this transformation began almost simultaneously with the first major influx of population and ran backward in many areas of the state where urban settlement rapidly outstripped the pace of agricultural development.

Although Northern California had developed first, the opening of the transcontinental railroads shifted the flow of immigration away from these areas of natural water abundance. The Southern Pacific had millions of acres to sell, and it turned its mighty promotional engines to touting the Mediterranean qualities of life in the semi-arid South Coast. Within a year after the golden spike was driven at Promontory Point, the rate of population growth in Southern California for the first time surpassed that of the north. By 1885, developers in Los Angeles were already building ahead of demand, relying upon long-term exclusive franchises from government or the railroad companies to minimize their risks. And so Los Angeles expanded, despite the absence of adequate schools or a host of other municipal services, a coastal city without a port, its growth fed by advertising, its development founded on the prospects for the future. And in 1890, the rate of growth in San Francisco for the first time fell behind the average for the state as a whole.

From the first complete California census in 1860 to the turn of the century, the population of the state increased by 290 percent from 379,994 to 1,485,053. During this period, the population of the San Francisco metropolitan area increased 540 percent, while that of Los Angeles grew to nearly seventeen times its size in 1860. As a result, by 1900 fully 40 percent of the state's people were concentrated in these two urban areas.[2] And at this point, both cities began to bump up against the limits of their indigenous water resources. Continued prosperity and development could not be assured without additional sources of supply. Thus confronting a common problem but acting independently and exclusively in their own interests, San Francisco and Los

Angeles set out simultaneously to develop distant watersheds in a race that would ultimately go a long way toward determining which city enjoyed supremacy among the commercial centers of the Pacific Coast.

There was little in contemporary law or practice to guide the cities in this endeavor. State and federal water development programs at this time were concerned primarily with flood control, drainage, the improvement of navigation, and the reclamation of swamps and marshlands—problems which have more to do with the abundance of water than its scarcity. Still more troubling, the practice of water law in California at this time rested upon riparian principles derived from English Common Law, which had little practical application to the problems of water development in the arid southwestern United States. Under the riparian doctrine, the primary right to the use of water in a stream belongs to those who own land touched by the stream. This right is not appurtenant to the land, but is part and parcel of it and cannot be transferred separately. By denying the transferability of water rights, the riparian doctrine vested the owners of lands adjoining the natural stream courses of California with a nearly eternal advantage over all other potential users of the state's limited water resources. A person owning lands not so well favored was permitted under California law to appropriate water from a stream for use elsewhere. But although these appropriative rights were exercised extensively by hydraulic mining companies in the northern part of the state, they remained at all times subsidiary to the riparian doctrine. Anyone who relied upon an appropriative right consequently ran the risk of seeing all his works and investments invalidated at some future time by an assertion of the superior rights of a riparian owner. Moreover, the riparian owner's right remained superior and inviolate regardless of whether he made no use of it at all.

Two essential aspects of the riparian doctrine held special consequences for the prospects of future development of Los Angeles and San Francisco. First, by tying the use of a water supply to the lands immediately adjacent to that supply, the doctrine went a long way toward assuring that development of the state would follow the natural distribution of water resources.

In other words, the communities of the North Coast and those cities situated on the great rivers of the interior possessed a legal and natural advantage for continued development which San Francisco and Los Angeles could not match. Ways around this restriction therefore had to be found, either by obtaining a federal grant to the use of a water supply lying within the public domain (the route chosen by San Francisco), or by buying out the interests of all the riparian owners along a stream (as Los Angeles was ultimately forced to do).

The second restrictive aspect of the riparian doctrine, however, had a more immediate and far-reaching impact on the operations and organization of the cities involved. For by making the law of waters a part of the rights of private property ownership, the riparian doctrine denied any role for the concept of a common public interest in the overall development of the state's water resources. Water, under the laws of California in the nineteenth century, was a private resource for private exploitation. An effort by the state legislature in 1880 to protect the flood-ravaged residents of the Sacramento Valley had been struck down by the state supreme court as an unconstitutional assumption by the state of an essentially private concern. Although the legislature was subsequently somewhat more successful in encouraging the formation of public irrigation districts for the enhancement of agricultural development, state law was virtually silent on the question of domestic water supplies to meet the needs of the cities. Even the federal Reclamation Act of 1902, which has done more than any other governmental program to remake the western waterscape, made no provision in its original form for the supply of domestic water needs. In confronting the problem of securing additional water resources to support their continued growth, San Francisco and Los Angeles consequently found themselves alone, left to their own devices, and forced to proceed in a legal and practical void.

It was the meeting of this challenge which separates the development of the water supplies of San Francisco and Los Angeles altogether from the traditions and practices of the nineteenth century. The construction of the Hetch Hetchy and Los Angeles aqueducts marks the true beginning of the modern water system of

California. This distinction does not lie simply in the scale of these municipal projects. Private capital had achieved great water projects in the nineteenth century, ranging from the successful irrigation colonies which produced thriving communities and abundant produce out of the arid wastes at Anaheim, Ontario, and San Bernardino to the gigantic water works of hydraulic mining, which were capable of breaking down whole mountainsides or shifting stretches of entire rivers from their streambeds in order to reveal the rich deposits of ore. But these projects did not require the movement of large quantities of water over great distances from one hydrologic basin to another; instead, they simply made systematic use of the water already available.

More important, although the development of the irrigation colonies and hydraulic mines required the concentration of large amounts of capital, the investments were made not for the development of the water itself but for the larger profits to be gained from the extraction of gold or the enhancement of land values which water development made possible. In the case of developing a water supply for domestic use, however, the water itself would be the principal object of the enterprise. And while private companies had successfully peddled water as a commodity for profit in numerous areas of the state where a water resource could be developed with a relatively small investment, no private water company could conceivably raise the capital required for the development of delivery systems of the size and complexity needed to sustain the long-term growth of San Francisco and Los Angeles. Thus, public officials in both cities realized that municipalization of the urban water supply, as the means to securing access to the far greater amounts of capital which government can raise through taxation and bond sales, was the essential first step toward securing the water they needed for the future.

This perception of the necessity for resorting to public finance was hardly a revolutionary insight. On a federal level, the need to assist in the improvement of harbors and inland navigation had been a recognized government responsibility since the adoption of the Constitution. The idea of municipalities controlling their own water systems and constructing works to tap distant sources of supply was a commonplace in other parts of the country. New

York City, in fact, was already launching an even more extensive delivery system than anything contemplated for San Francisco and Los Angeles at the same time that the movement toward municipalization was gaining momentum in California. And even in California, public assistance in the form of government grants of funding or rights-of-way had been crucial to the success of such grandiose schemes of nineteenth-century private enterprise as the building of the transcontinental railroad, the development of the harbor facilities at Oakland and San Pedro, and the construction of the Sutro Tunnel for the Comstock Lode.

But in the context of municipal organization and water development in California, the decision to turn to the public sector for the construction of water systems to supply the urban populations of San Francisco and Los Angeles marked a radical break with tradition. The extent of this departure can be measured most readily in how far the two cities had initially to come. For neither Los Angeles nor San Francisco possessed in 1900 an administrative structure capable of undertaking the kind of development project required to tap a distant water resource. In both cities, as in the other urban centers of California, the business of water supply was a private, not a municipal enterprise.

Nearly one hundred fifty years earlier, the first American municipal waterworks system had been installed at Bethlehem, Pennsylvania. The success of the major municipal systems subsequently constructed in Philadelphia and Cincinnati assured that by the middle of the nineteenth century private water systems, with few exceptions, were characteristic only of the smaller American cities. California was the home of one of these exceptions. Of the sixteen largest cities in the United States in 1860, San Francisco was one of only four that still lacked a municipally owned water system.[3] City officials steadfastly refused to take over the business of supplying water to San Francisco's residents during the nineteenth century. And even after the city charter was amended in 1900 to require the public development of an additional water supply, San Francisco's leaders persisted in treating their efforts with regard to the Hetch Hetchy project as a supplement but not a replacement for the services provided by the private sector. The city's break with the traditions of the nineteenth century was consequently halting, uncertain, and ultimately incomplete. In all, it took San Francisco thirty-four years to fulfill its charter mandate. And by the time it was through, Los Angeles had long since won its race for supremacy on the West Coast.

The Triumph of the Public Ethic

In Los Angeles the problems of water development were more acute than in San Francisco and the solutions were consequently more severe and more rapidly achieved. For Los Angeles in 1900 did not even have control of its local water supplies. This fact by itself is a measurement, first, of how poorly equipped the city was by the turn of the century to undertake a program of long-range municipal water development; second, of how deeply entrenched the nineteenth century's confidence in private enterprise had become in Los Angeles' city administration; and third, of how far the city had fallen from those benefits of its Spanish heritage which had enabled it to survive for more than a century. Los Angeles, after all, sits in the midst of a semi-arid coastal plain. The principal indigenous source of its water supply is the 502.5-square-mile basin of the Los Angeles River, whose tributaries in the San Gabriel, Santa Monica, and Santa Susanna mountains pour their often meager flows into the vast groundwater reservoirs of the San Fernando Valley. When the Spanish colonial authorities established the Pueblo de los Angeles in 1781 they located it on a low-lying alluvial terrace adjacent to the one part of the Los Angeles River where water could be expected to be flowing all year round.

Under Spanish colonial policy, the pueblo was invested with an exclusive right to the water of the river, a communal interest altogether different from the riparian principles of English common law. This Spanish notion of a public property in water, ideally suited to an arid area where waterworks had to be publicly managed to ensure their most efficient and equitable use, endured throughout the successive changes from Spanish to Mexican to American rule. And as the early water systems of the

Franciscan missions elsewhere in Southern California were secularized, ill-used, and eventually abandoned, irrigation and the development of water for domestic use continued without interruption within the borders of Los Angeles.

But as the city grew following the American conquest, it faced increasing problems in the management of its water system. In 1854, the city council established the position of water overseer to administer the distribution of irrigation water and enforce the city's ordinances relating to its use. This system worked well for agriculturists within the city limits but did nothing for improving the delivery of water for domestic use by the growing number of homeowners who drew their supplies each day from the common city ditches. And since these ditches were uncovered and had no bridges, the domestic supply was constantly polluted by bathers, teamsters, and animals of all sorts, as well as by use of the ditches for laundry and refuse disposal.[4] The city, however, rejected a proposal in 1853 by William G. Dryden to meet these problems by constructing a closed-pipe system to service homes directly. The Los Angeles common council regarded as excessive Dryden's request that he receive two square leagues of land and a twenty-one-year franchise for the construction and operation of the system. Instead, water carriers with jugs and horse-drawn wagons were allowed to serve the city's domestic needs by peddling their wares from door to door.

In 1857, the council relented and granted Dryden a franchise to deliver water to homes directly through underground mains beneath the city streets from the artesian springs that arose on his property. Dryden incorporated the Los Angeles Water Works Company, erected a forty-foot water wheel to lift water from the city's main ditch, and set a giant storage tank in the center of the city plaza. But his system served only a small portion of the city, and because he built his mains with wooden pipes it was constantly breaking down and turning the city's thoroughfares into muddy bogs. When heavy rains in December 1861 washed out the system entirely, Dryden withdrew and the city offered contracts to other local entrepreneurs who offered to improve upon his efforts. Jean L. Sainsevain entered into such a contract in 1863 but soon gave up. His works in turn were leased by the city in 1865 to David W. Alexander. Alexander admitted defeat after only eight months and reconveyed his lease to Sainsevain. With the assistance of former mayor Damien Marchessault, Sainsevain erected a dam, built a new water wheel, and in November 1867 began replacing Dryden's wooden pipes with iron ones. But severe flooding in the winter of 1867-68 again destroyed the system; Sainsevain gave up the job for good; and Marchessault was so embarrassed and discouraged by the whole venture that he committed suicide in the city council chambers.[5]

Against this backdrop of repeated failure and frustration, the council in 1868 decided to give up its precious right to the waters of the Los Angeles River and entrust its future development to the "enlightened selfishness" of private businessmen.[6] With an eye on the site of Marchessault's demise, the council gave up its waterworks, declaring, "It is well known by past experience that cities and towns can never manage enterprises of that nature as economically as individuals can, and besides, it is a continual source of annoyance."[7] The beneficiaries of the council's resignation were three of the city's more successful businessmen, John S. Griffen, Solomon Lazard, and Prudent Beaudry. Griffen and his associates had taken over Sainsevain's facilities, and in May 1868 they petitioned the council for a fifty-year lease on the entire water system of Los Angeles. The proposal they actually submitted to the council, however, constituted a quitclaim deed to the city's water rights and a prohibition of any control over water rates by the city in exchange for the payment of $10,000 in gold coin and the forgiveness of certain claims filed against the city by Griffen and his associates which were worth $15,000 in the aggregate. In addition, Griffen, Lazard, and Beaudry promised to construct a reservoir for the city, lay twelve miles of iron pipe, install fire hydrants at the major street crossings, provide free water to public buildings, and erect a $1,000 ornamental fountain in the city plaza.[8]

The council readily agreed to this remarkable proposal, but Mayor Christobal Aguilar, who had grown up in the city while it was under Mexican rule, vetoed the measure, commenting, "It has always been considered by my predecessors, as well as myself at the present time, that the prosperity of the City of Los Angeles depends entirely upon the proper management and distribution of the waters of the Los Angeles River . . . I cannot conceive the necessity of a Sale of this Water franchise in order to Secure a supply for domestic use."[9] Undaunted, Griffen, Lazard, and Beaudry responded with an offer to accept a thirty-year lease in exchange for the payment of $1,500 a year and performance of all the services enumerated in their original proposal.

By this time, the issue had become an emotionally political problem. Numerous other would-be water entrepreneurs offered proposals that were far more advantageous to the city. And while Griffen's latest proposal was under study, two new members were elected to the city council on campaign pledges to oppose the lease he had requested. The lease came before the council on July 20, 1868. All counter-proposals were rejected without a hearing, and the council president refused even to hear testimony from taxpayers, who had packed the hall to voice their concerns. Instead, the lease was summarily approved by a vote of four to two, and Mayor Aguilar reluctantly agreed to its adoption after insisting that the contract be amended to allow the city to continue to regulate water rates so long as they were not set below the levels in effect in 1868.[10]

Griffen, Lazard, and Beaudry incorporated as the Los Angeles City Water Company and promptly set about consolidating their control of the local domestic water supply by eliminating all potential competitors. Although the company eventually bought out virtually all the private sources of supply within the city, as well as the various private companies which serviced areas immediately outside the city limits, the operation which ranked first on their list for acquisition was that of Juan Bernard and P. McFadden.[11] Bernard and McFadden had taken over the original Dryden system and had irritated Griffen and his associates by offering to perform essentially the same services in exchange for only a twenty-year lease on which they promised to pay the city $2,000 a year. Once the new company had driven Bernard and McFadden out of business by forcing them to vacate their reservoir in the center of the city plaza, however, it delayed carrying through on its promise to replace Dryden's original tank with an ornamental fountain. After nearly two years of argument and threats of litigation, the company finally achieved a compromise under which it agreed to beautify the plaza in exchange for a reduction in the cost of its lease from $1,500 to $400 a year.[12] But this victory for the company did not result in any corresponding reduction in its customers' rates for water service.

The battle over the fountain was only the first of many conflicts between the city and the company. When the city first granted the lease, it believed that the company intended to develop its own water supply in the swampy area of Crystal Springs, just above the Narrows of the Los Angeles River. The lease, therefore, granted the company the right to take no more than ten miner's inches from the river.[13] But the company secretly drove a tunnel into the river itself and by the 1890s was taking as much as fifteen hundred miner's inches from it in a violation of the lease which the city felt powerless to prevent.[14]

When it came to appropriations of water by the city, in contrast, the company proved itself a stickler for strict adherence to the terms of the lease. Because the lease authorized the company to take water only for domestic purposes, the city made use of the water in the company's pipes for street sprinkling. The company sued for $2,500, which it estimated was the value of the water taken, and carried its complaint all the way to the state supreme court. But the court ruled that the company could not collect fees for water used for other than domestic purposes and therefore had no claim to any surplus water in its pipes.[15]

These were only minor skirmishes in comparison to the challenges the city faced to its precious pueblo rights. As soon as it was in operation, the Los Angeles City Water Company transferred its interest in the headworks of the water system to a new subsidiary corporation, the Crystal Springs Land and Water Company. This company then asserted its claim to the waters of the Los Angeles River on the grounds that it was a separate corporate entity and therefore not bound by the terms of the city's lease.[16] The company was not alone. After 1870, the city found itself in court repeatedly defending itself against similar claims by irrigators who tapped the river for use on their riparian lands. The city responded by securing from the legislature a statutory declaration of its pueblo rights.[17] Then, in 1881, the California Supreme Court issued the first in a succession of decisions affirming the city's historic claim to the river's flow.[18]

These problems combined with increasing demands for expansion of the community's irrigation works to force the city to assume a more active role in water affairs during the latter decades of the nineteenth century. In 1873, the common council directed the city engineer to begin surveying new reservoir sites that could be used to store the winter streamflows for agriculture. In 1877 a panel of engineers was formed to advise the city on ways to extend its irrigation system. But even as Los Angeles pressed forward with the construction of these new ditches and reservoirs, the agricultural lands they were built to serve were being subdivided and converted to homesites. The rapid growth of Los Angeles' population after 1880 made it increasingly clear to community leaders that domestic water use, rather than agriculture, would be the key to the city's future growth and development.

Consequently, as the expiration date of the Los Angeles City Water Company's lease drew near, popular support began to build for a return to complete municipal control of the local water supply. Amendments to the city charter in 1889 affirmed the city's authority to operate its own system and prohibited it from entering into any new leases that could not be canceled on six months' notice. In the local elections of 1896, both political parties endorsed the termination of the lease and a takeover of the waterworks by the city. Although the Democratic candidate for mayor, Meredith P. Snyder, won that year by outdoing his opponent in denunciations of the water company, the most ardent spokesman for municipalization was the chairman of the Republican City Central Committee, Fred Eaton, who proposed that the city provide free water service to its residents and pay for the operation and upkeep of the system from municipal tax revenues.

Eaton's opinion carried special weight because he was a former superintending engineer of the water company, as well as the brilliant scion of a family prominent in South Coast water development. His father, Benjamin, had taken his law degree at Harvard in one year and had arrived in Los Angeles with the first wave of immigration after the discovery of gold. Benjamin became one of the city's first district attorneys, but his greater interest lay in water engineering. After joining briefly in the struggle to develop a domestic waterworks system for Los Angeles in 1862, he moved to the San Pasqual rancho where he became founder and president of the Pasadena Colony. Although Benjamin experimented extensively with the development of nonirrigated vines, the financial success of the colony's orange groves was based on his demonstration of the value of iron pipes for irrigation. Following the success of the Pasadena Colony, Benjamin went on to build similar works for the Hermosa and Iowa colonies at Cucamonga, Jacinto, Marengo, Glendale, and North Pasadena.[19]

Fred Eaton, born in Los Angeles in 1856, shared his father's intelligence; but, in the words of one biographer, "Fred never attended school but little, preferring to shape his educational course himself and pursue in private such studies as were congenial to his taste." Under his father's tutelage, young Fred developed an abiding fascination with water and a determination to carry forward his father's achievements in water development. At the age of fifteen he went to work with the Los Angeles City Water Company, and by the time he was twenty he had taken over as its superintending engineer. During the nine years he held that position, Eaton supervised a dramatic expansion of the company's operations. In 1886, he was elected to the office of city engineer and devoted the next four years to designing the city's sewer system. He then returned to the private sector, working as chief engineer for the Los Angeles Consolidated Electric Company and directing the construction of the Los Angeles Railway Company.[20]

Eaton's expertise in water and his demonstrated devotion to the building up of Los Angeles propelled him easily to leadership in the drive to put an end to the Los Angeles City Water Company. More important, because his distinguished record of achievement had been rendered in both the private and public sectors, he was the perfect bridge to draw together the business and political communities behind a campaign for municipal takeover of the city's water supply. The movement for municipalization did not spring from some early impulse toward progressive reform. It originated in those historic principles of a community interest in water which had been a part of Los Angeles' heritage from its earliest founding, and as such it rapidly assumed a position above partisan political debate. The campaign, moreover, was not driven by assertions that government possessed some special expertise in the area of water development. On the contrary, the city government at that time possessed virtually no staff skilled in the management of such an enterprise, and the key question for the advocates of municipalization was how best to insulate the management of a public water system from political influence so that "good business principles" would still predominate.

Above all, the success of the effort to put the water company out of business did not represent in Los Angeles a wholesale rejection of free enterprise. Instead, the essential support for the movement came from the business community itself. The movement for municipalization emerged in the context of a greater effort by Los Angeles' business leaders to assert their independence in the stewardship of the city's social, political, and economic future. By the end of the nineteenth century they had succeeded, through puffery, advertising, and sheer force of will, in laying the foundation for a modern city in a spot where God clearly never intended large numbers of people to live. In addition, by the time the movement for municipalization began to gain momentum in the mid-1890s, the more forward-looking members of the business community had already united behind a drive by the Chamber of Commerce to build a harbor for the city that would be free of domination by the Southern Pacific Railroad and its allies in the gas, light, and telephone companies. They succeeded in their efforts to establish the harbor at San Pedro rather than at Santa Monica, where Southern Pacific's extensive landholdings would have given it a stranglehold on the city's commercial development as vicious as any the railroads held on the port of San Francisco and the trading centers of the interior valleys. Their victory over what came to be called "the associated villainies" was in part a hollow one in view of the fact that the Southern Pacific, Los Angeles, and Salt Lake railroad companies wound up controlling most of the harbor frontage at San Pedro.[21] But the fact that the battle had been fought at all, and fought so vigorously, signaled the appearance of a united community of business interests within Los Angeles who were determined to make certain that the course of the city's future development would be decided locally and not in a distant corporate boardroom.

Youthful, aggressive, innovative, startlingly handsome, and possessed of a charm which would win him the respect and even the affection of his adversaries throughout his life, Fred Eaton was the ideal exponent of the independent spirit of this assertive business community. And so he commanded their attention when he described with an insider's authority the limitations of the Los Angeles City Water Company and the potential benefits for the city's future development that would come from municipal management of the water supply. Continued operation of the city's waterworks by private interests constituted an intolerable obstacle to continued settlement, in Eaton's view. The rates the company charged were exorbitant, its services were inadequate, and the low pressure it maintained in its pipes was not sufficient for fighting fires. Rather than turning its profits back into improvement of the system, the company regularly declared 6-percent dividends for its stockholders, and Eaton estimated that it had earned an overall 10- to 35-percent profit on its investment over the full term of the lease.[22] A local engineer, Joseph B. Lippincott, declared that each family in Los Angeles paid five dollars a year for water service and ten dollars for the company's profit; and Eaton promised that the city could provide better service for only 10 percent of the company's rates.[23]

On January 20, 1897, the city council directed the city engineer to begin drawing up plans for a municipal waterworks system.[24] On February 25, the city advised the water company that the lease would not be renewed after its expiration on July 21, 1898. Early in 1898, the city opened negotiations with the company for the acquisition of its water system. And later that year, Eaton was elected mayor, fully intending to devote his term in office to the establishment of the new municipal system.

He was not to enjoy that satisfaction. The company refused to give up its monopoly even after the lease had expired, demanding $3 million in payment for a system the city estimated was worth only $1.3 million. A board of arbitration was established composed of one representative from the city, one from the company, and a third impartial member selected by the other two. When this panel issued its report in May 1899 declaring that the value of the system was even less than the city had originally estimated, the company refused to honor the panel's findings, declaring that it would abide only by a unanimous decision—and its representative to the panel had, of course, voted against these findings.

The major sticking point for the negotiations was the company's principal source of supply at Crystal Springs. The company demanded a million dollars for the springs and two million for the rest of its distribution system and refused to consider selling the system without the springs. Because the springs were fed by underground flows from the adjacent Los Angeles River, however, the city contended that it already owned the rights to all water in the springs and therefore would not pay for what it already possessed.

The controversy over acquisition of the waterworks thus came to turn on a question which has plagued Los Angeles in the courts almost throughout its history. The city's claim that its pueblo rights extend to the groundwater flows of the Los Angeles River Basin was first challenged by the Mission San Fernando in the early 1800s,[25] and similar litigation has been pursued by the residents of the San Fernando Valley to the present. In the midst of the controversy with the Los Angeles City Water Company, however, the California Supreme Court issued the first definitive affirmation of Los Angeles' claims to the groundwater of the Los Angeles River in a suit the city had brought against irrigators who had installed infiltration galleries to capture the subterranean flows of the river above the Narrows.[26]

This decision, rendered only a month after the issuance of the arbitration panel's findings, appeared at last to assure the city's complete authority over the Los Angeles River watershed. Armed on the one hand with the panel's recommendations and on the other with the supreme court's decision invalidating any claim the company might make to Crystal Springs, Eaton immediately called a bond election to provide the funds for purchase of the company's works and installation of extensive improvements to it. On August 23, 1899, these bonds, in the amount of $2,090,000, were approved by a margin of nearly eight to one.[27] But the company responded with further litigation which eventually succeeded in invalidating the election. It took two more years before a settlement was finally reached, and by then Eaton had left office. The company gave up its works for a compromise price of $2 million, and a new bond issue was approved at a special election August 28, 1901. On February 13, 1902, almost four years after expiration of the company's lease, the city finally regained control of its domestic water system.

Development of the city's newly acquired system had to wait, however, until a method could be devised to ensure that management of the water supply would be fully protected from political interference of any kind. At first, authority over the system was vested in a seven-member Board of Water Commissioners, which the city council established by ordinance on February 5, 1902. The members of this board were to be elected to two-year terms, the employees of the water system were to work under civil service, and the revenues from the system's operations were to be placed in a special fund for its maintenance and improvement. The city council, however, retained the authority to make all appropriations from this fund and to set the rates to be charged for water use. This arrangement, which left the management of the system almost completely exposed to the changing whims of the electorate, was immediately discarded. In its place, the city charter was amended to establish a newly reconstituted Board of Water Commissioners which would be almost entirely insulated from political considerations or public pressure.

The charter provisions adopted in January 1903 created a five-member board, none of whom would ever have to stand for popular election. All five were appointed by the mayor, subject to confirmation by the city council. Upon taking office, their control over the finances of the city's water system became almost autonomous. Although the setting of rates had still to be approved by the city council, the revenues were placed in a special account over which the commission exercised exclusive authority, subject only to the council's power to set aside certain funds for the payment of principal and interest on outstanding bonds, and subject as well to a general prohibition on expenditures for anything not necessary to the operation of the water system.[28] Although subsequent amendments to the charter have been adopted to address the expanded role of the commission in the area of electricity supply and distribution, these essential aspects of the commission's autonomy have never been eroded. And so its ability to pursue policies of its own making, without reference to popular reaction or the concerns of elected officials, has been protected.

The commission does, however, operate under one all-important restriction. At the same time the commission was created in its modern semi-autonomous form, Los Angeles took care to assure that the folly of its lease to the water company would never be repeated. The city charter was accordingly amended in 1903 to prohibit the sale, lease, or other disposition of any water or water right "now or hereafter owned or controlled by the city" without the consent of two-thirds of Los Angeles' voters. This constraint, the true bequest of the Los Angeles City Water Company, would be raised repeatedly as the principal obstacle to resolution of the controversies that swirled around the city's water program in the years that followed.[29]

William Mulholland

Along with the water company's works and facilities, Los Angeles acquired an asset that proved to be of far more enduring value: the company's superintendent, William Mulholland. No other individual has had so much to do with the creation of the modern metropolis of Los Angeles, and no other leader in California's water history looms quite so large as William Mulholland. A man of great vision and achievement, yet tragically flawed, his influence continues to shape the city's relations with the principal sources of its modern water supply.

When asked once in court to describe his qualifications as an expert in water engineering, Mulholland responded, "Well, I went to school in Ireland when I was a boy, learned the three R's and the Ten Commandments—or most of them—made a pilgrimage to the Blarney Stone, received my father's blessing, and here I am."[30] Mulholland was born in Dublin in 1855, the son of a postal clerk. Life on the coast made him impatient to set to sea, and after private tutoring in mathematics and navigation, he signed on as an apprentice seaman aboard the merchant ship *Clennifer* at the age of fifteen.[31] After four years of plying the trade routes between Glasgow, the United States, and the West Indies, he landed at New York City in 1874 and made his way to the Great Lakes, where he spent a winter in the lumber camps near Manistee, Michigan. For the next two years he lived in Pittsburgh, working at an uncle's drygoods store, and it was there that he read Charles Nordhoff's accounts of California and determined to move West.[32]

In December 1876, Mulholland and his brother Hugh booked passage on a ship bound from New York to Panama. Lacking the money for railroad fares, the two walked across the isthmus to Balboa, where they found work aboard a ship going to Acapulco. From there they shipped north to San Francisco, bought two horses in Martinez, and began the long ride through the San Joaquin Valley to Los Angeles. On this journey the brothers' paths diverged. Bill was determined to return to the sea; but on his way to San Pedro to ship out, he took a job on a well-drilling rig. "The first well I worked on changed the whole course of my life," he later observed. "When we were down about six hundred feet we struck a tree. A little further we got fossil remains and these things fired my curiosity. I wanted to know how they got there, so I got hold of Joseph Le Conte's book on the geology of this country. Right there I decided to become an engineer."[33]

Mulholland spent that summer of 1877 working on artesian wells near Compton and as a laborer on the installation of a water system for the town that is now Long Beach. But his new-found enthusiasm for geology carried him that winter to the Arizona Territory, where he tried his hand at prospecting near Erhenburg. The effort was a failure, and in the spring of 1878 he made his way down the Colorado River to Yuma and there caught a train back to Los Angeles. Late in life he recalled that spring, in an autobiographical sketch he never completed:

The world was my oyster and I was just opening it . . .
Los Angeles was a place after my own heart. It was the

most attractive town I had ever seen. The people were
hospitable. There was plenty to do and a fair compensation offered for whatever you did . . . The Los Angeles
River was the greatest attraction. It was a beautiful, limpid
little stream with willows on its banks . . . It was so
attractive to me that it at once became something about
which my whole scheme of life was woven. I loved it so
much.[34]

Here Mulholland began his enduring relationship with the
city of Los Angeles and the river that was its lifeblood. He took a
job as a ditch-tender for the Los Angeles City Water Company;
and when he was not pulling weeds or working with hoe and
shovel that summer, he spent the long hours of dusk striding the
river's banks, learning its peculiarities, and dreaming of the ways
he could fashion its uncertain flows to build a great city. Probably
no man has known the Los Angeles River as well as Mulholland,
and the lessons it taught him became the keystone of all his later
works.

Mulholland was no idle dreamer. He was a great, angular,
raw-boned sort of man, constantly in motion. Even in the official
portrait painted after completion of the aqueduct, when he was
nearly fifty years old, he appears lean and youthful. He posed in
fact as though for a camera flash that caught him in the midst of
work, and he appears on the verge of leaping up to rush off to
some new task. This great energy soon attracted the attention of
his superiors in the water company, and he moved rapidly up the
corporate ladder. Mulholland continued to live simply, however,
retaining an almost elemental closeness to nature in the midst of
the bustling city. In 1880, for example, he was put in charge of
the company's project to enlarge Buena Vista Reservoir from a
three- to a thirteen-million-gallon capacity; when the work was
finished, he erected a shanty on the water's shore and lived alone
in the Elysian Hills. And all the time he lived there, what money
he could save was spent on young trees which he planted himself,
numbering more than a thousand, around the reservoir.[35]

So rapid was Mulholland's rise within the ranks of the water
company that after only eight years this unschooled and un-
trained former laborer had emerged as Fred Eaton's protégé and
heir apparent for the superintendency of the company when Eaton

began to ready himself to run for public office in 1886. Although the two men were nearly the same age, they seemed to have little in common beyond their great energy and ambition. Eaton was elegant, well-born, and smooth in manner; Mulholland was gruff and direct, a lover of games and jokes who spent his Saturday afternoons at the baseball park and preferred the rough camaraderie of the field camp to the finer appointments of high office. Eaton throughout his life craved public attention and approval; Mulholland always claimed to love solitude and kept his private life strictly out of public view.

Instead of attending political events, social gatherings, and conferences at the city's more prominent clubs, Mulholland chose to spend his evenings reading. From the time of his arrival in Los Angeles, his friends remarked how he would sit up, long after others had gone to bed, bent over a lantern with a book. Most of his reading was devoted to scientific and technical studies. One friend who shared a room with him during these early years remembered, "His library at the time of his start in water works was little more than Fanning's *Treatise on Hydraulics*, Trautwine's *Engineer's Pocket Book*, Kent's *Mechanical Engineer's Pocket Book*, a Geometry, a Trigonometry, and Shakespeare's Works."[36] His passions in reading were those of a young man seeking to better himself. The subjects he pursued were those that excited his curiosity. Just as reading Nordhoff had brought him to California and Le Conte had turned his attention to water, his interest in trees inspired a lifelong fascination with botany. He was forever dabbling in specialized fields, picking up a bit of seismology here and a touch of hydraulics there, studying up on the latest mechanical inventions, and applying the fruits of his reading to innovations in his own work. Sometimes these experiments succeeded, at other times they failed miserably; but he was always open to new ideas and ready to dare a different way of doing things. "Damn a man who doesn't read books," he once exclaimed. "The test of a man is his knowledge of humanity, of the politics of human life, his comprehension of the things that move men."[37]

For one who loved reading so much, he abhorred writing anything down himself. While other engineers filled copybooks with their field notes and promoted their professional expertise with voluminous publications and reports, Mulholland kept no notes, relying instead on a memory so prodigious that few who knew him failed to remark on it.[38] His technical reports, with few exceptions, were prepared in conjunction with other engineers presumably more expert in the use of technical terminology. His business correspondence was invariably brief and expressed in the blandest officialese. And personal correspondence he avoided at all times, observing, "If you leave a letter in the basket long enough, it will take care of itself."[39]

As a result, Mulholland remains a somewhat elusive personality in retrospect. He married late, at 35, taking as his wife the former Lillie Ferguson, a native of Port Huron, Michigan. Though she bore him six children, five of whom lived to adulthood, almost nothing is known of his family life. His achievements, of course, are self-evident in the oceans of concrete that make up the Los Angeles of today and the hundreds of miles of water pipes and aqueducts that serve the city. But what made him angry, or afraid, is revealed only in his public statements. The brilliance of his mind can be seen only in its reflection upon his friends and associates. The force of his will can be measured only in his impact on those around him and in the shadow his accomplishments still cast today.

On the other hand, it was his phenomenal memory, his distaste for paperwork, and his refusal to "flare in the limelight"[40] that enabled him to survive the transition from private to public control of the city's waterworks. When the city government took over the system, it had no ability to operate it, so the more senior employees of the Los Angeles City Water Company were invited to remain at their posts under the municipal civil service system. But it was by no means certain that the same opportunity would be extended to the company's superintendent. He had, after all, been the company's spokesman during its long and often bitter negotiations with the city, and he was consequently not popular in many official circles. As one local commentator observed, "It was predicted that Mulholland would have to go because he was not a politician. In truth, his services were retained because of this very fact."[41]

As things turned out, the city probably had little choice but to accept Mulholland. As might be expected in an operation run by a man who preferred not to spend any time at his desk, the company's records were in disarray. When Mulholland had failed to produce the records and accounts the city's negotiators sought during the four years they spent dickering over the company's price, they assumed that this was just a reflection of the intransigence of the company's owners. As the negotiations drew close to settlement, however, they discovered that not only did these records not exist, the company lacked even a map of its distribution network. The city was thus in the position of buying a system it could not find. All of this information—the size of every inch of pipe, the age and location of every valve—Mulholland carried in his head. Once Mulholland had successfully demonstrated the total accuracy of his recall, the city realized it could not very well run the system without him.[42] And once his continued employment was assured, Mulholland promptly intervened with the company's principal stockholder, I. W. Hellman, advising him to accept the city's offer of two million dollars for the system.[43] "The city bought the works and me with it," Mulholland cheerily announced.[44]

There was no hypocrisy in Mulholland's conversion to the public sector, however; no breaking with an earlier faith in the virtues of private enterprise. Throughout his life, he exhibited little interest in ideological questions, keeping his viewpoint fixed instead upon the immediate tasks at hand. Municipal takeover for Mulholland meant access to funding for the expansion and improvements in the system which the tight-fisted private management had refused to support. The Los Angeles City Water Company had begun with a system of wooden pipes, a water wheel, and a storage tank in the city plaza and over the term of its lease with the city had gradually expanded it into a more modern distribution system including over three hundred miles of mains, infiltration galleries, pumping plants, and six important reservoirs, all servicing a population that had grown from fewer than 4,500 to more than 102,000 people. But the problems with the system were significant. It had been developed, after all, to provide minimal service at maximum profit. Its pressure was low and the consequent hazard of devastating fires within the city was very real.

In the agricultural areas served by the city's long-neglected irrigation system, the situation was not much better. The city employed a staff of only four to operate the system, although three more men were customarily added during the peak irrigation season from April to November. Measurements of the water delivered to individual irrigators were made on the basis of an imaginary unit called a "head," which was assumed to be equivalent to 100 miner's inches of flow but varied in fact from 50 to 150 inches depending on how much water was in the system at any given time. A team of federal experts who conducted a survey of irrigation practices in California in 1900 remarked upon these "astonishingly crude" methods, commenting, "It would be impossible to find another system in California—in the southern portion at least and probably not elsewhere in the State—where such unscientific means are still employed."[45] Confusion reigned as well among the city's records of water rights claims. Thousands of these vital filings were scattered throughout seventy-nine volumes of miscellaneous records. None were filed according to the actual location of use, and few even bothered to specify the location.[46] "The practice is simply the survival of the old-time, careless, Mexican method," the federal investigators complained, "little if any improved by the lapse of time."[47]

Mulholland made the conversion to public control with an enthusiasm that astonished many of his colleagues, and he immediately set about righting these conditions by putting into motion a flurry of projects and policies which had no doubt been forming in his mind for sixteen years as the water company's superintendent. First he cut the flat rates the city charged for water service by 10 percent and the metered rates by half. As a result, Los Angeles was able to offer its metered customers a rate of ten cents per thousand gallons as compared with charges of twenty-four cents in San Francisco, forty in Oakland, thirty-five in Berkeley, and thirty in Alameda.[48] At the same time, he began expanding the installation of meters within the city—which not only extended the benefits of these reduced rates more widely but also cut the city's average daily per capita consumption of water by one-third in only two years.[49]

In 1903, Mulholland completed the Elysian Reservoir, expanded the Buena Vista pumping plant, and bought out the West

Los Angeles Water Company, the sole survivor of the water company's campaign for an exclusive empire. The very next year he built the Solano Reservoir, installed still more pumps at Buena Vista, and laid a new supply conduit.[50] Meanwhile, he began driving a tunnel into the bedrock beneath the channel of the Los Angeles River which he proposed to run from a point just south of Huron Street all the way across the valley. His plan was that the city would then sink wells into this tunnel and pump off the groundwater that percolated into it.[51]

In the first three years of public operation, Mulholland succeeded in essentially rebuilding the entire water system of the city, paying for this reconstruction entirely out of the income from a drastically reduced rate structure. In fact, by the end of the 1904 fiscal year, he had actually turned a profit of $640,000 on his operations, and over the first four years he netted more than $1.5 million after meeting all operating expenses and debt service.[52]

An enthusiastic supporter of Mulholland's attributed the popular acclaim he now enjoyed to the fact that his breathtaking successes in these first three years "touched Mr. Citizen in two soft places, first the pocket book, and then civic pride."[53] But at the end of the 1904 fiscal year, Mulholland had an even more startling announcement to make. The city was growing rapidly, and new water connections had increased 75 percent in 1903 and another 25 percent in 1904.[54] After surveying the resources of the Los Angeles River, Mulholland declared, "The time has come when we shall have to supplement its flow from some other source."[55]

CHAPTER TWO

Competing
Public Interests

When William E. Smythe, first executive secretary of the National Irrigation Congress, editor of *Irrigation Age*, and author of the seminal history of the American reclamation movement, *The Conquest of Arid America*, surveyed the prospects for economic development in California in 1900, he saw no future for Los Angeles and the other communities of the South Coast. Though he applauded the success of the irrigation colonies of Southern California and the rapid pace of settlement they had encouraged, he noted as well that land values there had grown exorbitantly by the beginning of the twentieth century and that the region's water supply had been almost completely put to use. As a result, he concluded, "It is perfectly true that this charming district is not within the field of the largest future developments."[1] Instead, he looked to the eastern slope of the Sierra Nevada—to what he called the Undiscovered California, Plumas, Lassen, and Modoc counties in the north and the Owens Valley in the south —as the areas holding special promise for the state's future economic growth.

Smythe argued that these emerging communities, although isolated during the nineteenth century by the absence of railroad facilities connecting them to the major cities of the coast, "present today the finest field for development in California and one

of the finest in the United States. There can be no question that
during the next century they will become the homes of hundreds
of thousands of people and the seat of a manifold industrial
life."[2] His confidence was founded on the abundant water resources these areas naturally possessed. His optimism with regard
to the Owens Valley in particular was shared by other western
advocates of systematic irrigation and by the federal engineers
responsible for expanding agricultural development of the West
under the aegis of the newly formed United States Reclamation
Service. But in Los Angeles, William Mulholland looked to the
water riches of the Owens Valley and drew an altogether different
conclusion, one which would set him on a course in direct conflict with the public forces then gathering to aid the economic
development of the valley.

Smythe and his followers equated economic development with
the settlement of the land. In the semi-arid states of the American
Southwest, however, progress of this kind could be achieved only
through the development of systematic irrigation. And so the
promotion of irrigation became the motivating cause for a national movement which focused on California, whose abundant
rivers and climatic diversity made it a ripe field for a practical
demonstration of the benefits of irrigated agriculture. "As an
agricultural state, California stands alone," declared Elwood
Mead, head of the Irrigation Investigations branch of the United
States Department of Agriculture. "The usual limitations imposed by latitude are here set aside. Oranges ripen as early and
surely at Oroville, 100 miles north of San Francisco, as at San
Diego, 500 miles south of that City, and much of the State has
the unique distinction of being able to grow all the products of
New England and of Florida on the same acre of land."[3]

It was this very abundance of opportunities for agricultural
development which had worked to slow the advance of irrigation in California during the nineteenth century. "In much of the
cultivated portion of the State, irrigation is not a matter of
necessity but of choice," Mead observed, and most California
farmers chose not to bother. "Until quite recent years," commented one of Mead's investigators in 1900, "the people living in
the greater part of the State regarded irrigation in the same light

that eastern people generally view it, *viz.*, that it is a grievous hardship imposed by nature upon the inhabitants of certain ill-favored regions of the earth."[4] Instead of irrigated crops, cattle had dominated California's agricultural industry during the early years of settlement. And even when widespread drought conditions from 1862 through 1864 destroyed much of the state's herds and broke the dominance of the cattle industry, California turned to the cultivation of wheat, which Dr. Hugh J. Glenn demonstrated could be grown quickly and profitably without irrigation on vast acreages in the Sacramento Valley.

The rise of the great cattle and wheat empires in California assured the failure of state and federal programs put forward during the nineteenth century to encourage reclamation and the expansion of a diversified agricultural economy. When the federal government granted the state control of more than two million acres of swamp and overflow lands in the public domain under the Arkansas Act of 1850, on condition that the state administer these lands in such a way as to assure their reclamation, the California Legislature responded by removing the dispersal of these lands from all controls. By careless and sometimes fraudulent methods at the state level, the lands fell under the control of huge corporate ranchers like the Miller and Lux Land and Cattle Company, which used the federal program to establish an empire that ultimately came to embrace both banks of the San Joaquin River for a stretch of one hundred miles and the Kern River for more than fifty miles. Large portions of these lands were then withheld from settlement for speculative purposes and turned to grazing and pasturage instead of agriculture. The vast holdings of Miller and Lux along the rivers enabled the company to strangle agricultural development elsewhere in the San Joaquin Valley under the state's riparian water laws, a practice which the California Supreme Court upheld in a landmark decision in 1886.[5] Other efforts by the federal government to encourage agricultural settlement under the Desert Land Act of 1877 met a similar fate at the hands of the cattle interests.[6] And when California's first state engineer, William "Ham" Hall, used his state-wide surveys of water development to argue during the 1880s for greater efforts to encourage the expansion of irrigated agriculture, the legislature refused even to print the results of his studies and abolished his office.[7]

Despite intense opposition from the cattle and wheat interests in the interior valleys which are today California's richest areas of irrigated agricultural production, the movement for the expansion of irrigation did gain several significant footholds in California during the nineteenth century. The great public outcry that followed the supreme court's decision upholding the rights of the Miller and Lux company in 1886 encouraged the legislature to establish a mechanism the very next year for the formation of irrigation districts under the Wright Act of 1887. The Wright Act in its original and early amended forms, however, was ineffectual at ensuring the fiscal integrity of the districts formed under its provisions or at preventing fraud. Although dozens of districts sprang into existence immediately after its passage, few survived, with the notable exception of the Modesto and Turlock irrigation districts.

For the most part, irrigation succeeded only in those areas where it was a necessity and not a matter of choice, principally in the semi-arid wastes of Southern California. Here the success of the Mormon colony at San Bernardino in 1851 spurred the creation of similar small and carefully managed irrigation colonies at Anaheim, Riverside, and Ontario. The collapse of the cattle industry following the drought of the 1860s led to the conversion of great pasturages into small farms, a process that began with the division of two hundred thousand acres owned by Abel Stearns and Sam Brannan into forty-acre tracts in the Los Angeles area. As a result, 61 percent of the growth in California's rural population between 1880 and 1890 occurred in the seven counties of the South Coast.[8]

The uncertainties created by California's reliance upon riparian doctrines of law, the competing demands placed on the state's rivers for agriculture and navigation, suspicions that the widespread adoption of irrigation technology would unnecessarily undercut the state's self-image as an agricultural paradise, and the fear that the creation of great fields of standing water would provide an ideal breeding ground for disease-carrying mosquitoes were all effective barriers to the expansion of irrigated agriculture in California by the latter part of the nineteenth century. Moreover, the high costs of establishing irrigation works and the necessity of expending large sums of money on litigation to defend one's water rights virtually assured, in Elwood Mead's opinion, that "development of irrigation will be corporate and great aggregations of capital will control the water resources of the West."[9] But Mead, Smythe, and their followers also attributed California's resistance to the modern principles of irrigation to the Westerner's characteristic love of bigness. "The cowboy on horseback was an aristocrat; the irrigator on foot . . . a groveling wretch," Mead observed. "In cowboy land, the irrigation ditch has always been regarded with disfavor because it is the badge and symbol of a despised occupation."[10]

To counter these attitudes, the movement for irrigation began to assume an almost messianic fervor in which the expansion of irrigated agriculture came to be treated not only as a means to economic development but also as the driving wheel of social and spiritual progress. Smythe, for example, argued that the case for irrigation could be proven simply by comparing the quality of life in Southern as opposed to Northern California: "The one was born of the irrigation canal; the other of the mining camp and wheat ranch. The one is characterized by a high civilization; the other by a low one."[11] When the ruthless exploitation of the soil by California's one-crop wheat economy began to reduce the yields of grain, while competition from the Mississippi Valley and Russia set in motion the eventual demise of the great wheat empires in the 1890s, Smythe applauded the passing of the wheat barons as a blessing for California: "The fall in wheat prices has broken the land monopoly which kept labor servile and gave the most fruitful of countries to four-footed beasts rather than to men," he wrote in 1900.

> Not until nearly all the great ranches had been mortgaged to their full capacity, not until the failure of prices had made the debts intolerably burdensome and brought their owners face to face with disaster, was it possible to open the country for its best and highest uses. With the supremacy of wheat will go the shanty and the "hobo" laborer, to be followed in time by the Chinaman. In their places will

come the home and the man who works for himself. Civilization will bloom where barbarism has blighted the land.[12]

The ideal of the family farm thus became an integral part of a movement linking economic development, resource conservation, and social progress in an appeal which gradually gained support at the national level for programs designed primarily to benefit the West. In 1888, Congress authorized the first water resources investigations of the arid lands of the West. The United States Geological Survey began assembling a new cadre of engineers; unlike the self-taught entrepreneurs who specialized in water during the early years of western settlement, these men were professionally trained and brought up within the ranks of the governmental bureaucracies that came to dominate water development in the twentieth century. In 1894 Congress passed the Carey Act, granting a million acres of the public domain for each western state to sell in the expectation that the proceeds would be applied to state-financed reclamation programs. A Californian operating from Chicago, George H. Maxwell, united the National Irrigation Congress, the National Board of Trade, the National Association of Manufacturers, and the Businessmen's League in support of direct federal funding for western irrigation on the promise that irrigation could solve the nation's social problems by decentralizing population, creating new markets for eastern manufacturers, giving work to the unemployed, and returning the people to the land. By 1900, Maxwell's campaign, which enjoyed substantial financial support from the western railroad companies, who were always eager to bring new settlers to their domain, had been endorsed by the platforms of both major political parties. And in 1902, President Theodore Roosevelt fulfilled these pledges by signing the Federal Reclamation Act.

For a nation which had seen itself divided by intensifying class conflict during the 1890s and threatened by the rise of Bolshevism around the world, the reclamation program marked one of those masterstrokes of compromise by which Roosevelt would seek throughout his administration to bind his country together again. For unlike the efforts at land reform in other parts of the world, the federal reclamation program did not seek

to break up the holdings of western corporate interests and redis-
tribute their properties among a new class of resident farmers.
Instead, it was intended to extend opportunities for settlement
and self-reliance to the common people by creating a whole new
class of lands which would be made habitable through irrigation.

It was in this spirit of reforming agriculture to build the
nation and make homes for its people that the engineers of the
newly formed federal Reclamation Service set forth in the West.
They knew their efforts were on trial before a young and energetic
president. So they built quickly, forging ahead with new projects
in every western state so that their own skills and the benefits of
their expertise could be promptly demonstrated. Given Smythe's
earlier enthusiasm for its prospects, they soon found their way to
the Owens Valley.

Here nature had created a tiny island of green in the middle
of a wasteland. The valley is a narrow graben, approximately 100
miles long and an average of 5 miles wide, confined on the east by
the Inyo-White Mountains and on the west by the Sierra Nevada,
which rises abruptly thousands of feet above the valley's floor.
More than one and a half million years ago, when the vast granite
blocks that form the modern Sierra Nevada first pressed upward,
they carried the valley with them, lifting it to an elevation of nine
thousand feet before it broke away and fell back to its present
level. As they subsided, the blocks forming the valley's floor
twisted together, sealing the basin and closing its lower-lying
southern end with pinched bedrock. When particles of rock and
soil were washed down the mountainsides in the thousands of
centuries that followed, they were consequently captured in this
watertight basin, forming alluvial fans of granitic soil which eventually covered over 275 square miles of the area between Owens
Lake and the present site of Bishop. The mountains are thus the
source of all the valley's richness, for they have provided both the
soil that fills the valley today and the water to make it fertile.

In terms of climate, the valley is a desert. It lies in the rainless
shadow of the Sierra Nevada and shares the characteristics of the
barren lands to its south and east, which include the hottest,
driest regions of North America. But it lies as well within sight of
living glaciers and perpetual snow fields along the crest of the

Sierra. And every year the vast quantities of precipitation which the mountains capture from passing cloud masses pass down into the valley through rivulets and streams that run full in the summer months of June and July. Thus the valley flourished in the midst of what John Muir once described as "a land of pure desolation covered with beautiful light."[13]

The first men to apply the abundant waters of the Owens Valley to the growing of food were the Paiute Indians, who migrated to the valley each spring and summer to gather seeds, nuts, and grasses. To increase their harvest, the Indians applied techniques they had learned at Fort Tejon near Bakersfield to flood the fields around Bishop Creek. In the spring, they would dam the creek, turning its flows into a ditch that ran to two fields of natural vegetation which they harvested alternately each year. The women would then gather the fish stranded in the dry stream-bed, as well as the plants that flourished through the summer. In the fall the dam was taken down and the waters allowed to return to their natural course. The Indians would then gather the fish left in the fields and head south for the winter.[14]

Although white trappers and explorers had passed through the Owens Valley as early as 1833, there was no detailed written account of what they found there until 1859. In July of that year, Capt. J. W. Davidson entered the valley with a military column sent out from Fort Tejon to investigate charges that the Paiutes had been rustling cattle in the Santa Clara and San Fernando valleys. Proceeding north from Owens Lake, Davidson followed a river averaging fifty feet in width and running fifteen to twenty feet deep. "Every step now taken shows you that nature has been lavish of her stores," Davidson wrote. "The mountains are filled with timber, the vallies with water and meadows of luxuriant grass. Some of these meadows contain, at a moderate estimate, ten thousand acres, every foot of which can be irrigated." North of Oak Creek he noted, "The eye wanders over a sea of green." Of the soil, he reported, "Wherever water touches it, it produces abundantly. I should think it well suited to the growth of wheat, barley, oats, rye and various fruits, the apple, pear, etc. . . . To the Grazier, this is one of the finest parts of the State; to the Farmer, it offers every advantage but a market."[15]

Davidson exonerated the valley Indians of any involvement in the rustling further south and suggested that instead of punishing them the government should give the Paiutes the Owens Valley as a reservation. But his glowing accounts of conditions in the valley attracted the attention of white settlers, miners, and cattlemen, who began arriving in increasing numbers in the early 1860s and promptly made war on the Indians, nearly exterminating them altogether. The whites first came to mine the rich ore deposits of the mountains, and the Russ Mining District, established April 20, 1860, southeast of the present town of Independence, initiated civil government in Inyo Country. When the drought of the early 1860s crippled their industry, the cattlemen soon followed, driving their herds into the valley in search of greener pastures. Samuel Bishop first entered the valley on such a drive and remained to found the town that bears his name. In 1864, a sawmill was built at Bishop to serve the mines, and its logs were floated down the Owens River to build the towns that grew up around the mining camps. By the early 1870s, upward of two hundred thousand head of cattle were wintering regularly in the Owens Valley, and early signs of stable settlement soon began to appear: the first church in 1869, the first newspaper in 1870, regular mail service to Aurora in 1875, and a telegraph line in 1876.[16]

Efforts to develop the water resources of the valley for irrigated agriculture began almost as soon as the Indians had been subdued. In 1873, two speculators from the other side of the Sierra attempted to have 133,000 acres turned over to their control as swamp and overflow lands. The scheme was exposed in time to prevent its fruition, and the Owens Valley thus escaped the fate of the lower San Joaquin Valley, which had seen its richest croplands turned into cattle ranges by the Miller and Lux company.[17] The course of agricultural development in the Owens Valley was left to the enterprise of individual irrigation companies which began to extend their lines in the area of Bishop, Laws, and Big Pine in the late 1870s. By 1895, seven canals had been dug, totaling ninety miles in length. By the close of the nineteenth century, irrigation services had been extended to more than 41,000 acres of the valley, and orchards and vineyards had begun to appear on the high, relatively frost-free alluvial fans.[18]

Clarice Tate Uhlmeyer, an early valley resident, recalls the scene around Big Pine when she arrived as a small girl in 1901: "It was fall when we arrived and the orchards were loaded with luscious peaches, pears, plums, and apples, and the arbors hung heavy with ripening grapes. The creeks were running full, even so late in the year, and nearly every yard had an icy stream diverted from the main ditch."[19]

Farther south in the valley, where the river emptied into Owens Lake, the land was more sparsely settled. Here the soils were heavy with salts and soda which are commercially valuable but useless for cultivation. Because the river's flow has been diverted to Los Angeles, Owens Lake no longer exists. But one early settler, Beveridge R. Spear, remembers that the lake was once "alive with wild fowl, from the swift flying Teel to the honker goose . . . Ducks were by the square mile, millions of them. When they rose in flight, the roar of their wings . . . could be heard on the mountain top at Cerro Gordo, ten miles away . . . Occasionally, when shot down, a duck would burst open from fatness which was butter yellow."[20]

Other accounts of the lake are somewhat less glorious. Captain Davidson in 1859 called it "a perfect Dead Sea," though he admitted that it was populated by myriads of flies and "whole navies of aquatic birds, the Species of which is unknown to me."[21] T. E. Jones, writing in 1885, was more explicit:

> It is well to state some of the wonderful properties of the water, that for bathing, shampooing, and general cleansing powers it has no equal among artificial productions. It is believed by many to be a specific for catarrhal and lung affections . . . Though mild and agreeable for a short time, yet it will leave no vestige of bones or flesh of man or beast put in it for a few hours . . . No living thing abides the surface of this water, perfectly clear as ever it is, neither fish nor reptile nor anything save millions of small white worms from which spring other myriads of a peculiar kind of fly . . . Legions upon legions of a so-called duck . . . lived on the lake . . . They are web-footed but have a bill like a common chicken . . . they have no real wings or feathers and consequently cannot fly . . . It is the reasoned conviction of parties who have observed

the facts for years that these birds migrate from other regions, alighting on the Lake perfect birds, only soon to become bereft of feathers and even the physical power to prevent themselves from drowning whenever the surface of the water becomes ruffled by a continuous breeze.[22]

As the contrast between the idyllic paradise described by Spear and Jones' duck-eating lake may suggest, opinions on what the Owens Valley was like before the advent of Los Angeles can differ sharply. It became convenient in later years, for example, for officials of the Los Angeles Department of Water and Power to deny that the Owens Valley had ever had any significant agricultural production or potential.[23] Residents of the Owens Valley who oppose the city's policies, on the other hand, may tend to exaggerate the natural bounty of the valley before the water was removed. It is important, therefore, to fix with some precision the conditions which actually obtained for Owens Valley agriculture at the turn of the century.

The first comprehensive survey of the valley's soils was prepared for the United States Reclamation Service by Thomas H. Means in 1904. Means found that 75,000 acres of the valley lands were of the first class of soil quality and 50,000 of the second class. These lands, constituting 45 percent of the valley's arable area, Means concluded, were "all of value as soon as water is applied." In addition, Means found that another 80,000 acres, 29 percent of the area, could be brought into production with the installation of drainage systems.[24]

In addition to rich soils and abundant water, the Owens Valley possessed two other characteristics which made it particularly attractive to those working to expand irrigation in California: it was located in an area where irrigation was a matter of necessity, not choice; and the traditions of small family farm development were especially well rooted here. There was a total of 424 farms in operation on 141,059 acres of the valley in 1899, almost all owned by families who lived and worked on plots of 175 acres or less. Only 43,740 acres had actually been developed for growing crops, but 85 percent of the farms in Inyo Country and 94 percent of the improved acreage was under irrigation. One hundred ten miles of canals had been dug; and in terms of total irrigated area, Inyo ranked ninth among the 58 counties of

California in 1889, and twelfth in 1899. The percentage of improved lands under irrigation in Inyo in 1900 was exceeded only by tiny Alpine County, whose agricultural production was, of course, much less.[25]

Most of the 41,026 irrigated acres in the Owens Valley in 1900 were devoted to growing hay, alfalfa, and cereal grasses such as wheat, oats, and barley. Only seven counties in California had more acres in alfalfa and lucerne than Inyo in 1899, and Inyo ranked seventh among all the counties of California in the production of this crop, even though the somewhat shorter growing season at the valley's elevation restricted the number of cuttings that could be taken each year.[26] Despite this necessary concentration on the production of feed to support livestock in an isolated region which had retained a measure of economic dependence upon the cattle industry, Means noted that "corn of excellent quality is produced in sufficient quantity to demonstrate the capabilities of the valley."[27] In fact, Inyo ranked ninth among the counties of California in the number of acres devoted to corn and eleventh in terms of its production. And although it had scarcely begun to export its orchard products, the valley in 1900 already had 28,571 apple trees, 9,041 peach, 3,319 pear, and 2,387 plum, all of sufficient age to begin bearing fruit.[28]

The valley probably would have developed much faster before 1900 except for the absence of adequate transportation facilities to carry its products to a major metropolitan market. As it was, the major portion of its agricultural production was consumed locally in the mine fields, and the expansion of agriculture was consequently tied to the often radical rises and falls in the fortunes of the area's mining industry. In 1870, a railroad line was proposed to pass through San Bernardino to the Panamint Valley and thence to Independence in order to transport bullion from Darwin and the Cerro Gordo mines. But a widespread economic depression destroyed the market for silver in the 1870s, mine production dwindled, and the Southern Pacific decided to build an extension through Mojave to Bakersfield instead.[29]

Hard times then descended on the valley, and its roads to the south fell under the control of the bandit Tiburcio Vasquez in 1874 and 1875. In 1883, D. O. Mills built the Carson and Colorado Railroad line from Belleville, Nevada, through the mining camps to Keeler, where a marble quarry and soda works had been established on the shores of Owens Lake.[30] But the Carson and Colorado had been built for the mines, not for agriculture. Its operation was casual, its freight charges for agricultural products excessive, and the regularity of its service uncertain. Crews often stopped the train along its route so that those aboard could go hunting or refresh themselves with a swim in Walker Lake.[31] More important, the Slim Princess, as the Keeler train came to be known, ran on a narrow-gauge line, which meant that railroad cars loaded in the Owens Valley had to undergo expensive repacking once they reached the wider gauge lines going to Los Angeles. As a result, the San Francisco Bay Area and not the South Coast was the valley's principal urban market at the turn of the century, and only a few of the most valuable products of the valley could bear the high freight costs involved in shipping them east to Nevada and then north and back across the Sierra to San Francisco.

The argument that the Owens Valley had no agricultural potential rests in large part on this dearth of transportation facilities. Adherents of this argument point out that even with a railroad line to Los Angeles, Owens Valley produce would have had to travel 235 miles, whereas the Imperial Valley lies 60 miles closer to Los Angeles, apples and pears from the Victor Valley are only 100 miles away, and hay could be grown in the Antelope Valley, only 80 miles outside the city.[32] This line of reasoning, carried to an extreme by the city's most ardent defenders, has been extended to presume that railroads never would have reached the valley if Los Angeles had not constructed its own line to haul materials for the aqueduct, and that the valley residents should therefore be grateful to the city for bringing them a railroad line under circumstances which guaranteed they would not have much use for it.[33]

Might-have-beens are a poor basis for any argument, especially when the logic of such an equation could have been so easily upset by the action of a single railroad company. The Owens Valley with its rich soils and abundant water resources offered a far more likely prospect for agricultural development in 1900 than did the peat bogs of the Sacramento-San Joaquin delta, the barren lands of the west side of the San Joaquin Valley, or the forbidding wastes of the Colorado Desert, all of which rank today among the richest centers of agricultural production in California. The Owens Valley by the beginning of the twentieth century, moreover, seemed to have embarked upon a period of extended development. In 1900, Jim Butler discovered the Mizpah Silver Mine, thereby setting off a mining boom in the valley's principal market areas of Tonopah and Goldfield. Commercial activity in the valley suddenly began to flourish. The first banks opened their doors in 1903. The city of Bishop incorporated that year, erected a high school, and began laying plans for a domestic water and sewer system. And in 1904 several power companies, led by the Denver-backed Nevada Power Mining and Milling Company, announced plans for the construction of a series of five power plants in Bishop Creek Canyon to tap the enormous hydroelectric generating potential of the valley's water resources.[34]

Such experts in agriculture and water development as Smythe, Means, and the engineers of the Reclamation Service were therefore not alone in predicting a bright future for the Owens Valley at the turn of the century. With these rising expectations, the transportation problem seemed on the verge of solution. The Southern Pacific bought out the Carson and Colorado Railroad in 1900 for $2.75 million, and rumors began to circulate that the line would soon be improved.[35] In 1901, the *Los Angeles Times* enthusiastically reported that another company, the Randsburg Railway, which served the mining regions east of the Mojave and enjoyed financial support from a party of influential New York interests, had announced plans to extend its line to the Owens Valley. Thus, the *Times* assured its readers, "the trade of a rich agricultural and mining section" would soon be brought to the city.[36]

The Reclamation Service Project

So attractive was the Owens Valley for the purposes of the Reclamation Service that the new agency began laying plans for an examination of its potential for an irrigation project even before the service had fully organized for business. "Have you ever considered the advisability of an examination of Owens River Valley and the desirability of segregating public lands?" wrote the service's first director, Frederick Haynes Newell, to his chief of operations in California, Joseph B. Lippincott, on April 29, 1903. "If you think this is a good plan, I wish you would send a suitable man . . . and have a reconnaissance quietly made with the idea of withdrawing lands pending survey."[37] Newell's directive was issued fully four months before he convened his engineers in Orden, Utah, to formalize procedures, define the agency's goals, and launch the first wave of preliminary surveys. But by June 17 Lippincott had a man in the field, Jacob C. Clausen, a young Berkeley graduate who had worked the mines at Coeur d'Alene before joining the Reclamation Service. Clausen knew more about boats than about deserts—his parents had sailed to the United States in their own craft from Schleswig-Holstein and then had operated a ferry from Sacramento to San Francisco—but he readily accepted his new assignment. "The service was young," he later recalled, "looking everywhere for something to do . . . At that time nobody knew anything about the [Owens Valley]. We knew so little about it we hardly knew how to go in to make a report."[38]

For all their bright prospects, the communities of the Owens Valley which Clausen entered that summer were only barely removed from the primitive frontier. The streets of Bishop, the main town, were still muddy tracks, and for many residents this was still a "country of Lost Borders [where] not the law but the land sets the limit."[39] Organized vigilance committees were active in the valley as late as 1901, when nearly all the prominent citizens of Bishop joined to drive out a man suspected of selling liquor to the Indians; and lynchings were still taking place in the outlying mine camps in 1908.[40] But Clausen was so taken with the area that he would devote much of his life to its protection and improvement. "When I saw the lay of the land up there, I immediately recommended that they withdraw everything that we thought had anything to do with the project," Clausen later told an interviewer.[41]

Withdrawal was the first step in the establishment of any reclamation project. Under its enabling act of 1902, the service was empowered to protect lands in the public domain that might be useful for the construction of works or the extension of irrigation services under a proposed reclamation project by withdrawing them from entry under the various federal settlement acts. By prohibiting private parties from filing claims on these lands, the withdrawals protected the service from the possibility that speculators, learning of the government's interest in a particular area, might take over the lands to be served by a proposed project and thereby drive up the cost of their acquisition. The act provided that these withdrawals could be made before the government issued any public announcement of its interest. The mechanism was thus intended to provide a way of setting properties aside temporarily while detailed surveys could be conducted to determine whether a project would in fact be feasible.[42]

Clausen telegraphed Lippincott at the beginning of July to report that more than 110,000 acres in the valley were ideally suited for irrigation and that everything should be immediately withdrawn. Lippincott promptly set out for the valley to look over the situation after checking with Newell to make certain he had the authority to go ahead with any withdrawals that looked reasonable in his view. Newell was happy to trust Lippincott's judgment but urged him to make haste: "If there is an opportunity for government reclamation on a large scale I think that we should not let this opportunity go by."[43] With this encouragement, Lippincott withdrew 21,000 acres as soon as he arrived in the valley and made an enthusiastic report to Newell noting that the valley contained great quantities of high-quality public land which could be materially improved with a public works project that the local residents would heartily endorse.[44] On Lippincott's recommendation, another 544,480 acres of the valley were withdrawn in August, October, and December.

Once the initial withdrawals had been made in July 1903, it was necessary to begin the time-consuming work of mapping the area in detail, establishing gauging stations to measure the flow of waters into the project site, and researching the land and water rights of all the parties who might be affected by the proposed project. Newell was sometimes impatient with the pace of the work and wrote from Washington to complain about the time and money Lippincott was spending on surveys of the small glacial lakes in the mountains above Bishop, which Lippincott believed could be used to supplement the storage reservoir Clausen had tentatively proposed to be located in Long Valley.[45]

The research into private rights raised the specter of even more extended delays if the individuals holding these interests chose to resist the project and resorted to the courts to defend their claims. Of special concern in this connection were the lands held by T. B. Rickey and the Rickey Land and Cattle Company. Rickey owned 22,380 acres in the Owens Valley outright and controlled an even greater area through dummy titles made out in other names. Not only was Rickey the major landowner in Inyo County, but also, the Department of the Interior's district counsel, H. L. Holgate, reported, "He is practically proprietor of Mono County and there are few of the small population of Alpine County who are not in his employ."[46] Rickey's holdings in the Owens Valley included all the lands proposed for the reservoir at Long Valley, and he therefore held the key to the future of the government's project. But Rickey had not joined the chorus of support from the smaller ranchers of the valley when the government announced its project; as a cattleman, he did not look with favor on any transformation of the valley that would encourage irrigated agriculture.[47]

If Rickey opposed the project, Holgate reported, many of his land claims could be challenged and he might thereby be forced to vacate them. But to accomplish this would require extended litigation. "Much of the Rickey lands were doubtless acquired by legitimate purchase [although] legal would be a better term than legitimate, since many were forced to sell to Rickey after being coerced and hounded for months and sometimes years by Rickey and his men," Holgate told Lippincott. "A large part of the lands, however, was without doubt illegally acquired . . . There are thousands of acres fraudulently obtained by Rickey and now held by him which can be restored to the public domain only by legal proceedings in the courts."[48] Holgate warned that this would be a lengthy process because many of the defects in Rickey's titles were the result of misfeasance by state authorities, which would be both difficult and politically uncomfortable for the federal government to prove.[49] "To collect the evidence in the Rickey case will require good judgment, tact, patience, time and secrecy," Holgate advised. "Rickey has demonstrated his willingness and ability to injure those who oppose him, and there are few in the Valley who care to or can really afford to incur his enmity. On the other hand, there is hardly a man who does not greatly desire that Rickey be shorn of his illegal holdings."[50]

Holgate began to prepare his case while the other work on the project steadily progressed. By the end of 1903, the Reclamation Service was able to announce in its annual report that, although detailed surveys were still under way, the reservoir site which Clausen had identified in his first reconnaissance in June could provide ample water to double the irrigated acreage in the valley.[51] The following spring, Lippincott in an article in *Forestry and Irrigation* featured the Owens Valley prominently in a general accounting of the Reclamation Service's work in California and noted approvingly that the residents of the valley were "extremely anxious" to see the project completed.[52] On April 30, 1904, however, the same month his article appeared, Lippincott called a halt to further development of the project pending the arrival of a diamond-core drilling outfit and a skilled geologist, which he announced he needed to examine certain problems that concerned him about the Long Valley reservoir site. "The rocks at this point are of a volcanic nature," Lippincott told Newell, "and it is possible that the reservoir would not retain the water that might be impounded therein. I think it important that we should have a report on bed rock conditions and geology before we have spent too much money on surveys of other features of this project."[53] Although no one could have realized it at the time, this request marked the end of the Reclamation Service project in the Owens Valley. The drilling rig did not arrive that summer and by the time it was ready for use in the spring of 1905, the project had effectively been killed.

Part of the problem that would bring about this unexpected turn of events was revealed in a letter Lippincott wrote to Newell even before Lippincott made his first visit to the Owens Valley in July 1903. The consortium of power companies who had filed claims on Bishop Creek in hopes of developing hydroelectric plants for the mining camps in Tonopah represented a significant threat to the Reclamation Service project because their claims, of course, preceded and were therefore superior to any needs the government might have for its reservoir. Despite the fact that the government had not yet made any public announcement of its interest in the valley, and despite the fact that Newell had specifically instructed Lippincott to make his preliminary reconnaissance of the valley in secret, Lippincott, as soon as he had Clausen's recommendation for withdrawal in hand, had met with officials of the Edison Electric Company, a prominent partner in the power companies' plans, to discuss the potential for conflict between the two projects. Lippincott described this meeting in a letter to Newell written before his trip to decide whether to proceed on Clausen's recommendations: "I told him [the company representative] that I thought the situation was rather an embarrassing one; that they were principally after power developments and we were principally after irrigation developments . . . and I suggested that possibly we both could accomplish what we were after without mutual interference . . . This is, of course, a rather ticklish business, and it may be that it is wrong." Lippincott advised Newell that it would be better to proceed with the withdrawals and thereby strengthen the government's hand in any negotiations that might follow with the power companies.

In case a conflict with these private interests could not be avoided, however, Lippincott left little doubt where his sympathies lay as he concluded his letter:

> I consider that the Edison Electric people have done a very great deal for the development of the Southwest. They are the pioneers in long distance power transmission and have revolutionized the power business of the West by their enterprise and energy. They have induced Eastern capital to invest in this section large sums of money; the works that they build are permanent engineering structures of merit, and I hesitate greatly to either block or offend them in their enterprise.[54]

The question of whether the federal government should compete with private enterprise in the field of water development was the subject of intense debate in both Washington and the western states throughout the early years of the Reclamation Service. The matter was far from resolved, therefore, when Lippincott took over direction of the service's activities in California. His ambivalence on this point was a reflection of the experience he brought to the service and the peculiar arrangement under which he took over his post. Lippincott's early career had been spent straddling the two worlds of private and public water development. Born in Scranton, Pennsylvania, in 1864, he had studied at Dickinson College and the University of Kansas at Lawrence before taking his first job as a track engineer with the Santa Fe Railway. When Congress authorized the United States Geological Survey to undertake its first comprehensive hydrologic investigations of the West in 1888, Lippincott joined the rush of young engineers flocking to sign on with the new federal program. He worked as a topographer with the survey for three and a half years, but he was never able throughout this period to secure a permanent appointment. When a temporary shortage of funds in the summer of 1893 forced the government to furlough him, he resigned, taking a position as assistant engineer with the Bear Valley Irrigation Company, which was then developing a private project on the headwaters of the Santa Ana River.

Lippincott established a permanent residence in Los Angeles in 1891, and he soon had a lucrative consulting practice in partnership with another engineer, O. K. Parker. Lippincott's clients included a wide range of public and private agencies. He served as a resident hydrographer with the state of California and prepared water supply papers for the United States Geological Survey on the Gila and Santa Ana rivers and the San Bernardino artesian basin. He also assisted the communities of Santa Barbara, San Pedro, Pasadena, San Diego, Long Beach, and Fresno in developing waterworks of their own.[55] The city of Los Angeles, however, provided Lippincott with his most constant source of consulting fees. After representing the private irrigation interests who challenged the city's pueblo right to the underground flows of the Los Angeles River in the 1890s, Lippincott switched sides and served from the fall of 1897 through the spring of 1898 on a panel of engineers assisting the city in its litigation with residents of the San Fernando Valley. Thereafter, he undertook extensive surveys with Mulholland of the water supply of the Los Angeles River and the additional water resources that might be available to the city from outlying regions of the South Coast.[56]

Lippincott's close association with Los Angeles was well known to the officials of the United States Geological Survey when they retained him to perform hydrologic studies for them from 1895 to 1902. In fact, it was on the basis of the substantial fees the city paid Lippincott that Charles D. Walcott, director of the survey, specially requested that Lippincott receive a higher per diem rate than the government paid to any of its other consulting hydrographers.[57]

The Reclamation Service was placed under Walcott's authority upon its creation in 1902, and he promptly turned to Lippincott to serve as his supervising engineer for California. But Lippincott was reluctant to give up his private practice and insisted that he be permitted to retain an interest in his firm to supplement his income from the service. It was not an arrangement with which Newell, as head of the service, felt particularly comfortable. But the newly formed agency had not yet adopted any regulations on outside consulting by its employees, and as Newell pointed out in recommending Lippincott's appointment to the service, "It is not practicable, at present at least, to secure the services of men like Mr. Lippincott for a moderate rate of compensation, unless they be allowed to retain consulting practices in regions lying outside of the work they have in hand." An agreement was eventually worked out whereby Lippincott promised to exercise no more than a general supervision over the work of his partner and this only after regular working hours. Newell regarded this arrangement as only temporary, a necessary transition to enable Lippincott to extract himself altogether from the work of his firm. Lippincott, however, understood the agreement differently, and this confusion would be the cause of intense embarrassment to both men as events in the Owens Valley progressed.[58]

Lippincott's continued involvement with Los Angeles' water programs and his personal commitment to the improvement of that city soon led him into a far more "ticklish business" than the problems posed by the Edison Electric Company's interest in the

Owens Valley. For if Lippincott was of two minds when it came to conflicts between public and private development, there was no question which side he would join in case of a conflict between the Reclamation Service and Los Angeles. And the seeds of just such a conflict had been growing for some time in the mind of one of Lippincott's closest friends and associates, Fred Eaton.

Lippincott had worked closely with Eaton throughout the campaign for municipalization of the city's water supply. He had provided Eaton with facts and figures to support the call for termination of the lease which Eaton issued as chairman of the city's Republican Central Committee in 1896. In addition, he had represented Eaton's administration before the arbitration panel which was formed to fix a price for purchase of the Los Angeles City Water Company, and he had served on the campaign committee which Eaton formed to lead his drive for the bonds to buy out the company in 1899.[59]

Eaton's advocacy of municipal ownership of the city's water system, however, had been tied to a scheme of his own to bring the waters of the Owens Valley to Los Angeles. This was an idea he had borrowed from two private surveys performed in 1885 and 1891 which had shown it would be technically possible to construct a canal running 235 miles between the two regions in which water would flow entirely by gravity.[60] Eaton had been promoting the idea with Mulholland and anyone else who would listen since 1892, but no one had paid much attention.[61] Although the Reclamation Service had heard of the scheme, officials in Washington dismissed it as just another of the dozens of plans for bringing water to Los Angeles—"most of them chimerical"—that self-proclaimed experts in the South Coast had been producing for years. "Almost every possible or impossible solution of the water problem had been brought to the attention of the Geological Survey or the Reclamation Service at one time or another," wrote Arthur Powell Davis, Newell's assistant. Although Davis acknowledged that the survey's experts had examined Eaton's plan "in a more or less desultory way," he noted that "on the face of it, such a project is as likely as the City of Washington tapping the Ohio River."[62]

Recognizing that the Los Angeles City Water Company

lacked both the means and the desire to undertake a project of such mammoth proportions, Eaton had turned to municipalization as a way of gaining access to the far greater amounts of capital that public financing can provide. But he never conceived of the project as anything other than a private scheme that would work to his personal profit. He hoped to persuade the city to construct the aqueduct to a water supply in the Owens Valley which he would himself control. He intially proposed an aqueduct with the capacity to carry twenty thousand miner's inches of water, half of which would go to the city for domestic use under a long-term contract; the balance would be distributed by Eaton himself to irrigators and private companies outside the city limits. As the city grew after 1900, Eaton revised this proposal to increase Los Angeles' share to fifteen thousand inches, for which Eaton would receive an annual fee of one and a half million dollars.[63] Even though Eaton had made little progress with the promotion of his plan, the announcement of the Reclamation Service project for the Owens Valley threatened to end for all time the scheme he had been nurturing for more than a decade.

Eaton appeared in the valley in April 1904, just before Lippincott suspended work on the Reclamation Service project to wait for the arrival of a drill to test the bedrock at the Long Valley dam site. Although they were often seen together, both men later maintained that Eaton made no mention of his plans to Lippincott.[64] They soon returned to Los Angeles, while Eaton's son remained at Long Valley, conducting surveys and gathering stream measurements as he could. At the end of August the two men were back, nominally on a vacation trip with a small party of friends, although the Reclamation Service paid for their pack animals.[65] Lippincott led the party to Long Valley, where he showed them the proposed site of the government reservoir. Clausen had been brought along with the party, and although he did not know who Eaton was, he was concerned by the amount of information Eaton was being given. "Of course, Lippincott and I were talking all the time and Eaton was listening to everything we had to say and this probably was what Lippincott wanted to be done," Clausen recalled.[66]

Eaton then raced back to Los Angeles, where he persuaded

his former protégé Mulholland to return with him to the Owens Valley so that Mulholland could at least look over the resources of the area before it was too late and the water was committed to agriculture. Mulholland by this time had completed his studies of alternative water supplies the city might secure within its immediate area, and the results had not been encouraging. After examining the prospects for tapping Piru Creek in Ventura County and the Kern, Santa Ana, Mojave, and San Luis Rey rivers, Mulholland had concluded that all were either too small or already tied down by preexisting water rights claims to augment the water department's efforts to supply the city's growing population. He agreed, therefore, to examine Eaton's proposal, which he had dismissed many times before.

Together the two men set out for the Owens Valley by buckboard, traveling in secret and camping out along the way. The trip was not all hardship, though: it became a standing joke among the work crews along the line of the aqueduct in later years that they could trace the path Eaton and Mulholland had cut across the desert by following the trail of empty liquor bottles the two men left in their wake.[67] Once in the valley, Eaton was successful in convincing Mulholland that here lay a water supply capable of supporting a population of two million—ten times the number of people Los Angeles then contained. Mulholland returned to the city to confer with the members of the municipal water board while Eaton headed East to consult with Dillon and Hubbard, bond attorneys in New York, in a last fruitless attempt to form a private consortium to buy up water rights in the Owens Valley.[68]

Lippincott later swore that he did not learn of the city's interest in the Owens Valley until November 1904.[69] On September 17, however, he sent a confidential letter to Newell warning that "a situation has arisen with reference to the Owens project." Lippincott reviewed the limitations of the city's existing water resources and noted that the local officials had begun to look for an additional supply. "I find that they are looking towards the Owens River for a solution," Lippincott reported. "It will put us in rather an embarrassing position, however, with reference to the Owens Valley project. The matter has not at all come to a head, but I wish to inform you confidentially of what is under consideration."[70]

Lippincott's announcement of a potential conflict with the city was especially disturbing because the Reclamation Service officials as yet had no detailed information on which to determine whether the Owens Valley project was in fact feasible. Their soils engineer, Thomas Means, who had conducted his survey during the same trip on which Lippincott showed Eaton the Long Valley reservoir site, hurried a report of his findings to Lippincott on September 14. A study of geologic conditions in the valley was delivered to the Reclamation Service by Willis T. Lee on September 24. But the most important report, the one which Clausen as chief of the project would prepare, had still not been finished. Clausen by this time was back in Yuma, where the service had its first project in California already under construction. Newell was so concerned that he went to Yuma with Lippincott to urge Clausen to make haste in wrapping up his report.[71] Finally, on November 1, Clausen submitted his findings.

The Means and Clausen reports together presented a compelling case for the agricultural potential of the Owens Valley and the desirability of proceeding with a formal reclamation program. Means dwelt at length on the abundance of high-quality soils and warned that the valley offered more potentially valuable cropland than there was water to supply it. "There is more land than water for irrigation," Means reported, although he anticipated little difficulty in deciding where the water could best be used. He recommended leaving the low-lying alkaline lands alone because the salt grasses that grew there provided pasturage and were valued by the local ranchers as a source of winter feed. Instead, he advised, "if our irrigation systems were confined to the lands at present holding water rights and to such new lands as are in a good position for irrigation and which will require a minimum expenditure for drainage, I think all of the land for which there is water can easily be found."[72]

With regard to crops, Means noted the excellence of the hay and corn grown in the valley and the superior quality of its deciduous fruits. Because the success of the fruit crop depended on an absence of late spring frosts, however, Clausen concluded that fruits would never provide a certain source of revenue except for local consumption. Clausen held out great hope instead for the potential value of grapes and berries to the valley's economy whereas Means found the area ideally suited for growing hops. "Everything points to this," Means commented, "and should experimental work prove the adaptability to hop growing, the lands adapted to this crop can be made to produce large returns." Although both men acknowledged that hay and forage were still the principal crops of the region, Means noted, "We are, however, certain of the ability of the valley to produce excellent beef and this alone will warrant the expenditure of a large sum to improve conditions that the production may be doubled or trebled." With regard to the valley's isolation from its most proximate markets to the south, Clausen expressed confidence that "as soon as the traffic produced by the Owens Valley would warrant it the construction of [a] railroad would be almost sure to follow." Means summed up the case for both of them in his conclusion: "The Owens Valley seems to have many peculiar merits to favor it as an irrigation project. Among these may be mentioned abundance of water power, fertile soil, genial climate, nearby markets for all agricultural products in Tonopah and Goldfield, and a possible outlet to Los Angeles in the near future."[73]

One aspect of Owens Valley agriculture, however, came in for intense criticism, not only by Means and Clausen but also by numerous other visitors to the valley who knew something of irrigation techniques. This was the excessive use of water on many farms which was damaging the soil and turning some sections of the richest croplands into useless bogs. An independent report on agricultural conditions in Inyo County in 1905 noted: "The great majority of the farmers in the valley are very lax in their methods. It has been very easy for them to make a living, as about all they needed to do was pour the water onto their land and then harvest their crop . . . In many instances whole fields have been turned into quagmires."[74] This was in no way a new phenomenon. The white settlers had scarcely improved upon the primitive practices of their Indian predecessors, and as early as 1870 nearly all the cellars in Independence were flooding as a result of seepage from nearby drainage ditches.[75] So widespread had these practices become and so serious was their effect that by 1900 the Owens River ran dry in spring and later summer for fifty miles above the lake as a result of the ranchers' excessive diversions.[76]

The worst offenses in the way of profligate water use, according to Clausen, occurred on the lands of the Rickey Land and Cattle Company in Long Valley, where all the incoming streams were "unsystematically and wastefully spread over a large territory, thereby causing the growth of grass which is used as a summer range . . . In consequence of this so-called irrigation, much of Long Valley has been converted into an impassable swamp, and evaporation losses can only be estimated." Elsewhere in the valley, Clausen found that conditions were only slightly better:

> While some land, easily accessible by water, is suffering from drought, other lands due to wasteful use are being converted into swamps. Hundreds of acres once covered with sage brush and later by irrigation [which] were very productive have become either too wet for use or have become worthless due to the concentration of the alkali. In the vicinity of Bishop, the most extensively irrigated portion of the valley, the groundwater plane has risen to within two feet of the surface.[77]

Census records reveal that as a result of these destructive practices the total irrigated area of Inyo County declined by more than 5,000 acres between 1889 and 1899.[78] And in the face of so much waste, Clausen was unwilling even to venture a guess as to what the total appropriation of water for agriculture might be in the valley. On the few fields which he monitored closely he found the farmers applying enough water each year to cover their lands to a depth of seven to nine feet, more than double what he estimated was actually needed.[79]

Neither Clausen nor Means thought the situation in the valley was irredeemable. Means found a reason to hope for the future of the valley in the example of John S. Gorman, a former miner, sheriff, and tax collector who had been forced by poor health to settle on 150 acres of alkali land just north of Independence. Means reported that Gorman was one of the most enterprising farmers of the valley. A man who has demonstrated the feasibility of reclaiming the alkali lands and whose farm is an experimental demonstration of the profits of farming in Owens Valley . . . Mr. Gorman has yields of one to two tons of grain and five to eight tons of alfalfa on land which has been in salt grass and grease wood for many years. Such success is not the result of any peculiar circumstance which favors Mr. Gorman, but is entirely the result of intelligent application of well-known physical principles in his methods of farming.

Means was confident that other valley residents would be willing to learn from Gorman's example. "The general opinion among the farmers is that some system of drainage is as desirable as more extensive irrigation canals," he reported. "Drainage systems would reclaim large areas now swamped or only fit for pasturage and will enable any crop to be grown. The water developed by draining the upper lands will prove valuable for the irrigation of lands lower down the valley. For this reason it will permit the greatest area to be reclaimed if all possible lands are irrigated in the upper end of the valley."[80]

Clausen went even further in suggesting, "It is very probable that the efficiency of the present system with the existing canals and the present appropriation could be increased 50 percent by a judicious and economic management." Assuming that the farmers would agree to reduce the rate of their usage to an overall annual average of four acre-feet of water per acre, he estimated that the present water supply, without augmentation, would be sufficient to expand the irrigated area of the valley from its current coverage of approximately 40,000 acres to 97,223 acres in a dry year, 141,241 acres in a normal year, and 181,056 in a year of maximum streamflows.[81]

Some measure of Clausen's optimism was founded, no doubt, on the enthusiastic reception he had enjoyed in the valley. During his first summer there he had met the young lady he would marry, and he recognized that "Mr. Lippincott . . . knew that I had my heart and soul in Owens Valley."[82] He was careful to emphasize, therefore, that the valley residents were "very favorable to government aid and the sentiment now seems to be strongly in favor of having the Reclamation Service assume full charge of all existing canals."[83] And the people of the valley backed up Clausen's assurances on this score with a petition sent to the United States Secretary of the Interior at the same time that Clausen submitted his report. More than four hundred individuals owning a total of 102,433 acres signed this petition urging the government to proceed with its project "with all possible dispatch."[84]

This was the evidence Newell had to weigh in relation to Lippincott's report of a possible interest in the valley by the city of Los Angeles. On November 22, 1904, Newell joined Lippincott in Los Angeles and together they went to sound out the city's intentions in a meeting with Eaton, Mulholland, and the city attorney. The city's plans at this point were not yet formed; Los Angeles' officials needed more information to formulate a definite opinion. Lippincott proposed that the city be provided with a copy of Clausen's report, together with all the streamflow measurements and any other data the government had collected in connection with its studies. Most of this detailed information was available to the public in the regional offices of the Reclamation Service as soon as it was printed, and Lippincott regarded its direct delivery to the city officials as "only an ordinary and usual courtesy." The meeting was not inconclusive, however, because during its course Newell and Lippincott were emphatic in telling Mulholland and his cohorts that the government "would not step aside on Owens Valley unless the aqueduct was public owned from one end to another." Thus Eaton's dreams of private profit were dashed and the threat was removed that the city's future water supply might be held hostage to whatever he chose to charge for access to the Owens Valley.[85]

The Project Transformed

These arrangements, the steps Los Angeles took in the months following to determine its interest in the Owens Valley, and the Reclamation Service's involvement in that process were all matters of the deepest secrecy. Even the publishers of the Los Angeles newspapers were sworn not to report on the movements and activities of the city's water officials in relation to the Owens Valley. The fear was not simply that the Reclamation Service would be embarrassed by a report that it was considering abandoning its project in favor of Los Angeles. More important, the city officials were concerned that premature disclosure would result in a rush of speculators to the valley, thereby setting off an immediate upward spiral in land values as the local ranchers reacted to the threatened loss of their water. As Fred Eaton, who would act as the city's agent in acquiring lands for the municipal aqueduct, put it, "When our scheme gets out there is going to be an army of grafters in [the valley] filing upon and buying up water rights to my discomfort, and I must be given all the protection possible."[86]

Although these concerns more appropriately belonged to Los Angeles, the Reclamation Service was happy to go along with a policy intended to assure that the city's plans would not be queered before they got off the ground. Newell therefore answered the Owens Valley petitioners with a judicious degree of obfuscation, promising only that "the surveys and examinations will be pushed as rapidly as consistent with wisdom and economy, in view of all the conditions, and it is hoped that a feasible project can be worked out and constructed at an early date."[87]

But signs that the Reclamation Service's interest in the valley was declining were evident to anyone who looked closely. When the service first began operations in California, the Owens Valley ranked third among all the projects the agency was considering in that state. The Yuma project, which belonged as much to Arizona as it did to California, ranked first, followed by the Klamath River. All three, however, were rated as the service's "principal projects" in California, and all three were initiated simultaneously and carried forward in tandem, in the expectation that if one did not work out, construction on another could proceed without delay.[88] In contrast to the prominence given the Owens Valley in the service's second annual report at the end of 1903 and Lippincott's public report on the agency's activities in California in April 1904, however, the service's third annual report failed to mention the Owens Valley in a list of the principal projects the agency had under consideration, and Newell similarly ignored it in an article he published in *Popular Science* in December 1904.[89]

The problem was not all Los Angeles. Although the projects of the Bureau of Reclamation today depend upon vast taxpayer subsidies, the agency was originally intended to be self-supporting. The congressional fathers of the Reclamation Service imagined that the agency would operate initially on funds derived from the sale of public lands in the western states; the Reclamation Act of 1902 therefore specified that 51 percent of the funds derived in each state were to be spent there. Once the projects actually went into operation, the beneficiaries were expected to pay back the costs of construction. The first problem with this arrangement was that the states where large amounts of land could be offered for sale were not necessarily those which offered the most abundant opportunities for reclamation work. California's contributions to the reclamation fund, for example, ranked fifth among the western states in 1904, behind Oregon, North Dakota, Oklahoma, and Washington.[90] But in California the service was actively pursuing the prospects of developing new projects not only at Yuma, the Klamath River, and Owens Valley, but also in the valleys of the Sacramento River, the Kings River, Cache Creek, Story Creek, the Salinas River, and Puta Creek, at Clark Lake, and at Santa Barbara.[91]

The service's enthusiasm for initiating new projects soon outran its funding, and on November 1, 1904, Newell sent a confidential circular to his engineers announcing that the time had come to begin trimming back their operations in order to select carefully the projects they genuinely believed most deserved consideration. "It is evident there will not be sufficient funds for the construction of all of the projects which appear to be feasible," Newell declared,

> The first condition is that of the relative feasibility and benefit to the country as a whole . . . No project shall be considered feasible which is experimental in character, or in which the return of the funds is not guaranteed in the most effective manner. It is not intended to make experiments with this fund or to irrigate lands which may pro-

duce crops by dry farming in ordinary years, or to bring water to land, where, from any cause it is not probable that the lands will be continuously irrigated and cultivated."[92]

By these tests, the Owens Valley would still have ranked high on any list of desirable projects. In addition, the project was strikingly economical. Clausen had proposed the construction of a storage reservoir at Long Valley with a 260,000-acre-foot capacity which would service two parallel canals running down the east and west sides of the Owens Valley to a point south of the Fish Spring Hills. The total cost of construction was estimated at $2,292,398 for a project that would service 106,241 acres. This average cost of $21.58 per benefited acre compared most favorably with the other twenty-eight projects the Reclamation Service then had under active consideration; only two had a lower cost per acre than did the Owens Valley, and the average for all twenty-eight was $30.97 per acre.[93]

Simple economy, however, was not the only consideration for development. The requirement to spend 51 percent of the funds derived from each state in that state, for example, meant that the service would be compelled, as Newell pointed out, "to undertake and complete in Oklahoma a project which might not be considered on its merits in Colorado."[94] The service also had certain overriding priorities of its own. The Yuma project, for example, was pressed into construction ahead of all others despite the fact that it had the highest per-acre cost of all the service's fourteen active projects in 1904, in part because it was located on the Colorado River, which had been the geological survey's primary target for development ever since its first western irrigation studies in 1888.[95] In California, the Sacramento and San Joaquin valleys exercised a similar fascination for the federal reclamation engineers.

Would the Reclamation Service have abandoned the Owens Valley project even if Los Angeles had not interceded? The answer is almost certainly no. The funding problems of 1904 might well have delayed the project, but few areas offered as many opportunities as the Owens Valley for a dramatic demonstration of the benefits of systematic irrigation. And whereas farmers in other areas of the state, such as along the Kings River, were bitterly divided on the question of whether to accept federal assistance, the Owens Valley ranchers had welcomed the service with enthusiasm.[96] Having invested so much in preliminary surveys and obtained so favorable a recommendation from the project's chief engineer, it is hardly conceivable that the service would have simply withdrawn from the valley, particularly when the new agency had to work so hard in its early years to develop a political constituency among the often skeptical western legislators. As it was, however, the possibility of Los Angeles' interest provided an opportunity to cut back on the service's overextended finances in a way that Lippincott, at least, believed would reflect favorably upon the service. "I cannot see how the Reclamation Service could with propriety seriously oppose the City of Los Angeles in view of the fact that it cannot itself promptly proceed with the construction of the Owens Valley project. Moreover the greatest public necessity is certainly the use of the water in Southern California . . . So far as I am concerned, I certainly favor aiding them in their efforts," Lippincott told his superiors in Washington. "I believe that a connection with this enterprise on the part of the Reclamation Service or of its members will be considered as a marked public service."[97]

Lippincott was certainly sincere in his belief that he was serving some higher public duty by encouraging the Reclamation Service to abandon the Owens Valley in favor of Los Angeles. Eaton and Mulholland were his friends and closest professional associates, and as a result of his extensive experience on the South Coast, he knew as well if not better than they the severe limitations of that region's water supply. For years, he had been prominent as a spokesman for efforts to upgrade and expand the city's water system. And so, he readily accepted the wisdom of Eaton's proposal and soon went beyond a position favoring withdrawal by the service to one of actively working with Eaton to persuade the city to take up the project Eaton had suggested.

When the drilling rig he had ordered in April did not arrive during the summer of 1904, Lippincott suspended all work on the Owens Valley project as of September 3.[98] When the equipment became available the following spring, the question arose whether the service should reinstitute its surveys, given the prospect that the project was about to be abandoned anyway. Lippincott wrote to Newell on February 10, 1905, to ask that the drilling proceed on the argument that, although "there is some possibility of our not constructing the Owens Valley project but of our stepping aside in favor of the City of Los Angeles . . . there is a strong possibility that we may build the Owens Valley project at some later date." But it is evident that Lippincott did not seriously believe the Owens Valley project would ever be built because he proposed that, in light of the service's pinched financial condition, Los Angeles should be asked to pay for the cost of the drilling at Long Valley. Newell responded that he did not feel the Reclamation Service should be in the position of receiving payment directly from Los Angeles for its work, but that an agreement might be worked out under which the city would promise to pay an amount equivalent to the cost of the drilling into the reclamation fund for use in connection with other works in California.[99] Thus, within three months of Newell's and Lippincott's meeting with the city officials, and unbeknownst to the Owens Valley ranchers, the efforts of the federal engineers shifted from the development of an irrigation project for the agricultural improvement of the valley to the design of an aqueduct for Los Angeles.

Lippincott went even further three weeks later, when he signed a private contract with the Los Angeles Water Commission on March 6 to prepare a comprehensive survey with Mulholland of the possible sources the city could tap for additional water. This act by Lippincott naturally became the object of widespread condemnation when it was discovered later. Lippincott maintained in his defense that his work for the city included no confidential information obtained in connection with his work for the Reclamation Service and that the report in fact was composed simply of data he had already compiled and published in the course of his earlier studies for the city and the United States Geological Survey.[100] This assertion finds some support in the fact that Lippincott, only nine days after signing the contract, delivered the essence of his report to the city as a paper read before the Los Angeles Water Congress. Mulholland too tended to confirm Lippincott's depreciation of the report when he later testified that although the water commission's records show that Lippincott did not present his findings until May 22, 1905, the board had in fact been informed of the results of his study several months earlier. Mulholland advised that the water commissioners were usually sloppy in their record keeping.[101] But if the report contained little that was new, the city valued Lippincott's services highly. For his assistance, the city paid Lippincott $2,500, a somewhat spectacular sum for a set of warmed-over statistics, particularly in view of the fact that Lippincott's entire annual salary from the Reclamation Service was only $4,200.[102]

In order to avoid the charge that he was abusing his position with the Reclamation Service, Lippincott was careful in his formal report to cover all the possible sources of water for Los Angeles except the Owens Valley. But since the point of the report was to demonstrate that none of the alternative sources was viable, the connection to Eaton's plan was obvious to the city's water officials. Lippincott, in fact, could not resist emphasizing the obvious conclusion to be drawn from his study, and he ended his presentation to the Los Angeles Water Congress on March 15 with the remark: "While I cannot here present the details of a plan to meet this situation in and around the City of Los Angeles, I feel safe in saying that it can and will be properly met, and though the cost will be high, it can be made a paying business proposition. We should rather obtain and control a new supply than take by condemnation neighboring waters now required and used."[103]

When he came to submit his report formally to the city water commissioners on May 22, Lippincott appended a handwritten note at the end, under the admonition "Do Not Publish," which read, "Unfortunately these investigations and this report owing to possible conflict with other duties, must be confined to Southern California alone. The study of the Northern localities from which it may be possible to find relief, however, is assigned to other able engineers inspired with a full knowledge of the problem and the results to follow its accomplishment."[104] The water commissioners, in any event, were up to the mark and did not fail to recognize the connection. In their formal resolution accepting Lippincott's report, they noted that upon perusing Lippincott's findings, "It appears therefrom that, volume of water, cost of acquisition and delivery and engineering difficulties considered, the watershed of Owens River, among all possible sources of supply, affords the best for the purposes of the city."[105]

Before entering the contract with Los Angeles, Lippincott had asked for Newell's permission to accept the city's commission. Newell had advised against it, but Lippincott went ahead anyway without telling Newell. When Newell learned what Lippincott had done, he was livid.[106] Although the service had still not adopted a conflict of interest code, Newell in a meeting with his employees in El Paso in April 1905 had made a point of urging his engineers to drop all outside consulting and private employment immediately.[107] On May 17, he wrote to Lippincott:

> With reference to your taking up work in a consulting capacity for the City of Los Angeles, I regret exceedingly that my views as given on the subject have apparently not been taken in the spirit in which they were intended. The fact which we must all recognize is that there are certain laws and decisions on the subject of private employment which must be carefully considered, and beyond this there are questions of broad policy. The Reclamation Service and its men are constantly subject to attack and expect to be at all times. In my opinion it is better for you to know and anticipate the character of the attacks than to be taken unawares ... It has been my impression of earlier conversations that it was your intention to draw out absolutely from private business, until at least some one of the great irrigation works was successfully concluded. If you ask my advice, or invite suggestions, I must of necessity advise you to keep out of entanglements such as that of the City of Los Angeles . . . My feeling is that the amount you receive from the City of Los Angeles will not compensate you for the future difficulties.[108]

Lippincott's response on May 26 was less than satisfactory. After assuring Newell that his private work was not interfering with the time he devoted to government service, he lied by telling Newell that he had not yet submitted the report which the city water commissioners had formally accepted four days earlier. He then went on to review all the reasons why he felt the water of the Owens Valley was more valuable if used in Los Angeles, and he advised Newell, "I took the matter up with Senator [George C.] Perkins in San Francisco. He said he considered it not only a privilege for us to assist California municipalities in their water problems, but an obligation that we owed to the cities and to the state."[109]

Lippincott's thinly veiled threat to summon the senior United States senator from California in his defense if Newell threatened to pursue the question brought an immediate reaction. On June 3, Newell answered that although he appreciated the senator's position,

> the question, as I see it, is not so much as to this obligation, but as to how it should be carried out . . . As an officer of the Government [each engineer] is spending Government funds for a specific purpose and he must see that that purpose is carried out. He cannot of his own motion discharge other public functions or duties, otherwise, confusion would result . . . He has no right to divert reclamation funds or time to the study of this city water supply, nor as an individual has he the right to utilize his position to assist the city and obtain from the city a fee for such assistance . . . Our men have these opportunities. There is no question but that they can greatly assist in the development of city water supplies . . . At the same time this is not the work for which they are employed by the Government, and any departure from this work should receive the full acquiescence of the Secretary [of the Interior], otherwise we will be open to the very serious charge of utilizing public information and experience acquired in public employment for private gain.[110]

Lippincott was unimpressed. He sent a brief letter complaining that he was too busy to prepare a detailed reply and pointedly reminded Newell that he was just then making arrangements to take a party of congressmen on a tour of reclamation projects in California in the middle of June.[111] It was not until the end of that month that Lippincott got around to submitting a formal request for permission to accept the city's offer of a contract, and by then the work had long since been done.[112]

Lippincott had gone even further in assisting Eaton's plan.

Three days before he signed his contract with Los Angeles, he asked Eaton to investigate a series of applications for rights-of-way across the public lands in the vicinity of the Long Valley reservoir site that had been filed by various companies interested in power development. This act confused Lippincott's superiors in Washington. "I fail to understand in what capacity he is acting in connection with the Department that he should be called upon for such a report," commented Newell's chief assistant, Arthur Powell Davis, when Lippincott told him what Eaton would be doing. Lippincott explained that since all the Reclamation Service engineers in the Owens Valley had been reassigned to Yuma following his suspension of their work the preceding fall, he had no personnel available to determine whether these applications would interfere with the service's irrigation plans. Since Eaton was engaged in negotiations of his own with the principal applicant, T. B. Rickey, and planned to be in the valley that summer anyway, Lippincott wanted his advice in an unofficial capacity. Eaton had asked for a formal commission from the Reclamation Service, but Newell had vetoed that request; so Lippincott gave him a letter directing him to prepare a personal report.[113]

Lippincott, of course, knew that Eaton was working to undermine the Reclamation Service project in the Owens Valley by buying up options on lands in the valley that would be needed for the city's aqueduct. Eaton promptly made use of Lippincott's letter to gain access to the detailed records at the federal land office in Bishop. In addition to the letter, Eaton carried with him the official maps that the service's survey parties had prepared for the irrigation project; he directed the officials at the land office to make tracings of these maps, which he then used as a guide in selecting the properties to buy. At the land office, Eaton was careful never to say that he was acting as an employee of the Reclamation Service, but only as Lippincott's agent in the matter of the right-of-way applications. Nevertheless, the fact that Eaton and Lippincott were known to be close friends, the fact that they had often been seen together touring the project site, and the fact that Eaton seemed to have an insider's knowledge of the project led many people in the valley to conclude that Eaton was working on behalf of the government in some way in his land purchases.

Eaton not only did nothing to correct this misapprehension, he even boasted that he was personally directing the Reclamation Service decisions on which lands to withdraw on behalf of the irrigation project.[114]

Eaton's most important use of the Lippincott letter was in connection with the Rickey lands. Because Rickey owned the Long Valley reservoir site, keystone of the government project, the fact that Eaton was most interested in buying him out only underscored the impression in the valley that Eaton was working for the federal government in an effort to remove the principal opponent to the Reclamation Service's plan. But Rickey's lands were just as important to Los Angeles as they were to the service. It was not that the city needed to build a reservoir at Long Valley; Mulholland included such a reservoir in his early plans for the aqueduct but soon dropped it as unessential to the operation of the city's system. The lands the city needed instead lay far to the south, below Independence, where the city planned to install the intake of its aqueduct to capture the flows of the Owens River after the needs of the agricultural communities in the upper end of the valley had been met. Here the lands were useless for agriculture, and Eaton was able to buy them cheaply for the city. But the Rickey lands at Long Valley headed Eaton's list of properties for acquisition because once the city had control of that key site, with its valuable water rights, the Reclamation Service plan would be finished.

On March 23, Eaton gleefully informed the city that the prize was his; Rickey had given him an option the night before, "after a week of Italian work."[115] Eaton did not specify what offer he had made that Rickey could not refuse, but it seems clear that the key was Eaton's putative authority in connection with the power company applications. It was known that Rickey had been interested for some time in selling out his land and cattle interests in Inyo County, and Eaton had been dickering with him over a price.[116] But Rickey was not withdrawing from the valley altogether; instead, as a partner in the Nevada Power Mining and Milling Company, he was vitally interested in the success of that company's efforts to develop a hydroelectric project on Bishop Creek to deliver power to the mining fields at Tonopah and

Goldfield.[117] This project, however, was threatened by a competitive interest in hydroelectric power development by the Owens River Water and Power Company, backed by Edson F. Adams, president of the Farmers and Merchants Exchange Bank of Oakland. The Owens River Water and Power Company enjoyed an advantage in the race to develop the area's resources because it held a water rights filing on the Owens River which predated and was therefore superior even to the claims of the Reclamation Service.[118] Eaton had been associated with both these companies in connection with his earlier efforts to develop the aqueduct as a private venture. As he explained his original plan, "My idea of the method for working out the idea [for the aqueduct] was to organize a strong company, which should develop the great water power of the streams . . . and then combine with the electric features, the project of bringing the water to the San Fernando Valley, this city [Los Angeles], and the tributary lands."[119]

Because Eaton could legitimately claim he had been invested with the authority to recommend whether the government should approve the right-of-way applications filed by both the Nevada Power Mining and Milling Company and the Owens River Water and Power Company, he could thus offer Rickey a measure of assistance which no other potential purchaser of Rickey's holdings at Long Valley could match. Eaton had, in fact, told Rickey on February 24, 1905, that the government was referring all of Rickey's power applications to him for a report; Lippincott's letter of March 3, therefore, simply gave Eaton the tangible evidence he needed to prove his claim to Rickey.[120] On March 16, Eaton followed through with a recommendation to Lippincott that the Nevada power company's application be approved and that of the Owens River company be denied. This letter marked the beginning of Eaton's "week of Italian work" with Rickey, which culminated on March 22 in Rickey's agreement to sell the lands to Eaton.

Eaton's claim in his recommendation to Lippincott that the Nevada company's project would not interfere with the Reclamation Service's irrigation project was, however, vigorously denied by Clausen when Lippincott asked him to check over Eaton's report. Eaton advised in connection with the Nevada company's application, "I cannot see in what way this enterprise will interfere with any plans the government may have for utilizing this creek to best advantage." Clausen, however, demonstrated on the basis of the service's streamflow records that the Nevada company's project would destroy the viability of the government's proposed reservoir and severely reduce the water available for agriculture in the very months it would be most needed. As for the application of the Owens River company, Eaton acknowledged that "the right of way they now ask for offers no interference in itself"; but he warned that at some future date, if the project were fully developed, it would interfere with irrigation below the proposed dam site at Long Valley. Therefore, Eaton argued, "It is well to give them notice at once that the Government will not permit their irrigation plans to be obstructed and set aside by speculations of this character." Eaton's reasoning on this point was somewhat specious, and the irony of his stalwart defense of irrigation for the Owens Valley certainly appears cruel in light of the fact that he was himself the foremost obstruction to the Reclamation Service plans. But Clausen had no idea of Eaton's relationship to the city, and he found no fault with this recommendation. In fact, Clausen went even further in his response to Eaton's report and suggested that a host of other applications not even considered by Eaton also be denied and the lands of the Owens River Gorge be placed under government withdrawal. Lippincott, however, ignored Clausen's protests, and on May 29, the same day the Los Angeles water commissioners appropriated the funds to take up Eaton's option on the Rickey lands, Lippincott recommended approval of the Nevada Power Mining and Milling Company application.[121]

Perhaps the most remarkable aspect of Eaton's maneuverings is that it took the city two months from the time he had secured an option on Rickey's lands to decide whether to take up the option and commit itself to the construction of an aqueduct of its own. In fact, in the six months that elapsed between the city's first tentative confirmation of an interest in the Owens Valley in the meeting with Lippincott and Newell and the decision at the end of May to take up the Rickey option, it was Eaton and Lippincott, not Mulholland, who were most vigorous in urging the water commission to accept the plan for the aqueduct. Eaton's frustration with this turn of events is evident in a letter he wrote on March 25, 1905, urging the city to take up the Rickey option and forward him the necessary funds to secure the other lands needed for the aqueduct in the lower half of the valley: "If the City had money, I could buy up the entire river in 60 days, before anyone could get on to our curves, but when they commence to impress the people [of the Owens Valley] with the idea that this is their only supply, in order that the officials may escape a roast Eaton gets smacked right in the eye (excuse the expression) unless he is strongly entrenched with the city against the get-rich-quick man."[122]

Part of the reason for the city's hesitancy was that it had no legitimate way of investing public funds secretly in a venture which was still very speculative. The city paid out a total of $233,865 for the options Eaton secured at Long Valley in March and downstream on the Owens River in April and May.[123] But the city had no funds set aside for this purpose; in essence, it was borrowing the funds against the hope of being able to repay them from the proceeds of a future bond issue that the voters would have to approve to pay for the aqueduct. The water commission, moreover, was concerned that the city charter prohibited its expenditure of any funds outside the city limits. But as one member of the commission, J. M. Elliott, later commented, "At the time I was on the Water Board I did not altogether comply with the law strictly; when I saw that an act tended in a good business way to make money for the city, I did it."[124] The problem ultimately boiled down to the reluctance of the city treasurer to authorize the expenditure of funds for which he would be personally liable if the future bond issue should fail. A party of private businessmen was therefore gathered who agreed to cover the treasurer's potential liability with an indemnity bond of $300,000.[125]

Once the city had determined to go ahead, it found that Eaton had one more trick up his sleeve. The dashing of his scheme for personal profit from the aqueduct by Lippincott and Newell in their meeting in November, 1904, still rankled with Eaton. The project had to be turned over to the city, and, as Eaton later commented, "This I disliked to do, for it would deprive me of what I believed to be a splendid opportunity to make money, and one which I had had in view for a dozen years."[126] But Eaton's dreams of a water empire had gradually shifted to a vision of himself as a cattle baron, and he had the means to realize this new ambition in the option he held on the lands at Long Valley. The city had to have those lands to stop the Reclamation Service project, and so long as he held the option he could dictate his own terms. The city, moreover, could not bypass him and open negotiations of its own with the valley landowners without breaking the veil of secrecy which they regarded as essential to the protection of the project.

The water commission first approved Eaton's plan for the aqueduct in concept on May 22, 1905, the day it formally accepted Lippincott's report. At this time, Eaton offered the city an option for all the Rickey lands in Long Valley. Payment for the option was to go directly to T. B. Rickey, who would pay Eaton a commission on the sale. On May 29, the water commission appropriated $50,000 to be paid out in accordance with Eaton's option agreement. On June 2, however, Eaton produced a new option agreement altogether different from the one he had presented to the board ten days earlier. The new agreement provided for payments directly to Eaton, and only a part of Rickey's land at Long Valley was offered to the city. In the words of an auditor who investigated this startling development for the city several years later, "The evidence of both Mr. Mulholland and Mr. Mathews [the city attorney] shows that Mr. Eaton's attitude was unexpected, was not in accordance with any arrangement that they may have had, and that for two days they fought at swords' points in securing from Mr. Eaton the property needed for the aqueduct . . . notwithstanding the fact that . . . the necessity of Mr. Eaton in the deal was only for the use of his name to forestall public knowledge."[127]

The city ultimately acquired options on 22,670 acres of the Rickey lands. But Eaton fought to retain the Long Valley reservoir site. Under the terms of the agreement Eaton finally struck with the city, Los Angeles promised to pay him $450,000 for water rights and an easement allowing the eventual construction of a small reservoir on the land he had an option to purchase for

$500,000. If Los Angeles failed to make payment in full by the end of 1905, the price would go up to $475,000. And if for any reason the project were not built, all the land would revert to Eaton. Eaton retained control of the rest of the property, a total of 22,850 acres, together with 5,000 head of Rickey's cattle, 100 horses and mules, and all Rickey's farm equipment—by 1912 estimated by the city to have a combined value of $500,000. The cattle alone were worth $7-10 per head.

Eaton was thus paid the entire purchase price of the property, 90-95 percent in cash and the balance in livestock, while still retaining control of half the land. All this he obtained for a total cash outlay of only $15,000 by his own estimate. In addition, he made another $100,000 on commissions paid by the city for the other lands he transferred to it. For the future, moreover, Eaton looked forward to a steady expansion of his new cattle empire as the other ranchers downstream in the valley were driven out of business by the aqueduct and forced to sell their cattle at reduced prices to him.[128] Finally, and in the long run most important, Eaton retained control of the reservoir site. On this point he was emphatic; he told the water commission, "I want you to understand I am not giving you any right to the Long Valley reservoir site, except the right to overflow it, and if you are not going to take it, I am going to use it for my own."[129] Eaton's foresight in this respect would spark bitter conflict twenty years later.

The Way Out

The agreement with Eaton was formally accepted by the water commission on June 5, 1905. By this time the city realized it had to make haste to complete its acquisition of properties needed for the aqueduct; the secrecy which had enshrouded the plans could not be guarded much longer. Eaton, for one, had been indiscreet in his activities in the valley. He had coerced some ranchers into selling their properties to him with the threat that the Reclamation Service was about to withdraw from its project, and he had boasted to others that their lands would soon be returned to desert conditions and so their only choice was "to sell out or dry out."[130] Lippincott's remarks to the Water Congress in March had hinted broadly at the existence of a plan, and his speech was scheduled to be reprinted in the July edition of *Out West*. In addition, Lippincott had another article appearing in the August issue of *Forestry and Irrigation* in which he presented the "General Outlook for Reclamation Work in California" without mentioning the Owens Valley project at all.[131] Clausen, though he had been reassigned to Yuma, had learned from Newell that "there was something else in the wind."[132] And friends of the water commission members had been privately advised not to invest in Owens Valley; Mulholland had even been quoted as telling one associate, "Do not go to Inyo County. We are going to turn that country dry."[133]

Newell, in particular, was anxious to get matters resolved. The Reclamation Service project in the Owens Valley, after all, had been in a state of suspension effectively since April and officially since September 1904. The government, therefore, was vulnerable to the charge that, by continuing to hold the lands it had withdrawn from entry, it was acting to protect Los Angeles' interests by blocking private development of the valley. Newell's problem was complicated by the fact that the city's plans were still a secret, and Los Angeles had not made any formal declaration of its interest in the Owens Valley even in confidence. Newell, therefore, had to find a way to extricate the Reclamation Service from the Owens Valley in such a way as to avoid the appearance of double-dealing.

On May 24, Newell advised Lippincott that he wanted to establish a panel of engineers to review the status of the Owens Valley project and make a formal recommendation to the secretary of the interior to abandon in favor of the city. "The matter is apparently one of public discussion," Newell complained, "and in view of this fact early action should be taken . . . Please inform me as to the earliest practicable date when Mr. Clausen can make his report for submission to a board for final decision. This should be as soon as possible after July 1."[134] Lippincott, however, waited to act on this urgent instruction until after the matter of Eaton's contract had been resolved and the Long Valley site was safely under the city's control. On June 7 he wrote to Clausen, "I desire you to bring your report on the Owens Valley situation up to date, and to submit this report to a Board of Engineers for final decision as to what course should be taken with respect to the Owens Valley Project. This matter is urgent and should be attended to as soon as possible after the 1st of July."[135]

Newell initially felt that Lippincott, as supervising engineer for the region, should sit on the panel. But Lippincott's involvement with the city of Los Angeles was already the matter of some gossip and considerable condemnation among the Reclamation Service engineers. Consequently, one of the other engineers Newell had designated for the panel, W. H. Sanders, refused to sit with Lippincott. "Sanders is greatly disturbed at being assigned to consider with Lippincott the Owens Valley matter," Newell told his chief assistant, Arthur Powell Davis. "I advised him to attend . . . and if he was not thoroughly satisfied, to hold the conclusions out to another meeting to be held later on . . . He is greatly annoyed by Lippincott's attitude . . . [and] if Lippincott insists on rejecting the Owens Valley in favor of the City of Los Angeles, Sanders will probably refuse to assume the responsibility and ask for another board of men wholly impartial."[136]

Two days after he wired Clausen to prepare a report for presentation sometime after July 1, Lippincott changed his mind and wired Newell to propose that the meeting of the board be moved up to June 20 and that it be held in Los Angeles, with Clausen sitting on the panel together with himself and W. C. Mendenhall, a hydrologist with the United States Geological Survey who had just completed a study of the groundwater resources of the South Coast and who had already endorsed Eaton's plan for the aqueduct.[137] "For some reason Mr. Lippincott is in a great hurry with this matter," Davis commented. "There is strong evidence that Lippincott is determined to railroad through a preconceived idea of his own."[138]

Newell's first reaction to this problem was to temporize. "Ample time should be taken to appoint a strong board," he wrote to Davis from the western states, where Newell was on tour.

> Lippincott being, in popular opinion at least, an employee of the City of Los Angeles, should not serve on the board or any man who has worked under him. The matters to be discussed are very delicate and there should be no

question arise such as might if any of Lippincott's men, Mendenhall, Clausen, or anyone connected with the City of Los Angeles, were on the board. In other words, its absolute impartiality should be guarded with great care or we will be exposed to criticism, possibly of spending Government funds for city or corporate purposes. If an unquestionably impartial board decided to withdraw in favor of Los Angeles, then there can be no points brought against us. On the other hand, a board on which are Lippincott, Clausen, and others would be open to charges of being packed in favor of Los Angeles, whether true or not."[139]

Davis agreed that delay was desirable under the circumstances and proposed that D. C. Henny be appointed to chair the panel. Newell readily agreed because Henny, as the Reclamation Service's supervising engineer in North Yakima, Washington, was well removed from the situation, and he was, moreover, one of the most respected members of the service. On June 13, Davis wrote to Henny to ask him to serve:

It seems that the Reclamation Service has been placed in a very embarrassing position in regard to these investigations. The Service having been already committed to the projects in the Yuma and Klamath valleys, it would not be possible to take up the Owens Valley project for some time to come . . . If the project is to be held for the Reclamation Service, it is not necessary to go into any great detail with surveys for several years, as it cannot be taken up for some time. If the project is to be taken up by the city, any expenditure of reclamation funds there is illegal and will lead to scandal, if persisted in. The situation is therefore a delicate one, and it is the desire to have it handled with a firm hand by persons entirely loyal to the Service, without any personal interest. For this reason, Mr. Lippincott, who is consulting engineer for the city of Los Angeles, will not serve on the board, and I am instructed to exclude all engineers who have had any connection with the work.[140]

Henny conferred with Sanders and then advised Davis that they would both accept the assignment, given the new conditions Newell had stipulated. "Our opinions of the principles which should govern employees in the Service agree," Henny wrote on June 20, "it being illegal and vicious, if not destructive in its effects, besides as appears now, leading to serious embarrassment, if employees are permitted to engage in any outside employment."[141]

By this time Newell was also revising his opinion on the necessity for haste. While traveling in California on June 17, he had been approached by Governor George C. Pardee and the state's newly elected United States senator, Frank P. Flint. Both men emphasized their support for Los Angeles in the matter, expressing emphatically their belief that "in the interests of the greatest good to the greatest number, the Government should not interfere with any possible use of the water by the City of Los Angeles."[142] Newell already knew that Lippincott had brought in Senator Perkins on his behalf; clearly, the circle of people privy to the secret of Los Angeles' activities was expanding rapidly and prompt action was needed. But although Newell was willing to accommodate the city and its powerful political friends, he still hoped to obtain a public proposal from Los Angeles on which to base a decision against the Reclamation Service's plan for the Owens Valley. He wrote to Davis on June 21,

> It was my idea that we should bring this matter to an early close, but . . . as matters have turned out, I think it would be preferable to wait until the City of Los Angeles makes a formal request to the Secretary [of the Interior] to turn the work over to the city. Such a request will probably be coupled with the statement that the city will refund to the reclamation fund the cost of the work accomplished. If this is done, we will be in a far better position than for our engineers to take the initiative in withdrawing from the project.[143]

Newell had already attempted to extract such a declaration of its intentions from the city in the course of berating Lippincott for his contract with Los Angeles. "The solution of this question," Newell told Lippincott on June 3, "lies in the very simple expedient of referring the city authorities to the Secretary of the Interior, who in turn has it in his power to consider the equities of the case and instruct [the Reclamation Service] to give such assistance as may be necessary and desirable."[144] But the attempt misfired badly. Although the Los Angeles Board of Water Commissioners responded promptly to Newell's suggestion with a formal letter on June 5, the letter went to Newell, not to the secretary, and it made no mention of any promise to pay for the Reclamation Service's work. Still worse, the wording of the letter virtually assured that Newell would be unable to show it to anyone without embarrassing himself. "Fully recognizing the valuable assistance rendered the City of Los Angeles by the United States Geological Survey Department through your intercession in its efforts to obtain an additional water supply from the Owens River Valley," the letter began portentously, "we deem it necessary in order to show our good faith in the matter to keep you informed of the progress being made by us to that end, so that it may be shown that we are not uselessly hampering the work already begun in that valley by the reclamation branch under your direction." The board then went on to review its purchases in the valley, and concluded by pointing out that although their work to date had been kept secret, "All our actions in this business will be held open to the scrutiny of your Department at all times, as considering the helpful and accommodating spirit in which we have been treated by you we consider such confidence your due."[145]

With this tortured prose, the commission could scarcely have created a more perfect impression that Newell had been as closely allied with them as Lippincott in the effort to subvert the Reclamation Service's plan for the Owens Valley. This point was amply demonstrated by the fact that the Owens River Water and Power Company—disgruntled at the shabby treatment they felt their application for a right-of-way had received at Lippincott's hands —filed suit to secure a copy of this letter as soon as they learned of its existence.[146] Newell consequently gave up any hope of persuading the city to declare its intentions openly; Davis named a third, disinterested member to the panel of engineers; and a meeting of the panel to review the Owens Valley project was called for the end of July in San Francisco.[147]

Because the meeting would be public, and because it would be held in a city where the newspapers had not been sworn to secrecy, this decision effectively set the deadline for the city to complete its preparations to take over the Owens Valley project. Eaton and Lippincott immediately stepped up their efforts. With Lippincott's assistance, Eaton was provided with mules and a packer at federal expense to take a photographer around the Owens Valley, taking pictures of the streams and government gauging stations.[148] Lippincott's partner, O. K. Parker, was rushed out to complete the city's surveys in Long Valley, and Fred Eaton soon had another party of surveyors working their way down the line of the aqueduct in July.[149] Mulholland and Eaton meanwhile pushed ahead with their land purchases.

But the illusion that Eaton was working for the Reclamation Service could no longer be maintained because the city's acquisitions had by now reached Haiwee Point, far south of any conceivable interest in irrigation on the part of the federal government. Suspicions in the valley of Eaton's true intent now began to approach certainties, and with that the effort to maintain secrecy started to fall apart. On July 12, Stafford W. Austin and Richard Fysh, register and receiver, respectively, of the local federal land office, wrote to the commissioner of the General Land Office in Washington:

> Within the last two months, a prominent businessman of Los Angeles, Mr. Fred Eaton, claiming in certain matters to be the representative of J. B. Lippincott . . . has purchased to the extent of about $1,000,000 . . . all the patented lands within the government's withdrawal for reservoir purposes and also riparian and other rights along the Owens River for over fifty miles. This purchaser now practically controls the waters of the river. The well-known friendship between the purchaser and Engineer J. B. Lippincott made it easy for these valuable rights to be secured as it was generally understood that they were to be used for the benefit of the government project. There is now, however, a rapidly growing conviction in the minds of the people that this purchaser has secured this large supply of water in order to take it to Southern California . . . and furthermore that he has acted upon information received as to the ultimate intention of the government . . . which if made public at all, ought surely to be given first to the people of this district who are most

nearly concerned in it . . . We are not making any charges whatever but are simply advising you of the important events which have taken place here in order that the proper authorities may be placed on their guard in case these purchases are antagonistic to the government project.[150]

In the weeks to come, the statements of Austin and Fysh would become more precise and pointed, but this letter set the tone for all that would follow. They concluded with a warning that if the government abandoned its project now, Los Angeles would be left in full control "and in a position to destroy the future prospects of the valley . . . Such abandonment at this time will make it appear that the expensive surveys and measurements of the past two years have all been made in the interests of a band of Los Angeles speculators, and it will result in bringing our reclamation service into disrepute."[151] Although no newspaper had yet printed these reports, the secret was out; the embarrassment Newell had hoped to avoid had begun.

The week after they mailed this report to Washington, Austin and Fysh journeyed out to the Kearsarge Pass, where Senator Perkins was on an outing with friends from Fresno. They presented their charges to him, together with a more detailed account of Eaton's activities; Perkins suggested they bring the matter to the attention of the secretary of the interior.[152] On July 24 they made a similar presentation to W. H. Sanders, who was touring the Owens Valley to prepare for his participation on the panel of engineers reviewing the project. Sanders immediately sent a wire to Arthur Powell Davis in Washington in which he posed a single question: "Has Fred Eaton the right to claim he represents the Reclamation Service in Owens Valley?"[153]

The opening session of the panel was now only three days away, and Lippincott had to race to separate himself from Eaton and get onto the record a denial of his culpability in Eaton's affairs. The night before the panel met, Lippincott wired Eaton, "Reported to me and publicly accepted that you had represented yourself as connected with the Reclamation Service and acting as my agent in Owens Valley. As this is entirely erroneous and very embarrassing to me, please publicly deny it or the service will be forced to do so."[154] Lippincott attempted to soften the blow to his old friend with a letter he sent to follow up the wire that same day: "I regret to take this matter up with you at all, but it has been presented to the Service in such a way that I am compelled to do so. I understand that it has been unadvisable heretofore for you to let the people of Owens Valley know really what you were doing, but I trust that the time has arrived when you can soon explain the situation to them and relieve me of the misconception I am placed in." Nevertheless, Lippincott instructed Eaton not only to give him a letter of denial but also to deny the charges publicly. He further directed Eaton to see Austin "and if you can possibly do so, convince him that he is in error both as to his conclusion and his premises."[155]

Eaton was furious. Richard Fysh in a deposition later described Eaton's arrival in the land office at Independence the morning he received Lippincott's wire: "Eaton said he had a telegram from Mr. Lippincott and it was a damned hot one and he, Eaton, did not like it a little bit, as it put him in a wrong light."[156] Eaton nevertheless made all the denials Lippincott asked for and even arranged to have a statement of his true purpose in the valley printed in the local newspapers.[157]

The panel of engineers opened its hearing into the Owens Valley project on July 27. Once he had been denied a place on the panel for himself, Lippincott had attempted to dissuade Clausen from even appearing to testify on behalf of the project.[158] But Clausen made the journey from Yuma nonetheless and was the first to speak in the morning session, where he essentially reviewed the findings he and Means had made in their earlier reports.[159] Lippincott was next to speak, but before he could begin, the statement of charges that Austin had left with Senator Perkins was read into the record. Lippincott submitted his own written statement in response to the charges, but because Austin dealt principally with Eaton's activities, Lippincott limited his remarks on this score to a denial that he had given Eaton any information about the government project in the spring of 1904 and an affirmation that he had never appointed Eaton as an agent of the Reclamation Service. "I know nothing of Mr. Eaton's general statements and I do not consider that I am responsible for them," Lippincott said. "Mr. Eaton, however, is a friend whom I have known for many years."[160]

Lippincott began his testimony on the Owens Valley project

by agreeing with Clausen: "I believe that there is a good project in the Owens Valley and that it is worth careful consideration." He went on, however, to argue that the water of the Owens Valley would be far more valuable if used in Los Angeles, "the home of about 200,000 energetic, prosperous, and cultured people . . . undoubtedly one of the most delightful residence cities in the United States." He pointed out that there was not currently enough money in the reclamation fund to undertake the project at this time, and he contended that even if the money were available, it could be better spent elsewhere rather than in a remote valley where only staple crops could be grown. He concluded by asserting that the question was closed, in any event, because the land and water rights purchases by the city of Los Angeles had already rendered the government project impossible. "The whole motive and spirit of my relation to this subject simply was to aid the City of Los Angeles as a municipality," Lippincott told the panel, "because I thought it was for the public good, and I have no occasion to change my mind on the subject."[161]

Senator Perkins attended the afternoon session to urge the panel to recommend abandonment in favor of Los Angeles. "The question now is, is it in the public service to supply the water to great municipal and suburban interests rather than to a mere local interest," Perkins told the panel. But the bulk of the senator's remarks were devoted to a ringing defense of Lippincott: "I know Mr. Lippincott is above any wrong action . . . He has the confidence and respect of all who know him and his integrity and faithfulness to his trust, I think, cannot be questioned."[162] The panel finished the day in a vain effort to induce the president of the Owens River Water and Power Company to make a clear statement as to whether he actually intended to proceed with his project.

The panel spent all the next day in executive session, preparing its report. The engineers accepted Clausen's and Means's estimates of the value the project would have for the Owens Valley and concluded that "the project appears to be attractive and deserves further study and investigation." But they noted as well that the project would be rendered infeasible if the Owens River Water and Power Company proceeded with its plans, if the local farmers could not be convinced to reduce their waste of water, or if a reservoir could not be built at Long Valley as a result of the city's purchases there. They recommended, therefore, an immediate investigation of the legal rights of both the power company and Los Angeles to interfere with the project. If these investigations revealed that the federal government's rights were superior, then the panel concluded that the Reclamation Service should proceed with final cost estimates and negotiations with the local farmers to reduce their rate of water use. On the most important point of the city's interest, the panel recommended that the service refuse any request from the city to withdraw from the valley except on the specific order of the secretary of the interior. In sum, the panel proposed that the entire project should be placed in suspension, with the federal government retaining all its rights and the lands it had withdrawn from entry "until either the project has been proven infeasible or other good reasons become apparent for such surrender and restoration."[163]

Los Angeles' interest in the Owens Valley was now a matter of public record. But the city had won its race to complete the preparations for its project before the panel released its findings. On the same night the engineers adjourned in San Francisco, Mulholland returned to Los Angeles from a final round of buying in the valley. "The last spike is driven," Mulholland announced. "The options are all secured."[164] The next morning, the *Los Angeles Times* breached the veil of secrecy which had surrounded Eaton's aqueduct with a massive report on the city's plans to bring the Owens River south for storage in the San Fernando Valley. In characteristically exalted prose, the *Times* proclaimed, "The cable that has held the San Fernando Valley vassal for ten centuries to the arid demon is about to be severed by the magic scimitar of modern engineering skill."[165]

CHAPTER THREE

The Politics
of Appropriation

　　　　The Reclamation Service, apart from Lippincott's active encouragement, had stood until this time as the principal obstacle to Los Angeles' plans for the aqueduct. The decision of the review panel did not remove this obstacle; it simply placed the federal government's project in suspension. The city's land and water rights acquisitions had effectively nullified any threat that the Reclamation Service might proceed with its project in the Owens Valley. But even so, Mulholland could not afford to have the service as his adversary because federal approval of the aqueduct was essential, both to remove the service altogether from the Owens Valley and to secure the critical rights-of-way the aqueduct needed to cross the federal lands lying between Los Angeles and the Owens Valley. In his campaign to win Washington's blessing for the aqueduct, however, Mulholland had to contend with the fact that Los Angeles had not yet declared its intention to proceed or demonstrated its ability to fund such a project. The solution to both these problems lay in the promotion of a bond issue which would demonstrate the community's commitment to the project while providing the funds to take up the options the city had secretly acquired. Before turning to the federal government, therefore, Mulholland had to win the support of the voters of Los Angeles for a bond issue to finance a project which few city residents understood was even needed.

His efforts in this regard were complicated initially by the abruptness of the *Times'* disclosure of his plans. But Mulholland was not the only promoter of the aqueduct to be upset by the sudden revelation. The appearance of the *Times'* report that morning left Fred Eaton unprepared and trapped in the Owens Valley, where he had to stare down an angry crowd of ranchers before beating a hasty retreat on the first train to San Francisco.[1] More important for the long-term prospects of the project, by breaking the gentleman's agreement among the other newspaper publishers and scooping every paper in town, the *Times* stirred the editorial ire of William Randolph Hearst's *Los Angeles Examiner*. At first the *Times* gloated over its coup. While the *Examiner* ran a front-page apology from Mayor Owen McAleer condemning the *Times'* perfidy, the *Times* chuckled that the *Examiner's* editor, Henry A. Loewenthal, was "flying around all day like a loose button on a barn door."[2] But the *Times'* publisher, Harrison Gray Otis, and the other supporters of the aqueduct soon had reason to regret Loewenthal's discomfiture. For the *Examiner* was new to the city; it had begun operation on December 12, 1903, as the seventh in Hearst's expanding chain. And whereas the older newspapers in town shared the booster gospel of the business community, the *Examiner* had been started with financial backing from the local typographer's union and had quickly revealed an enthusiasm for muckraking. And so, while the other papers rallied in uniform praise of the proposed aqueduct, the *Examiner*—with a circulation that on Sundays, at least, far exceeded even that of the *Times*—initiated its coverage of the issue with an air of suspicion that rapidly deteriorated into outright hostility.[3]

The *Examiner's* initial line of inquiry focused sharply on the awesome haste with which the water board and city council were proceeding with the project. The water commissioners, as their first order of business on the Monday following the *Times'* Saturday morning revelation, passed a resolution asking the city council to call an immediate election on the issuance of $1.5 million in bonds to pay for land and water rights purchases in the Owens Valley.[4] Although it was understood that a far greater bond issue would be needed later to pay for the actual construction of the aqueduct, the commissioners were unable to specify what would ultimately be involved in the project or how much it was likely to cost. The commissioners, at first, could not even provide a map of the proposed line of the aqueduct. The *Examiner* eventually developed a map of its own by piecing together federal topographic maps and published it with a warning that the project could not be completed for less than $50 million, more than twice what Mulholland was vaguely estimating.[5] Despite these shortcomings and the fact that the city council's own finance committee had recommended delaying any election until the water department developed a detailed cost estimate of the project, the city council before adjourning to a champagne luncheon with the water commissioners on August 14 called for the bond election to be held only three weeks later, on September 7.

Mulholland attempted at first to drown all questions in a flood of statistics. If the city had no detailed studies of its own to offer, he could at least produce the voluminous reports of stream measurements by the Reclamation Service which Newell and Lippincott had provided, as proof that technical studies of the Owens River had been performed, at least by someone. But in the heat of the campaign, Mulholland often tried to make more claims for the project than these reports could support, and as his promises proliferated, they tended increasingly to stray from any serious relation to the predictable nature of the project he was promoting.

Mulholland promised the *Times*, for example, that the entire project would be finished in only four years.[6] And he assured one public meeting that the aqueduct could be built without storage reservoirs of any kind; instead, he promised that by releasing twenty thousand inches of Owens River water a year for three years into the groundwater basin of the San Fernando Valley, the flows of the Los Angeles River would be enhanced sufficiently to provide for all the city's needs. Loewenthal answered that prospect with the argument that if that much water were poured into the San Fernando Valley for three years, "the valley would be floating gaily to the sea."[7] As the campaign progressed, the *Examiner* leaped on the inconsistencies, real and imagined, in Mulholland's public statements, pointing out that Mulholland could not even give a definite figure for the amount of water Los Angeles would receive from the project.[8] The *Times* attempted to come to Mulholland's defense with a five-part series of articles on the project which it labeled as an investigative report; but the articles were nothing more than a promotional broadside on behalf of the aqueduct, and their author, Allen Kelly, left the *Times* staff soon after to handle public relations for the city water department.[9]

Mulholland's other efforts to explain his inordinate haste met with no better reception on the editorial pages of the *Examiner*. He warned, for example, that private investors would take over the development of the aqueduct if the city failed to act promptly. This was a threat Fred Eaton was happy to corroborate, telling reporters, "There would be no disappointment to me if the city should decide that it does not care to proceed with the deal for I have no fear of my ability to capitalize the venture as a private corporation."[10] Even though the city had from the beginning used the specter of private speculators lurking in the Owens Valley to justify the secrecy of its proceedings, Mulholland never disclosed just who these potential competitors might be. "They didn't get away with it, and that ends it," Mulholland grumped when pressed on the question. "I got away with it."[11] The *Examiner*, in any event, dismissed Mulholland's argument by pointing out that Eaton had been trying for thirteen years to interest private investors in the project without success and that the federal government's withdrawals in the valley would prohibit a private takeover at this point anyway.[12] Similarly, when Mulholland maintained that the bond issue had to be passed to meet the first $50,000 installment due on October 1 on Eaton's contract for Long Valley, the *Examiner* charged that committing $1.5 million in public funds for the sake of $50,000 was patently absurd.[13]

Mulholland ultimately resorted to exaggerations of the city's need for water as a way of encouraging voters to approve his bonds, and, in the weeks before the election, the *Times* began to print almost daily predictions of the dire consequences which would be visited on Los Angeles if the aqueduct were not built. One of the most enduring stories fabricated as part of this scare campaign involved the so-called drought which descended on

Southern California at a time variously cited as 1892 or 1895 and which reportedly persisted until 1904. Modern historians still refer to this drought even though it seems to have originated with Mulholland in the election of 1905. For example, Erwin Cooper's *Aqueduct Empire* recalls on Mulholland's authority that the average rainfall in Los Angeles from 1895 to 1904 dropped to only six inches per year; in fact, National Weather Bureau records reveal that Los Angeles' annual precipitation in this period averaged 11.52 inches.[14] Similarly, Remi Nadeau in his history of the Los Angeles aqueduct reports that Mulholland first traveled to the Owens Valley in September 1904 because that summer's "water famine" had set the city "reeling."[15] In fact, Los Angeles in 1904 received a perfectly average rainfall of 11.88 inches and in August experienced a record downpour for that month which was not even approached in the entire forty-year period from 1891 to 1930.[16]

Los Angeles did experience two successive years of extremely deficient rainfall in 1898 and 1899. But in the years after the turn of the century the levels of precipitation steadily increased, and by the summer of 1905, when Mulholland discovered his drought, the city was in the midst of an especially wet year, with precipitation running more than 25 percent above normal—a level exceeded only six times in the forty years between 1891 and 1930.[17] Mulholland consequently had a difficult case to make, and his sudden announcement of a lingering drought must have come as something of a shock to any residents of the city who had been following the water department's affairs. For even in the worst months of the real drought in 1898-99, the *Times* had assured its readers that there was no cause for concern. "It is evident that the possibilities of the future are ample to meet all requirements," the *Times* commented in 1899. "There is no need for precipitancy of action."[18] In the altered circumstances of 1905, however, the *Times* promptly stepped in to back Mulholland's claims with the declaration on July 31 that there were new "facts relating to water development which have been kept secret lest they create a panic."[19] The city's water commissioners followed suit on August 8 with the announcement that the municipal water supplies were dangerously low, a situation which the board explained it had been reluctant to announce earlier for fear of endangering the city's prosperity.[20]

Mulholland warned that the city's existing water supply was incapable of supporting more than 220,000 people, a number only slightly larger than the current population of 206,000.[21] He warned, moreover, that at the rate the community was consuming its water supplies, Los Angeles could run dry in only a few weeks.[22] Soon all the newspapers in town were giving prominent play to the "water nightmare" Mulholland had conjured up with the prediction, "If Los Angeles runs out of water for one week, the city within a year will not have a population of 100,000 people."[23] "If the bonds don't pass," the *Los Angeles Herald* warned in a direct appeal to the *Examiner*'s constituency in labor, "building will stop and workers will have to leave the city."[24] And it was in the context of these bleak visions of water famines, drought, and economic collapse that Mulholland produced with special effect the photographs of the Owens Valley's abundant streams, which Eaton had arranged to have taken with Lippincott's cooperation the month before.[25]

If anyone had been inclined to doubt Mulholland's extravagant claims, there was little he or she could have done to challenge them, because the city water department held all the numbers and there was no alternative source of hydrologic data. The *Examiner* could pick up inconsistencies in Mulholland's claims for the Owens Valley water supply, but Loewenthal was less willing to challenge him on statements about conditions in the city. So when Mulholland told the *Examiner* that the flow of the Los Angeles River had dropped to only thirty-three or thirty-four million gallons per day in a city that was consuming more than thirty-eight million gallons on a hot day, the *Examiner* simply reprinted the numbers without question.[26]

It was not until the bond election had long since been settled that the city water department began quietly revising these figures in later reports as part of an apparent effort to correct the most obvious exaggerations employed in this first promotion of the aqueduct. Thus, Mulholland himself in his first annual report as chief engineer of the aqueduct in 1907 acknowledged that the city's rainfall had been perfectly normal since 1900 and revised without comment the streamflow figures he had given the *Examiner* to state that the river's flow on July 1, 1905, had actually been forty-six million gallons per day, or 71.5 cubic feet per second, rather than the nearly 30-percent lower number he had proffered in 1905.[27] In his final report on the construction of the aqueduct in 1916—and again in 1924—however, he dropped the streamflow figures for 1905 back down to below 45 cubic feet per second because by then the project was once again embroiled in controversies to be described in succeeding chapters.[28] In 1928, when these controversies seemed to have been resolved, the department of Water and Power issued a comprehensive set of statistics on its available water supply in which the streamflow measurements for the Los Angeles River in 1905 went back up again by nearly 20 percent over the figures the department had given out to one of its own consultants only four years earlier.[29]

Unfortunately, it is impossible to fix with any certainty what the real flow of the river in 1905 may have been because there are no independently recognized comprehensive streamflow records for the Los Angeles River prior to 1929 other than the department's own, and, as indicated, the department's statistics sometimes vary with the occasion.[30] The degree of divergence in the records the department uses can be measured, however, in the fact that in 1924 its records showed the river's flow steadily decreasing from 1902 through 1906, whereas in 1928 the records showed the river not only carrying more water but carrying it in steadily increasing amounts during the same period.[31]

An even more glaring example of the department's efforts at revisionism after the fact involves Mulholland's claim in 1905 that the city's indigenous water supply was not capable of supporting more than 220,000 people. It became increasingly obvious that this estimate had been calculated from whole cloth during the next eight years that it took to complete the aqueduct, a period in which the city's population rose to more than 500,000 without experiencing a water shortage of any kind. Although Mulholland later observed somewhat lamely that when the aqueduct water finally arrived in 1913 it did so "in the nick of time," his estimate of the number of people the Los Angeles River could support gradually floated upward in successive department reports and publications from his original assertion of 220,000 in 1905 to 250,000 in 1928, 300,000 in 1936, and 500,000 in 1939.[32]

Mulholland's exaggerations notwithstanding, there is no question that Los Angeles' available water supplies were declining in 1905; but the problem was overuse and not the more compelling threat of Mulholland's fabricated drought. The real drought of 1898 and 1899 had only a slight effect on the flows of the Los Angeles River. Lippincott, in a report prepared for the United States Geological Survey in 1900 using figures he and Mulholland had developed, remarked with some enthusiasm that despite the extreme shortage of precipitation in the two preceding rainy seasons, "the discharge of the Los Angeles River has been exceptionally constant, the decrease in 1900 being not more than 20 percent of the average."[33] Even so, the drought of 1898 and 1899 did force many irrigators on the south coastal plain to sink wells which brought a rapid acceleration in the depletion of the groundwater basins that are the principal source of supply for the area's rivers and streams.[34] When precipitation returned to normal after 1900, these wells were not shut down; instead, they were continued in operation to serve an everextending range of agricultural activities in Corona, Ontario, Redlands, Riverside, San Diego, Los Angeles, and the San Fernando Valley. As a result, groundwater levels continued to decline after 1900, especially in the area of Los Angeles and Anaheim, where more than a hundred thousand acres of land were receiving irrigation services.[35]

The United States Geological Survey estimated that there were twenty-five hundred flowing artesian wells on the south coastal plain in 1904 draining the area's groundwater basins at a minimum rate of three hundred cubic feet per second.[36] The destructive effects of this excessive depletion began to appear in 1904, when the overall artesian area of the plain dwindled to an estimated 73 percent of its original size.[37] Groundwater levels in the San Fernando Valley, principal source of the Los Angeles River, reached a heretofore unprecedented low in 1905, and Mulholland later estimated that the flows of the river itself dropped by one-third the next year as a result.[38]

Los Angeles would probably have experienced the adverse

effects of these groundwater overdrafts in the areas outside its borders much earlier than 1905 if Mulholland's new water management programs had not been so effective in achieving greater efficiency in the city's overall use of water. As a result of the metering program and improvements in the city's internal distribution system which Mulholland initiated after the municipal takeover of the water system, Los Angeles' rate of per capita daily consumption was dropping in the years 1902 through 1905 at a rate five times faster than the flow of the Los Angeles River was increasing.[39] These increased efficiencies, in turn, enabled the city to absorb new growth in its population without experiencing a proportionate increase in its overall water use. In the first four years of municipal ownership, from 1902 to 1905, for example, Los Angeles' population grew 61 percent from an estimated 128,000 to 206,000. The overall demand for water services, however, increased only one-tenth as fast, from an average demand for 30,976,000 gallons per day in 1902 to 32,960,000 gallons per day in 1905, a growth of only 6.4 percent.[40]

Mulholland attributed this success to the fact that "the organization of the Water Department has been kept entirely free from politics and subject to civil service rules."[41] Nevertheless, improved management techniques could only go so far in meeting the problems posed by agricultural development on the South Coast. To defend its water supply from depletion, the city had to resort first to litigation to establish its pueblo right to the groundwater of the San Fernando Valley, then to a temporary suspension of irrigation services during the spring of 1904; and by the summer of 1905, it was suing two hundred ranchers in the San Fernando Valley to cut off their access to wells altogether.[42]

These events simply confirmed the conclusion William E. Smythe had reached in 1900: the indigenous water supply of the South Coast had already been stretched nearly to the limit. Further growth, especially in Los Angeles, could not be achieved except at the expense of agriculture within the basin as a whole. This was the central point of the report the city had paid Lippincott to prepare in 1905, and others had long since reached the same conclusion. Numerous schemes had been offered for new waterworks within the region, and each had its supporters. The

Examiner, for example, favored the idea of tapping Piru Creek, which would have been far less expensive than the aqueduct Mulholland was proposing.[43] But J. M. Elliott, a member of the city water commission, knew as a stockholder in the Piru Land and Water Company that the creek "amounted to absolutely nothing as a supply for this city." For his part, Elliott was enamored of the idea of tunneling through the San Bernardino Mountains to take water from the Mojave River near Victorville, and he had even authorized funding for the preparation of preliminary plans for such a project.[44]

The value of Lippincott's report to Mulholland lay precisely in the fact that it gave him a document, invested with the sanction and authority of the top Reclamation Service official in California, which he could use to cut through all these counterproposals by demonstrating that it was impossible to obtain a sufficient new water supply for the city within the South Coast.[45] In the same fashion and to make the same point, Mulholland referred frequently throughout this first campaign for the aqueduct bonds to the United States Geological Survey reports on groundwater conditions in the South Coast, which had been prepared by Walter C. Mendenhall, the same official Lippincott had hoped to have appointed to the panel of engineers reviewing the Reclamation Service's Owens Valley project. Although more limited in scope than Lippincott's report, the Mendenhall studies were in one respect even more valuable to Mulholland. For whereas Lippincott felt constrained by his connection to the Owens Valley project not to mention potential supplies outside the South Coast specifically in his report, Mendenhall had no hesitation in drawing the conclusion Lippincott demurred to set in print. "So far as the groundwater situation is concerned," Mendenhall wrote, "the policy of the City in going to a distant source for its water supply is not merely wise, but is absolutely necessary if the City's future growth is not to be at the expense of neighboring communities."[46]

For all the exaggeration Mulholland may have employed in his efforts to convince the voters of Los Angeles to support the aqueduct, the essential point he was making was true. The city needed the aqueduct, but it was a need founded in prospect. The

city had to have the aqueduct, not to meet any actual and immediate needs, but to serve the prospective demands of a greatly
increased future population. Without the aqueduct, Los Angeles
and possibly the entire South Coast would be condemned to the
static economic conditions Smythe had predicted in 1900. Fred
Eaton, although no longer as enthusiastic an advocate of the
aqueduct as he had been when it promised to provide him with a
perpetual source of personal wealth, made this point when he
spoke with reporters following the *Times'* initial disclosure of the
project: "In my opinion, this is not the greatest thing that could
be done to build up Los Angeles, but it is the one thing that it is
necessary to do if the city is to become greater than it is now."[47]
Other backers of the project were more fulsome in their predictions of the aqueduct's future benefits. The *Times* promised that,
in the Owens Valley, Los Angeles had found a supply of water
"ample for all the needs of the City and its suburbs for all time to
come."[48]

Mulholland never claimed that the city would be able to put
all the water from the aqueduct to use immediately; instead he
predicted sales of at least half the aqueduct's supply to support
irrigation projects outside the city.[49] Charles A. Moody in *Out
West* magazine quoted one city water official as promising: "We
can put under cultivation all the lands from Duarte to Santa
Monica and practically all the lands in the San Fernando Valley.
We can make half a dozen Riversides in this country that is
surrounding us." And this roseate vision in turn encouraged
Moody to make the seemingly preposterous suggestion that,
with the advent of Owens Valley water, there might someday be
more people living within thirty miles of the Los Angeles City
Hall than the more than one and a half million people then
residing in all of California.[50]

The *Los Angeles Examiner* might quarrel with Mulholland's
haste to get the project under way, but it certainly had no desire
to put down the dream Moody and others described of a greater
Los Angeles stretching one day from San Gabriel to the Simi
Pass. Progress in Los Angeles was measured in land sales and
population growth. No member of the commercial community
could question so fundamental an article of faith, and even the

Examiner printed a daily list of real estate transfers, building permits, and new mortgages. Major land purchases merited full articles. But even so, Loewenthal and his cohorts at the *Examiner* could not suppress their curiosity as to who would benefit most from the new economic prosperity the aqueduct promised to bring to Los Angeles. And so, the *Examiner* continued digging for a more pecuniary reason behind the city's rush to judgment at the polls.

Although the *Examiner* declared editorially that it had long supported the idea of a water project for Los Angeles, it maintained from the outset that "there must be no politics and no graft."[51] The *Examiner*'s first question to Mulholland when he announced the project was whether the possibility existed for graft. "None at all," Mulholland answered. "The only man who could graft is Fred Eaton, and I know that he never made a dirty dollar in his life and never will."[52] Despite the fact that they had been "at swords' point" only a month before, Mulholland was always very protective of Eaton and often went out of his way to help him. "A man like Mr. Eaton," Mulholland once declared, "people can't comprehend his character, because few people have a character like his, his whole soul, a big man."[53]

In large part, Mulholland's affection for Eaton was no doubt due to their long association in the early part of Mulholland's career, when he had been Eaton's friend and protégé. But there was an element too of self-defensiveness in Mulholland's comments on Eaton. He could hardly have answered the reporters otherwise in 1905; and when a formal municipal investigation of the aqueduct project in 1912 began looking closely at Eaton's financial relationship with the city, Mulholland again responded with a stalwart defense of his former mentor, declaring, "There isn't a straighter man in money matters on God's footstool."[54]

For all the promises made in the course of the municipalization campaign to bring tough business principles to the administration of the city water department, Eaton had driven an embarrassingly hard bargain for the Long Valley lands, the full ramifications of which would not become clear for another twenty years. In addition, at the time of the first bond issue election, Eaton was being paid his commissions on the land purchases he arranged for Los Angeles out of the sellers' proceeds. It did not occur to the water commissioners for another year that such an arrangement was not likely to encourage Eaton to negotiate the lowest possible price for the city.[55] Mulholland was consequently careful in all his reports on the aqueduct never to specify in detail the provisions of Eaton's sale of Long Valley, preferring instead to maintain the illusion that the results had been "favorable to the city and only just to him."[56] Eaton was happy to go along with this policy. In the midst of the bond election of 1905, for example, he told the *Times* that he had only been paid $40,000 for both the land and the cattle at Long Valley and not a dollar for his expenses—even though he had retained all the cattle and had signed a contract with the city only two months earlier that provided him with all expenses plus $10 a day for his services.[57]

Although Eaton's financial relationship with the aqueduct successfully escaped close scrutiny in 1905, rumors were soon circulating that others stood to profit from the project. When the resolution to call an election sailed through the city council on August 14, the only dissenting councilman, A. D. Houghton, himself the product of a political reform movement led by J. R. Haynes and J. B. Irvine, observed ominously, "It almost looks as if some of these men [the other council members] whose character and integrity are above reproach, had been let in on this deal three or four months ago, had purchased arid lands, and are in haste to have them made valuable by this water project."[58] The *Examiner* picked up the insinuation of corruption and played it coyly on the editorial page, observing of the city council, "They are all men, who, like Jim Fisk's legislators, 'do not stir around for nothing' . . . They are the same men who obey the behests of the trolley and gas monopolies. How far is the water project allied with the interests which control their actions?"[59]

The reference to the monopolies was a cut at a favorite *Examiner* adversary, Henry Huntington. Before the aqueduct story broke, the *Examiner* had been campaigning against Huntington and the city council for lax municipal ordinances which permitted the unsafe operation of the trolley cars in Huntington's municipal railway company to claim several hundred casualties each year. For a newspaper committed to muckraking, reform, and the ongoing battle against malefactors of great wealth, Huntington made a large and inviting target. He had once been heir apparent to his uncle Collis Huntington's control of the Southern Pacific Railroad Company. But when a party of stockholders led by the president of the Union Pacific, E. H. Harriman, managed to block his succession for five months after his uncle's death, Huntington retired from the combat, selling out his interest in the Southern Pacific to Harriman while retaining his position as a vice president and director. With the profits from this sale, he moved to Southern California in 1900, where he rapidly established himself as a masterbuilder and first among the financial giants of the Los Angeles business community.

Huntington founded his new financial empire on trolley companies, beginning with the Pacific Electric Railway company, which he formed in 1901 out of the bankrupt remains of the city's first consolidated trolley system, the Los Angeles Railway Company. Within two years he had expanded his system into a major network linking forty-two incorporated cities within a thirty-five-mile radius of Los Angeles. Unlike most municipal railway systems, which ran on narrow-gauge tracks through city streets, Huntington laid his tracks standard-gauge on private rights-of-way. As a result, he could move freight and passenger cars directly from the transcontinental lines, and in this way, he was able to cut deeply into the local traffic of the Southern Pacific, thereby irritating his old nemesis Harriman. When Harriman struck back in 1903 by buying out Huntington's associates in the Pacific Electric Railway, Huntington responded by forming a new system, the Los Angeles Inter-Urban Railway Company, which he threatened to develop into a direct competitor with the Southern Pacific for all traffic on the South Coast.[60]

Huntington's acquisitions extended as well to light and gas utilities, real estate, and development companies. Wherever Huntington ran his tracks, land sales spiraled upward and development soon followed. And as the *Times* noted, "Wherever the Huntington railways extend their lines, the Huntington electric and gas companies are preparing to furnish fuel and light."[61] Huntington actually made money in three ways: first from land sales, then from ticket fares, and finally from utility services to the communities which grew up on his properties at Alhambra, Oak Knoll, San Marino, Venice, Glendale, Seal Beach, Huntington Beach, and Olinda.[62]

As soon as Mulholland announced his plans for the aqueduct, Huntington emerged as "a most enthusiastic advocate."[63] His active support of the aqueduct bond issue, however, quickened the *Examiner*'s suspicions for several reasons. In the first place, whereas the other local power companies opposed the project because they feared the competition with municipal power the aqueduct would generate, Huntington's Pacific Electric and Power Company endorsed the project.[64] In addition, Huntington had recently extended a transit line into the San Fernando Valley, a sure sign that his development companies would soon follow. But this move would put Huntington at odds with the city water board for the meager water reserves available in the valley. The revelation that a massive new water project was planned which would deliver water in great quantities for storage in the San Fernando Valley seemed an uncanny stroke of good luck for Mr. Huntington.

Equally curious from Loewenthal's point of view was the fact that the *Times*' enthusiastic coverage of the aqueduct had, from the outset, dwelt more upon the potential benefits the project would have for the San Fernando Valley than upon any municipal needs it would serve. It was the San Fernando Valley and not Los Angeles, after all, which the *Times* predicted "the magic scimitar of modern engineering skill" would unleash. "To put it mildly, the value of all San Fernando Valley lands will be doubled by the acquisition of this new vast supply," the *Times* observed in its first report on the project. "With the great increase in population that will follow, the increased productivity of lands, there will be ample demand for every acre of land . . . Prices will need no other bolstering."[65] Indeed, by August 10 the *Times* reported that land values in the valley were already "skyrocketing" on the *Times*'s promise that "the San Fernando Valley can be converted into a veritable Garden of Eden. Vast areas of land, devoted now to grazing and grain, will be converted into orchards and gardens, the peer of any in the world."[66]

The *Times*' endorsement of the project was all the more peculiar because Harrison Gray Otis, its publisher, had at all other times opposed the principles of municipal ownership and had vigorously campaigned for an extension of the lease to the Los Angeles City Water Company in 1898 and 1901. Having built a one-quarter interest in the floundering weekly *Times* in 1886 into complete control of the most profitable daily newspaper in the West by 1900, Otis was a ferocious defender of free enterprise and had no patience with unionization or governmental regulation. In addition, as all new reporters at the *Times* soon learned, Otis, in the words of one of his editors, "was a believer in, and apostle of personal journalism. Purely objective writing was frowned upon as 'weak and vacillating.'"[67]

When the *Times* first scooped the other papers with its announcement of the aqueduct, the *Examiner* sniffed "an impression that the old grafter . . . Harrison Gray Otis either had or hoped to get his paw in the pie."[68] Otis refused to rise to that bait. But when Councilman Houghton began to suggest there was corruption in the city council, the *Times* attacked with a violent denunciation of this "braying ass, a stench in the nostrils of decency" and his reform-minded friends Haynes and Irvine, "freaks and pests who see no good in the existing order." When Houghton rose to question Mulholland during a presentation to the Municipal League on the night of August 15, he was hooted down by the distinguished business leaders gathered there, and the *Times* observed approvingly: "If Councilman Howton [*sic*] had not been born by reason of a miscarriage (of justice) the city of Los Angeles would have escaped the annoyance and humiliation to which it has been subjected through his fool antics, his innumerable and disgusting monkeyshines, and his asinine performances in and out of the council chamber."[69]

Otis had a special reason to dislike Houghton. In 1904, the city council had awarded the *Times* the exclusive contract to print the city's advertising, even though the *Times*' bid for this contract was 50 to 100 percent higher than all others. The advocates of municipal reform had then mounted a recall campaign against Councilman J.P. Davenport, charging that he was Otis' henchman. In the election held September 16, 1904, Davenport became the first official ever recalled in a United States city, and

Houghton, with strong backing from organized labor and the *Examiner*, had been elected in his place. Two other councilmen who supported the *Times'* contract were subsequently defeated in regular elections, and the *Times* consequently lost the contract for several years to come.[70] But the vicious personal attacks on Houghton, and the business community's refusal even to listen to his questions, were a reflection of more than just Harrison Gray Otis' vituperative spirit. "It is one of the things that happens in Los Angeles," the *Examiner*'s editor Henry Loewenthal later reflected. "It is unfortunately a village method of looking at things, that whenever anybody disagrees with you in opinions, and the other persons are strong enough, they will either boycott you or do something else to you. That is part of that spirit of lawlessness that prevails here, that I have never seen anywhere else."[71]

Otis was unable, in any event, to stifle all the questions that began to grow up about the project as the date of the election drew near. On August 22, 1905, the *San Francisco Chronicle* ran an editorial pointing to the value of the proposed aqueduct to Los Angeles commerce and noting the recurrence of rumors, in *Brandstreet's Financial Report*, to the effect that the project was linked to a land development scheme for the San Fernando Valley. The *Examiner* waited two days to allow Otis to prepare his response; then, on the same day that the *Times* attacked the *Chronicle* in an editorial entitled "Baseless Rumors," the *Examiner* struck with the revelation of an organized land syndicate which had purchased sixteen thousand acres in the San Fernando Valley for thirty-five dollars an acre, an investment which would return millions once water arrived from the Owens Valley. The *Examiner* named ten syndicate members, each of whom held a thousand shares in the San Fernando Mission Land Company at a par value of one hundred dollars per share. The list included Henry Huntington, of course; E. H. Harriman, president of the Union Pacific; W. G. Kerckhoff, president of the Pacific Light and Power Company; Joseph Sartori of the Security Trust and Savings Bank; L. C. Brand of the Title Guarantee and Trust Company; G. K. Porter, a San Fernando land speculator who owned the land bought by the syndicate; and, best of all from the *Examiner*'s point of view, the owners of the three leading news-

papers of the city, E. T. Earl of the *Express* and Harrison Gray
Otis himself, publisher of the *Times* and "its vermiform appendix," the *Herald.*

The next morning, Otis leaped to attack the Hearst "yellow
atrocity," declaring, "The insane desire of the *Examiner* to discredit certain citizens of Los Angeles has at last led it into the
open as a vicious enemy of the city's welfare, its mask of hypocrisy dropped and its convulsed features revealed."[72] In subsequent issues Otis asserted that the company had been formed two
years earlier, before the aqueduct was anything more than a
gleam in Fred Eaton's eye, a claim which the *Examiner* promptly
demonstrated to be false. Though it was true that Brand had
taken an option in his own name on the Porter ranch on October
13, 1903, in hopes that Huntington's railway lines would someday reach the area, the syndicate had not been formed and its
stock subscribed until November 28, 1904—less than a week after
Newell and Lippincott had met with the city's water officials and
agreed to suspend the Reclamation Service project while the city
completed its investigations of the Owens Valley. Also on November 28, Otis had issued a check for fifty thousand dollars to
secure the option on the Porter ranch, which formed the core of
the syndicate's holdings. On December 3, 1904, the syndicate had
incorporated as the San Fernando Mission Land Company, and
a company charter had been duly issued. The syndicate did not
proceed with full purchase of the property, however, until March
23, 1905, the very day Fred Eaton's telegram arrived announcing
his success in securing the Rickey Lands at Long Valley.[73]

"This is the prize for which the newspaper persons . . . are
working and the size of it accounts for [their] tremendous zeal,"
the *Examiner* crowed. "The mystery of the enterprise is how it
happens that Messrs. Huntington and Harriman, who let no one
into their land purchasing schemes, but bought up everything for
themselves, consented to let eight others in on the 'ground floor'
so to speak."[74] The mystery is not hard to understand. Together
the principal partners in the San Fernando land syndicate made
up a representative cross-section of the most powerful development interests in the Los Angeles business community. Their
support would be needed to put across the aqueduct to the voters.

And their influence was further strengthened by the later addition to their ranks of Moses Sherman, a member of the city's board of water commissioners. Even at a time when the perception of conflicts of interest by public officials was less restrictive than today, Sherman's involvement drew censure among his colleagues on the water commission. Another member of the commission, J. M. Elliott, later explained why he did not follow Sherman's example and begin buying up lands in the San Fernando Valley as soon as he knew the aqueduct was being planned: "I had a perfect right to buy land anywhere but I didn't want any question to come up afterward whether I did or did not, and I determined that I wouldn't and I didn't . . . I took that attitude because I would know earlier than anybody else of the possibility of that water coming down through there, and I knew that its coming down there would make that land very much more valuable."[75]

So tightly interwoven were the interests of the principal partners in the syndicate that as a group they reflected in miniature the complexity of both the business community itself and Huntington's influence within it. Sherman, for example, in addition to providing the syndicate with a voice in the water commission's secret deliberations, had built up the first trolley system Huntington bought in Los Angeles.[76] Brand sold Huntington the Los Angeles and Glendale Electric Company in 1904.[77] Similarly, Huntington's Pacific Light and Power Company had been incorporated on March 6, 1902, as the successor to Kerckhoff's San Gabriel Electric Company, and Huntington and Kerckhoff were its principal stockholders.[78] Kerckhoff, moreover, was one of the state's most active conservationists, and as president of the Forest and Water Society he provided a powerful organizing force within the business and political communities for the new principles of scientific conservation which Gifford Pinchot was fighting to establish in federal forestry programs. And Pinchot's support, in turn, would be essential to the city's efforts to gain federal approval of its aqueduct.[79] Harriman, as president of the Southern Pacific, controlled lands along a hundred miles of the line of the aqueduct, and his cooperation in granting a right-of-way was therefore equally important to the success of the city's project.[80]

And Huntington even owned the building to which Lippincott had moved the regional offices of the Reclamation Service on June 25, 1905.[81]

As a microcosm of the greater Los Angeles business community, the divisions within the syndicate were as revealing as its alliances. Huntington despised Sherman personally, for example, and would be betrayed by him in a business deal only a year later.[82] Otis had fought Huntington bitterly over the issue of the city's harbor at San Pedro.[83] Otis also regarded E. T. Earl as his most deadly competitor in the local newspaper industry, and the two devoted ten years of their lives from 1901 to 1911 trying to drive one another out of business.[84] And Huntington and Harriman, of course, had been at war since 1900, if not before.

Given all the personal animosities among its members, it is not surprising that the syndicate never actually met as a group.[85] But as intense as these internal rivalries became, the individual members of the syndicate, like the greater Los Angeles business community, could unite on issues where their own best interests were involved. Even when he was working hardest to undercut the Southern Pacific's business in Southern California, for example, Huntington never gave up his position as its vice president and member of the board of directors. The general growth and economic development of Los Angeles and the South Coast provided such a unifying issue. An observation of the *Times* on the rivalry between Huntington and Harriman might therefore serve to describe the essential relationship between the diverse business interests which united behind the aqueduct bond issue: "Their hate for each other was so terrible as to be less intense than only their love for their business interests."[86]

The revelation of the syndicate's existence appeared at first to pose a serious threat to the prospects for passage of the bond issue. Although Otis attempted to dismiss the *Examiner*'s charges as a "Plain Case of Hydrophobia," with only two weeks to go until the city election the campaign for approval of the aqueduct was beginning to unravel.[87] Otis' denials of guilt did not prevent other newspapers in the state from picking up the *Examiner*'s reports on the syndicate. Huntington rushed back to the city from business elsewhere and closeted himself with his advisors at the Jonathan Club. On August 30, the temperature fortuitously rose to 101 degrees, the highest in twenty years, thereby lending credence to Mulholland's claims of an impending water famine; but the incipient heat wave broke the next day. Worst of all, business leaders outside the circle which stood to gain most from construction of the aqueduct began to comment in public that there was no need for such haste in approving the project. The president of the Merchant's National Bank, I. W. Hellman, and C. Seligman of M. A. Newmark and Company, for example, joined in calling for the creation of a "committee of large tax-payers" to investigate the project.[88] The local Chamber of Commerce promptly dispatched a committee of three businessmen to the Owens Valley with orders to prepare a report. And Houghton proposed that the United States Army Corps of Engineers be called in to review the proposal, a suggestion the *Times* greeted with the wish that "the Sixth Ward Spook ... will soon be thrown over in disgust by his constituency like a pair of useless bloomers."[89]

On August 30, the *Examiner* commented favorably on the growing likelihood that approval of the aqueduct would be delayed. "Of one thing the people of Los Angeles can be assured and that is that they will be in no danger of a water famine in the future, even if the present scheme fails. No one else will acquire the water of the Owens Valley if the city needs it. And, maybe, if it is otherwise acquired there will be less suspicion of graft in the matter, and there will be competent engineers employed to devise a plan for impounding the water and bringing it here."

This was close as the *Examiner* would ever come to outright opposition to the aqueduct. There were, after all, larger interests at stake than those of Otis and his partners in the land syndicate. A new harbor was being built at San Pedro to accommodate the traffic expected from the new canal in Panama. On the Fourth of July that year, Huntington had opened the "Venice of America" with great fanfare and had followed up that achievement a few days later with the announcement of another new development at Redondo, thereby setting off a feverish land boom on Santa Monica Bay in which some properties changed hands six times in a single day. Elliott, who was president of the Municipal League as well as a member of the city water commission, had led the consolidation of the First National Bank in August, the largest merger of financial institutions the city had ever seen. These and dozens of other commercial ventures depended for their success upon a growing metropolis with the water to serve a vast new population.

On September 2, the city's business leaders invited William Randolph Hearst, owner and publisher of the *Examiner*, to Los Angeles for private consultation. Hearst was by now a congressman embarked at full sail upon his vain quest for the presidency. Political ambition had intruded upon the quality of his journalism by 1905, causing his editors across the country to be considerably more circumspect in their exposure of graft, deception, and public scandal than had previously been their practice. Hearst's biographer, W. A. Swanberg, described conditions in the Hearst chain during the summer of 1905:

> Every Hearstman from Boston to Los Angeles knew how the Chief had been bitten by the Presidential bug, and it subtracted something from their already limited integrity in reporting the news. Most of all, it affected the Chief himself. Before politics seized him he had taken a fierce pride in his journalistic achievements, outlandish though they often were. Now, Politician Hearst subtracted something from Editor Hearst. While it would not be quite fair to say that he now considered his newspapers simply as a means to reach the White House, that would be an important part of their function.[90]

After his meeting with the businessmen, Hearst appeared at the offices of the *Examiner*. Henry Loewenthal recalled the scene: "Mr. Hearst himself was here and came in about as I was shifting and he said to help them along on the bond issue. That was public policy. Now that was all there was to it." Hearst then sat down and personally wrote a front-page editorial endorsing the project for the next morning's edition.[91]

The editorial began by reiterating all the charges the *Examiner* had made against the project. Hearst damned the water commission's haste in pushing the election and its profligacy in spending public funds for land purchases without authorization.

He dismissed as "veriest bosh" the claims that the project would be taken over by private speculators if the city did not act promptly. And he pointed out that no private company would ever build the aqueduct so long as the city had the power to fix water rates within its borders. The *Examiner* found an excuse for its apparent change of attitude toward the project in the recommendation made on September 2 by the Chamber of Commerce's committee that any funds derived from the sale of municipal bonds for the aqueduct not be spent until an independent panel of engineers had approved Mulholland's plans at some point after the election. The water commissioners had readily agreed to this suggestion. Therefore, the editorial concluded, "The Board's promise not to embark deeply in the venture until the best expert advice is obtained, removes its most objectionable features."[92]

The *Examiner*'s justification for its change of position thus called upon city voters to approve the commitment of funds for a project they did not understand; its dimensions, direction, and utility would all be revealed after they had agreed to buy this multimillion-dollar pig in a poke. Hearst's decision to endorse the project, however, was recommended by more than mere political gamesmanship. For all the *Examiner*'s revelations of double-dealing and deceit in the promotion of the bond issue, the fact remained unalterable that the entire community stood to benefit from construction of the aqueduct. The existence of the San Fernando land syndicate had been revealed to the people. If the *Examiner* had sought to embarrass Otis for scooping the Hearst paper, that objective had been achieved. Personally, and as a matter of his public policy in Congress and the press, Hearst supported the principle of municipal ownership of utilities.

With the most vocal opponent of the aqueduct thus silenced, Otis and his partners in the syndicate dropped any pretense that their schemes were not connected to the aqueduct. On the same morning Hearst's editorial appeared, the *Times* published the first advertisement for the San Fernando Mission Land Company. "Have a Contract for a Lot in Your Pocket When the Big Bonds are Voted," the ad urged, identifying Pacoima as "the first gun in the opening of the San Fernando Valley . . . its glorious future assured by abundant water."[93] The land office at Pacoima opened September 4, offering individual lots at prices ranging from $75 to $250. On the day before the election, the land company's advertisement in the *Times* promised to give full refunds to purchasers if the aqueduct bonds failed but warned that prices would go up ten percent if the bonds carried.[94]

On September 7, the first issue of aqueduct bonds was approved by a margin of fourteen to one. The fact of the syndicate's operation was apparently a matter of relative indifference to the voters, and the prospect that certain private interests would profit personally from the city's water project did little to discourage support for a proposal that most people believed would bring prosperity for all. Even more remarkable, the voters were apparently equally indifferent about the election itself. Less than half the number of voters turned out to vote on the aqueduct bonds as had cast ballots in the city's municipal elections in December 1904 and on an anti-saloon proposal in June 1905. As a result, a total of 11,500 voters, a little more than 5 percent of the city's population in 1905, decided the future of what would become the principal metropolitan trading center on the West Coast.[95]

A Clearing of Skirts

While the *Los Angeles Times* first revealed the news of the aqueduct with the headline, "Titanic Project to Give City a River," the initial reports of the city's plans in the *Inyo Register* ran under the heading, "Los Angeles Plots Destruction, Would Take Owens River, Lay Lands Waste, Ruin People, Homes, and Communities."[96] Throughout the campaign for the first aqueduct bonds, no voice was ever raised in Los Angeles on behalf of the Owens Valley. In fact, in the absence of maps or other specific information, few residents of the city probably had any detailed idea where the Owens Valley is or what the development of the aqueduct might mean for its future. When the project was first announced, reporters asked Los Angeles City Librarian Charles F. Lummis about the history of the valley. After a quick search, Lummis responded, "The resources of the City Library have been exhausted but nothing has been found to give the desired information."[97]

If anyone in Los Angeles were likely to know about the valley it would have been Lummis, for he was probably the city's most prominent litterateur, local historian, and publisher of travelers' guides to Southern California. He had been the first city editor of the daily *Times* and was the only member of its local news staff in 1884—a position he had stepped into after walking across the country from Ohio, contributing accounts of his journey to the *Times* along the way. Having retired from the *Times* in 1886, he founded the California Landmarks Club and became editor of *Land of Sunshine* magazine.[98] Lummis, as an enthusiastic advocate of public control of water rights and distribution, was especially familiar with the city's need for an additional source of supply.[99] If the city library contained no information on the Owens Valley, he could easily have written for details from a former member of the writing group he conducted, Mary Austin, who, as a resident of the valley, was deeply involved in the reaction there to annoucement of the city's plans.[100]

Mary Austin was the wife of Stafford Wallace Austin, the register of federal lands in Independence, whose letters to the General Land Office in June 1905 complaining of Fred Eaton's activities in the valley had forced Lippincott to disassociate himself as best he could from the city's agent. As an author, she had established for herself a stature far surpassing that of her husband. The appearance in 1903 of her *Land of Little Rain*, a collection of word sketches of life on the high desert lands of the Owens Valley, had won her wide acclaim in Europe and America and established her reputation as a major figure on the American literary scene. Articulate, imperious, and extraordinarily gifted, she became, in Carl Van Doren's words, a "matriarch in a desert" who "had again more mind than her daily existence could occupy. It was the surplus which made her poet and prophet ... The desert put its mark on her ... Her desert knowledge ripened to a wisdom that formed and colored all her later experience ... Her books were wells driven into America to bring up water for her countrymen, though they might not have realized their thirst."[101] Seeing the valley threatened by Los Angeles' plans in 1905, she joined her husband in leading a defense of the country where her talents had matured.

The Austins' early life together had been marked by poverty and hardship. "Nothing in Mary's married life turned out as she expected it," she later observed in her autobiography.

> She had been brought up in a university town where people of intelligence and taste contrive, on incomes little better than those of highly skilled labor, to achieve for themselves security and certain of the appurtenances of good living . . . What she had to discover was that to her husband these things were unheard of and strange . . . Brought up on a huge, carelessly kept plantation [in Hawaii], in assumptions of social superiority such as accrue to Nordics living among brown peoples . . . he had never heard of such things as budgeting the family income, of competence achieved by cumulative small sacrifices and savings. Now that he did hear of it, he thought it all rather cheap and piffling.[102]

Modest, intellectual, gentlemanly, and ineffectually ambitious, Wallace brought Mary to Lone Pine in 1896, where he and his brother hoped to found an irrigation colony. "Mary at 26 was far too desperately displaced from the true center of her being not to feel obliged to go somewhere."[103] The project was a total failure, and the couple was turned out of the hotel where they were living, even though Mary was by then carrying a child. Wallace found a cabin near George's Creek, and there the baby, Ruth, was born retarded. Mary, her health failing, fled first to Bishop, where she taught at the private Inyo Academy, and then to Los Angeles, where she worked with Lummis.[104]

When Wallace obtained his appointment at the land office in Independence she joined him once again, and it was here that her writing skill began to blossom. The Owens Valley at this time was populated by a wide diversity of peoples, cultures, and races. In Lone Pine she had become friendly with the cattlemen and sheep drovers, Mexicans, Basques, and English émigrés, "people of gentility, old world grace, and idleness."[105] In Independence, she came to know the Indians and spent long hours with them, walking in the desert and learning its secrets. With her affection for the Indians, her often distracted manner, and her liberal enthusiasm for women's suffrage, free silver, and juvenile court reform, she seems never to have fit in well with the more conventional white farming families who were settling the Owens Valley in increasing numbers by the turn of the century. Many of the neighboring wives later recalled with horror rushing to Mary's house at night after hearing Ruth cry for hours, only to find the child strapped into a chair screaming while her mother paced the floor, hair streaming down her back, composing some new bit of writing.[106]

Life in the Owens Valley was rapidly changing in those years. "With the slow decline of mining, agricultural possibilities came to the fore . . . and there between the old era and the new the Valley hung," she later wrote. Everyone who came there seemed filled with an expectation of impending prosperity. "This was an attitude prevailing among men of Inyo; one on which they constantly reassured one another. *Something* was due to happen soon," she observed. "Once they had exposed themselves to it, they spent their lives going around and around in it, always keyed to the expected, the releasing discovery."[107] Wallace Austin had certainly been infected by this spirit, and it seems to have deepened the gulf between them. The more time she spent walking in the desert and writing about what she found there, the further apart they became. When she mailed in the manuscript of *Land of Little Rain*, her publishers in New York asked her for a biographical sketch describing her artistic method, to print with the book. "There is really nothing to tell," she responded. "I have just looked, nothing more . . . and by and by I got to know when and where looking was most worthwhile. Then I got so full of looking that I had to write to get rid of some of it and make room for more."[108] The theme of sight is also prominent in the description she later gave of her relationship with Wallace: "Once he had given himself to me, my husband never looked at another woman; but also he never looked with me at any single thing. He never, any more than he could help, afforded me a clue as to where he himself might be looking."[109] As a result, Mary found herself "widowed so far as physical resources and mental and spiritual cooperation, soon after her marriage to Wallace Austin."[110]

And so, when the occasion arose to make a common cause with Wallace against Los Angeles' aqueduct, she threw herself into the effort, perhaps as much to save her marriage as to preserve the Owens Valley. She went to Los Angeles, where she interviewed Mulholland and came away with the conviction that, despite his protestations to the contrary, construction of the aqueduct would mean the end of all the dreams Wallace and the other men of Inyo nurtured for a future of prosperity and growth in the valley. "By God, that woman is the only one who has brains enough to see where this is going!" Mulholland exclaimed after she had gone.[111] She poured all of her findings and convictions into a long article for the *San Francisco Chronicle* denouncing the Reclamation Service for its assistance to Los Angeles:

> Every considerable city in the State is or is about to be confronted by a water problem. But what is to be gained by the commonwealth if it robs Peter to pay Paul? Is all this worthwhile in order that Los Angeles should be just so big? . . . It is worthwhile for other cities to consider that as this case proceeds their own water problems are likely to be shaped by it more or less. Shall the question of domestic water in California be determined by craft and graft and bitterness and long-drawn wasteful struggles, or conducted with rightness and dignity to an equal conclusion? . . . Heaven send in the interests of decent government that they will not make good the boast of the promoters [of the aqueduct] to have their private ears. In a republic, government is not supposed to have a private ear.[112]

At the same time, Wallace Austin made a similar shift in the letters he wrote to Washington, focusing his attack on Lippincott and the Reclamation Service rather than on Eaton. Whereas his earlier correspondence in June had been directed to his superiors in the General Land Office, warning them of Fred Eaton's activities without making any charges, Austin now wrote directly to the president charging that Lippincott had connived with Eaton "to betray the Government" in exchange for secret payments from Los Angeles. "The whole outrageous scheme is now made plain," Austin wrote to Theodore Roosevelt on August 4, 1905.

> Mr. Lippincott while drawing a large salary from the Government was employed by the City of Los Angeles to assist in securing this water for the city. He agreed to turn down this project at the critical moment when the Los Angeles men had secured other rights here which they wanted ... The connection between Mr. Lippincott and Eaton deceived the people of this valley ... [who] could not believe that a plan to rob the valley of its water and turn down the Government's irrigation project was being carried out with the consent of the Supervising Engineer.[113]

Austin clearly overstated his case. He could not prove that Lippincott had been employed by the city for the purpose of assisting in its land acquisitions; the Reclamation Service had not yet abandoned its irrigation project; and his estimate elsewhere in this letter that there were two hundred and eighty thousand acres in the valley that could be served by irrigation was far too high. But Austin soon followed up his letter to the president with a petition from the valley residents asking for a formal investigation by any agency other than the Reclamation Service.[114]

Ironically, Austin had had his attention turned to Lippincott's role in the city's plan by the *Los Angeles Times*. In its first reports of the aqueduct, the *Times* included an article under the heading "Good Grace of Government" in which it injudiciously commended Lippincott for his "valuable assistance" in "looking after" Fred Eaton's purchases and for his help in arranging an initial survey of the route for the aqueduct by federal engineers. "Without Mr. Lippincott's interest and cooperation, it is declared that the plan never would have gone through," the *Times* concluded. "Any other government engineer, a non-resident of Los Angeles and not familiar with the needs of this section, undoubtedly would have gone ahead with nothing more than the mere reclamation of arid lands in view."[115]

Damned by such avid praise, Lippincott moved quickly to cover himself with his superiors. "Many of the statements are true and some are not," he wrote in a letter enclosing the *Times* article on the same day it appeared. "I certainly never had any of our men locate a line for the city," he protested, while acknowledging that "there are some men who were employed at one time on a level line for the topographic division and who on my recommendation were afterwards employed by the city." Otherwise, Lippincott assured Davis, "I have never told anyone that the Government had withdrawn from Owens Valley but I have stated that I thought they ought to under the circumstances as a matter of best public policy." Lippincott then concluded with a cheery observation which Davis may well have taken in a way Lippincott never intended: "I think you will see how vital the people of Southern California consider this is to them. You will note that they have paid well for what they have got."[116]

Lippincott had no way of knowing at the time that Austin was not his only problem. Before leaving for a tour of the western states, Newell had submitted to the personnel committee of the Reclamation Service Lippincott's formal request for permission to accept a private contract with the city. The service's recommendation, submitted to Newell on July 12, denounced not only Lippincott's involvement with Los Angeles but also his private contracts with the city of Santa Barbara:

> Not only is private work in violation of law and regulation, but the two engagements which he proposes to continue are peculiarly repugnant to his duties in the Reclamation Service. At the present time it is understood that the City of Los Angeles desires the Reclamation Service to relinquish an attractive irrigation project on which extensive investigations have been and are being made, and Mr. Lippincott, while acting as the Government adviser on this project, is accepting pay from the city for his services, including the exertion of his influence to have the Government retire from the field. The City of Santa Barbara is using expensive boring machinery belonging to the Government which was loaned on the recommendation of Mr. Lippincott who is receiving pay from the said city and proposes to continue in that relation. These are conditions which if publicly exploited by the enemies of the Reclamation Service would lead to great scandal. We have therefore to urgently recommend that in obedience to the orders of the Secretary of the Interior, and the requirements of the law, Mr. Lippincott be required to take a leave of absence until such time as he shall have closed up his private engagements or to resign his commission in the Reclamation Service.[117]

At the same time Lippincott was writing to disavow the *Times'* report, D.C. Henny wrote to Davis to confirm the story in his final report of the board of engineers that had been called to review the Reclamation Service's Owens Valley project. Henny, however, unlike the *Times*, regarded the extent of Lippincott's assistance to the city as a matter deserving contempt rather than praise. At the time of their hearing, the board had seen only Austin's earlier charges of July, which dealt primarily with Eaton's activities rather than with those of Lippincott. On the charge that Eaton had claimed to represent Lippincott, the panel nevertheless concluded that "the allegations are probably true in a general way." Furthermore, Henny advised, Austin's assertion that many valley residents had consequently been misled into selling their land cheaply to Eaton "seems a plausible one to this Board."[118]

Henny refused to comment further on Lippincott's involvement with Los Angeles in his formal report, observing that it was the board's opinion that this was a matter that did not seem "necessary or desirable to touch upon" in public. In a separate, personal letter to Davis, however, Henny warned, "The real danger in the entire matter does not lie so much in any action on the part of the officers of the Reclamation Service taken independently, as in the fact that in Mr. Lippincott's personal case he has represented two interests which are clearly antagonistic, and that Mr. Lippincott has allowed the United States Geological Survey and the United States Reclamation Service to be made use of for the private purposes of the City of Los Angeles." With regard to Lippincott's future employment by the service, Henny advised, "I have little doubt regarding an attractive offer likely to be made to Lippincott by the City of Los Angeles possibly as a reward for past services . . . All these connections and alliances I think are vicious and must bring disrepute upon the Service." Henny concluded on an even more disquieting note for Davis and the other officials in Washington: "This, of course, is a very delicate matter and one which I believe Mr. Newell and yourself had a full understanding of."[119]

It had been Newell, and not Davis, who negotiated the initial plan for cooperation with Los Angeles, and it was to Newell that Lippincott had revealed his employment with Los Angeles. But Newell was on tour when Austin's letters first began to arrive in

Washington, so it was Davis who had to contend with the controversy that followed public disclosure of Lippincott's activities. But neither Davis nor Newell understood the significance of Lippincott's selection of Eaton as his agent for the right-of-way investigations until Austin's letters revealed what Eaton had been doing.[120] On July 29, Lippincott sent a telegram to Davis, warning: "City Los Angeles has made public its intentions towards Owens Valley. Have referred newspaper correspondents to your office for information."[121] That night, Davis wrote to Newell to request instructions and to offer some advice:

> The crucial question is whether [Eaton] has been authorized by Mr. Lippincott to represent himself as a reclamation official . . . Apparently some property owners have sold him property much cheaper than they otherwise would owing to his supposed power of condemnation in the Reclamation Service. It is likely that some of these property owners will endeavor to make it warm for the parties concerned. I think we cannot clear the skirts of the Reclamation Service any too quickly nor completely.[122]

Newell's first reaction, typically, was to temporize. "I think it will be wise to defer action so we can discuss matters with Mr. Walcott" (head of the Geological Survey), he wired Davis two weeks later.[123] Davis did his best to keep matters under control until Newell's scheduled return on September 12. But once Los Angeles' bond election broke into full cry in August, with charges and countercharges of municipal corruption flying, the situation developed too quickly for Davis to contain. Letters and telegrams began to pour in from Owens Valley residents and from western congressmen and senators, either protesting the Reclamation Service's abandonment of the valley or urging it to proceed with abandonment. The ensuing furor rose rapidly from the offices of the Reclamation Service to the Geological Survey and thence to the secretary of the interior, who began inundating Davis with demands for a clarification of the service's position.[124]

Newell, at his great distance from the storm center, persisted in believing that the problem involved nothing more than a relatively straightforward question of Lippincott's conflict of interest. On August 6 he promised to get together with Walcott upon his return to Washington to discuss a formal prohibition on outside consulting by federal engineers.[125] Davis was at first inclined to agree with this limited view. "The mix-up in the Owens Valley project ... would have caused little or no embarrassment if we had adhered to the law which requires our engineers to abstain from outside practice," he confided to Henny on August 14.[126] Certainly there was no question that Lippincott had failed to honor his promise to Newell, when he had first accepted his assignment as supervising engineer, to withdraw from private practice. Even though Lippincott was still renewing this pledge to Newell as late as the end of June, he had, as the personnel committee pointed out in July, continued his private involvements with Los Angeles and Santa Barbara.[127] Instead of cutting back on his private practice, Lippincott, as Davis and Newell discovered, had been using his position with the Reclamation Service to secure still more contracts for his firm. Lippincott even went so far as to arrange a contract with the city of Bishop for the construction of its water and sewer system at the same time as he was secretly working to divert the Owens Valley's water to Los Angeles.[128]

But the controversy ignited by disclosure of Lippincott's indiscretions soon expanded to threaten other parts of the pattern of federal land and water policies which the Reclamation Service had been struggling to establish. The city of San Francisco, for example, was quick to pass a resolution commending the federal government for its assistance to Los Angeles in the Owens Valley matter and observing caustically that it wished the government would exhibit the same spirit of cooperation in granting approval to its own Hetch Hetchy project, which was at that time being held up by the Department of the Interior.[129] Other officers of the service similarly began to complain of the damage they feared Lippincott's entanglements would do to the good works they were striving to accomplish. This concern had, of course, been foremost in the minds of Henny, Sanders, and Taylor as they reviewed the Owens Valley project. A rodman working for the Geological Survey in the Owens Valley, for example, wrote on August 2 to denounce Lippincott's efforts to convince Los Angeles to take the water needed for Owens Valley agriculture in order that "a pleasure loving city of wealthy idlers may add to her welth [*sic*] by forever condemning to absilute [*sic*] desert these same thousands of acres."[130] Similarly, George Wisner, a construction engineer working on the service's other projects in California, wrote on August 19 to urge that Lippincott's office as supervising engineer be shut down altogether: "With good construction engineers in charge of the Yuma and Klamath projects, I see no reason for maintenance of an expensive supervising engineer's office at Los Angeles ... To abolish the office of supervising engineer in this State will in my opinion greatly simplify the rather serious complications which have arisen in the Los Angeles office."[131]

On a broader and potentially more threatening level, the so-called mix-up in the Owens Valley called into question the integrity of the entire process of withdrawal by which the Reclamation Service sought to set aside large sections of public domain for the eventual construction of public irrigation projects. Western irrigators complained that the federal government, by withdrawing vast tracts of land from settlement, was stifling economic development for its own purposes. Although western irrigators had pioneered in the theories of watershed protection through forestry management which had led to the creation of the first federal forestry reserves, western political leaders were still sharply divided on the question of whether the federal government should set itself up as a competitor with private enterprise in the development of natural resources. By investing the Reclamation Service with the power to have withdrawals made on its behalf, the Reclamation Act of 1902 had given public agencies an insurmountable advantage over any private water developer. And even before the advent of the Reclamation Service, federal officials had often demonstrated a readiness to pursue the creation of reserves without regard for the wishes of state political leaders. Defenders of free enterprise and states' rights therefore joined readily with private water and power companies to oppose the work of the service. The annual meetings of the National Irrigation Congress became their battleground and the influential publication *Irrigation Age* their spokesman.[132]

Newell had shown himself generally unsympathetic to these

concerns, and he resisted attempts by western political leaders to achieve modifications in the projects being built by the Reclamation Service in their states. A major reorganization of land management programs in the Departments of Interior and Agriculture in 1905 did nothing to assuage western fears of federal interference and indifference; rather, it exacerbated them by tightening Washington's control of the public domain with a plethora of new rules and regulations on land use and leasing policy. Fees for the first time were assessed for grazing and irrigation rights on federal lands; new reserves were created; and local field agents were replaced with officials from Washington. These changes, of course, ranged far beyond the limited sphere of Newell's authority, so he was not the only or even a principal object of the hostility they engendered. But when it became clear in the summer of 1905 that his enthusiasm for making withdrawals had far exceeded the ability of the Reclamation Service to fund the many projects for which the lands had been withdrawn, western congressmen took to attacking his integrity as well as his arrogance.[133]

As the personnel committee had warned, Lippincott's difficulties now offered the enemies of the service a prime opportunity to demonstrate the defects in Newell's leadership. The problem was not simply the mix-up in the Owens Valley project or the fact that Newell had chosen for his supervising engineer in California an imperfect vessel for the public trust. For at the same time Lippincott and Newell were attempting to justify abandonment of the Owens Valley on the grounds that the Reclamation Service lacked the funds to construct a project there, they were coming under increasing pressure to explain why Lippincott, with Newell's encouragement, had also withdrawn huge areas of the San Joaquin and Imperial valleys, where the service had no conceivable expectation of constructing any projects for decades to come. Overall, Newell in his first three years as head of the service withdrew more than 40 million acres in the western states, 2,666,860 of which lay in California. And yet, out of all these 40 million acres, he conceded that only a million might ultimately be reclaimed within the foreseeable future.[134]

The Reclamation Service field officers in California were in the best position to appreciate the potential for embarrassment which these conditions posed, and so they readily made use of Lippincott's enthusiasm for excessive withdrawals to reinforce their calls for his dismissal. George Wisner, for example, pointed to the withdrawals in the Imperial Valley to support his advocacy for the abolition of Lippincott's office. And Henny privately advised Davis that as difficult as abandonment of the Owens Valley might prove to be politically, "the same delicate situation exists in regard to the so-called San Joaquin Project, which Mr. Lippincott has admitted is practically not under consideration, but upon the strength of which large withdrawals have been made." Henny dwelt at length upon the risks of Newell's and Lippincott's policy of making premature withdrawals:

> Such withdrawals under the Reclamation Act can only be justified by a bona-fide project for whose benefit they are made, and the question has arisen and was frankly discussed [among the members of the review panel] whether restoration should not be in order as soon as such a project is practically abandoned, and whether, if such restoration is not made and the withdrawal maintained, such action can be justified, as it cannot have been the object of the Reclamation Act to make withdrawal under it merely for what may be claimed to be general public policy, and what in effect may be the favoring of the interests of one public body as against those of another public body or of a private corporation.[135]

In addition to these general defects of a policy of widespread withdrawals, the specific case of the Owens Valley project presented an especially heinous example of an abuse of Reclamation Service authority. For Lippincott had been taking money from another public agency whose interests were directly antagonistic to those of the irrigators on whose behalf the withdrawals had been made in the first place. As Henny observed in his catalogue of the risks of premature withdrawal: "All of this, even, may seem justified so long as there cannot exist a financial relation between any of the public bodies interested and officers of the Reclamation Service making recommendations."[136] More important, whereas withdrawals in the San Joaquin and Imperial valleys only affected principally barren lands which could not be made productive without the kind of massive water importation projects that only public agencies could afford, the service's involvement in the Owens Valley had interfered with the economic growth of a rapidly developing region where irrigation development was already well advanced. Having interrupted the pace of private development of the valley with its withdrawals, the service had then kept the valley's lands in suspension while another entity readied itself to initiate a project which would at best severely curtail the prospects for further agricultural growth there. Through Lippincott, therefore, the Reclamation Service could be charged with actively working to undermine the very purposes for which it had been created.

Newell and Davis knew they would not have to wait for these complaints to be raised in the West; some of their most ardent enemies were right in Washington. The United States Army Corps of Engineers had opposed the formation of the Reclamation Service, just as it had fought any form of federal involvement in water programs for any purpose other than the enhancement of navigation. The officers of the corps not only opposed the principle of coordinated water resource development, they rejected the theory that forestry land management could have any effect on watershed protection and even denied that floods could be contained by reservoirs. In the Department of Agriculture, western interests opposed to Reclamation Service policies had found a champion in Elwood Mead, the head of that department's irrigation investigations, who urged the cession of more federal lands to the states so that private commercial interests could take the lead in western resource development. Mead had sought the authority to implement the Reclamation Act of 1902 for his own agency rather than the Geological Survey; and following that defeat, Newell had worked to have Mead's office abolished. The greatest threat to Newell and the Reclamation Service in the case of the Owens Valley controversy, however, lay in the General Land Office, which resented the intrusion of this new agency upon its historic role of supervising the public domain. The General Land Office enjoyed a far broader base of support within the western states than Newell or anyone else in the Department of the Interior at that time, and the lands commissioner consequently could expect the attention and cooperation of the president. And it was to this agency that Austin had directed his complaints against the Reclamation Service.

Newell and Davis, moreover, could not rely on the Department of the Interior to defend them from attack. If anything, the Secretary of the Interior, Ethan A. Hitchcock, was more profoundly disturbed than anyone else by charges of corruption. A Chicago industrialist, Hitchcock had been appointed to his post by President McKinley on a pledge to rid federal lands programs of the frauds and scandals which had plagued them throughout the last decades of the nineteenth century. He suspected anyone associated with land and water resource development and promised to stamp out corruption wherever he found it, observing in his first annual report, "The higher the offender, the greater the crime against society and law, because of the force and influence of the higher example." Hitchcock had little interest in convoluted theories of resource management; he believed federal lands should either be preserved from any form of use or opened to settlement. His strict sense of legality and high moral purpose left little room for halfway measures, and he therefore opposed commercial leases on the public domain for limited grazing or recreational uses.[137]

Confronted with the multiple charges against Lippincott and the Reclamation Service in the Owens Valley case, Hitchcock declared his determination "to go to the bottom of this matter and to ascertain the exact facts in the case whatever they may be."[138] Davis was consequently inundated with inquiries from the secretary's office demanding to know when Lippincott had learned of Los Angeles' interest in the Owens Valley, how he had acted to favor the city, and how much he had told Newell about what he was doing. Davis, in Newell's absence, tried to put the best face possible on Lippincott's activities. Though he acknowledged that "it is well known that the desires of the City of Los Angeles have been favored by Mr. Lippincott," he hastened to point out that "Mr. Lippincott, as a resident of Los Angeles, has at all times known of the desires of the citizens for a better water supply and, in fact, has been one of the chief advocates of a better

supply for Southern California, being the authority on this subject . . . As to how much or how little Mr. Lippincott knew . . . it
is impossible to state at this time." If Lippincott had been secretly
informed of the city's designs on the Owens Valley, Davis argued
with tortured logic, "he unquestionably respected that confidence
as a matter of public duty and of personal integrity."

In early August, Davis was willing even to go so far as to
support Lippincott's position. "Conceding that the Owens Valley
Project . . . is feasible both from the point of view of the water
supply and of the cost of the work," he told Hitchcock on August
11, "it is nevertheless the fact that the use of this water supply for
the City of Los Angeles is probably more important to the growth
of the southern section of California than the development of the
Owens Valley Project."[139] Within two weeks of this endorsement,
however, Davis changed his mind. In the spring of 1905, Newell
had come as close as he ever would to providing the city with
direct assistance when he permitted Lippincott to reinstitute surveys in the Owens Valley even though he knew that this work
would be used by Los Angeles in its planning for the aqueduct.
Newell had hoped to preserve the appearance of legitimacy for
this decision by encouraging Lippincott to extract a promise
from the city that it would pay the costs of any work performed
by federal engineers. Lippincott had never obtained such a pledge
from the city in writing, but Newell nevertheless expected this
understanding to be honored. When Davis learned in the latter
part of August that Lippincott had betrayed even this confidence
he turned irrevocably against Lippincott.

Lippincott had told the city's water officials that the costs for
which they would be expected to reimburse the government
would not exceed $12,000. In reviewing Lippincott's accounts,
however, Davis discovered that Lippincott had attributed a total
of $13,888.26 in direct costs to the Owens Valley project and
nothing at all for the usual overhead expenses which were customarily distributed among all projects in order to cover the costs
of maintaining the Reclamation Service offices in Washington
and Los Angeles. In addition, Lippincott had charged not a
penny to the city's account for the costs of Mendenhall's study of
groundwater conditions in the South Coast, even though these

reports, as Davis pointed out to Newell, "had a very direct, intimate, and important bearing on the possible water supply of the City of Los Angeles, and consequently upon the desire of that city to acquire the Owens Valley Project."[140]

On August 24, Davis informed Newell that he was calling for a formal audit, although a preliminary analysis had revealed that the actual amount Los Angeles should repay was $17,853.39, and Davis believed the total might rise to $20,000.[141] "The facts ... clearly show that Mr. Lippincott has been biased in the distribution of expenses ... [although] it will probably be impossible to unearth all of the [costs Lippincott charged elsewhere]," Davis fumed. Davis announced that he was withdrawing his endorsement of a proposal Newell had earlier favored to increase Lippincott's salary "liberally" as a way of persuading him to give up his private consulting practice. Davis told Newell:

> So many things have come to my attention during the past summer, which I can describe to you verbally, that are of a similar nature to the above that I am convinced that Lippincott is so blind to the public interest and so biased by private and selfish considerations that it will be impossible to secure loyal service from him; and I believe the only safe way for the Reclamation Service is to encourage him to devote his time to private practice and give up his connection with the Reclamation Service ... I have the highest appreciation of the ability and energy of Mr. Lippincott; but I believe that loyalty to the interests of the Service is just as essential as ability, particularly in a position so high as he will demand for continued service.[142]

Accordingly, on August 31, Davis delivered a mass of records and correspondence concerning Lippincott's activities to the Secretary of the Interior with the declaration, "I intend to go to the bottom of this matter, if possible, and think I will succeed."[143] It was too late. Hitchcock had determined by this time to take the matter out of his hands and honor Austin's request for an independent investigation of the Reclamation Service. The same day Davis delivered his pledge, Hitchcock sent a telegram to his top special investigator S. F. O'Fallon, in Sheridan, Wyoming, ordering him to proceed immediately to the Owens Valley, where written instructions would be waiting.[144] Upon his arrival in Independence, O'Fallon—who throughout his long career with the Department of the Interior had distinguished himself as one of the government's most trusted Indian agents and all-round troubleshooters—found eight pages of instructions detailing Austin's charges and directing him to begin immediately gathering depositions and sworn affidavits from everyone involved. "The Department wishes to impress upon your mind that it wants the exact facts in this matter, so that it may be enabled to do exact justice to all parties concerned," O'Fallon's instructions warned. "You will readily understand that if the charges made against Mr. Lippincott, the Supervising Engineer, are true, that he should not be in the public service; and that if the charges made by Mr. Austin against him are not true, then Mr. Austin ought not to be in public service."[145]

Austin received a similar directive from Hitchcock's office. "The charges made . . . against Mr. Lippincott are of so serious a nature that the Department cannot afford to ignore them," Austin was advised. "What the Department desires is evidence; not conclusions or inferences or mere allegations."[146] Austin responded enthusiastically to this announcement and urged that the federal investigator be given full authority, free rein, and a liberal travel budget because much of the evidence against Lippincott was in Los Angeles, and other facts were known only to employees of the Reclamation Service who had since been transferred out of the Owens Valley. He especially emphasized the need for speed. "Every delay can but work further injury to the people here," he warned, "by giving to the Los Angeles promoters time to perfect their plans."[147]

Lippincott was less happy to learn of O'Fallon's arrival on the scene. On September 8, he wrote to Newell and Davis demanding that the Reclamation Service defend him against Austin's charges.[148] On September 12, he wrote Hitchcock to ask that he at least be provided with a copy of Henny's final report for the board of engineers reviewing the Owens Valley project. "This is due me," Lippincott complained with a remarkably impolitic argument, "not only because we are carrying on work under my direction in Owens Valley but also because of the intense interest and financial obligation that the City of Los Angeles is assuming in that valley at present."[149] These appeals were unavailing, however, and on September 19 Lippincott requested permission to speak out in his own defense. "I think that these statements should be publicly denied," he told Newell. "If you feel that it is improper to issue any statement from the Washington office—which would be preferable as far as I am concerned—I wish you would permit me to make a statement myself."[150] This request too was turned down.[151] And when Lippincott complained that, as a result of Mary Austin's article in the *San Francisco Chronicle*, "I am having my first experience along the lines of an attack on my motives and integrity in connection with the Owens Valley matter," Newell suggested he bring a libel suit against Mrs. Austin if he felt he had been wronged. Lippincott quickly backed away from this challenge, advising Newell, "I am reminded of my father-in-law's advice—'Sue a beggar and catch a louse' . . . I have felt that the thing for me to do concerning this Owens Valley situation is to await with as much patience as I can the outcome of the investigations that are being carried on by the Secretary. A few words from Washington will do more to put the Reclamation Service, and particularly myself, straight along these lines than anything else."[152]

Newell by this time was too busy defending himself to bother with Lippincott's problems. And just as Lippincott had attempted to disassociate himself from Eaton when their activities were first revealed, so too did Newell find that his best line of defense lay in disavowing any knowledge of Lippincott's activities. At first, Newell denied knowing anything of Los Angeles' interest in the Owens Valley before Senator Flint and Governor Pardee had approached him on June 17, 1905, during his western tour.[153] When he discovered upon his return to Washington that his earlier meeting with Mulholland in November 1904 had been revealed to the Secretary of the Interior, he turned to complaints that his memory was faulty because "I have not given much personal thought to the Owens Valley situation."[154]

Newell soon found that his protestations of ignorance were continually running afoul of the avalanche of correspondence which Lippincott was sending to officials in Washington in an effort to defend his own actions. In each letter, Lippincott seemed to come up with another meeting or directive from Newell which Lippincott used to argue that he had been acting in the best interests of the Reclamation Service. Each letter, in turn, produced a brusque demand from the secretary's office for copies of the correspondence or records to which Lippincott had just referred. Newell's correspondence files for the latter part of 1905 consequently began to fill with laborious responses to Hitchcock's detailed inquiries.[155] Exasperated, Newell wrote to Lippincott at the end of September complaining,

> This has been a source of considerable annoyance and embarrassment . . . it would be well for you, if you feel that you must make some reply, to write a very concise, specific letter to me covering the principal points, flatly contradicting the assertions made, making no admissions or qualified statements which can be misconstrued, and not entering into lengthy explanations. Such a letter given out from this end will, I think, be far more effectual than anything which can be seized upon as the subject of controversy.[156]

Lippincott did not comply, and Newell again warned him, "You have made so many voluminous statements and explanations that the effect is not of the best."[157] When this had no effect, Newell ordered Lippincott to stop referring to other letters in his correspondence. "Special pains should be taken in reports to strike out all allusion and references which are not perfectly clear," he complained of Lippincott's letters. "Their vagueness makes them a subject of suspicion."[158]

So distracted did Newell become by the painstaking thoroughness of the secretary's investigation that he even berated Henny for preparing a transcript of the board of engineers' hearing on the Owens Valley project. "I think a mistake was made in permitting [a] stenographic report," he remarked in a personal letter, "as it furnishes material to a pettifogging opponent to weave an elaborate argument on some phrase or word taken from this context." Henny promptly assured Newell that he would not make the same mistake again.[159]

Finding himself abandoned by his superiors in Washington, Lippincott resolved to mount a political campaign on his own behalf. As soon as O'Fallon commenced his investigation, Lippincott began gathering endorsements of his actions. On September 8, the Engineers and Architects Association of Southern California unanimously adopted a resolution expressing "the personal esteem in which Mr. Lippincott is held by the members of this association and . . . its belief that Mr. Lippincott's action in the matter of the acquisition of a water supply by the City of Los Angeles from Owens River Valley has been entirely straightforward and honorable to himself and the Government which he so ably serves."[160] Lippincott sent this resolution to Newell together with a report that, at a meeting of the Los Angeles Realty Board the next night, "the expressions of friendship and compliments towards the Reclamation Service were so pronounced as to be almost embarrassing."[161] Lippincott soon secured a similar endorsement, specifically urging that he be retained in his current position, from the Los Angeles Chamber of Commerce.[162] And Mulholland and the board of water commissioners were equally cooperative in providing reports to O'Fallon which completely exonerated Lippincott of any wrongdoing.[163]

For more influential endorsements, Lippincott turned to Senator Flint and Governor Pardee. Flint was unwilling to intervene on Lippincott's behalf, but Pardee was more than helpful.[164] Pardee's assistance was especially useful to Lippincott because, as president of the National Irrigation Congress, Pardee was the Reclamation Service's most valuable western ally. In his first inaugural address, Governor Pardee had committed his administration to the development of a comprehensive forest and water resource conservation program, and he soon followed through by reestablishing a board of forestry at the state level.[165] On September 15, Pardee wrote to Hitchcock asking to know what charges had been brought against Lippincott. Though he assured Hitchcock that "the only interest I have in the matter is an official one," he requested that no action be taken to dismiss Lippincott until he had been granted the opportunity to plead Lippincott's case as part of his own "great official interest in the whole subject matter of irrigation." Hitchcock, to his credit, rejected all

Pardee's requests, advising that Lippincott already knew what charges had been brought against him.[166] Thus rebuffed, Pardee tried again, this time sending Newell a copy of an appeal from Austin for Pardee's assistance and asking for details. Newell responded confidentially with a blanket denial of all Austin's allegations.[167]

These efforts did not deter O'Fallon from his course. On October 5, he completed his report. In a fifty-seven-page study buttressed by dozens of sworn affidavits and exhibits, he meticulously reviewed the evidence Austin had produced against Lippincott, together with a considerable number of additional details which had only been brought to light as a result of his investigation.

On the subject of Lippincott's employment by Los Angeles, O'Fallon acknowledged that he had never reported specifically to the city on the Owens Valley project. O'Fallon pointed out, however, that "his action in this matter injures the reputation of the Reclamation Service and places him in an equivocal position, and when he now advises the Department that the Owens Valley Reclamation Project be abandoned in favor of the City of Los Angeles, it has the appearance of coming from a paid representative of the City." He noted, moreover, that Lippincott's acceptance of this contract violated the promises he had given Newell at the time he was employed by the Reclamation Service. In his defense, Lippincott had argued that he could scarcely have opposed the city's plans except by going to the Owens Valley and urging people not to sell their water rights to Eaton, and he would not have done this in view of the fact that he personally believed the water would be put to better use in Los Angeles. O'Fallon dismissed this argument by pointing out that Lippincott could easily have told his friends in Los Angeles not to interfere with the Reclamation Service project. O'Fallon further observed, "I do not believe that either the promoters or the City would have spent a dollar in acquiring land or water rights in the Owens Valley if they had not known that Supervising Engineer Lippincott was favorable to their enterprise, and that at the proper time would recommend the abandonment of the Government project.

His conduct in this entire matter in my opinion deserves the severest condemnation."[168]

O'Fallon was equally critical of Lippincott's selection of Eaton as his agent for investigating right-of-way applications in the Owens Valley. Although O'Fallon agreed that this decision would not have been improper under other circumstances, he pointed out that "it was well known [to Lippincott] that Mr. Eaton was more deeply interested than any other single person in defeating the government's project . . . It seems almost farcical to have the promoter of a scheme that was antagonistic to the government project reporting on other applications that they should be refused on account of interference with the plans of the Reclamation Service." But O'Fallon found no evidence to suggest that Lippincott had directly assisted Eaton in securing options for the city, or that Eaton had ever directly misrepresented himself. He even conceded that Eaton had been at least partially honest in telling prospective sellers that he was interested in their land for a cattle ranch. O'Fallon noted, however, that the people of the Owens Valley were confused and misled by their knowledge of Eaton's close association with Lippincott, and by the fact that Eaton had in his employ certain former employees of the Reclamation Service. As a result, O'Fallon concluded, "There is no doubt . . . that if the people of the valley had realized the true situation they would have obtained much more for their property than they actually received." And, if Lippincott did not directly assist Eaton in securing options, O'Fallon expressed his certain conviction that "Mr. Lippincott evidently knew that Mr. Eaton was obtaining these options, and he is alleged to have connived at it, which, no doubt, is a proper conclusion from his entire conduct in the premises."[169]

Although O'Fallon refused to concur in all the allegations and conclusions Austin had made in his various letters, he defended both Austin and the federal lands receiver, Richard Fysh, from any charge of misrepresentation.

> So far as the statement of facts in [their] communications is concerned, they are true. Mr. Austin . . . is a first class official, honest, upright, and in the conduct of the office

cannot be commended too highly . . . I believe, under all
the circumstances, that their conduct has been justified,
and while probably somewhat hysterical, as would be
natural under the circumstance, they were influenced in
these communications by proper motives and a desire
that the full facts be brought to the attention of the President and Department in this matter.[170]

On the question of Lippincott's motives, O'Fallon was equally
resolute. "After considering the whole matter, I can arrive at no
other conclusion than that Supervising Engineer Lippincott's
action in the matter is indefensible, and for the good of the
Reclamation Service he should be separated from it. He is no
doubt a capable official and could have rendered valuable aid to
the Reclamation Service, but his conduct in this matter has been
such as, in my opinion, would destroy his usefulness as a public
official."[171]

Having pressed the investigation so vigorously, Hitchcock
was slow to act on its conclusions. Three months passed before
Davis instructed Lippincott to come to Washington for a meeting with Hitchcock and the director of the Geological Survey,
Charles Walcott. "The Secretary sent for [Walcott] on the 24th,"
Davis informed Lippincott at the end of January, "and informed
him that he had read every word [of O'Fallon's report] and carefully considered the correspondence in the Owens Valley matter,
and had come to the conclusion that your usefulness to the Reclamation Service was at an end."[172] Lippincott called on his
friends once more in a last effort to stave off dismissal. The Los
Angeles Chamber of Commerce sent another letter to Walcott in
his defense.[173] And Governor Pardee vigorously protested his
impending dismissal in a letter to Hitchcock. With regard to the
problems of the Owens Valley, Pardee acknowledged, "I have
not, as yet, been able sufficiently to inform myself to arrive at an
opinion"; but he considered that question irrelevant to Lippincott's situation.

Our people believe in him, and were his connection with
the Reclamation Service now to terminate, I am firmly of
the opinion that our people would feel that they had been
deprived of the very greatly needed services of a compe-

tent, energetic, and conscientious man . . . His loss from the Service, for any cause, would be a serious setback to the work of the Reclamation Service in this State . . . The enemies of the Service would regard it as a distinct victory . . . the introduction of the thin edge of a disrupting wedge.[174]

Charges of corruption in a public agency are commonly answered with the promise of prompt investigation. When it comes to exacting punishment, however, it is often easier to tolerate the excesses of an individual rather than risk the reputation of the agency as a whole by condemning them. It would have been difficult to take action against Lippincott without tarnishing Newell, who enjoyed the active encouragement of the White House in his efforts to establish a comprehensive water resource program for the West. Pardee had effectively described the consequences for the nascent federal reclamation program that would follow upon an incautious passion for justice in Lippincott's case. In the face of that danger, Hitchcock softened his attitude.

In a memorandum recording his meeting with Lippincott and Hitchcock at the end of February, Walcott attempted to minimize the embarrassment for all concerned. "It appears that Mr. Lippincott erred in being overzealous in the interests of Los Angeles . . . I feel convinced, however, that it was not with the intention of wronging the people of Owens Valley, or of taking undue advantage of his position as an engineer of the Reclamation Service."[175] Hitchcock, however, was not satisfied with this account of their meeting. "To make the record somewhat clearer," Hitchcock wrote, "he practically admitted the substantial correctness of Mr. O'Fallon's report, and replied with the statement that his action as criticized was not only erroneous and much to be regretted, but [would] not be in any case repeated."[176] On Lippincott's solemn promise that he would sever all connections with his consulting practice and avoid any business relations "that will in fact or appearance connect him with any private or public project that will bring him in any pecuniary or personal advantage, or bring any reflection upon the Reclamation Service," Hitchcock agreed that Lippincott could remain with the service.[177] Hitchcock had gone to the bottom of things as he promised, but the skirts of the Reclamation Service remained uncleared.

The Issue Is Joined

Lippincott remained with the Reclamation Service only long enough to see Los Angeles' project through the process of obtaining the federal rights-of-way it required. So long as Lippincott's status with the service was unresolved, the city did not press its claims in Washington. Throughout all the long months of Hitchcock's investigations, therefore, the lands in the Owens Valley remained in suspension. The year 1905 was a particularly difficult time in the valley. The opening of the gold fields to the east severely overloaded the local railroad facilities, with the result that by that summer an embargo had been placed on all freight moving in and out of the valley except for clothing and food so as to make room for the equipment the miners needed and the precious ore they were producing.[178] With Lippincott's case decided in the spring of 1906, the contending interests of the city and the valley moved rapidly toward a direct confrontation before the United States Congress.

Los Angeles' reticence with regard to its plans created additional complications for the Reclamation Service's efforts at skirt-clearing. Although the service had not taken over any storage rights in the Owens Valley or made any promises that it would proceed with an irrigation project there, Hitchcock of course was anxious to learn what course it intended to pursue once the storm of controversy had broken in the late summer of 1905. Davis argued that "it is up to the City to show that the project should be surrendered to it."[179] And though the acquisition of land and water rights were for Los Angeles "the first vital obstacles to be overcome," Davis was quick to point out to the secretary that the service would not have to address the question of whether the city's purchases had rendered its irrigation project infeasible until a host of other problems had been resolved. "Since these vague rights attach to the lands to be benefitted, and are, under usage sanctioned by the Department, merged or blended or recognized in the operation of reclamation," Davis contended that the city would either have to extinguish the federal government's pre-existing claims through legislation or render them "innocuous" through a system of water storage that would benefit the valley as well as Los Angeles.

While Lippincott, always the activist on the city's behalf, was pressing his superiors in Washington to make an early announcement that the government would abandon the Owens Valley project, Davis saw no need for precipitate action, at least not until the bond election had been concluded in Los Angeles. "The purpose of the city can only be ascertained by a vote of its citizens," he told Hitchcock.[180] The service thus refused to recommend any course of action on the Owens Valley project other than waiting to see what Los Angeles would do next. Newell's attitude was encapsulated in an article on the Owens Valley project that he published in October 1905 in *Out West*. Whereas in another article only two months earlier he had listed the Owens Valley as one of the service's three most promising projects in California, he now admitted that the project was being held in abeyance pending a decision by higher authorities for which he would not be personally responsible. "These are matters," Newell declared, "which in their finality must be dealt with by other branches of the Government than the Reclamation Service."[181]

As much as Newell might have wished to pass the problem elsewhere, the course he chose was scarcely neutral in its effect. For as Austin had warned, the longer the federal government delayed, the more time the city had to perfect its plans. And when the election passed and still no action had been taken, some legal experts within the Department of the Interior expressed concern that any rights the federal government might have in the valley would lapse because the Reclamation Service had not been diligent in exercising them.[182] While Austin turned his attention to the gathering of facts and affidavits for O'Fallon's investigation, other citizens of the Owens Valley began appealing to their representatives in Washington for assistance in obtaining a prompt resolution of the situation. "We have braved the hardships, builded our homes, laid many a loved one to rest here," wrote one longtime valley resident to the president, "and now to think of being robbed of our water by a few moneyed men. I appeal to you to help us . . . and as speedily as possible."[183] Similarly, in a unanimous action, the Board of Supervisors of Inyo County petitioned Hitchcock to "earnestly request that the government prosecute with all due and reasonable diligence, its investigations and work on [the] Owens Valley Reclamation Project."[184] The most persistent pressure for prompt action came from the Owens River Water and Power Company, which sent its attorneys to Washington, where they met with the president to protest the Reclamation Service's interference in their plans for private development.[185]

Although Newell, at Hitchcock's insistence, did write to Los Angeles' Mayor Owen McAleer in late September asking for a complete report of the city's land and water rights filings and an outline of the plans for the aqueduct, McAleer deferred the request, promising a formal statement at a later date.[186] Instead, the city officials appealed to Senator Flint to exercise his influence to assure that the Department of the Interior would refuse any applications from other public or private interests for federal rights-of-way in the Owens Valley. Hitchcock flatly refused to suspend all the federal right-of-way statutes for Los Angeles' convenience, particularly when he had no way of knowing which applications would conflict with a project the city had so far failed to define.[187] This rebuff finally produced the desired effect. On October 23, 1905, the city of Los Angeles filed its first notice of appropriation from the Owens River, laying claim to one thousand cubic feet per second of the river's flow at a point well south of any agricultural activity in the valley.[188] McAleer promptly followed up with a formal request on November 2 that the Reclamation Service abandon its plans for a reservoir at Long Valley, promising: "When this project is executed, the City of Los Angeles will have obtained a permanent, unfailing water supply adequate for all its future needs."[189] And on December 11, the Los Angeles City Council formally petitioned the California congressional delegation to join in persuading the Department of the Interior to abandon the Owens Valley project and deny all applications for rights-of-way which might conflict with the city's aqueduct.[190]

Until Lippincott's case was resolved, the city refused to go further than this request for abandonment and the continued suspension of the Owens Valley lands. The detailed description of the aqueduct project was not forthcoming. Mulholland and the other promoters of the aqueduct had been able to push the project past the voters of Los Angeles without ever having to define the size or nature of the facility they proposed to build, and they clearly hoped to repeat the success of this tactic in Washington. The Chamber of Commerce's board of expert engineers, which would ultimately determine the components of the aqueduct, was not even formed until after the federal rights-of way had been secured. Rather than weakening Los Angeles' appeal for federal approval, the resulting confusion over the size and purpose of the aqueduct and its potential effects upon the Owens Valley worked to the city's advantage. Austin and his allies in the valley, for example, warned that Los Angeles' plans would result in the destruction of the valley's economy. Charles Lummis, writing as editor of *Out West*, countered these predictions with the assurance that "the city must go to Inyo County courts and juries in any condemnation it attempts, consequently the rights of that locality will be amply protected."[191] But as Lippincott privately pointed out to Newell, it was precisely to avoid the Inyo courts that Los Angeles had chosen to buy its rights in the valley outright rather than pursue the more conventional and presumably less costly course of condemnation proceedings.[192]

Although the Reclamation Service's authority under the 1902 act did not extend to the development of municipal water supplies, its parent agency, the United States Geological Survey, was inclined on general principles to favor domestic over agricultural water use. In justifying their actions, the federal water officials explained that they tolerated Los Angeles' interference in the Owens Valley irrigation project in part because they understood that the city intended to use the valley's waters for domestic purposes and not for agricultural development in the San Fernando Valley.[193] "The injection of the City of Los Angeles into the problem raises the question whether the Service would be justified in using for irrigation water that is required for domestic purposes," the survey pointed out to Hitchcock. "It is not believed that it would be wise to insist upon such use until the present and probably future requirements for domestic purposes have been provided for, as this is usually considered superior to use for irrigation."[194]

The problem was that Los Angeles had neither the intention

nor the ability to use its aqueduct exclusively for domestic purposes. The city would not be large enough for years to absorb the total supply of the aqueduct. This was another reason why Los Angeles could not resort to condemnation of the Owens Valley lands it required, because it could not make the requisite proof that it actually needed the water for domestic use.[195] But this did not mean that the city intended to take only enough water from the Owens Valley in the first years of the aqueduct's operation to supply the city's actual and immediate domestic needs. Instead, Mulholland intended to operate the project at full capacity from the very beginning for the benefit of agriculture in the San Fernando Valley. In Washington as in the bond election in Los Angeles, the use of the aqueduct for the San Fernando Valley consequently became the critical issue in the debate over acceptance of the city's plans.

Use of the Owens Valley water in the San Fernando Valley was essential to the project's success. Mulholland's basic conception of the aqueduct depended upon the use of the San Fernando Valley's vast underground reservoirs to store the water from the Owens Valley and enhance the flows of the Los Angeles River. The ardent endorsement the local newspapers gave to the project had focused almost exclusively upon the future growth and development which aqueduct water would bring to the San Fernando Valley. And the recognition that the project would be operated primarily for irrigation even won for the aqueduct the enthusiastic support of William Smythe, who five years before had predicted a bright future for the Owens Valley but not for the South Coast. As a result of the aqueduct, Smythe estimated that a minimum of a hundred thousand acres could be irrigated, the entire area divided into small farms under intensive cultivation. From these developments would flow a multifold prosperity: armies of labor, great manufacturing establishments to produce the equipment needed for irrigation, highways laced with electric railroads, and thousands of new homes and public buildings. "In a word," Smythe wrote, "it means that the City of Angels will . . . in an economic sense . . . be sufficient unto itself . . . without very much regard to what may happen north of Tehachapi or east of San Gorgonio."[196]

The San Fernando Valley was equally important to the economic viability of the aqueduct. Although numerous cities around Los Angeles expressed interest in purchasing the surplus waters of the aqueduct as soon as the project was announced, and Mulholland welcomed their applications, the city's legal counselors soon determined that the city charter provisions prohibiting alienation of any part of the city's water supply without a vote of the people would effectively block the sale of aqueduct water to agencies outside the city limits.[197] The city could not pay for the construction, therefore, by peddling the water it could not use; instead, it would have to rely entirely upon its own ability to raise funds through the sale of municipal bonds. But state law at that time prohibited any California city from incurring indebtedness greater than 15 percent of its total assessed valuation. Under this formula, the permissible limit on Los Angeles' bond sales in 1906 was $23,499,286. And the city already had $6,968,725 in bonds outstanding, leaving only slightly more than $18 million available to pay all the costs of constructing the aqueduct.[198] This was less than even Mulholland's most conservative estimates of the cost of the project and far short of the even greater quantities of funding that other experts predicted the aqueduct would require. If the city could not consume all the water from the aqueduct within its borders or sell the excess outside them, the solution obviously lay in expanding those borders because that would also increase the city's assessed valuation and thereby enhance its ability to raise funds. Mulholland never hid the fact that completion of the aqueduct would involve massive annexations to the city.[199] And although the process of annexation did not, in fact, turn out to be necessary until after the aqueduct's completion, it was generally assumed in Los Angeles in 1905 that the San Fernando Valley would have to be annexed immediately simply to get enough assessed valuation within the city's borders to float the bonds for construction of the aqueduct.[200]

If the San Fernando Valley was the key to the aqueduct's success, it was also the one aspect of the project most vulnerable to attack. The *Examiner* had fastened upon the profits that would accrue to the San Fernando land syndicate as a result of the aqueduct's construction during its assault on the project during the bond election. And Austin, too, focused upon the use of the aqueduct's water supply for agriculture in the San Fernando Valley in his efforts to block federal approval of the project. The residents of the Owens Valley did not object to the use of their water for the city's domestic needs, Austin assured President Roosevelt, "so long as this can be done without prejudice to the Government's reclamation project and to the vested rights of our property owners."[201] But when it came to a project which would effectively sacrifice the future of the Owens Valley for the sake of economic growth in the San Fernando Valley, there Austin drew the lines of his opposition. The choice in his view was clear: "In Owens Valley [the water] will make homes for 100,000 people of moderate means, while in the San Fernando Valley it will be accessible only to the rich and the land and water will be in the control of speculators and middle men."[202]

It was in blunting this line of attack that the purposeful obscurity within which Los Angeles draped its project proved most effective. As long as the size of the aqueduct and the extent to which it would be used for agriculture remained unknown, the damage it would do to the Owens Valley could not be measured. The Geological Survey at first was completely in the dark. "This office is not prepared to state the magnitude of the needs of the city of Los Angeles," the survey advised Hitchcock at the beginning of September 1905, "but it is believed that the city will not require the entire water supply available for development in the Owens Valley, at least for a great many years."[203] Faced with Mulholland's intransigence and unwilling to trust the judgment of either Lippincott or Newell, Walcott retained a consulting engineer, C. E. Grunsky, to provide an independent assessment of the probable size of the city's project. But Grunsky was stymied as well. "No information is available," he reported a few weeks later, "nor is it likely that any definite information can be obtained at this time as to what other uses the city would make of Owens River water, if it has secured rights to more than required for ordinary municipal purposes. This is not the time to express any final conclusions in this matter."[204] Even three months later, Grunsky could do no more than guess at the city's intentions. He noted that the aqueduct would have to have a very large capacity in order to justify its expense, and he estimated on this basis that the project would not be worthwhile if it carried less than eighty-four thousand acre-feet of water a year. Such a system, Grunsky pointed out, would only remove approximately one-fourth of the total water supply of the Owens Valley. Since the Owens Valley farmers were then using only half the available water supply, Grunsky concluded with remarkable optimism that the irrigated area of the Owens Valley could still be expanded by half its current size even after the aqueduct went into operation.[205]

Although Grunsky noted that without Los Angeles' cooperation any irrigation project for the Owens Valley would be "practically out of the question," other federal officials familiar with the situation were far less sanguine about the Owens Valley ranchers' prospects. Henny, Sanders, and Taylor, the panel of engineers who had reviewed the Reclamation Service irrigation project, concluded that it was "probably true" that abandonment of the project would lead to the destruction of the Owens Valley.[206] O'Fallon, in his report to Hitchcock on Lippincott's activities, advised that "the City at present will ruin the lower half of the valley including the towns of Lone Pine and Independence, and if the system contemplated is built, they will finally reduce the entire valley into an arid plain."[207]

The city attempted to counter these grim predictions with promises to protect the interests of the Owens Valley. A special representative of the Reclamation Service, A. E. Chandler, whom Newell sent to treat with the city officials regarding their water rights claims at the end of 1905, happily reported back that Los Angeles intended to pursue "a broad and liberal" policy which would protect all of the Owens Valley's presently vested rights. "The general plan is to enter into an agreement with the farmers whereby the City will construct a large canal to replace the many small ditches now in use," Chandler told Newell. "This will give the farmers far better service than at present and also result in a saving of water supply to the City." Chandler, however, was not prepared to trust the city's assurances entirely; instead, he proposed that the Reclamation Service should maintain its claims to the water of the Owens Valley by continuing to hold the lands it had withdrawn from settlement until Los Angeles actually entered into such an agreement with the Owens Valley ranchers.[208] Newell advised Hitchcock of Chandler's findings, but he did not pass along to the secretary any of Chandler's recommendations for compelling the city to deal fairly with the residents of the Owens Valley.[209]

O'Fallon, however, advocated even stronger measures for forcing Los Angeles to adopt an equitable policy toward the valley, and because his report went directly to the Secretary of the Interior, Newell was unable to stifle O'Fallon's recommendations. "Southern California needs all the water of the Owens Valley," O'Fallon wrote, "and rather than let them destroy the property rights in the valley by piece meal, I believe it would be preferable for the city to purchase the entire valley." O'Fallon proposed the appointment of an impartial arbitrator to determine the fair market value of the properties not yet purchased by the city. "Of course, no one in the valley could be compelled to sell at the price fixed or any other price, but he could be given the opportunity of obtaining a fair valuation for his property." In order to force Los Angeles to accept this arrangement, O'Fallon suggested that the government should refuse to grant the city any rights-of-way "until adequate protection has been extended to the property owners in the valley."[210]

Though Hitchcock was not inclined to accept O'Fallon's idea of initiating a cumbersome process of arbitration, Newell and Walcott were offering no recommendations of their own as to the course he should pursue with respect to Los Angeles' rights-of-way. It was therefore O'Fallon's suggestion to use the rights-of-way as a lever to force the city to protect the interests of the Owens Valley that prevailed in determining Hitchcock's position once the issue was finally joined in the summer of 1906.

The vehicle for obtaining federal approval of the city's project was a bill carried by Senator Flint to give Los Angeles title to the public lands required for the aqueduct at a rate of $1.25 an acre. All the lands presently withdrawn from settlement by the federal government would remain in reserved status for three years while the city made its selections. Certain lands belonging to Indians and the properties along Bishop Creek where the private power companies already had their projects under way were exempted on the promise that the power companies would not oppose the bill.[211] As a local matter affecting only Senator Flint's constituents in California, the bill did not encounter significant resistance from his colleagues in the Senate. On its route to enactment, however, it had to pass through the House Public Lands Committee; and there, for the first time, Los Angeles confronted the Owens Valley interests directly in the formidable presence on the committee of Sylvester C. Smith, congressman for Inyo County.

In keeping with the attitude Austin had first enunciated, Smith acknowledged Los Angeles' need for an additional domestic water supply. It was on the question of using the surplus waters from the aqueduct for agriculture in the San Fernando Valley that Smith's concerns with the bill were directed. He argued that until the city had grown to the point where it could use all the water its aqueduct would provide for domestic purposes, the excess water would be better used irrigating public lands in the Owens Valley rather than benefiting private interests in Los Angeles.[212] Smith therefore proposed a compromise in the form of an amendment to the bill which would enable the Reclamation Service to proceed with its irrigation project for the valley. Under the terms of the amendment, the Owens Valley would have first claim to its own water supply. Any water left over after the valley's needs had been met could be diverted to Los Angeles, but only to serve the city's domestic needs. And any excess water the city could not use would revert to the valley's control.

Although Walcott personally doubted that Smith's idea could ever be implemented in practice, the amendment offered a superficial appearance of utter reasonableness.[213] Smith's proposal would protect the survival of the valley while at the same time allowing enough water for Los Angeles to meet those "needs" Mulholland had described in such desperate terms during the campaign for the bond election. But, by granting primacy to the Owens Valley claims on the water, the Smith amendment was anathema to the as-yet-unspoken intentions of the city, which looked ahead to the day when it would tap the entire flow of the Owens River. Under the Smith amendment, as the city's need for water grew with its population, it would have to fight the valley in court for every additional drop it took from one year to the next. Alternatively, if agriculture in the valley blossomed, Los Angeles would have to begin looking elsewhere for a new water supply.

The dilemma which the Smith amendment posed for the city as a whole was even more extreme in the case of the interests of the San Fernando land syndicate. The success of the syndicate did not depend upon immediate settlement of the lands it held in the San Fernando Valley. Instead, the syndicate looked forward to years of profitable agricultural production made possible by the new water for these otherwise useless lands until the tide of urbanization would eventually reach out and claim their property. But, if use of the water for agriculture were prohibited under the Smith amendment, the syndicate would lose both the promise of income in these intervening years and, more important, its claims on the water once settlement did begin. The private interests of Huntington, Otis, and the rest thus joined with the greater public interest served by Mulholland. As before, the need for water as perceived by both sides was founded in prospect rather than on the existing conditions of the Los Angeles water supply. No conspiracy was necessary; their objectives were the same.

Mulholland traveled to Washington to meet the challenge. The predominating influence of the local business community in Los Angeles' public affairs in general and the aqueduct in particular was evident in the fact that he took with him, in addition to the city attorney, the president of the Los Angeles Chamber of Commerce and the chairman of the chamber's investigating committee, which had endorsed the aqueduct in the critical closing days of the bond election.[214] Finding that Smith's proposal enjoyed the support of the Secretary of the Interior, Mulholland initially agreed to accept the amendment in a meeting he had with Smith and Flint on June 21, 1906.[215] Senator Flint, however, was not so ready to concede defeat, and he turned for assistance to President Roosevelt's close personal friend and chief of the Forest Service, Gifford Pinchot. On the night of June 23, Flint obtained an audience with Roosevelt, and with Pinchot's help he succeeded in convincing Roosevelt to oppose the Smith compromise.[216] Hitchcock and Smith did not learn of this turn of events until June 25, when Roosevelt, despite their strenuous protests, sent a formal request to the House Public Lands Committee asking that the Smith amendment be removed. The committee reported Flint's bill out the next day drawn according to the president's instructions, and the House promptly approved. On June 28, five days after Flint's first late-night call, the bill went to the president's desk for signature.

Roosevelt's decision to side with Los Angeles and the special interests which stood to profit from the city's scheme to exploit the water of a small agricultural community would seem to mark a significant lapse in policy for a president who is remembered today as a trustbuster, friend of the little man, and early champion of the modern conservation movement. As Henry Pringle notes in his biography of the president, "Roosevelt's passionate interest in the national forests, in reclamation of arid western lands by irrigation, in conservation of water power and other natural resources, may well be considered as part of his campaign against the malefactors of great wealth . . . His opposition to exploitation of water power was based on the conception, novel in that day, that this was the property of the people and should redound to their benefit."[217]

But, as John Morton Blum observes in *The Republican Roosevelt*, Roosevelt's policy was informed not so much by love for the weak as by a vision of Spencerian progression, the principles of Social Darwinism, and an overriding desire to establish order in a period of rapidly changing social relations. His objective in battling the moneyed interests while favoring the formation of labor unions and agricultural associations was not the destruction of corporate wealth but rather the creation of "an equilibrium of consolidated interests over which government would preside." Although his vision encompassed the details of individual cases of hardship, his eye was fixed ultimately upon the greater benefits for the nation which would proceed from such a balance of competing interests. Thus, Blum argues, "Roosevelt sponsored conservation not so much to preserve a domain for agriculture as to preserve and enhance the strength of the whole nation."[218]

The conservation policies which Roosevelt and Pinchot initiated during the president's first term in office were informed by an almost boundless confidence in the efficacy of scientific bureaucracies which left little room for consideration of local interests or concerns. As Samuel P. Hays points out in his seminal study *Conservation and the Gospel of Efficiency*,

> Conservation neither arose from a broad public outcry, nor centered its fire primarily upon the private corporation . . . Conservation, above all, was a scientific movement . . . Its essence was rational planning to promote efficient development and use of all natural resources . . . It is from the vantage point of applied science, rather than of democratic protest, that one must understand the historic role of the conservation movement . . . The political implications of conservation, it is particularly important to observe, grew out of the political implications of applied science rather than conflict over the distribution of wealth. Who should decide the course of resource development? . . . Since resource matters were basically technical in nature, conservationists argued, technicians, rather than legislators, should deal with them . . . Conflicts between competing resource users, especially, should not be dealt with through the normal process of politics. Pressure group action, logrolling in Congress, or partisan debate could not guarantee rational and scientific decisions . . . Conservationists envisaged, even though they did not realize their aims, a political system guided by the ideal of efficiency and dominated by technicians who could best determine how to achieve it.[219]

In the case of Los Angeles' aqueduct, the locus of the national interest seemed clear to Roosevelt. While he acknowledged that the concerns of the Owens Valley were "genuine," he concluded that this interest "must unfortunately be disregarded in view of the infinitely greater interest to be served by putting the water in Los Angeles." In a formal letter to Secretary of the Interior Hitchcock drafted June 25, 1906, in the secretary's presence as "a record of our attitude in the Los Angeles water supply question," Roosevelt argued: "It is a hundred or thousandfold more important to state that this [water] is more valuable to the people as a whole if used by the city than if used by the people of the Owens Valley."[220] In the name of efficiency, Roosevelt had established the Reclamation Service and set it to the task of planning for the use of whole watersheds in the West, without regard for state boundaries and local jurisdictional rivalries. Protests were to be expected when the water of one state or community was proposed for use elsewhere, and the outcry that had arisen in the Owens Valley was only a small reflection of the much greater controversies that would come when the Reclamation Service set about dividing the waters of the Rio Grande and Colorado rivers.

For his part, Hitchcock focused on the evils of the San Fernando syndicate, warning that the passage of Flint's bill without the Smith amendment would enable the city "to use the surplus of water thus acquired beyond the amount actually used for drinking purposes for some irrigation scheme."[221] But Hitchcock's opinion carried little weight with Roosevelt. Hitchcock had consistently opposed Pinchot's efforts to put the public domain to use through grazing leases and commercial concessions in the national parks.[222] His moralism and lack of concern for possible political embarrassments to the president resulting from his efforts to root out fraud in the federal lands programs disgusted Roosevelt.[223] The president was therefore inclined to accept Flint's argument that Los Angeles had to possess the surplus in order to retain its rights to that surplus in the future. When Flint suggested, moreover, that Los Angeles' primary concern with the Smith amendment was that it might prohibit the city's residents from using aqueduct water on their gardens at home, Roosevelt readily agreed to the elimination of the proposed compromise.[224]

Roosevelt resolved the problem of the San Fernando land syndicate's interest after a fashion by insisting on an amendment of his own to the Flint bill which prohibited Los Angeles from selling the surplus to any private interest for resale as irrigation water.[225] But, as the congressman who carried Flint's bill in the House observed, it was clear to the Public Lands Committee that the Roosevelt amendment "could not prevent the Los Angeles City Council from doing what it chose with the water. This water will belong absolutely to Los Angeles and the city council can do as it pleases with it—sell directly to private individuals or corporations for irrigation purposes, or sell to Pasadena or other surrounding towns for the same purposes, or for a water supply, or use it in any other way the council chooses." Smith himself agreed that "it did not make any difference what became of the water after it was taken to the Los Angeles neighborhood."[226]

Roosevelt found further cause for his support of Flint's bill in the fact that it was opposed by "certain private power companies whose object evidently is for their own pecuniary interest to prevent the municipality from furnishing its own water." The Southern California Edison Company and the Los Angeles Gas and Electric Corporation, seeing their interests threatened by the proposed aqueduct, had joined in the back-room lobbying against the Flint legislation. This unfortunate identity of interest with the power companies proved fatal for the future of the Owens Valley, for, as Roosevelt observed of the power companies, "Their opposition seems to me to afford one of the strongest arguments for passing the law."[227]

In the years that followed, those who opposed the city's policies in the Owens Valley would expend much of their energies in searching for an appropriate forum at the state or national level in which to gain a fair hearing for their case. In that one meeting on June 25, 1906, they had the best and arguably the last opportunity to obtain such a hearing in the highest office in the land. The fate of the Owens Valley was sealed the moment President Roosevelt determined that the greater public interest would be served by a greater Los Angeles. They lost without even having had the opportunity to have their representative present. When Congressman Smith protested his exclusion from this meeting at which his amendment was dismissed, Roosevelt feigned ignorance of his interest in the matter. "You have been guilty of laches and of failure in your duty both to your constituents and to the Department [of the Interior] in not laying before the Department and myself any information as to why we should not approve the bill," Roosevelt wrote angrily to Smith. "Of course we cannot divine what men wish to be heard."[228]

"The victory for Los Angeles is complete," crowed the *Los Angeles Times* in its report of the approval of Flint's legislation.[229] Mulholland and the other members of the city's delegation to

Washington had been successful even on the relatively minor matter of the amount of money Los Angeles would have to pay the Reclamation Service for its work on the Owens Valley project. This had been Newell's primary concern in his dealings with Los Angeles and the cause of Davis' final break with Lippincott. But even though the service's final accounting showed expenditures on the project totaling more than $26,000, Flint's bill specified that the city of Los Angeles could not be charged more than $14,000 for access to all the service's maps, surveys, field notes, and river measurements in the Owens Valley.[230]

With Flint's legislation enacted into law and the development of the aqueduct thereby assured, Lippincott promptly resigned his position with the Reclamation Service to take the far better-paying job which Henny had predicted the city would have waiting for him. For the rest of his life he would be plagued by charges and allegations concerning the partisanship he had shown for Los Angeles while serving the federal government. But despite the fact that his official record of employment with the Reclamation Service bears the notation "resigned under pressure," he had few regrets. Looking back on these events five years later, he was resolute in defense of his virtue: "I would do everything over again, just exactly as I did it, if that proposition came up again in the same form," he commented.[231]

Governor Pardee, however, apparently suffered some second thoughts about his ardent defense of Lippincott. "I don't think the man is intentionally a rascal," he told an interviewer in 1908, "but he has shown damn poor judgment. I suppose he could not resist the temptation to get his fingers in the municipal pie."[232] But to Newell, Lippincott confided, "As far as my record with the Government in Owens Valley is concerned, I can most emphatically state that in everything I did I was guided by a desire to accomplish the greatest public good. There were absolutely no personal ambitions that controlled me, and while my judgment may have been wrong in some cases, my conscience is absolutely clear." Indeed, Lippincott had no reason to feel repentant, for, as he pointed out to Newell, "The policy which Congress, the President, and the Secretary of the Interior ultimately adopted . . . was exactly in line with the views which I had in the matter."[233]

Newell could scarcely make a similar claim to vindication.

The reputation of the Reclamation Service and his management of it had been severely blemished, and the Owens Valley affair would be raised time and again by his opponents in the western states as an example of the shortcomings of his administration. But he had at least survived, and the Reclamation Service in fact emerged from the controversy with its authority significantly enhanced. Recognizing that the problems raised in the conflict between Los Angeles and the Owens Valley were inherent to the service's limited mandate and would therefore be likely to arise again, Congress, at the same time it adopted Flint's legislation, also passed a companion bill amending the Reclamation Act of 1902 to permit the Secretary of the Interior to extend the benefits of federal water project development to municipalities as well as irrigators. In order to assure that the Owens Valley conflict would not be repeated, however, Congress was careful to stipulate that any arrangements for the delivery of domestic water supplies from federal reclamation projects cannot compromise the commitments made for irrigation water from those projects.[234]

Throughout his career in Washington, Newell displayed a remarkable ability to retain his job despite the hostility of the various secretaries of the Interior he served. Roosevelt removed Hitchcock in 1907 and replaced him with James Garfield, another of Pinchot's protégés, who worked well with Newell. President William Howard Taft's Secretary of the Interior, Richard Ballinger, however, effectively excluded Newell from policy decisions. But even after Newell testified against him in the congressional investigations of Ballinger's celebrated break with Pinchot, Ballinger was unable to remove him. Ballinger's successor, in turn, Walter Fisher, similarly tried to fire Newell, but without success. It was not until the advent of Woodrow Wilson's administration that Newell was finally persuaded to leave. And even then he was permitted to resign after his control of the reclamation program had been turned over to a five-member commission. Newell then spent the balance of his career as head of the civil engineering department at the University of Illinois.[235] His chief assistant, Arthur Powell Davis, succeeded him. But after nine controversial and crisis-packed years as the head of the program, Davis was dismissed. He enjoyed greater success in California, where he took over direction of the East Bay Municipal Utility District and promptly retained William Mulholland as one of his principal consultants in the development of new municipal water supplies.[236]

Among all the principal players in the controversy over federal approval of the aqueduct, the only real loser was Wallace Austin. Despite the fact that O'Fallon's investigation had completely vindicated his role in bringing charges against Lippincott, Austin found himself entangled in Lippincott's desperate efforts to save his job in the closing months of 1905, when it seemed that O'Fallon's recommendation for Lippincott's dismissal might actually be implemented. Austin himself provided Lippincott with the opportunity to discredit him. Having heard Fred Eaton's assurances that the Reclamation Service was about to abandon the Owens Valley, Austin in July and August 1905 joined with several other local residents in filing claims on the surplus waters of the valley. Their plan was to hold these rights until an association of Owens Valley irrigators could be organized to assume control of the rights on behalf of all the residents of the valley. As the association later explained:

> The people were advised by able attorneys to make a location upon the surplus waters for their own benefit and to hold said location until it was known what action would be taken by the government upon the Owens River Reclamation Project . . . As the people on all sides had the utmost confidence in Mr. S. W. Austin, and as he was interested with us as a property owner in the valley, he was naturally selected to make the location and hold it in trust for the people.[237]

Austin received no payment for his assistance, and as soon as the association had perfected its organization, he turned the filings over to it with the stipulation that they should be transferred to the federal government or abandoned in case the Reclamation Service's irrigation project ultimately proved feasible.[238]

When Eaton discovered these filings in October, he immediately announced to the newspapers, "Grafters are at work in the valley and that Government Agent Austin and his associates are among the worst."[239] Although Eaton was unable to identify any of the corrupt interests he charged were in league with Austin or define just what their purpose might be, he promised, "I have my suspicions. When the proper time comes I shall expose everything."[240] Lippincott pounced on these ridiculous allegations and had no difficulty in coming up with the name of one possible conspirator. He mailed off copies of the newspaper reports of Eaton's charges to his superiors in Washington together with an assurance that Austin was working on behalf of George Chaffey, one of the most prominent and controversial water developers in California. Chaffey had achieved his greatest success in founding the water colony at Ontario; his efforts to establish a similar project in Australia, however, had been undone by a financial crisis in the Australian government. Returning to California, he had the misfortune of joining Charles Rockwood in his largely fraudulent efforts to develop the Imperial Valley. Although Chaffey resigned from Rockwood's California Development Company before its collapse, his reputation suffered from this brief alliance. Chaffey had appeared in the Owens Valley in 1905, laying plans for the establishment of a new water colony at Manzanar, and Lippincott did not hesitate to tie Austin in with this man, who, Lippincott claimed, "is said to have left Australia for the good of the country."[241]

Lippincott's charges against Austin had no basis in fact; but the entire undertaking had been a foolish and pointless exercise on Austin's part. An immediate investigation by the Reclamation Service revealed that the filings Austin and his friends had entered, "Are of no value except in so far as they show enthusiasm on the part of the claimants."[242] The city officials had not been concerned. Mayor McAleer dismissed the filings as "a bluff" and assured the press, "I don't anticipate any trouble." Mulholland similarly declared, "The city is not in a position to be held up. Austin's alleged filings don't amount to anything, I am sure. Austin has placed himself in a ridiculous position."[243] The incident demonstrated nothing more than Austin's ignorance, but the experience profoundly embarrassed him, and the ridicule Eaton heaped upon him in the press, combined with the repeated failures of his efforts to prevent the fulfillment of Los Angeles' plans, convinced him to resign his position as the federal lands register in the Owens Valley.

THE POLITICS OF APPROPRIATION 147

"After a year of somewhat aimless clawing, he reverted to the desert, even deeper into its desolation, at Death Valley," his wife Mary later recalled. "Although he had actually a competent income, he never managed it competently so as to make a frame of life secure for me and comfortably patterned ... The proposal for a divorce came from me. I was grieved to find how grieved he was, but I thought there was still a chance that if he were free he might make a more satisfactory marriage. That expectation was never fulfilled."[244]

Mary too fled the valley. The retarded infant, Ruth, was placed in an institution, and Mary went alone to Carmel, where she worked and wrote steadily in a less hostile climate. Following her death in 1934, the women's club of Inyo County proposed the construction of a fountain in her memory, "a low pool where even the smallest desert creatures might come to drink." But the county supervisors vetoed the project. "Too many of the men I have known have not been able to forgive me for having a mind and life of my own," she once complained to a friend.[245] In her autobiography, Mary wrote of the last months of her struggle against Los Angeles' plans in the Owens Valley and the apocalyptic vision that precipitated her departure:

> Mary did what she could. And that was too little ... She walked in the fields and considered what could be done. She called upon the Voice, and the Voice answered her— Nothing. She was told to go away. And suddenly there was an answer, a terrifying answer, pushed off, deferred, delayed; an answer impossible to be repeated; an answer still impending; which I might not live to see confirmed, but hangs suspended over the Southern country. Mary went away ... She knew that the land of Inyo would be desolated, and the cruelty and deception smote her beyond belief ... She sold her house in Inyo; she meant not to go there again.[246]

CHAPTER FOUR

Forging the Link

       In many respects, Los Angeles' victories on behalf of the aqueduct until this point had been won on a long bluff. The way was now clear for construction to proceed, but the project had not yet been defined, the funds to build it had not been raised, and the technical capability of the city to undertake an endeavor of such magnitude was very much in doubt. Most important were the state-mandated limitations on the amount of money Los Angeles could raise through the sale of bonds. The city did not have a sufficient amount of assessed valuation in the 1905-1906 fiscal year to issue enough bonds to pay for the project, and these conditions were not substantially improved in the next fiscal year, even though the federal rights-of-way had by then been granted. It was not until the beginning of the 1907-1908 fiscal year, in July 1907, that the city auditor estimated that Los Angeles' total assessed valuation would rise to a level enabling it to commit a total of $24.5 million to the project.[1]

Further progress in the form of a second bond election to raise the funds for construction consequently had to be delayed for a year after enactment of the Flint legislation in order to allow the city's assessed valuation time to float up to the level projected for the beginning of the 1907-1908 fiscal year. Even then, the city would be taking a terrific gamble on the assurances of one man, William Mulholland, who had no training as an engineer and no experience in the management of construction projects of any significant size. The issuance of $24.5 million in bonds would push the city's permissible indebtedness to the limit. The cost simply of servicing so great a public debt would mean a tax of $88 on every resident of Los Angeles.[2] And failure of the project once the bonds had been issued could have placed the city in receivership.

Mulholland's initial plans called for a project that included 60 miles of canals and 140 miles of conduit linking three storage reservoirs, one at Long Valley and two in the San Fernando Valley.[3] The bond issue of 1905 had raised $1.5 million for the acquisition of land and water rights; that left $23 million which the city could commit for construction of the aqueduct. Although Mulholland assured his supporters that his initial design could be realized for less than $23 million, the Reclamation Service fixed the cost at $36 million, and experts consulted by the *Los Angeles Examiner* during the bond election of 1905 estimated that the price would rise much higher, to more than $50 million.[4] Paring Mulholland's concept to fit within the city's budgetary constraints would consequently be the principal task of the panel of consulting engineers convened by Los Angeles to review the project at the end of 1906.

The formation of this panel represented fulfillment of the city's pledge during the bond election of 1905 not to embark too deeply upon the project until the wisdom of the enterprise had been independently and reliably confirmed. This promise had been given to the Chamber of Commerce; how the panel members were selected further demonstrated the extent to which the aqueduct was regarded as a joint venture of Los Angeles' public officials and its business leaders. The appointment of each member of the panel had to be approved not only by the City Council, the Board of Water Commissioners, and the Board of Public Works, but also by the Chamber of Commerce, the Municipal League, and the Merchants and Manufacturers Association. Recognizing that the prosperity of the city was at stake in the venture, the authorities responsible for nominating the panel members ranged far beyond the readily available circle of local engineers and aqueduct enthusiasts in making their selections. Of the three members of the panel, only one, James D. Schuyler, had had any extensive experience in the American Southwest.

Schuyler had served as California's assistant state engineer from 1878 to 1882 and was responsible as well for the construction of the Sweetwater and Hemet dams in Southern California. But while Los Angeles had employed him frequently over the preceding ten years as a consultant in the litigation to protect its water rights, Schuyler's work extended well beyond the limits of the South Coast to include projects throughout the western states and Hawaii. As the other two members of the panel, the city chose eastern engineers of international stature: Frederic P. Stearns, chief engineer of the Metropolitan Water Board of Boston and a former president of the American Society of Civil Engineers, and John R. Freeman, a former president of the American Society of Mechanical Engineers who had served as a consultant with Stearns on the construction of the Panama Canal and the municipal water systems of Boston and New York City.[5]

The panel devoted more than a month to its study of the project, spending twelve days in the field along the line of the aqueduct. Henry Loewenthal, editor of the *Los Angeles Examiner*, later took satisfaction in claiming that the consultants "knocked Mr. Mulholland's plans into a cocked hat."[6] Their report of December 22, 1906, did not go quite that far, although the changes they made in Mulholland's original design were substantial. For the sake of economy, all three storage reservoirs at Long Valley and in the San Fernando Valley were jettisoned. Many of the steel siphons which Mulholland had planned to use were also deleted on the observation that these materials were expensive and it was doubtful that anyone could supply as many siphons as Mulholland estimated he would need. In addition, the consulting engineers altered the route of the aqueduct. Rather than coming through Lancaster and Palmdale and then west to burrow through the San Gabriel Mountains to a terminal reservoir in the Big Tejunga Canyon, as Mulholland had planned, the panel directed that the aqueduct should skirt the Antelope Valley and enter the San Fernando Valley through San Francisquito Canyon.[7] Although the city had already spent more than $28,000 to buy lands it would now never use at Palmdale, these changes shortened the overall length of the project by twenty miles and substituted one five-mile tunnel near Elizabeth Lake for two six-mile tunnels through the San Gabriel Mountains.[8]

The project that emerged from the panel's deliberations was thus a peculiarly amputated version of Mulholland's once-grand conception. It was essentially no more than a long ditch connecting two points which, for reasons of economy, had to be deleted. There would be no reservoir at the upper end of the aqueduct to store the peak flows of the Owens River for later use in dry periods and there would be no reservoirs at the lower end of the project to receive the waters when they arrived. Most important, the design made no provision at all for getting the water to the city and distributing it after it reached the San Fernando Valley. Those problems, the Board of Public Works declared in a grand stroke of bureaucratic legerdemain, were not its concern; let the Board of Public Service decide how to store and distribute the water once the aqueduct had carried it across the desert.[9] As strange as this design was, it was all the city could afford. The aqueduct alone would cost $18,221,300, the consultants estimated. The expense of building a cement plant and a railroad to transport construction materials, plus a 15-percent allowance for contingencies would bring the total to $24,485,600, once the funds for land and water right acquisitions were added in.[10]

It later became part of the personal legend of William Mulholland that he completed the aqueduct within the budget set for him, a remarkable achievement for any engineering enterprise of such magnitude. The project Mulholland built for $24.5 million, however, lacked storage reservoirs, power plants, and a distribution system—in short, all the components of the aqueduct that would actually make it useful to the people of Los Angeles. These parts of the project had instead to be funded from other sources. And even so, Mulholland had to make further reductions in the scale of the project in order to stay within the funding available.

The most significant of these was the elimination of the railway system which the consulting engineers had included in their cost projections for the project. A total of 127 miles of broad-gauge track would be needed for the project, and the city estimated that the costs of building and operating such a system for the five years the aqueduct was under construction would exceed $1.4 million.[11] Not only was the railway line essential for the aqueduct, the system would also provide long-term benefits to the merchants and growers of the Owens Valley, and, as Mulholland

acknowledged, "It would be to the interests of this City to have
. . . the benefits of this trade." Nevertheless, Mulholland eliminated the system from his own plans in the spring of 1907, arguing
that the city charter would prohibit the city from conducting a
general freight-hauling business after the aqueduct was built despite the fact that the state legislature that March passed a bill
specifically authorizing the city to engage in such an activity.[12]
Instead, the contract for building and operating the railway line
was turned over to the Southern Pacific. Although other railroad
companies offered lower bids to perform the same work, Mulholland needed the Southern Pacific's cooperation in gaining a
right-of-way across a thousand acres of land the company controlled along the line of the aqueduct. And in exchange for the
city's lucrative contract to haul over a million tons of freight for
the project, the Southern Pacific made these lands available at a
nominal price of five dollars an acre.[13]

In their concern for the economic aspects of the aqueduct, the
panel of consulting engineers did more than simply restrict its
length and scope. They also altered the design of the system to
place a greater emphasis on its hydroelectric-power-generating
potential. The decision to bring the aqueduct into the San Fernando Valley through the San Francisquito Canyon, for example,
added three power drops to the project, aggregating 1,842 feet, at
which municipal power plants could be located. With all the
modifications to the plan which they recommended, the consulting engineers estimated that the aqueduct would be capable of
generating a maximum load of ninety-three thousand horsepower, more than all the electrical energy then being consumed
in the cities of Los Angeles, Long Beach, Pasadena, and Santa
Monica. And the sale of this electrical energy could return, by the
engineers' estimate, upward of $1.4 million in annual revenues to
the city.[14]

This emphasis on hydroelectricity reflected Stearns' and Freeman's backgrounds in the more sophisticated and technologically
advanced engineering circles of the East, where the idea of using
the proceeds from the sale of public power to pay for the development of public water projects was just then gaining currency in
the Roosevelt administration.[15] Whereas Eaton had found the

power-generating potential of the aqueduct its most attractive feature, Mulholland had been generally unaware of how great this potential might be when he first introduced the project to the people of Los Angeles. He assumed simply that whatever electrical energy the system developed would be consumed in pumping the water over barriers that would otherwise have to be circumvented or tunneled under.[16] Once the opportunities for revenue to the city were pointed out to him, however, Mulholland was quick to endorse the principle: "I believe that the people have in the possible power development from the aqueduct an investment which 20 years hence will turn back into the city treasury the entire $24.5 million provided for the construction of the aqueduct with interest," he declared.[17]

Although the establishment of this linkage between public water development and power sales at the federal level provided the means of financing new water projects throughout the nation, it also posed a direct threat to the livelihood of private power companies who have fought mightily throughout the twentieth century to prevent competition from the public sector in the distribution and sale of domestic power. The consortium of private power companies in Northern California which gathered under the banner of the Pacific Gas and Electric Company, for example, fought the developers of San Francisco's Hetch Hetchy system to a standstill; as a result, that system today operates under an arrangement for the sale of power within San Francisco which is in direct conflict with the terms of the legislation under which Congress authorized the project in the first place.[18]

Mulholland and the supporters of the aqueduct in Los Angeles did not face so formidable an adversary in their efforts to realize the power-producing potential of their project. In place of the united strength of the Pacific Gas and Electric Company, with its vast financial resources and political influence, Mulholland had only to deal with three poorly coordinated and noncompetitive private companies which had divided the city's power markets among themselves. The Los Angeles Gas and Electric Company, a subsidiary of Pacific Lighting, provided most of the power for the city's business district. Pacific Light and Power operated principally for the benefit of Huntington's railway system and his development projects in the southern and northeastern portions of the city. And Edison Electric provided a little less than half of the city's domestic power supply.[19]

These companies recognized from the outset the threat to their operations posed by the aqueduct. The Edison company, for example, mounted the only formal opposition the aqueduct bonds in 1905 ever faced from within Los Angeles' business community.[20] And the companies' efforts behind the scenes in Washington to block the federal right-of-way for the aqueduct in 1906 backfired by providing President Roosevelt with an additional reason to support the project. But power generation was never an important feature of the political controversies surrounding the aqueduct in 1905 and 1906. With the increased emphasis the consulting engineers placed on this aspect of the project in their report at the end of 1906, however, this latent issue moved to the fore.

Although the local power companies might have hoped to share in the general prosperity which aqueduct water would bring to Los Angeles, they feared more the competition from municipal power that the project would generate. The dilemma posed by the aqueduct was especially acute in the case of Pacific Light and Power, which was owned by Henry Huntington and William Kerckhoff. Both were members of the San Fernando land syndicate, and their interests were consequently divided between a proprietary fear of public power and the private gain they stood to make through the land syndicate upon the project's completion. They reasoned that their problem could be resolved if the private power companies retained control of the power distribution system within the city. After the Flint bill had passed, Kerckhoff accordingly approached Mulholland to discuss a long-term lease of the power facilities on the aqueduct. But Mulholland's view of the aqueduct as a wholly municipal enterprise did not allow for such a compromise. He viewed Kerckhoff's proposal in the same light as Eaton's earlier advocacy of private ownership of the water, and he rejected Kerckhoff's overture just as firmly.[21]

Mulholland's stand on behalf of both public power and public water left the power companies with no other option than to throw their weight openly against the second municipal bond election to provide the $23 million needed for construction of the aqueduct. The election was scheduled for June 12, 1907, so as to take full advantage of the increased assessed valuation in the city that would apply after the beginning of the new fiscal year, July 1. As the vehicle for their opposition, the companies secured control of a struggling new newspaper, the *Los Angeles Evening News*, whose editor was Samuel T. Clover. The entire effort was doomed from the beginning. Every other business institution in the city supported the bonds, and the opposition lacked a creditable issue on which to hang its case. The project had already been approved by the panel of engineers called for in the 1905 bond election. The companies could scarcely attack Otis, Huntington, and Kerckhoff on the issue of a syndicate conspiracy, and public arguments for their own self-interests predictably carried little weight with the electorate. From the perspective of the Los Angeles voters, it was one thing for a group of special interests like the San Fernando land syndicate to profit from a project which would yield greater benefits for all, and quite another for the special interests combined in the power companies to stop the project altogether.

Mulholland for his part was careful to blunt the main line of the companies' attack by divorcing the issue of power development from the aqueduct bond proposal which actually lay before the voters. None of the revenues from the sale of these bonds would be used for power plant construction, Mulholland pointed out. The question of what should be done with the power that might ultimately be generated by the aqueduct was consequently treated by Mulholland as "wholly independent of the proposition of supplying water and should stand on its own merits."[22] Mulholland went even further to remove himself personally from any position that might bring him into direct confrontation with the private power interests. On his recommendation, E. F. Scattergood was retained as the aqueduct's electrical engineer and placed at the head of a separate bureau exclusively responsible for the distribution of aqueduct power.[23]

Thus denied the real grounds for their opposition, the leaders of the resistance to the aqueduct bond issue of 1907 resorted to charges that the Owens River was polluted by unnatural concentrations of alkali. Though the consulting engineers had noticed the presence of a brown stain in the river water, they expressed complete confidence in their report that the quality of the water was more than adequate for all domestic and agricultural uses and that any sedimentary pollutants would be removed in the small settling reservoir the city proposed to construct at Haiwee Point and by subsequent aeration.[24]

In debunking the charges made in the *Evening News* by "Alkali Sammy" Clover, Harrison Gray Otis at the *Times* was never moved to the rhetorical heights he had reached in promoting the initial bond issue in 1905.[25] Gone too were the dire predictions of impending drought with which Mulholland had animated the drive for passage of the first aqueduct bonds. In the campaign of 1907, Mulholland restricted his case for the aqueduct to a more accurate depiction of the city's prospective needs for the project, an attitude he summed up with the observation, "If we don't get the water, we won't need it."[26] And as the campaign for the bonds gathered steam in the early weeks of May 1907, the *Times* devoted more attention to train wrecks and labor issues than to water for the city. The bond campaign of 1907 was consequently only a pale shadow of the controversy generated by the *Examiner* two years before.

The only real excitement was that created by Otis when he made the mistake of publishing a declaration that he had sold his interest in the San Fernando land syndicate in February 1905 and defied the "allegators" to prove him wrong.[27] It was stupid for Otis to raise the issue of the syndicate at all, particularly for the sake of making a claim which Clover could so easily disprove by checking the public records of the syndicate's incorporation. In fact, Clover was able to turn up a report that had appeared in the *Times* itself on August 23, 1906, admitting to Otis' continuing interest in the syndicate.[28] The resulting personal embarrassment to Otis was unnecessary in view of the ineffectuality of Clover's campaign, although the flap did produce an unexpected benefit for Mulholland's efforts to secure passage of the bonds. For once Clover turned to attacking the syndicate, Kerckhoff formally withdrew from the fight he could not truly have wished to win.

Without the contributions from the power companies which had kept Clover's paper afloat after the other elements of the business community had withdrawn their advertising in protest of his anti-aqueduct policy, he went out of business.[29] On May 28, both Edison Electric and the Los Angeles Gas and Electric Company joined in endorsing the aqueduct proposal. And by the end of May, the *Times* reported, the only corporate opposition to the bond issue was being raised by one J.D. Hooker, who had been one of the original litigants over the city's pueblo rights and now feared Mulholland would not make use of the steel pipe his company manufactured when the aqueduct was actually begun.[30]

As the election date drew near, the question was not whether the bonds would pass but by how wide a margin. The *Times* launched a contest for the best guess on the total number of votes that would be cast for the bonds.[31] Children's clubs and civic groups throughout the city were decked out with banners and buttons in a get-out-the-vote campaign. "We have got to have water or quit growing," Mulholland told a cheering crowd of supporters two days before the polls opened.[32] The election was novel in that it marked an early appearance of the automobile in the strategy of modern campaigning. For the first time, wealthier members of the community donated their new horseless carriages to ferry voters to and from the polls. "Cast a vote and prove that you are fit to be a citizen of Los Angeles," the *Times* commanded on election day, and the turnout was the largest yet recorded for a special election in Los Angeles.[33] Out of a total of 24,051 ballots cast, the bonds passed by a margin of better than ten to one. Every one of the city's 143 precincts approved the project. "The antis were as rare as a ham sandwich at a picnic of the sons of Levi," the *Times* observed wryly.[34]

A Ditch in the Desert

The burden of responsibility for the aqueduct now descended squarely upon Mulholland, whose judgment and ability had been made an issue in the campaigns of both 1905 and 1907. Those who doubted the desirability of the project had been quick to point out not only his lack of training or experience but the fact as well that, for all the sixteen years he had served as superintendent of the Los Angeles City Water Company, he had scrupulously hewed to the company line that there was no need for a water project of the kind he now proposed to build. But the people of Los Angeles had supported him, and beginning in September 1907 he moved rapidly to fulfill what he regarded in large measure as a vote of confidence in himself.[35] For all the brilliance of his success in two political campaigns in which the local press had played a crucial role in delivering victory, Mulholland had no patience for the niceties of politics. "I do not pay much attention to the press anywhere because they have fits at irregular periods," he remarked. "A man trying to do useful work cannot be paying much attention to what the press says or does; only occasionally, as he needs their help, he might go after them and encourage them, and get away with it."[36] But he savored combat of any kind, and in setting out to bring a river across more than two hundred miles of mountains and deserts he saw himself embarked upon the greatest battle of his life: "Nature is the squarest fighter there is, and I wanted this fight."[37]

Public concern about his lack of experience and technical background was not entirely misplaced. The problem was not simply that Mulholland had never been schooled in the science of engineering, but rather that he had little or no regard for the very skills that the new schools of professional engineering valued most highly. "A mathematical mind does not denote a fine mind in any way. It is a trait or gift that a few people are born with," he complained. "The trouble with a great many men who are brilliant at mathematics is that they don't or can't broaden mentally in other directions . . . I know very few engineers that read books outside of the technical stuff of their profession, and consequently their views are not broad and their outlook on life is restricted."[38] This was the bluff, unorthodox man who now found himself in charge of the fourth largest engineering project in American history to that date, an endeavor surpassed in scope and complexity only by the building of the Panama Canal, the New York Aqueduct, and the Erie Canal.[39]

What Mulholland brought to the project in place of the fine-honed precision of an engineer were the skills of a builder and organizer. He did not supervise; he directed. He had no time for office work; instead, he spent every moment he could in the field, alongside his working men. He kept no notes on his work and had no patience for detail.[40] When confronted with a problem of construction, he preferred to stoop down and sketch a solution in the dirt where he stood and then move on, leaving his subordinates to work out the specifics.[41] He was never cold or distant in dealing with his men; rather, he visited frequently in the work camps and more than once stopped to show new mothers in the camps the proper way to change a diaper.[42] His constant presence, accessibility, and confidence in his fellow workers generated a remarkably cohesive spirit within the aqueduct's work force. Visitors to the construction sites remarked upon "this sympathetic placing of himself in the other fellow's place, the large democracy, simplicity, and withal the square dealing of the man."[43] The tireless dedication of "the Chief" soon spread to his employees. Pilferage, for example, a common problem on any construction site, was almost nonexistent on the aqueduct.[44] And John Gray, who had charge of the hard-rock digging at the north portal of the Elizabeth Tunnel, once stayed on his feet through six straight shifts, two days and nights in all, when his crews struck water in the tunnel.[45]

The breadth of vision Mulholland honored so highly was reflected not only in his dealings with his men but also in the spirit of innovation which he brought to the project. Without question, the most radical departure he made from customary practice was his determination to use municipal workers rather than private contractors whenever possible. In its original form, the aqueduct extended over 233 miles and required the construction of 142 tunnels totaling 53 miles in length, 120 miles of railroad track, 500 miles of highways and trails, 2 small power plants to service the construction work, 169 miles of transmission lines, and 240 miles of telephone wire.[46] With the exception of the railroad line, public employees built all but 11 miles of the canal and 1,485 feet of the tunnels.[47] In addition, the Bureau of the Los Angeles Aqueduct constructed its own cement manufacturing plant at Monolith and developed special mixes of cement utilizing the tufa stone available in the Owens Valley and desert regions in place of clay. Such a policy was recommended by more than Mulholland's determination to keep the aqueduct a public project from end to end; sheer economic necessity dictated it. The bids the city received from the private sector for cement alone would have bankrupted the project, and city officials, after looking at the costs projected for private construction of the Jawbone Division, estimated that the aqueduct would have cost over $40 million to complete if it were forced to rely on private contractors.[48]

At first, there was some concern that the city would never be able to find enough skilled workers to construct the project.[49] A fortuitous financial panic originating in the eastern markets in October 1907, however, brought about the closure of scores of mining operations in the western states just as construction on the aqueduct was getting under way. As a result, more than four thousand trained tunnelers and diggers from the gold fields of California, Nevada, and Colorado suddenly became available. Some were over fifty years old and had worked the original Comstock Lode.[50] Nevertheless, anyone who needed a job found a welcome on the aqueduct, which operated under special provisions waiving the city's usual civil service requirements for all but supervisory positions.[51] Americans of Greek, Austrian, Serbian, Montenegran, Hungarian, and Italian extraction made up the bulk of the labor force.[52] Japanese and Chinese workers were rare.[53] Most numerous of all the ethnic groups were Irish-Americans, who arrived in dungarees held up with a bit of fuse tied for a belt, hobnailed boots, and derby hats which could absorb the impact of a falling rock in this age before the introduction of hard hats.[54]

The conditions under which these men worked were demanding in the extreme. Temperatures in the desert ranged from 10 degrees Fahrenheit at night to more than 110 during the day. Those who chose to work in the tunnels, where the temperature remained constant, faced the constant danger of falling rock and cave-ins. With the exception of the cement plant at Monolith, where the city employed 250 men, the buildings in the camps did little to protect workers from the elements. Most structures were built of wood and canvas so that they could be moved easily; only the equipment storage sheds merited corrugated iron. Insulation was rare and refrigeration altogether unknown. The meat in the commissaries was usually rotten and maggot-ridden, and eggs and cheese arrived in an inedible condition.[55]

The Los Angeles Young Men's Christian Association did its best to lighten the workers' lot with regular shipments of books, magazines, games, movies, and bags of candy sent to the club rooms it established in the work camps. Nevertheless, few men could stand exposure to these conditions for long. As a result, the work force was constantly fluctuating. As many as one hundred thousand men worked on the aqueduct, but the labor force never numbered more than six thousand at a time, and three thousand was the average.[56] A general exodus from the camps occurred each summer as the men fled the Mojave Desert to find work in the Northwest or on the other side of the Sierra; when winter returned, the aqueduct labor force swelled again. For shorter respites, each man would save up a small stake of cash and head for Los Angeles; few got past the saloons that sprang up in the towns of Cinco and Mojave, however, and alcoholism became an acute problem in the camps at the southern end of the project.[57]

Health and sanitary conditions were primitive, though no worse than was customary for the period. The hundreds of men working the Saugus Division, for example, had only one bathtub among them, and when it wore out from constant use it was not replaced.[58] All employees contributed to the cost of medical care. If a worker was injured but did not require hospitalization, he was allowed to return to work once he signed a release absolving the city of Los Angeles of any liability for subsequent complications. Those who did go into the camp hospitals received no pay at all unless they signed similar waivers, in which case they were provided with free board and half pay. Settlements for the survivors of men killed on the project were rarely paid and never generous. Of the forty-three deaths that occurred during construction of the aqueduct, only eight resulted in the payment of benefits to survivors. The total paid to these eight families was no more than $3,928, and only three of the eight received cash settlements greater than $500. The city of Los Angeles did contribute $75 automatically toward the burial expenses of anyone killed on the project.[59]

Casualties were rare, however, and the aqueduct set records

in its time for a remarkably low death rate. This achievement was all the more distinctive in view of the numerous tunnels called for in Mulholland's design. Mulholland's preference for going through rather than around natural barriers was standard practice in a period when construction materials were more expensive than labor. "When you buy a piece of pork you don't have to eat the bristles," Mulholland pointed out in explaining this approach to the difficulties posed by the terrain he had to cross.[60] In all, only 5 men were killed during the course of an overall tunneling and excavation effort which consumed five or six million pounds of blasting powder—a figure which compares most favorably with the 160 deaths in New York in the course of construction of the Catskill Aqueduct. The city's record can be attributed at least in part to Mulholland's determination to use modern high-grade German fuses and blasting caps which left little powder unexploded and thereby reduced the risk of unexpected detonations that all tunnel workers in the United States had faced theretofore.[61]

Mulholland not only kept his men alive, he kept them working. Given the tight economic tether on which he was forced to operate and the generally predictable cost of construction materials, the greatest risks he faced were delays which might drive up his projected budget for labor. His determination to employ municipal workers rather than private contractors angered the forces of organized labor elsewhere in the state, and no sooner had the project begun than the unions rallied in Sacramento to put forward legislation that would have increased the minimum wage for day labor on all public projects to $2.50 a day. This represented an increase of 25 percent and would have boosted in one stroke the costs to the city of building the aqueduct by $5 million.[62] Although the bill was defeated, Mulholland took to heart the threat it posed. He instituted a system of quotas for the work to be done and paid bonuses to each man who exceeded his daily quota. In this way, he was able to increase the pay to his best workers while ensuring that the project as a whole would remain on schedule and under budget. In order to collect their bonuses, some crews were encouraged to work as much as twelve hours a day. The system also helped to assure that a high quality of workmanship would be maintained because progress was measured on the basis of the number of rivets driven, and no team wanted to be delayed by having to go back and redo poor work.[63]

The benefits of this system were not immediately apparent to Mulholland's overseers in the business community who were less familiar with the practical realities of construction work. Mulholland initially limited the application of the bonus system to construction of the Elizabeth Tunnel, the longest tunnel on the project, twenty-five thousand feet. The consulting engineers had noted in their review of his design that the pace of work here would determine how quickly the project as a whole could be completed.[64] Mulholland had therefore commenced work on the Elizabeth Tunnel before any other part of the aqueduct, though he had assembled a work force of only 327 men for the entire project when the tunneling began on September 20, 1907.[65] Two teams of a hundred men each were set to work at the north and south portals of the tunnel, laboring around the clock in three shifts. Even so, the tunnel progressed at the rate of only eight to twenty feet a day, and twenty pounds of dynamite were needed for every foot driven into the rock.[66] When fifteen months had passed and the tunnel was still not finished, the Chamber of Commerce, in December 1908, demanded an accounting from Mulholland of his progress. "Well, we have spent about $3 million all told, I guess, and there is perhaps 900 feet of aqueduct built," Mulholland responded. "Figuring all our expenditures, it has cost us about $3,300 per foot. But by this time next year, I'll have 50 miles completed and at a cost of under $30 per foot, if you'll let me alone."[67]

What the Chamber of Commerce failed to appreciate was that the crews working under the enticements of Mulholland's bonus system on the Elizabeth Tunnel were setting and resetting records for hard-rock tunneling. When the tunnel was finally completed in 1911, it turned out to have taken only two-thirds the time and two-thirds the cost originally estimated by the city's panel of consulting engineers.[68] Mulholland's bonus system proved such an unqualified success that it was soon extended to the other tunnels on the project, then to the construction of siphons in 1911, and finally to most of the other components of the aqueduct.[69] So popular was the system with the work crews that the professional engineers who did not share in its benefits became disgruntled. "This is a great thing for the underdog but where does the engineer come in?" they complained in a demand for higher wages. "His only reward is to work himself out of a job as quickly as possible while the men under him reap the benefit in increased wages."[70]

Mulholland also achieved savings in time and labor through the introduction of electric shovels and air-driven drills, which replaced the old-fashioned two-man teams working with sledge hammer and stem.[71] But not every innovation he tried out on the aqueduct was successful. In 1908, for example, he imported twenty-eight caterpillar tractors from the Holt Manufacturing Company in Stockton at a total cost of $104,250. These track-laying vehicles, forerunners of the modern tank, had been developed for use on the peaty soils of the Sacramento-San Joaquin Delta farmlands. Mulholland thought they would perform equally well in hauling pipe sections and equipment across the desert. But blowing sand damaged the engines, and unskilled operators, working under the pressure of Mulholland's bonus system, soon wore them out. As a result, the caterpillars were reduced to junk, and Mulholland suddenly found himself in the position of having to assemble on short notice more than fifteen hundred mules to replace them.[72]

Similar problems cropped up at the city's cement plant in Monolith. The tufa mix the city developed was adequate for constructing canals where the water moved slowly and there was consequently less risk of abrasion. But in sections of the aqueduct where the rate of flow increased under pressure, the cement quickly broke down and could be used only as a liner.[73] The problems Mulholland encountered with the tractors and cement were not brought to public view for several years, however; for the most part, the city honored his request to be left alone to do his work. Mulholland's greatest difficulties during the first four years of the aqueduct's construction in fact arose from the very success he achieved in pushing the project forward ahead of schedule.

The first of these crises involved the city's bonds. The same

financial panic in October 1907 that released the army of unemployed miners Mulholland needed to construct the aqueduct also
destroyed the market for the bonds the city had to sell to pay for
the work. As a result, the city was able to issue only $1,020,000 in
aqueduct bonds that year, and none found buyers in the troubled
money markets of the East. Instead, half the bonds issued in 1907
were sold to the state of California, and the balance were picked
up by various financial institutions in Los Angeles. The city's
efforts to raise another $340,000 by issuing aqueduct bonds in
$200 denomincations for public sale failed to produce more than
a few thousand dollars, and by the spring of 1908 the project was
running out of money. The bond revenues were sufficient to
carry the work forward to June, but the city by that time would
have no funds to pay more than a million dollars owed to the
suppliers of its materials.

On July 1, the city failed to meet its payroll on the aqueduct.
On July 10, all purchasing for the project was suspended. July 16
was set as the deadline for a resolution of the problem; if more
bonds had not been sold by that date, Mulholland declared the
project would have to be shut down.[74] By this time, however, the
panic of 1907 had blown over, and three bond houses in New
York expressed interest in taking over the sale of the nearly $22
million in aqueduct bonds the city still had outstanding. In the
desperate circumstances in which it found itself by the middle of
July, Los Angeles chose to forego competitive bidding. The city
attorney declared two of the offers invalid in a ruling later overturned by his immediate successor.[75] The entire unsold portion of
the aqueduct bond issue was turned over to a syndicate of investors headed by A. B. Leach and Company and the Kountze Brothers of New York. Under the contract the city struck with the New
York syndicate, Los Angeles would have to pay 4.5 percent interest on its aqueduct bonds, whereas all its previous bond issues
had been at 3.75- and 4-percent interest rates. But as damaging as
this arrangement might prove to the long-term financing of the
project, the syndicate was ready at least to put up $4,085,000
immediately to bail Los Angeles out of its most pressing difficulties. The balance of the unsold bonds, nearly $18 million in all,
would be picked up at the syndicate's option according to a fixed

schedule of payments on each succeeding February 1 over the next five years.[76]

Precipitate haste had been a hallmark of the city's handling of water bonds ever since the first issue to pay the costs of buying up the works of the Los Angeles City Water Company. On that occasion, the city treasurer had sat up all night signing the bonds on the day they were issued so they could be rushed immediately to the market for sale.[77] Mulholland refused to take heed of the crisis he had faced in mid-July 1908 and pressed ahead with construction of the aqueduct regardless of the schedule of financing established in the city's contract with the syndicate. As a result, his expenditures soon outstripped the funding available to the project. And every time Los Angeles was forced to issue more bonds ahead of the schedule established with the syndicate, the city lost money on the interest rates the syndicate charged for the sale.[78] For Mulholland, it was a maddening dilemma. If he pushed the project at the pace his work crews were capable of achieving, he ran out of funds in the short term; if, on the other hand, he delayed work to stay within the limits of his short-term financing, he ran the risk that labor costs and inflation would push the overall cost of the aqueduct beyond his $24.5 million maximum. "I don't know why I ever went into this job," he complained to a reporter in the spring of 1909. "There is more in a private practice, but I guess it was the Irish in me . . . When I saw it staring me in the face I couldn't back away from it. I know the necessity better than any man . . . I didn't want to have to buckle down and admit I was afraid of the thing, because I never have been—not for a second."[79]

By the beginning of 1910, Mulholland was operating with only enough cash reserves to pay for thirty days of continued construction. So long as the bond market remained healthy, he was safe. But when it came time for the syndicate to pick up its next installment of $4,896,000 in bonds on February 1, it demurred. Officially, the syndicate complained that since Mulholland was by this time nearly $10 million ahead of the schedule it had established with the city, the market for municipal securities simply could not absorb more of the aqueduct bonds at this time. Under these circumstances, the syndicate declared its intention to wait until the "excess" bonds which the city had pressed into its hands for sale ahead of schedule had been fully absorbed. In other words, the syndicate had decided to adhere rigidly to the schedule fixed in its contract for any future sales, and in view of the quantity of bonds it had already received, it could not be required to exercise its option on any additional bonds for another year.[80]

The financial disaster Mulholland had been skirting for two and a half years was finally upon him. With the aqueduct nearly two-thirds complete, the project had run out of money. An estimated four thousand men, constituting 80 percent of the aqueduct's work force at that time, had to be laid off in May.[81] The close-knit organization of working men and skilled supervisors Mulholland had built suddenly lay in a shambles, its members scattered. After a fruitless trip to New York at the end of May to plead with the bond merchants to relent, Mulholland announced that he was suspending all work on those parts of the aqueduct which were farthest advanced in order to concentrate his remainin resources upon those sections which were lagging.[82]

Mulholland believed there were more sinister forces at work in his troubles than simply a lull in the bond market. "This action [by the syndicate], whatever the reasons for taking it may have been, was calculated to seriously embarrass the city in its efforts to keep construction work going on the aqueduct," he declared.[83] Behind the intransigence of A. B. Leach and the brothers Kountze, Mulholland saw the fine hand of the local power companies, who had worked to block the project three times before. Foremost among these opponents was the Los Angeles Gas and Electric Company. Unlike Kerckhoff and Huntington at Pacific Light and Power, Los Angeles Gas and Electric had no prospect of sharing in the impending prosperity of the San Fernando Valley, so it suffered from no division of interests where the aqueduct was concerned. As the supplier of 87 percent of the power for lighting in the city's business district, it was more directly threatened by the advent of municipal power than either of the other two local companies. And as a subsidiary of Pacific Lighting, which was a member of the Pacific Gas and Electric consortium, it shared in that organization's wealth, influence, and determination to oppose public power in any form.[84]

The city began preliminary planning for a power distribution system in 1909, and a new Bureau of the Los Angeles Aqueduct Power was established by municipal ordinance that year. Although the local companies renewed their offer to build the power plants along the aqueduct themselves in exchange for a lease to distribute the power within the city, it was again rejected; and the city council called a bond election for April 19, 1910, to provide the first public funds for the construction of municipal hydroelectric plants.[85] It seemed a little too neat that this announcement should be followed immediately by the New York syndicate's decision to suspend funding for the aqueduct. And when the syndicate offered to revise its stand if the city would agree to a set of conditions for further bond sales that would have effectively prohibited the city from entering the business of selling power, Mulholland resolutely declared, "I would rather see the work on the desert stand just the way it is for fifty years than accept the terms."[86]

Mulholland was able to resolve his most pressing cash shortages by tapping the city's own sinking fund, which had been established in connection with the aqueduct bond issue, and by peddling a million dollars worth of bonds to the Metropolitan and New York Life Insurance companies. Although these arrangements were completed in August 1910, the New York syndicate continued to attempt to block the city's maneuvers until November, at which point it relented and agreed to purchase $530,000 in bonds.[87] This left the city with $2.9 million in unsold aqueduct bonds which the syndicate still controlled even though it could not be compelled to offer them for sale until the beginning of 1912. This time the syndicate did not waver in its determination to adhere to the schedule set forth in the contract. It delayed announcing its intentions until January 10, 1912, when it declared it would not take up its last option on the aqueduct bonds. The city would have to raise this final bit of the financing for the aqueduct by itself.[88]

Mulholland's problems during these long two years of financial travail were further complicated by a strike which swept the aqueduct soon after the massive layoffs of May 1910. The issue that ignited this conflict with labor was the food service, always a sensitive point for the men working along the aqueduct. During the early planning stages of the project, Los Angeles provided its

survey crews with a commissary service supplied from the Owens
Valley. When the time came to assemble the much larger work
force needed for construction, the city withdrew from the food
business and contracted instead with D. J. Desmond, a conces-
sionaire whose services were popular with the local railroad companies. Desmond had been awarded special commendations from
the United States Army for the excellence of his service to the
refugees after the San Francisco earthquake, but on the aqueduct
his work found little favor.[89] Riots in the mess halls were not
uncommon, and many of Desmond's cooks quite rather than
serve his food.[90]

Desmond's original contract of August 1908 called for the
provision of food at a cost to the workers of $.25 per meal, or
twenty-one meals for $5.00. The bargain rate of $5.00 was
dropped at the beginning of March 1910. When the number of
workers Desmond had to supply dropped precipitously as a result
of Mulholland's layoffs that summer, Desmond on November 1
attempted to cover his losses by raising his price to $.30 a meal.
The city, however, did not offer the workers any compensating
increase in wages.[91] The resulting dissatisfaction among the labor
force played directly into the hands of Ed Crough and James
Cowan, organizers for the Western Federation of Miners, who
had been working for months to unionize the crews on the Elizabeth, Little Lake, and Grape Vine tunnels. Within two weeks of
the announcement of Desmond's new rates, seven hundred men
walked off the job and work on the Elizabeth Tunnel came to a
standstill. And when Mulholland refused even to discuss a pay
increase, the metal workers and steam shovel operators joined
the miners on the picket lines.[92]

The union men could not have chosen a worse time to call a
strike. Since Mulholland lacked the funding in the winter of 1910
to employ a full work force, he was in no hurry to achieve a
settlement. When the aqueduct's financial situation improved the
following spring, Mulholland still did not have to grant any
concessions; he simply accelerated the spread of his bonus system
to satisfy the workers on sections of the project which had not yet
received its benefits. But his intransigence in dealing with the
unions brought the aqueduct into the midst of a far greater labor
controversy which was by that time raging in the city.

The Election of 1911

Los Angeles business leaders had been locked in battle with organized labor ever since the typographers' union strike of 1890. Defense of the open shop was the particular passion of Harrison Gray Otis, publisher of the *Los Angeles Times*, and the Merchants and Manufacturers Association was his favored weapon. In the strike of 1890, the printers who made up Los Angeles' oldest union struck the *Tribune, Express, Herald,* and *Times* in a dispute over wages. Although the other publishers exhibited a willingness to negotiate, Otis refused even to discuss a settlement. Instead, he cut his printers' salaries by 20 percent, locked the union men out, and began importing new men from as far away as Kansas City. When the typographers' union responded with an unsuccessful effort to institute a boycott against his paper, Otis organized a counterboycott of his own in association with his largest advertiser, A. Hamburger, proprietor of the People's Store.[93]

Otis soon found a more powerful agent for his anti-union zeal in the Merchants and Manufacturers Association. Originally formed on June 26, 1896, to promote tourism and to stage the annual Fiesta de las Flores, the association within six months of its creation found itself drawn inexorably into the city's emerging labor problems. At first its activities in this respect were limited to efforts to put the unemployed to work on municipal beautification projects. On August 1, 1897, however, the association elected F. J. Zeehandelaar as its secretary, and for the next twenty-seven years he built the organization into one of the most powerful advocates of the open shop in America. Within two months of his election, Zeehandelaar led the group into a conflict which, as the association's official history points out, "forecast its historic place as the advocate of better employment relations." The labor unions in San Francisco had organized a boycott against the Maier and Zobelein Breweries of Los Angeles, and the association leaped to the breweries' defense with a resolution declaring that the unions' action was "against all principles of the American Institution and a serious menace to the freedom of action guaranteed to every citizen under the Constitution of the United States."[94]

As the city's labor leaders escalated their efforts in the years that followed, the association quickly lost its distaste for the device of the boycott. Businessmen who refused to join the association found their credit cut off at the local banks, and members who weakened in the face of union demands had their products boycotted by the association.[95] For members who faced labor difficulties, however, the association provided a ready source of funding, strike breakers, and special police. After 1905, Zeehandelaar later testified, the mayor and chief of police regularly permitted men paid by the association to be sworn in as special deputies to assist in labor disputes.[96] In the view of the *San Francisco Bulletin*, "The Merchants and Manufacturers Association has one confession of faith, one creed: 'We will employ no union man.'"[97] And the unquestioned head and field marshall of this virulent campaign was Harrison Gray Otis. As Frederick Palmer observed of the association in 1911, "Otis has taught it strictly military principles. His Adjutant General is the secretary of the Association, Felix J. Zeehandelaar. A soft-spoken, suave man is 'Zee' there in his office all day looking after tactical detail. Back of 'Zee,' always alert, is Otis with his daily newspaper ready to beat any laggard into line . . . Few businessmen would choose to run athwart the hidden forces of the 'M and M' and the open attacks of Otis and the *Times*."[98]

The division of Los Angeles' Republican Party into conservative and progressive factions and the resulting ascendancy of the progressive reformers during the first decade of the twentieth century did nothing to blunt the confrontational tactics that Otis and the Merchant and Manufacturers Association pursued with such vigor. The progressives campaigned for civil service reform, nonpartisan elections, introduction of the initiative referendum and recall in municipal elections, and the elimination of graft and corruption in city government. These proposals alone were enough to win them the opposition of Harrison Gray Otis and the *Times*. Otis' son-in-law and heir apparent, Harry Chandler, even went so far as to get caught forging four thousand ballots in an effort to defeat the reformers' candidate for mayor in 1907.[99]

But the progressives' enthusiasms ran only to technical adjustments in the way government was run in the city. They represented no fundamental break with the corporate ideals which had guided Los Angeles' municipal administration for decades. Rather, the progressives enthusiastically embraced the business community and saw their efforts at reform as an attempt "to apply to city government the techniques of systematization and administrative control being developed in business and the professions."[100] When the progressives' Good Government League elected its first mayor, George Alexander, in 1909, its chief ideologue, Meyer Lissner, promised, "We are going to have a real business administration . . . [which] will do public business like great private business is done."[101] And in keeping with this spirit, the progressives eschewed any contact with organized labor, with the result that the union men uniformly opposed the Good Government League's reform candidates.

The threat George Alexander's election posed to the established order in Los Angeles consequently amounted to little more than a changing of the guard. The progressives railed against the continued influence of Henry Huntington and Walter Parker of the Southern Pacific in municipal affairs, and one of Alexander's first acts as mayor was an attempt to throw Otis' associate in the San Fernando land syndicate, Moses Sherman, off the board of water commissioners. But Alexander immediately sought a rapprochement with Otis by appointing the *Times*' assistant city editor, Edward Dishman, as his chief of police. In large part, the reformers were members of the same establishment they appeared to be fighting: they were simply the upwardly mobile young attorneys and newly arrived businessmen who had been denied positions of leadership within the regular Republican organization by Otis and the other major domos of the party's conservative wing. Alexander, moreover, proved to be singularly ineffectual in his efforts to achieve even limited reforms. The city council refused to back up his attempts to remove Sherman, although Sherman eventually resigned at his own behest. Dishman, who had no experience for his position other than a brief assignment early in his career as a crime reporter, fell to warring with the police commission and was fired by it. Meanwhile, the members of the city's fire, parks, and health commissions all resigned, and Alexander had great difficulty finding anyone willing to replace them in their unsalaried positions.[102]

While Alexander fumbled to gain control of his administration, the unions drew new battle lines. In 1910, the American Federation of Labor announced the establishment of a unified labor council in Los Angeles to fight against the open shop in what they called "the scabbiest town on earth." A general strike committee was organized; by June 1, fifteen hundred workers were manning the picket lines, and the city's breweries, metal shops, and leather works were almost entirely closed down. Mayor Alexander and his progressive allies on the city council struck back with an ordinance drawn up by the Merchants and Manufacturers Association banning picketing of any kind. Mass arrests followed; and in the mayoralty campaign of 1911, the union forces drew up behind the candidacy of Job Harriman, Socialist nominee for governor in 1898 and for vice-president in 1900 and an early critic of the aqueduct during the bond election of 1907. In the primary election on November 1, Harriman led the field and looked to be an easy victor over the incumbent Alexander in the general election scheduled for December 5.[103]

This startling turn of events occurred as part of a general surge of support for radical reform which swept more than five hundred Socialists into local, state, and federal offices around the country during 1910 and 1911. It is very doubtful, however, that the Socialists could have achieved this much success in so resolutely conservative a community as Los Angeles without the bitterness sown by Otis' excesses and the artful use Harriman made of Mulholland's aqueduct as a symbol of all that was wrong and corrupt in the existing order. Harriman once again brought out all the charges raised in the bond elections of 1905 and 1907 concerning the financing of the project, the adequacy of its design, and the quality of the water it would deliver. More important, he charged that the project was unnecessary, that the flows of the Los Angeles River were sufficient to serve the city's needs, that Mulholland's drought of 1905 had been fabricated, and that the aqueduct had been promoted in the first place for no other reason than to benefit the San Fernando land syndicate.

As troubling as these charges were, the threat which the anti-cipated election of Job Harriman posed to Mulholland's project was indirect at best. With less than fifty miles of the aqueduct yet to be constructed, Harriman could scarcely have ordered a halt to its completion. But he warned from the stump that if the San Fernando land syndicate ever received any water from the Owens Valley, the city would lose forevermore its right to regain that water for municipal use. He accordingly promised that if he could not stop the project, as mayor he would make certain that the syndicate never received a drop of water from the aqueduct.[104]

The mayoralty campaign of 1911 was thus considerably more significant to the party of interests behind the aqueduct than either of the bond elections of 1905 and 1907 had been because it raised the prospect of a complete change in the administration of public policy under a political movement in no way allied with the business community and its objectives. The challenge to Har-rison Gray Otis was made even more specific in an initiative that appeared on the same ballot proposing the establishment of a publicly financed weekly newspaper so that Los Angeles would for the first time have an honest and impartial source of informa-tion on municipal affairs.[105] As a result, the issues in the election of 1911 were clearly drawn from the point of view of the *Los Angeles Times*: "The forces of law and order against Socialism—peace and prosperity against misery and chaos—the Stars and Stripes against the red flag."[106]

The business community accordingly drew together to meet the threat in full force. Otis dropped his customary line of edi-torial vituperation against the progressives. The operations of the Good Government League were suspended after the primary, and its leaders were absorbed back into the ranks of the regular Republican organization. In its place, William Garland, presi-dent of the local realty board and chief sales agent for Henry Huntington's properties, agreed to lead with Bradner Wells Lee, chairman of the county Republican committee, "a great strictly non-partisan general committee unshackled by any partisan ties, embracing Democrats, Republicans, and Independents into one great party—the People—to crush in defeat the Socialist move-ment that is declared to be threatening the city's progress."[107]

   While Harrison Gray Otis patroled the streets in his private limousine with a cannon mounted on the hood and held forth daily against the "anarchic scum" who challenged his Campaign to Save Los Angeles, the city council set to work striking the names of more than twelve hundred registered voters who were listed as living in lodging houses. At the same time, the major newspapers in town imposed a virtually total blackout on any news of Harriman's campaign events. Harriman's name appeared only in conjunction with predictions of the dreadful cost for the city if he were elected. Newspaper editorials warned variously that eastern investors would withdraw their support from municipal projects if a socialist took office; that the "American Home" would be undermined by hordes of "aliens" poised to rush into the city at the moment of Harriman's victory; that the city under Harriman would be no better than San Francisco, which was just then undergoing the revelation of scandals by Abe Reuf and the Union Labor party; and finally, that since Harriman had won the primary in the first election at which women in the city had been permitted to vote, his victory would mean the death of women's suffrage as other states saw how women abused their franchise.[108]

   Mayor Alexander gave up trying to answer every charge against his conduct in office and barricaded himself in City Hall, explaining that the press of public business left him no time for speeches. Similarly, all other city officials declined repeated requests from the Harriman camp to debate the question of "political and financial manipulation for the private interests of a few capitalists" in the construction of the aqueduct.[109]

   The aqueduct, however, was not the only issue in the campaign of 1911. Of equal importance on the local scene, and of far greater significance nationally, was the trial of two brothers, James B. and John Joseph McNamara, on charges of having dynamited the offices of the *Los Angeles Times* on the night of October 1, 1910. Harriman himself was a member of the team of defense attorneys, headed by Clarence Darrow, and throughout the city workers bore campaign buttons reading "McNamaras Innocent! Vote for Harriman!" May Day 1911 was declared McNamara Day, and huge supportive parades were organized in every major city across the country. Small contributions to the

McNamara Defense Fund poured in from laboring men and women throughout the nation, and thousands came to Los Angeles for the trial. Darrow's problem, though few could be sure of it at the time, was that his clients were guilty. With the *Times* charging that Harriman was a member of the dynamite conspiracy and that Darrow was financing the Harriman campaign from the McNamara Defense Fund, Darrow realized that the election and his case were fatally intertwined and that any negotiated plea for his clients would have to be approved by Otis' allies in the business community.[110]

Darrow sent as his agent in these negotiations the muckraking journalist Lincoln Steffens. The idea of seeking a settlement was first raised by E. W. Scripps on November 19 during a weekend Steffens and Darrow spent at Scripps's ranch at Miramar, near San Diego. Darrow went there to recuperate from the rigors of preparing for the trial; his health was poor, and he had already entered semiretirement when Samuel Gompers personally appealed to him to take the McNamaras' case. Steffens was delighted by the discomfiture which Harriman's election would cause the bankers and businessmen of Los Angeles: "They feared that socialism was coming to Los Angeles and think what that news out in Iowa would do to all their real estate plans!" he exclaimed.[111] But Steffens also shared Scripps' concern for the effect a prolonged trial would have on Darrow's health. So after securing Darrow's blessing for the venture, Steffens set out to establish contact with the business leaders surrounding Otis.

The prospect of negotiating a plea to save the McNamaras' lives intrigued Steffens as a chance to prove that Christian charity could flourish in even so hostile an environment as he regarded Los Angeles to be. Steffens went directly from Miramar to Meyer Lissner, one of the most prominent of the city's progressive leaders, and demanded a list of the men who could arrange a settlement. "Write the names of the few men who actually govern this town, the big, bad men," he told Lissner. "I mean the kind of men who act off their own bats, don't have to consult others, and who, when they set out to do something, good or bad, put it over. Imagination, courage, strength we need, not goodness. If you get a single good citizen . . . a reformer or a heeler on the list, we'll be done . . . Only men, now; hard-boiled, unscrupulous fellows who act."[112] Thus Steffens found his way to the most powerful men in the Merchants and Manufacturers Association and set them to the task of obtaining the acquiescence of the district attorney and of Harry Chandler of the *Times*.

By his own account, Steffens secured the backing of twenty of the city's leading capitalists at a meeting on November 29 when he assured them that mercy for the McNamaras would be the only way to restore order to the city's troubled labor relations. The next day he met with four other "leading citizens who were regarded as necessary to complete the list of insiders to put the matter over on the city." Among these four were William Mulholland and his chief lieutenants, J. B. Lippincott and W. B. Mathews. "They were for the proposition at the first statement of it, 'of course,'" Steffens recalled. "But they were too public-spirited to count big in my experiment . . . to justify my theory that there is enough good will in all men of imagination and power to do any good, hard job, even if it is not obviously in their own selfish interest."[113]

Harrison Gray Otis was not so constrained. When he learned what was afoot, he was livid. Accounts differ as to how he was ultimately persuaded to forego the pleasure of seeing the McNamaras hang, but both LeCompte Davis and Harry Chandler later reported that he gave his consent only on the assurance that a confession would surely discredit the labor movement in Los Angeles.[114] While the negotiators wrangled over the length of the prison terms the brothers would serve, there was never any question that the price the business leaders demanded for their support of a settlement was the defeat of Job Harriman. An agreement therefore had to be reached before election day. The negotiations nearly broke down altogether when the district attorney's men at the last minute arrested one of Darrow's investigators on charges of attempted jury tampering. But on December 1, four days before the voters were scheduled to elect their next mayor, Darrow rose in court to announce a change of plea to guilty.

The shock of Darrow's action was immediate and devastating. Darrow walked out of court that day on streets littered with discarded Harriman campaign buttons. Harriman himself had never been consulted on the settlement or even informed that negotiations were under way. He was left instead to read the doom of his hopes for election in the press the next morning. Darrow expressed considerable regret at this effect of his decision, but he later explained, "The lives of my clients were at stake, and I had no right or inclination to consider anything but them. I could not tell Mr. Harriman; it would place him in the position of either deserting his party or letting one client go to almost certain death, which he could not do."[115]

Steffens too had reason later to regret his participation in the settlement. None of the objectives he had sought were achieved: there was no rapprochement between labor and capital; the sentences handed down to the two brothers were longer than expected; the district attorney did not suspend his pursuit of other suspects in the bombing; and, worst of all, the city proceeded to prosecute Darrow for compliance with the jury tampering charge. Steffens blamed the failure of his experiment on the reaction of the city's religious leaders to Darrow's change of plea: "That Sunday, the churches spoke . . . and what they preached was hate and disappointed revenge . . . the local churches did not grasp the 'Golden Rule.'"[116]

Certainly there was no trace of charity in Otis' editorial treatment of the outcome of the trial and Harriman's subsequent defeat. "Yesterday, in the city of Los Angeles, God's people spoke and the enemies of God stand confused," the *Times* proclaimed in its account of the McNamaras' sentencing, which took place the same day Harriman was buried at the polls. "Scoffing, anarchistic Socialism has been crushed—as far as this city is concerned—with the same swift merciless annihilation that the heel of a giant crushed the head of a reptile."[117] In one stroke, Otis and his political allies had turned back the Socialist threat and emerged from the conflict stronger than before. The labor movement was discredited. The progressives had been forced to fall back upon the regular party machinery in their hour of need, and neither they nor the Socialists would ever mount a significant electoral challenge again. And even though the initiative creating a public news service for the city did pass in that election, Otis

warned his advertisers that they would be blacklisted and boycotted if they ever took their business to it; the newsboys hired to
distribute the city's new weekly were beaten in the streets; and the
entire project was abandoned sixteen months later when funding
was withdrawn.[118]

For Mulholland, however, the battle was far from over. While
the most immediate danger to the operation of his aqueduct had
been defeated, a great wound had been opened in the community
he served, and he and his associates at City Hall now faced an
electorate that was divided in a way it had never been in the bond
elections of 1905 and 1907. The charges Harriman leveled against
the aqueduct had not been answered in the campaign of 1911,
and they would be raised again, first by the embittered Socialists
and later from a quarter Harriman had all but ignored, the
Owens Valley.

CHAPTER FIVE

Years of Excess

The year 1912 was not a good one for William Mulholland. It began with the decision by A. B. Leach and the Kountze Brothers not to take up their final option on the city's bonds, thereby further complicating Los Angeles' troubled financing of the aqueduct. The disgruntled Socialists and local power companies meanwhile stepped up their attacks on the project, forcing a formal municipal investigation by midyear These problems in turn intertwined with the continuing debate over disposition of the surplus waters the aqueduct would provide. And it was in the resolution of this last question that the future of the city's relations with the Owens Valley was finally and fatally fixed.

Although it had been clear from the outset that the aqueduct would provide far more water than Los Angeles could immediately absorb, the amount of the surplus and the city's policy for its distribution had not been defined. Vagueness on these points had worked to Los Angeles' advantage in the bond election of 1905 and the campaign for congressional approval of the project in 1906. But as the aqueduct neared completion, the city had finally to come to terms with the problem of what it would do with the water it had gone so deeply into debt to acquire.

Three years after construction of the aqueduct had begun, the city council initiated a series of public hearings, in September and October 1910, to solicit opinions on the question. The charter provisions adopted after the municipalization of the city's water system in 1902 prohibited any alienation of Los Angeles' rights to its new water supply without the approval of two-thirds of the city's voters. The amendment President Roosevelt had inserted into the 1906 legislation granting a right-of-way for the aqueduct across federal lands forbade the sale of these excess waters to any private corporation. Within these general limitations on the city's action, the hearings revealed at least three distinct bodies of opinion on how Los Angeles could apply the surplus to its best advantage. Mayor George Alexander favored the broadest possible distribution of the aqueduct water as a way of eventually bringing about a consolidation of city and county governments in Los Angeles. As soon as the city council had completed its hearings, the mayor went so far as to form a special commission of his own to press for this grandiose scheme.[1]

As great as the surplus would be, however, it could not be stretched to serve all of Los Angeles County, and the idea of consolidation met with vigorous opposition from the fiercely independent communities of Pasadena and Long Beach.[2] A more moderate position called for the extension of surplus water only to those areas which could be most readily annexed to the city, especially in the San Fernando Valley. This proposal, of course, enjoyed the enthusiastic support of the influential members of the San Fernando land syndicate and other major developers in the valley.[3] They had always regarded the aqueduct as a project beneficial to their interests, and the city government was by 1910 acknowledging that irrigation of the valley was one of the major purposes of the project.[4] In addition, many unincorporated communities near Los Angeles' existing borders had been encouraged to apply for immediate absorption by the city upon the publication of assurances by some members of the Board of Public Works that the revenues from the sale of water and power from the aqueduct would eliminate the need for any other tax collections in Los Angeles.[5]

Overarching the drives for both annexation and consolidation was the general conviction that, however the surplus waters were used, they must be administered so as to obtain the greatest possible immediate financial return to the city in order to pay back the costs of constructing the aqueduct. This emphasis on profitability, an objective which would not necessarily be served by annexation or consolidation, was a particular article of faith for the efficiency-minded progressives who had put George Alexander into office. For them, Los Angeles was "simply a huge corporation . . .[whose] citizens are stockholders and [whose] purpose is not to produce dividends but to promote the well-being of the community and to conserve the interests of the people as a whole."[6]

As the controversy over distribution heated up, Mulholland at first attempted to maintain his distance. The consulting engineers who reviewed his project in 1907 had severed the aqueduct from its distribution system for reasons of economy. The Department of Public Works, as the agency responsible for construction of the aqueduct, consequently contended that its jurisdiction stopped at the north end of the San Fernando Valley, and it refused even to assist in surveys for a distribution system.[7] "That is a matter of business management afterwards," Mulholland declared. "We have nothing to do with that."[8] The responsibility for these questions was eventually taken up by the city's newly created Public Service Commission, which set up its own board of consulting engineers in early 1911 to develop a plan for the distribution of the surplus waters of the aqueduct without regard for the mayor's commission on consolidation.

In their report of 1911, the consulting engineers, John Henry Quinton, W. H. Code, and Homer Hamlin, estimated that the aqueduct upon its completion would provide the city with eight times as much water as it could immediately consume, and four times as much as it would ever be able to use once all the lands within its existing borders were fully developed. The resulting surplus, assuming full development of the city, was an amount sufficient to irrigate an additional 135,000 acres of land each year. Although this was enough to serve the needs of the Owens Valley twice over, such an application of the surplus was never seriously entertained by the panel. Instead, the consulting engineers recommended a general policy of municipal expansion under which any area outside the city limits desirous of sharing in the surplus would have to agree to annexation as a condition for receipt of the water. Water would not be supplied to those areas where there was not a "reasonable assurance" of ultimate annexation. Any area that met this test for delivery of aqueduct water would be required to pay in advance the cost of constructing a distribution system according to the city's specifications, and to assume as well a proportionate share of the tax burden for the cost of building the aqueduct. Los Angeles, the engineers argued, should retain ownership of all facilities with the exception of distribution systems built within already incorporated cities. Consolidation was rejected outright on the grounds that the city would not have enough water to service so large an area. But Quinton, Code, and Hamlin did hold out the prospect that the city could eventually grow so large through annexation of the lands it served with water that it could establish itself as a county in its own right, leaving the semi-arid fringe areas that were too expensive to reach with water delivery lines to the existing county administration.[9]

The appearance of this report stirred immediate controversy, not for the general policies it advocated, but for the engineers' specific recommendation that the San Fernando Valley should receive first consideration in the allocation of surplus waters. Quinton, Code, and Hamlin proposed that fully three-fourths of the surplus—double the amount they estimated the city itself would ever need—should be devoted to irrigation in the San Fernando Valley. This recommendation was firmly founded upon hydrologic conditions within the South Coast. Wilmington, San Pedro, and the so-called Shoestring annexation connecting the city proper to its harbor at San Pedro had no need for aqueduct water because pumping was cheaper in those areas than purchases of water from the city could ever be. Although Pasadena, South Pasadena, Alhambra, and the Bairdstown district could benefit from aqueduct deliveries, the engineers recommended that only small quantities of the surplus should be allocated to these areas because water used for irrigation there would never seep back into the Los Angeles River basin. In contrast, one-fourth of every drop of water used for agriculture in the San Fernando Valley, according to the engineers, would enter the vast groundwater reservoirs that supply the Los Angeles River and thus be returned to the city for subsequent use elsewhere. In sum, the engineers estimated that the advent of aqueduct water would increase the city's supply from an average of 80 cubic feet per second to 480 cubic feet per second; and by applying 275 cubic feet per second for irrigation in the San Fernando Valley, the city could expect to gain back in return flows an additional 80 cubic feet per second each year, an amount equivalent to its total natural supply without the aqueduct.[10]

There was a compelling logic to the panel's recommendations. The consulting engineers were in essence simply reciting the perceptions that had moved the San Fernando Valley to the center of the city's planning for the aqueduct almost from the beginning. Nevertheless, the suggestion that the San Fernando Valley should receive twice as much water from the aqueduct as Los Angeles gave sudden new credence to the old charges that the project had been conceived and promoted for the purpose of benefiting the influential members of the San Fernando land syndicate. Job Harriman used these charges to great effect in his campaign for the mayoralty in 1911. And following his defeat, they were recast into a broader indictment of municipal corruption and deceit in a potent tract published by the Alembic Club of Los Angeles in 1912, W. T. Spilman's *Conspiracy*.[11]

Although rarely cited by modern historians, Spilman's slim volume must surely rank as one of the most influential documents ever published on the controversy over Los Angeles' aqueduct to the Owens Valley. The author not only dredged up again the evidence first uncovered by Loewenthal's *Examiner* in 1905 regarding the San Fernando land syndicate's operations, he surrounded this information with a wealth of seemingly authoritative data to support a host of new allegations of fraud and malfeasance in the development of the project. Spilman was not a Socialist, and he bore no allegiance to either the labor unions or the private power companies which had formed the backbone of the opposition to the aqueduct within Los Angeles after 1906. He was acting out of the purest self-interest. As president of the private Spilman Suburban Water Company, which dominated water services in the heart of the San Fernando Valley, he recognized that his company would soon be absorbed by the city's water program under the annexation policies which Quinton, Code, and Hamlin proposed.[12] He wrote, therefore, with the venom of a dedicated and canny capitalist who saw his means of livelihood threatened. Where Loewenthal in 1905 had merely questioned the necessity for haste in approving the initial bonds for the aqueduct, Spilman denied that there was any need at all for its construction. And where Samuel T. Clover in 1907 had attempted to show that the water of the Owens Valley was polluted by high concentrations of alkali, Spilman charged that it was absolutely poisonous.

To support his claims, Spilman constructed an elaborate conspiracy in which Mulholland and Lippincott were seen fabricating drought conditions in 1904 by secretly draining the city's reservoirs through the sewers, while the San Fernando land promotors raced to sell off their properties before the polluted aqueduct water arrived to render them worthless.[13] In Spilman's view, however, Mulholland, Lippincott, and Eaton were mere "cat's paws" for unidentified men "who, from under their vile covering, guide and manipulate the great corrupt political machine which has become so powerful that it is impossible to convict one of their protégés."[14] Although much of his reasoning was specious and his statistical references ranged from incomplete to irrelevant, Spilman's charges not only made up the substance of the formal municipal investigations of the aqueduct that soon followed, they can be found echoing as well through all the attacks on Los Angeles' policies in the Owens Valley that in later years made up the popular legend of the "rape of the valley."

In the years since the first revelation of its existence, the syndicate against which Spilman directed his main fire had grown richer, more deeply entrenched in the San FernandoValley, and more narrowly concentrated in its leadership. The giants of the Southern Pacific, whose great personal wealth set them apart from all the other members of the syndicate, were gone by 1912. E. H. Harriman was dead. Henry Huntington, having sold off his local railway empire for a second time to the Southern Pacific in 1910, was slipping into a comfortable semiretirement in which he would devote his remaining years to books and art and a marriage of the widow of his Uncle Collis whereby he regained the

inheritance Harriman had earlier denied him.[15] Harrison Gray
Otis and Moses Sherman were still active, but the leadership
in the group now belonged clearly to Otis' son-in-law, Harry
Chandler.

Chandler, born in New Hampshire in 1864, had cut short his
college career at Dartmouth by jumping into a vat of starch on a
dare, an incident which severely damaged his lungs. Forced to
seek a drier climate for the sake of his health, he arrived nearly
penniless in Los Angeles in 1883 and was promptly turned out of
his boardinghouse into the streets because the other roomers
could not bear his endless coughing. Chandler's subsequent rise
from this unhappy beginning in Southern California would have
made Horatio Alger blanch. He supported himself initially by
picking oranges and delivering newspapers. In time, he was able
to use his control of newspaper circulation within large areas of
the city to strangle Harrison Gray Otis' primary rival, the *Los
Angeles Tribune*. Having secretly bought the *Tribune*'s printing
plant, he turned it over to Otis in exchange for a position as
circulation manager of the *Times*. Upon his marriage to one of
Otis' daughters in 1894 he was promoted to business manager,
and his future with the *Times* was made secure.[16]

Chandler flirted briefly with progressive reform. In 1900 he
was even elected to the Board of Freeholders, where he worked
to introduce the initiative, recall, and referendum to city elections. But the *Times* adamantly opposed charter revisions along
these lines, and Chandler soon found another outlet for his energies in real estate development.[17] Moses Sherman first approached
Chandler for assistance in establishing a project Sherman had
begun with Hobart J. Whitley to run a railway line to the unset-
tled area northwest of the city. Chandler responded by forming a
syndicate of investors headed by his father-in-law to back Sherman's Los Angeles Pacific Boulevard and Development Company, which underwrote the subdivision of what is today Hollywood. Chandler and Sherman were thereafter nearly inseparable,
although Chandler's facility for assembling vast quantities of
investment capital seems always to have made him the senior
partner in their joint ventures. By the outbreak of World War I,
Chandler headed the largest real estate network in California.[18]

In 1926, the *Saturday Evening Post* surveyed the bewildering complexity of his corporate maneuvers and concluded approvingly, "He is mixed up in so many ventures that nobody with the possible exception of himself has ever been able to count them."[19]

With the creation of Hollywood, Chandler laid the foundation for a personal fortune that was estimated at his death to range from $200 to $500 million. But it was in the San Fernando Valley that he established his family's enduring influence over Los Angeles and the South Coast. At the beginning of 1909, Chandler and Otis were concentrating their investments in downtown Los Angeles. Here they were joined by Sherman and by William M. Garland, Henry Huntington's land agent who later headed the drive to defeat Job Harriman.[20] Chandler had already bought his way into the original San Fernando land syndicate by delivering into the hands of the San Fernando Mission Land Company an additional 2,300 acres, which made the company's holdings predominant in the upper valley.[21] In September 1909 Chandler moved to extend the syndicate's interest into the southern portion of the valley. With Otis and Sherman, he acquired an option on 47,500 acres held by the Los Angeles Farm and Milling Company at a total purchase price of $2.5 million. For this enterprise the three members of the northern syndicate formed a new company, the Los Angeles Suburban Home Company, in partnership with thirty-seven smaller investors including, most prominently, Sherman's associate in the Hollywood venture, Hobart Whitley, and the vice president and general manager of the Title Insurance and Trust Company, Otto Brant, who had acted as the front man for Otis' secret purchase of the *Los Angeles Herald* in 1904.

The company exercised its option in 1910 and on March 14, 1911, filed a subdivision map for Tract 1000, the largest single land development in Los Angeles history until that time. The Pacific Electric Railway immediately began construction of an extension to this vast new subdivision, while Chandler, Otis, Sherman, and Brant raced still farther afield to form yet another syndicate which acquired 300,000 acres of the Tejon Ranch in Los Angeles and Kern counties.[22] In June 1912, Henry Huntington withdrew from the original syndicate, selling at a profit of

$115,000 the one-tenth interest in the San Fernando Mission Land Company that he had bought for $15,000 in 1905.[23] Thus by the middle of 1912 the syndicate's holdings had come to embrace the greater part of the valley as a whole while the comparatively diversified consortium of interests Henry Huntington had formed in 1905 had been transformed into little more than a creature of Harry Chandler and the *Times*.

With Harriman defeated and land sales in the valley booming, Chandler saw neither a pretext nor a purpose for continuing to deny his family's involvement in the San Fernando Valley. The other members of the syndicate were, in any event, already well embarked upon a grotesque public display of profit-taking. In addition to the general profits of their land companies, individual members of the syndicates north and south drew subsidiary benefits through construction and the provision of support services to the new towns springing up throughout the valley. One of the first official acts of the city of Burbank following its incorporation on July 8, 1911, for example, was to extend a contract for the supply of power for home and street lighting to L. C. Brand, one of the charter members of the northern syndicate.[24] When they were not enjoying the fun of naming streets and townsites after one another, the syndicate members began carving out choice tracts for themselves like feudal princes dividing a conquered territory. Sherman, for example, appropriated 1,000 acres at the site of what is now Sherman Oaks; Otis received 550 acres which he later sold to Edgar Rice Burroughs, who renamed it Tarzana; Brant took 850 acres to form his Brant Rancho; and Chandler and Whitley secured smaller tracts for themselves near Sherman Way and Van Nuys Boulevard.[25]

But by this time the excesses of his father-in-law were beginning to haunt Harry Chandler and his associates. Harrison Gray Otis' uncompromising hostility to municipal reform and social change had eroded the *Times*' influence over public affairs. Politicians in increasing numbers were finding that they could not only attack Otis with impunity but that it was often to their advantage to do so. Hiram Johnson, in his first campaign for the governorship in 1910, marked this change most clearly in a memorable rhetorical attack that he delivered on Otis' home ground. "He sits there in senile dementia with gangrened heart and rotting brain, grimacing at every reform, chattering impotently at all things that are decent, frothing, fuming violently, gibbering, going down to his grave in snarling infamy," Johnson declaimed to a mass meeting in Los Angeles' Simpson Auditorium. "He is the one thing that all California looks at when, in looking at Southern California, they see anything that is disgraceful, depraved, corrupt, crooked, and putrescent."[26] By 1912, even so respected a leader as Theodore Roosevelt was denouncing Otis as

> a consistent enemy of every movement for social and economic betterment, a consistent enemy of men in California who have dared to stand against corruption and in favor of honesty . . . a curious instance of the anarchy of soul which comes to a man who in conscienceless fashion deifies property at the expense of human rights. The *Times* has again and again shown itself to be such an enemy of good citizenship, honest, decent government, and every effective effort to secure fair play for the workingman and woman as any anarchist could show itself.[27]

In these altered circumstances in the city's political life, the appearance of the Quinton, Code, and Hamlin report, with its recommendation to turn over the greater part of the aqueduct's water for the benefit of the San Fernando speculators, spurred the Socialists and labor unions to rally their forces once again in calling for a formal investigation of corruption in the promotion of the aqueduct. The Chamber of Commerce refused at first to take part in such a proceeding, but the city council, acting on a recommendation offered by Mayor George Alexander soon after his reelection, appointed a five-member investigating committee that included two Socialists—a number deemed proportionate to the number of votes cast for the Socialist candidate in the last election. Almost immediately, the council reconsidered this egalitarian gesture, removed the two Socialists, and attempted to force the resignation of a third, left-leaning appointee. The Socialists responded with an initiative ordinance, passed May 29, 1912, which established a new committee funded separately from the council's control. This panel included two Socialists as well as the apostate council appointee, plus two members approved by the council and the Chamber of Commerce.[28]

The investigating committee set up its own office and opened its doors three days a week to receive complaints from anyone who cared to offer them. At the same time, it commissioned a team of special investigators and auditors to prepare reports on specific aspects of the project and announced that it would commence public hearings on July 9. The hearings had scarcely begun, however, when the two original council appointees, Edward S. Cobb and Edward Johnson, resigned, declaring that they "could not retain their self-respect and remain of the body." As for the results of their investigation, Johnson and Cobb told the *Times*: "There is not a single thing the matter with that aqueduct except the knockers who are attempting to bring discredit upon a magnificent undertaking and upon men who wrought even better than they know."[29]

Mulholland had at first welcomed the call for a formal investigation in hopes of clearing the air and, no doubt, in a certain confidence that he would obtain just such an exoneration as Johnson and Cobb at first seemed to offer. On March 22, before the Socialists took over the investigation with their initiative, he had gone so far as to join in the popular denunciations of the syndicate, declaring, "Arable lands which should be selling at about $100 an acre have been seized by a few capitalists who have forced prices to $1000 an acre. Instead of being developed as agricultural lands, the property has been subdivided into town lots and small 'rich men's country estates' at prohibitive values. The capitalists have stolen the unearned increment for the next 20 years."[30] And even with the Socialists in control, he initially attempted to couch his testimony in terms that would be pleasing to their ears. "This is a socialistic problem, this aqueduct," he told them, "the biggest socialistic thing ever done in this town."[31]

But as the scope of the investigation ranged beyond the question of the syndicate's involvement, and the panel members began to probe ever more deeply into the details of his management of the project, Mulholland's patience wore thin. The board pursued at particular length one of the central theses of Spilman's *Conspiracy* that there was ample water available in the groundwater reservoirs of the San Fernando Valley that Mulholland should have developed first before seeking an additional source of supply. Mulholland had encountered this argument before, when Samuel

Clover raised it during the bond election of 1907, and he had dismissed it then with the remark, "That is tantamount to putting a tube in your flour barrel, using the bottom flour first, and thus making it last forever."[32] But when the investigators now presented Mulholland with United States Geological Survey reports, prepared by a hydrographer Mulholland had later hired onto his own staff, that suggested there was more water available in the Los Angeles River watershed than Mulholland had earlier allowed, he rejected the reports as inaccurate.[33] Similarly, when pressed on the question of why he had not increased pumping from the groundwater reservoirs around the Narrows, he snapped, "If anybody can show me that he can go in there and get ten inches more water than we are getting, I will buy him a new hat."[34]

Even more troubling to Mulholland in the long term were the charges raised against some of his technological innovations and the quality of the water the aqueduct would ultimately deliver. His principal nemesis on these questions was not a member of the panel of investigators but a private consulting engineer, F.C. Finkle, who had been working for Edison Electric when it launched its unsuccessful campaign against the aqueduct bonds of 1907 and who had since taken up the denigration of Mulholland's project as a personal cause. Finkle attacked the folly of building the aqueduct without storage or distribution facilities and decried the money Mulholland had wasted bringing caterpillar tractors to the desert. With regard to water quality, his accusations were little more than a reprise of the specious claims Clover had made in 1907. Mulholland by this time could produce authoritative studies by the United States Geological Survey based on three years of scientific sampling that concluded, "The water is well adapted to irrigation and is suitable for a municipal supply . . . [although] not particularly well adapted for the greater number of manufacturing industries."[35] But the charge that the aqueduct water would be fit only for irrigation was a central point in proving the Socialists' theory that the project had been built exclusively for the benefit of San Fernando speculators, so the investigators ultimately paid little attention to Mulholland's protestations on this score.

Finkle's most determined attack in 1912 was directed against the cement the city had fabricated at its Monolith plant. Finkle had secured the backing of the Association of American Portland Cement Manufacturers that year to conduct a study of the inadequacies of the city's product. And although Mulholland refused to provide any samples to Finkle's analysts, the little bit they had been able to cadge on the sly was sufficient for them to conclude that the city's cement was definitely inferior.[36] At this, Mulholland lost his temper. It was true that his work crews were encountering difficulties with the cement. Some of it was already breaking down, although the full extent of the problem would not be revealed until water was actually released into the aqueduct. But Mulholland was loath to admit that any problem existed, and his reaction to the charge was purposefully offensive to the political affinities of the investigators. "I might promise you that the concrete of the aqueduct will last as long as the Pyramids of Egypt or the Parthenon of Athens, but I will not," he exploded. "Rather I will promise you that the aqueduct work will endure until Job Harriman is elected mayor of Los Angeles."[37]

Mulholland was not the only one to suffer embarrassment at the investigators' questions. Fred Eaton's contract for the sale of the Long Valley properties received especially critical scrutiny; and J. B. Lippincott was dismayed to find the whole tawdry history of his entanglements with the city while serving with the Reclamation Service being dredged up again. "It is a pretty severe thing for a man to spend 25 years in building up a reputation and then have it destroyed in an unnecessary and ruthless way," Lippincott protested.[38] But the more widely the investigators ranged in their probing, the further they moved from the central question of syndicate corruption. The bulk of complaints the board received, for example, related to the poor quality of the food and living quarters provided for the workers and the fact that dark blue rather than white enameled tableware was used in the mess halls.[39]

None of the principal members of the syndicate even deigned to appear before the panel. Lacking the power of subpoena, the investigators were stymied. Only E. T. Earl, a member of the original syndicate, offered substantive testimony, and it was immediately clear that he had been only a minor partner in the scheme. Not only had he never been invited to join in any of Otis' or Chandler's subsequent investments, but he also found that his continued publication of the *Los Angeles Express* was by this time facing a united assault by Otis and by Hearst's *Examiner*.[40] Earl's one real contribution to the investigation was to deny that the syndicate could ever have expected to profit from the aqueduct because the original plan for the project, before the panel of consulting engineers changed it, would have brought the water into the San Fernando Valley at the lower rather than the upper end of their property. The members of the investigating board promptly concluded from this peculiar bit of reasoning-by-hindsight that the panel of consulting engineers had been somehow bought off by the syndicate as well.[41]

Neither Mulholland nor his project fared well in the results of this investigation. Johnson and Cobb, the dissident members of the panel, filed a minority report agreeing to the unreliability of the city's cement and the failure of the caterpillar tractors and pointing out a number of deficiencies in the aqueduct's overall design and siphon construction.[42] To these charges, the other three members of the panel added their conclusions that the funding of the project and the arrangements for the bond sales had been irregular, that the water of the aqueduct was unfit for anything but irrigation, and that construction should begin immediately on a storage facility at the upper end of the project. On the question of the overall need for the project, the majority concluded that Los Angeles' indigenous supplies were sufficient to support a city of one million. But when it came to the San Fernando land syndicate, the panel could do no more than affirm that the syndicate existed and that it stood to profit immensely from the project's completion. To forestall this possibility, the members of the majority recommended that no water from the aqueduct should be provided to the San Fernando Valley.[43]

On the all-important question of municipal corruption, however, all five members of the panel were in essential agreement. Johnson and Cobb in their report asserted, "There was not a statement submitted nor any evidence unearthed to indicate that any criticism of the integrity, business ability, or loyalty of effort for the best interests of the City of Los Angeles could be maintained to the slightest degree."[44] And although the members of the majority did call for the immediate indictment of Fred Eaton to punish him for having negotiated so favorable a contract for his properties at Long Valley, they nevertheless concluded "that no direct evidence of graft has been developed." They qualified this exoneration of Mulholland, however, with the protest that if they had only been allowed a little more time to conduct their investigations, "men would have been found who had succumbed to temptation."[45]

Mulholland Rampant

The confusing outcome of the investigation satisfied none of the participants in the controversy. Although Mulholland had been cleared of any wrongdoing, the debate over syndicate corruption continued. The cumulative effect of the majority's conclusions and recommendations was to advise the voters of Los Angeles that they owned a project they had not needed in the first place and which they could not use now, but one which they nonetheless would have to supplement with an additional storage facility. Mayor Alexander dismissed the majority report as "unimportant . . . most of it the veriest rot."[46] And the city council refused even to print it.

But the repercussions from the investigation were felt almost immediately. The public airing of so many charges against the administration of the project and the eventual use of its water disrupted the city's efforts to sell off the outstanding aqueduct bonds. The president of the Investment Bankers Association of America, for example, wrote to Mayor Alexander at the end of September to express the concerns of the investment community on this score. Although Alexander attempted to reassure the bankers, his efforts were not entirely successful—with the result that by the end of the year Mulholland had to go begging to the city council for a loan of $325,000 simply to finish the project.[47]

More important for the long-term prospects of the aqueduct's operation, the investigating panel's recommendation to deny water to the San Fernando Valley encouraged a member of Mayor Alexander's special commission on consolidation and the water surplus to offer an alternative to the policies advocated by Quinton, Code, and Hamlin. Rather than apply the surplus in a way that would directly benefit syndicate speculation in the San Fernando Valley, S. C. Graham proposed that the city simply sell the surplus for the highest rates it could get and turn a profit on the aqueduct as quickly as possible. The proposal offered a number of superficial attractions. It satisfied the Socialists by implementing the principal recommendation of the investigating board and fulfilling a promise Job Harriman had first made in his campaign for the mayoralty in 1911. By requiring anyone outside the city who wanted the water to pay full fare for its benefits, the Graham Plan would stifle the persistent rumors then circulating to the effect that the San Fernando syndicate had arranged to receive the water from the aqueduct at specially reduced prices. And by maximizing the city's profits on the project, the plan appealed to the progressives' affection for good business practice. Within two weeks after it was first proposed, the city council approved the Graham Plan for submission on the ballot as a referendum at the next regular election, on November 5. And, with the support of Mayor Alexander's progressives, the plan was approved by the electorate two to one.

In contrast to the Quinton, Code, and Hamlin proposal, which would have required recipients of the surplus water to build their own distribution systems, implementation of the Graham Plan depended upon the approval of $8.4 million in municipal bonds to build conduits to the outlying regions that could afford the city's rates. Under the proposed construction plan approved by the Public Service Commission, one conduit would extend through the Santa Monica Mountains at Franklin Canyon to service the Providencia, Cahuenga, Inglewood, and Glendale areas. A second major conduit would supply forty thousand acres in the Mission, Fernando, and Chatsworth districts of the San Fernando Valley. On January 8, 1913, the city council approved the submission of the bond issues in a special election called for February 25. On January 25, however, in a letter to the chairman of the Public Service Commission, Mulholland denounced the Graham Plan as "audacious rapacity" and launched his own crusade to defeat the bonds.[48]

Thus Mulholland's extended attempts to remain personally

aloof from the debate over distribution of the aqueduct water came abruptly to an end. His efforts in this respect had never really been more than an illusion. The policies recommended by Quinton, Code, and Hamlin reflected the same principles Mulholland had advocated for years. Quinton, in fact, was an especially close associate of both Mulholland and his chief lieutenant, J. B. Lippincott, and the three of them joined as a consulting panel to assist Lippincott in his continuing professional work for the city of Santa Barbara.[49] But even in his testimony before the Aqueduct Investigation Board, Mulholland sought to maintain his neutrality on the question of distribution. "I hope the people of Los Angeles City will be wise enough and generous enough to sell the water for its cost, just as they do now," he told the investigators. "Let the poor devil who has to make a living off the land, let him have the water at the lower end. That's my idea."[50] When the Graham Plan was first submitted to the voters as a referendum, Mulholland did not oppose it directly, although he did permit Lippincott to speak out vigorously against it.[51] Following the approval of the plan in principle by the electorate, he initially asked simply that the Quinton, Code, and Hamlin proposal be placed on the same ballot with Graham's bond issue as an alternative. It was only after this request had been denied that Mulholland committed himself to campaigning actively against the bonds.

This was a bold move for a public employee, and one that seemed to come too late for any prospect of success. In opposing the bonds, Mulholland was taking a stand against the policies already adopted by the Alexander administration and his employers on the Public Service Commission. He consequently had no doubt of the risk he was taking. Above all else, he had displayed consummate skill as a survivor throughout his career. His talent in this respect had enabled him to retain control of the city's water programs over nearly three decades of political conflict and change. His longevity in office, it is true, was due in large measure to the independence of mind and deed which he had exhibited at all times. But there was little question that, in opposing the Graham Plan, he was now entrusting his career to the public confidence and respect his long years of service had won for him.

Confronted with this unexpected break in the ranks at City Hall, the city council set back the date for the election, first to March 25, then to April 15. Graham himself chose to lead the battle for the bonds in association with the president of the Public Service Commission, F. G. Henderson. Their campaign emphasized the economic benefits the city would be able to reap in short order if the plan were implemented. But Mulholland advocated a broader vision for the municipal enterprise he had begun with construction of the aqueduct. In an article prepared many years later, Lippincott disclosed that there were three "unwritten rules" governing Mulholland's policy on the surplus: "First, when water was once put upon an area there never should be the necessity of its removal; second, that the area of the city should not be expanded beyond that which could be permanently supplied; and third, that surplus water above the requirements for domestic use should be applied to irrigation of such areas at a price farmers could afford to pay."[52] In this way, Mulholland argued, the surplus could be applied to sustain the long-term growth and expansion of the city through annexation of the areas benefited by the delivery of aqueduct water.

Annexation, which would require the granting of long-term rights for the use of the municipal water supply, was antithetical to the Graham Plan. Rather, the genius of the Graham Plan lay in "an automatic process" by which any person who contracted to receive surplus water could be subsequently priced out of the market "whenever the Public Service Commission desired to receive the water." By forcing such "voluntary" withdrawals of service, Graham contended that the city would be able to recover its water at any time "without controversy and without the payment of damages for improvements."[53] Mulholland denounced the cruelties implicit in such a proposal as "one of the most conspicuous acts of insatiable greed that it has ever been my experience to witness." He focused his concern upon the consequences this policy would have for future generations in the communities that initially contracted for water from the city: "In putting water there we would be practicing a base deception on the people who will later come there as innocent purchasers and from whom it is the declared intentions of the [Graham Plan advocates] to take the water away after they have probably made millions of dollars worth of improvements dependent on the water."[54]

Implementation of the Graham Plan would, in the view of Mulholland and his supporters, play havoc with the future development of the region. The delivery systems Graham and the Public Service Commission proposed would service 227,000 acres, an area Mulholland claimed was 70 percent greater than the aqueduct could serve. He predicted, therefore, that development along these delivery lines would necessarily have to follow a checkerboard pattern. And Lippincott forcefully described the consequences of this kind of growth:

> We will have an area surrounding the city with one-half the land irrigated and one-half desert. The city in its rapid growth will extend its boundaries to cover the adjacent regions, semi-irrigated, and the city water supply then will be inadequate to serve the domestic requirements of this newly annexed region . . . It therefore will be necessary to take away the water from the more remote districts in order to obtain an adequate supply for the city. There will inevitably follow bitterness and strife . . . litigation will ensue as a matter of course, and under the letter of the contracts, the city will get judgment . . . but the withdrawal of the water will be difficult, if not impossible.[55]

The debate over distribution of the surplus thus went to the heart of the aqueduct's purpose. For the business interests who had first rallied to promote it, the project was seen as the means of continued economic growth. For Otis and Chandler at the *Times*, as for Huntington, Sherman, and the commercial bankers with their widespread investments, the economic life of the community depended on the stimulation that continued expansion of the population provided to real estate values in general and suburban development in particular. For the Socialists and labor leaders who had gained ascendancy in the political life of the city only after the aqueduct had been begun, however, this kind of unrestrained growth was seen as the means by which the business establishment maintained its power over the working men and women of Los Angeles. Carey McWilliams succinctly stated this proletarian perspective in his history of Southern California in 1946:

> From 1890 to 1910, wages were from 20 to 30, and in some categories, even 40 percent lower than in San Francisco. It was precisely this margin that enabled Los Angeles to grow as an industrial center. Thus the maintenance of a cheap labor pool became an indispensable cog in the curious economics of the region. For the system to work, however, the labor market had to remain unorganized; otherwise, it would become impossible to exploit the homeseeker element. The system required—it absolutely demanded—a non-union, open-shop setup. It was this basic requirement, rather than the ferocity of General Otis, that really created the open-shop movement in Los Angeles. Once lured to the region and saddled with equity in a cheap home, most of the homeseekers had no means of escape. Just as the open-shop principle was essential to the functioning of the cheap labor market, so the continued influx of homeseekers made possible the retention of the open shop. If the influx had ever stopped, the workers stranded in the region might have organized, but they could never organize so long as the surplus existed. In effect, the system was self-generating and self-perpetuating; once started, it could not be abandoned.[56]

Mulholland certainly did not see himself as an oppressor of the working class. But the unfortunate consequence of his stand against the Graham Plan was that it placed him firmly on the side of the San Fernando land syndicate. Graham, Alexander, and the progressives had designed their proposal specifically to deny the syndicate the fruits of their enterprise. In the political climate of widespread hostility to the syndicate and its leaders that had developed since 1910, not even the *Times* had been willing to take a strong position against the Graham Plan when it had first appeared on the ballot as a referendum at the end of 1912. It had opposed the proposition, of course, but only in a few very brief and uncharacteristically muted editorials just before the election.[57] With so popular and respected a leader as Mulholland acting as the champion of the cause, however, the *Times'* editorial writers cranked up into high gear and began denouncing the Graham Plan with all their former vigor as "near-socialism, graft and corruption."[58] Editorial cartoons showing Mulholland cutting a tightrope out from under the hated reformers in Mayor Alexander's administration blossomed on the front page. And the campaign rapidly began to take on the aspect of yet another test of strength between the *Times* and the goo-goos of municipal reform.

One of the great ironies of the campaign was the use Mulholland made of the amendment President Roosevelt had inserted into the federal legislation granting the city's right-of-way for the aqueduct in 1906, prohibiting any sale by the city of the aqueduct water to any private interest for subsequent resale. In his letter denouncing the Graham Plan on January 25, 1913, Mulholland was careful not to say that the proposal to sell the water to public agencies outside the city limits violated this legal restriction, but he did contend that such a policy would be against the spirit of the promises he had given the federal authorities in 1906.[59] Even this was an overstatement of the case. And, as the election campaign heated up, the Roosevelt amendment began to be cited as an affirmative requirement for annexation to the city as a condition for receipt of water from the aqueduct.[60] Thus the restriction Roosevelt intended to prevent the syndicate from profiting from the project was twisted into something that gave the appearance of compelling delivery of the surplus to their lands.

Mulholland's great gamble ultimately paid off. When the votes were counted on April 15, the bonds on which the Graham Plan depended went down to defeat. "We wonder now," the *Times* crowed jubilantly the following day, "if the grafters, booze-absorbers, and satyr-politicians will keep hands off this great, this devoted, this pursued and pestered but patient city-builder, William Mulholland, and let him complete his great work."

Any joy Mulholland found in his victory was short-lived. The aqueduct by this time was complete. The small reservoir at Haiwee Point in the Owens Valley, where the water would be temporarily stored long enough to allow suspended solids to settle out before it was moved south, had been filling since the middle of

February. The official ceremonies marking the arrival of the water in Los Angeles were scheduled for July. At last the time had come to turn the water into the aqueduct. This was the first real opportunity Mulholland would have to test the quality of his construction. The result was a spectacular disaster. When the water was released into the Sand Canyon siphon on May 16, great slabs of concrete sheared off, the entire mountainside began to slide, and the roof of the tunnel was blown skyward, releasing a great shower of water and debris. Repairs were hastily begun and the welcoming ceremonies put off until November.

The delay afforded Mulholland time to complete the resolution of the problem of distribution before the water actually arrived. In the mayoralty election in June, Henry Rose emerged victorious after campaigning on a pledge to restore the Graham Plan and oppose widespread annexation.[61] Within a month of taking office, however, Rose reversed his position, declaring all criticism of the aqueduct to be "captious," and promptly formed his own annexation commission.[62] On August 29, the Public Service Commission formally adopted the Quinton, Code, and Hamlin report as city policy, thereby opening the way to a decade of massive annexations to the city of Los Angeles.

The water finally arrived on November 5 at a celebration held at the city's Exposition Park. "Not since the days of Caesar and his Roman Aqueduct has the world recorded an engineering accomplishment aqueductorial equal to this gathering of waters . . . [for] the salvation of the half million souls which now are and the added half million soon to be in that incomparable City of the Golden West," trumpeted the official invitations. The *Times* too had its eye firmly fixed on future growth when it hailed the event: "And a great river has been turned from its course—a course that it followed since the hand of God raised the mountains and laid the oceans in their place on the morn of creation—and brought down to serve the people of Los Angeles who are here today, and the millions more who are to come tomorrow, and tomorrow, and tomorrow."[63] Secretary of the Interior Franklin K. Lane urged President Woodrow Wilson to make an official statement on the aqueduct's completion on the grounds that this event was "encouraging to all students of civic enterprises and to citizens

who are especially concerned in the upbuilding of civic conscious-
ness."[64] Mulholland, however, was less florid in marking his
achievement aqueductorial: as the water thundered down the
spillway for the first time, he shouted, "There it is! Take it!"

The mighty work force Mulholland had assembled in the
desert now began to disperse. Many of the laborers with Eastern
European backgrounds returned to their countries of origin to
fight in World War I.[65] Some of their supervisors found new
employment immediately on the Hilo Railroad in Hawaii.[66] And
J. B. Lippincott resigned to devote himself to the private consulting practice he had never discontinued during all his years in
public service.[67]

The arrival of the water did not, however, bring an end to
Mulholland's problems. Within three months of the project's
completion it had broken down again. Three days of torrential
rains in the Mojave Desert in February 1914 pressed so heavily
on the siphon at Antelope Valley that two miles of ten-foot pipe
were squashed flat. It would cost an estimated $250,000 to dis-
mantle the pipe and rebuild the siphon. But Mulholland had
neither the time nor the money for such an undertaking. Instead,
he welded the pipe where it had broken and then began pumping
water under gradually increasing pressure back into the collapsed
pipe. Within a month the pipe had been pressed back into its
original shape, and Mulholland was so taken with this unheard-
of solution that he devoted an entire page of his final report on
the aqueduct's construction to pictures of the pipe progressively
repairing itself.[68]

Mulholland's critics were undaunted. F. C. Finkle continued
to spew out articles and pamphlets attacking the aqueduct as "a
practical illustration of the working of municipal ownership carried to unreasonable extremes," which he illustrated with abundant photographs of concrete crumbling along the aqueduct's
walls.[69] More troubling was the persistent opposition of the Socialists, lead by Henry A. Hart, a former member of the Aqueduct Investigation Board. Hart brought suit on August 15, 1914,
to enjoin the city from making any use of the aqueduct water on
the grounds that it was unfit for human consumption. He buttressed his case with a chemical survey of the Owens Valley and

aqueduct waters by Dr. Ethel Leonard. In her report, Dr. Leonard listed outbreaks of anthrax and typhoid in the Owens Valley and described barnyards, pigpens, and slaughterhouses draining into the Owens River. At the city's Haiwee Reservoir, she found the shoreline piled deep with the carcasses of dead wild animals, which she reported had to be hauled away each morning. And on the basis of her findings she concluded, "Any use of Owens River water is absolutely impossible."[70]

Leonard began her report by quoting from Dr. Stockmann's famous speech in Henrick Ibsen's *Enemy of the People*: "What I want to speak about is the great discovery ... that all the sources of our Moral Life are poisoned and that the whole fabric of our civic community is founded on the pestiferous soil of falsehood." To this, Peter Stockmann in the play responds, "The man who can throw out such offensive insinuations about his native town must be an enemy to our community."[71] Mulholland replied in kind, declaring that "The filing of this petition ... is the most astonishing example of unpatriotic action that I know of in the history of Los Angeles."[72] Mulholland in fact devoted a great deal of space in his final report on the aqueduct to denunciations of Hart as the "leader of the malodorous majority of the People's Aqueduct Investigation Board" who, as the secret ally of "selfish interests" and "malefactors of great wealth," had "waged a battle from ambush" and "used the knife in the dark."[73] The trial itself consumed forty working days and covered 6,312 pages of testimony—one of the longest trials on a water quality issue ever held in the United States until that time. When it was over, however, the judge rendered his decision almost immediately, rejecting Hart's claims and concluding that the Owens River was not polluted in any way that would not be characteristic of any other rural area.[74]

The Enemies of Conservation

As the months passed and the aqueduct continued in successful operation and the people of Los Angeles drank from it and did not die, these disputes eventually withered away and were forgotten. Not so easily dismissed were the complaints of the Owens Valley. All the years the aqueduct was a-building, the residents of the valley continued to rail against the project. But their anger was directed more against the federal Reclamation Service than against Los Angeles. It was in Washington that they felt they had been betrayed, and it was from Washington that they sought succor for their wounds.

At first these efforts focused on an attempt to persuade the Reclamation Service to develop a small irrigation project at Fish Slough in the Owens Valley as an alternative to the much larger reclamation plan rendered infeasible by Los Angeles' purchases at the Long Valley reservoir site. At the beginning of 1906, while the city's right-of-way bill for the aqueduct was still pending in Congress, the Owens Valley Water Protective Association, composed of the principal officers of the valley's major private irrigation ditches, retained a San Francisco engineer, J. D. Galloway, to develop a plan for the Fish Slough project.

Galloway's plans for the comprehensive development of the Sierra streams that drained into the Central Valley had already established his place among the company of forward-thinking engineers who saw California's future writ in water. Crossing the Sierra Nevada now at the behest of the Owens Valley ranchers, he was able after only a month's study to offer a report calling for the construction of a 45,000-acre-foot capacity reservoir behind a 55-foot dam which would, in his estimation, be capable of servicing upward of 100,000 acres of Owens Valley land through a five-and-a-half-mile-long canal. All of this, Galloway promised, could be accomplished without interfering with either power development upstream or the aqueduct's intake downstream. Best of all, because the proposed reservoir would benefit lands already served by existing irrigation ditches, Galloway estimated the Fish Slough project could be built for only a tenth of the cost of the Reclamation Service's original plan. "This would be a cheap proposition for the Government and a safe one, but beyond our means to undertake as a private enterprise," the association president, Willie Arthur Chalfant, told Secretary of the Interior Ethan Allen Hitchcock, as he submitted Galloway's report. After reciting once again all the injustices the valley residents felt they had suffered at the hands of the service through its agent, J. B. Lippincott, Chalfant concluded, "There is but one hope for the future of Owens Valley, and that is in Government protection by the control of the water . . . Under the circumstances, we feel that it would be but simple justice for the Government to specially interest itself in our behalf."[75]

The association was careful to make its appeal directly to the Secretary of the Interior, bypassing the uncertain ground of the Reclamation Service. And because J. C. Clausen had first urged the valley ranchers to organize themselves into such an association in his initial report for the service on the Long Valley project, the association soon followed up its submission of the Galloway plan with a request that Clausen be called to Washington immediately in order to present the valley's case in detail.[76] Hitchcock ignored this request and instead turned the Galloway report over to the head of the service, F. H. Newell, who in turn promptly sent it along to J. B. Lippincott.

Lippincott at this time was still on the federal payroll, although he was devoting most of his efforts in these last few months of federal service to behind-the-scenes lobbying for Los Angeles' right-of-way bill. His reaction was immediate and ominously revealing of what he believed were the city's real but as yet unspoken intentions with regard to the Owens Valley. "The use of this reservoir [at Fish Slough] to *extend* the use of irrigation water in the valley would probably lead to a suit with the city," he warned Newell. "If the city builds a conduit to Los Angeles . . . and the conduit has the capacity to carry all the water, I do not believe the water will be long used in Owens Valley."[77] Lippincott's conviction that any agricultural development in the Owens Valley should be stopped as anathematic to the city's interest certainly went much further than any policies contemplated in the spring of 1906 by government officials in either Washington or Los Angeles. But it was a view that would soon insinuate its way into the thinking of the city's water planners.

When Lippincott first wrote to Newell in opposition to the Galloway report on February 15, 1906, he included a cautionary but altogether unnecessary observation: "I may be biased in this matter."[78] Five days later he offered further corroboration of this suspicion in a letter to Newell in which he reported variously that any bitterness in the Owens Valley toward the Los Angeles project had subsided, that the Fish Slough proposal had been concocted purely as a speculative venture, and that the Owens Valley ranchers supporting the proposal had already offered to sell out their rights in the Fish Slough site to Los Angeles for $20,000.[79] Arthur Powell Davis, Newell's assistant, reviewed these claims, which were artfully designed to undercut any sense of need for serious consideration of the Fish Slough proposal, and then wisely assigned Leon H. Taylor to the task of preparing a detailed study of the Galloway proposal.[80]

As a member of the panel of engineers that reviewed the Reclamation Service's Owens Valley project in 1905, Taylor had been one of Lippincott's most vocal critics; and by the spring of 1906, he had been appointed the service's Supervising Engineer for Nevada. In his report on the Galloway proposal, Taylor took pains to point out that all of Lippincott's claims were utterly false. Instead, Taylor found the Fish Slough plan "an attractive and inexpensive enterprise." He quibbled with some of Galloway's calculations, estimating that the cost would be closer to $300,000 than the $255,597 Galloway had projected and that the service area of the reservoir would probably be no more than 75,000 rather than 100,000 acres. But even so, Taylor pointed out that the project offered the prospect of "fully doubling the present cultivated area and still leaving an abundance of water—from 75 million to 100 million gallons per day—for diversion to Los Angeles," an amount which, Taylor argued, would be "ample" for all the city's future needs.[81]

Despite Taylor's glowing report, the Reclamation Service recommended rejection of the Galloway Plan.[82] By the time Taylor had submitted his report the city's right-of-way bill had passed into law, and caution with respect to the Owens Valley seemed the best course for the service until Los Angeles more clearly defined its plans for the aqueduct. Taylor, in submitting his report, had urged that whatever action was taken on the Fish Slough proposal, the Owens Valley residents should be promptly advised of the Reclamation Service's intentions. Newell and Davis vigorously seconded this aspect of Taylor's report and called on Hitchcock to inform the Owens Valley Water Protective Association that the project would not be undertaken. Hitchcock, however, by the latter part of 1906, was in the process of being shuffled out of his position at the Department of the Interior. Thus preoccupied, he took no action of any kind on the Fish Slough proposal.

The result was complete confusion. Neither the Owens Valley representative, Sylvester C. Smith, nor the ranchers' other friend in Congress, Francis G. Newlands of Nevada, could extract from the Department of the Interior any statement of the government's intentions at Fish Slough.[83] Los Angeles' water officials, having been informed of the Galloway plan by Lippincott, were meanwhile in a panic about the potential threat Lippincott warned the Fish Slough project would pose for the aqueduct.[84] When they ran up against the same wall of silence as Smith and Newlands had, they turned for assistance to their United States senator, Frank P. Flint, who wrote directly to Charles D. Walcott, Newell's nominal supervisor as head of the United States Geological Survey. Despite Flint's forceful reminder to Walcott that, as a member of the Senate Committee on the Geological Survey, he certainly should be privy to any projects that might be under consideration, Walcott stonily replied that Taylor's report was a private matter still pending with the Secretary of the Interior.[85] Not even Taylor knew what the Reclamation Service had recommended with respect to his report, although Newell did advise him in December not to "push this matter."[86] After waiting in the dark for nearly a year, he wrote angrily to Newell, "I am not advised of the real attitude either of your office or the Interior Department toward the Owens Valley or Fish Slough projects ... However, I assume ... that it has been decided to withdraw entirely from that territory. In view of the foregoing, I respectfully ask that I be relieved from any further connection of any nature with the projects."[87]

Taylor's desire to remove himself from the Owens Valley controversy expressed an attitude that was becoming increasingly prevalent among Reclamation Service officials. The valley's economic development had been effectively placed in a state of suspension ever since the service had withdrawn large portions of its most irrigable lands from settlement pending the study of its own project. So long as the service failed to announce that it was formally abandoning the project, all applications for the use of these public lands were automatically set aside. Thus, the special authority to make withdrawals which had been accorded to the service as a means of protecting its projects from interference by potential competitors was being applied in the peculiar circumstances of the Owens Valley to protect the interests of one such competitor, the city of Los Angeles. And in this way, continued inaction by the Department of the Interior worked to keep the service at the center of the controversy. As the agency responsible for creating this situation, the service by mid-1906 was clearly uncomfortable with further perpetuating it.

Outside pressures for restoration of the withdrawn lands came not only from the Owens Valley ranchers but also from the various private power companies whose lawyers kept up a steady drumfire of demands for permission to proceed with their plans for hydroelectric power development in the valley. As soon as Los Angeles' right-of-way bill became law, Newell pressed for an immediate reopening of the power development applications filed by the Owens River Water and Power Company, which had been held up pending a decision on the Reclamation Service's Owens Valley project.[88] Both Newell and Davis, when they forwarded Taylor's report on the Galloway proposal, urged Hitchcock to restore all the withdrawn lands. And by the end of 1906, Walcott, in his increasingly urgent efforts to persuade Hitchcock to take action, even proposed a rationale for abandonment of the Owens Valley, pointing out that since the Reclamation Service was by this time committed to the development of the Orland and Truckee-Carson projects, Hitchcock could explain rejection of the Owens Valley proposals on the grounds that there were no more funds available for new works in California.[89]

Los Angeles' officials understandably had no desire to see the protection of the Reclamation Service removed and the Owens Valley lands reopened to the development of agricultural and hydroelectric projects that might ultimately interfere with the operation of the aqueduct. When the service, for example, sought to press the issue by urging the immediate approval of certain hydroelectric power development applications filed by the Mono

Power Company, Los Angeles begged for a delay in order to allow time to negotiate a settlement with the power company which would assure that the power project would not interfere with the use of Long Valley if the city ever chose to build a reservoir there. But the city refused to initiate the promised negotiations. When the service threatened to go ahead with the applications in March 1907, Lippincott responded on the city's behalf with a counter-threat "to begin construction on Long Valley dam this year if necessary to preserve our rights."[90] Newell, of course, knew that Los Angeles could barely afford to build the aqueduct even without the Long Valley reservoir, and this empty gesture of belligerence by Lippincott infuriated him. But despite his repeated complaints against the "efforts of the city to place upon the Reclamation Service the burden of assisting in adjusting various questions relating to its conflicts with other parties," Newell's superiors in the Department of the Interior continued to delay taking any action.[91]

Apart from bluster, Los Angeles had only one significant means of assuring delay, and that was by withholding the money it had promised to pay the service in compensation for the surveys the federal engineers had conducted on its behalf in the Owens Valley. Newell had insisted on this payment as a face-saving device when he acquiesced in the secret agreement of 1904 to allow the city's project to take precedence over the federal government's plans. Now he found the device being used against him. The requirement for repayment had been included in the city's right-of-way bill, albeit at a figure which the Reclamation Service estimated was far below its actual cost. Until Los Angeles met the requirement for repayment, the service could not formally abandon its Owens Valley project. "The City has on several occasions undertaken to have the Government protect its interests through the Reclamation Service," Newell grumbled to Walcott when Los Angeles asked for delay on the Mono Power applications, "but there have been no overtures from the City toward the payment of the sum stipulated in the Act."[92]

At the end of April, Newell once again appealed, this time to the new Secretary of the Interior, James R. Garfield, to restore the withdrawn lands and allow the service to withdraw from the

Owens Valley.[93] Although Garfield readily agreed, Los Angeles was able to prolong Newell's agony for another two months. Finally, with the passage of the bonds for the aqueduct's construction and the beginning of the city's new fiscal year on July 1, 1907, Los Angeles officials could find no additional excuses for delay, and a check was dispatched. On July 12, 1907, the Department of the Interior announced the abandonment of the Owens Valley reclamation project.[94]

This announcement did not immediately restore any of the lands withdrawn from settlement by the service. Under the terms of its right-of-way bill, the city had been given three years—until July 1, 1909—to determine which of the withdrawn lands it would actually need for the aqueduct. At first, Los Angeles' attorneys argued that this provision required that all the lands withdrawn by the Reclamation Service and all the applications for private projects on those lands should remain in suspension for the entire three-year period unless the city agreed that a specific project would not interfere with the aqueduct. Newell and Walcott vigorously disagreed with this interpretation of the act. After Mulholland, accompanied by the mayor and the president of the Board of Public Works, had come to Washington to press the city's claim, Garfield determined to strike a compromise. Los Angeles under its right-of-way bill had first claim to the withdrawn lands, and none that might be needed for the aqueduct would be restored to entry without the city's consent. But the processing of applications for use of public lands in the Owens River drainage basin would go forward. Any proposed projects that did not appear to conflict with the aqueduct would be permitted, although Los Angeles would be given the opportunity to protest.[95]

Chalfant, speaking on behalf of the valley ranchers, later charged that "the government held Owens Valley while Los Angeles skinned it."[96] But it is not true that Garfield and his successors at the Department of the Interior simply acceded to every one of Los Angeles' demands. Garfield's policy with respect to the withdrawn lands required the city to argue against each application on its merits, and a departmental investigation in 1909 failed to uncover a single instance in which an application for use of the withdrawn lands had been improperly denied.[97] Faced with Garfield's refusal to suspend these applications, the city's second line of defense lay in the assertion that it was the intent of Congress in enacting the right-of-way bill to give Los Angeles sole authority to determine which lands were actually needed for the aqueduct, and that the Department of the Interior's only responsibility in this connection was to check over the city's maps to assure that they were correctly drawn.[98] Such a policy would, of course, have granted Los Angeles an outright and unquestionable veto authority over every application, and Garfield rejected out of hand the city's claims on this score. When the city, for example, attempted in 1908 to prevent the granting of a permit for the opening of a saloon to serve the aqueduct workers, the commissioner of the General Land Office ruled that this application did not conflict with the operation of the aqueduct in any way that Congress could ever have intended to prevent.[99] In later years, the General Land Office similarly rejected the city's claims to thousands of acres of land in the Owens Valley which it determined were not directly needed for the aqueduct.[100]

But if the Department of the Interior was determined to pursue a more even-handed policy toward the Owens Valley after 1907, Los Angeles could always count on a more cordial reception from Gifford Pinchot and his friends in the Department of Agriculture. As soon as it became clear at the beginning of May 1907 that the Department of the Interior intended to proceed with abandonment and the reopening of the applications for use of the withdrawn lands, a recommendation surfaced in the Department of Agriculture calling for withdrawal of an additional 211,840 acres of the Owens Valley as federal forest preserves.[101] On July 2, 1908, President Roosevelt acted on the recommendation by executive order. Although many of the lands affected by this action had already been withdrawn for forestry purposes under earlier orders dating back to the creation of the Inyo National Forest in 1893, a series of subsequent executive orders brought the area under the department's protection to a total of more than 298,000 acres of the Owens Valley.[102]

The extension of the national forest to embrace large parts of the treeless Owens Valley was especially galling to the valley ranchers. Chalfant later claimed that Pinchot had to send three foresters to the area before he could find one who would sign a report recommending withdrawal.[103] Not only had none of the lands withdrawn by the Reclamation Service been restored, but now a whole new area had also been closed to settlement. Although limited uses of the forestry lands were permitted under law, Pinchot insisted that all applications for the use of the Owens Valley lands had to be submitted to his office in Washington rather than being handled by the local federal land office. This assured that applicants had to wait three to six months for any action on their requests. And, because there were no records available in Bishop or Independence, a local applicant had no way of knowing whether others had already filed applications on the same tract.[104] "This is not a government by legislation," fumed Sylvester Smith on the floor of Congress. "It is a government by strangulation."[105]

If abandonment had proved ineffectual in freeing the lands of the Owens Valley, it was no more successful in relieving the Reclamation Service of criticism for its role in the affair. Western opponents of federal land use policies found in the plight of the Owens Valley a supreme example of "how the Reclamation Service is robbing the settler" through arrogant attempts to "satisfy the inordinate ambitions of the officials to create something great, even though the country be strewn with the wrecks of the pauperized families and bankrupted irrigation companies that have a right to the protection of the Government they are taxed to support."[106] In September 1907, a delegation of valley ranchers carried their appeal for relief from what they described as an "utter perversion of the purposes of the Reclamation Act" to the fifteenth convention of the National Irrigation Congress in Sacramento. "Our only hope now," they told the delegates, "is that Congress will take cognizance of the matter, will perceive that maladministration of the reclamation laws is not merely a false step of the moment but a defect in the very foundations upon which the future of the whole system is builded [sic]."[107]

They could scarcely have chosen a worse forum for the presentation of their case. An organization formed to promote comprehensive reclamation programs under the slogan "Save the Forests, Store the Floods, Reclaim the Deserts, Make Homes on the Land" that was meeting that year in the capital city of one of the Reclamation Service's most stalwart champions, Governor George C. Pardee, had little time to hear complaints. The ranchers were derided at the meeting and in the press as "kickers" of a worthy principle, and, as the *San Francisco Call* observed of the debates, "Anybody here who plays tennis at the White House can have anything he wants from these people and the kickers had no more chance than a snowball."[108]

The intervention of the Forest Service in 1908, however, elevated the Owens Valley to the status of a cause célèbre among the broad party of interests who saw in Gifford Pinchot the evil genius behind the most hated aspects of President Roosevelt's conservation policies. The creation of federal forestry reserves had been a sore point with private development interests in the western states ever since President Grover Cleveland had withdrawn the first twenty million acres of forest lands in the closing weeks of his second administration. Opposition was, of course, never uniform within the West. Western irrigators had been among the first to recognize that proper forestry management, by slowing runoff, shepherding groundwater reserves, and retarding erosion, could have a direct effect on the protection of indigenous watersheds. In California, where steep slopes and torrential rainstorms made floods and erosion control a perennial problem, the enthusiasm for Pinchot's new theories of scientific resource management was particularly high; and Californians organized under the aegis of Adolph Wood's Water and Forest Association had successfully petitioned the Cleveland, McKinley, and Roosevelt administrations for vast extensions of the state's forest reserves.[109]

But Pinchot's brand of conservationism was fundamentally a scientific movement; its gospel was efficiency and rational planning; its apostles were scientists and technicians who had little patience with the need to curry popular support and attend to legal niceties. Their purely technical enthusiasms did not countenance aesthetics, recreational development, or the needs of local economies. As a result, the cry of one Washington state legislator came gradually to be raised across the land: "Why should we be everlastingly and eternally harassed and annoyed and bedeviled by those scientific gentlemen?" Popular hostility to Pinchot's policies reached a high point in 1907, when Congress enacted an outright prohibition on the creation of new forestry reserves without congressional approval in all the western states except California, Nevada, and Utah.[110]

The extension of a federal forestry preserve into the treeless Owens Valley was therefore not a unique or especially egregious example of federal arrogance but one that was altogether in keeping with the zealousness Pinchot had elsewhere demonstrated in the pursuit of his objectives. It was one that was recommended, moreover, by the fact that Los Angeles was engaged in a practical demonstration of the benefits of scientific water development on a scale far greater than anything the Reclamation Service was at that time equipped to undertake. And if the law did not provide specific authority for federal intervention in such a case, Pinchot was never a man to be hung up by such trifling technicalities. But the fact that these questionable actions had been taken in California, which had heretofore provided Pinchot with a solid front of official support, made the example of the Owens Valley's plight all the more attractive to the private power companies and local land speculators whose schemes had been upset by Pinchot's policies.

The Owens Valley ranchers consequently found themselves swept up in a movement which was pursuing objectives that were not only far grander but also in large part irrelevant to their own limited interest in relief. *The Irrigation Age*, principal organ of the opposition to federal conservation programs, began a series of spectacularly inaccurate reports on the Owens Valley's plight in which the editors sought to prove collusion between city and federal authorities in a program of systematic law-breaking.[111] Similarly, the ranchers' simple appeal for restoration of their lands to settlement became transformed into a demand that the entire federal reclamation program should be turned over to the War Department, whose Army Corps of Engineers represented the one contingent of hydrologic engineers within the Roosevelt administration that steadfastly refused to admit any connection between forestry management and watershed protection.[112] And Willie Arthur Chalfant eventually took to presenting his own efforts on behalf of the Owens Valley Water Protective Association in the terms of a crusade against "hysterical conservatism." Years later he wrote of Roosevelt's resource policies,

> In the stages of novelty, it ran so far toward hysteria that there was danger of all being conserved for the future with little regard for the necessities of the present . . . Pinchot, who has stated that he did what he could to help Los Angeles, was able to read into his authority the power to assist the city by preventing settlement. He has since asserted that "the end justifies the means." So might the highwayman say as he blackjacks his victim into helplessness; the end itself is not justifiable.[113]

If the Owens Valley ranchers hoped to persuade the Forest Service to restore some of its lands to settlement, these were certainly not the sentiments or the alliances best suited to accomplishing that purpose. Pinchot remained in office after Roosevelt's departure in 1909, and even if the protection of Los Angeles' interests did not command his constant vigilance, Senator Flint was always at hand, ready to meet any suggestion for restoration of the Owens Valley lands with angry protestations that every square inch of the withdrawn property was "absolutely necessary" to the success of the aqueduct.[114] In fact, the outgoing Roosevelt administration in its closing hours withdrew an additional 496 tracts totaling forty thousand acres for the Inyo National Forest.[115]

Ironically, in light of the scandals that later swept the Department of the Interior during his administration, President William Howard Taft entered office determined to redress the excesses of Roosevelt's conservationist policies and restore the operation of the federal lands programs to a strict basis of legality. His Secretary of the Interior, Richard Ballinger, an opponent of Pinchot's attempts to achieve federal coordination of western resource development at the expense of private enterprise and the rights of the western states, went even further in urging restoration of all the withdrawn lands to state control and the outright repeal of the federal Right of Way Act of 1901. Although Ballinger did cut back those programs of the Reclamation Service which did not have a clear authority in law, he was unsuccessful in his attempts to remove Newell, and his efforts to reopen the western lands to private development ended in stalemate.[116]

With Pinchot and Ballinger locked in combat over the future of federal resource policies, the renewed petitions from the Owens Valley ranchers for a substantial restoration of their lands continued to go unanswered for nearly another two years.[117] By the beginning of 1910, however, the ongoing conflict in Washington removed the principal obstacle to a resolution of the valley's appeal: "Pinchot has fallen," the *Owens Valley Herald* proclaimed on January 14, 1910. "A false prophet and wooden idol could no longer endure."[118] Finally, on February 23, 1911, President Taft issued his Executive Proclamation 1117, eliminating 270,000 acres from the Inyo National Forest and reopening these lands to settlement. And by the end of the decade, the need to increase domestic food production during World War I had persuaded the succeeding administration of Woodrow Wilson to open another 105,293 acres of desert lands in the eastern Sierra for irrigation development.[119]

Closing Sesame

The reopening of the Inyo County lands to settlement produced a flood of promotional brochures touting the prospects for economic development in the Owens Valley. That vague expectation of impending prosperity which Mary Austin had seen activating the ranchers and businessmen of the valley ten years before seemed now at last to be on the verge of fulfillment. "Inyo is a land of superlatives. All of its attributes, physical and industrial, exist in the greatest degree," trumpeted *Sunset Magazine*'s Homeseekers Bureau in a pamphlet describing the valley as "one vast sweep of tillable land, only one-fourth of it as yet under cultivation, the remainder holding forth immense opportunities to homeseeker and farmer great and small."[120] The *Inyo Register* in a promotional broadside sang the praises of the valley's "unequaled hay" and "fruits of perfection" and pictured the area around Bishop as a sonic paradise where "the music of a hundred streams is ever upon the air; the harmony of swaying trees and brimming life is an endless accompaniment to the song of rivers and brooks, all telling of the life to be lived, of happiness to be gained, in the bosom of nature."[121]

Although the valley in 1911 might have appeared to the un-schooled visitor to be largely an arid expanse of sagebrush, the promoters were quick to point out that "it has always been an acknowledged fact among farmers that where sagebrush grows the richest, there is the most fruitful soil, if water can be put upon it." And on the all-important question of water availability, these brochures were brimful of confidence for a certain and bountiful future. "As there is plenty of water," *Sunset* assured its readers, "Owens Valley is an open sesame for all that can delight the heart and fill the pocketbook of a homeseeker."[122]

The aqueduct appeared to pose no threat to these roseate prospects. The water resources of the valley seemed ample for all, and the aqueduct's point of intake lay far downstream of the principal areas of agricultural and urban development at a place called Charley's Butte, so named for a Negro, Charley Tyler, who died there in 1863 when an Indian attack persuaded the white family with whom he was traveling to escape on their wagon horses, leaving Charley behind.[123] Even as late as 1928 the city maintained in its official publications that, in building the aque-duct, Los Angeles "sought only to use the surplus waters of Owens River after the needs of the ranchers had been fulfilled."[124] When asked by the Aqueduct Investigation Board in 1912 whether there was any basis for dissatisfaction among the Owens Valley ranch-ers, Mulholland declared that there was "absolutely none."[125] And when he came to prepare his final report on the building of the aqueduct in 1916, he assured his readers that the ranchers' "fears of prospective injury due to the action of the City of Los Angeles in their valley [are] groundless." As for the agricultural activities in the northern part of the valley, Mulholland com-mented, "It is not expected that it will be necessary or desirable to interfere with them."[126]

Even so, the arrival of the aqueduct was scarcely welcomed with open arms in the Owens Valley. When Dr. Ethel Leonard made her investigation of water quality conditions in connection

with the Socialists' suit against the project in 1914, Willie Arthur
Chalfant and his friends were happy to regale her with tales of
outbreaks of typhoid among those who had been so foolhardy as
to drink from the river, which they called "the sewer of Owens
River Valley."[127] And when the aqueduct opened, Chalfant as
editor of the *Inyo Register* printed no notice of the event beyond
a passing sneer to the effect that the project was leaking so badly
that the ten thousand bottles of water the city gave away as
souvenirs had had to be filled from other sources.[128] But throughout their prolonged battle to obtain restoration of their lands, the
valley's spokesmen were careful, as they had been from the outset, to make it clear that they did not begrudge the city water for
its true domestic needs. Their fight, as they saw it, was with
Pinchot and the Reclamation Service, not with Los Angeles.

As a result, outright conflict with Los Angeles in the years
immediately following approval of the right-of-way bill cropped
up only when the city sought to use its influence in Washington
to extend its hold over the valley's lands. In 1909, for example,
the city sought to acquire several thousand additional acres of
federally protected land in the valley which it hoped might eventually be used for groundwater storage. At the public hearing on
this application in Independence, the presiding local lands register, Galen Dixon, who had been appointed to replace the unfortunate Stafford W. Austin, became so abusive toward the city's
representatives that the entire matter had to be remanded to
Washington for a decision. Although Dixon was fired as a result
of this display and John Gorman, the local farmer whose careful
water management had so impressed Means and Clausen on
their earlier visits to the valley, was appointed in his stead, the
greater part of Los Angeles' request was ultimately denied upon a
finding by the federal government's hydrologists that the city
already owned more than enough water-bearing land to satisfy
its needs under all but the most adverse drought conditions.[129]
Similarly, attempts by the city in 1911 and 1912 to obtain an
extension until 1916 of its right to select additional lands for use
in conjunction with the aqueduct were successfully opposed by
the valley's representative in Congress.[130]

In only one instance in the years before 1920 did the city take
action in accordance with the extreme view voiced by J. B. Lip-

pincott that any agricultural or economic development in the Owens Valley should be opposed as a threat to Los Angeles' eventual need for all the valley's water. This effort, initiated by Lippincott, was directed against George Chaffey's attempt to establish an irrigation colony at Manzanar. Chaffey was one of the foremost water developers of his generation and a prime example of the successful engineer as private entrepreneur. In his early years, he had supervised the construction of the first hydroelectric power plant in California and the first electrically lighted house west of the Rocky Mountains. His greatest contribution to the course of water development in the West came with his founding of the water colonies at Etiwanda and Ontario, where he introduced a system for the mutual ownership of water resources which was later widely adopted to open large sections of Southern California for settlement. His subsequent efforts to repeat these successes in Australia and the desert wastes of the Imperial Valley had all come a cropper. He therefore came to the Owens Valley in 1905 in the hope of fulfilling the wish he described to his son "to do one more big thing before I die."[131]

Here was a worthy contender for the water resources of the valley that Lippincott regarded as all too limited, and Lippincott's fear and hatred of Chaffey's prowess are evident in the viciousness of his attack. Although Lippincott had falsely charged that Stafford W. Austin was working for Chaffey when Lippincott sought to secure Austin's dismissal, it was Chaffey whom Lippincott meant to destroy; and he set himself to this task with a dedication that stretched out over five years. Chaffey originally filed an application in September 1905 for the right to construct a reservoir on Cottonwood Creek. His objective was to establish a desert irrigation colony to be served by the reservoir and an attendant hydroelectric power plant which he hoped might also be used one day to supply an electric railroad line running to Los Angeles. Chaffey's application was routinely referred to Lippincott, who was then still working for the Reclamation Service, to determine whether the proposed project would interfere with the service's plans for an irrigation project in the Owens Valley. Because Cottonwood Creek lay well downstream of the service's project and the federal government had no plans to use the creek, Lippincott was forced to acknowledge in his official report to

Newell that no conflict existed between the two projects and that Chaffey's application could therefore not be held up. Lippincott, however, immediately notified Mulholland of Chaffey's plan. And in a separate confidential letter to Newell with his report, Lippincott enclosed a protest from Mulholland and recited for Newell all the gossip then circulating about possible fraud in Chaffey's endeavors in Australia and the Imperial Valley. "While these charges may not have any official bearing on his application," Lippincott noted, "practically I think it has."[132]

When this initial effort had no effect and Chaffey filed new applications for additional water resources, Lippincott stepped up his program of character assassination with another confidential letter to Newell alleging that Chaffey was acting only as a speculator with a view toward ultimately selling out his interests to Los Angeles. He urged Newell to reject Chaffey's application "for the best public interest."[133] Chaffey, however, continued to press his cause, and because his applications posed no threat to the Reclamation Service project, they had to be approved in this period preceding passage of the city's right-of-way bill. Lippincott nevertheless continued his attempts to strangle Chaffey's project even as he prepared to leave the service for the more remunerative position Los Angeles had waiting for him. "I do not believe the applications are made in good faith," he wrote to Newell in one last effort. "If we are to consider only the technical form of the applications, I know of no reason why they should not be granted. If we are to consider public interest and public policy, I think they certainly should be rejected."[134] In the absence of any legal authority for rejection, however, Newell was unwilling to intervene any further on the city's behalf.

As soon as he had been formally entered on Los Angeles' payroll, Lippincott filed an official protest for the city seeking the denial of Chaffey's applications. This protest was just as promptly dismissed by the federal government, with the result that by the beginning of 1907, Chaffey's plans ranked in the view of the city's water officials alongside the claims of the private power companies in the Owens Valley as the only significant obstacles to development of the aqueduct.[135] Chaffey, meanwhile, pushed ahead with the building of Manzanar. More than five hundred acres around the fledgling community were planted in apples, pears, peaches, prunes, and grapes. A packing house, general store, garage, blacksmith shop, school house, lumber yard, and ice cream parlor all sprang into existence. By 1910, a sophisticated drainage system of concrete and steel was under construction and twenty-acre tracts were available to new settlers at prices of $150 and up.[136]

But Lippincott refused to relent, and by 1912, with the aqueduct nearing completion, Newell was inclined to be somewhat more accommodating. "Again imposing on your good nature," Lippincott and Mulholland wired Newell on January 16, 1912, "we think you could substantially aid us in the Chaffey contest on Cottonwood Creek." Newell this time answered that he would be happy to help, and the aqueduct's top legal counsel, W. B. Mathews, was promptly dispatched to Washington with a request for Newell's assistance in speeding the approval of an application the city was filing under the right-of-way bill of 1906 to buy up the bottomlands on which Chaffey's project depended.[137]

This effort, buttressed by the extended litigation with which the city repeatedly buffeted his endeavor, eventually forced Chaffey to withdraw. The attacks on his integrity which had been an integral part of Lippincott's campaign from its beginning had wearied him, and he had no taste left for the battle. He left, embittered, to turn his energy to his last great development project in East Whittier and the La Habra Valley.[138] On February 10, 1912, the president of the Los Angeles Board of Public Works wrote to Newell in a flowery expression of the city's thanks:

> The Los Angeles Aqueduct has appealed to you so often and you have been so generous in your aid and so solicitous for the welfare of our enterprise that in view of your last intercession in our favor we feel it incumbent upon us to express our most hearty thanks for all those liberally rendered services. It is but natural, of course, for you to perform these acts as they no doubt appeal to you as being in the line of duty, the nature of your own work being such that it has, like ours, a special and intimate relation to the broad public welfare.[139]

The destruction of George Chaffey's project, however, was an isolated instance, one springing more from Lippincott's mean spirit than from any considered policy of the city's water administrators. In general, relations between Los Angeles and the Owens Valley in the years between the passage of the right-of-way bill and the end of World War I were marked by the serenity of studied indifference. Residents of the valley did not see themselves as existing in the city's shadow; and Mulholland and his colleagues were for the most part uninterested in events in the valley. To the extent that the two communities engaged one another at all in this period, their relations seemed to hold more promise of partnership than of adversarial conflict. The completion of the aqueduct's railroad line north from Mojave in October 1910 tied them more closely together than ever before. For the first time, the valley had a reliable transportation route to the markets of Southern California. "Los Angeles is sending up a cry for a greater milk and cream supply," proclaimed one of the valley's advertising brochures. "This demand Owens Valley can and will largely meet. In time milk trains will run from here as they do into New York City."[140] When the acquisition of large tracts of land by a distant but nonetheless tax-exempt municipal agency posed a serious question with regard to the county's continued property tax revenues, the city was quick to resolve the problem by promising not to oppose the collection of taxes on its holdings in the valley.[141]

By 1916, William Mulholland could assert with pride that "the valley has developed at an accelerated rate both in population and wealth from the time of the advent of the City."[142] And Mulholland even sought to add to the valley's bountiful production by pressing forward a plan while the aqueduct was under construction to plant twenty-five million eucalyptus, locust, and walnut trees on fifty thousand acres lining the aqueduct. These trees, he estimated, could be harvested and sold after ten years for a hundred million dollars. It was a beautiful if slightly screwy notion, and one especially appropriate to a man who had spent the nights of his youth planting trees in the Elysian Hills. But in the end, leveler heads prevailed in pointing out the vast quantities of water these trees would absorb which might otherwise flow to Los Angeles, and the dream was stillborn.[143]

Even without Mulholland's trees, the Owens Valley, in the words of a survey conducted by the California Development

Board in 1917, was a region "just awakening to its limitless possibilities, both agriculturally and industrially."[144] According to a
visitor in the summer of 1916:

> From the railroad station at Laws to the town of Bishop
> and west to Red Hill one travelled tree-lined roads
> through a district almost continuously cultivated; green
> fields bordered by wide irrigating canals alternated with
> stretches of damp pasture lands. Creeks brimful of spar-
> kling water dissected the piedmont sloping to Owens Riv-
> er. A verdant land, Owens Valley presented a scene of sub-
> stantial economic well-being and human contentment.[145]

Hay, especially alfalfa, remained the principal agricultural
commodity, accounting for two-thirds the total value of all the
valley's crops in 1920. But wheat production, mainly for export,
expanded dramatically in the years between 1910 and 1920. While
corn production declined, more than twenty-eight thousand orchard trees reached bearing age in this decade. The valley's apples
and honey consistently took prizes at the San Francisco Mid-
winter Fair and the Lewis and Clark Exposition in Portland.
And though most of the 124,929 acres then owned by the city of
Los Angeles were left fallow as grazing lands, even some of these
tracts were turned to the growing of alfalfa, corn, wheat, barley,
and vegetables to feed the city's work crews along the aqueduct.[146]

Changing conditions and the opening of new markets brought
a number of developments in valley agriculture. By 1917, 6,500
head of cattle were being shipped out of the valley each year.
Wartime demands encouraged the Holly Sugar Company of
Huntington Beach to import seeds, machinery, and labor for
the production of sugar beets, and the new railroad line was
soon hauling 150 tons of this new crop each day during harvest
time. Despite the promise of Los Angeles' growing market,
dairying remained a form of agricultural industry with more
potential than real profitability. Although Bishop established a
cooperative creamery with the capacity to produce eleven hundred
pounds of butter each day, the lack of reliable refrigerated shipping restricted further expansion of the operation.[147]

Poultry offered the greatest potential for development, in the view of at least one prominent valley resident, Fred Eaton. Despite his involvement in the city's land purchases, Eaton had remained to make a home for himself in the valley, and his great personal charm gradually overcame much of the ill will his earlier activities had inspired. By 1915, his acceptance in the valley had risen to the point that the *Big Pine Citizen* was moved to berate those who criticized him. In a front-page profile of the man it concluded, "If we had a few more Fred Eatons in the Owens Valley and the people would work with them instead of against them, this valley would grow by leaps and bounds."[148] Eaton's land and cattle operation in Long Valley, however, had failed to prosper, and by 1912 he had ceased to dream of becoming a cattle baron and imagined himself instead a chicken czar. Always the plunger, Eaton could not begin with a modest chicken ranch but established instead a General Motors of poultry processing. With an initial $100,000 investment and the cement which he was able to persuade Mulholland to provide from Monolith, Eaton installed a 440-acre "chicken plant" surrounded by steel fencing set in concrete. Steel cars running on tracks that led out of a mill containing nine hundred tons of grain carried feed to more than sixty thousand Leghorns housed variously in twenty-four maturing houses, sixty laying houses, and a brooder house that was an eighth of a mile long. "Recognition of the superior quality of a strain systematically and scientifically developed in the favorable climate and conditions of this valley is a future certainty," Eaton proudly predicted of his pullets.[149]

These were prosperous years for other forms of industrial enterprise as well. The value of mineral production in Inyo County increased 137 percent between 1910 and 1920. In Keeler, the richest industrial community in the county, three plants with a combined capability of processing 47,000 tons of soda ash and bicarbonate each year extracted more than half of all the soda products consumed annually in the United States. And by 1911, one visionary group of investors in Bishop was laying plans for the construction of a thirteen-mile aerial tramway to tap the salt deposits lying on the other side of the White Mountains. Bishop, of course, remained the principal trading center in the valley, but Lone Pine and Coso Hot Springs were both moving actively to establish themselves as resort communities.[150]

Life in the towns was losing much of its frontier roughness. Bishop could boast of both a musical and a literary society, as well as three hotels, two newspapers, its own electric power plant, and a Women's Improvement Club. The streets were still mud and heavy hauling had made the road between Bishop and Laws the worst in the county, but concrete sidewalks were beginning to appear in the residential areas, and most of the town leaders were united in pushing for construction of a local library. A new state fish hatchery was under construction near Independence. Big Pine not only had a weekly newspaper but a community swimming pool as well. And Lone Pine offered the visitor a drug store, two garages, a new hotel, four restaurants, and a movie house. Every town in the valley had its own baseball team, and games were played every summer Sunday after church.

By 1916, two Union High School districts had been created at Lone Pine and Independence to complement the schools already established at Big Pine and Bishop. Fifty-one teachers ministered to the more than one thousand students enrolled in public schools throughout the valley, not counting the Indian schools at Bishop, Big Pine, and Independence. The graduates of these schools were accredited to the University of California and the University of Southern California without having to take entrance examinations. And there was a private college under development at nearby Deep Springs where students could pursue a three-part program of work, academics, and student government in a location so well removed from normal diversions that its founder, Lucien Nunn, hoped that "petty pedagogic surveillance . . . which retards the development of self-control and self-reliance" would be wholly unnecessary.[151]

With all its efforts at self-promotion and development, however, the Owens Valley achieved only a modest rate of growth between 1910 and 1920. Moreover, what gains it achieved proved to be for the most part illusory in relation to the establishment of a basis for sustained growth. For example, the value of crops grown in the valley nearly tripled in this period, rising from $523,643 in 1909 to $1,503,195 in 1919. But this dramatic increase simply reflected in large part the temporary boost that all agricultural commodities enjoyed as a result of wartime demand. The number of farms operating in the valley increased from 438 to

521, and the land area included in them registered a corresponding increase of 27 percent from 110,142 to 140,029 acres between 1910 and 1920. But the acreage actually improved for agricultural production increased by only 3 percent.

The records of increase in the assessed value of all the properties on the Inyo County tax rolls provide a similar picture of diminishing expectations. Whereas the total assessed value of the county nearly quadrupled in the fifteen years following the advent of the city in 1905, the greatest growth occurred in the first five years of this period, when the city was making its major land purchases. In the next five years, 1910 to 1915, the rate of growth in assessed value dropped by more than a third from 94 to 58 percent. And from 1915 to 1920, when the valley's promotional efforts should have been displaying their effect, the rate of growth in assessed value dropped again by nearly half, to 33 percent. Perhaps most discouraging of all, the population of the valley, which had swelled almost 60 percent in the decade 1900 to 1910, leveled off abruptly, with the result that there were only 57 more people living in Inyo County in 1920 than a decade earlier, an increase of less than 1 percent.[152]

These minor gains were completely overshadowed by developments at the other end of Mulholland's project, where, as the *Los Angeles Times* reported, "Under the Mighty Aqueduct A Fruitful Valley [Was] Unfolding."[153] Here Mulholland was moving rapidly to reinforce his victory in the battle over municipal policy for the distribution of surplus waters from the aqueduct. With the annexation of the first major sections of San Fernando and Palms on May 22, 1915, Los Angeles more than doubled in size from 108 to 285 square miles. Subsequent additions in 1916 and 1917 brought the city's total land area to more than 350 square miles, a rate of expansion supported entirely by the introduction of aqueduct water.[154]

Not every fledgling community in the San Fernando Valley was enthusiastic about surrendering its identity to be absorbed by Los Angeles in exchange for water deliveries, and the annexation campaigns in some areas were consequently acrimonious. But where resistance to annexation was stiffest, the community of interests tied up in banking and real estate could always be relied upon to deliver a winning margin at the polls. In some areas about to vote on annexation, for example, homeowners received little bottles of evil-smelling liquids labeled as if they came from the local water distributor, with notes attached, reading, "This is the water you drink."[155] The profitability of annexation was irresistible. The city's tax rolls soared; the lands held by the Los Angeles Suburban Home Company increased in value from an average of $20 to $2,000 an acre, giving the syndicate a profit on that company alone in the neighborhood of $100 million; and even J. B. Lippincott, once he had secured his release from municipal service with the completion of the aqueduct, found a lucrative practice in handling the formation of irrigation districts and annexation proceedings as a private consultant.[156]

The city adjusted its policies on the sale of aqueduct water in order to assure the rapid development of its newly acquired territories in the San Fernando Valley. Other areas of the city were able to expand irrigated farming by tapping underground reservoirs which had been needed to meet domestic requirements before the arrival of the Owens Valley water. But the San Fernando Valley was unique in its development as an integral part of the aqueduct project. Thus, while other areas were charged a flat rate for water to be used for domestic purposes or a somewhat lower rate for water to be applied for both domestic and irrigation uses, the San Fernando Valley alone enjoyed the benefits of a split-rate system which charged $43.56 per acre-foot for domestic water but only $6.10 for irrigation water.[157] As a result, the total irrigated acreage in the area of the San Fernando Valley served by the aqueduct expanded from 3,000 acres in 1914, the last year before aqueduct water was available, to 10,000 acres in 1915, 18,000 acres in 1916, and 30,000 acres in 1917. Although the city's water experts expected this area under irrigation to double again the next year, wartime demand for foodstuffs brought an even greater expansion to 75,000 acres in 1918.[158] By this time, the mean daily consumption of water within the city's boundaries was double what it had been in the last year before the aqueduct opened, and the Board of Public Service Commissioners, which was charged with overseeing Mulholland's activities, began to question the wisdom of a pricing policy which returned to the city only $200,000 on crops bearing a gross value of not less than $7.5 million.[159]

There was good reason for concern over more than the city's revenues because it was clear by the end of 1918 that the development of the San Fernando Valley was not proceeding at all in the manner Mulholland had planned. From the outset, Mulholland had assumed in preparing his projections for use of the aqueduct supply that domestic and irrigation uses would be roughly the same per acre and that the agricultural economy of the San Fernando Valley would continue to be based on tree crops which require only intermittent irrigation over a long growing season. But instead of trees, large sections of the valley in the war years were given over to the water-intensive production of beans, potatoes, and truck garden crops. As a result, during periods of peak irrigation demand, the consumption of water in the valley equaled the entire flow of the aqueduct and at times exceeded the total mean flow of the Owens River itself.[160] And although the publications of the Public Service Commission in 1919 continued to speak hopefully of a time when the majority of the irrigated lands in the San Fernando Valley would be devoted to the production of oranges, lemons, walnuts, apricots, and peaches, with beans being raised "only as a rotating crop," in fact, conditions in the valley that year were exactly the reverse. Beans continued to be the principal crop, and citrus acreage was only half what the commission had projected under its most favorable assumptions.[161]

Behind the immediate problem posed by the vastly underestimated demands of the San Fernando Valley for irrigation water lurked a more troubling potential difficulty for the operation of the aqueduct: population growth. Here, too, the projections upon which Mulholland had predicated his plans for the project had gone completely awry. Mulholland had assumed in 1905 that the rate of population growth in the city would continue along the lines established in the preceding ten years. On this basis, he had predicted that the city would grow from 200,000 residents to 250,000 in 1912 and 390,000 in 1925, by which time the city would require a mean daily supply of ninety cubic feet per second of water or 58 million gallons per day. By 1910, however, the city's population had reached 319,000, the level predicted for

1918. By 1913, the year the aqueduct went into operation, it had surpassed 500,000, a number Mulholland had not expected would be attained until 1936. And by 1925, Los Angeles would be more than three times the size Mulholland had predicted for that year.[162]

Annexation was not at fault in this case. The areas the city absorbed in this period were for the most part sparsely populated, and the 266 square miles added to the city between 1915 and 1920 added only 12,701 people to Los Angeles' population. Of the 1,192,000 people residing in the city by 1925, only 45,782 could be directly attributed to annexation.[163] But the combination of errors in Mulholland's projections for both domestic and irrigation water demand meant that, by 1919, rather than the 90 cubic feet per second of water Mulholland had planned to supply, the city was consuming a mean of 220 cubic feet per second each day.[164]

As the second decade of the twentieth century drew to a close, the prospects for a future of mutual prosperity for Los Angeles and the Owens Valley were thus growing very dim. While the opening of the railroad line had linked the two, the railroad had been built, after all, for the convenience of the aqueduct, and it was the aqueduct which bound the future of the Owens Valley inextricably to the course of development in the San Fernando Valley. The project which the city's officials had confidently predicted only seven years before would be sufficient to supply the needs of Los Angeles for all time to come was already strained to its limit. The hope for continued good relations between the city and the valley consequently hung in a fragile balance which could be abruptly upset either by a sudden increase in population or by an unexpected decrease in the available supply of water resulting from the onset of a prolonged drought. As luck would have it, both occurred.

CHAPTER SIX

The Politics
of Exploitation

In 1920, William Mulholland was sixty-five years old. He stood now at the pinnacle of his career. The controversies of the past were all but forgotten; as one admiring reporter put it in recalling the attacks on the concrete used for the aqueduct, "If Bill Mulholland should say that he is lining the aqueduct with green cheese because green cheese is better than concrete, this town would not only believe the guff but take oath that it was so."[1] To the city he had served for more than forty years, he was "the most indispensable citizen."[2] For this was the year that Los Angeles won its race with San Francisco for supremacy among the port cities of the West Coast. Thanks to the new development an abundant water supply made possible, Los Angeles in only twenty years had grown to five times its size at the beginning of the century. In the same period, the population of the San Francisco Bay Area had barely doubled; and after years of controversy, expenditures, reversals, and indecision, the water project San Francisco had begun at the same time as Los Angeles' was still fourteen years away from completion.[3]

Mulholland's aqueduct was the largest water project in the West. As an irrigation project for the San Fernando Valley it had firmly fixed Los Angeles' position as the number one agricultural county in the nation. As an urban delivery system it had laid the basis for a modern metropolis. The manifest benefits of public water development had in turn prompted the city to begin establishing its own distribution system for the electrical power the aqueduct would generate, a process which would eventually make Los Angeles the largest municipal electric utility in the country. And the clean hydroelectric power the aqueduct produced enabled the city's boosters to tout their community as America's "smokeless city" in this age before freeways.[4]

In this spectacular success lay the proof of the benefits of public water development, and Mulholland, as its progenitor, stood therefore not only as the perfect embodiment of the city's water policies but also as the supreme example of "what the applied scientist can do for his state when he holds his brief for the people."[5] Los Angeles' triumph brought a new age to California, an era marked by the construction of massive public water projects that would reshape the environment of the state and establish California's preeminence as the richest and most agriculturally productive state in the union. In Sacramento, the success of the aqueduct inspired renewed efforts to develop a comprehensive program for development of the state's water resources. And Mulholland, appropriately, was called to advise in this effort—just as he had served as a consultant in the development of public water projects for San Francisco, Oakland, Seattle, and the East Bay Municipal Utility District.[6]

With his achievements in the field came the professional distinctions he had never won in the classroom. In 1914, to mark the completion of the aqueduct, the University of California awarded him an honorary doctorate of laws. Honorary memberships in the American Water Works Association, the National Association of Power Engineers, and the Tau Beta Pi engineering fraternity soon followed. As a result of his activities outside Los Angeles, he by this time had also achieved particular renown among hydraulic engineers for having supervised the construction of twenty-five dams.[7] But for all the acclaim, Mulholland never aspired to any other position than the one that had been his since 1886. When the Los Angeles progressives in a desperate bid to regain power in 1913, for example, offered to nominate him as their candidate for mayor, he turned them away, declaring stoutly, "Gentlemen, I would rather give birth to a porcupine back-wards than be Mayor of Los Angeles."[8]

Mulholland had grown wealthy in the public service. He was by this time reputed to be the highest paid public servant in California.[9] In addition to his salary and the fees for his consulting services, he drew a comfortable income from the real estate investments he and Lippincott had made in the San Fernando Valley in 1908 and 1909.[10] But despite the attempts of scandal-mongers to link him with the wealthy financiers of the San Fernando land syndicates, he never really belonged to their world, their clubs, or their way of life. He lived modestly, dressed simply, and seems in general to have been rather careless about money. His friends and colleagues frequently came upon uncashed pay-checks that he had stuffed into a desk drawer or coat pocket and forgotten.[11]

"The dollar I spend I consider to be the greasy, dirty dollar of the workingman," he once declared.[12] It was this common quality so carefully nurtured throughout his life that no doubt endeared Mulholland most to the people of Los Angeles. For like so many of them, he had come to the city with nothing more to recommend himself than a strong back and a willingness to work. Since he shared their roots, they shared in a way in his success and drew confidence from his example. And so, when his wife Lillie died in 1915, Mulholland was not left alone. He lived on happily with his son Thomas and his adoring spinster daughter Rose, basking in the affection of his fellow Angelenos.[13]

But the city he had helped to build had changed as it grew. Its people were now more diverse, its politics more complex, its ambitions less clearly ascertained. And William Mulholland was sixty-five years old in 1920. If he had retired this year and left the management of the city's water system to younger hands, to a mind less inclined to see in every problem an occasion for self-righteous conflict, to someone whose sense of identity was not so completely wrapped up in the city as a whole that he saw each challenge as a personal affront, perhaps then the history of Los Angeles' relations with the Owens Valley would have been very different. But Mulholland stayed on, and in only seven years he destroyed his own career, embarrassed the city, devastated the

Owens Valley, and undermined the ideal of public water development he had labored so long to establish.

Ever since the passage of the aqueduct right-of-way bill in 1906, Mulholland had not had to concern himself with developments in the Owens Valley or with the aspirations of its citizens. While Lippincott looked ahead to a day when the city would require all the water of the valley, Mulholland had dreamed of planting trees, confident that there would be enough water to guarantee prosperity for all. But the public statements in which Mulholland spoke generously of the future for the Owens Valley had all been made before the full effects of his distribution policy for the San Fernando Valley became clear. The unprecedented and wholly unexpected growth that came with the construction of the aqueduct now compelled him to look again at the Owens Valley and to begin planning for a formal division of its waters.

There had been one attempt before this to negotiate an agreement by which the long-term supply of the aqueduct would be assured and the interests of the Owens Valley irrigators protected. The city had initiated discussions with the owners of the valley's major irrigation ditches in 1910, when the prospects for a settlement were especially favorable because Los Angeles' water officials were only just then beginning to confront the question of what should be done with the excess waters the aqueduct would provide. Detailed maps of the areas served by the existing ditches were drawn up, and on April 5, 1913, a tentative agreement was struck specifying that irrigation in the future would be limited to these areas already served. In exchange for thus proscribing their future expansion, the ranchers would be given unlimited use of the valley's groundwater supply and storage rights on Big Pine Creek and north of Fish Springs, and the city further promised to withdraw its opposition to settlement on the public lands of the Owens Valley.

Ten days after this agreement was reached, the Graham Plan for the distribution of the surplus water from the aqueduct went down to defeat, thereby opening the way to intensive development of the San Fernando Valley along the lines Mulholland had advocated. The city nevertheless pressed ahead in July with its efforts to formalize this agreement with the valley through the device of a so-called friendly suit intended to secure a judicial confirmation of its terms. But Henry Hart, the most outspoken of Mulholland's Socialist opponents on the Aqueduct Investigation Board, having been disappointed in his attempt to have the aqueduct's water declared unfit for human consumption, immediately filed a countersuit contending that the proposed agreement would further contaminate the aqueduct supply by perpetuating agricultural water use in the Owens Valley. The agreement, moreover, in Hart's view, violated the city charter by alienating the city's rights to the flow of the Owens River, despite the fact that the city at this time neither asserted a claim to the entire flow of the river nor desired one.[14]

Hart's suit was dismissed on May 23, 1914. But the city fathers had begun to have second thoughts about the wisdom of entering into any agreement with the Owens Valley ranchers. The distribution policies proposed by Quinton, Code, and Hamlin had by this time been adopted and massive annexations were being planned. Abruptly, the city refused to pursue the agreement any further, declaring that the city charter provisions on alienation which had been adopted by the time of municipalization to prevent the city from entering into another private contract for its water supply might well, as Hart claimed, prohibit it from entering into the settlement Mulholland had negotiated. Or at least, the city officials observed, the matter deserved further study. This was not the first time the city had invoked these charter provisions to avoid doing something it found distasteful, and it would certainly not be the last. These legalisms notwithstanding, Mulholland proceeded with exact measurements of the diversions the Owens Valley irrigators were making with a view toward using these measurements as the basis for an eventual settlement. And by 1919, the city's concerns for the charter were promptly forgotten, as Mulholland moved to negotiate just such an agreement.

It was not so much a renewed need for additional water supplies as the city's growing appetite for electrical energy that brought Mulholland back to the Owens Valley in 1919. Part of the beauty of Mulholland's project is that it flows entirely downhill, falling eight thousand feet in the 360 miles from the top of the Owens River watershed to Los Angeles. This means that its flow can be used to generate hydroelectric power while no power has to be consumed in getting the water to the reservoirs in the San Fernando Valley. Mulholland had been slow to recognize the hydroelectric generating potential of the aqueduct when he first conceived of the project, and he had thereafter maintained his distance from all questions involving development of the city's municipal electric system. These matters were left to E. F. Scattergood, head of a separate bureau of aqueduct power. This separation of powers was not only appropriate, given Mulholland's lack of expertise in the field of hydroelectric generation, it was also convenient to Mulholland politically. For Scattergood's efforts to establish a municipal power system met with intense opposition from the same elements of the business community that could always be counted upon to provide Mulholland with his most vigorous support. The embittered resistance of the local private power companies, the Merchants and Manufacturers Association, and the *Los Angeles Times* had consequently delayed Scattergood's efforts to set his sytem into operation, and actual construction of the municipal power system had not begun until the spring of 1916, when the first overhead poles were set.[15]

The original surveys for the aqueduct indicated that the city could expect to generate within the system a reliable supply of 200,000 horsepower.[16] The city had begun installing generating plants as early as 1908 with the construction of a small plant on Division Creek which was used to operate a floating power shovel needed to dig the aqueduct.[17] But by 1919, with an installed generating capacity of only 37,500 horsepower, the system was still a long way from realizing its promised potential. The city's engineers, moreover, had determined by this time that no substantial expansion of the aqueduct's hydroelectric power generation could be achieved without extending the system to make use of the precipitous twenty-two-hundred-foot power drop the river makes along fourteen miles of the Owens Gorge below Long Valley.[18] Development of the gorge would require the acquisition of additional water-bearing lands in the Mono Basin and the construction of reservoirs to regulate flows through the new power plants. And the prospect of these modifications to the aqueduct, in turn, brought Mulholland onto the scene.

Los Angeles was not alone in recognizing the opportunities

for hydroelectric power generation on the Owens River and its tributaries. Between 1910 and 1918, sixteen separate withdrawals of public lands had been made in the Owens Valley for the purpose of locating potential power sites.[19] The Southern Sierras Power Company, which had emerged by this time as the principal private developer in the area, had five plants and 125 miles of transmission lines in place by the time the aqueduct opened. And by 1919, the company had expanded its overall generation from only 5.5 million kilowatt hours in 1906 to 200 million.[20] In addition, development interests in Inyo and Kern counties and the Mojave Desert had announced somewhat vague plans to bring all the water from the Mono Basin down through the Southern Sierras Power Company's plants in the gorge to a point near the aqueduct's intake and then over the Haiwee Summit south to Owens Lake and Indian Wells Valley.[21]

A far more immediate problem for the city was posed by the owners of the principal irrigation ditches in the northern end of the Owens Valley. Having been left to their own devices since the collapse of the proposed agreement of 1913, they were now attempting to establish a combined power and irrigation project for themselves by reviving J. D. Galloway's plan for a reservoir at Fish Slough. Originally prepared as an alternative to the Reclamation Service's plans for a reservoir at Long Valley, Galloway's Fish Slough project had lain more or less dormant since the service's formal abandonment of the Owens Valley in 1907. A local rancher, William Rowan, announced his intention to proceed with the project in 1911 and applied to the federal government for the necessary easement across public lands. Rowan's claim was based on a water rights filing he had posted at the site of the proposed reservoir on November 4, 1905, which he declared predated and was therefore superior to any claims the city might make to the water he intended to divert into his reservoir. Rowan had offered to relinquish his water rights under this filing in favor of the Reclamation Service's project at Long Valley, but he retained the authority to reassert his rights once the service withdrew.[22]

Rowan's claim was taken up by Galen Dixon, whose brief career in the local federal lands office had been cut short as a result of his abusive treatment of Los Angeles' representatives. To lead the drive to resuscitate the Fish Slough project, Dixon approached Delos A. Chappelle, an official of the Hillside Water Company outside Bishop who also served as president of the Nevada-California Power Company. With Chappelle's financial backing and the legal assistance his companies could command, Dixon next set to work encouraging others who had filed on the valley's public lands to assert their claims. By "out-generalling the Department of the Interior" and inundating Washington with applications for use of the public lands, Dixon hoped to pressure the federal government into relaxing its grip on the Owens Valley and restoring the lands withdrawn on Los Angeles' behalf.[23]

Chappelle was agreeable, and Rowan was happy to have him as his champion. But Chappelle began buying up many of these claims for his own use. By December 1913 Chappelle and his associates held enough options on lands in the Fish Slough area to offer a deal to the Owens Valley irrigators. If the ranchers would pool their claims with his, Chappelle proposed to build an eighty-thousand-acre-foot capacity reservoir at Fish Slough capable of delivering four hundred second feet of water. In exchange for their rights and a promise to contribute up to $5,000 for the court costs Chappelle expected to incur in defending the project, he agreed to give the ranchers half the water from the project for use in the Owens River and Bishop Creek watersheds.[24] The irrigators refused and promptly banded together to prevent Chappelle from expanding his holdings in the area.[25] Chappelle then dropped the project and died soon after, leaving Rowan's application in limbo until it was taken up by the Owens Valley ditch owners themselves in 1919.[26]

The leader in the renewed effort to build the Fish Slough reservoir was George Watterson, a local rancher, hardware store owner, and secretary to the Bishop Creek Ditch Company. Backing him were the owners and presidents of seven of the valley's eleven major private irrigation canals, whose combined operations reached 48,852 acres, or 93 percent of all the irrigated acreage in the Owens Valley. Their plan, although only vaguely defined at the outset, was to develop a project at Fish Slough that would expand their operations 60 percent by irrigating an additional 30,000 acres. To aid them in the difficult task of securing all the federal grants and approvals the project required, the associated ditch companies retained the Washington law firm of Charles F. Consaul and Charles C. Heltman, who had formerly been very active in pressing the claims of the Nevada Power Mining and Milling Company and the Silver Lake Power and Irrigation Company for development projects in the Owens Valley.[27]

The federal authorities were initially incredulous. When Rowan first applied for an easement for the project in 1911, the commissioner of the General Land Office expressed amazement at the "enormous" size of the 91,500-acre-foot reservoir Rowan proposed to build. The United States Geological Survey had no idea how he could ever fill it if Los Angeles proceeded with construction of its own reservoir at Long Valley, twenty miles upstream.[28] When the ditch companies asked the Reclamation Service in January 1919 to reconsider building the Fish Slough reservoir, Arthur Powell Davis, as head of the service, turned them down flat. After reviewing all the official reasons for the government's original decision to reject the project, Davis noted drily that "subsequent developments in the Owens Valley seem to have rendered it even less desirable as a field for federal work."[29] And to quiet the fears of Los Angeles officials when they learned of the companies' request, Davis repeated the reasoning he had laid out for the ditch owners and added, "I therefore feel safe in asserting that I do not regard the Owens Valley irrigation project as feasible and it certainly is not contemplated for construction by the Reclamation Service."[30] The Owens Valley irrigators similarly had no success in their efforts to have the survey work for the dam site performed by no less prominent a figure than Elwood Mead—formerly the leading spokesman for private water development within the Department of Agriculture and now teaching at the University of California.[31]

As improbable as the project may have seemed, Mulholland could scarcely ignore any plan to interfere with the flows south to the aqueduct's intake, especially when the advocates of the Fish Slough project sometimes took to airy descriptions of a 100,000-acre-foot reservoir servicing new agricultural enterprises covering 200,000 acres of the Owens and Indian Wells valleys and Mono

Basin.[32] But if he could not dismiss it, neither could he simply oppose it, because the Owens Valley ranchers had one important lever at their disposal with which to move Mulholland toward a spirit of accommodation. The city had a vital piece of legislation pending in Congress at the beginning of 1919, and acquiescence of the valley's residents was essential to its passage.

This bill had been offered to correct certain variations between the specific description of the public lands the aqueduct actually crossed and those that had been granted for the project in the city's right-of-way bill of 1906. These deviations from the course Congress had originally defined for the aqueduct came about in large part as a result of Mulholland's preference for going through, rather than around natural barriers whenever he felt he could tunnel more cheaply than he could lay pipe. Although essentially technical in nature, the legislation was vital to the city's interests because without perfect title the legal authority for the continued operation of the aqueduct could be challenged. But Los Angeles had used the occasion of the bill's introduction to attempt to go much farther.

The city had lost its right to continue selecting lands for use in conjunction with the aqueduct, and its attempts to reestablish a preferential claim to the public lands of the Owens Valley had been turned back in 1911 and 1912. Although the Department of the Interior had since exercised its discretionary authority to give Los Angeles great latitude in the continued acquisition of properties in the public domain, this bill, as introduced, would have renewed the city's specific legal authority for asserting first claim to any public lands it determined were needed for the aqueduct at the rate of $1.25 per acre. And though the bill specified a termination date for this authority on December 31, 1922, it also gave the Secretary of the Interior five years to complete his review of any maps filed by the city at the end of 1922. As a result, the city's opponents claimed, the effect of the bill would be to block any power and irrigation projects proposed by anyone other than the city of Los Angeles for the next eight years.[33]

As soon as they learned of the bill, the owners of the associated ditches rushed off individual telegrams to Washington and Los Angeles protesting this attempted interference with their water and storage rights.[34] Watterson and Dixon were immediately dispatched to Washington to present their case to the California delegation and particularly to the two California congressmen on the Public Lands Committee, William Kettner and John E. Raker. Raker proved an especially valuable ally because he represented Mono County and had worked closely with Sylvester Smith in that gentleman's rarely successful efforts to defend the Owens Valley against perceived threats from Los Angeles. Dixon and Watterson soon sent back glowing reports of their success: "With every member with whom we talked, we found that they were practically ignorant of the matter or had grossly erroneous views, and repeatedly expressed their surprise before the Committee as to the manner in which they had been deceived."[35]

Faced with this onslaught impugning their motives and honesty, the city's representatives began backtracking quickly. Testifying for the city was William B. Mathews, chief counsel for the city water bureau, of whom Mulholland had once remarked, "I did the work but Mathews kept me out of jail."[36] Under fire before the Public Lands Committee, Mathews repeatedly declared that the city had no intention of acquiring additional water rights in Inyo or Mono counties and that its only interest in the provisions of this bill that Kettner and Raker found so offensive was for power development.[37] The bill was promptly amended to eliminate the authority the city had proposed for itself to select lands on Bishop Creek and the Fish Slough reservoir site, as well as in large sections of Mono County and areas as far-flung as San Diego.[38] When Congressman Kettner proposed an amendment on behalf of the Southern Sierras Power Company that would have denied priority to Los Angeles' claims, Mathews demurred. But when Raker proposed inserting specific permission for continued homesteading and other filings for entry on public lands in the Owens Valley and Mono basin, Mathews agreed, averring stoutly, "We do not ask you to hamstring them."[39]

In Los Angeles, meanwhile, invitations were hastily extended for a reopening of the negotiations for a long-term water agreement. As part-owner of the Sanger Ditch, H.S. Beckman was delegated to represent the associated ditches because he maintained a residence in the city. The initial meeting on February 5 was cordial but inconclusive. Mulholland complained mightily about the opposition to the city's bill in Congress and expressed amazement that the Owens Valley interests would object to "such an innocent bill." Although Beckman presented the broad outlines for an agreement, it did not sit well with the city officials. "Nothing much was accomplished," he reported back. "After debating the conditions of our agreement, they seemed to change their attitude and stated that they were willing to come through with the agreement but could not handle the matter just now."[40]

The city continued to avoid further discussion for more than three months. Finally, on May 21, 1919, Beckman was able to reestablish communication with "the city gods," as he called them. "I put it to them plainly that my only mission was to know their attitude," he explained in a letter to Dixon. Scattergood, whose interests were most at stake in these discussions, was "especially cordial" and promised to do all he could to expedite an agreement. But Scattergood warned that there would be trouble with Mulholland, who dismissed the Fish Slough reservoir site as impractical, contending that "it would not hold" and would leak like "a cane-bottom chair." Beckman, however, reported that he had been approached by Fred Eaton, who, sniffing an opportunity for profit by trading on his relationship with Mulholland, had presented himself as "the only person who could manage our affairs judiciously and diplomatically through the Water Department." Eaton, Beckman advised, was angling for a contract to do surveys for the Fish Slough dam site, as well as "to convince Mr. Mulholland he has been hasty in passing judgment."[41]

The achievement of a settlement involving the Fish Slough reservoir site was not simply a two-way affair. The Southern Sierras Power Company, as the successor in interest to the smaller water and power companies that had sprung up in the Owens Valley in the early part of the century, constituted a third party whose interests could upset any plan Los Angeles and the ditch owners might devise. For in addition to five thousand acres held in the name of the Hillside Water Company, Southern Sierras had acquired the rights to three key water filings that had earlier been bought up by Edson F. Adams, head of the now defunct Owens River Water and Power Company. All three filings were located in the heart of the Fish Slough reservoir site and were antedated only by Rowan's own claim.[42] As a result, the ditch owners could not construct a reservoir at Fish Slough without encountering certain opposition from the power company for infringement of its rights and from Los Angeles for interference with the aqueduct.

Relations between the ditch owners and the power company were touchy. Before the construction of the power company's plants upstream of their operations, the irrigators had relied primarily upon spring floods for their water. This meant that excessive quantities of water had to spread during the peak of the floods, damaging the croplands, whereas the water supply was insufficient at seeding time before the floods and again when the crops began reaching maturity after the floods had passed.[43] The release of water from the power company's regulating reservoirs was far more constant than the natural flow had been, but the ditch owners were always demanding that more water be released to them when they needed it most. This continuing controversy came to a head in the midst of the ditch owners' maneuvering for the Fish Slough project. Drought came to the valley that summer, and on June 11, 1919, a band of angry downstream farmers stormed one of the power company's reservoirs and turned its water back into the stream for irrigation.[44]

Beckman was insistent in advising his colleagues that they had to resolve their differences with the power company if they were to have any hope of constructing the Fish Slough reservoir. First, he told them, they would have to incorporate. Although the association had existed under a loose agreement adopted on September 22, 1900, first as the Owens Valley Associated Ditches and later as the Owens Valley Water Protective Association, they had no legal identity. Second, Beckman urged them to secure an option on the power company's holdings. "Nothing should stand in the way of taking this important step at once," he wrote, "for if we do not, it gives the city an opportunity to acquire that interest and then insist upon terms that otherwise we might not have to consent to." These two actions, Beckman promised, "will put the Associated Ditch Company in a position to negotiate direct with the City." On such a firm footing as this, Beckman believed even more glittering prospects might be theirs. "It is no secret among the City's department heads," he wrote after his meeting with the gods in May, "that if we had the Fish Slough proposition in shape, they will not only negotiate with us but have even intimated that they would help us finance it."[45]

With this encouragement, the associated ditches moved quickly to act on Beckman's advice. Articles of incorporation were filed in July, $500,000 in capital stock was issued at $10.00 a share, and George Watterson and Galen Dixon were elected as president and secretary, respectively.[46] Because Dixon had worked for the Southern Sierras Power Company, he was delegated to negotiate an agreement with A. B. West, president of the Hillside Water Company and vice president and general manager of the power company. Although West was happy to quote a purchase price of $39,000 for all of the company's interests and survey data, the negotiations soon stalled on questions involving the control of Bishop Creek and the compensation due to the various individuals who had filed entries on the power company's behalf.[47] Consaul and Heltman meanwhile pressed ahead in their efforts to obtain federal approval for the project before Los Angeles' bill came up for a final vote in the Public Lands Committee.[48] The Washington attorneys considered this timing vital because, as they explained to Dixon, "We know that various power companies have found the city officials very difficult to deal with and that the City has at times evinced a disposition to drive very hard bargains with those whom it found to be at its mercy."[49]

At the end of October, these disparate activities began to come together. Consaul and Heltman secured the Secretary of the Interior's authorization for the Fish Slough reservoir just one day before the congressional committee acted on the city's bill. The secretary's formal blessing afforded a greater protection for the project than the amendments to the bill could ever provide. Even so, Consaul and Heltman reported, "We have not advised Mr. Mathews, city attorney, of the approval of your application because it can do the Fish Slough no harm to have the existing exclusion in the city bill."[50] Within a month, an agreement with the Hillside Water Company had been concluded.[51] Preparations were made to begin construction immediately on a temporary dam for the reservoir.[52] And Dixon was able to report happily to

Arthur Powell Davis at the Reclamation Service that the city, having recognized that it might need to use the Fish Slough reservoir for secondary storage in connection with its planned power plants in the gorge, had endorsed the project "and doubtless will aid in its construction."[53]

But the prospects for the project were not nearly as bright as Dixon described them to Davis. The drought which had driven the ranchers to seize the Southern Sierras Power Company reservoir in June had shaken the resolve of the ditch company owners. As a result, the entire complex scheme began to come apart. Fearing that the next winter would be as dry as the past one, William Symons, as president of the McNally Ditch, announced in October that his members would have all the water they needed so long as no one tampered with the streams. Symons therefore threatened to sue the association if it attempted to proceed with the construction of a dam. George Watterson raised a similar threat on behalf of the Bishop Creek Ditch Company. Because these two companies alone accounted for more than 40 percent of all the acreage served by the association, their defection could cripple the project.[54]

To make matters worse, the association had no funds to begin work on the damsite. The corporate stocks had not sold, and the individual ditch companies refused to contribute to the association's expenses. As a result, Consaul and Heltman could not be paid for their successful labors on behalf of the project. Because all payments to the association were voluntary on the part of the individual ditch companies, Consual noted drily that they were operating like the Continental Congress, with the power to incur debt but no authority to raise taxes to pay for it.[55] Galen Dixon, as the association's only paid employee, was in particularly severe financial straits. At the beginning of October, he wrote plaintively to Beckman in a vain attempt to receive some sort of reassurance:

> If as a result of my efforts, the right of the associated ditches can be secured to an extent which will aggregate many millions of dollars within the present generation and protect them for all time, [and] they cannot now protect me as I have protected them . . . I am deceived,

and if all the others . . . are intending to profit . . . without recognizing that I am to have an equitable interest in the results and a fair opportunity to look after the interests of myself and my family for the balance of my natural life, then of course I must proceed to look out for my own interests and of course shall do so.[56]

But Beckman could not help. A few months later Dixon was dead, and with him died the last real hope for private irrigation development in the Owens Valley.

Long Valley

The desperate financial condition of the association made Los Angeles' participation in the Fish Slough reservoir not only a desirable augmentation of the project but an absolute necessity for its success. Symons and Watterson, whose threats to withdraw from the association had helped to bring about this situation, now replaced Beckman as the principal negotiators for the valley ditches with Los Angeles. The city's attitude toward the project, however, had by this time hardened. Beckman had reported in October that "Mulholland is very decided in his views about the Fish Slough Reservoir and claims there is no possibility of the slough holding water . . . and that a 30-foot dam would make it leak like a sieve." Mathews, in his meetings with Beckman, had taken the position that not even a reservoir at Long Valley would satisfy the needs of the Owens Valley. And Scattergood, the third member of the committee the city named to meet with the valley representatives, had by this time been silenced and refused to express any opinion.[57] Symons' and Watterson's negotiations with the city in 1920 thereafter shifted from discussions of the Fish Slough site to planning for the construction of a reservoir on the city's lands at Long Valley.

The Long Valley reservoir site had been the city's first acquisition in the Owens Valley. Initial surveys for the Reclamation Service by J. C. Clausen had identified the site as the most favorable location for a major reservoir, which Clausen estimated would be capable of storing 240,000 acre-feet of water behind a

140-foot dam.[58] Subsequent surveys revealed that a dam of this height would in fact store upwards of 260,000 acre-feet of water, making it by far the largest reservoir ever built in California to that time. Even after the Reclamation Service withdrew its project, Clausen's proposal remained an essential element in the city's original plans for the aqueduct, although Mulholland toyed at various times with the idea of building the dam at 100, 120, or even 160 feet.[59]

Possession of Long Valley, however, had been important to the city not so much as a potential reservoir site but rather as the essential means of blocking the Reclamation Service's plans for its own irrigation project to benefit the Owens Valley. "For that reason alone, if for no other, it was wise for us to take every precaution to protect the City in the future," testified J. M. Elliott of the city water commission in explaining the purchase of these lands to the Aqueduct Investigation Board.[60] The panel of consulting engineers retained by Los Angeles in 1906 to review the project eliminated the proposal for a reservoir at Long Valley from the city's plans for the aqueduct on the grounds that it was too expensive and of too little immediate value to the city.[61] Thereafter, Mulholland had adopted as his own the position that the Long Valley reservoir would be developed only when the city's need for water exceeded the 400-second-foot capacity of the aqueduct. Even then, Mulholland maintained, the reservoir would be built only as a last resort. He testified before the Aqueduct Investigation Board in 1912 that neither Long Valley nor the smaller reservoir site the city owned at Tinemaha was essential to the aqueduct: "As a matter of precaution they were taken in. Neither one of them cost us much . . . Personally, I have been very confident that the City will not want that dam [at Long Valley]. I mean for the next 50 years."[62]

In 1920, however, Mulholland was ready to reconsider construction of the Long Valley reservoir both as an alternative to the ranchers' project at Fish Slough and, far more important from the city's point of view, as a necessary component in the power system it was planning for the gorge. On June 5, the city's bill to amend the right-of-way act of 1906 passed into law, thereby assuring Los Angeles' ability to proceed with the purchase of water rights in the Mono Basin that would be needed for the power project.[63] By September, preliminary studies for the city's power project confirmed the need for a reservoir at Long Valley to regulate flows into the city's proposed power plants.[64] Under the water rights laws of the time, however, Los Angeles could not construct the dam and interfere with the river's natural flows downstream from Long Valley without the consent of the irrigators who depended upon those flows. The associated ditch companies had already stated their opposition to any diversions in Long Valley. Mulholland therefore accepted their request for formal negotiations, and by April 21, 1921, the outline for an agreement had taken shape.[65]

The deal Mulholland offered to Watterson, Symons, and their colleagues promised that construction on a dam at Long Valley would begin within twelve months and be completed within three years, and that the city would thereafter provide the irrigators with a regulated supply of 374 cubic feet per second apportioned over a six-month growing season that began on April 1. Although the dam would be built with a foundation capable of supporting a 150-foot structure, Mulholland proposed to raise it to a height of only 100 feet. As a result, the reservoir would contain only 68,000 acre-feet of water, and a supplemental storage facility for another 15,000 acre-feet of water would have to be provided on Rock Creek in order to meet the irrigators' needs.[66] At this reduced size, the project would be of doubtful value for irrigation or power development. Clausen, who had been retained by the associated ditch companies to review the proposal, warned that if the project had been built earlier, the storage the city proposed would have been inadequate for irrigation in seven of the preceding seventeen years. In addition, he contended that the supplemental facilities on Rock Creek would be used to drive the city's hydroelectric power plants, so there would be no assurance that there would actually be any water available when the ditch companies needed it most.[67] Nothing less than a 150-foot dam would suffice, according to Clausen; and in this view he was joined by the authors of the city's own plans for the power project.[68]

The problem was that the city owned only enough of Long

Valley to construct a hundred-foot dam. Though Los Angeles' water officials had intended initially to acquire the entire site, their agent, Fred Eaton, once he held an option on the property, had reneged on his original contract with the city and withheld for himself everything at Long Valley above the hundred-foot contour line. This betrayal of the city's confidence had led to violent exchanges between Mulholland and Eaton, and the re-negotiated contract by which Eaton was paid the full purchase price for the Long Valley property in exchange for turning over only 20 percent of the land had been the one aspect of Mulholland's project which the Aqueduct Investigation Board had considered a genuinely indictable offense.

Even so, Mulholland had remained loyal and generous in his dealings with his former mentor. When the aqueduct investigators pressed him in 1912 on the propriety of the agreement with Eaton, Mulholland stoutly declared, "The 100-foot contour looked pretty good to me [when the deal was struck], and a long time has elapsed, and it looks very good to me right now . . . I am positive that the 100-foot contour is as high as that valley will ever have to be flooded."[69] Of Eaton, he proclaimed, "God bless him. I would like to see a monument to him a mile high when this city gets the Aqueduct through."[70] When Eaton set out to establish his mammoth chicken ranch, Mulholland was there to help, first by supplying him with concrete from the aqueduct's Monolith plant and later by agreeing to buy up some of the excess lands of Eaton's poultry company at an average of $26.57 an acre even though properties all around it were selling at an average price of only a fourth as much.[71]

Eaton, however, did not return these kindnesses. When the aqueduct was finally complete, he did not deign even to attend the dedication ceremonies. He was the same age as Mulholland, after all, and while all his schemes for personal wealth and power had gone awry, he had watched his former protégé rise to fame. In the city's need for the rest of the Long Valley property Eaton saw what would be perhaps his last chance for riches. At first he fixed a price of $900,000 for the lands above the hundred-foot contour line that the city estimated were worth no more than $255,000. When Mulholland balked at this demand, Eaton increased the price to $1.5 million and then to $3 million. Mulholland refused even to discuss the matter and determined instead to make do with a hundred-foot dam which he would build with a foundation capable of supporting an eventual expansion of the reservoir after Eaton was dead.[72]

Although an arrangement whereby Mulholland would gain control of Long Valley only over his dead body may have been perfectly acceptable to Fred Eaton, it was not so to the other irrigators whose livelihood depended upon an abundance of water below the dam site. Watterson and Symons vigorously defended the product of their negotiations as an agreement that would be "the salvation of the valley" by bringing jobs and prosperity to the Bishop region while postponing indefinitely any additional demands by the city upon the valley's water resources.[73] But the other owners of the associated ditch companies would have none of it. On October 21, 1921, they sent a formal protest to the city's Board of Public Service Commissioners advising that they would "permit no interference" with the waters of Long Valley and demanding that the city cease all work on the proposed reservoir.[74]

H. S. Beckman deplored this action, warning that Mulholland had no serious intention of proceeding with the Long Valley project but was using the reservoir instead as a foil for his much grander plans to tap the hydroelectric potential of the Colorado River at Boulder Canyon. "The City, in the propaganda for the Boulder Canyon project, are making excuses for not proceeding with Long Valley and I am sure would be only too glad to say to the people of the City at this time that the water users of the Valley had protested," he wrote in November. "I am led to believe that the City is desirous of having this protest and, if served at this time, it seems to me we would be playing right into the City's hands."[75] Beckman's counsel came too late; even Watterson and Symons acknowledged, "This agreement is dead—dead as a doornail."[76] Rather than promoting the agreement, they were busy by the end of 1921 simply trying to dissuade the other ditch owners from further burdening the doubtful finances of the association by suing for an injunction against the Long Valley project.[77]

Such an action by this time was unnecessary, for the collapse

of the Long Valley project had already been assured by the intervention of the Southern Sierras Power Company. The ranchers'
seizure of the power company's reservoir in the summer of 1919
had led to a formal determination that the irrigators on Bishop
Creek did in fact have first claim to its flows. Any power development there would consequently require the unanimous consent of
the ranchers, which was now clearly impossible. The power company in the meantime had secured control of another of Edson
Adams' filings, this one located at the site of the greatest power
drop in the center of the gorge. Fred Eaton, acting as Adams'
agent, had once offered this property to Los Angeles, but the city
had rejected the price Eaton demanded. Once title to the property
passed into the hands of the power company on February 4,
1920, the company gained the same pivotal influence over the
Long Valley reservoir project which it had possessed with regard
to the Fish Slough plan. Without the control of this key site, Los
Angeles could not proceed with full development of the hydroelectric power potential of the gorge, nor could it regulate the
flow of water through the gorge without interfering with the
rights associated with the power company's holding. Rather than
negotiate a price for the property it now had reason to regret
rejecting, the city sought to condemn the power company's water
rights and right-of-way. When the United States Circuit Court of
Appeal denied the city's suit in 1922, Mulholland lost the only
reason he had ever had for contemplating construction of the
Long Valley reservoir, and the project was abandoned.[78]

In later years, critics of Los Angeles' policies in the Owens
Valley would find in the collapse of the Long Valley project the
origin of the conflict that followed. Had the reservoir only been
built in 1921, so this argument runs, the needs of both the city
and the valley could have been met and the subsequent devastation of the valley's land and economy would never have been
necessary.[79] To a limited extent, the argument borrows from the
Socialist attacks on the aqueduct of a decade earlier. Job Harriman, for example, had called for the construction of the Long
Valley dam in the mayoralty campaign of 1911, and the Aqueduct Investigation Board repeated this demand in its report of
1912. But the provenance of the argument is somewhat more

tortuous than this, depending as it must upon a confirmation in retrospect of George Watterson's contention that the agreement he and Symons negotiated meant salvation for the valley. In the context of the events that followed Los Angeles' withdrawal from Long Valley, Watterson's argument for the proposed agreement was taken up by the same people who had been most vociferous in rejecting the agreement itself. Thus Willie Arthur Chalfant, editor of the *Inyo Register*, zealously denounced Watterson and his agreement in 1924 as a betrayal of the valley's interests; then in 1933 he came round to speaking of the Long Valley project as the simple expedient by which the valley might have been preserved.[80]

As the legend of the Owens Valley conflict grew, the decision not to proceed with the Long Valley reservoir became the proof not only of Mulholland's perfidy but of his incompetence as well. Thus Thomas Means, one of the city's most trusted independent consultants, declared in 1941: "Nothing but negligence and reckless disregard of the consequences can explain the failure to immediately construct Long Valley reservoir."[81] And by the time Carey McWilliams wrote his *Southern California Country* in 1946, the memory of events in the Owens Valley had become so blurred that McWilliams wound up describing the Long Valley dam as a superior alternative to the aqueduct itself.[82]

The argument for Long Valley's significance as casus belli fails on several points. It presumes first that the Long Valley project was offered as a means of preserving irrigated agriculture in the Owens Valley. But it was never intended for this purpose. First and foremost, the reservoir was conceived as an essential element in the city's long-term plans for power development in the gorge. Irrigation supply was only a marginal function of the project, included simply as a means of securing the acquiescence of the downstream irrigators in its development. The ditch owners, moreover, had no difficulty in recognizing the inadequacy of what the project offered them. And although the matter never came to a formal accounting, it seems doubtful in the extreme that a dam even at 150 feet could have supplied the conflicting demands of the city, the power company, and the associated ditches. At best, the project might have delayed but not prevented the day when Mulholland realized the city would require all the water of the Owens Valley. But such a delay, especially when it would have had the effect of more deeply entrenching irrigated agriculture in the Owens Valley, could scarcely have been in the best interests of Los Angeles, if the city was in fact already committed to the destruction of the valley by 1921. The argument that abandonment of the Long Valley project demonstrated Mulholland's animosity toward valley agriculture consequently implodes as a result of its failure to explain why, if this was Mulholland's attitude, he ever considered development of the project at all.

More important, the overemphasis which later commentators placed on the Long Valley project failed to grasp the essential genius of the project Mulholland had built and the way he imagined it could be operated. For the real significance of the abandonment of Long Valley as an index of the city's attitude lies in the fact that Mulholland did not consider it very significant at all. Ever since the reservoirs had been excised from the original plans for the aqueduct in 1906, Mulholland had consistently expressed his indifference toward the need for surface storage facilities at either end of his project. It was convenient, of course, for him to speak in this fashion; since he could not afford to construct the reservoirs anyway it was just as well to downplay their importance. But there was an element of conviction as well in Mulholland's argument, drawn from all he had learned of water supply conditions in Southern California.

His experience, after all, had been limited to the South Coast, where groundwater pumping had been a way of life almost since the first white settlements. The one hydrologic system he knew really well was that of the Los Angeles River. And this was a river which, as he often joked, ran upside down; the greater part of its flows occurred beneath the ground and the river itself surfaced at irregular intervals and then only at certain times of the year. But from the years of his youth spent studying this river and its quirks, this elemental man had evolved a singular appreciation for the advantages of groundwater development. "On this coast we do not hesitate to build up great communities on water supplies of this character," he wrote in 1912. "In fact, we believe that underground water supplies stored in gravel beds of this character are the more reliable, freer from contamination, and usually are not subject to evaporation losses."[83]

"I don't like impounded water myself," he told the Aqueduct Investigation Board when they criticized his failure to plan for reservoirs for the aqueduct in the San Fernando Valley. Rather than building dams, he counseled them to look to the Tujunga Wash, where the waters of the Los Angeles River enter a vast bed of sand and gravel: "If you will go there in the winter time, you will find that there is a natural reservoir already constructed by nature. You will find that the water is going into a reservoir that nature made that beats anything that could be built by human hands, in point of capacity, safety, and security from contamination."[84] If no rain fell for seven years, Mulholland declared, the groundwater reservoirs of the San Fernando Valley would still be capable of supporting the city of Los Angeles at its size in 1905.[85]

With this perception that groundwater reservoirs could be used not simply as a supplemental source of supply but more importantly as a far superior substitute for surface storage, Mulholland intuitively grasped the basic elements of a concept for the coordinated development of surface and groundwater resources. It was an idea well in advance of its time. The members of the Aqueduct Investigation Board, for example, dismissed Mulholland's theories as "not worthy of serious consideration."[86] And indeed, the principles of conjunctive use are still today a new, intensely controversial, and only imperfectly realized element in California's water resource planning. But it was this central idea which animated Mulholland's vision of how the aqueduct could be operated as a link between the great groundwater reservoirs of the Owens and San Fernando valleys.

Edwin T. Earl, publisher of the *Los Angeles Express* and a member of the first San Fernando land syndicate, claimed credit for first turning Mulholland's attention to the groundwater potential of the Owens Valley. Earl had grown up in the Owens Valley, and he recalled a meeting with Mulholland soon after the aqueduct was proposed at which he told Mulholland, "You take a well rig up in that valley . . . And along the line of the Aqueduct, between Lone Pine and Charley's Butte . . . you put down a

well, and if I am not mistaken, you will get a spouter every time."
A year or two later, Mulholland came back to Earl to report,
"Well, I tried it; I put down eleven wells . . . Every one is a
corker."[87]

It had not been that simple of course; rather than racing off
with a drilling rig on Earl's unsolicited assurance, Mulholland
had relied heavily upon the United States Geological Survey to
scout the prospects for groundwater development in the valley.
The initial investigations were not encouraging. In its first report
based on field studies conducted in 1904, the survey concluded
that "the only place within Owens Valley where conditions of
flow worthy of note are now known to exist is at Keeler." And
even here, the Inyo Development Company had had to drill 465
feet before it obtained a strong artesian flow.[88]

Undaunted, Mulholland personally took charge of a second
series of field studies conducted from June 1908 to June 1911
under the aegis of the survey. A total of fifteen test wells were
sunk in 1910, and as a result, four major groundwater regions
were identified at Long Valley, Owens Lake, Independence, and
the Bishop-Big Pine area.[89] The Independence field alone, Mulholland claimed, was capable of supplying 17 percent of the
aqueduct's total capacity on a continuous basis, or 55 percent of
all the water the system could carry when intensively pumped for
short periods at times of extreme emergency.[90] While these surveys were going forward, Mulholland kept his hopes to himself.
But once the preliminary reports were in, and after further consultation with the survey's groundwater experts, he was able to
announce confidently that the Owens Valley offered "one of the
greatest artesian reservoirs in the world."[91]

Nothing more was done to develop the groundwater potential
of the Owens Valley until 1918, when the demands of agriculture
in the San Fernando Valley compelled the city to begin seeking
ways to supplement the flows of the aqueduct during the peak of
the irrigation season. Thirty-two wells were sunk in the Owens
Valley in 1918, 1919, and 1920, and air compressors were installed
to augment the artesian flows at eighteen of these sites in 1919.
Even though pumping was necessary for only a few months of
the year, these first wells by the end of 1920 had produced nearly

twenty-five thousand acre-feet for the aqueduct. "Since that time," as one employee of the city water department observed in 1930, "the city has been drilling wells almost without interruption." Even with all this intense activity, however, the *Western Construction News* noted in 1926 that it remained "a little known fact" that Los Angeles was operating one of the largest groundwater management projects in the United States, the water yield of which was exceeded only by Brooklyn's pumping on Long Island.[92]

At the other end of the aqueduct, steps were taken to assure that the abundant flows from the San Fernando Valley's groundwater reservoirs would be maintained. In 1909, the state supreme court granted Los Angeles' request for a halt to the sinking of wells by private irrigators in that area.[93] In 1915, J. B. Lippincott was appointed to the board of engineers laying the initial plans for the spreading of floodwaters captured in the collecting reservoirs of the newly created Los Angeles County Flood Control District; by 1928, these floodwaters accounted for an estimated 10-30 percent of the total groundwater supply of the South Coast.[94] In 1920, the extent of irrigated agriculture in the San Fernando Valley reached a peak of 80,000 acres and thereafter began to decline, to 77,000 acres in 1921 and 73,000 acres in 1922.[95] With pumping virtually eliminated, the valley's groundwater reservoirs, which had been severely depleted in 1905, regained their maximum levels by 1922.[96] And because 20 to 35 percent of all the aqueduct water used in the San Fernando Valley eventually filtered down into the Los Angeles River, the river's flows by 1917 were running consistently higher than they had ever been since the early 1890s.[97]

The success of Mulholland's water management policies at both ends of the aqueduct shaped in turn his attitude toward agriculture in the Owens Valley. The quality of irrigation in the valley had not improved since Clausen and Means decried the waste and inefficiency of local farming operations in 1905. If anything, irrigation practices had become even more primitive by the early 1920s. Because the water was free, it was allowed to run untended for days at a time, washing out roads and turning the lower-lying croplands into swamps. The greatest acreages were given over to pasture and alfalfa, and in these areas waste was especially excessive. Little or no attempt was made to dig furrows to guide the irrigation water released onto these fields. Even in the corn fields, the furrows were dug too long to be efficient.

On the average, the Owens Valley farmers applied water to their fields six to nine times in a normal irrigation season, usually to a depth of two feet for every acre at each application. As one survey of the valley's agricultural practices in September 1919 noted, one such application in some areas of the state would have been sufficient for the entire irrigation season.[98] The California Conservation Commission in 1912 had called on the farmers in the Bishop area to improve their practices, noting that the "present use of water is excessive and it is considered probable that by economical methods the water at present diverted can be made to irrigate most of the agricultural lands in this portion of the valley."[99] By 1920, however, a special report for Los Angeles estimated that the efficiency of agricultural water use among the twenty-eight ditches diverting water from Bishop Creek alone had declined to only 20 percent.[100]

"Gross negligence in handling water is abundantly evident," announced the soils expert Thomas H. Means after a three-day field study in the Bishop area in 1919.[101] According to an agricultural and industrial survey conducted by the California Development Board in 1917, the fields were old and few had been reseeded. The irrigation ditches were overgrown and clogged with weeds, but no effort was made to clear them. Foxtails were spreading throughout the fields unchecked. Residents of the area were bedeviled by infestations of mosquitoes that bred in the large fields of standing water outside Bishop.[102] In addition, the repeated flooding of the fields for irrigation was more than the natural drainage system could manage. Large areas of otherwise productive land were rendered unusable by the concentrations of alkali which so much water carried to the surface of the soil. By 1920, water stood within four inches of the surface on four thousand of the ten thousand acres Means examined in the vicinity of Bishop.[103]

Although the United States Department of Agriculture had proposed the installation of a modern drainage system for the area and the state had offered to supply half the funds needed for its construction, the Bishop ranchers had rejected the suggestion. Only at the site of George Chaffey's settlement at Manzanar could an efficient drainage system be found; elsewhere, as the California Development Board observed, "old times, small farmers, and non-progressive thinking" prevailed.[104] An artificial drainage system would not have been needed, Means contended, if the excessive use of irrigation water could have been curbed. But in the absence of any restraint on the part of the ranchers, the most productive soils became saturated, thereby limiting the selection of crops which could be grown on them. And the few crops which could be planted developed shallow root systems, which meant that still more irrigation water was required to sustain them.[105]

The refusal of the Owens Valley ranchers to improve their operations had been one of the reasons cited by Arthur Powell Davis of the Reclamation Service in support of his decision not to assist with the Fish Slough project.[106] More important, the demands of the ranchers for irrigation water lay at the root of their conflicts with the Southern Sierras Power Company. Thomas Means investigated this conflict following the seizure of the power company's reservoirs in the summer of 1919, and his conclusions were unequivocal: "The shortage heretofore experienced [by the ranchers] is due to wasteful and inefficient methods of use." Means noted that although the operation of the company's power plants provided the downstream irrigators with a better regulated and more dependable water supply than would obtain naturally, the ranchers always needed more. He contrasted the "gross negligence" of their farming practices with the efficiency the power company had brought to its management of the stream flows. "No expense has been spared which would save water or enable a higher efficiency to be obtained from its use," Means noted approvingly of the power company's operations. "It would seem justice," he therefore observed, "to require some attempt on the part of the farmers toward economy of water use to meet at least in a measure the efforts of the power company."[107]

As troubling as agricultural conditions in the Owens Valley

may have been for the Southern Sierras Power Company, from Mulholland's point of view they were ideal. For all the diversions made by the ranchers above the aqueduct intake at Charley's Butte simply acted to regulate the flows of the Owens River into his system. "Just think of it," Mulholland enthused in testimony before Congress in February 1924, "at the present time there is a flow of 400 cubic feet per second in our system, without any snow on the mountains, as a product of the irrigation of those lands last summer." What the ranchers were providing, in effect, through the inefficiency of their operations in the Owens Valley was the same sort of water-spreading which Mulholland was instituting in the San Fernando Valley in the name of greater management efficiency of that region's groundwater reservoirs. Rather than regarding agricultural development in the Owens Valley as inimical to the operation of the aqueduct, Mulholland therefore welcomed it as an essential aid in achieving his conception of the aqueduct as a link between two groundwater reservoirs. And rather than deploring the wasteful and excessive use of water for irrigation in the Owens Valley, Mulholland applauded it because it served his purposes so well. He explained:

> We take all the water there is in the valley for seven months in the year. It all runs through our net; it does not matter whether they use it or not ... That water soaks through the ground and goes right into our system; it gives us a regulated flow into the river. So that the existence of those farming lands there gives us an advantage ... If those lands were not there, the stream would come down in torrents in the summer time, and some of it might get by us.[108]

When asked specifically whether there would be any advantage to the city in curbing irrigation waste in the Owens Valley or acquiring additional water rights there, Mulholland answered,

> Very little. There is some little work that can be done there yet, which I have in mind ... but as a general source of supply, we have about exhausted that resource ... We have already devastated—if the public use of water may be called devastating—more than 80,000 acres in that valley ... marked it down as desert land ... There are still 10,000

or 12,000 acres there that is land capable of being irrigated; but I am in no hurry to deprive them of that water.

As for building reservoirs above the intake, Mulholland considered the idea not worthy of consideration. "If we had had reservoirs up there," he pointed out in 1924, "there would have been long periods when we could not have put any water in them." And though he acknowledged that there might be "occasional waters" at Long Valley, "they would not be of any permanent value; it would be like leaning on a reed . . . There would have been many times when there would be no water of any kind in that reservoir; and a reservoir of that kind is of no earthly use."[109]

When his proposed agreement with the ranchers collapsed in 1922, Mulholland therefore confidently dismissed the Long Valley reservoir as a project that would be wholly superfluous to the water management policies he was already implementing. Its only value lay in its connection to the city's plans for power development in the gorge. And since these plans would take years to reach fruition, Mulholland felt certain that the city had plenty of time to wait for Fred Eaton to die before construction of a dam at Long Valley or any disruption of Owens Valley agriculture would be necessary. Within a year of the abandonment of Long Valley, however, Mulholland was embarked upon an aggressive campaign of land and water rights purchases in the Owens Valley that would bring armed resistance and eventual disaster for the city and the valley.

Things Fall Apart

It was an accumulation of constants rather than any sudden change that brought about this abrupt reversal in Mulholland's thinking. One such constant was the city's continued growth. After a brief lull following the end of the war, new people began pouring into the city at a rate of a hundred thousand a year. In just two and a half years after 1920, more people moved into Los Angeles than in the entire preceding decade. By 1925 the city's population was twice what it had been only five years earlier, and assessments were up 120 percent. Oil fields were booming, the movie industry was firmly established, and the annual tonnage passing through Los Angeles' port soared past that of San Francisco. But real estate remained the city's principal commodity. From 1921 to 1928, 3,233 subdivisions covering nearly fifty thousand acres were formed and 246,612 building lots were created. Tourism was the lure, and Harry Chandler's All Year Club was the mechanism by which millions from the Midwest were drawn to the South Coast, where tens of thousands of real estate agents waited to minister to their needs. "The community is thus a parasite upon the great industrial centers of other parts of America," wrote Upton Sinclair. "It is smug and self-satisfied making the sacredness of property the first and last article of its creed ... Its social life is display, its intellectual life is 'boosting' and its politics are run by Chambers of Commerce and Real Estate Exchanges."[110]

The city's growth rate after 1920 worked to upset all the calculations on which Mulholland had predicated his plans for the aqueduct. Not only were people arriving faster than he had originally predicted, but they were also settling more densely than he had expected. This meant that his estimates of the intensity of water demand in the urban areas were now proving to be just as wrong as his estimates for irrigation demand in the San Fernando Valley had turned out to be by 1917. His basic premise had been that agriculture and urban development would consume the same quantity of water per acre. Under this assumption, the pace at which agricultural lands were converted to urban settlement would not make any difference in the city's water deliveries. The city could therefore afford to embrace thousands of acres in the newly annexed territories without fear that the demand for water in these areas would increase as they were settled. But the assumption was wrong. People were settling at densities of fourteen to the acre and higher, while industrial water demands were running far beyond anything Mulholland had expected.[111] "The tendency from now on will be rather to intensify the density of population," Mulholland observed. "We are rapidly approaching an age of almost universal apartment houses."[112] As a result, each passing year of continued urban expansion intensified the demand for water and increased the disparity in Mulholland's projections.

The aqueduct meanwhile was failing to deliver water in the quantities the city had once hoped. Mulholland had originally assumed that the aqueduct would not be operated continuously, so he had designed the system to allow for some losses due to seepage in order to give him a net capacity of 400 cubic feet per second. In actual operation, however, seepage losses were negligible, with the result that the aqueduct had a somewhat higher capacity than planned.[113] But by 1920 it had delivered a mean annual flow of only 260 cubic feet per second, or approximately 60 percent of its designed capacity.[114] Although aqueduct deliveries increased somewhat in the water year 1921-22, they plummeted again the following year. By 1923, the city was entering the sixth straight year of deficiency in the operation of the aqueduct, and studies revealed that the project would have suffered similar deficiencies in nine of the preceding 19 years.[115]

It was evident by this time that the Owens Valley was in the grip of the worst drought on record. The flows of the Owens River that year dropped to 56 percent of normal, and those on Bishop Creek declined to 46 percent. And to make matters worse, precipitation in Los Angeles dropped to less than half of normal in 1923, thereby marking the beginning of a succession of the driest years the city had experienced since the late 1890s.[116] To meet the deficiency, pumping in the Los Angeles area was abruptly renewed, with the result that groundwater levels which had risen an average of twenty feet under seventy-five thousand acres of the San Fernando Valley by 1922 began to drop fifteen to fifty feet over the next three years.[117]

These conditions did not prove that Mulholland had made an error in rejecting the Long Valley project; there would not have been enough water flowing into the Owens Valley to fill that reservoir in any event. But they did serve to focus attention on the waste within Mulholland's system at the lower end of the aqueduct. These inefficiencies resulted in part from the operation of the city's power plants, but they were to a far greater extent the product of the wide disparity in the demand for irrigation water in the San Fernando Valley at different points in the year. Agriculture in Los Angeles required a quantity of water equivalent to the entire 400 second-foot capacity of the aqueduct for the three months of summer. But in the winter its needs dropped to only 20 cubic feet per second. As a result, Mulholland explained, "For half the year, water from the hydro-electric plants on the Owens River Aqueduct to the extent of about 200 cubic feet per second is wasted into the Los Angeles River because of a lack of irrigation demand."[118]

Mulholland's efforts to improve the storage system at the lower end of the aqueduct through a three-million-dollar bond issue were rejected by the voters in 1921. When the city engineer subsequently proposed treating the city's sewage water for use in irrigation, Mulholland opposed the idea, pointing out that the groundwater reservoir of the San Fernando Valley was already filled to capacity, and in the absence of adequate surface storage facilities in the valley, there would consequently be no way of holding the purified sewage until it was needed.[119] But the dumping of water into the Los Angeles River, which continued for as long as three hundred days out of the year in 1917 and 1918, had grown so excessive by the early 1920s that property owners in the lower end of thc San Fernando Valley complained that their lands were being swamped.[120] Some of this water was recaptured in the sand and gravel beds of the river, but a significant portion of it simply flowed out to sea. Mulholland estimated that in March and April of 1923, more than 15,000 acre-feet of Owens Valley water was turned into the ocean. And by 1925, when the city's needs for water were turning critical, Los Angeles' overall discharge of wastewater into the ocean at Hyperion had risen to 89,100 acre-feet a year.[121]

As these conditions combined and the evidence of their significance mounted, it must have seemed to Mulholland that the work of a lifetime was beginning to come apart at the seams. The result, in the view of one of his closest advisors, was that "hysteria seized the Water Department."[122] New projections of the city's growth rate and water needs were hastily ordered up. Estimates of the future population of Los Angeles differed by as much as 50 percent from one report to the next. Some predicted that the city would exhaust its current water supply by 1928; others were more sanguine where the city was concerned but promised disaster for the metropolitan area as a whole by 1933.[123]

To meet the threat, Mulholland began jettisoning one aspect of his water management program after another. In July 1922 he called for restraint in any future annexations to Los Angeles and recommended instead that any further extension of the city limits should be limited to those territories which would "tend to make the city's outline more symmetrical."[124] On August 8, 1923, he abruptly shut off all deliveries of aqueduct water for the irrigation of alfalfa in the San Fernando Valley and imposed strict limits on water use for all other crops, thereby preventing any winter planting.[125] At the same time, he began throwing up reservoirs at the lower end of the aqueduct. Construction on the Hollywood Reservoir began in August 1923, and water storage commenced there the following June even though the dam for the reservoir would not be completed for another six months. And in the San Francisquito Canyon, Mulholland ordered a 25-percent enlargement of a small regulating reservoir which was already under construction for use in conjunction with the city's power plants.[126]

Restricting nonurban water use and reducing waste were logical and predictable management techniques. But at best they were only stopgap measures which could delay but not prevent the crisis Mulholland now believed was impending unless the city's water supply could be dramatically increased. For the long-term needs of the city, he directed his attention toward the Colorado River.

Los Angeles had been deeply involved in the negotiations for development of the Colorado since 1920, but its interest heretofore had focused exclusively upon securing the hydroelectric power that would be generated at the proposed Boulder Dam. Even with so limited an interest, the city's intercession in the lobbying effort to gain congressional approval of the project had been deeply disturbing to the other parties in this campaign. San Diego, which had initiated the drive for development of the Colorado through the formation of the League of the Southwest, had already been muscled out of its leadership position in California by Los Angeles. The well-known coziness of relations between Mulholland and the head of the federal government's reclamation program, Arthur Powell Davis, quickened the fears of the other states in the Colorado Basin that Los Angeles meant to secure for itself a preferential right to all the power generated by the Boulder Canyon project. And the example of what Los Angeles had already done to the Owens Valley was prominent in the minds of many in the Imperial and Coachella valleys who viewed the city's interest with alarm. "I am skeptical of Los Angeles," declared one representative from San Bernardino at a meeting in 1921 at which Mulholland and Scattergood attempted to assuage these concerns. "She has always been inimical to the interests of the back country when she should be the reverse." Given the choice between Los Angeles' participation in the project and development of the Colorado for the benefit of private power companies, many applauded the view expressed by a Riverside official at the same meeting: "I would rather pay $1.27 per kilowatt hour and get it than have Los Angeles take it all and we get nothing."[127]

Mulholland had visited the Colorado in his youth and had learned more about it from his long association with J. B. Lippincott. Lippincott had surveyed the lower Colorado for Arthur Powell Davis in 1902 and had erroneously identified Boulder and not Black Canyon as the best potential dam site. In 1902, however, Lippincott had dismissed the lower Colorado as an unlikely site for development, arguing that bedrock conditions there would make long-term water storage impossible. Mulholland sent Lippincott back to the area in 1912, and this time he returned with a glowing report in which he described the lower Colorado as "an American Nile awaiting regulation" that would be capable of supporting "a large and prosperous population."[128] Mulholland toured the area early in 1921, but put aside any thought of tapping the Colorado's flows until water supply conditions in the city had so deteriorated by mid-1923 that he was encouraged to readjust his attitude. On October 23, 1923, he obtained the backing of the Board of Public Service Commissioners for a new series of exploratory surveys, and within a week he was back on the Colorado himself conducting what he called a "brush clearing expedition" from two rowboats.[129]

As with the preliminary investigations of the Owens Valley twenty years before, these surveys were conducted quietly, and no bonds had yet been submitted to the voters to support the expenses incurred. But on February 15, 1924, Mulholland appeared before the congressional committee reviewing plans for the Colorado to announce, "I am here in the interest of a domestic water supply for the City of Los Angeles, and that injects a new phase into this whole matter." To quiet the fears of the other basin states, Mulholland promised to "take a noble part, I can assure you, in any project that will be helpful to the country around there generally." As for the ranchers of the Imperial Valley, he declared grandiloquently, "Our need is their need ... Our sympathies are with the people of the Imperial Valley. The people in Imperial Valley are our customers and they are our citizens. They live in Los Angeles, they have to go out there to Imperial Valley and nearly roast themselves to death trying to raise crops for us; and they are as welcome as the flowers in May to come to Los Angeles to cool off."[130]

On the key question of how much water Los Angeles intended to take from the river, Mulholland refused to be specific. And when the city's behavior in the Owens Valley was raised, he became positively obscure. "Everything that we got we got peacefully," he declared stoutly. "We got all the water of Owens Valley that we wanted and never had a lawsuit, never had a condemnation suit ... and never transgressed the rights of anyone." He admitted that he had "only sketchily" discussed the idea of a new aqueduct to the Colorado with the members of his city council. But he assured the congressmen, "Among the old people who know best about the necessities and needs, and among the thinking people there, new or old, the thing has been ratified heartily ... I am the authority there ... when it is shown to them that there is no other means of existence, then they will ratify the proposition without any doubt."[131]

Popular support for Mulholland's policies in Los Angeles after 1920, however, was not nearly so hearty as he had become accustomed to expect. The bond issue proposed in 1921 for improvements to the water system in the San Fernando Valley had marked the first time he had had to turn to the electorate in nearly a decade, and they dealt him his first defeat. Even though the bonds were passed at a second election the following year, the total of votes recorded in opposition was greater than Mulholland had ever encountered.[132] His actions since in cutting off irrigation supplies to the San Fernando Valley had even more deeply divided his reservoir of potential support. For the ranchers of the San Fernando Valley could no longer be treated as outsiders poaching on the city's water rights; since annexation, they were voting citizens of Los Angeles itself. In addition, the labor-oriented *Los Angeles Record* had by this time adopted an editorial policy that was as resolutely opposed to Mulholland's programs as the *Los Angeles Times* had once been supportive. And to top matters off, Mulholland's vehement support of the Boulder Canyon project had now set him at odds with Harry Chandler and the *Times*.

The grounds for Chandler's opposition to the project lay for the most part in Mexico. There Chandler, in association with his ever-constant coinvestors Harrison Gray Otis, Moses Sherman, and Otto Brant, had established a vast ranching operation which eventually embraced 860,000 acres and an additional 1,000 acres on the American side of the border. Chandler had used the editorial pages of the *Times* to promote the Díaz regime in Mexico and to urge American intervention in the Mexican insurrection of 1910, which had threatened to disrupt his ranching operations. He and his associates had subsequently been indicted in 1915 by a United States grand jury on charges that they had conspired to foment a revolution in Baja aimed at overthrowing the Carranza regime, which favored land reforms. The case was eventually dismissed in 1917 on a directed verdict to a jury whose venire was made up principally of Los Angeles businessmen and advertisers in the *Times*.[133]

Chandler did, of course, support flood control on the Colorado, which would have the effect of regulating the flows onto his Mexican holdings. In 1910, the *Times* had led a drive to persuade the Taft administration to construct a system of levees on the Chandler lands above the international boundary. But under an earlier agreement between Mexico and the private development company that first opened the Imperial Valley to settlement, Mexico could claim half the water the ranchers in the Imperial

Valley diverted into the Alamo Canal, an overflow channel of the Colorado which crossed Mexican lands on its way to the valley. As a result, Chandler paid only eighty-six cents per acre-foot in Mexico for the same Colorado River water other ranchers in the Imperial Valley received for eight dollars. Construction of the high dam and the All-American Canal to the Imperial Valley called for in the plans for the Boulder Canyon Project, however, would have put an end to Chandler's competitive advantages and interfered with the flows south to his Mexican holdings. He consequently opposed the project with the same vigor and for much the same reason of self-interest as his father-in-law had formerly supported the aqueduct to the Owens Valley.[134]

Hatred of Harry Chandler had been one of several factors which rallied the Imperial Valley ranchers in support of the Boulder Canyon Project and its All-American Canal. Quite apart from the advantages Chandler enjoyed in Mexico, the ranchers resented his preference for leasing his holdings to Mexican, Japanese, and Chinese farmers, thereby giving water to "Japs and Chinamen" which they felt properly should go to "red-blooded free Americans."[135] Philip Swing, cosponsor of the project in Congress with Senator Hiram Johnson, consequently welcomed Chandler's hostility, claiming that Chandler was "building Boulder Dam by his opposition to it."[136] In Los Angeles, Chandler threw his support behind the mayoralty campaign of George E. Cryer in 1921 while at the same time opposing a $35-million bond issue for the distribution of hydroelectric power from Boulder Dam. Cryer won and the bonds were defeated. But once in office, Cryer switched his position and began supporting the Boulder Canyon project. Chandler's efforts to remove Cryer from office in 1923 were unsuccessful. So at the time Mulholland declared his support for the high dam and the All-American Canal in 1924, Chandler was already organizing a strong conservative alliance to defeat Cryer at the next election and replace him with a candidate who many feared would allow Chandler himself to name the city's water and power commissioners.[137]

Mulholland therefore faced an especially complicated political situation as he set out to reach the Colorado. To succeed, he needed not only to hold the support of the city but also to persuade its outlying communities to join in underwriting the costs of the endeavor. In this way, he could avoid the state-mandated limitation on the amount of indebtedness an individual city may incur which had delayed the start of his first aqueduct for nearly two years. His call for a reduction in new annexations to the city, of course, aided this undertaking because each area that was denied access to aqueduct water by reason of his new policy of symmetry became a ready candidate for enlistment in the new metropolitan water district Mulholland was trying to form. But even so, the course would be long and time-consuming. Once enough cities with a combined assessed valuation sufficient to meet the limitation on indebtedness were lined up, he needed to secure the approval of the state legislature to form the district. And then he had to lead the district in lobbying the authorization for the project through Congress.

To meet the challenge, Mulholland fell back on the tactics of panic which had served him so well during his first campaign for the aqueduct. He now warned that a "disastrous water shortage" was looming. He recalled the conditions which had necessitated construction of the aqueduct to the Owens Valley, and then confirmed: "We are today facing a similar situation . . . an additional supply will be required, and if not at hand, Los Angeles will have reached the limit of its growth."[138] These were the "unvarnished facts," and the "half-baked objections" of those who opposed the project were "utterly foolish."[139] When this disaster would occur did not seem to matter much. By 1928 Mulholland was using deadlines of eight, ten, and twelve years interchangeably, depending on his audience. Whatever date he picked, however, he always assured his listeners that "every minute" of the time period specified would be needed to make the additional water available.[140]

A definition of how much water would be needed was equally hard to come by. On the Colorado, Mulholland had originally asked for a thousand cubic feet per second, but he formally filed in June 1924 for fifteen hundred.[141] The city's studies suggested that the overall needs of the South Coast would rise to roughly twice this amount by 1950.[142] By 1927, the state engineer was vaguely predicting an even greater need. "In order that growth and expansion may continue to the full limit of the natural resources other than water," he wrote, "the Pacific Slope of Southern California will require three times the volume of water that can be obtained from nature's allotment to this territory. Unless this additional water can be secured, the future must face a curtailed growth incommensurate with the opportunities offered by the other natural endowments of this remarkable territory."[143] In the end, however, the backers of the project settled for the filings Mulholland had already made on the Colorado. As the economist W. C. Yeatman observed in 1932:

> The extremely rapid growth of Los Angeles immediately after the World War created in some minds the idea of indefinite expansion, with the vision of a future tremendous city, lacking only an adequate water supply to become the largest in the World . . . The quantity fixed on was 1,000,000 acre-feet, or in round numbers, 1,500 second-feet, which became traditional and irrevocable as time went on. All studies of the [Metropolitan Water District] have been made on this basis, though some have been admittedly guided to justify this preconceived idea.[144]

Whatever the amount of water the city might need, and whenever it might be needed, Mulholland recognized that the new supplies from the Colorado would not be available any time soon. By the time all the necessary approvals had been secured and the canal built, the water crisis Mulholland imagined looming might already have struck Los Angeles. An interim source of additional water would therefore have to be found. Such a supply was available in the Mono Basin, and the revisions in the aqueduct's right-of-way bill had opened the way to its acquisition. But development of the Mono Basin and the extensive construction needed to bring its water resources down to the aqueduct would also take years to accomplish. So, as the mood of hysteria in the city water department mounted following the dry winter of 1922-23, Mulholland began to rethink his attitudes toward the Owens Valley.

The outlines for a new policy in the Owens Valley were provided by a series of three reports prepared for the city in October and November 1923 and January 1924 by the independent consultant Thomas H. Means. A soils expert, Means had taken his engineering degrees at George Washington University and then worked with the United States Department of Agriculture and the Reclamation Service before setting up his own consulting practice in 1910. Having served as the first Reclamation Service engineer on the Newlands project outside Reno, Means was indeed familiar with the water resources of the eastern slope of the Sierra, and his subsequent work in private practice had involved him with numerous irrigation projects in Shasta and Tehama counties.[145] In the Owens Valley region he had been part of Clausen's initial survey for the Reclamation Service, and he had since been retained frequently to prepare hydrologic studies for both Los Angeles and the Southern Sierras Power Company.[146]

Ever since his first visit to the valley with Clausen, Means had deplored the wastefulness of the ranchers' irrigation practices, and he had expressed his belief that agriculture in the valley could operate effectively on half the water it was presently consuming.[147] He was convinced, moreover, that Los Angeles faced certain disaster; and to support his case, he prepared projections of the city's future water needs showing a 42-percent increase in total consumption over the next five years leading to a critical shortage as early as 1928. "The limit of water is the limit of growth," he forcefully reminded Mulholland.[148]

Means was critical as well of Mulholland's operation of the aqueduct. "The supply [from the Owens Valley] has proven deficient—the aqueduct cannot be kept full," he stated flatly. The problem, he argued, lay in Mulholland's tolerance of continued agricultural activity in the valley. Whereas Mulholland estimated that the loss of water from the ranchers' irrigation practices amounted to no more than 10 or 12 percent of the total amount they spilled over their fields each year, Means contended that fully two-thirds of the water they used to flood their fields evaporated before it had a chance to seep into the ground and eventually trickle down to the aqueduct.[149]

The solution, Means felt, was obvious. For the long term, he recommended acquisition of the total water supply of the Mono Basin and construction of a second aqueduct to carry the resource south to Los Angeles. He admitted that such an undertaking might cost the city $56 million once the power plants in the gorge were added in but expressed confidence that this development would guarantee Los Angeles enough water to supply a population of 4.7 million.[150] For the immediate future, he advocated an aggressive expansion of the city's groundwater pumping program. He called on Mulholland to extend his operations northward into the Bishop area, where Means proposed to sink two hundred new wells which he estimated would be capable of supplying the entire flow of the aqueduct. "The City of Los Angeles can protect its water supply for all time and insure the full aqueduct supply if it will take the precaution of drilling wells in this territory," Means promised. And the cost would be minor: only $120,000 a year in operating expenses to secure an assured supply of 750,000 acre-feet of water.[151]

An extension of the city's land acquisitions into the Bishop area in order to deplete its groundwater supply would, of course, mean devastation for Owens Valley agriculture. But Means considered this cost to be similarly negligible. "The logic of the situation is so clear that there is no question about what the business judgment of the managers of the city's affairs will dictate," he concluded. "This fertile region will be nearly depopulated in the future in order to make more water available for the rapidly growing city."[152]

But implementation of such a policy for the maximum exploitation of the water resources of the Owens Valley would not be easy. For just as Mulholland was facing a higher level of organized opposition in the city, he had a new set of adversaries to contend with in the Owens Valley as well. The rejection of the Long Valley agreement of 1921 had put an end to the prominence of George Watterson and William Symons among the associated ditch owners. Leadership of the irrigators' interests had subsequently passed to Watterson's nephews, Wilfred and Mark Watterson. And they brought to the task a far greater measure of financial acumen and organizational skill than Mulholland had ever encountered in his dealings with the valley.

The Manx People

The Watterson brothers were the scions of one of the valley's older and more distinguished families. Their parents, William and Eliza, had grown up together on the Isle of Man and married just before they set sail for California in 1869, accompanied by William's brother Mark. The two men found work as sheepherders, first in Stockton and then in Kern County, for which they were paid in room, board, and a portion of the increase of their flock. In time, they built up a flock of their own, which they brought across the mountains from Delano to graze on the slopes above Bishop each summer. In 1886, the family took up permanent residence in the valley, on adjoining ranches three miles north of Bishop. Profits did not come quickly; freight rates ran as high as three cents a pound on wool that sold for only ten cents in San Francisco. But the family grew its own alfalfa, corn, and other grains to feed their animals in winter, and over the years they prospered. Mark returned to the Isle of Man, but William's other two brothers, James and George, as well as two sisters eventually joined the family, and they all settled on the eastern side of the Sierra in Bishop, Benton, and Virginia City.[153]

William was a courtly man of modest learning and upright character, "a man to be loved, firm, steadfast, and a man respected."[154] Mary Austin knew him when she taught at the Inyo Academy with his two sons Wilfred and Mark and daughter Isabella. And she described him fondly as the Manxman in her book *The Flock*: "In time I grew to know the owner of the flocks being the Three Legs of Man, and as I sat by his fire, touching his tempered spirit as one half draws and drops a sword in its scabbard for pleasure of its fineness, being flockwise I understood why the herders hereabout gave him the name of the Best Shepherd."[155] Eliza complemented his quiet strength with a quick mind and a love of books which she instilled in her children along with her devotion to temperance and the Methodist Church.

They had seven children in all, three sons followed in succession by four daughters, although the third son, Eldred, died while very young. Wilfred, the eldest, was born within a year of his parents' arrival in California and so grew up traveling with the flocks. He was an astonishingly handsome man with fine aquiline features and an elegance of bearing which he liked to show to its best effect when touring as a young man in the first automobile in the valley. But there was a sadness to him as well. He married unhappily to a woman whose father went mad and whose mother moved in with them. His wife soon took to her bed and then to a clinic in Battle Creek, Michigan, from which she returned a Seventh Day Adventist. The costs of caring for his wife and maintaining her mother imposed a burden, while his wife's extended illnesses forbade the kind of socializing he most enjoyed.

His brother Mark, seven years the junior, though lacking Wilfred's elegance and good looks, was by far the happier of the two. Along with his sunny disposition, Mark maintained careful habits and profound convictions. Their friends recalled Wilfred as "high strung and quick of action," whereas Mark was "slower but nonetheless decisive."[156] Despite the contrasts in their temperament, the two were devoted to one another and worked well together. In their assorted business ventures, it was usually Wilfred who assumed the outward appearance of leadership, while Mark, in his capacity as treasurer and accountant, tended to the real work of running the family's investments.

Their mother encouraged Wilfred and Mark to open a hardware business in 1896 and provided her own small inheritance to get them started. The boys kept a safe in the store and a bank account in San Francisco, and their neighbors became accustomed to bringing their savings to the Watterson brothers for safekeeping. In 1902, again with their mother's support and encouragement, the brothers founded the first bank on the eastern Sierra, with Wilfred as president and Mark as treasurer. Although others soon followed with banking ventures of their own, all were eventually absorbed by the Wattersons' Inyo County Bank. And by 1912, when their father died, the brothers' bank was flourishing, with total assets listed in excess of $700,000.[157]

Their success in banking and hardware encouraged the two men to extend their interests into other areas of the valley's economy. They opened the first gasoline station in the valley and invested heavily in the tungsten mines below Owens Lake. Wilfred took a special interest in the soda works that Captain James M. Keeler had first established on the lake. Wilfred's Natural Soda Products Company, however, ran into difficulties almost from the start. With the diversion of the Owens River flows into the aqueduct in 1913, the lake began to dry up. And although the city paid $15,000 to cover his damages, this barely made up for the expenses he incurred in bringing in new machinery to accommodate the different methods of extraction the receding lake level made necessary. Once the plant had been retooled, in time to take advantage of the higher prices that came with the outbreak of World War I, it promptly burned down. But the Wattersons rebuilt the plant and adhered strictly to the contracts they had signed, even though this meant that by the end of the war they were supplying soda products at a fifth of the price they could have commanded.[158]

A later involvement in the valley's tourist industry fared even less well. Efforts began in 1917 to tout the curative powers of the valley's "volcanic mineral water," and by the early 1920s the brothers were bottling mud and water in five-gallon jugs for Coso Hot Springs, Incorporated. Although an office was opened in Los Angeles to sell the water on the claim that it "builds blood, aids digestion, and salves stomach ailments," the products apparently lost their powers in shipment, and the business floundered.[159]

Despite these setbacks, the brothers gained a reputation in the valley for scrupulousness, fairness, and competence in their business dealings.[160] When Bishop incorporated in 1903, Wilfred served on the first town council and Mark was treasurer.[161] And when the valley ditch companies had formed their association in 1900, Mark had been elected chairman.[162] Since that time, however, the brothers had remained for the most part at the periphery of the valley's struggle with Los Angeles. They did, of course, join with all the other major landowners in signing the mass petition in November 1904 endorsing the Reclamation Service's plan. But their names were noticeably absent from the later petition of August 1905 asking for a formal investigation by the Secretary of the Interior of the service's dealings with Los Angeles.[163] Mark Watterson, in fact, is listed by the city as one of the first landowners to have offered the city two hundred acres for the aqueduct.[164] Later, when Galen Dixon was promoting the Fish Slough reservoir, Wilfred Watterson wrote to Arthur Powell Davis on the ditch owners' behalf asking the service to consider funding the project.[165] But when his uncle George took over the negotiations with the city, Wilfred's attitude turned sour, and Dixon eventually came to regard Wilfred as his enemy.[166]

Whatever their previous attitudes toward Los Angeles may have been, Wilfred and Mark Watterson were peculiarly well equipped to lead the valley in meeting the new onslaught of acquisitions the city launched in 1923. Los Angeles in its drive to secure the water resources of the Owens Valley had always enjoyed the advantage of a single-minded sense of purpose which had enabled Mulholland to divide the valley's interests and deal with them piecemeal. The Watterson brothers, however, brought to the situation an essential ability to unify the valley in a way it had never been before. Through their extensive involvement in agriculture, mining, industry, and mercantilism, the Wattersons dominated the commercial life of the valley. Their Inyo County Bank, moreover, provided what Willie Arthur Chalfant, publisher of the *Inyo Register*, called "the strong right arm on which the business of Owens Valley has confidently leaned . . . the balance wheel of Inyo County whenever one was needed." Apart from Chalfant's newspaper, in fact, the Wattersons' bank, with mortgages outstanding on more than a third of the local farms, provided the one common element that linked all the far-flung communities of the valley.[167]

Equally important, as the developing situation would reveal, was the membership of the family itself. For as wide as Wilfred's and Mark's interests were, their sisters' marriages extended the family's reach still farther. J. C. Clausen, the lonely champion of the Reclamation Service's original project in the Owens Valley and a frequent consultant to the associated ditch owners in their negotiations with Los Angeles ever since, married Elizabeth Watterson. Mary Watterson married into the Gorman family, whose farm outside Independence had first inspired Thomas Means in 1904 to recognize the potential of the Owens Valley for systematic irrigation.[168] And Isabel Watterson married Court Kunze, a gifted publicist who, with Carl Glasscock, had founded the short-lived *Inyo* and *Chuckawalla* magazines and the more enduring *Owens Valley Herald*. Control of the *Herald* by this time had passed to Carl's son Harry, but Court Kunze retained a lively interest in the paper's editorial policy, and Harry Glasscock proved an invaluable ally to the Wattersons.[169] The fourth sister, Elsie, never married, and Mary was absent from the valley during the 1920s. But all these individuals had played a part in the historical development of the valley and its water resources; and their experience in turn worked both to inform and to reinforce the response Wilfred and Mark Watterson would make to the city's new program.

Among those who achieved particular prominence in the resistance to Los Angeles in the conflict that followed, only Willie Arthur Chalfant was not directly connected to the Watterson family, and his hostility toward the city and its aqueduct had been unrelenting from the first. It is, of course, not uncommon to find so many liaisons among the prominent members of a community when people in the valley as a whole numbered only seven thousand during the 1920s. But this in no way diminishes the significance of the fact that the Wattersons could gather around their family table the same sort of concentration of influence and expertise that the members of the San Fernando land syndicate had earlier applied with such effect in Los Angeles.

One member of the family, however, stood apart, and that was the uncle, George Watterson. He was much younger than his brother William and only ten years older than his nephew Wilfred. Like Wilfred, he was a proud man with a strong will and a taste for show. He had come from the Isle of Man alone, at the age of seventeen, and had studied at the University of Southern California and tried his hand at mining before he threw in with the family's growing livestock business. George always kept a part of himself distinct from the life of the family. He flaunted his education and clung doggedly to his English heritage, maintaining a subscription to the London *Times* throughout his life. In time, he came to resent the success of his brother's eldest son. When Wilfred was twenty, he and George both filed applications with the public land office for use of the same plot of mountain land, Wilfred for grazing and George for mining. Wilfred won the contest, and that victory opened a breach between the two men which never healed.

George soon opened a hardware store in Bishop to compete with Wilfred. Although both prospered, their differences remained unresolved. Wilfred established his home on the north side of Bishop, George on the south side, and the rivalry continued. When George found success with cattle, Wilfred established a herd of his own; and although Wilfred soon discovered that it is impossible to run a cattle ranch from a bank office, in most of their competitive endeavors the younger man proved himself the better. Perhaps the rivalry had something to do with Wilfred's opposition to the Long Valley agreement George Watterson negotiated in 1921. But there is no question that, once that agreement fell apart, Wilfred leaped at the opportunity to take over where his uncle had failed.

With the enthusiastic support of both Chalfant's *Register* and Glasscock's *Herald*, Wilfred proposed that the ditch owners and the ranchers they served should form an irrigation district to deal with Los Angeles in united strength. Since the district would have the authority to issue bonds based on the assessed valuation of the lands it embraced, this new form of organization would enjoy the strong financial base that the ditch owners' incorporated association lacked. George Watterson and William Symons denounced the proposal as "a delusion and a snare" which would "overwhelm the taxpayer with a burden too heavy to bear, the weight of which . . . [will] eventually force him to sell (if he has anything left) on the City's own terms."[170] But on December 26, 1922, the proposal was approved by a popular vote of 599 to 27. And a week later Wilfred Watterson was installed as the new district's president with his brother Mark as treasurer.[171]

The Owens Valley Irrigation District covered all the arable lands between the Owens River Canal on the west and the McNally Ditch on the east, an area of nearly fifty-four thousand acres with an assessed valuation in excess of five million dollars. All eleven of the major canals and ditch companies in the upper valley eventually joined the district. In a year of average precipitation, the district's members drew 156,000 acre-feet from the river and its tributaries, an amount slightly more than half the total demand of the aqueduct, and they asserted claims to more than 180,000 acre-feet.[172] As a governmental entity, however, the district existed for the most limited of purposes. From its inception, its officers declared that they had no intention of investing in a drainage system or making any other improvements to the existing irrigation system beyond the minor expenses of maintenance required to sustain the district's legal existence. Instead, its principal function was to act as a bargaining unit which would "effect unity of purpose and mutual protection . . . [from] encroachments of interests other than agricultural."[173]

The chief counsel to the city's water department, W. B. Mathews, had initially encouraged the ranchers to form such an organization in order to give the city a single point of contact for its negotiations with the valley. Mathews had even proposed where the district's boundaries should be fixed.[174] Once the district had been formed, however, Mulholland promptly began to reconsider the wisdom of Mathews' initiative. A policy of dealing with the Owens Valley interests individually had worked well for him when Eaton made his initial acquisitions for the city, and Mulholland had no desire to make any change now. The determination was therefore made to destroy the district before it could firmly establish itself. Any hope of persuading Eaton to act as the city's agent in this undertaking had been lost with the collapse of the Long Valley agreement. But George Watterson and William Symons had shown themselves to be more than amenable to the city's purpose in their negotiations over Long Valley. At the beginning of March 1923 Watterson and Symons, accompanied by their attorney, Leicester C. Hall, were invited to return to Los Angeles for the purpose of receiving a new proposal.

Symons, Hall, and Watterson held key positions with three of the largest ditch companies in the new district. Symons was president of the McNally Ditch; Watterson was secretary of the Bishop Creek Ditch; and Hall was treasurer of the Owens River Canal Company. Together, the three companies accounted for 56 percent of the acreage, 62 percent of the assessed valuation, and 65 percent of the water diversions made by the district as a whole. If the city could buy out these three companies, the district would be broken and the deficiency in the aqueduct's intake would be largely made up.

Together they agreed to strike first at the McNally Ditch, oldest and largest in the valley. Using Symons' influence among the company stockholders, the three men were able to secure options for the city on two-thirds of the company's land and water rights within a single day. Hall was heard to boast on the streets of Bishop that "they had broken the right arm of the irrigation district."[175] A stockholders' meeting was called immediately to review the situation and to exercise the city's proxies to rescind the action by which the company had earlier turned over its water rights to the irrigation district. Symons presided, but Hall held the floor with bitter denunciations of Chalfant and the Wattersons and praise for Mulholland as the "Moses of Los Angeles." Those who refused to let the city vote their stock were warned that their options would not be taken up, and indeed, almost all who did not vote with the city at that meeting found that their lands were in fact left unpurchased for a year and a half. As for the unfortunate third who had not yet given options on their land, they were warned to settle quickly or they would be left "high and dry."[176]

With this victory behind them, Symons, Watterson, and Hall pressed on through the summer of 1923 extending the city's reach into the Owens River, Bishop Creek, and Big Pine canal companies. As with the McNally Ditch, their efforts were focused on the key properties which controlled the points of access to the river, so that the less favorably situated ranchers inland could be cut off from their water supply if they refused to negotiate. Their actions were denounced as "nothing short of criminal" by the local papers, and Hall was dismissed from his position as treasurer of the Owens River Canal Company.[177] But before he left, Hall gathered up the company records showing the indebtedness, interest rates, and mortgage due dates of every rancher on the canal, and this information became a powerful lever in his attempts to pressure the ranchers into selling.[178]

Symons profited hugely from his work for the city. The land and water rights which he sold for himself and his family brought in nearly $500,000, and for his properties under the McNally Ditch he was paid nearly twice as much per acre as the average price the city paid for all the other lands served by that company.[179] On top of this, he received a 3-percent commission on all the other sales he negotiated for Mulholland. But profit was not the only motivation for the three men. Watterson, for example, received a comparatively modest $48,000 for his lands and no commissions. Hall had no lands to sell but was paid an undisclosed amount of attorney's fees by the city.[180] For Hall and George Watterson, however, there was compensation in the satisfaction they drew from injuring the enterprise of Wilfred and Mark. George had married into Symons' family and so was able to bring him along with ease. Hall was more of a misfit. An Amherst graduate with a love for music, he had traveled in Alaska before deciding to stand for the bar in the Owens Valley. He had once courted Elizabeth Watterson, but that was before Clausen had arrived in the valley and won her heart. Although he later married Nevada Butler, step-daughter of the founder of Tonopah, she died while he was away in the war. Thereafter he grew lonely and resentful. Chalfant once suggested that Hall, in the midst of these purchases, proclaimed his determination to "ruin the valley if it's the last act of my life."[181] And as events progressed in 1923, it very nearly was.

Wilfred and Mark Watterson responded to the loss of the McNally Ditch with a redoubled determination to blunt the city's advance. On March 20, four days after Symons disclosed his purchase of the McNally stock options for the city, the district's board of directors announced its intention to issue $1.65 million in bonds.[182] On May 29, the California Bond Certification Commission authorized the bond issue to be put to a vote, although it expressed its alarm at the deteriorating situation in the valley and the city's "possible tendency to favor a minority local group."[183]

Mathews meanwhile persisted in his efforts to negotiate a settlement with the valley as a whole which would release for the aqueduct the same quantity of water Mulholland was bent on buying up bit by bit. The need for a general settlement seemed obvious. For each time Mulholland acquired water rights in the upper part of the valley, the ranchers downstream simply recaptured the additional flows to the aqueduct by increasing their diversions from the river. Mathews' proposal ran into the same problem in July when the ranchers on the Owens River and Big Pine Canal objected to the effect Mathews' plan would have on their diversions. Mathews arranged to meet with them on August 13, three days before the district bonds were scheduled to come to a vote. But Mulholland was infuriated by the ranchers' interference with the water rights he had bought and paid for, and his precipitate response once again undercut Mathews' attempt to achieve a negotiated settlement. On the same Sunday afternoon Mathews was scheduled to meet with the ranchers, Mulholland sent work crews to cut the intake of the Big Pine Canal. Farmers on their way to see Mathews came upon this work in progress and soon rallied with guns to drive off the city's men. The meeting was a shambles, and the district bonds were approved by a vote of 702 to 80.[184]

Mulholland followed up his attack on the Big Pine Canal by ordering the destruction of a small dam which stored water for Fred Eaton's lands at Long Valley. But this act too only had the effect of strengthening support for the Wattersons' district. Fred Eaton, finding himself in the unfamiliar role of defender of the valley, urged the residents of the upper valley to join behind the district. He proclaimed:

> The people of the Owens Valley Irrigation District have it in their power at the present time to protect their homes, the homes of their friends and neighbors, and this section as a whole if they will ... bend all their efforts ... immediately to turning over these rights to the district ... Failure to do this spells nothing but ruin for this country for wherever the hand of Los Angeles has touched Owens Valley it has turned it back into a desert.[185]

Where direct action had failed, the city soon proved the courts could prevail. Before any bonds could be issued, George Watterson protested to the state bond commission. A suit was filed in the name of two local ranchers to enjoin the sale, and Watterson and Symons guaranteed the men who brought the suit against any financial loss. Symons and his wife, meanwhile, sued to have the district itself declared null and void in an action brought by Hall. And the city entered its own action asking for a delay in the issuance of any bonds until a formal determination of water rights could be made in the valley as a whole. Technical deficiencies in the bond sale were found and a restraining order was issued. Although $470,000 in bonds were eventually sold at a discount of 88.5 cents on the dollar, the district's financial future had been effectively strangled by litigation.[186]

The defeat of the district's bonds brought an incendiary reaction from Chalfant. "In such days as those when J. B. Lippincott did not dare to show himself in Bishop," Chalfant commented editorially at the beginning of 1924, "persons who followed the course taken by Hall, Watterson and Symons would have found some other place much safer than the one in which they have made their living for so many years, and where today they are generally execrated . . . How long must this community have within it these men whose activities mean loss and injury to every property owner?"[187] Watterson and Symons bitterly protested this "lawless appeal to passion and mob violence" and denied that their actions would ruin the valley, claiming, "there has been nothing left to ruin" since the defeat of the Long Valley agreement.[188] "Those who believe that George Watterson and Symons are actuated by . . . any regard for the community's welfare, will rub their right ears with their left elbows," Chalfant retorted.[189] Hall's defiant attitude, meanwhile, made him a particular object of resentment; and on August 27, 1924, he was seized by a band of angry ranchers in Bishop, driven out of town, and told never to return.[190]

The Wattersons were far from finished. Rather, the loss of funding for the district helped bring them to the same conclusions Thomas Means had already reached. They recognized that the valley was now engaged in a contest it could not possibly win. As a bargaining agent, their district could not prevent the city from absorbing all the water resources of the Owens Valley. That had been inevitable—as Lippincott had realized almost twenty years earlier—ever since President Roosevelt had determined that the greater public interest would be served by a greater Los Angeles. But the district could be used to make the city's inevitable conquest expensive. Their strategy henceforth assumed that the valley would have to sell out, and it was geared, in consequence, at extracting the highest price possible. That vision of impending prosperity Mary Austin described had at last materialized, and its shape was certain destruction for the Owens Valley.

The accuracy of their perception could be read in the steadily escalating prices the city had to pay for its new acquisitions in the Owens Valley, and the success of their strategy could be measured by the same standard. When the city made its initial round of purchases in 1905 and 1906 it had paid an average of $14.89 an acre and grumbled then that the properties cost more than they were worth for any other purpose.[191] By the end of 1923 the city was negotiating at prices more than four times higher than the values fixed on the county assessment roles. For the properties on the McNally Ditch, the city in March paid an average of $145 an acre. Six months later the prices had jumped again, and the city found itself laying out more than $250 an acre for its acquisitions on the Bishop and Big Pine canals. And for the lands served by the Owens River Canal, the city was offering to pay $279 an acre.[192] In the early months of 1924 the Wattersons, speaking for the business interests of the upper valley, offered to sell the entire town of Bishop and all its surrounding lands within the irrigation district for a total of $8.75 million. The ranchers who supported the district were no longer fighting for their homes, only for money.

This was not a viewpoint that was widely shared, of course, at least not at first. Many valley residents continued to dream of a brighter future and to build for its arrival. The county erected a new courthouse in 1920. Between 1922 and 1925, Bishop constructed a new high school, an American Legion hall, and a Masonic temple. Even the Wattersons invested in a new commercial block for the town; and in Laws the local farmers' cooperative put up a large new warehouse for their crops. The years 1921 through 1923, moreover, had been good for valley agriculture. Although the cattle market was somewhat depressed, the sheep business was flourishing. The agricultural depression that swept other parts of the nation during the 1920s did not reach California until the end of the decade. And many in the valley looked forward to a great expansion in the acreage devoted to the growing of corn that would eventually displace alfalfa as the county's principal commercial crop.[193] Even Willie Arthur Chalfant concluded a history of the valley he wrote in 1922 on a hopeful note, praising the aqueduct as "a wonderful enterprise worthy of an ambitious city," and promising, "We shall gladly list with [Los Angeles' achievements] the professions of amity, whenever by meeting the just and reasonable demands of Owens Valley the city shall show that any consideration it may extend arises from the sense of equity, and not merely as an incident in securing some further concession."[194]

But by 1924, the confusion of the city's policies and the uncertainties it created had begun to take their toll. Crop production declined by half as more and more farms were taken out of operation by the city's advance. A total of sixty-six farms had been purchased by the city in 1923 alone. National and state banks which could have provided farm relief withdrew from the area, explaining that there could be no loans until economic conditions within the valley stabilized. Even the Veterans Welfare Commission advised its applicants that they could receive loans up to $7,500 for settlement anywhere but in Inyo. Schools began to close in Laws, North Inyo, and Poletta. The Alfalfa Growers Association closed their warehouse in Bishop and the pear growers disbanded their association altogether. The economy of the Owens Valley was further damaged by an outbreak of hoof and mouth disease in 1924 which required the imposition of a strict quarantine that cut tourist traffic by an estimated 75 percent.[195]

"Effort after effort was made by Owens Valley's people, during these trying years, to have Los Angeles announce a definite program, whatever it might be, so that the future might be planned," Chalfant later wrote. "The lack of such an understanding was one of the most injurious facts of the whole controversy."[196] In May 1924, Wilfred Watterson told a gathering of businessmen from the city's Chamber of Commerce, "Los Angeles should deal collectively with the Owens River Valley, buy up all the farms and pay the towns an indemnity for their losses, and then take all the water. Or Los Angeles should leave the valley absolutely alone and tell the world about it so we can go ahead. As it is, the uncertainty has ruined all confidence."[197]

Mulholland, however, resisted the policy of wholesale devastation which Means had urged upon him and which the Wattersons sought to compel him to pursue. He continued to cling instead to the remnants of his earlier policy toward the valley. Los Angeles and the Owens Valley, in his view, had coexisted comfortably and prosperously ever since the aqueduct began, and he saw no reason why that relationship should not continue, albeit under somewhat altered circumstances. Although he agreed that the issue for the valley involved a choice between development or destruction, he genuinely saw himself as the opponent of destruction.[198] His objectives in the valley were consequently limited. He hoped to secure through his purchases clear title to one-third of the river's flow and increased access to the valley's most productive groundwater pumping areas. And by the end of 1923, when the city held nearly all the ranches served by the McNally, Russell, and Big Pine ditches, the end appeared to be in sight. Means estimated that Mulholland needed only another twelve thousand acres of principally poorer and swampy lands to accomplish his purpose.[199]

But Mulholland's attitudes were dangerously outmoded. He consistently failed to appreciate the depth of the anger his policies were creating among the ranchers. Instead, he dismissed the "widespread spirit of bitter antagonism" he was encountering as the product of propaganda. "Dissatisfaction in the valley? Yes, a lot of it," he commented in response to an inquiry from the *Times*. "Dissatisfaction is a sort of condition that prevails there, like the foot and mouth disease . . . There are those in the valley like Tam O'Shanter's wife, who nursed her wrath to keep it warm."[200] More important, by refusing to deal with the ranchers collectively as they demanded, Mulholland's program of limited acquisitions became vulnerable to the reactions of individual irrigators. Purchase of the McNally Ditch, as Mulholland learned, in no way assured that the ranchers on the Big Pine Canal would allow any additional water to flow past their lands to the aqueduct. The ranchers' persistent diversions consequently upset Mulholland's policy and compelled him repeatedly to extend the range of his acquisitions.

Mulholland's drive to increase groundwater pumping had the same effect. By 1930, Los Angeles had drilled a total of 171 wells in the Owens Valley to depths ranging from 100 to 850 feet. In the Independence region alone, Mulholland between 1923 and 1926 installed 52 new wells throughout a zone one mile wide and twenty miles long running along the west side of the aqueduct. All were outfitted with the new electric turbine pumps, and by the beginning of 1924 they were running continuously at a maximum pumpage rate of 325 cubic feet per second. But, by operating at this intensity over extended periods of time, Mulholland soon found that his estimates of the potential yield from pumping had been grossly overoptimistic. Groundwater levels began dropping rapidly; production decreased to 247 cubic feet per second as the shallower wells ran dry. At their peak, the wells never yielded more than 72 percent of their total installed capacity. And these disappointments forced Mulholland to extend his pumping operations farther north into the Bishop and Big Pine regions. His protestations of good will toward the valley, moreover, ignored the effect that intensive pumping would have on agricultural activities in the croplands surrounding his well fields. As the water table dropped ten and twenty feet, the ranchers called on their supervisors to act on behalf of the county as a whole. And when these appeals failed, the ranchers brought suit individually to halt this interference with their water supply. Rather than allow these cases to come to trial, Mulholland had to buy out each of the protesting landowners.[201]

The Wattersons and their allies could shred Mulholland's policies so easily because they knew they had time on their side. As the drought persisted and Mulholland whipped himself and his city into a frenzy over the water crisis he imagined was looming, their advantage increased. At the beginning of 1924, Los Angeles' population soared past the one million mark, while aqueduct deliveries dropped 20 percent to slightly more than half the system's capacity. The next year the aqueduct supply declined still farther, to the lowest level since the project had gone into full operation in 1917.[202] The city now found it had invested an overall total of $39.5 million in a project which was failing to deliver even half the water Mulholland had promised.[203]

In addition, the diseconomies of Mulholland's confused and ineffectual policies in the Owens Valley were becoming more apparent. The cost of acquiring additional water rights in the Owens Valley had risen in little more than a year from an average of $1,000 a miner's inch to a projected $1,500 an inch for some of the better lands on Bishop Creek—precisely the price Los Angeles charged for use of this water in irrigation once it reached the San

Fernando Valley. New land acquisitions by the middle of 1924 had cost the city $3.5 million, and there was still no end in sight. Not only had these acquisitions failed to increase the city's water supply, they were also costing more money each year to maintain. Revenues to Los Angeles from the rental of its Owens Valley lands and the sale of the products grown on them declined from $45,250 in 1921 to $35,768 in 1922 and $27,496 in 1923 as the city withdrew more and more land from production. The expenses of operating these ranches in 1923, however, totaled $17,277 exclusive of taxes. Thus, while Mulholland tried to obscure these facts in his annual reports, the city discovered it was earning an annual net profit of 9.5 cents an acre for land that was costing an average of 20 cents an acre in taxes.[204]

The Wattersons meanwhile were moving to increase the pressure on Mulholland. In March 1924 they bypassed the city water department and opened negotiations for the sale of their district's water rights directly to the San Fernando farming interests whose water Mulholland had cut off. At this point they also introduced a new element to their demands; in addition to the price of their land and water rights, they insisted on the payment of reparations to compensate the valley's merchants for the business lost as a result of the city's depredations. In April, Court Kunze persuaded the Hearst press to return to the story it had once discarded. Under the heading "Valley of Broken Hearts," he prepared a twelve-part series for the *San Francisco Call* in which he detailed the plight of the Owens Valley at the hands of Los Angeles and condemned the aqueduct as a scheme hatched by the San Fernando land syndicate.[205]

Mulholland returned from negotiations in Washington over the Boulder Canyon project to deal severely with this multifold challenge to his authority. He blocked the proposed deal with the San Fernando Valley interests and continued in effect his prohibition on the use of irrigation water for their lands. He declared his adamant opposition to the payment of reparations. And on May 10 he filed suit against eighteen Owens Valley canal companies to prevent the ranchers from continuing their diversions. In the early morning hours of May 21, less than two weeks after the announcement of Mulholland's suit, a band of forty men broke into the Watterson brothers' warehouse in Bishop and stole three boxes of dynamite which they used to blow a hole in the aqueduct.

Civil War

The effect of this attack was electric. Kunze's series in the *Call* had helped awaken the general public to what was happening in the Owens Valley; the first explosion on the aqueduct now brought a flood of reporters from all over the state to study the situation. The *Los Angeles Times* blamed Hearst for inciting the violence, likening the series in the *Call* to Hearst's infamous involvement in promoting America's war with Spain. But even so, the *Times* wavered in its support of Mulholland, noting, "There is an essential conflict between the life of the aqueduct, which is the life of the city, and the agricultural prosperity of the Owens River Valley."[206] The *Los Angeles Record*, meanwhile, stepped up its attacks on Mulholland and the aqueduct, urging as a solution to the controversy Mulholland's immediate resignation, a fair settlement with the ranchers, and the construction of Long Valley dam.[207]

For the very first time, Mulholland's policies in the Owens Valley were the subject of public debate in Los Angeles. The Wattersons did all they could to isolate Mulholland and his superiors on the Public Service Commission. They pursued their negotiations for a settlement, not with the city's water officials, but instead with the Los Angeles Chamber of Commerce. "Whenever possible the city's agents have assumed the attitude of unscrupulous hirelings, with no sense of decency or right," the ranchers asserted.[208] "The development of one of the best parts of California has been crippled, possibly killed, by the whims and the contemptuous faithlessness of these men," declared Chalfant.[209] "We won't deal with the Public Service Commission because they are not decent men," Harry Glasscock told a meeting of Los Angeles businessmen. "And if we have to, well then, we won't deal at all."[210]

On June 26, the Wattersons proposed to the chairman of the chamber's Power and Reclamation Committee, C. S. Whitcomb, that a committee of five disinterested businessmen be established to fix a price for the lands included in their water district.[211] The Public Service Commission immediately intervened to suppress Whitcomb's subsequent report, which was critical of Mulholland, arguing that Whitcomb's understanding of the situation was unbalanced.[212] But Mayor George E. Cryer could not be so easily silenced. In July he returned from a personal tour of the valley, recommending the immediate purchase of all the valley's lands either through direct negotiation or by appointment of an arbitration commission.[213]

Only the Municipal League remained constant in its support of Mulholland. In a report also published in July, it recited the many benefits the aqueduct had produced for the landowners in the southern portion of the Owens Valley, such as increased tourism and the inexpensive delivery of electrical power. It blamed the resistance the city had encountered among the more populous and prosperous communities of the upper valley upon a "legacy of sectional jealousies" involving the Wattersons, Fred Eaton, and the Southern Sierras Power Company. "It is well for Los Angeles citizens to remember," the league admonished, "that while the water department through its agents may have been tactless at times in dealing with the ranchers, it has never been charged with treachery to the city's interests." For the future, the league advised, "the first consideration of Los Angeles should be to get right and stay right, not with the Wattersons . . . the Eatons, or the Southern Sierras Power Company, but with the actual wealth producers of the valley, the dirt farmers."[214]

This report so perfectly stated Mulholland's attitude that it might as well have been dictated by him. He rejected altogether Mayor Cryer's call for an immediate purchase of the Owens Valley. Instead, all purchases of valley lands were suspended. Unlike his insubordination in the case of the controversy over distribution of the aqueduct surplus ten years before, Mulholland this time enjoyed the support of the Public Service Commission. On the day before the Wattersons first appeared before Whitcomb's committee at the Chamber of Commerce, Mulholland commissioned a study which would give his program of limited acquisitions one last airing.

Hastily prepared for submission in August, this *Report on*

the Available Water Supply of the City of Los Angeles and the Metropolitan Area offered for the most part little more than a reworking of the figures Thomas Means had already provided in his various submissions to Mulholland and the commission. Though its conclusions were somewhat less strident than Means' with regard to the immediacy of a water shortage in the city, it recommended, as Means had, the immediate acquisition and development of the water resources of the Mono Basin and the construction of a second aqueduct to handle this additional water. In his current extremity, Mulholland had called back J. B. Lippincott to prepare the report with the assistance of two other independent consultants, Louis Hill and A. L. Sonderegger. Lippincott's longstanding conviction that the entire water supply of the Owens Valley would be needed for the city was clearly reflected in the report's central conclusion that, if these recommendations were followed "after destroying all irrigation" in the Owens Valley, the city would have enough water to last for the next thirty-five years of continued growth. "If irrigation in Owens Valley is not destroyed and a second aqueduct not built," the report warned, "the deficit [in the city's water supply by 1950] will be about 900 second-feet."[215]

Unlike Means' reports—which had been limited exclusively to the Owens Valley and Mono Basin—Hill, Lippincott, and Sonderegger took cognizance of Mulholland's newfound enthusiasm for development of the Colorado River water supply. Recognizing the opportunity for making up any deficits in the aqueduct supply with Colorado River water, their report consequently offered four alternatives for city policy toward the Owens Valley, three of which would have allowed some limited irrigation activity to continue in areas ranging from 18,500 to 36,000 acres. Two of the four proposed alternatives also called for construction of the Long Valley reservoir. And all the alternatives providing for continued irrigation in the Owens Valley would have required substantial reductions in the amount of water used by the valley ranchers.[216]

In keeping with Mulholland's announced determination to limit his purchases in the valley and preserve some form of agriculture, Means had offered a similar proposal for keeping thirty-three thousand acres of the valley green that same year. On October 14, the Public Service Commission adopted that alternative which was most closely aligned with Mulholland's existing policy: thirty thousand acres of the valley would continue under limited irrigation and the Long Valley reservoir would not be built. The commission's plan departed significantly from Means' earlier proposal principally in the commission's pointed exclusion of most of the lands in the Wattersons' district from those areas proposed for municipal acquisition. In addition, the commission noted that the Municipal League in its report had quoted one merchant in the lower end of the valley as saying, "This country's future lies in developing the Los Angeles tourist trade. We make more money setting here and selling the tourists gas and other things than we could make raising cheap alfalfa."[217] In the hope, therefore, of making their package offer more attractive, the commission added to its announcement the promise to lend its support to the construction of a "hard road" for the convenience of tourists.[218]

It was an utterly hopeless gambit. Given its authorship by Lippincott, the first betrayer of the valley, the report could not have been received by the ranchers with anything other than suspicion. The people of the Owens Valley, moreover, had heard promises of compromise from the city before, in 1913 and 1921, and this one came too late. The commission's apparent confidence that the attitudes of the few remaining residents of the lower valley could be taken as indicative of the goals and aspirations of those who lived in and around Bishop reflected nothing so much as Mulholland's complete failure to understand current conditions in the valley. Acceptance of the proposal would have meant the denial of reparations and the destruction of the Wattersons' irrigation district. The offer ignored the ranchers' growing confidence that they could make a much better deal by working through the mayor's office and the Chamber of Commerce.

Most important, the effort failed to appreciate the fact that Mulholland's steadfast refusal to deal with the ranchers in concert had already destroyed any hope he might have had of negotiating a general settlement now. By seeking consistently to divide the ranchers and deal with them separately, Mulholland had not only driven up the ultimate cost to Los Angeles for each of its successive acquisitions, he had also made the valley "a hotbed of suspicions, prejudices, and hatreds." As a later report for the city noted, "Suspicions are mutual and widespread. The Valley people are suspicious of each other, suspicious of newcomers, suspicious of city men, suspicious, in short, of almost everybody and everything . . . Owens Valley is full of whisperings, mutterings, recrimination and suggestion of threat of one kind and another."[219] This attitude of profound distrust had even infected the city's employees working in the valley, who came to regard the policies of their superiors in Los Angeles as hopelessly misguided. His inability to rely upon his own workers, in turn, compelled Mulholland to rely all the more upon the independent reports he commissioned with increasing frequency throughout this period.[220]

On November 16, the ranchers responded to the commission's new proposal by seizing the Alabama Gates, which control the main flow of water into the aqueduct. The gates were shut and the water sent spilling back into the river bed. Mark Watterson, who led the assault, was joined at the gates over the next four days by crowds of five hundred to eight hundred valley residents. It was a festive event. Businesses throughout the valley closed as shopowners left to join their friends at the aqueduct. Families came with picnic lunches. And the movie star Tom Mix, who was shooting a film nearby, sent over an orchestra.[221]

Local law enforcement authorities were powerless to intervene. When Los Angeles demanded that the leaders of the insurrection be arrested, Sheriff Charles A. Collins warned that if two men were indicted, two hundred would step forward to stand with them. Instead Collins called upon Governor Friend W. Richardson to send in state troops, arguing that guardsmen were the only authority the unarmed mob would be likely to obey. Richardson demurred and urged Collins instead to demonstrate his "manhood and courage."[222]

The pressure on the city was immense. News reports of events at the Alabama Gates were reprinted around the world. The judge sitting in Mulholland's suit to block the ranchers' diversions withdrew, declaring that he could no longer take an objective and dispassionate view of the city's case. The Los Angeles papers at first denounced the Wattersons as mobsters and printed false stories linking them with the Ku Klux Klan which even their own correspondents denounced. But they were alone in their defense of Mulholland's policy. "If the people of Los Angeles knew what their political agents were doing in Owens Valley they would be fired," declared Harry Glasscock in a statement that gained wide circulation.

On November 18, the *Los Angeles Times* deserted Mulholland in an editorial noting that the ranchers were not anarchists but honest citizens of the hardy stock of pioneers who had made California great: "They have put themselves hopelessly in the wrong by taking the law into their own hands, but that is not to say that there has not been a measure of justice on their side of the argument." In the view of the *Times*, the need for an amicable settlement was clear, and it called upon the Public Service Commission to pay for the suffering its policies had caused. "It is not a time to drive the hardest possible bargain," the *Times* concluded. "The city can afford to be liberal in its settlement with these pioneers whose work of half a century it will undo." As the *Literary Digest* observed, "The reputation of Los Angeles for decent dealing throughout the entire country now hangs in the balance."[223]

The public embarrassment prompted Los Angeles' bankers to come forth with an offer to intercede with the city government to achieve a settlement. On November 20, Wilfred Watterson emerged from a meeting of the bankers' Joint Clearinghouse Association and wired his brother Mark with the good news:

> If the object of the crowd at the spillway is to bring their wrongs to the attention of the citizens of Los Angeles, they have done so one hundred percent and further defiance of law will injure the Valley cause beyond all possibility of remedy. The press and minds of the people here will be open from now on and I feel sure that the wrongs done will be remedied . . . I have the assurance that strong influences here will be brought to bear on the situation to see that justice is done.[224]

The ranchers accordingly dispersed, and on November 29 the Wattersons submitted their terms for settlement to J. A. Graves, president of the clearinghouse association. Wilfred proposed that the city should either pay $5.3 million in reparations and leave the valley alone or buy out their district as a whole for $12 million, reparations included. If neither course was acceptable, Watterson renewed his suggestion for the appointment of an independent board of arbitrators.[225]

It became immediately apparent that the promised negotiations would fail. Graves made no comment on the Wattersons' proposal; he simply acknowledged receipt and scheduled no furthur meetings on it. City officials meanwhile were declaring that the mob's dispersal constituted a "complete moral victory" for Los Angeles. "The backbone of the publicity stunt was broken," trumpeted the *Los Angeles Examiner* in an editorial that mocked Wilfred Watterson for sending "the embattled farmers back to the homes they were trying to force the city to buy and destroy."[226] On December 5, Graves denounced the Wattersons as leaders of a "junta" of bankers and capitalists "willing to graft equally upon the poverty of the Owens Valley farmers and of the municipal treasury of Los Angeles."[227]

State Engineer Wilbur F. McClure, who had been dispatched by Governor Richardson to review the situation, attempted at this point to intervene. On December 9 and again on December 24, he presented the Wattersons' proposal to the city's officials and requested the opportunity to meet with the members of the Public Service Commission. But McClure met with the same silence Graves had shown the Wattersons' offer. Finally, on December 29, the commissioners consented to see McClure, and he emerged from the meeting shaking his head in discouragement. "While in Owens Valley I heard some severe criticisms of the chief engineer and Board of Public Service Commissioners," he reported to the governor, "but none of them exceeded in caustic utterances and bitterness statements made around the table in the Public Service Commissioners' room concerning the people of Owens Valley."[228]

On January 19, the Public Service Commission rejected the Watterson proposal without discussion, rescinded its offer to keep thirty thousand acres of the valley green, and ordered Mulholland to renew his land purchasing program. Graves later

William Mulholland

(Photo courtesy of the Los Angeles
Department of Water and Power)

The three fathers of the aqueduct meet to consider their plans; from left to right in the photograph above, Joseph B. Lippincott, Fred Eaton, and William Mulholland.

(Photo courtesy of the Los Angeles Department of Water and Power)

At left, Henry Huntington, first among the financial giants of Los Angeles, whose interest in the aqueduct helped to unify the support of the local business community.

(Photo courtesy of the Security Pacific National Bank)

Three of the major beneficiaries
of the aqueduct's construction:
at right, Harrison Gray Otis,
publisher of the *Los Angeles
Times*; below, Otis' mild-
appearing heir, Harry Chandler;
at right below, Moses Sherman,
a frequent partner in Chandler's
various investment schemes.

(Photos courtesy of the Security
Pacific National Bank)

In the photograph above, Mulholland leads the panel of expert engineers reviewing the aqueduct on a tour of the proposed route; from left to right above, John R. Freeman, Joseph D. Schuyler, Lippincott, Fred P. Stearns, and Mulholland. Mulholland.

(Photo courtesy of the Security Pacific National Bank)

At left, Mary Austin, whose passionate appeals first drew public attention to the Owens Valley's objections to the city's project.

(Photo courtesy of the Eastern California Museum)

Within a decade of the first opening of the intake to the aqueduct shown below, Wilfred Watterson, at right, had emerged at the head of a united band of valley ranchers opposed to Los Angeles' policies during the 1920s.

(Aqueduct photo courtesy of the Los Angeles Department of Water and Power; Watterson photo courtesy of Mrs. Mary W. Gorman)

Mark Watterson, at right, led
the seizure of the Alabama
Gates above, which controlled
the flow of water into the
aqueduct.

(Aqueduct photo courtesy of the
Los Angeles Department of Water
and Power; Watterson photo
courtesy of Mrs. Mary W. Gorman)

City crews at work repairing
a siphon on the aqueduct blown
up during the conflict of 1927.

(Photo courtesy of the Security
Pacific National Bank)

The collapse of the Watterson banks brought the withdrawal of the city's armed guards, like the ones shown above in this obviously retouched photograph from the Los Angeles Department of Water and Power. The restoration of peace made possible a new kind of leadership within the valley by Father John Crowley at left.

(Crowley photo courtesy of Curtis Phillips).

blamed the offensiveness of the Wattersons' proposal for the failure of the bankers' peace-keeping mission. "With a friendly spirit toward the Owens Valley people," Graves wrote to Wilfred, "I desire to inform you that your veiled threats of further violence and damage to the aqueduct will injure your cause with any fair-minded people. The blustering, swaggering bully of the old days has passed away and it ill becomes you . . . to resort to such tactics."[229]

The failure of the bankers' efforts at mediation scarcely mattered to the ranchers. Thanks to the attention their so-called civil war had focused on the valley's plight, they no longer had to deal exclusively with Los Angeles but could instead carry their complaint to the larger forum of public opinion. Their efforts would now be directed toward obtaining relief from the state government. On January 9, 1925, their cause received a crucial boost from the publication of the state engineer's report on the controversy. McClure was a dour, self-righteous man who knew the Owens Valley, having worked there as a young man. He had even served as a lay preacher in one of the Bishop churches. He had tangled as well with the water developers of the South Coast in his capacity as California's representative to the negotiations for the Colorado River Compact in 1922. Their attacks on him during the course of these negotiations had become so extreme, in fact, that the compact conference itself had almost dissolved as a result.[230]

In his report to the governor, McClure made no attempt to "pronounce judgment," but he expressed confidence that the appropriate "notions of justification, censure, or excuse . . . [could be] gathered from a statement of facts and a reading of valley history over the past eighteen or nineteen years." He traced the record of the city's involvement in the valley and asserted that "no one need argue" with the ranchers' belief that the Owens Valley would by now have had seventy-five to one hundred thousand acres in production and two or three times as many residents if the city had not intervened with the Reclamation Service. "The people of the valley are not anarchists, criminals, or thieves, as has been stated, but on the contrary, are ordinary industrious American citizens," he wrote. Their bitterness he ascribed to the city's circumvention of President Roosevelt's restrictions on the operation of the aqueduct in order to develop the San Fernando Valley. And with regard to the present controversy, he concluded, "The commission's attitude seems to be that of playing the part of big brother to the valley. The valley does not desire to be big brothered but to go its own way and insists that if the parental idea is to be insisted upon, the would-be big brother should be willing to pay well for the privilege of exercising such domination."[231]

Governor Richardson was unwilling to intervene in the conflict. An arch-conservative elected on a promise of "sweeping retrenchment" by the fanatically antiprogressive wing of the Republican Party, he had distinguished himself in office principally by the frequency of his vetoes and by his enthusiastic efforts to close schools and colleges and cut government services of all kinds.[232] The legislature, however, followed through on McClure's report by knocking out the principal prop of Mulholland's intransigent resistance. Until this time, Mulholland had justified his refusal to consider the Wattersons' offers of settlement on the grounds that the city had no legal authority to pay the reparations claims they insisted upon. In May, the legislature passed a bill specifically allowing the payment of reparations for damages caused by the loss of water but not for those arising from the construction or operation of the aqueduct.[233]

Reparations associations promptly formed in Bishop and Big Pine, and the residents of the Owens Valley began adding up their claims. Bishop eventually submitted 431 claims totaling $2,272,978 and Big Pine came up with 117 claims covering $540,378 in estimated losses. All the claims were neatly segregated into losses suffered by businesses, occupational and professional services, and real and personal property. The Watterson brothers and the members of their immediate families produced claims totaling $387,356, or 18 percent of the total for Bishop.[234] The city, however, continued to refuse to pay anything, contending that the law passed by the legislature was of dubious constitutionality and that damages should, in any event, be fixed by courts and not simply paid on demand. It refused, moreover, to acknowledge any responsibility for the losses the valley residents claimed to have suffered. "If the City did wrong in buying, they did wrong in selling," argued a Department of Water and Power pamphlet responding to the Wattersons' proposal. "Such losses, while very regrettable, are among the hazards which all must take in buying property or establishing a business."[235]

Rather than softening their stand, Mulholland and his colleagues responded to the increasing isolation of their position by mounting a public relations campaign of their own. Pamphlets, broadsides, and articles began to pour out of the Department of Water and Power, all seeking to present a very different view of conditions in the Owens Valley than the one presented by the city's critics. To a large extent, this effort involved an artful rewriting of history. In the department's publications, the Owens Valley never had more than thirty thousand acres under irrigation, although in some documents this figure was increased to thirty-five thousand acres and the adverbial modifier was changed to rarely.[236] The valley's farmers had survived, according to the department, only by dint of the exorbitant prices they were able to extract from the mines in the area. When the mines consolidated and developed their own sources of supply, all that saved the valley from economic collapse was the advent of the aqueduct, which sprang from an "unsolicited offer" by Fred Eaton.[237]

The department strove to depict the aqueduct as an endless source of benefits for the Owens Valley. "Never in its history has Owens Valley prospered and increased in wealth as it has in the last twenty years," one departmental publication quite accurately pointed out before going on to attribute this increase somewhat less accurately to the aqueduct's development. The city pointed to the jobs the aqueduct had created and the taxes it had paid to Inyo County. "Where the city has purchased water bearing land adjoining privately owned land, the rancher without a single exception has continued to divert his full share of water," the department pointed out, without mentioning its suit to prevent that practice from continuing. Any drying up of the ranches the department attributed to the drought, and any decline in the value of the valley's produce was ascribed to an undefined but nevertheless generalized slump in agricultural prices. To support its contention that the valley was prospering, the department relied principally upon two indices: the registration of automobiles, which were of course a necessity for the residents of the far-flung communities of the valley; and bank deposits, which had risen since 1920 quite naturally as a result of the quantity of money the city was pumping into the local economy through its widespread land purchases.[238]

As for the current controversy, the department asserted that McClure was unfit to comment because of his previous employment in the valley. It presented the conflict instead as a unique example of "a rural community attempting to compel a city to buy its lands, and in addition to pay it large sums of reparations under threat of forcibly destroying . . . the very life of its existence if the coin was not promptly forthcoming." The hostility of the ranchers was ascribed to "the mental reactions of a pioneer community . . . uninformed and unaccustomed to the ways of the outside world," who had fallen victim to "schemers and unscrupulous individuals" in their own midst. As a result, the ranchers were unable to understand "city representatives who are pressed by the necessities of the moment and bound by the legal requirements imposed upon public servants."[239]

This genteel presentation of the Owens Valley residents as bumpkins and dupes only appeared in some departmental handouts. In others, the ranchers were depicted as "outlaws" working "to milk the people of Los Angeles out of millions of dollars on the claim that the City of Los Angeles has damaged them." Such claims, the department asserted, were unfounded because Los Angeles only took that water which would otherwise be wasted into Owens Lake. The purchases on the McNally Ditch, which of course were at variance with this assertion, had been undertaken "with the view of disturbing the situation in the Valley as little as possible" because the lands it served were on the east side of the river and therefore "detached in a great measure" from the rest of valley agriculture. The city had only crossed the river in its purchasing program when "forced" to do so by "Bishop businessmen" who organized themselves into pools to demand more for the land than it was worth. The continued resistance of the ranchers was laid to a mistaken "belief" that "the time will come when every available drop will be needed in Los Angeles, even if a second aqueduct must be built to obtain it." To allay this fear, "city officials point to the active steps which Los Angeles and other Southern California communities are taking to obtain an adequate future supply from the surplus waters of the Colorado River."[240]

The department reserved its most creative analysis for questions concerning the Long Valley dam. Chalfant, the *Los Angeles Examiner*, and others were by this time blaming the violence in the valley on the collapse of the agreement of 1921. The reservoir Mulholland refused to build at Long Valley was consequently being presented as an enterprise that would have been capable not only of supplying the ranchers' needs, but also of saving the city from the water crisis Mulholland was fomenting as part of his promotion of the Boulder Canyon project. Recognizing that his most important audience was in Los Angeles, Mulholland at first took the tack of belittling the project's importance to the city. "Such a dam was not needed particularly so far as the City was concerned since large storage capacity was already available along the line of the aqueduct," one departmental publication claimed. "The principal beneficiaries of the Long Valley dam, it was shown, would be the Owens Valley irrigators who would be provided with a regulated water supply."[241] To support this contention, Mulholland even went so far as to assert that the city suffered no water shortage in 1924 that would have required either the construction of the dam or any additional land purchases in the Owens Valley. "Los Angeles people were using 12.5 million gallons MORE each day than during the previous year," he proudly pointed out in denying that the city's water supply was in any way precarious.[242] The collapse of the agreement of 1921 was therefore blamed entirely on the shortsightedness of the ranchers who would have been its beneficiaries.[243]

This line of argument may have been sufficient to meet local criticism of his abandonment of the project, but it did nothing to answer the charges originating in the Owens Valley as to the importance the project would have had for their needs. For this purpose, Mulholland announced that the 150-foot dam the ranchers wanted had not been built because the soil at the Long Valley dam site was too porous to support a structure of that size. This disclosure must have come as a startling revelation to the various engineers who had studied the reservoir site and pronounced it fit for a high dam. Clausen's first report for the Reclamation Service in November 1904 had noted that the volcanic tufa in the area of the proposed reservoir was so soft it could be hewn and shaped with a broadax. But he reported that it hardened quickly upon exposure and presented no obstacle to the construction of the 140-foot dam he proposed.[244] The city's panel of consulting engineers on the aqueduct had examined Long Valley in 1906 and found it "admirably adapted" for use as a reservoir, concluding that "a stable and safe dam can be built" of any kind that would prove most economical.[245] Mulholland himself, in the course of his testimony before the Aqueduct Investigation Board in 1912, had expressed complete confidence that a high dam could be built there, noting that "as a matter of fact, the explorations that we have since made bear that out."[246] And by 1916, he was even toying with the idea of building the Long Valley dam to a height of 160 feet.[247] Studies conducted for the city at Long Valley by the Reclamation Service in 1921 and by Thomas Means in 1923 had similarly discovered no difficulty with the use of the area for a major storage reservoir.[248]

In fact, the only reservation that had ever been publicly expressed concerning the use of the Long Valley reservoir site had been a concern for its vulnerability to earthquakes noted by a United States Geological Survey report in 1906.[249] In July 1924, however, the report which Lippincott prepared for Mulholland in association with Hill and Sonderegger had for the first time observed that fissures on the rim of the reservoir site might result in leakage. Even so, Lippincott and his colleagues expressed confidence that any height of dam could be safely built there.[250] It was this slight observation that Mulholland fastened upon in defending his refusal to build the high dam at Long Valley. Lippincott had used the same excuse in the summer of 1904 to halt all work on the federal project for the Owens Valley while he made arrangements to spike the project in favor of Los Angeles. And Mulholland had adopted a similar argument in opposing the ranchers' plans for Fish Slough. The pretext served as well again. It consequently became departmental policy that any dam above the 100-foot contour at Long Valley would spring leaks and run dry in no time.[251] The extent of the deceit is evident in the fact that the department in later years built a dam at Long Valley that was 126 feet high, and in 1960 they pronounced it "feasible from engineering and geologic standpoints" to raise this structure another 30 feet.[252] But so long as Mulholland remained in control of the city's water department, no consideration to the construction of the Long Valley reservoir would ever be given again.[253]

Final Accounting

The long drought ended in 1926. Precipitation levels in Los Angeles ran 20 percent above the long-term average that year, and aqueduct deliveries began to return to normal. But the pressure on the city to expand its water supply did not diminish. The population of Los Angeles continued to grow, and Mulholland by this time was issuing feverish predictions of a crisis within ten years as part of his continuing campaign to secure the Boulder Canyon project. The city therefore pressed doggedly ahead with its land and water rights purchases in the Owens Valley. By the end of 1926, 166 separate acquisitions had been negotiated involving 32,625 acres. Los Angeles' holdings now included almost all the land irrigated by nine of the valley's major ditch companies, plus 75 percent of the lands served by the Owens River Canal, all of Round Valley, and a substantial portion of the acreage watered directly by Bishop Creek. In all, the city owned or was negotiating for 90 percent of all the land and water rights on the Owens River.[254]

In an effort to win the valley's confidence and at the same time hold down the prices the city was paying, the Los Angeles water commission established a board of appraisers composed of the chairman of the Inyo County Board of Supervisors and the current and former Inyo County assessors to fix the values of the properties it sought.[255] But it continued to resist the Wattersons' demands for the payment of reparations. The renewal of the city's purchasing program following the withdrawal of its offer to keep thirty thousand acres green in January 1925 consequently brought fresh outbreaks of violence. And the city's steady northward advance into the water-rich lands of the Bishop area were punctuated by intermittent explosions along the aqueduct.

Mulholland's public relations efforts had accomplished nothing in the way of eroding the popular view of the Owens Valley as the victim of the city's aggression. "Remember the Owens Valley" became the slogan under which rural and north state legislators rallied to defeat both a reapportionment bill designed to increase Los Angeles' political representation in 1924 and the enabling act for the Metropolitan Water District in 1925. The example of Los Angeles' exploitation of the Owens Valley's water resources meanwhile encouraged popular support for direct state intervention in the management of California's water resources. The *Santa Barbara Press* voiced an increasingly widespread concern when it warned, "Other communities in California will sooner or later find themselves in the same predicament unless some agency tackles the task of conserving the waters of the state which now go to waste or which are now not utilized as fully as possible."[256]

With the arrival of 1927, events began to converge which worked to the valley's advantage. In Washington and Sacramento, the authorization for federal funding of the Boulder Canyon Project and the enabling act for the Metropolitan Water District were each coming to a vote once again. Arrayed against these efforts were the state's private water and power interests, allied with the most ardent editorial defenders of the free enterprise system. For them, the Owens Valley controversy was an invaluable aid. In the view of the *Sacramento Union*, for example: "The City of Los Angeles cannot be trusted with the privilege of diverting a single gallon of water from the Colorado River; there is the tragic lesson of Owens Valley."[257] At the same time, the publication of a new state water plan and the popular reaction to a recent state supreme court decision unfavorable to orderly water management had forced the issue of public versus private water development to the forefront of political attention. A movement was now under way to amend the state constitution to reverse the dominance of private water rights and to affirm for the first time the public's interest in the water resources of California.[258] In the midst of these disputes stood the Owens Valley, a model of the dangers of Mulholland's policy and an example of the need for overhauling the state's outmoded water laws.

The Wattersons, now at the head of a unified resistance group titled the Owens Valley Property Owners Protective Association, seized the occasion of the legislative hearings on the proposed constitutional amendment as an opportunity to present the valley's case directly to the people of California. On March 20 and again on March 22, the association bought full-page advertisements in each of the state's major newspapers in which they detailed the plight of the Owens Valley, "a name writ in water . . . its characters salt with tears and stained in blood." This passionate appeal was immediately echoed in a series of articles printed in the *Sacramento Union* from March 29 through April 3.

Although they were extreme examples of the purple rhetoric popular in journalistic prose of the period, the association advertisements together with the *Union* articles marked a sophisticated departure from the appeals of old. Gone were the fatal associations with the interests of private power companies and the unpopular opposition to "hysterical conservationism" which had proved so detrimental to the valley's interest in the past. Instead, these articles found more common strains with which to sound the heartstrings of their readers. They described an authentic American tragedy, rich with Biblical overtones, which touched one of America's fondest cultural themes: conflict between the city and the frontier, the strong, sophisticated society against the weaker primitive, the machine run rampant amid the primeval garden.

In the advertisements, the Owens Valley became a democratic Eden threatened by the aqueduct, "an evil serpent, bringing ruin as another serpent did to the earliest valley in human history." The advertisements further described how "the sturdy winners of the wilderness, whose fibre made America great . . . pushed back the disputing sands and reared the homes of their families, the halls of their democracy, and the altars and thanes of their God—until happy, lovely Owens Valley was a fairyland of beauty surrounded by peaks and desert and dotted with monuments to human industry."

Through this frontier paradise the *Union* stories followed "the trail of the wreckers," presenting "a record of political ownership run rabid, the record of a great city which raised itself above the law." Here the *Union* watched the destruction of the

fruit orchards by city tractors: "Shame-faced Los Angeles removing the traces of civilization in the hope that the future will not
curse her." There the *Union* found an abandoned schoolhouse
with flag still flying, "its blood-red stripes now twined and twisted
with the halyard . . . tired of neglect . . . the last thing to yield to
the decree of abandonment." Mulholland was presented throughout as the cruelest of villains, chief architect of "a policy of
ruthlessness, of 'sink without trace,' of brutality and sharp practice which leads crooks to jail or makes them fugitives from
justice." When asked by the *Union* what justice he felt was due to
the Owens Valley ranchers, Mulholland was quoted in reply,
"Justice! Why there are not enough trees in the valley to give the
— — — [*sic*] justice!"[259]

The impact of this appeal was felt even before the *Union*
series had run its course. On March 31, Assemblyman Dan E.
Williams of Chinese Camp announced that he would ask Governor Clement C. Young to allow the legislature to arbitrate the
controversy. When this effort failed, Williams headed a special
assembly investigating committee, which set out on April 16 to
visit the valley. The assembly delegation, as guests of the Wattersons' protective association, met with two hundred ranchers in
Bishop on Saturday night, April 17. The following Monday, the
committee convened again in Sacramento for hearings on a resolution introduced by Williams which damned Los Angeles and
all its works in the Owens Valley.

Williams' resolution declared that Los Angeles' policy of
"ruthless destruction" constituted "a menace to the peace and
welfare of the entire state" and called upon the city either to
restore the Owens Valley to its former agricultural status or give
the valley residents and businessmen proper compensation for
their damages.[260] After seven hours of bickering, the representatives from Los Angeles refused to participate further in the committee's hearings. Before the chief legal counsel for the city left
the hearing room, however, he warned the committee members
that, regardless of what had happened in the Owens Valley, Los
Angeles would enter any other part of the state, including the
San Joaquin Valley, if it needed the water. He concluded with the
declaration that Los Angeles had the money to do what it

pleased.[261] In response, eight members of the Assembly, mostly from rural, well-watered counties but including one from Orange, joined in declaring publicly, "We deplore the policy of the city which abandons its municipal functions and enters into extensive activities of a private nature, to the ruination of another political subdivision."[262] On April 22, after a tumultuous debate highlighted by a fistfight on the floor of the assembly chamber, the Williams resolution passed by a vote of 43 to 34.

Although the resolution next went to the Senate Committee on Conservation, chaired by Senator Herbert J. Evans of Los Angeles, where it died without a hearing, their success in Sacramento encouraged the valley ranchers to stand firm against the city. The Wattersons had launched their advertising campaign in response to an announcement by the city at the beginning of March that it would refuse to honor the prices set by its board of Inyo appraisers for any lands not sold by May 1. The ranchers ignored the deadline, and on May 13 the protective association again demanded that the city submit to arbitration, denouncing Mulholland's employment of "imported gumshoe men" to guard the aqueduct as an un-American practice which "can have but one effect, namely to inflame real American citizens to violence."[263]

On May 27, one of the largest siphons on the aqueduct was blown up. The next night, sixty more feet of pipe were destroyed. Night riders now plied the back roads of Inyo, preying upon the aqueduct and threatening those they suspected of opposing the Wattersons and their district. Los Angeles assembled six hundred reservists at the city police headquarters and dispatched a contingent of private detectives to the valley armed with Winchesters and tommy guns with orders to shoot to kill anyone found loitering around the aqueduct. Undeterred, the ranchers blew up portions of the aqueduct again on the nights of June 4, 19, and 24. On June 10, Los Angeles sent an entire trainload of guards to the valley bearing sawed-off shotguns.[264] No blood had been shed in the so-called civil war of 1924, but, in the superheated atmosphere of the valley in the summer of 1927, the stage was set for a violent confrontation of major proportions.

The level of violence in the Owens Valley compelled the gov-

ernor at last to intervene. Clement Young had been elected the
year before on a pledge of strong support for development of the
Colorado River. On May 10 he redeemed his promise by signing
into law the legislation creating the Metropolitan Water District.
With this aspect of Los Angeles' water problems resolved, he
turned his attention to the conflict in the valley. Although he had
earlier rejected appeals from the city's water commission to appoint an impartial investigator and from Assemblyman Williams
to allow the legislature to arbitrate the controversy, on June 23
he traveled to Los Angeles to offer a solution of his own. Following a closed-door meeting with the water commissioners, he called
for an immediate cessation of violence. Young noted that the
only significant point at issue betwen the city and the ranchers
involved the payment of reparations. He proposed, therefore,
that both sides submit to a review of their conflicting claims by
the state supreme court. The court could then decide whether the
state's new law authorizing the payment of reparations was in
fact constitutionally valid.[265]

Los Angeles readily agreed to this proposal and promptly
issued a warning that any employee who agreed to the payment
of a claim for reparations in advance of the court's decision
would be held personally liable. Wilfred Watterson, however,
emerged from his own meeting with the governor in Sacramento
on July 1 offering no comment. Two weeks later, the Wattersons'
protective association and the reparations associations of Bishop
and Big Pine rejected the governors' suggestion, contending that
Los Angeles would use the court case as an excuse for delay.
"Time is a very valuable aid to the Water and Power Board in
carrying on this campaign of destruction," they observed in a
joint letter to the governor, "and it seems to us that a prolonged
court litigation ... would be very welcome to the Water and
Power Board and for that reason is looked upon with fear and
distrust by our people."[266] Although they thanked the governor
for his concern, the Wattersons had nothing else to offer as an
alternative.

The passage of the Williams resolution in the assembly
marked the high point of the Owens Valley resistance, and time
now was indeed running out for the Watterson brothers. Because

their investments and commercial activities made up so much of the local economy, they had suffered most from the hard times that had descended on the valley after 1923. Recognizing these difficulties, their uncle George had launched an attack the preceding October against the heart of their financial empire by filing an application for a bank of his own to compete with Wilfred and Mark. In this effort, George had been joined by the presidents of the Bishop Creek and Owens River ditch companies, who had been among the first to desert the brothers' irrigation district.[267] At first, the application seemed certain to succeed. Clement Young, in his primary campaign, had received massive support from A. P. Giannini's Bank of Italy (later the Bank of America), which hoped to secure through his election an end to the restrictions on branch banking which Governor Richardson had imposed. One of Young's first acts upon taking office was to install Will C. Wood as the state's banking superintendent, and Wood had immediately revoked Richardson's restrictions, with the result that the number of Giannini's branch banks increased nearly threefold from 98 to 289 in 1927 alone.[268]

George Watterson's application had, of course, been filed in the name of the Bank of Italy, and to meet the threat, Wilfred and Mark had begun diverting funds from their own bank in a desperate effort to shore up their various enterprises. In this way, they later explained that they hoped to resuscitate the valley's economy and thereby sustain the resistance to Los Angeles, at least until the reparations payments arrived, which would presumably make right any imbalance in the bank's assets. When the brothers began their peculations that October 1926, they initially applied the funds only to support their failing resort and mineral water business at Coso Hot Springs. But in the months that followed, the drain on the bank's resources increased, and by the summer of 1927 fully half of the bank's assets had been secretly committed to the Watterson brothers' own investments.[269]

Los Angeles' program of devastation, however, had succeeded too well in undermining the valley's economy. Not only were the funds Wilfred and Mark diverted insufficient to sustain the family's various enterprises, but George Watterson's application was also turned down by the United States Comptroller of the Treasury on the grounds that there was not sufficient business in the Owens Valley any longer to justify the establishment of another bank. Similarly, the state bank commissioner refused George Watterson's application following a hearing on March 31 at which Wilfred testified that the new bank was only a front for the city which intended to drive the brothers out of business and thereby secure all the mortgages outstanding in the valley.[270]

Nevertheless, the process of application did reveal certain discrepancies between the amount of money the Watterson brothers' financial statements indicated their bank had on deposit in San Francisco and the amount which the banks in San Francisco reported to be in their possession. William B. Mathews, chief counsel to the city water department, accordingly brought these problems to the attention of the state banking commissioner on August 2, and a bank examiner set out for Bishop that night. The banking commissioner himself followed the next day to take charge of the investigation personally. When confronted with the evidence of their crimes, Wilfred and Mark made no effort to deny anything. Mark even joked that the bank examiners would probably be surprised when they calculated the total amount of the deficit. Mark especially saw nothing wrong in what they had done. The brothers argued sincerely that they had been working in the best interests of their friends and neighbors, and Mark pointed out proudly that not a penny of the missing funds had ever left the Owens Valley.[271]

At noon on August 4, all five of the Watterson brothers' banks closed their doors. At each a sign was posted stating, "This result has been brought about by the last 4 years of destructive work carried on by the City of Los Angeles." The bank examiners immediately tore the signs down. The residents of the valley, most of whom had their life savings tied up in the Watterson banks, were stunned and confused. The water commission, however, was well prepared and immediately issued a statement denying any responsibility for the closure and advising that the banks' problem appeared to be internal. To ease the burden on the valley ranchers, the city also offered to delay the collection of rents on the properties it leased. Will Wood joined in absolving the city of any blame and gave the brothers until August 10 to make up the deficit. Rallies were held throughout the valley at which the Watterson brothers attempted to explain their actions. Hundreds came to cheer them and vigorously denounce Los Angeles. The residents of Bishop alone pledged $600,000 to cover the brothers' losses. But Wood announced that the deficit amounted to more than $800,000, and although this estimate later proved excessive, the pledges could not have been fulfilled in time to meet his deadline. On August 13, Wilfred and Mark Watterson were arrested and charged with thirty-six counts of embezzlement and grand theft amounting to $450,000.[272]

At their trial, which began November 1, 1927, Wilfred appeared gaunt and drawn, but Mark was relaxed. They did not attempt to deny the evidence against them, and any inference that their actions had been prompted by Los Angeles' actions in the valley was ruled inadmissible and irrelevant. When even the question of what had been done with the missing funds arose, the judge refused to allow it, declaring "I'm not trying a war between Los Angeles and Inyo County." In their defense, the brothers offered only a brief parade of character witnesses, and the district attorney conceded that he too would have testified to their good character if he had not been prosecuting the case. As the district attorney presented his closing argument, he broke into tears, and the judge and jury wept with him. The jury was out for only six hours and convicted the two brothers on all counts. When they appeared for sentencing on November 14, the Wattersons made no appeal for probation. They had said goodbye to their wives and children that morning, before they left for the courthouse. They received concurrent terms of ten years in San Quentin and departed for prison immediately. With the ranchers' life savings lost and their homes now forfeit, the resistance to Los Angeles was broken. After the brothers were sentenced, someone posted a sign on the north side of Bishop reading, "Los Angeles City Limits."[273]

Although the war was over, the city persisted in its pursuit of those responsible for the attacks on the aqueduct. Two men had been arrested just before the Watterson banks closed, but both were released for lack of evidence. Six more were indicted in March 1928, and although one confessed, the case was dropped when his testimony proved contradictory. There was one last bombing in November 1931, but that was attributed to a disgruntled employee and not to the Owens Valley ranchers.[274] As a result, the Watterson brothers were the only people to receive criminal penalties for the activities arising from the valley's struggle with Los Angeles.

When the Wattersons were sentenced, their friends and supporters hoped for an early parole. The district attorney, in fact, gave "most emphatic promises" of his support for parole after they had served one year, and on the strength of these assurances, the president of the Los Angeles Soap Company advanced $100,000 to keep the brothers' investment in the Natural Soda Products Company intact.[275] But the years passed, and the brothers remained behind bars. In 1930, the new state banking superintendent expressed the opinion, "For my own part, I do not believe that either of these men concealed money and, while I am not condoning what they did, I sympathise with them."[276] And in 1931, the president of the College of the Pacific lent his voice to those appealing for parole of the two brothers. "My conviction is that in order to bolster Inyo County industries and have available funds to loan to ranchers who were struggling to maintain themselves," he wrote to the state board of prison directors, "they were not acting as criminals although the results were those of criminals."[277]

Not until March 1933 were the brothers finally released. Their businesses by this time had long since been liquidated by the court-appointed receivers. Their uncle George had therefore won the last round of his long competition with Wilfred. But he found no pleasure in this victory. Although the charter for his bank was eventually granted, and the Bank of America by the end of 1934 had taken over all the valley's banking business, George drifted between Los Angeles and the Owens Valley and died in 1935, sitting quietly over a copy of the London *Times*. Wilfred, destitute and broken, returned to his son's home in Long Valley, where he died in 1943. Mark, however, retained his buoyancy and reestablished himself in Los Angeles, where he headed a firm manufacturing paper shredders (of all things) at the time of his death in 1948.[278]

The conviction of the Watterson brothers was received in Los

Angeles as a harbinger of better times to come. "The propaganda which for years has been directed against the city is now shown not only to have been financed by stolen money but to have been motivated by the necessity the Wattersons had of covering up their own criminal acts," observed the *Los Angeles Times*. "This poison spring is now dried up and the two communities will be the healthier for it."[279] The failure of the valley's banks had removed almost all of Mulholland's most prominent adversaries in the valley. Fred Eaton and J. C. Clausen lost everything when the banks closed. Harry Glasscock of the *Owens Valley Herald* was similarly left penniless and eventually committed suicide. Mulholland therefore felt confidence in the future. "For twenty years the consummation of [a program of development for the valley] has been thwarted by those who have preached hatred and violence against the City," declared a publication of the water and power department early in 1928. "But the failure of the Watterson banks apparently has marked the passing of the nightrider and the dynamiter. And now, perhaps, the time has arrived when the City and the Valley will be permitted to join hands in peace and mutual helpfulness."[280]

But Mulholland's problems were far from over. When he abandoned his earlier policy toward Owens Valley agriculture in 1923 and initiated the city's new program of land and water rights acquisitions, Mulholland had done more than set off a war with the valley ranchers; he had also created problems for the operation of the aqueduct itself. By eliminating irrigated agriculture in the upper part of the Owens Valley, he had lost the benefits of the regulation of flows into the aqueduct which the ranchers' farming practices had formerly provided. To compensate for this loss, he had to establish within the aqueduct system the additional storage capacity he had never needed before. As a result, the steady northward progression of the city's purchases in the Owens Valley had been marked by the continuous construction of new reservoirs to receive the increased flows that the devastation of the valley released. The Mulholland and Saint Francis dams were completed in 1924 and 1926, and by 1927 Los Angeles had another reservoir under way at Tinemahah and was accepting bids for a fourth new project at San Gabriel.[281]

The Saint Francis project, however, had already been under

construction when Mulholland began switching his policies. Although it was initially designed for use in connection with the city's power plants in San Francisquito canyon, Mulholland had announced successive expansions of its planned storage capacity in 1924 and 1925, thereby increasing the size of the project by one-fourth. The militancy of the ranchers and the bombing attacks on the aqueduct spurred Mulholland to make these last-minute changes in order to obtain a secure facility capable of storing a full year's supply of water for the city far from the scene of battle in the Owens Valley.[282] But in contrast to the deficiencies in the Long Valley reservoir site which he belatedly claimed to have discovered in 1926, Mulholland had identified very real geologic weaknesses at the site of the Saint Francis project as early as 1911.[283] These concerns he chose to ignore in his desperate haste to bring the new reservoir into service.

Water from the aqueduct began pouring into the new reservoir on March 1, 1926, two months before the dam was completed. By the time the Owens Valley ranchers blew up the No-Name Canyon siphon on May 27, 1927, the reservoir was nearly full, and withdrawals to replace the lost flows from the aqueduct began immediately. That winter the reservoir began to fill once again, and by March 7, 1928, the level of water reached the full capacity of the reservoir for the first time. But the dam had begun to spring leaks almost as soon as water was placed behind it. With the full weight of the reservoir now pressing against it, the rate of leakage increased. On the morning of March 12, Mulholland inspected the structure and pronounced it safe. That night the dam collapsed. A hundred-foot wall of water bearing huge chunks of concrete on its crest swept down the Santa Clara Valley and obliterated three towns and more than four hundred lives along its path.[284]

The Saint Francis Dam disaster prompted no fewer than nine independent investigations, most of them hastily performed and incomplete in their conclusions. The reason for the dam's collapse has never been authoritatively determined, although Charles Outland's *Man-Made Disaster*, first published in 1963, presents a far more thorough and convincing analysis of the structure's failure than any of the official reports. At the time of the disaster, rumors began to circulate almost immediately to the effect that the dam had been blown up by saboteurs from the Owens Valley. Mulholland did nothing to discourage these suggestions and even appeared to subscribe to them in his statements to the press and testimony during the city coroner's investigation. Members of the city water commission were even more outspoken in blaming the ranchers for the dam's collapse, and on March 20, the commission pointedly announced that it was placing the entire aqueduct under armed guard.

The strongest evidence in support of a sabotage theory was submitted by a Stanford University zoologist who reported finding no live fish below the fallen dam. From this he concluded that the fish in the reservoir had been killed by the concussion of a bomb. But as Outland observes, the emotional antipathy toward the city water department in general and Mulholland in particular was so intense following the disaster that "even an unimpeachable sabotage case would have had little chance of acceptance." Endorsement of the sabotage theory eventually collapsed under an intensive editorial barrage from the *Los Angeles Record*, which declared, "We are inclined to believe that there MAY be a dead fish involved in this matter—a fish SO dead that it smells to high heaven. And we think that this fish may be a red herring the Water Board would like to drag across the trail that leads to those responsible for the Saint Francis Dam disaster."[285]

In the end, Mulholland accepted full responsibility for this, the greatest unnatural disaster in California history. His career was now at an end. In Washington, the future of the legislation which would open the way to construction of the Boulder Canyon project was suddenly in doubt. The governor of Arizona, George W. P. Hunt, saw the collapse of the Saint Francis as a boon to his efforts to defeat the Boulder Canyon bill, and he rushed his own investigators to the scene of the destruction.[286] The plight of the Owens Valley thus combined with the Saint Francis Dam disaster to cause the city's supporters in Congress a degree of embarrassment they could ill afford in the midst of their negotiations. As the architect of both the dam and the city's policy toward the Owens Valley, Mulholland had become a liability the city could no longer sustain. "I envy the dead," he told the coroner's inquest on the dam disaster.[287] At the end of November 1928, nearly a year to the day after the Watterson brothers entered San Quentin and only a month before President Coolidge signed the Boulder Canyon act, William Mulholland resigned in disgrace.

With Mulholland gone, the city moved swiftly to settle accounts with the victims of the Saint Francis dam and the remaining landowners of the Owens Valley. A $38-million bond issue was passed in 1930 to pay claims arising from both quarters. The selective purchasing policy Mulholland had pursued in the valley was cast aside in an effort to put an end to the controversy. On February 15, 1929, the water commissioners announced their readiness to purchase every outstanding piece of private property, including town lots which carried with them no water rights. Rather than risk a renewal of the disputes over reparations, the city agreed in this last round of acquisitions to increase the 1929 market prices set by its own panel of appraisers according to a schedule of percentage adjustments designed to reflect the depreciation of market values that had occurred as a result of the city's policies since 1923. The city paid a total of $5,798,780 for the town properties: for Bishop $2,975,833; Big Pine $722,635; Independence $730,306; Laws $102,446; and Lone Pine $1,217,560. Only the claims of Keeler, which was by that time disappearing beneath shifting banks of sand, alkali, and soda from the dry bed of Owens Lake, were ignored by the city. Most of the remaining farm properties were purchased for a total of $1,120,087. No payments were made for estimated business losses or for the value of fixtures and equipment, and all sales were conditioned upon a release of the city from liability for any reparations claims. On these terms, the city by 1933 had expanded its holdings in the valley to include 95 percent of all farmlands and 85 percent of the town properties.[288]

In the years of the Great Depression, these generous settlements were a great aid to the valley's refugees. But many longtime residents chose to remain. Some continued to work their former lands under leasing arrangements with the city. Others found work with the aqueduct or with the local district offices of the state highway commission or the federal Indian and forestry services. Overall, the population of Inyo County by 1930 declined only 6.8 percent from its level in 1920. In the northern part of the Owens Valley, however, the loss of population was closer to 20 percent.[289] Those who left what Willie Arthur Chalfant called "the impending desolation that was Owens Valley" suffered "the wrench that the expatriate feels on being driven from his homeland." In 1934, Will C. Parcher and his wife, who purchased the *Owens Valley Herald*, published a slim volume of poems describing the valley in this period. They depicted one man closing up the store his father had founded: "A pioneer once more—a pioneer with his life behind him." Their most evocative phrase, however, was one with double meaning which they attributed to a mother comforting her children: "For land's sake, don't start to cry."[290] One fifth-generation valley resident later recalled, "For a while, the valley was still green, even after city bulldozers knocked down the farmhouses. The soil is so good and water so plentiful, that the grass kept coming back each spring as if the farms were still there. But it got drier and drier, until the sagebrush took over."[291]

Mulholland meanwhile entered a life of enforced obscurity. His fall from public affection could scarcely have been more complete. He was blamed not only for the hundreds who had perished below the Saint Francis Dam but also for the suffering of the Owens Valley. His critics fastened upon the Saint Francis Dam disaster as proof of his incompetence, noting that two other dams for which he had acted as consultant had subsequently collapsed and that the city had abandoned his last dam project at San Gabriel after five million dollars had been spent.[292] Mulholland's example reflected negatively upon the entire engineering profession. The fears that sprang from the Saint Francis disaster engendered a new state program for the certification of dam safety. And when Mulholland died on July 22, 1935, the *Western Construction News* took care to distinguish his career from its own vision of what a professional engineer should be. It happened that D. C. Henny passed away at nearly the same time as Mulholland. Henny had served as chairman of the panel of engineers that first reviewed the Reclamation Service's plans for the Owens Valley, and he had thereby played a key role in giving the aqueduct its start. In its obituary of these two prominent western water engineers, the *Western Construction News* contrasted Mulholland's methods with the ideal of professionalism it found in Henny's example. Henny was portrayed as an analyst who studied a problem in all its phases, "patiently eliminating errors and inaccurate deduction." In Mulholland's case, however, "the accent was heavy on the urge to overcome obstacles and accomplish results. One, the judge weighing the evidence of the case before arriving at the verdict; the other, the prosecutor, driving, always driving to get things done."[293]

The harshest judgment of Mulholland's actions lay in the damage he had done to the principle of public water development. More than any other individual, William Mulholland, through the building of the aqueduct and the formation of the Metropolitan Water District, established the principle of public ownership of water indelibly on California's history. But the furor that followed upon the mistakes made in the last seven years of his public service discredited the man and thereby gave aid to the enemies of the ideal he had labored all his life to establish. As the *Sacramento Union* noted in concluding its series of articles on the Owens Valley controversy in 1927, "There is a warning to be heeded. Here is a case where political ownership of public utilities had full sway for demonstration. The city concerned reverted to ruthlessness, savage disregard for moral and economic equations, to chicanery and faith-breaking ... The municipality became a destroyer, deliberately, unconscionably, boastfully."[294]

Mulholland's friends and colleagues, many of whom had found their own reputations tarnished by his disgrace, mounted a desultory campaign to restore his good name both before and after his death. Especially active in this effort was J. B. Lippincott because he suffered most from the criticism in the press of the city's treatment of the Owens Valley, which inevitably rehashed his intervention on Los Angeles' behalf a quarter-century earlier. The memoirs and tributes to Mulholland that appeared in this period consequently attempted to portray him as a figure larger than life, fighting Apaches on the Colorado River as a youth and poring over copies of Carlyle, Pope, and Shakespeare by the light of a coal oil lamp at night.[295] It also became customary at this time when writing biographical sketches of Mulholland never to mention the Saint Francis Dam.[296]

The old man took little interest in this foolishness. He started an autobiography but dropped it. He returned to the city water department from time to time to offer his advice and made his last public appearance at a celebration at Cabazon marking the commencement of construction on the city's new aqueduct to the Colorado.[297] For the most part, he was content. Just before his death, he took H. A. Van Norman, his successor as head of the city water department, to the top of a hill overlooking the burgeoning San Fernando Valley. "The fact that the valley has developed as it has is compensation enough for all of us," he said quietly.[298] After his passing, the Department of Water and Power set a plaque beneath his portrait that concluded, "The hours flow on without him, yet the years to come will bear the record of his will."[299]

CHAPTER SEVEN

Legacy

There is no statue of William Mulholland at the Department of Water and Power today. His portrait has been relegated to an obscure corner outside the commissioners' meeting room at the department headquarters. But the building, like the agency it houses, is a testament to his achievement. Its seventeen stories command the top of a hill overlooking the complex of local, state, and federal offices in downtown Los Angeles. Whereas the other government structures in the city center are clad in white stone, the department has chosen to sheath itself in black glass. The main entrance is approached by a black slate bridge over a 4.75-acre pool that borders the building. As a result the overall effect is of a dark tower guarded by a moat, brooding over the city like some ancient battlement in a fairy tale.[1]

In keeping with its medieval aspect, the Department of Water and Power building is framed by the main court of the Chandler family pavilions, which house the city's major cultural events. It is especially fitting that the monuments of these two great institutions, the *Times* and the department, which have played so large a part in the development of Los Angeles in this century, should be thus paired on a special prominence, with all the other agencies of government appropriately arrayed at their feet.

Each structure expresses something of the contributions its builders have made to the modern metropolis. The department's headquarters, for example, is studiously impersonal, bureaucratic, its interior spaces divided by seven and a half miles of entirely movable partitions. Its design, rather than emphasizing individuals, stresses the commodities the agency has brought to the building up of Los Angeles: the structure is powered entirely by electricity, and the conspicuous display of water abundance in the vast exterior pool and ornamental fountains is its principal architectural feature.[2] The Chandler pavilions, by contrast, stand as monuments to the ego of their patrons. The pavilions are built in that style peculiar to Southern California which confuses empty space with opulence. But here the barren expanses of marble walls have been turned to listing the names of every individual or corporation who contributed significantly to their construction. Where these congratulatory graffiti give way, floor-to-ceiling mirrors take their place. And in the center of the main pavilion, the gown Dorothy Chandler wore to the building's opening has been enshrined on a mannequin whose flesh is money green and whose eyes are opals.

If the physical presence of William Mulholland has been all but expunged from the Department of Water and Power headquarters, his influence there is undiminished. None of his successors has ever dominated the city's water programs or captured the public imagination as he did. The public works he initiated remain the principal source of the city's water supply. And the policies and attitudes he originated with regard to the Owens Valley have been pursued without significant alteration or even serious reconsideration throughout the half-century since his fall.

The most obvious and immediate aspect of Mulholland's legacy that the department had to contend with was the enduring bitterness of relations with the Owens Valley. Even after the backbone of the resistance to Los Angeles had been broken by the collapse of the Watterson banks, the valley's partisans continued to wage battle with the city in print. As a result, the Owens Valley controversy came to be one instance in which the history of a conflict was not written by the victors. The most prominent formulator of the legend of the valley's victimization was Willie Arthur Chalfant, the lone survivor among the leaders of resistance in the 1920s. Chalfant's love for the Owens Valley was deeply rooted. His father, Pleasant Arthur Chalfant, founded the valley's first newspaper, the *Inyo Independent*, in 1870. From 1889, Willie was sole owner of his father's second paper, the *Inyo Register*.[3] Having grown up with the valley, Chalfant resolved to stay on to write the history of the city's conquest. In 1933 he published a revised version of his *Story of Inyo* in which he depicted the valley's plight with all the sentimental flourishes Court Kunze had introduced in his advertisements for the protective association in 1927. Los Angeles was presented unquestionably as the aggressor, and the problems of valley irrigation and the role the Wattersons and their district had played in the conflict were accordingly given little notice.

The readership for county histories is usually quite limited. But the same year Chalfant's revised *Story of Inyo* appeared, Morrow Mayo published his own version of the controversy in a trashy and sensationalist history of the city called *Los Angeles*. The thrust of his analysis was encapsulated in his title for the chapter dealing with "The Rape of the Owens Valley," a phrase that has endured in the public memory of these events long after Mayo's book has been forgotten. "The City of Los Angeles moved through this valley like a devastating plague," he wrote. "It was ruthless, stupid, cruel, and crooked ... For no sound reason, for no sane reason, it destroyed a helpless agricultural section and a dozen towns. It was an obscene enterprise from beginning to end."[4]

Both Chalfant and Mayo relied heavily upon the research of Andrae B. Nordskog, whose *Gridiron* newspaper in Los Angeles had taken up the valley's cause. An opera singer manqué and aspiring politician, Nordskog ran as the Liberty party's vice presidential nominee in 1932 on a platform calling for abolition of the electoral college, monetary reform, and America First. Water policy and the denigration of the Department of Water and Power, however, were his special passions. Through the pages of his newspaper and his radio talks on the "Gridiron Hour," Nordskog poured out a steady stream of abuse against the "political plutocrats" who shaped the city's water programs. He fought the Metropolitan Water District, the state's plan for development of the Central Valley Project, and the Los Angeles County Flood Control District's efforts at water conservation, arguing in all instances that salt water conversion would be cheaper than these programs for freshwater development. As president of the Southwest Water League, he gave a new platform to another self-appointed crusader against the Department of Water and Power, F. C. Finkle, who had denounced Mulholland's concrete fifteen years earlier. And in Washington, he burrowed into the early records of the Reclamation Service to unearth much of the documentary evidence of J. B. Lippincott's perfidy.[5]

The works of Chalfant, Nordskog, and Mayo drew together the separate threads of controversy that had grown up around the aqueduct since the first bond election in 1905 and wove them into the popular perception of Los Angeles as the devastator of a fabulously productive agricultural community. Thus the pundit Will Rogers observed caustically of the Owens Valley in 1932, "Ten years ago this was a wonderful valley with one quarter of a million acres of fruit and alfalfa. But Los Angeles needed more water for the Chamber of Commerce to drink more toasts to its growth, more water to dilute its orange juice, more water for its geraniums to delight the tourists, while the giant cottonwoods here died. So, now, this is a valley of desolation."[6] In a similar vein, Cornelius Vanderbilt commented in the *Reno Journal*, "Probably in all Western history there has not been a more flagrant example of one part of the country, politically and financially powerful, destroying a weaker section. And doing it without regard to obligations, moral or financial."[7]

So compelling was this simple story of noble farmers in conflict with the malevolent city that it passed readily into the realm of popular fiction. In 1935, Republic Pictures sent a youthful John Wayne and the Mesquiteers riding to the aid of New Hope Valley in the film *New Frontier*.[8] The valley is threatened by a water project for Metropole City, and when the ranchers prove reluctant to give up their homes, the city's construction chief, Murdoch MacQuarrie, an obvious stand-in for Mulholland, turns belligerent. "Say, mister, you don't know the kind of people you're dealing with," John Wayne warns MacQuarrie—while his sidekick, Windy, chuckles toward the camera, "But he'll find out." In the ensuing conflict the ranchers reveal themselves to be "a bunch of fighting fools." The city nevertheless bests these "mule-headed hicks" with "lowdown Injun tricks." In the end, Wayne punches out the Mulholland character and the city is compelled to resettle the ranchers and provide them with an irrigation project in a nearby valley, Devil's Acres.

George Palmer Putnam and Frances Gragg tell a similar story in their novel of the Owens Valley conflict, *Golden Valley*. Here J.B. Lippincott makes a brief appearance as a double-dealing liar, and Wilfred Watterson is depicted even more briefly in the person of Frank Master, a proud but stubborn banker who is destroyed "trying to fight Los Angeles with dollars—the city that had a hundred thousand dollars to his one." Rather than resisting the city, most of the ranchers simply go off and commit suicide in this story. There are some incidents of night riding and there is an attempt to dynamite the aqueduct, which the hero easily deflects. But in the end the violence is revealed to be the work of land speculators who have been fomenting armed hostilities in the hope of persuading the city to buy up their properties. Since the ranchers extract confessions from these evil-doers by torture and then dispose of the bodies, the moral perspective of the novel is somewhat confused.

The strongest character is that of Mulholland, here portrayed as Angus MacAndrew, a great, hulking brute of a man with huge hands and a pitted face who speaks in a comic-opera Scottish burr. Although MacAndrew and the ranchers are eventually reconciled, his best scene involves a confrontation with the heroine who owns the lands at Haiwee that MacAndrew must have as a reservoir site for his aqueduct. When she refuses to negotiate, MacAndrew becomes apoplectic (something he does frequently throughout the book) and rises to waggle a massive finger under her nose. "As for ye, Miss," he thunders, "ye've had yere fair chance. From now on this is war. Sine it takes one year or ten, we'll have yon Haiwee. In the whilst, I'll dig my ditch to its very edge. When th' courts gie the final worrd, I'll droon ye under forty foot o' water. Come hell or high water, my city drinks. Come on, men!"[9]

These presentations contrast markedly with the two other fictional treatments of the controversy that appeared before the little civil war of the 1920s broke out. Peter B. Kyne used the

Owens Valley as the scene of his 1914 western adventure story *The Long Chance*. After three impressive opening chapters in which the author demonstrates how well he can write, the novel settles into a conventional potboiler that turns on a water scheme of bewildering complexity. The roguish hero McGraw is set against an eastern land speculator who is told by one of the valley's residents early on, "This country is mine and I love it, and I won't have it profaned by any growling, dyspeptic little squirt from a land where they have pie for breakfast." There is governmental corruption here, but it is located in the General Land Office in Sacramento. The villains are all private speculators. The city's project is mentioned, but only in passing, and then as a potentially beneficial alternative to the hero's plans to use the valley's water "to make thirty-two thousand acres of barren waste bloom and furnish clean, unsullied wealth for a few thousand poor, crushed devils that have been slaughtered and maimed under the Juggernaut of our Christian civilization."[10]

The city is similarly blameless in Mary Austin's novelization of the controversy, *The Ford*, published in 1917. Just as she fled the conflict in her own life, Austin backs away from it in her book. The valley she describes is imaginary, and the water project that would devastate it is proposed as an alternative to the Hetch Hetchy plan for San Francisco. In all other respects, the location of her story is clear. Long Valley here becomes Tierra Longa, Round Valley is Terra Rondo, the Hillside Water Company is the Hillside Ditch Company, and so forth. Eaton and Lippincott appear as minor characters, the one dressed all in black with an evil eye, and the other as an alcoholic engineer who has fallen prey to "that cult of Locality, by which so much is forgiven as long as it is done in the name of the Good of the Town." The Lippincott character sustains himself in his treachery with alcoholic delusions of being honored as "San Francisco's most public spirited citizen . . . He had looted the wilderness; he had led a river captive. It was a tremendous thing to have done, a man's-size thing. The sort of thing a Man's Own Town expected of him, as a witness to its superiority over all other towns."[11]

But Lippincott is not the villain of Austin's piece, nor is the proposed water project the real threat to the valley's survival.

Austin's attention is focused instead upon the weaknesses of the ranchers themselves. Their true adversary is the local financier Timothy Rickart, who dominates Tierra Longa in the same way T. B. Rickey ruled Long Valley in the years Mary Austin lived in Owens Valley. The first half of the book is steeped in the sadness of her own life with Stafford W. Austin as she follows the tribulations of the Brent family, whose patriarch is perpetually unable to "get into" any profitable line of employment: "Things hovered, bright, irreducible promises that seemed about to fold their wings and rest upon the fortunes of the Brents, only to sail high over them at last and fix on the most unlikely quarters." Brent is no different from the other men of Tierra Longa, who stand in awe of Rickart's superior skill in business and pursue their own petty schemes of riches in hopes that they shall by some lucky stroke not "fall for him . . . but fall in with him." Their refusal to recognize their own best interests and work together, of course, plays directly into Rickart's plans. "These men of Tierra Longa plotted without knowledge and imagined childishly. They were as much the victims of their own limitations as they were likely to be of the machinations of Rickart . . . producers rather than players of the game."[12]

The hero of the story eventually gives up his own career to lead the ranchers in opposition to Rickart's scheme, but they refuse to follow him. As Austin observes, the ranchers knew that Rickart "was the enemy, no doubt, but he was also illusion, the satisfaction of that incurable desire of men to be played upon, to be handled." The hero's efforts, nevertheless, succeed in delaying the project long enough so that the city decides to go to Hetch Hetchy for its water supply instead. The ranchers then turn against the hero for besting Rickart. The whole book has built toward this bleak conclusion. But Austin's resolve again gives way, and she tacks on a last ten pages of unrelentingly gratuitous happy endings: after a considerable passage of time, the ranchers come round to join in erecting an irrigation project of their own; Rickart and the hero are reconciled and Rickart tells the hero where oil can be found; and his fortune now assured, the hero goes back to the valley to find his girlfriend waiting on the riverbank, where she has apparently been standing for several months in expectation of his eventual return.[13]

Austin and Kyne wrote at a time when relations between the city and the valley were at their best and it still seemed possible to imagine a future of prosperity for the valley. But in their novels, as in the later works of Chalfant, Mayo, Nordskog, and Putnam and Gragg, and the other books and films which have treated the controversy in passing, there is a common theme in the brutality and deception employed by the enemies of the Owens Valley.[14] This all-pervading popular perception of the Department of Water and Power as an unscrupulous agency whose word cannot be trusted has plagued Los Angeles' water programs to the present day. But in the 1930s, hostility toward the department posed more than a simple problem of public relations. It threatened as well to interfere with the department's ability to carry forward the new projects Mulholland had initiated to meet the water famine that he had convinced the city was looming.

The torrent of criticism of the department that had been unleashed by the collapse of the Saint Francis Dam was not stopped by Mulholland's departure. Instead, with Mulholland gone, the department was swept up in a divisive political controversy which persisted for the next dozen years. In the mayoralty election of 1929, the *Los Angeles Record*, which for years had condemned the city's water and power commissioners as "traitors to Los Angeles," threw its support to John C. Porter, who campaigned on a promise of strong support for public ownership and sweeping reform of the Department of Water and Power.[15] Upon taking office, Porter demanded the resignations of all the commissioners, declaring, "The public has lost confidence in the administration of these utilities and is demanding that politics be eliminated from the department and that conservative business methods be substituted throughout."[16]

Porter's objective was to bring the department back under municipal control. Having sought to insulate its administration from political influence when it was first created under the city charter, the Los Angeles voters now recognized that they had created within the department a distinct political entity whose influence was unchecked by the other agencies of local government. Mulholland had been a power unto himself and had not hesitated to oppose the commissioners or the mayor on questions involving his own policy. In 1923, the Public Service Commission had begun appropriating funds to cover the political expenses of its various campaigns for municipal bond issues, a practice the state supreme court halted in 1927. Following the supreme court's action, the department employees had taken to marshaling their great numbers to provide the candidates and issues which their association supported with an immensely influential block of campaign workers and votes.[17]

Porter's efforts to dismantle what had come to be called the Water and Power Machine focused on E. F. Scattergood's administration of the power bureau. Despite the opposition of the local private utilities and successive defeats at the polls with his bond issues, Scattergood by 1928 had built his organization into the largest public utility in the nation, and he bid fair to replace Mulholland as the dominant figure in the politics of water and power in Los Angeles. To prevent this, Porter at first consolidated the power bureau under the general administration of Mulholland's successor at the water department. He then dismissed Scattergood's key political operatives when he discovered they were removing the political campaign files of the employees' association to prevent disclosure of their contents.[18] The attack on Scattergood was hailed by conservative business interests in Los Angeles as a step toward taking the city out of the public power business, and it was damned on the same score by the progressive supporters of municipal ownership. As a result, the department's employees joined with the progressives to form a Municipal Power and Light Defense League, which elected a new majority on the city council that was pledged to oppose Porter's policies. In the ensuing struggle, which raged throughout the successive administrations of Porter, Frank Shaw, and Fletcher Bowron, the department was repeatedly reorganized, appointees to the commission were regularly blocked, removed, and reappointed with stunning alacrity, key departmental personnel were dismissed to be replaced by cronies of whichever administration happened to be in power at the time, and Scattergood was variously removed, brought back, placed on contract, suspended, and ultimately bivouacked to Washington.[19]

Although criticism of Los Angeles' treatment of the Owens Valley certainly encouraged distrust of the department, concern for the well-being of the valley residents played little part in the political opposition to the department within Los Angeles. On the contrary, Mayor Porter's efforts to restore "conservative business methods" to the administration of municipal water and power programs generated a concern that the city was in fact being too generous in its settlements with the valley. When the city first announced its intention to buy out the valley at the end of February 1929, the purchase price for the outstanding properties was estimated at $8 million.[20] By the time municipal bonds were approved to pay for these acquisitions on May 20, 1930, however, the estimated cost had risen to $12.5 million. And since the department was continuing to take farm lands out of production in order to maximize the yield of water into the aqueduct, the city had no expectation of being able to generate any income on much of the property it was acquiring, a point of vital concern to many of the more economy-minded members of the water and power commission and city council.

The confusion that infected the department as a result of Porter's attempts at reform ensnarled the process of negotiation with the valley's representatives. Special problems in Bishop brought further delay. Each of the five towns of the Owens Valley appointed two representatives to a Committee of Ten for purposes of negotiating the purchase prices of the town lots. In addition to naming its own delegates to the committee, B. E. Johnson and C. H. Rhudy, Bishop retained a consultant appraiser whose estimates of the worth of the Bishop properties differed drastically from the values attached to them by Los Angeles. To resolve the impasse, Johnson and Rhudy proposed that the value of the Bishop properties be calculated on the basis of the growth rates achieved by the counties of the South Coast since 1923. But since assessed valuation on the South Coast had expanded at a rate ten times greater than that experienced by Inyo County in this period, the suggestion was unacceptable to Los Angeles. Instead, Harlan Palmer, representing the water and power commission, persuaded the Committee of Ten to accept a schedule of purchase prices that would increase the appraised market values of the town properties in 1929 by 40 percent for Bishop, 34.5 percent for Laws, 30 percent for Big Pine, 25 percent for Independence, and nothing for Lone Pine. Johnson's and Rhudy's objections were overridden, and Johnson responded by joining with a former state senator, Joe Riley, to organize a pool of thirty-one Bishop businessmen who demanded double the adjusted price Los Angeles was offering for their commercial parcels.[21]

Porter regarded this as an attempt to reap speculative profits at the City's expense, and he was so incensed that he immediately directed the department to advise all the land owners in the Owens Valley that "they will not require, in any particular, the services of legal advisors or land brokers in dealing with the city ... I shall seriously question any land purchase transaction that may have been presented to the city through the medium of a third party, whether that third party be an individual broker, a so-called legal advisor, or a syndicate."[22] In trying to deny the valley residents their legitimate right to counsel, Porter was successful neither in speeding the purchasing program nor in quieting the fear of speculation. By the beginning of 1931, the members of the water and power committee of the city council were blocking the acquisition program on grounds that the prices the department had agreed to pay were excessive.[23] And these delays in turn encouraged many valley residents to throw in their lot with the Southern Sierras Power Company, which had brought suit to block operation of the city's wells and had also formed the Municipal Water Supply Company of California for the express purpose of buying up properties in the Owens Valley in speculative competition with Los Angeles.[24]

The need to achieve a speedy settlement with the valley residents was especially acute because the city's faltering acquisition program had by this time stirred renewed interest in the state legislature in the problems of the Owens Valley. The senate formed a special investigating committee to examine the water situation in Inyo and Mono counties in the spring of 1931, and its hearings provided Andrae Nordskog with the forum he had been seeking to present his charges against the city. On the basis of his research into Lippincott's activities with the Reclamation Service, Nordskog had developed an elaborate indictment of the aqueduct project, claiming variously that Lippincott was corrupt, Roosevelt had been misled, the project was a tool of the San Fernando land syndicate, and the taxpayers of Los Angeles were being robbed. He blanketed local, state, and federal authorities with demands for a formal investigation. Successive grand juries in Los Angeles, however, ignored his requests. The same appeal to Washington had brought a bemused response from the Secretary of the Interior, noting, "Upon consideration of your letter, it would appear that the events described occurred some 25 years ago, and that under present facts and conditions, there is nothing therein which would form a basis for action by this Department."[25] In Sacramento, however, Nordskog's testimony was so well received that extraordinary arrangements were made for it to be printed in the legislative record.[26]

In its report in May, the special investigating committee agreed that the prices Los Angeles was paying for the Owens Valley properties were fair. But it deplored the city's refusal to honor reparations claims or make any allowances for fixtures or business losses resulting from the devastation of the valley. Since the remaining claims for reparations amounted to less than $500,000, the committee urged Los Angeles to be generous. These problems aside, the committee's principal concern was with the future, and particularly with finding the means to assure that the hardships suffered by the Owens Valley would not be visited upon the Mono Basin as Los Angeles proceeded with its plans to extend the aqueduct there. To prevent a repetition of the Owens Valley conflict, the committee recommended adoption of legislation similar to the statutes in New York requiring that a municipality which seeks to extend its water system to a distant source of supply must first submit its plans to a state commission which would also receive and adjudicate all claims for damages arising from that development.[27]

The heritage of bitterness toward Mulholland's policies in the Owens Valley, however, ran deeper than the committee imagined. For in addition to the means for mediating disputes that the committee had called for, the legislature that year went a step further and enacted an outright prohibition against the draining of one region of the state for the sake of development in another. Water resources planning for California would henceforth proceed under the strictures of this fundamental guarantee that the water-rich rural areas of the state could never again be threatened with the loss of the water needed for their own future development.[28] This so-called County of Origin law thus became part of Mulholland's legacy. But for the Mono Basin, as for the Owens Valley, its protection came too late.

The Mono Extension

The threat of state intervention in the department's plans for tapping the water supply of the Mono Basin was the first new wrinkle in a process which had otherwise been conducted as an almost perfect carbon copy of Mulholland's development of the original aqueduct. Although Los Angeles began acquiring lands and water rights in the Mono Basin as early as 1912 and 1913 for eventual use in conjunction with its plans for power development in the gorge below Long Valley, no serious effort was committed to the project until Galen Dixon and the associated ditch companies of the Owens Valley threatened in 1919 to scotch the project with their own plans for the Fish Slough reservoir.[29] At this point, Mulholland turned to the Reclamation Service for the same assistance in preparing the detailed surveys for the Mono project that they had provided for the original aqueduct.

Considering the intense embarrassment its first involvement with Los Angeles had caused the Reclamation Service, it seems incredible that the responsible federal officials would have been willing to risk a second engagement. But Mulholland had maintained his close personal relationship with Arthur Powell Davis, who succeeded Newell as the head of the service, and on March 29, 1920, an agreement was struck. The device for federal involvement in the project was a cooperative contract whereby the service, in exchange for the reimbursement of costs by the city, promised to prepare detailed plans, surveys, and cost estimates for an extension of Los Angeles' aqueduct to the Mono Basin. Since Los Angeles was paying for the study, the bureau took the extraordinary position that this was a private matter between two public agencies; the results of the work performed by the federal engineers were never published but were deemed instead to be the property of Los Angeles, which exercised exclusive control over their distribution.[30]

The report, which was prepared by Harold Conkling, appeared in both preliminary and final forms, which differed dramatically in content. Both focused on the prospects for development of Rush and Lee Vining Creeks in Mono County, which Conkling estimated were capable of delivering 142,000 acre-feet of water annually into the headwaters of the Owens River for diversion south to the aqueduct. The third major stream in the southern portion of the Mono Basin, Mill Creek, was dismissed from consideration because its flows were too small and the costs of tapping it through a six-mile tunnel would be too high to justify its development. Also, as in the Owens Valley, these initial plans did not address the possibilities of developing the upper portion of the basin because the waters there were already in use. The Southern Sierras Power Company and its subsidiary, the Cain Irrigation Company, controlled all the waters above the point of the proposed diversion, principally for power development. So the Mono extension, like the aqueduct before it, was planned initially to operate on the discharge from these preexisting activities without interfering with them in any way.[31]

As with the development of the aqueduct, the survey work of the Reclamation Service was conducted in the name of irrigation for the Owens Valley. In view of the fact that the city's only interest in the project in 1920 was for power development and augmentation of the aqueduct supply—interests which had nothing to do with the mandate of the Reclamation Service at that time—such a pretext was essential in order to invest the federal government's involvement with even a patina of legitimacy. The pretext was all the more important because the plan, though it would not interfere with the Southern Sierras Power Company plants, would take approximately three thousand acres of land presently irrigated in the Mono Basin out of production. These were marginal irrigation operations, however; and in Conkling's view the water could be better used in the Owens Valley.[32]

The harsh climate and rugged terrain of the Mono Basin does

not lend itself to agricultural development, and for this reason, federal officials had long recognized that applications filed for irrigation development on the public lands of Mono County would most likely be used instead for power development. Because the generation of hydroelectric power was considered a more desirable application of the basin's water supplies, the government had displayed a willingness since 1910 to overlook irregularities in the actual uses made under the permits it issued. Even so, development of the basin had been delayed by a long-running competition between the Southern Sierras and Cain Irrigation Company on the one hand and the California-Nevada Power Company and Rush Creek Mutual Ditch Company on the other.

The controversy over the rights of these companies to develop Rush and Lee Vining Creeks had been marked by incidents of fraud and bad faith by all parties. And the litigation of their conflicting claims had culminated in a judicial decree which gave the Cain and Southern Sierras companies the upper hand in a decision which appeared, at least to the state officials who reviewed it, to conflict not only with the facts in the case but also with the established principles of water law in California.[33] As a result, at the time Conkling made his studies, the Rush Creek company was scarcely operating at all, whereas the Cain company was growing nothing but native hay. Cain, moreover, was dumping as much as six acre-feet of water a year on each acre it had in production. And although the company attempted to justify this excessive usage as a means of controlling weeds, the practice seemed clearly intended simply as a method of protecting the company's water rights rather than for any real agricultural purpose.[34]

It was in explaining how this proposed power project for Los Angeles would be used to benefit agriculture in the Owens Valley that the Conkling study changed most dramatically between its preliminary and final versions. In his initial report, Conkling estimated there were 137,000 acres of potentially irrigable land in the area of Bishop and Independence, although only 46,000 acres were at that time irrigated. The additional supply from the Mono Basin, once the needs of the aqueduct were deducted, would be enough to bring 60,000 acres into production. For the short term, Conkling proposed applying most of the benefits of this new system to the lands outside Bishop. Development of the Independence region could follow later, provided there was enough water available. "The importance of not jeopardizing the aqueduct supply is the paramount consideration in this," Conkling noted. If, however, the Bishop landowners balked at the installation of the drainage system Conkling considered essential for the efficient management of these lands, then development of Independence could begin immediately; Los Angeles owned most of the lands there, and the city, Conkling felt certain, would agree to anything.[35]

Conkling, of course, recognized that the project was intended principally for power development. He was acting too under the false impression that Los Angeles had already begun building its proposed plants in the gorge. He consequently included the Long Valley reservoir as the key regulating facility upon which the entire operation of his plan depended. But in trying to build an irrigation element into his proposal, he had to strain to make the numbers fit. Conkling estimated in his 1920 report that the project as a whole would cost $8 million to construct. He could assign only $1.6 million of this to the benefits of irrigation in the Owens Valley. The rest would consequently have to be borne entirely by Los Angeles for the power and additional water supplies it would be receiving. And even to justify the $1.6 million figure for the irrigation share of the project, Conkling had to make two heady assumptions that the landowners in Bishop would be able to bear the $100 per acre cost the new water supply would impose on them, and that they would somehow magically reduce their rate of water use to only two acre-feet per acre each year.[36]

It was no doubt useful to Mulholland to be able to tell the owners of the associated ditch companies that he was sponsoring surveys for expanded irrigation in the Owens Valley when he was trying to head off their plans for the Fish Slough reservoir and assuage their opposition to his right-of-way bill in the first half of 1920. But by the time Conkling's preliminary report was complete, the city's bill in Congress had been enacted and Mulholland had no real desire to improve the situation of his adversaries in Bishop.

So he commenced construction of the small dam at Long Valley to demonstrate his good faith with the Reclamation Service and meanwhile set to work preparing a new contract for the continuation of their work. On March 9, 1921, Conkling was sent back to his drawing board to come up with a new plan.

What he produced was much closer to the city's wishes, but it included some unsettling elements for Mulholland as well. In the final report Conkling submitted in September 1921 it was proposed that the agricultural lands of Bishop be bypassed almost entirely. Instead, the properties the city already owned in the vicinity of Independence were slated to receive the bulk of the benefits of irrigation water from the Mono extension. In exchange, the city proposed to turn over title to these lands to the federal government, free. And by avoiding the privately held lands of Bishop, Conkling explained, the risk of local resistance to the installation of a drainage system would be obviated.[37] In addition, Conkling revised his cost estimates for the project downward to $6 million while increasing the share attributed for irrigation to $2 million. And since all these costs would presumably have to be borne by the federal government as the new titleholder to the lands to be benefited, there would be no risk that any landowners would balk at the expense of the development or protest at having to get by on only two acre-feet of water per acre per year.[38]

Conkling, however, had by this time realized that the operation of the Long Valley reservoir for power generation at the reduced size the city proposed to build it would not be compatible with the delivery of irrigation water at the times in the growing season when it would be most needed. To safeguard agricultural development, his revised plan therefore called for the expansion of the Long Valley project and either the construction of the Fish Slough reservoir or the dedication of a portion of the storage capacity of the Long Valley reservoir for irrigation. None of these proposals, of course, was especially appealing to Mulholland.[39]

The illusion that the Reclamation Service's investigation for Los Angeles had anything to do with irrigation for the Owens Valley had never been particularly persuasive in any event. Conkling himself acknowledged in his preliminary report that development of the project for the sake of irrigation would have made no fiscal sense except for the much larger benefits in the form of hydroelectric power generation that would also accrue.[40] In August 1921, even before Conkling turned in his final report, the Mono Grand Jury demanded an investigation of the entire undertaking by the state engineer. Progress on the investigation, however, was delayed because the chief engineer of the Reclamation Service, Frank E. Weymouth, refused to make any portion of Conkling's work available to state authorities. On Los Angeles' sufferance, Weymouth eventually provided State Engineer W. F. McClure with a copy of the report; but though Weymouth granted this concession in May 1922, he sent McClure only the preliminary report of 1920. Access to the final report, with its far more favorable conclusions with respect to Los Angeles, was strictly prohibited.[41]

Even operating with this limited information, McClure's investigator, Sidney T. Harding, concluded, "This project is feasible, if at all, only because of the power possibilities involved . . . Its margin of attractiveness seems small . . . [and] entirely dependent on the willingness of the City of Los Angeles to carry the cost of diversion from Mono Basin for the value of the power which may be secured." Since Harding regarded the city as the only real beneficiary of the plan, he chided the Reclamation Service for its involvement, noting, "The City can be presumed to be able to finance the development without the aid of Federal interest-free funds."[42]

Any possibility that the service might have acted on Conkling's plan ended with Arthur Powell Davis' dismissal on June 20, 1923, in a sweeping attempt at reform of the federal reclamation program. Thoughts of expanded irrigation in the Owens Valley, if they had ever been seriously entertained, submerged in the hysteria that was simultaneously sweeping Mulholland's department. And Mulholland's steadfast refusal to give any further consideration to development of the Long Valley reservoir meant that the city's plans for power development had also to be set aside. The Mono extension was henceforth regarded first and foremost as a water supply project for the aqueduct.

The contract with the Reclamation Service had nonetheless

been far more than an idle exercise from the city's point of view.
For in addition to Conkling's detailed surveys, Mulholland had
secured a benefit of far greater value: the assurance that no further
development could occur within the Mono Basin which might
conflict with the city's eventual construction of the aqueduct
extension. And the federal government continued to hold the
basin in suspense, just as it had held the Owens Valley, for as
long as Los Angeles took to get its plans in motion.

Obtaining this measure of protection was undoubtedly Mulholland's primary rationale for pursuing the contract with the
Reclamation Service in the first place. The city had attempted in
1913 and again in 1915 to block proposed developments on Rush
and Lee Vining Creeks, arguing that the power they could generate would be needed in Los Angeles. But the appeals of the public
service commissioners had been flatly rejected. As the district
engineer of the federal Forest Service commented at the time,
"The protest was not taken seriously by either the State Water
Commission nor [sic] the District Office since the City had never
gone to the trouble of making applications or surveys of the
various reservoir sites until after the [applicants] had filed the
necessary plans and applications and also after [they] had been
granted easements on the various reservoirs."[43]

As soon as the terms of the contract with the city had been
agreed upon, and even before the contract was approved, Arthur
Powell Davis began withdrawing from settlement the lands that
would be covered by Conkling's investigations. When his superiors in the Department of the Interior noted that these same
lands were involved in the city's right-of-way bill, which was then
pending before the Congress and encountering "very strenuous"
opposition from the power and irrigation interests it would affect,
they demanded to know whether Davis' recommendations for
withdrawals constituted an attempt to get around the amendments to the bill that Los Angeles had already accepted. If so, the
Board of Appeals for the Department of the Interior observed,
"It would seem to be contrary to the spirit, intent, and purpose of
the bill mentioned and the agreement on the part of . . . the city."
Davis responded cryptically, "While this withdrawal will prevent
homestead and desert entries, etc., it will not embarrass the Sec-

retary in granting any easement that seems desirable."[44] On this assurance, the withdrawals were approved on April 5, 1920, and then modified at Davis' request on April 19 to remove those lands which lacked potential for power development. A week later, however, Davis was back with a series of massive new withdrawals affecting the irrigable lands of the basin, and these were quickly approved on April 27.

Harding considered the suspension of the Mono Basin lands the most offensive aspect of the Reclamation Service's intervention on the city's behalf. But he recognized as well that it constituted the central purpose of Mulholland's appeal for federal assistance. Stung by criticism originating in the Owens Valley and elsewhere of Newell's and Davis' abuse of their power to withdraw lands in the public domain from settlement, Congress had restricted the Reclamation Service's authority in this regard. The authority to withdraw lands needed in conjunction with power development projects had been specifically denied to the service and assigned instead to the Federal Power Commission. But as Harding pointed out, if the city had followed the normal course of procedure, it would have had to submit a detailed application for power plant construction with the commission together with water rights filings with the appropriate state authorities. And all these proceedings would have been subject to public hearings.

The city's problem was that it had no definite plan for its project. In 1920, it simply wanted to prevent anyone else from interfering with whatever use Mulholland might eventually decide to make of the Mono Basin waters. By creating the pretext of an interest in irrigation and getting Davis to go along with him, Mulholland was able to avoid the necessity for public hearings and put off the time when he would have to make up his mind. "In this case," Harding observed,

we have these rights more effectively preserved for the City of Los Angeles than they could be under any regular procedure by the withdrawal placed on them by the Reclamation Service in advance of their own investigation and without any opportunity for hearing on the part of any other interested parties. By the payment of $19,500 of the cost of the investigation, Los Angeles has secured a greater

protection of its prospective rights than could have been
given to it by the action of the only Federal Office [the
Federal Power Commission] to which responsibility has
been given by Congressional action.

On this basis, he concluded:

There does not appear to be any justification for the action
of the Reclamation Service in this instance . . . While the
principle of cooperative investigation . . . is a useful one,
its use where an individual interest contributes the entire
cost and secures the use of privileges reserved only for the
Government in its own undertaking is considered to be
an abuse of such cooperative undertakings and outside
the proper functions of the Reclamation Service.[45]

The private parties affected by Davis' withdrawals were quick
to make their feelings known. Consaul and Heltman, the attorneys
for Galen Dixon and the Owens Valley irrigators, bitterly protested the April 27 order and charged that Davis' action "for the
purpose of aiding the city to engage in a quasi-private power
scheme is wholly unwarranted, either in law or fairness."[46] Davis'
superiors in the Department of the Interior were sympathetic to
this complaint. The April 27 order was suspended within a week
of its issuance, and further modifications were subsequently made
in the withdrawals approved on April 5 in order to allow the
private power companies to proceed with their projects.[47]

With Davis gone and Mulholland distracted by visions of a
water famine, the Mono project, by the end of 1923, had entered
a kind of limbo. But the lands of the Mono Basin remained in
suspension. On January 8, 1924, the Mono Board of Supervisors
asked that Davis' order of withdrawal be lifted. The First Assistant Secretary for the Department of the Interior E. C. Finney
responded by denying that the newly renamed Bureau of Reclamation had been exploited by Los Angeles. Instead, Finney
charged that the supervisors were motivated by a desire to keep
all the Mono waters within their own basin rather than allowing
them to be put to a higher use in the Owens Valley. Since the
Conkling reports had demonstrated that an irrigation project for
the Owens Valley would be "meritorious," Finney argued that
the withdrawals should remain in force until the Bureau of Rec-

lamation decided whether to proceed with the project. The supervisors, however, informed Finney that, rather than pursuing any alleged interest in irrigation, the city had already applied to the state for rights to appropriate all the waters of the Mono Basin for domestic use in Los Angeles. This revelation rocked the Department of the Interior. Finney conceded that the city's action "indicates the possibility both of the depletion of the possible water supply of the Owens Valley project and the loss of the cooperation of the city in the undertaking of the project, either of which would render its construction infeasible."[48]

Finney immediately dispatched a blistering letter to the Los Angeles Public Service Commission noting that its action "is wholly inconsistent with the purported project to reclaim arid land as pretended in [the Conkling] contract." Because the Mono supervisors were complaining that the withdrawal of their lands was retarding the county's growth, he demanded to know the city's true intentions.[49] Los Angeles refused at first to respond, and the question was held in abeyance for six months. When the city finally acted to mend its fences with the federal government, it went again to its friends in the Bureau of Reclamation and not to their superiors in the Department of the Interior. On July 10, W. B. Mathews, chief counsel for the municipal water department, wrote a long letter of apology to the bureau's chief engineer, F. E. Weymouth, in which he attributed Los Angeles' change of heart to the fear of an impending water shortage. "Being in the midst of an unusually dry season, and confronted with an unprecedented rate of increase in population, [we] became more than ever impressed with the necessity for making immediate provision for an augmented water supply to meet future requirements," Mathews explained. "It also appeared that the surplus and return waters from the proposed irrigation project would be insufficient for the City's domestic needs."[50] Mathews followed this up with a personal visit to Finney in September.

Weymouth had earlier intervened on Los Angeles' behalf when the private power companies sought to soften the restrictions on their operations imposed by Davis' withdrawals. And he came through for the city once again with a strong recommendation for the continuation of withdrawals in the Mono Basin. As soon as this recommendation had been accepted, Weymouth left federal service in order to be rewarded, like Lippincott before him, with a well-paid position high on Mulholland's staff. For his kind assistance, Weymouth was placed in charge of the city's planning for the aqueduct to the Colorado, and when this project had been completed he moved on to become the first general manager and chief engineer of the Metropolitan Water District.[51]

Private citizens in Mono nevertheless continued to call for a restoration of the public lands in their county, and the question was reopened by the Department of the Interior in 1926 and again in 1928. Although Weymouth's successor as chief engineer of the Bureau of Reclamation consistently recommended a suspension of Davis' original order, the matter was always resolved in Los Angeles' favor. These disappointments prompted one basin resident to appeal directly to the president. "Please do not send an investigation committee here to investigate," he wrote with exasperation. "They are just as useless to this valley as an umbrella would be to a nine-eyed eel."[52]

The problem was particularly troubling to Elwood Mead, who had taken over as commissioner of the Bureau of Reclamation with a strong mandate for reform and a deep personal commitment to redressing the injustices of his predecessors to the interests of private development in the West. He ruminated in a memorandum to the secretary of the interior in 1928,

> The question arises, should the Interior Department continue this withdrawal when it has been definitely settled that no reclamation works are to be carried out? The only reason for so doing is the fact that there seems no question that the water of this region will soon be needed for domestic and industrial purposes in the City of Los Angeles, and its value for these purposes is far greater than for agriculture.[53]

Mead therefore set out to resolve the question by forcing Los Angeles to take action on its project under the threat that the withdrawn lands of the Mono Basin would otherwise be restored to entry.[54]

Mead could not have picked a more opportune time to bring pressure upon the city. So long as Mulholland remained in control, his continuing feud with Fred Eaton prevented the water department from building the Long Valley reservoir, which would be the linchpin for any development of the Mono Basin. Even as late as 1928, when the California Department of Public Works was reporting that an extension of the aqueduct to the Mono Basin would be capable of delivering one-fourth of all the water the South Coast would need for the foreseeable future, Mulholland steadfastly refused to consider the construction of new storage facilities in the Owens Valley.[55] But with Mulholland gone in 1929 and Eaton's lands now in receivership, the way to Long Valley was open at last. Beginning in May 1929 and continuing through the end of 1930, Los Angeles began filing requests for a massive series of new withdrawals affecting 365,894 acres in Inyo and Mono counties in order to clear a path for the new project. Despite the opposition of the Bishop Chamber of Commerce, the new Secretary of the Interior, Ray Lyman Wilbur, invariably lent his assistance to securing the necessary executive orders to make these withdrawals. And his help in turn drew a special note of thanks from Los Angeles for having "conferred a lasting benefit upon the Department of Water and Power and the people of this City."[56]

Mead and Wilbur did not have to be persuaded of the value of the project. The real problem for the city government lay in explaining to its voters why they should provide funds for yet another new water supply project when they were already being asked to commit themselves to the expenditure of hundreds of millions of dollars for an aqueduct to the Colorado. After all, Mulholland himself, in attempting to secure congressional approval of the Boulder Canyon project, had denigrated the Mono extension, testifying, "It is not a promising prospect to go after that water."[57] In an excess of enthusiasm and a complete lack of appreciation for the mood of the electorate, the Department of Water and Power tried to pass $40 million worth of water and power bonds for this project and several others in 1929. But in the wake of the Saint Francis Dam disaster the people were in no mood to give the department their support, and the bonds fell well short of the two-thirds majority approval required.[58]

The following spring the department tried again, this time with a $38.8 million bond issue, to complete the purchase of the Owens Valley properties, buy out the interests of the Southern

Sierras Power Company, build the Mono extension with a reservoir at Long Valley, and expand the local distribution system. To put the issue across, the department fell back on Mulholland's tried and tested tactics of terror. The Mono extension was presented to the voters as a vitally important interim device to save Los Angeles from a water famine until the aqueduct to the Colorado could be completed. In its first attempt to pass the bonds in 1929, the department had predicted a disastrous water shortage within six years if the extension were not built.[59] Since that had not proved frightening enough, the *Los Angeles Times* now took to threatening a shortage within the next two years.[60]

The campaign for the 1930 bond issue presented a naked display of the power of the Water and Power Machine. The Chamber of Commerce and every other major commercial association lined up in support. The Department of Water and Power sent its employees as speakers "into every nook and cranny" of the city "to properly inform the public." The local railways and downtown merchants blanketed the city with brochures, posters, and advertisements promoting the bonds. Pepsodent was importuned into giving up its radio time on the "Amos 'n' Andy Show" so that a pitch for the bonds could be presented instead. Uniformed firemen and policemen patrolled the precincts on their off-duty hours, soliciting support for the bonds, passing out brochures, and making arrangements to transport voters to the polls.[61] On election day, the bonds passed by an overwhelming margin of almost eight to one.

After this victory, however, nothing went well for the project. Negotiations for the acquisition of private holdings needed for the new system in the Owens Valley and Mono Basin dragged on for more than four years. Although $7 million of the proceeds from the bond sales had been set aside for the purchase of water rights and lands controlled by the Southern Sierras Power Company, the deal was not completed until 1933. Relinquishment of the rights held by the Owens Valley associated ditch companies to the Fish Slough reservoir site similarly took until the middle of 1934 to accomplish.[62] Construction was further delayed by the peculiar problems posed by the terrain the project had to cross. To bring the Mono Basin waters down to the Owens River and thence to the intake of the aqueduct, the department had to tunnel 11.3 miles through the craters of an extinct volcano—the first time such an endeavor had ever been attempted. Men experienced in hard-rock mining, however, were not so common in the 1930s as they had been when Mulholland built the first aqueduct. And with all the controversy aroused by charges of political manipulation in the management of the department, the project engineers could not bypass local civil service requirements as easily as Mulholland had done in order to attract the men they needed. Once the crews had finally been assembled, in 1934, their progress on the tunnel was slowed again by cave-ins and by the steam, hot water, and volcanic gases they encountered.[63]

Planning for the project, moreover, had been confused from the outset. The Mono extension had been conceived originally as a power project and then had been converted to a water supply system with subsidiary power benefits. When the bonds for its construction were approved in 1930, only $750,000 was provided for erecting Mulholland's 100-foot dam at Long Valley. Since this would be wholly inadequate for the department's purposes, the plans had to be changed to provide for a much larger reservoir behind a 167-foot dam, 50 feet of which were sunk beneath the level of the streambed. But the extra cost of this change could be covered only by deleting expenditures for other aspects of the project.

Thomas Means, in a series of preliminary studies of the project that he prepared for Mulholland in 1923 and 1924, had warned that the water supply available in the Mono Basin so far exceeded the capacity of the city's aqueduct that a second aqueduct, even larger than the first, would have to be built to carry the water to Los Angeles. The department achieved a marginal increase in the original aqueduct's capacity from 400 to 490 cubic feet per second even before the Mono extension was begun. But the design of an entirely new delivery system would take years to prepare, and the acquisition of the necessary rights-of-way would have further delayed its development. With the Boulder Canyon project only just beginning and the Great Depression deepening, the department was not anxious to try the patience of the voters with a proposal for yet a third aqueduct. And so, the problem was simply put aside. This seemed reasonable so long as the city's water planners regarded the Mono extension as an interim device which would stave off a water famine until the completion of the Boulder Canyon project by bringing the original aqueduct's deliveries up to its designed capacity. The question of what should be done with the surplus waters of the Mono Basin could therefore be addressed at some later date.[64]

Delay and confusion further complicated the department's efforts to secure congressional approval of the undertaking. The city's right-of-way bill in 1920 had given the department access to the Mono Basin. But in the view of the Department of the Interior, that bill had been so heavily amended that it provided nothing more than "a sort of preference on the part of the City of Los Angeles to utilize any site it might desire."[65] This "sort of preference" was clearly an insufficient legal basis for the department to commit millions of public dollars. The withdrawals made on the city's behalf in 1929 and 1930 had been supported by the Department of the Interior in the expectation that Los Angeles would follow with legislation authorizing the outright sale of these lands to the city for use in connection with its project.[66] But the defeat of the water bonds in 1929 had stalled the department's new bill to accomplish this purpose. And by the time the city was able to renew pressure for its passage in 1931, the memory of the Owens Valley controversy had begun to haunt Los Angeles in the halls of Congress as well as the State Capitol.

The passage of the County of Origin law in Sacramento that year did not directly threaten the department's project because the lands it needed were almost entirely under federal jurisdiction and therefore would not be affected by any restrictions imposed by state statutes. But the Department of the Interior was also beginning to feel the pressure of public protest over its interference with the economic development of the Mono Basin. The Secretary of the Interior therefore withdrew his support of the city's bill. And although he would not oppose the legislation, he did join with the Secretary of Agriculture in calling for amendments to allow the lands which the city needed to be used for other purposes as well. "The taking over of the water [of the Owens Valley] by the City of Los Angeles has converted a prosperous community into a waste, and the landowners [of Mono] should be given consideration," the Department of the Interior noted.[67]

Congressman Phil Swing, coauthor of the Boulder Canyon legislation, was carrying the new right-of-way bill for the city. Since his district included Mono County, he readily agreed to amendments restricting the bill's effect to a codification of the withdrawals that had already been made. In this way, title to the lands would be denied to Los Angeles and the area affected would remain under federal jurisdiction. "I would not be in favor of withdrawal of it from entry if there was any reasonable hope of its being used for the settlement and development of a community," he told his colleagues when the legislation reached the House of Representatives. "The people in my district are unalterably opposed to either selling this or giving it to the City of Los Angeles. We want the title to remain in the United States for public purposes." What Swing did not tell his fellow congressmen was that although the Bishop Chamber of Commerce and the other communities of the Owens Valley had endorsed the bill in this form, the Mono County Board of Supervisors remained bitterly opposed to it.[68]

The city got its right-of-way on March 4, 1931, but the lands granted to it remained open to grazing, recreation, and mining development under federal authority.[69] The Department of Water and Power by this time was encountering extensive litigation from private developers along the line of the extension; to undercut this opposition, Los Angeles determined that it would need still more land. Two months after the right-of-way bill placed 370,000 acres of the public domain at Los Angeles' disposal, the city secured additional withdrawals of another 67,760 acres for a canal route from Mono Lake.[70] In 1932, the Rush Creek Mutual Ditch Company sought repeal of the city's right of way.[71] In 1933, Los Angeles obtained the withdrawal of another 212,000 acres near Owens Lake and filed additional applications for an enlargement of its planned reservoir at Grant Lake. At this point, the Federal Power Commission stepped in to oppose Los Angeles' Grant Lake applications on the grounds that the city should have first applied for a license from the commission. Los

Angeles responded by seeking a new and expanded authorization from Congress to eliminate the grounds for the Federal Power Commission's intervention. Meanwhile, work on the Mono extension commenced in 1934 under a special use permit from the federal Forest Service. This second right-of-way bill did not pass until 1936, and by that time the Federal Power Commission had dropped its opposition to the city's project. But Los Angeles continued to press for the bill's enactment because it included an authorization for the city to continue acquiring additional lands in Mono County for a payment of $1.25 an acre.[72]

The Department of Water and Power did not obtain the entirely free hand in the Mono Basin which it sought under the second right-of-way bill. The act did not codify the withdrawals made on the city's behalf in 1931 and 1933, and these lands consequently remained subject to recession to the federal government. In addition, all the sales of land to the city authorized by the act were made subject to the approval of the Secretary of the Interior. The secretary was empowered as well to impose whatever restrictions on the city's use of the lands seemed most appropriate. Although it had achieved an incomplete victory, Los Angeles nevertheless emerged from this extended struggle with the lands and water resources of the Mono Basin firmly in hand. In fact, city officials conceded in 1970, the efforts to secure a right-of-way for the Mono extension resulted in the placement under Los Angeles' control of 603,000 acres in Inyo and Mono counties which were of no practical use to the project's development.[73]

The department's fitful progress on the project had meanwhile created new problems from a wholly unexpected quarter. Long Valley is crossed by a thermal belt of hot springs, geysers, and fumaroles which emit water containing boron at levels ten to twenty times greater than that found in any other part of the watershed. Throughout the winter and summer months, gas bubbling up in the marshes along this belt produces immense concentrations of boron, which are then washed down into the Owens River with the spring thaws and autumn rains. The resulting discharges into the river system can reach four tons of boron a day. The spreading of water for irrigation in the Bishop region had removed the greater part of these natural contaminants. But as Los Angeles steadily cut back on agriculture in the Owens Valley, these boron-charged waters began flowing directly into the aqueduct.[74] As Thomas Means observed, "The real trouble seems to have come in the dry years after irrigation ceased, at which time the volume of water in the aqueduct reservoirs was so low that the low flow of springs carrying boron became an appreciable part of the water going to San Fernando."[75] Boron had not posed any great threat to the particular crops grown in the Owens Valley. But in the San Fernando Valley, damage to the lemon, avocado, and walnut crops due to boron pollution in the aqueduct's water supply began showing up as early as 1928 and increased in the years following.[76]

The United States Department of Agriculture set up an experiment station at Rubidoux in 1929 to locate the source of the problem, and on March 3, 1931, government scientists began testing the aqueduct supply. By July of the following year they had identified Hot Creek and Hot Lake in Long Valley as the source of 90 percent of the boron, which by that time was entering the water supply of the upper San Fernando Valley at a rate of sixteen hundred pounds a day during the peak of the summer irrigation season. The Department of Agriculture immediately condemned Hot Creek and ordered the city to develop a means of disposing of its water elsewhere. At first, the Department of Water and Power attempted to spread the Hot Creek waters on nearby rocky plateaus which soon proved incapable of absorbing them. Alternative plans to convey the polluted waters to Round Valley or the Chidago Canyon were given up when the city's water officials determined that it would be too expensive to construct the necessary conveyance facilities, and then defend against the damage suits that would inevitably follow the commencement of dumping operations in those two locations.[77]

The boron concentrations did not interfere with domestic use of the aqueduct's water supply, and the problem as a whole would be resolved once the aqueduct extension was complete and the purer waters of the Mono Basin began to dilute the tainted discharges in the Long Valley reservoir. For the interim, the Department of Water and Power chose to do nothing more than increase water-spreading around Bishop and allow limited wastage into Owens Lake during the months of March and April. As the levels of boron in the San Fernando Valley's irrigation water continued to increase after 1932 and the damages claimed by orchardists in Los Angeles rose to more than a million dollars a year, the department took to denying that any problem existed at all. The tests for boron were unreliable, the department steadfastly maintained; the safe limits for boron concentration had not been fixed; and there might be other factors responsible for the sudden defoliation of the city's citrus crops. Rather than agree to participate in any further control efforts which might reduce the quantity of water moving through the aqueduct, the city assumed an angry defensive posture, charging that the local orchardists were simply being "egged on by prejudiced advisors."[78]

Only the resolutely supportive attitude of the local newspapers saved the department from what might have been the ultimate embarrassment resulting from the development of the Mono extension. Construction of the project was delayed so long that it did not go into operation until the new aqueduct to the Colorado River was also complete. No enterprising reporter bothered to point out, however, that the water famine which had driven Mulholland to devastate the Owens Valley and launch the Colorado and Mono projects never materialized. And by the time the Mono extension was finished at the end of 1940, the department had come round to regarding the project not as an interim stopgap for the Boulder Canyon development but as a substitute for it.

It is uncertain when the city's water planners discovered that they would not need the new water supply from the Colorado that the taxpayers of Los Angeles had paid to secure. Perhaps the realization dawned in 1936, for that was when J. B. Lippincott began proposing methods for disposing of the surplus waters from Boulder Canyon.[79] But the warnings that this would be so had been sounded long before. State Engineer W. F. McClure had commented as early as 1925 that, even if the Colorado River water was immediately available, "It would be good business to secure the supply from Owens Valley and Mono Lake Basin because of its superior quality and delivery by gravity."[80] The city's own Bureau of Municipal Research had similarly opposed the

Colorado project as unnecessary and expensive, arguing instead for a more intensive development of the water resources of the Owens Valley.[81] And in 1932, the economist W. C. Yeatman had produced a devastating analysis of the population projections used by the Metropolitan Water District and the Chamber of Commerce to promote the Boulder Canyon project. Whereas the proponents of the project estimated that the city's population would reach 4.2 million by 1960 and 5.1 million by 1970, Yeatman pointed out that these calculations were founded upon a set of assumptions so faulty that, if they were extended far enough, they would project the entire population of the United States eventually residing in the four counties of the South Coast. As an alternative, Yeatman predicted that the population of the city of Los Angeles would be only 1.9 million in 1960 and 2.1 million in 1970.[82]

Los Angeles in any event was not alone in discovering that it had no use for the Colorado water when it finally arrived. In its first five years of operations, the Metropolitan Water District could find customers for only 2 percent of the water it was capable of delivering. After the first ten years, this figure had risen to only 18 percent. And even as late as 1952, when the district had vastly expanded its service area in an effort to bring in new customers, its pumps drawing water from the Colorado were still operating only half the time.

In the years since, most of the charter members of the Metropolitan Water District have eventually come to rely on the system they have paid to build. But not Los Angeles. The alternative supply the city derives from the Mono Basin is of far superior quality to the waters of the Colorado. And because the Mono waters flow downhill to Los Angeles through the aqueduct, it is much less expensive than are the Colorado supplies, which must be pumped over intervening mountain ranges. As a result, the city has taken only 7 percent of all the water it has been entitled to receive from the Metropolitan Water District since 1941. The city's taxpayers, meanwhile, have paid out more than $335 million over the same period to develop this water supply they scarcely use.[83] Completion of the two projects Mulholland left unfinished thus fulfilled his fondest wish of assuring

Los Angeles an abundant water supply for the future. But the hysteria of his last years at the water department also left the city saddled with an immense debt for a water system it never needed.

Homes for the Homeless

The expectation that Los Angeles would soon receive more water from the Colorado than it could possibly consume prompted some hope in the Owens Valley that the city would use its excess supply to recharge the valley's groundwater basins and restore agriculture in the Bishop region. In this way, valley optimists argued, the city would be able to boost the value of its holdings in the Owens Valley and sell them off at a profit. Willie Arthur Chalfant did not share in this speculation. "If there is to be a coming back," he wrote in 1933, "it must be well into the years ahead, when those who have given Inyo their devotion are beyond its enjoyment."[84] And in Los Angeles, the idea of applying the surplus for the benefit of the Owens Valley was given no more consideration than it had received under similar circumstances in 1912.

In deciding what should be done with the Owens Valley properties, however, the city's officials faced a problem almost entirely without precedent under the United States federal system of government. The wholesale land and water acquisitions that followed the collapse of the Watterson banks had created an anomalous situation whereby one public entity, the city of Los Angeles, had become the virtual owner of another public entity, the county of Inyo. The modern history of relations between the city and the valley has consequently been shaped by Los Angeles' sometimes faltering attempts to come to terms with its responsibilities under this essentially colonial relationship.

Even as late as 1927, spokesmen for the Department of Water and Power were predicting "renewed prosperity" for the Owens Valley and promising support for a larger railroad line to carry the valley's produce south from Laws.[85] But once the ranchers' resistance had been broken, such promises were no longer necessary. And, as Los Angeles became the principal landowner in the valley, the focus of the city's concern shifted accordingly. "It is essential to determine the manner in which the Owens Valley region may be used in the best interest of the people who have paid for it," observed Clarence Dykstra for the department in 1928.[86]

Dykstra had served as a member of the board of commissioners overseeing Mulholland's work from 1923 to 1926. In his subsequent employment as director of personnel and efficiency for the Department of Water and Power, he had become intimately involved with the department's efforts to reach a settlement with the valley ranchers. Dykstra regarded the question posed by the city's ownership of valley lands as essentially "an agrarian problem." The solution for the city, in Dykstra's view, lay in determining which agricultural activities would least interfere with the city's use of the valley's water supply. "Whatever [the city] does in the valley cannot and must not jeopardize this supply," Dykstra acknowledged. "The central fact of water and its control dominates the situation." He suggested, therefore, that stock raising and dairy farming might be the best use for the city's lands.[87]

Having just won their war with the valley ranchers, the water and power commissioners had little desire to reestablish their former adversaries on the lands the city had bought. Dykstra's limited plans for "rehabilitating" valley agriculture consequently gave way to an alternative idea proposed by another member of the commission, W. P. Whitsett, who had just returned from a European tour flush with visions of converting the Owens Valley into "an American Switzerland . . . a vacation and tourist land supreme."[88] The announcement that the state of California intended to commence a substantial improvement of the highway north and south of Bishop in 1932 lent considerable strength to this plan for using the department's lands as "a great park and playground" governed exclusively by the city of Los Angeles.[89] But for the short term, the department could do no more to realize this objective than arrange a lease for the establishment of a duck-hunting refuge.[90]

The ability of the water and power commission to pursue any consistent program for development of the Owens Valley in the early 1930s was undercut by the increasing pressure it encountered from the mayor's office to turn an immediate profit on its properties. By forcing the abandonment of once-productive farmlands in order to increase water deliveries to the aqueduct, the department was both reducing its revenues and increasing the share of Inyo County taxes it had to bear. Dykstra's plan for a limited agricultural program had the advantage over Whitsett's grandiose design in that Dykstra had always regarded "making the valley yield some revenue" as one of the central purposes of his proposal.[91] By leasing the lands back to the Owens Valley ranchers, the department realized it could shift the entire burden of taxation on these properties to the leaseholders. In addition, the rents paid by the lessees would satisfy the mayor's demand for income to the city, while the policy as a whole would quiet the state legislature's concern for the treatment the ranchers had received at Los Angeles' hands.

The essential problem for the city was one of devising a leasing program that would not allow agriculture to become so deeply entrenched that it would ever pose a threat to the operation of the aqueduct again. In the case of its duck-hunting refuge, the city had leased out sixty-four hundred acres at a return of less than one-third of 1 percent on the value of the land.[92] The terms offered to the Owens Valley ranchers were considerably less favorable. In addition to assuming all the taxes due on the property, the lessee paid an annual rent equivalent to 6 percent of the inflated price at which the city had purchased the land originally. Each lease could be canceled at any time by the city, and none were issued for terms longer than five years with no guarantee of renewal. Though these terms assured that no one would be able to secure financing for any substantial improvements, the leaseholder was permitted to apply up to 10 percent of his annual rent to repairs and maintenance of the property. Most important, the granting of a lease carried with it no assurance of a continued water supply. Los Angeles made the perils of such an agreement immediately clear when it abruptly canceled nearly all its leases in 1930 and diverted the entire flow of the Owens River to the San Fernando Valley during the peak of the irrigation season.[93]

One group of ranchers, however, did not suffer from the

city's policies of forced impermanence. The 811 Paiute Indians who remained in the Owens Valley in 1930 held their lands and water rights under federal grants with which Los Angeles had no power to interfere. Since 1902, a portion of the former military reserve at Camp Independence had been set aside for use of the Indian population. A few families owned their own lands outright under patents perfected before 1884. Others held patents which were kept in trust by the federal government until such time as they had demonstrated to the satisfaction of the federal authorities that they were "competent to manage their own affairs."[94] As a federal report in 1912 observed, those who preferred not to live on the reserved lands but who owned none of their own led "a precarious existence, depending almost entirely upon the goodness of their white neighbors or friends of their race for shelter."[95]

When the massive withdrawals made on Los Angeles' behalf were lifted in 1912 and the lands of the Owens Valley began to be reopened to settlement, the Department of the Interior set aside nearly 69,000 acres of land at widely scattered sites for the use of these homeless Indians.[96] The largest was a 67,164-acre tract on volcanic tablelands north of Bishop which the local Indian agent, C. E. Kelsey, believed was located atop an undiscovered artesian field.[97] The lands, however, were in fact worthless; and the federal government was slow in providing funds for the establishment of irrigated homesites on these new properties. As a result, the Indians continued to wander through the valley. "During the years of waiting for assistance from the Government," the Bureau of Indian Affairs reported in 1919, "they have pitched their tents and temporary huts wherever they were allowed to do so, in many cases on waste land and under such conditions as to render it impossible to maintain healthful conditions or to obtain subsistence from the land."[98]

Those who left the barren homesites cut themselves off from any prospect of government assistance. "The scattering bands of Indians in the State of California have for some time been considered as citizens and the responsibility for their care when indigent devolves upon local or state officials rather than upon this Service, just the same as if they were white persons in similar circumstances," an assistant secretary for the Department of the

Interior explained to a valley resident who had written to express concern for the destitute condition of the Paiutes.[99] As a result, the local Indian community had played no part in the conflict between their white neighbors and the city of Los Angeles. Similarly, they had not benefited from the generally high prices Los Angeles offered for the purchase of lands in the Owens Valley. Nineteen individual Indian homesites aggregating 1,336 acres were sold to the city for a total cost of $72,262. But the federal government set aside the proceeds from these sales to buy new homesites for the families involved. And when it discovered that only three families could be relocated within the valley, the others were encouraged to remove themselves to the Walker River Reservation in Nevada.[100]

The Department of the Interior, however, was powerless to sell the majority of the Indian lands set aside by executive orders and congressional appropriations, which could not be altered except by an act of Congress. This extreme action was in fact taken in the case of thirty acres at Manzanar which the city was particularly anxious to obtain.[101] But for the most part, Los Angeles' officials expressed indifference toward the Indian lands, and the prices they offered for them were in some cases only a fourth of what they were paying for similar lands owned by whites.[102]

The collapse of the valley's economy and the subsequent devastation of local agriculture afflicted the homeless Paiutes with particular severity. Many had drifted to the Bishop area, where the men had worked in the fields and the women found ready employment in the households around town.[103] With the opportunities for farm labor gone and the population of Bishop in sharp decline, these Indians were suddenly rendered destitute once again. Their plight prompted renewed concern at the federal level. At the end of May, 1932, the Secretary of the Interior sent a special representative, Louis C. Cramton, to study the condition of the Indians in the Owens Valley, "With only a few exceptions," Cramton reported,

> they have been identified with agriculture, some farming their own lands or leased lands, but more generally as laborers for whites. A few are very well advanced in capac-

ity and industry, but many are lacking in initiative and unequal to responsibility. By destroying almost entirely their labor market, the City of Los Angeles has upset their world and done them very serious injury. They are now in serious situation, with a desolate present and an an uncertain future.[104]

Cramton's report went on to describe how the Indians were being excluded from the few opportunities for employment that remained in the valley by laborers imported from Los Angeles. He expressed concern as well for the impact the city's policies would have on the character of the Paiutes. "While their economic welfare has been jeopardized, their moral welfare is likewise endangered by lack of responsibility which seems to obtain in the city administration of this valley which it is turning back to desert after four score years of progress," Cramton observed. "An old school building now rented for dance hall purposes and other buildings rented to bootleggers and other undesirables are bringing very bad conditions for the Indians."

Cramton's view of the city's program seems to have been colored somewhat by the fact that he was dealing with A. J. Ford, the chief right-of-way and land agent for the Department of Water and Power. Cramton was frank in expressing his suspicion that Ford lied frequently to him about specific city policies. Ford similarly did not take well to Cramton's investigation and responded to the charges raised in the report with the assertion that: "In a perusal of the early history of the Owens Valley situation, it is obvious that the Indians were badly treated by the National Government, and had such agency used the proper vision and tolerance for an ignorant race then, the Owens Valley Indians would have been happy and contented on this date by being self-supporting and law-abiding."[105]

Part of Ford's irritation sprang from the fact that the city had been acutely conscious of the Indian problem well in advance of Cramton's arrival in the Owens Valley. The number of indigent families of all races in Inyo County had of course increased dramatically since the collapse of the Watterson banks. In the case of whites, the county had had to assume the full cost of their care through the payment of rents to the Department of Water and Power for the use of the houses where these families lived. Los Angeles then prosecuted any family which Inyo County determined was not deserving of charity.[106] In the case of the Indians, however, the Department of Water and Power had, since the winter of 1931-32, begun appropriating its own funds to employ the Paiutes on maintenance crews for city-owned ranches, roads, streams, and ditches. In exchange for this work, the city provided the Indians with cash, provisions, clothing, and medical assistance.[107]

The need for a long-term solution to the problem was obvious to the city. The Indian lands were scattered throughout Los Angeles' holdings in the Owens Valley and disrupted the city's efforts to consolidate its control of the watershed. Those Indian lands which held water rights under federal law had to be supplied by the Department of Water and Power, even though this meant the loss of a significant quantity of water which might otherwise be going into the aqueduct.[108] And the deteriorating condition of the Paiutes posed a potential threat both to the peace of the valley and the operation of the aqueduct. As A. J. Ford observed in one of his reports in 1932:

> A large percentage of the Owens Valley Indians are living in shacks, tents, wickiups, and hovels that are generally too small for the number of occupants, unsanitary, in violation of the housing laws, impossible to properly heat in the winter, constituting not only a menace to the Indian, but to the entire population of Owens Valley, and particularly threatening contamination of local community water supplies and the municipal water supply for the City of Los Angeles ... Execution of some plan to place the Owens Valley Indians upon a self-supporting basis at an early date is essential ... Continued unemployment, and the consequent lack of funds, works toward crime and lawlessness ... Furthermore, it is a fact that under their present environment they are not able to correct this condition on their own account, as it has been necessary to care for many of them under welfare plans during the past two winter seasons. A continuation of such procedures will tend to more firmly set the Indians against any move to establish them on a self-supporting basis.[109]

The solution Ford had in mind involved the complete elimination of the Indians from the Owens Valley and the delivery of their lands into the control of the city of Los Angeles. But his plan for moving the Paiutes to another agricultural community on the other side of the Sierra was acceptable neither to the federal government nor to the Indians. A similar attempt to relocate the Owens Valley Indians to the San Sebastian Reservation in 1863 had failed completely, and the Indians had fled the forced march to Fort Tejon and made their way back to the valley.[110] Ford recognized the acceptance of his plan would not come quickly. He therefore proposed that new homesites be temporarily established within the valley for those Indians who refused to leave. But he set an absolute limit of twenty years for the continued maintenance of the Paiutes in the area. He promised:

> The problem can be solved successfully to all concerned at the end of a twenty-year period through the assistance of education, natural elimination by death, and other eliminations due to the decision of some of the Indians to relocate voluntarily in other sections. If a program of education were inaugurated, it is felt that the middle-aged and younger Indians could be so educated over a twenty-year period that they would have voluntarily concluded that their interests could be best served by attaching themselves to another location where labor and water supply conditions were more favorable and permanent.[111]

The further development of Ford's program for coercive education ended with his dismissal in 1933 during one of the purges of departmental personnel that repeatedly beset the city's water program during the 1930s. Responsibility for Los Angeles' policy toward the Indians now passed to his former deputy, E. A. Porter, who had already dismissed the idea of a forced relocation of the Paiutes as impractical. "Many of the Indians have never been out of the Valley and all of them are attached to the local natural environment of the region," Porter had observed in an oblique dissent from one of Ford's reports in 1932.

> They know where and how to fish; many have summer camp grounds in the high mountains close by; others are more or less influenced by their native religion so closely

connected with the local country. So while it may be possible to pick a group of Indians up bodily and transfer them to a new location, which would no doubt be to their advantage in the long run, it might prove to be a heartless move on the part of those responsible and probably an unsuccessful venture for those in charge.[112]

Under Porter's more sensitive direction, the Department of Water and Power gradually hammered out an agreement with the Department of the Interior for the maintenance of the Owens Valley Indians. Porter's plan called for the establishment of three new homesite areas on city-owned lands and the addition of 120 acres to the existing federal reservation at Camp Independence. In exchange for turning over its properties to the federal government to hold in trust for the Indians, Los Angeles obtained control of all the remaining Indian homesites. Although the city received 2,914 acres for the 1,392 acres it offered under this plan, the lands Los Angeles provided were far superior to the ones the Indians were being asked to give up. For example, only 103 acres of the Indian lands were prime quality, while 340 acres of the lands they received met this standard.

With these lands, the city provided first-class water rights to 6,046 acre-feet a year. The negotiations on this point nearly collapsed in 1937 when the city abruptly asserted that it would be unable to deliver the rights per se because its charter prohibited alienation of its water supply without a two-thirds vote by the electorate. But sufficient latitude was granted to the Secretary of the Interior under the congressional legislation authorizing this exchange to enable him to accept the city's guarantee that water in these amounts would be delivered in perpetuity. For its part, the federal government agreed to provide these new homesites with sewer systems, efficient irrigation, and adequate housing.

The plan was accepted by all the Owens Valley Indians except those residing on the Camp Independence Reservation. Those aspects of the exchange affecting their lands and water rights were consequently severed from the deed executed by the Department of the Interior on June 26, 1939. But a subsequent review of the land exchange conducted for the tribal councils of the Owens Valley and Mono region in 1976 confirmed the generosity of the city's terms, and the Department of Water and Power continues today to hold open its offer to complete the exchange with the Camp Independence Indians on the same basis fixed in 1939.[113]

The land exchange of 1939 achieved a remarkable balance of the interests of the city and the Owens Valley Indians. The Paiutes obtained superior lands and a guaranteed water supply. In addition, as Porter noted in his final report on the exchange, the new consolidated homesites were closer to the existing towns of the Owens Valley, "where moral, school, health, labor, market etc. conditions can be better met." At the same time, the city was relieved of paying taxes on the lands it turned over to the Indians and received in exchange a large block of tax-exempt federal land. More important, the Department of Water and Power achieved a greater efficiency in the use of water within the valley for the support of the Indian lands. And the settlement as a whole represented, in Porter's view, a responsible "discharge of a possible moral duty on the part of the City in assisting the Indians." Completion of the land exchange, he concluded, "will at least place the Owens Valley Indians on a basis which will offer them the maximum of success under present and future more or less limited market and labor conditions in the Valley."[114]

The department in this period displayed a similar spirit of generosity in offering the use of its lands for the benefit of another displaced part of Creation. The Tule Elk once roamed the Central Valley and coastal regions of California in vast herds that numbered in the aggregate an estimated 500,000. Early settlements from 1800 to 1840 displaced the elk from their natural habitats, and after 1840, they were hunted for their hides and tallow. In only twenty years, the herds were all but eliminated. When the state government finally prohibited the killing of the elk in 1873, it was generally believed that none were left. One surviving pair, however, was found in the marshlands of the Buena Vista Basin, which were then part of the vast empire belonging to the Miller and Lux Land and Cattle Company. Henry Miller put the animals under his personal protection and offered a reward of five hundred dollars for anyone who dared to disturb them. By 1905, a herd of 145 elk had established itself at Buttonwillow, and by 1923 their numbers had increased to over 400. From 1923 to 1927, the

Miller and Lux lands began to be subdivided into 40- and 160-
acre lots, and the Tule Elk seemed to be facing extinction once
again. Efforts to transplant them to Yosemite National Park
failed in 1927 when they were caged to cut down their damage to
park forage and to reduce the hazard they appeared to present to
park visitors. At this point, G. Walter Dow, a businessman in
Lone Pine, took up the elk's cause and persuaded the Department of Water and Power in 1933 to bring the entire Yosemite
herd to the Owens Valley. In 1934, a second herd of elk were
brought to the valley from a refuge at Tupman where the animals
had been fenced and nearly starved as a result.[115]

The Tule Elk flourished in the Owens Valley, and separate,
smaller herds have subsequently been established at Tupman,
Cache Creek, and San Luis Island. Their arrival in the valley,
however, was vigorously opposed by the local cattlemen operating
on rangelands leased from Los Angeles. For them, the introduction of the elk represented another hardship imposed by the
Department of Water and Power on the profitability of their
activities. The department's concern for preservation of the Tule
Elk thus created a conflict between Whitsett's vision of the valley
as an open parkland and Dykstra's plan for the limited restoration
of valley agriculture. In 1943, the California Department of Fish
and Game responded to the cattlemen's complaints about the
damage the elk were doing to their fences and pasturelands, and
for the first time in seventy years, hunting permits were issued to
cull the Owens Valley herd. A total of forty-three bulls were
killed in that first hunt, and four subsequent hunts organized by
the state at roughly six-year intervals took an additional 400 elk.
By 1969, the opportunity for slaughter had become so popular
that the Department of Fish and Game held a lottery for the 80
available permits from among the eight thousand applications it
had received. With the blessing of state authorities, the elk were
tracked with helicopters and shot from jeeps. Many wounded
animals were left to die on the range. At this point, conservationists and sportsmen rallied to put an end to this grotesque
display.[116]

The ad hoc Committee for the Preservation of the Tule Elk
first proposed that the entire southern end of the valley should be

fenced off for the exclusive use of the elk. But a wildlife specialist later retained by the Department of Water and Power pointed out that this would have led to overpopulation of the elk within a limited area, destruction of their habitat, and the possible loss of the entire herd in case of a single outbreak of disease. In 1970, the state legislature intervened by imposing a prohibition upon the taking of Tule Elk except when their population within the Owens Valley exceeded four hundred and their numbers statewide had risen above two thousand. Subsequent administrative practices adopted by the Department of Fish and Game in cooperation with the Department of Water and Power, the Bureau of Land Management, and the National Forest Service have limited the taking of Tule Elk to trained personnel and encouraged the movement of the elk population to other areas when their numbers become excessive.[117]

Resettlement

Dow's success in persuading Los Angeles to provide a home for the Tule Elk, and the generosity the city displayed in its negotiations with the Paiute Indians after 1932, encouraged other residents of the Owens Valley to hope that the Department of Water and Power might grant its favor to other efforts to rejuvenate the local economy. The energy and initiative for turning this hope into reality came from two relative newcomers to the valley, Ralph Merritt and Father John Crowley. Merritt was a gifted agricultural organizer who had served as president of the state's rice growers' association and later as president of the Sun Maid raisin growers' association in Fresno. Stricken with polio, he had come to the Owens Valley in the early 1930s to recover and had there taken up speculating in various silver and lead mines.[118] Crowley too arrived in the valley in 1933 in ill health, but unlike Merritt, he had been there before.

From 1919 to 1925, Crowley had served as the valley's first resident priest. Because there were only a handful of nominal Catholics in Inyo County when he began, his first parish had been expanded to include the communities of Bishop, Lone Pine,

Randsburg, and Barstow in Inyo, Kern, and San Bernardino counties—a thirty-thousand-square-mile area equal in size to his native Ireland. In a Model T Ford especially outfitted to provide him with sleeping quarters, Crowley had run the circuit among his scattered parishioners every month, logging 50,000 miles in little over one year. After eighteen months, the Barstow congregation had grown large enough to have its own pastor, and six months later a mining boom had the same effect on Randsburg. With his parish now reduced to only ten thousand square miles, Crowley was able to concentrate on construction. A new church in Bishop was completed in time for the celebration of Christmas 1921. The remains of an Episcopal church in Randsburg were trucked into Lone Pine and fitted out with a bell tower. The grading of the highway between Bishop and Lone Pine enabled Father Crowley to begin offering mass in both towns on the same day by the beginning of 1923. And soon thereafter he had a chapel under way at Keeler.[119]

Crowley's success in the erection of edifices prompted his superiors to bring him to Fresno in 1925, where he was named a monsignor and appointed chancellor of the Monterey-Fresno Archdiocese. Although he was removed from the valley during the denouement of its conflict with Los Angeles, he retained a lively interest in its affairs. And when the Watterson brothers went to jail, he joined with other prominent current and former residents of the Owens Valley in appealing for clemency on their behalf. "In all my experience with the Wattersons," he wrote to the chairman of the state crime commission,

> I never knew them to seek for personal gain at the cost of the inhabitants of the Valley who trusted them . . . On the contrary, they lived modestly, even frugally, and fought consistently for the people against the encroachments of the Los Angeles Water Board . . . It has never been proved that the money was used otherwise than for the protection of the farmers in Owens Valley and for the extension of the life of the industries which kept the Valley alive.

And though he did not condone the brothers' actions, he observed, "I can readily understand how the Wattersons could yield to the temptation of 'borrowing' money from their banks to keep the

Valley alive while the City of Los Angeles browbeat and dragged through every court in the land, the poor and practically defenseless ranchers."[120]

Although his perception of the conflict had thus been shaped by his sympathy for the Watterson brothers, Crowley did not seek to renew the struggle with Los Angeles when he gave up his elevated title and administrative responsibilities in Fresno to return to the valley in 1933. Instead, he joined with Merritt in forming an independent organization, the Inyo Associates, to press for economic development in the valley through cooperation with the Department of Water and Power. This involvement in the commercial life of his parish Crowley regarded as a natural extension of his ministry. For, as one reporter later remarked, "He knew what every missionary knows; that it is easier to save a man's soul when he is prosperous and happy than when he is worried by adversity and embittered against the world and against God."[121]

Merritt's reputation for sharp practice, and rumors that the two men had been closely associated in Fresno, cast a shadow over their initial enterprise. Only $2,500 could be raised locally to launch the Inyo Associates, and the county supervisors refused to provide any support at all. All county officers were accordingly excluded from membership in the new organization.[122] The officials of the city water department were at first no more enthusiastic than the supervisors. "Father Crowley, we own Owens Valley. We propose to have no interference. There are no issues for discussion," Mulholland's successor, H. A. Van Norman, reportedly declared at his first meeting with the Inyo Associates. On another occasion, Crowley claimed to have locked Van Norman into a room until he agreed to the concessions the doughty father prayed him to grant.[123]

In time, however, Van Norman and his colleagues realized that Crowley posed no threat to their operations. Rather, the priest was in fact working tirelessly to lend form and substance to the department's own vague ideas on recreational development in the Owens Valley. To realize this dream, Crowley once again took to the highway, touting the valley's recreational opportunities wherever he could raise an audience, eating with friends and parishioners along the way, and sleeping by the roadside when no lodging could be found. To pay his expenses, he organized street carnivals and community plays, sold off church properties, and rented out unneeded areas of the churches and rectories in his parish for use by undertakers, doctors, dentists, and even a gas station.[124]

The seemingly boundless energy he had once directed toward the construction of new church facilities he now focused upon fish. There are no native sport fish in the Owens Valley, only suckers, chubs, dace, and pupfish. But as early as 1876, packers began transplanting trout from the Kern River to Cottonwood Creek. In 1909, the California Fish and Game Commission began to plant golden trout intensively throughout the lakes and streams of the Sierra Nevada. And in 1917, the state constructed its Mount Whitney fish hatchery outside Independence. Local officials had been slow at first to recognize the potential economic benefits that might come from recreational fishing. When the Mount Whitney hatchery was built, the state Fish and Game Commission had to prod the Inyo supervisors not to be so short-sighted as to deny the new facility an adequate access road for tourists. Even after it had been pointed out to them that the hatchery would be "a showplace for Independence for all time," the supervisors put up only $500 for a road, and private citizens in Independence had to raise the other $1,850 needed to complete the improvement.[125]

Crowley, in contrast, saw the transplanted fish as an immediate source of income for the valley residents. To bring fishermen and tourists to the area, he hired a publicist and began staging promotional events. When a road was laid between Mount Whitney and Bad Water in Death Valley, linking what were at that time the highest and lowest points in the United States, Crowley organized an elaborate ceremony to mark its completion at which runners carried vials from one end of the road to the other for a "wedding of the waters." By 1940, when more than a million tourists visited the Owens Valley, Crowley had firmly established May 1, the opening of the trout fishing season, as a valleywide holiday. The schools were closed so that all could come see the indefatigable father bless the fishermen's flies and rods at an early morning mass for which collections were taken in a creel.[126]

The promotion of recreational development in the Owens Valley was only the first step in Father Crowley's far grander plan to restore ownership of the valley's lands to its residents. In this endeavor, he was aided immeasurably by the relentless pressure to show a profit on its acquisitions which the Department of Water and Power faced in this period from its economy-minded critics in Los Angeles. Support for continued city purchases in the Owens Valley ended with an abortive attempt by the department in 1936 to persuade the residents of Bishop to disincorporate their community. Disincorporation offered Los Angeles a way of reducing its tax assessments while at the same time further concentrating its control of the valley's affairs. In exchange, the department offered to buy up the commercial properties which the Bishop merchants had organized into a pool and held out for sale at an exorbitant price. On August 22, 1936, the citizens of Bishop rejected the proposition at a special election. "With God's help," Crowley declared, "we're going to persuade the City of Los Angeles to let us buy back our property and use our water on it and own our valley once again."[127]

It would have taken nothing less than divine intervention to persuade Los Angeles to give up the water-bearing lands it had gone through so much to obtain. But the town properties presented an entirely different matter. For the most part these lands carried with them no water rights, and they had been acquired by the city in a hasty, charitable gesture aimed at bringing a swift end to the controversy after the collapse of the Watterson banks. By 1938, the long struggle over municipal control of the city's water programs was entering its final phase with the election of Fletcher Bowron as mayor of Los Angeles. Having come to office as the reform candidate in a recall election, Bowron immediately set out to obtain the resignations of the entire board of water and power commissioners. In place of the policies of the past, he promised to bring efficiency, economy, and accountability to the operation of the department. And as part of this effort, he accepted an offer from the Inyo Associates to visit the Owens Valley with his newly appointed water and power commissioners for the purpose of discussing the resale of town properties owned by Los Angeles. On August 29, 1939, the first group of town lots was offered for sale, and by February 1944 the Department of Water and Power had disposed of 637 parcels representing nearly 50 percent of all the town properties the city had acquired.[128]

The return of the town properties to private control proceeded without Father Crowley. In the early morning hours of March 17, 1940, while returning to Lone Pine from San Francisco, he struck a steer that had wandered onto the roadway. The impact hurled his car into the path of an oncoming lumber truck, and he was killed instantly. More than six hundred people attended his funeral mass, overflowing the chapel at Lone Pine. The entire Inyo County Board of Supervisors came to pay their last respects. Los Angeles was represented by Van Norman, the chairman of the water and power commission, and two city councilmen. Mayor Bowron sent flowers; so too did a group of grateful valley residents, who included a note reading, "These flowers were not bought from a florist. We picked them ourselves at our homes because it was Inyo water that made them grow."[129]

At the time of Crowley's death it seemed that the bitterness of a decade before had at last come to an end. The following year, Los Angeles completed the Long Valley project; and in recognition of all that Father Crowley had done to improve relations between the city and the valley, the Department of Water and Power chose to name the new reservoir for him. Willie Arthur Chalfant, who was by this time nearing the end of his own long life in the valley, was invited to speak at the dedication of Crowley Lake. He too saw in the city's gesture of good will the hope of better times to come. "It is a promise of the end of dissensions," he remarked, "and we welcome its implied pledge that hereafter city and eastern Sierra shall work hand in hand for upbuilding. We cannot but regret that this enterprise was not constructed long ago; there would have been less of history to forget."[130]

Crowley's death, however, left unresolved the problem posed by the agricultural lands still held by the Department of Water and Power. Unused, they represented either a potential for continued conflict or an opportunity for Los Angeles to demonstrate its commitment to the improvement of the valley. Crowley, Chalfant, and Merritt had regarded a limited restoration of valley agriculture as the ultimate objective of their efforts. And though the impetus for the development they dreamed of took hold much sooner then they had expected, it came about for reasons no one could have foreseen or desired.

In the wake of the Japanese attack on Pearl Harbor, the United States Army on March 7, 1942, formally advised the Department of Water and Power that it was taking over 4,725 acres of the city's holdings in the Owens Valley "for so long as the present emergency requires." Along with the land, the army assumed control of four wells, three creeks, and as much water as the army determined would be necessary to support an agricultural community in the valley composed of Japanese-Americans who were being removed from coastal areas under the president's Executive Order 9066.[131] The area selected for this installation was the site of George Chaffey's stillborn water colony at Manzanar, where the drainage system and concrete conduits Chaffey had so carefully constructed still waited to be put to use.

The announcement at first stirred great consternation in the valley. Surveyors for the Army Corps of Engineers had appeared there a week before the announcement, circulating rumors that a hundred thousand Japanese internees were on the way. Strident opposition was expressed in several communities, and the town of Independence formed a militia to protect its citizens from these Americans it presumed were disloyal. Despite the impression created by popular fiction that every Western ranch house had its Chinese cook, Orientals were almost wholly unknown in the Owens Valley at this time.[132] And although the relocation of the Japanese-Americans was prompted by America's entry into World War II, it marked as well the fulfillment of a stridently racist campaign conducted for two decades by the publisher of the *Sacramento Bee*, V.S. McClatchey, to exclude Asian-Americans from any role in the economic life of California.

The principal engine of McClatchey's exclusionary program was the California Joint Immigration Committee, composed of the state attorney general and representatives of the American Legion, the California Federation of Labor, the Grange, and the Grand President of the Native Sons of the Golden West. Although the Joint Immigration Committee also condemned the granting of citizenship to Negroes after the Civil War as a "grave mistake," the principal object of McClatchey's vitriol was the Asian community, which he argued was incapable, for cultural reasons, of ever functioning as a loyal component of American society.[133] The seeds of hatred sown by McClatchey soon blossomed in the weeks after Pearl Harbor into hysterical reports that Japanese-American employees of the Department of Water and Power were plotting to poison the city's water supply. As a result, fourteen employees of the water department and ten members of the Los Angeles police force were summarily dismissed. And Owens Valley residents suddenly began recalling earlier visits by Oriental tourists who had been seen painting and photographing elements of the aqueduct delivery system.[134]

In contrast to this atmosphere of hostility and mistrust, responsible leaders in the Owens Valley regarded the establishment of the Manzanar relocation camp as a great boon to the community which could bring about an abrupt reversal of the valley's declining economic condition. "Let's Look at this New Development with a Long Range View," the *Inyo Independent* proposed in a special edition announcing the project. The publisher of the *Independent*, George Savage, had been included in the planning for the camp from its very inception, along with Ralph Merritt, Bob Brown, and Douglas Joseph of the Inyo Associates. In their view, the establishment of the camp afforded the Owens Valley a chance "to play a part in history in the making." More important, it offered "an opportunity to permit a part of our land and natural resources to be used for defense production, possibly of foodstuffs and other needs." Through the opening of the camp, Savage pointed out, the valley would gain "a large reservoir of labor" at no cost to county government. The army had asked Savage and his colleagues to develop a program for the activity of the camp that would be beneficial to the valley, and in this context, Savage proposed that the internees should be employed in building a broad-gauge railroad north from Owenyo, upgrading the county roads, and improving the valley's forest lands for postwar recreational use. The establishment of the camp was a matter of national defense, Savage emphasized, "one that cannot be displaced by local feeling or political reaction." The task for the Owens Valley, he therefore argued, was to make certain that the work performed at the relocation center would be "of permanent value in results attained."[135]

The opening of Manzanar did indeed bring the prosperity Savage and his colleagues promised. Safeway, J.C. Penney, and Sprouse-Reitz opened branch stores to handle the increased commercial trade from the camp, and Savage himself began publishing the *Manzanar Daily Free Press* for as long as the relocation center was in operation.[136] Within only two weeks of the announcement of the army's plans, Savage reported approvingly of the envy expressed by residents of Mono County at Inyo's good fortune. The *Bridgeport Chronicle Union* in Mono County observed editorially, "The chances of any of these Japanese doing misdeeds or costing the county extra money is negligible, and the amount of revenue it will bring to the businessmen and merchants should be astounding. We are only sorry that the heavy snows in the winter months and other terrain conditions prevent having one of these camps in this county."[137]

Local resentment of the camp, however, could not be entirely eradicated. Plans to employ the internees in maintaining the Haiwee Reservoir were dropped when local residents expressed their fear at any proposal to let the Japanese-Americans out of the camp. Similarly, a request by twenty-two Lone Pine businessmen to allow the residents of the camp to shop in their stores was stopped by a counterpetition drive which garnered five hundred signatures. "We ought to take those Yellow-tails right down to the edge of the Pacific and say to 'em: 'Okay boys, over there's Tokyo. Start walkin','" commented one Lone Pine barber. Inyo county officials also rejected a proposal to bring the schools set up within the camp under the aegis of the local school district, even though this action would have substantially increased revenues to the county schools. "We don't need any Jap money," declared one county supervisor. Another pontificated, "A Jap's a Jap, and by God I wouldn't trust one of 'em further'n I could throw a bull by the tail."[138]

On June 1, 1942, responsibility for the operation of the internment camps was shifted from the army to the newly created War Relocation Authority. Ralph Merritt was appointed director of the Manzanar facility, and he used the monthly meetings of the Inyo Associates to report on conditions within the camp, dispel rumors, and emphasize its value as a "war asset" to Inyo County.[139] Despite Merritt's best efforts, points of conflict continued to arise. Guards and other employees of the camp frequently encountered the same hostility that local residents directed against the internees. The fact that ham and bacon were being provided to the camps at a time when other Americans faced strict rationing of these foodstuffs sparked particular resentment, and in time it became an article of faith within California that all food shortages were due to the generosity of the War Relocation Authority. "It makes one's blood boil, and some of us feel like taking a tommy gun and cleaning that lot out," complained one impassioned resident of Huntington Park.[140]

The *Los Angeles Examiner* fanned the fires of reaction by reporting that the residents of Manzanar would be paid more for their work in the relocation center than the base pay for army recruits. The *Examiner* failed in its report to take account of the money deducted from the internees' wages for food and rent. But the pay scales for the internees were nonetheless adjusted downward, and even after army base pay had been increased from twenty-one to fifty dollars per month, the residents of Manzanar were never paid more than nineteen dollars a month for their labors. Even more damaging was the work of Congressman Martin Dies and his House Un-American Activities Committee, which persistently issued sensational reports of Japanese army officers lurking in the relocation centers and food caches buried in the desert outside Manzanar for the use of invading paratroopers.[141]

The worst fears of the valley residents seemed to be coming true on the night of December 6, 1942, when a major disturbance broke out within the Manzanar camp grounds. Similar conflicts had occurred at other camps, but the Manzanar incident marked the first occasion on which military police guarding the camp opened fire on the internees. Two men were killed. Although the disturbance was sparked by a labor dispute involving divisions deep within the Japanese-American community, the *Inyo Register* was quick to report falsely that it had come about as the result of a celebration of the anniversary of the bombing of Pearl Harbor. Dissident elements within the Manzanar community were promptly moved to other camps, and Merritt was able to restore order to the center on December 18 by persuading the military police to withdraw. But even with the armed guards gone, the incident had shattered the vitality of the community. The internees kept to their barracks; no work crews reported for assignment; no children were allowed to play outdoors; no lights were turned on at night. On Christmas Eve, Merritt and his wife gathered the orphans of the camp to go caroling. As they wound their way through the dusty streets of Manzanar, other children came out to join in the singing, and one by one, the lights came on again.[142]

The endurance of the internees, and their abiding faith in a nation that had disowned them, was the hallmark of life within the Manzanar community. When they first arrived, they had been told that the area was populated with poisonous snakes and thieves, and that United States warplanes would bomb the camp if Japan invaded California.[143] What they found was dust. "The desert was bad enough. The mushroom barracks made it worse. The constant cyclonic storms loaded with sand and dust made it worst," observed one internee. All accounts of Manzanar agree that dust was the central fact of life. "Nothing is more permanent about Manzanar than the dust which has lodged on its tar-papered barracks," noted one contemporary account of the camp. In their haste to open the facility, the army engineers had used bulldozers to scrape away all the existing surface vegetation and topsoil. As a result, an internee recalled, "We slept in the dust; we breathed the dust; and we ate the dust. Such abominable existence one could not forget, no matter how much we tried to be patient, understand the situation, and take it bravely."[144]

Despite these hardships, the residents of Manzanar fashioned a community which at its peak numbered 10,026 people. They established their own system of local government, their own police and fire departments, and their own shops, offices, farms, medical services, schools, parks, museums, libraries, and concerts. And it was in working the land that they fulfilled the promise that George Chaffey had first seen in this part of the Owens Valley. When they began in March 1942, only a few apple and pear trees still stood as gaunt reminders of Chaffey's ambition. They planted 325 acres in vegetables and 115 in alfalfa and meadow hay. By the end of 1943, twenty-two miles of lined irrigation ditches were in operation. The camp farm that year produced eighteen hundred tons of vegetables with a wholesale value of $110,000, and the camp as a whole contributed $900,000 to the local economy. That January, the United States Supreme Court ruled against the detention of loyal citizens, and the War Relocation Authority announced plans to close its camps within the year. At the end of June 1944, when the Manzanar population had already declined to 5,567, the remaining internees kept 368 acres in production, and their gross sales that year exceeded $309,000.[145]

The Department of Water and Power had not opposed the army's appropriation of its land and water as a matter of wartime necessity. By the same token, the department had not been criticized by those residents of the valley who feared the arrival of the Japanese. With the closing of the camp now in prospect, however, Los Angeles' officials focused their attention on making a profit from the arrangement. The federal government had originally placed $30,166.67 on account for use of the Manzanar property, and by mid-1944 Los Angeles had drawn a total of $27,500 in rents. At this point the city began demanding more, estimating that the combined value of its land and water merited rental payments totaling $44,000 a year. The federal authorities wisely retained Thomas Means to prepare an independent accounting. The key point at issue involved the water used for domestic purposes in the camp: the city at this time was asking ten times what the War Relocation Authority regarded as a fair price for this water. Means attacked Los Angeles' contentions, pointing out that the water involved was for the most part surplus to the city's needs, and very little of it ever reached the aqueduct in any event. "It does not seem that water in a mountain stream at some distance above the aqueduct can be considered domestic water," Means argued. "The stream is unregulated, varies greatly in flow, freezes in winter, is subject to contamination, and is not safe for human consumption unless it is treated." Since the federal government was providing this treatment at its own expense through a $147,000 sewage plant it had installed at Manzanar, Means concluded that the city was entitled to no more than $25,000 a year in overall rents.[146]

Of far greater importance from the department's point of view was the question of the ultimate disposition of the camp after the last internees had left. Manzanar had been the first of the detention camps to open, and it was one of the last to close. The resettlement rate of internees from Manzanar was only half that of other camps. Although none of the residents of Manzanar wished to remain, they were reluctant to enter a greater society which still regarded them with hostility. In Utah, the American Federation of Labor was campaigning to prohibit the issuance of business licenses to former inmates of the internment camps. In Colorado, the *Denver Post* advocated denying them the right to own land. Arizona forbade shopkeepers from selling any commodity to Japanese-Americans without first filing a declaration of intent with the governor's office and publishing an announcement in the press a day in advance. And in California, the racist tirades of the American Legion and the Native Sons of the Golden West were agumented by ad hoc groups such as No Japs Incorporated of San Diego, the Home Front Commanders of Sacramento, and the Pacific Coast Japanese Problem League in Los Angeles.[147]

So long as the internees remained at Manzanar and continued to work the land, their success created a troubling reminder of what might have been in the Owens Valley. Proposals were already being put forward by valley leaders in the middle of 1944 to keep the camp open after the war to provide veterans' housing or a home for senior citizens. Los Angeles would have no part of these plans. As soon as the last resident of Manzanar departed on November 21, 1945, and the land returned to the city's possession, the fields were torn up once again, the sewage treatment plant dismantled, and the barracks cut up and trucked away for use as extensions to the hotels in Lone Pine. Merritt remained long enough to supervise the destruction of the camp, then moved to Los Angeles, where he worked at establishing a rapid transit system.[148]

In the absence of any definite program for the management

of its lands in the Owens Valley, Los Angeles had drifted for ten years toward a policy of allowing its properties to be used as a haven for the displaced. Its generosity toward the Paiutes, the Tule Elk, and the residents of the valley towns had done much to dispel the bitterness of Mulholland's legacy in the valley. But these acts had posed no threat to the supply of water entering the aqueduct. The opening of the Manzanar relocation center, by contrast, had brought the city to the brink of reestablishing the very conditions of intensive agricultural development which it had fought a war to eliminate. A more definite policy was clearly needed to assure that henceforth Los Angeles' lands in the Owens Valley would remain in large part closed to resettlement.

CHAPTER EIGHT

The Ties That Bind

In his last annual message to Congress, Theodore Roosevelt reflected upon the changes occurring in American life as a result of the growth of giant corporations, national labor organizations, and the new urban metropolises. "The chief breakdown is in dealing with the new relations that arise from the mutualism, the interdependence of our time," he wrote. "Every new social relation begets a new type of wrong-doing—of sin to use an old-fashioned word—and many years always elapse before society is able to turn this sin into crime which can be effectively punished."[1]

In the case of the Owens Valley, the evolution of legal and social principles which Roosevelt predicted began almost immediately. The amendment to the state constitution in 1928 affirming the public interest in water and the enactment of the County of Origin statute three years later brought an end to the system of law under which Los Angeles had first entered the valley. Water in California no longer belonged to anyone with the money and the political muscle to take and defend it. And water development would henceforward proceed within the context of an adjudicative process whereby the needs of all would be balanced. These protections assure that nothing like the exploitation of the Owens Valley can ever occur again; and their adoption proved to be of critical importance in securing the state's participation in the construction of the Central Valley Project.[2] But because the rights of Los Angeles secured in the Owens Valley predate these fundamental changes in the law of water for California, their provisions have not been applied retroactively to protect the valley itself. As a result, the Owens Valley has become an island in time and law where the principles of another age still apply.

The completion of the Mono extension and the new aqueduct to the Colorado provided Los Angeles with a water supply far greater than it could ever absorb. After World War II, therefore, the concerns of the Department of Water and Power shifted from planning for the construction of new projects to the formulation of management strategies designed to achieve the greatest possible efficiency in the use of the water resources at its disposal. In pursuit of this objective, the department has sought to ward off interference with the administration of its land and water rights in the Owens Valley. But the Department of the Interior's insistence on a settlement program for the Paiutes, Father Crowley's campaign for resale of the town properties, and the army's establishment of the Manzanar relocation center had already demonstrated that the city could not truly operate in isolation. The modern relationship between Los Angeles and the Owens Valley has consequently been shaped by the city's continuing struggle to preserve its independence of action from the growing mutualism and interdependence which characterize water development in the rest of California today.

By the time the closure of the Manzanar facility had been announced, Los Angeles was already facing a far more serious threat of interference with its management of the aqueduct. The problem originated in the spring of 1937, when an unusually wet winter poured more water into the Owens River than the aqueduct was capable of carrying south to Los Angeles. Because the Long Valley reservoir had not yet been constructed, the city had no place to store the excess water. And because the orchardists of the San Fernando Valley were complaining mightily of the damage the boron-charged waters of Long Valley were doing to their crops, the department determined to waste the excess into Owens Lake.

The lake, however, had been dry since 1924 as a result of the city's diversion of its natural inflows to the aqueduct. And in the intervening years, the Natural Soda Products Company had secured the necessary permits from the state to establish a new plant in the dry lake bed. Control of the company had by this time passed to Stanley Pedder, formerly the principal customer for the soda products manufactured by the Watterson brothers at the lake. Pedder had prospered since acquiring the company in 1932, and in 1935 he began sinking wells and installing new pumps and other equipment to improve the efficiency of his operation and double the capacity of his processing plant. But even before the new plant could open, Los Angeles began releasing 50,000 acre-feet of water into the lake, inundating Pedder's facilities to a depth of three to four feet and destroying the commercial value of the chemical brine his company extracted from the lake bed.[3]

The city continued dumping water into the lake for the next five months, and the following year it added another 221,000 acre-feet to Pedder's problems. In December 1937 Pedder filed suit to recover his damages and enjoin the city from continuing its depredations against his commercial operations. The trial court in Inyo awarded the Natural Soda Products Company $154,000, and Los Angeles promptly appealed to the state supreme court. But by the time the supreme court rendered its judgment in November 1943, Pedder had persuaded the State Lands Commission to join his suit for the recovery of royalties the state had lost from the destruction of his works.[4]

Los Angeles at first contended that the company's suit should be dismissed because Pedder had not acted promptly in filing his claim against the city. The supreme court rejected this argument, pointing out that Pedder had been unable even to secure access to his facilities to begin totting up his losses until after the waters had subsided in October. The heart of Los Angeles' defense subsequently came to depend upon a savagely ironic interpretation of its duties under the constitutional amendment of 1928, which had been adopted in part to protect other communities from the fate of the Owens Valley. Los Angeles' attorneys now read its provisions as compelling the city to take the action it had, even though this meant the destruction of one of the valley's last surviving major industries. Because the constitutional amendment requires water to be conserved for its highest beneficial uses, and because Los Angeles contended that it had no ability to store or use the excess water itself, the city argued that it was obligated to allow the water to flow on to its natural resting place, the bed of Owens Lake.

The supreme court was neither amused nor persuaded. "It is generally recognized that one who makes substantial expenditures in reliance on long-continued diversion of water by another has the right to have the diversion continued if his investment would otherwise be destroyed," the court pointed out. The evidence in the case, moreover, amply established to the court's satisfaction that Los Angeles "could easily have found an outlet for the surplus water instead of causing it to flow into the lake." And the constitutional provisions upon which the city relied "have never been construed as requiring a particular disposition of surplus water, least of all a disposition harmful to the recipient." On the contrary, the court concluded, these constitutional provisions actually prohibit the city from disposing of the surplus in a way that would be destructive to other natural resources.[5]

This loss had a far greater significance for Los Angeles than the monetary damages awarded to Pedder and the State Lands Commission. For the court's decision now compelled the Department of Water and Power to include flood control within the Owens Valley as one of its functional considerations in the operation of the aqueduct. And this requirement in turn restricted the amount of water that could be brought down from the Mono Basin during periods of high runoff in the Owens River watershed. The necessity to provide sufficient storage facilities to capture excess runoff at flood times thus created a fundamental conflict with the city's desire to keep its reservoirs full at all times for use in the event of a drought.[6]

Pedder went still further by suggesting that the city should be compelled to apply any water it could not use to the restoration of valley agriculture.[7] The result was the enactment in 1945 of a new state statute prohibiting Los Angeles from wasting the water it derives from the Owens and Mono basins in any way.[8] Although the city subsequently secured from the courts a limited right to waste excess waters into Owens Lake under specified conditions, these restrictions resulting from the Natural Soda

Products case represented the most severe limitations imposed on Los Angeles' operation of the aqueduct since President Theodore Roosevelt's amendment to the right-of-way bill of 1906 prohibited the city from selling aqueduct water outside its borders.[9]

For the residents of the Owens Valley, the case presented an ominous warning that the era of good feelings and mutual prosperity predicted by Chalfant and Crowley had not truly been taken to heart by the officials of the Department of Water and Power. Even admitting all of the city's protestations of constitutional good faith and concern for the orchardists of the San Fernando Valley, the willful destruction of Pedder's plant was an act of breathtaking arrogance which suggested that at best Los Angeles' officials regarded valley industry with an indifference verging on contempt. At worst, the city's action suggested a determination to prevent an economic resurgence of any kind in the Owens Valley.

Further evidence that the city's attitude had changed since Father Crowley's death came within a few months of the supreme court's decision in the Natural Soda Products case. Ever since the first sale of town lots in 1939, Los Angeles had given preference to leaseholders in the sale of its properties in the Owens Valley. In this way, the dislocation of families and businesses resulting from the sales was kept to a minimum, and those who improved the properties they rented were assured that they would have the opportunity to benefit from their investments. Such a policy, moreover, was consistent with the position adopted by the water and power commission only a year after the destruction of Pedder's plant that "the existing spirit of good will and cooperation . . . [should] be in all proper ways promoted and fostered and, particularly, by such aid and encouragement to . . . settlement and development as the City of Los Angeles can afford through the disposal of its lands . . . on terms that, while safeguarding the interests of [the] City, will assure settlers and developers of permanency in their respective tenures and investments."[10]

In the wake of the supreme court's decision, however, the city abruptly reversed this policy at the beginning of 1944 and announced that henceforth all lands offered for sale would go to the highest bidder in a sealed bid competition. When the valley lease-holders protested, the city responded by increasing the rents on all its properties in the Owens Valley, effective January 1, 1945. Both the change in sales procedures and the increase in rents could be seen as part of the continuing pressure upon the depart-ment to turn a profit on its properties in the valley. But the timing and method chosen by the department once again signaled either complete disregard for the effect of its actions on the valley residents or a purposeful cruelty. For the announcement of the rent increases came at a time when federally enforced rent con-trols were in effect across the country, and the notices of the increase were mailed to arrive during Christmas week 1944.[11]

The city's action drew an immediate response from the state legislature. The state senator representing Inyo County, Charles Brown, rushed legislation through that required the city to give its leaseholders first option on the valley properties it offered for sale. The act additionally prohibited Los Angeles from charging more in rent for any property than the value of the use to which it was put by the leaseholder. The city retaliated in March 1945 by announcing a virtual halt to all its land sales in the valley. Under Brown's legislation, sales by sealed bid would still be permitted where the purchaser was a public agency or where the property involved was unoccupied and run down. In all other instances, the city declared, its charter prohibited compliance with this new statute, and no sales would therefore be possible.

Brown's legislation did reinforce its provisions with a decla-ration of statewide interest in the exercise of the state's police power, which is the conventional method by which the legislature signals its intent to void a conflicting provision in a city charter. And the Los Angeles city charter itself permitted a suspension of the requirement for sealed bids whenever such an action would be "compatible with the city's interests." But the city attorney ruled that the goodwill of the residents of the Owens Valley was not a sufficiently valuable consideration to justify waiving the requirement. Coming as it did after more than six hundred town lots had already been sold, the city's sudden discovery of the charter restrictions carried a gratuitously punitive air. But the decision held, and a deadlock was created. Although many lots which met the requirements of both the charter and the Brown act continued to be put up for sale through 1967, Crowley's program for returning the communities of the Owens Valley to the possession of their residents came to a complete halt thereafter, and no properties were offered for sale by the city again until 1979.[12]

The uproar Los Angeles had fomented in the Owens Valley created problems for the city in Washington as well as in Sacramento. Progress on Los Angeles' power plants in the Owens Gorge had been delayed by wartime shortages of labor and materiel. To aid in the war effort, moreover, the Department of Water and Power had converted its machine shops to the production of airplane parts, batteries, switchboards, and gasoline tanks. But America's entry into the war had also brought a massive influx of skilled workers to Southern California; and with peace restored, they could now be employed in construction of the power plants which had once been the principal purpose of the Mono extension. The state supreme court's decision in the Natural Soda Products case lent a special urgency to this effort because the power plants would provide the regulating capacity the city needed to comply with the court's prohibition on dumping.[13] And in order to prevent any additional conflicts with existing uses of the land and resources of the area, Los Angeles in October 1944 exercised its authority under the right-of-way bills of 1931 and 1936 to apply for control of an additional 23,851 acres of the public domain in Mono County.

The application stirred immediate resistance. In Sacramento, Charles Brown, as chairman of the Senate Committee on Local Governmental Agencies, launched an investigation of the city's relations with the valley, focusing particularly on the 1936 act, which gave Los Angeles the power to acquire lands in the Mono Basin at $1.25 an acre. In Washington, meanwhile, California's Congressman Clair Engle and Nevada's Senator Patrick A. McCarran introduced legislation to repeal the 1931 and 1936 acts altogether. The point at issue was not the desirability of the project but whether Los Angeles in fact needed to hold title to the lands it had requested. Brown, Engle, and McCarran contended that it did not and that the permits and licenses customarily issued by federal agencies for the use of public lands would be ample for the city's purposes. In this opinion, they were joined by the County Supervisors Association of California, the California Cattleman's Association, Mono County District Attorney Walter Evans, and the head of the Bishop Chamber of Commerce, Roy Boothe. Brown dismissed the city's argument that it needed title to the lands to prevent later claims from being filed as piling speculation upon speculation. "It does not appear to this committee," he concluded, "that the city needs the fee title to any of the land which it has selected for any of the purposes which it has indicated."[14]

Faced with this opposition, the Department of the Interior determined to hold Los Angeles' applications in abeyance until the fate of the Engle and McCarran bills was decided. A total of five thousand acres of the land Los Angeles proposed to purchase under the 1936 act lay within the Inyo National Forest, and that portion of the city's application was rejected out of hand by the Secretary of Agriculture. There were concerns as well that acceptance of the city's request would interfere with the use of these lands for grazing, recreation, and residential development which had already been authorized under permits issued by the responsible federal agencies. And Brown's committee pointed out that three commercial sites lying within the town of Lee Vining, which Los Angeles later dropped from its application, had a higher assessed valuation than the city would have to pay for the entire 23,851 acres it proposed to buy.[15]

The controversy ultimately centered on distrust of Los Angeles. "The thing that we fear mostly," the Mono district attorney testified, "is the fact that we will go through the very disheartening and heartbreaking conditions and happenings that the people in Inyo County have gone through."[16] Similarly, Roy Boothe, speaking for the Bishop merchants, expressed concern that acceptance of the city's applications would further undermine the Owens Valley economy and destroy what seemed at the time to be a promising prospect for a substantial boom in second-home development throughout the eastern Sierra.[17]

To assuage these fears, the city promised that no one currently residing on the lands affected by its applications would be moved and that their lease payments or permit fees would remain the same. Moreover, the city's representatives pointed out, its leases were extended for five years, whereas the existing federal permits had to be renewed annually. The all-important difference in Brown's view, however, lay in the fact that the federal government always renewed its permits as long as the fees were paid, whereas the city would give no assurance that such a policy would be maintained. Brown, therefore, focused on Los Angeles' "conflicting proprietary interest in the very lands which it undertakes to administer in the public interest." And he argued forcefully that the history of the city's actions in the Owens Valley "furnishes no basis for expectation that it could and would in Mono County consistently pursue the policy which it now announces."[18]

On May 12, 1947, Brown succeeded in persuading his colleagues in the state senate to endorse Engle's efforts to repeal the 1931 and 1936 acts. One month later, the State Lands Commission asked the Department of the Interior to suspend further consideration of the city's applications and then filed its own application for control of all the public lands within one mile of the meander line of Mono Lake.[19] The newspapers in Los Angeles had by this time taken to attacking Congressman Engle as a "cow-county prophet . . . gazing into a somewhat dusty crystal ball."[20] The *Los Angeles Times* made its contribution to public misunderstanding by blaming the opposition to the city's applications on an unidentified band of private speculators who were allegedly plotting to establish a chemical industry on the shores of Mono Lake. Unless the city were allowed to proceed, the *Times* warned, water shortages would soon occur in Los Angeles and groundwater pumping in Burbank and Glendale would have to be stopped.[21] The conflict, of course, had nothing to do with the city's water supply, and even the Department of Water and Power by this time was acknowledging that there was enough water available to support eight million people, double the current population of the entire metropolitan area.[22] Nevertheless, the city's champion in Congress, Norris Poulson, denounced all suggestions that Los Angeles' water supply was more than sufficient as "asinine."[23]

What the city's officials found particularly irksome was the fact that rural legislators like Engle and Brown could exercise so much influence even though they represented very small constituencies. In this age before the one-man-one-vote rule, the entire county of Los Angeles sent only one state senator to Sacramento, and that single seat was held by Jack Tenney, whose influence in the legislature was diminished by his enthusiasm for charging his fellow senators with communist sympathies.[24] The *Los Angeles Daily News* angrily pointed out that the three senators who voted against the resolution endorsing Engle's bills represented more people than the thirty legislators whose votes passed it. And the Department of Water and Power threatened to retaliate for the passage of Brown's resolution by ordering an immediate halt in the sale of any properties it still offered in the Owens Valley.[25]

The beginning of 1948 brought a brief attempt at compromise. The Department of Water and Power had already agreed to the repeal of the 1936 act if the lands it had requested in 1944 were delivered into its control.[26] Congressmen Poulson of Los Angeles and Carl Hinshaw of Pasadena introduced legislation to this effect, claiming the support of Brown's committee and Inyo and Mono counties. But the effort collapsed amid a flurry of charges and countercharges that Poulson had reneged on the terms of the compromise and was trying to rush much more through Congress than the local county representatives had agreed to. And with that, the controversy ended in stalemate. The stakes were simply too high for the city to persist in trying to secure what amounted to a marginal degree of protection for its interests. The 1936 act consequently remained intact, albeit little used, and the city went ahead with its power plants without the lands it had sought.[27]

For half a century, individual officials and agencies in Washington had provided Los Angeles with the essential support it required to secure an abundant municipal water supply. But the battle over the Engle and McCarran bills demonstrated that the city's ability to rely upon federal assistance was now at an end. George Savage, the new owner of the Chalfant newspapers, had warned of this coming change. In a guest editorial in the *Times* at the end of the war, he had argued that Los Angeles could no longer afford to ignore the concerns of the Owens Valley. "If it does," he wrote, "it need not be surprised if the rest of the State reacts in support of Inyo; further publicity will result, and Washington will lend an ear." The city's successive defeats in the courts, the state legislature, and the Congress proved the accuracy of Savage's prediction. The need to achieve an accommodation through the development of a consistent policy for the valley's development was greater now than ever before. Further strife, as Savage pointed out, could only lead to "more and more legislative control."[28]

The Department of Water and Power was in a better position in 1948 to fix a new policy toward the Owens Valley than it had been at any time in the two decades since Mulholland's fall. For the long-running attempts to break the so-called Water and Power Machine and bring the department's activities under tighter municipal control had effectively ended in 1944 with a general strike by the employees of the Bureau of Power and Light.[29] After suffering repeated disruptions of its policies and programs, the department had emerged from the controversy stronger than ever. And in 1947 it had secured a far greater measure of political independence through the promotion of a successful charter amendment that relieved it of ever having to obtain the voters' approval of another bond issue. Thenceforward it could be able to finance new projects from its own revenues.

"We can't always be certain that we will have a two-thirds vote to carry the bonds . . . We can't afford an uncertainty," the new general manager, Samuel B. Morris, pointed out at a kickoff rally for the department's employees who would be working to pass the charter amendment. His deputy, Charles Garman, enthused, "Many of us have wished that there was some way to finance ourselves. Gentlemen, this is it! This is the answer we have been looking for for a long time. If it goes over, we will have the time to make the Department grow and less time to worry about financing."[30] Fewer than four-fifths of the voters who went to the polls that year bothered to cast a ballot on the department's proposition. But those who did approved the measure by a margin of two to one.[31] "It just proves again," commented the chairman of the department's political action committee, "that the All-American employee department team does not specialize in failures."[32]

The Water and Power Machine had not been broken. Its multiple victories, capped by passage of the charter amendment of 1947, simply obviated any need for its continued operation. The resistance to municipal ownership of the city's water and power resources had been vanquished. The department had succeeded in establishing a unified management system in defiance of the policies of the Board of Water and Power Commissioners.[33] The board's authority would hereafter be limited to the broadest oversight of general policies; no further interference in the day-to-day management of the department's affairs would be attempted. The end of the controversy thus signaled more than a victory for the principle of public ownership. More important, it reaffirmed the essential autonomy which the founders of the Department of Water and Power at the turn of the century had regarded as the primary requirement for its successful operation. The charter amendment of 1947 perfected the department's insulation from political influence. "The task of the great creators was finished," Vincent Ostrom noted approvingly in a scholarly study of the department published in 1953 under the aegis of the foundation named for one of Los Angeles' most prominent progressive reformers, John Randolph Haynes.[34]

Ostrom's book was the second of two laudatory histories of Los Angeles' water programs that appeared at the beginning of the 1950s. Three years earlier, Remi Nadeau had produced *The Water Seekers*, which emphasized the multiple benefits the aqueduct had brought not only to Los Angeles but also to the Owens Valley. For the first time since 1920, the department seemed to be putting the controversies of the past behind it. The rent increase of Christmas 1945 and all the setbacks that had flowed from it now appeared in retrospect as an aberration, a last gasp of assertiveness by an economy-minded Board of Water and Power Commissioners. Any clumsiness in the handling of the department's relations with the Owens Valley since the end of World War II could be laid to the fact that the department had then been headed by a new general manager who had been brought in from outside the departmental ranks and so was less well attuned to the sensitivities peculiar to the city's relations with the valley. But now, with its autonomy restored, the department by 1950 could look forward to setting about the task of restoring calm to its dealings with the Owens Valley.

The Modern Relationship, 1950-1970

"The policy of Los Angeles has been and is admittedly against the development of Inyo and Mono counties," Clair Engle asserted in 1948, "because the basis of their philosophy . . . has been that one more person in Inyo County is one more problem."[35] The head of the city's water program, H. A. Van Norman, acknowledged the essential truth of Engle's observation in testimony before Senator Brown's committee in California: "If we start in and dedicate a lot of water into the Owens Valley for general farming purposes and build up the towns and build up the communities on the expectation that there is a permanent plan, then we are going to have more senate investigating committees some time in the future when we have to take the water away."[36]

Van Norman's remarks affirmed the perception Lippincott, Means, and the Watterson brothers had all shared from the first, that Los Angeles and the Owens Valley were essentially adversaries in competition for a limited resource. The city's interest in the protection of its own water supply therefore dictated opposition to the further growth and development of the valley. But if restraint was the logical objective of any plan Los Angeles might formulate for the future of the valley, it was not a plan itself. The events of the past two decades had shown that inaction could be as dangerous to the city's interest as too forthright a policy of opposition to valley development. Simply leaving the lands idle invited interference. With the end of the controversy in Los Angeles over the management of the Department of Water and Power, the pressure to show a profit on the city's lands in the valley diminished. A far greater need clearly existed to develop some method for assuaging the concerns of an increasingly restive valley population whose protests could now be heard in Washington as well as Sacramento. The avoidance of controversy therefore became an objective for city planning in the valley that was second in importance only to the necessary resistance to development.

The pattern of land ownership within the Owens and Mono basins created a further restraint upon the city's freedom of action. Privately held lands, where the opportunities for development would be most likely to occur, constituted only 3 percent of the 2.4 million acres lying within the two basins, according to a survey by the state Department of Water Resources in 1960. In contrast, the city of Los Angeles owned 12 percent of the overall land area outright and controlled another 27 percent under federal land withdrawals made for the protection of its water supply. State lands, including the beds of Owens and Mono lakes, amounted to another 5 percent. But 52 percent of the total land area, lying principally within the Inyo National Forest, fell under the jurisdiction of federal agencies whose acquiescence in the city's programs could no longer simply be taken for granted.[37] The Inyo Forest supervisor pointed out in 1965 that fully 60 percent of Los Angeles' water supply originated within his domain. Accommodation with federal land management programs consequently became another essential element in the city's policy toward the two basins. And as a result, Los Angeles after 1950 dropped its earlier opposition to the issuance of permits for domestic and commercial use of these federal lands.[38]

The limits of the city's new spirit of cooperation were first defined with respect to its approach to valley agriculture. In 1945, Los Angeles negotiated an agreement with the local cattlemen which for the first time made some formal provision for the delivery of water to irrigate grazing lands under five-year leases that would be renewable without competitive bidding. Two types of leases were offered. Approximately 85 percent of the lands the city leased for agricultural purposes were made available without water at rates as low as six cents per acre. On the remainder, the value of an individual lease varied according to the water supplied and the value of the commodity grown. Although the leases ran for five-year terms, the determination as to whether any water would actually be delivered was made annually, depending upon the amount the city had available after the needs of the aqueduct had been met. The amount of irrigated acreage consequently fluctuated widely from as much as 30,000 acres in some wet years to as little as 3,000 acres in dry periods.[39]

This uncertainty, combined with the five-year limit on any single lease, made any investment in crop production "exceedingly precarious," according to a study for the University of California in 1964. Dairying, orchards, and a wide range of water-dependent crops were thus effectively excluded from valley agriculture. "The net effect of city leasing policies," the university researchers observed, "is to place a premium on lack of development by making long-range capital investment in crop production too risky."[40] As a result, even the irrigated acreage within the valley was turned over for the most part to grazing, with some small areas set aside for the production of alfalfa, oats, barley, hay, and other livestock fodder. In 1963, for example, when an abundant seasonal water supply allowed 30,700 acres to be irrigated, fully 28,000 acres were left as pasture.[41] The days when Inyo exported its fruits and vegetables to the markets of Los Angeles were gone, never to return.

The city's leasing program thus effectively restored valley agriculture to the primitive conditions of a century before. The publications of the Department of Water and Power have subsequently sought to foster the impression that this is the natural order of things, and that no brighter prospect of agricultural prosperity ever beckoned.[42] There is a significant difference, however, between cattle ranching then and now in the Owens Valley. For the limitations imposed by the city's leasing policy have severely diminished the likelihood that livestock can be raised as anything other than a supplemental source of income or as part of a larger corporate enterprise. Those who initially rushed to secure the city's leases soon had reason to regret their haste. After steadily expanding the amount of irrigated acreage from 1950 to 1959, the department began cutting back on valley water deliveries when a series of dry winters set in. In 1961, the area of irrigated agriculture in the Mono Basin dropped from a high of 2,100 acres to nothing at all, while in the Owens Basin, irrigated acreage was diminished by half. Since the leases themselves could not be sold, it became customary for a faltering farmer to sell his livestock at a price inflated to reflect the value of his lease. As a result, possession of the vast proportion of the city's leased agricultural lands gradually passed to a handful of agricultural corporations, and the proportion of valley residents actually employed in agriculture dwindled to less than 2 percent of the total work force by 1970.[43]

For purposes of restricting the economic growth of the Owens and Mono basins, these developments could scarcely have been more favorable. Most of the city's lands were now committed to agriculture, thereby insulating the Department of Water and Power in large measure from any external pressure to convert these lands to more productive uses. And the dependence of the lessees upon the department's readiness to provide water from year to year created an influential constituency whose members would be more likely to favor accommodation for the sake of their annual balance sheets than to risk loss of the city's goodwill in the interest of pressing for long-range improvements in the valley's overall economic condition.

Most important, the department's agricultural leasing policies effectively restricted any prospects for new commercial or residential growth to the existing town boundaries. Within the towns, Los Angeles' ability to effect its will was more limited than on the agricultural lands it controlled. The city, after all, had sold off many of its holdings here and continued to do so throughout this period. Nevertheless, it became popular in some local quarters to blame the failure to attract new industry upon the city's opposition. "Whenever we propose any development of the valley, it is blocked by the Department of Water and Power," complained one county official in 1964. Critics of the city pointed especially at the department's refusal to make water and power available for aircraft, sugar beet, and ski lift manufacturing plants which expressed an interest in locating new facilities in the valley. In their defense, departmental officials argued that water rights could still be purchased in some parts of the valley and that power supplies could be obtained from the Southern California Edison Company, which in 1964 succeeded to the interests of the older power companies that had formerly served the communities of the Owens and Mono basins.[44]

Certainly the department did nothing to encourage economic development in the valley. The reluctance Van Norman had expressed in 1945 about making any long-term commitments for the delivery of water and power in the Owens Valley became all-important in fixing the department's attitude. As a result, industrial developers interested in opening new plants in areas of the valley not served by the Southern California Edison Company were advised that power would not be available on anything other than a stand-by or temporary basis. Further obstacles to development were erected by the department's insistence that any new industrial installation in the valley must be prepared to accept the costs of providing its own water treatment facilities. And in Bishop, fully one-fourth of the town's total land area and one-third of its taxable lands were kept as vacant lots let for the grazing of horses and sheep.[45]

During the period of drift and indecision in the city's land management programs from 1930 to 1950, Inyo County's population grew by 78 percent; and the population of Bishop nearly doubled from 1940 to 1950. With the resurgence of departmental authority after 1950, however, the rate of population growth in Inyo came to a complete halt which endured throughout the next decade. Mono's population, meanwhile, remained virtually fixed from 1930 to 1960.[46]

But the department was not actively conspiring to strangle the economic vitality of the valley. Los Angeles had no more of a plan or program for the future of the Owens Valley than Mulholland had ever had. Mulholland's successors were content with the status quo, and they simply responded to events and proposals originating in the valley in accordance with their own interest in protecting the city's water resources. Whatever influence Los Angeles exercised over the development of the valley towns derived in part from the acquiescence of local officials. A report for the Izaak Walton League in 1971 decried the fact that "up to the moment, there exists no public agency or planning institution capable of formulating a comprehensive, multiple-purpose, resource use master plan." The consequence, in the author's view, was the assignment of local responsibility to "single-purpose, absentee decision-making in the allocation of water."[47] The city of Bishop, for example, as late as 1966, did not impose any zoning restrictions of its own, leaving land use regulation generally to the Department of Water and Power.[48] Similarly, the formulation of a general plan for Inyo in 1968 was prompted by the county's belated recognition that it would not be able to obtain federal and state subventions without one.[49]

In some instances, the city's interests impelled Los Angeles to provide assistance to the valley towns in correcting problems which local officials were unable or unwilling to confront. This was especially true in the case of the valley's neglected water and sewage systems. By the late 1960s, only 80 percent of Bishop was served by the local municipal water utility, and only 50 percent of the community's area received sewer service. Less than 30 percent of Lone Pine was served by sewers, and Big Pine had no sewer system at all. And as the county general plan noted in 1968, the steady deterioration of the generally outmoded local systems and septic tanks posed a growing threat not only to the water resources of all the valley communities but also to the aqueduct supply.[50]

Los Angeles has actively sought to improve these conditions, and the Department of Water and Power today provides water to Big Pine and Lone Pine and water and sewer services to Independence. In addition, when the city acquired the Bishop power distribution system at the end of World War II, it began rewiring homes throughout the community at its own expense, with the result that service was restored to many people who had stopped using their appliances because the voltage was so poor.[51]

The limits of the city's control over economic development in the Owens Valley is indicated by the fact that even though the department's policies did not change after 1960, the rate of growth in Inyo and Mono counties certainly did. In the next decade the population of Inyo County increased by a third and Mono County's numbers nearly tripled. Increased tourist traffic to the recreational resources of the eastern Sierra was the principal spur driving this new growth. State officials had already identified this potential for economic development and had predicted in

1958, "It appears evident that the Mono-Inyo area is on the threshold of substantial additional growth in the development and use of this recreational resource."[52] By 1963, recreational use of the Inyo National Forest had increased 34 percent over the levels of ten years before, and fishing at Crowley Lake was up 123 percent. Assuming that this contemporary popular enthusiasm for summertime travel and recreation would continue unabated, state agencies began projecting a sevenfold increase in the demand for water recreation facilities over the next thirty years.[53]

Some local officials expressed misgivings about the valley's increasing dependence upon "a two-month economy based mostly on recreation."[54] But in the absence of an alternative, it became increasingly popular to imagine that tourism offered a better potential for prosperity than agriculture or more conventional industrial development ever had.[55] As a result, services to tourists came to constitute a steadily increasing component of the activities of the civilian work force, retail sales tax revenues assumed a disproportionately large part of the burden of municipal financing, and an estimated 85 to 90 percent of the Bishop economy shifted to reliance on the tourist industry.[56] The influx of visitors, in turn, enhanced the popularity of the region as a site for the construction of vacation or retirement homes. And older residents consequently became a disproportionately large component of the local population when compared with statewide averages, whereas the number of children in the valley dwindled.[57]

The median income in Inyo and Mono counties, however, continued to lag behind the statewide mean. The valley's labor force consequently declined as unemployment rose.[58] The increasing vulnerability of the local economy to a shift in tourist travel habits had produced a marked disparity by the mid-1960s among the projections various population experts made for the future growth of the area. Thus, while the state Department of Water Resources and Department of Finance, the telephone company, and the county's own planners persisted in predicting a near doubling of the Inyo County population by 1990, the Los Angeles Chamber of Commerce and the University of California Center for Planning and Development Research projected minimal expansion or a decline.[59] And in 1968, the Inyo general plan observed that the valley's economy was in a state of "relative stagnation."[60]

The Department of Water and Power generally encouraged the development of the local tourist industry as part of its historic but undefined dream of converting the Owens Valley into a playland for the swelling population of the South Coast. Glossy departmental brochures touted the area's recreational attractions, and city officials exercised their authority wherever possible to protect the scenic resources of the valley. Billboards, for example, were prohibited on city-owned lands along the local highways. The department's commercial leases for town properties similarly reserved to Los Angeles the power to restrict the size, type, and placement of signs. And in some cases, the department even refused to grant leases within the towns for uses which it considered incompatible with the surrounding environment.[61]

There were limits, of course, to how much the department was willing to do. It made some of its lands available for local parks at low lease rates and opened Crowley Lake to anglers. But the work of planting more than two hundred thousand fish in the lake each year was handled by the state Department of Fish and Game and the city's Department of Parks and Recreation. And apart from investing an estimated $500,000 a year in advertising Crowley Lake to fishermen, the department committed little of its own financial resources to the improvement of recreational opportunities in the valley.[62] A state survey of the area's water recreation facilities in 1964, for example, found that Los Angeles provided only 6 of the 48 boat launches and 150 of the 2,950 feet of public beaches available in the valley, even though the city's lakes and reservoirs made up more than a quarter of the total water surface area in the region.[63]

The growing enthusiasm of the local residents for tourism as a basis for their economy inevitably generated pressure on the department to do more. The fact that Los Angeles had opened 75 percent of its lands in the valley for public access but not for camping was criticized as an "empty gesture" in the absence of any plan to attract and sustain game and water fowl which might entice daytime visitors into traipsing away from the roadsides.[64] The city's practice of allowing its agricultural lessees to burn or spray cottonwoods and willows along stream banks as a way of increasing their grazing area was similarly attacked because the resulting breakdown of the banks contributed to erosion and thereby interfered with the spawning beds of brown trout.[65] And the diversion of water below Crowley Dam into the city's power plants was condemned as a direct assault on the local fish population. Because these diversions dried up a fifteen-mile stretch of the riverbed containing a trout fishery worth an estimated $400,000, representatives of the Bishop Chamber of Commerce charged, "The complete destruction of fish population in this stretch of matchless fishing waters established a new low in the principles of conservation of natural resources . . . [which] will be long remembered."[66]

Crowley Lake, as the valley's principal recreational resource, was open for fishing only ninety days out of the year, and camping and water contact sports were at all times prohibited. When the state legislature in 1960 for the first time officially designated recreation and fish and wildlife enhancement as beneficial uses of water under the terms of the state constitution, the valley residents promptly applied to Sacramento for assistance in expanding its recreational facilities and resolving the problems of the fisheries. A study was duly ordered in the 1961-62 fiscal year, and the state Department of Water Resources soon after announced the discovery of an "urgent need for additional reservoirs for recreational purposes."[67] Aubrey Lyon, president of the local chapter of the Izaak Walton League, meanwhile began pressing for the construction of a network of warm water ponds and lakes which would serve to enhance the fish habitat and improve the quality of grazing lands along the sloughs in the upper part of the valley.[68] A reconnaissance study for the Department of Water Resources in 1960 identified sixteen potential sites within the valley for the installation of new recreational reservoirs, as well as five existing lakes which could be expanded to provide additional storage for recreational purposes and the maintenance of downstream flows.[69] The state subsequently filed for water rights on all these sites, which were to be held in trust until funds could be found to develop the proposed projects.[70]

Although the state water planners hoped to begin with a series of small reservoirs, Inyo County urged the Department of

Water Resources to focus instead on the largest of the proposed reservoir sites at Fish Slough. Any of these projects would have increased the loss of water from the valley due to evaporation. So each would have constituted exactly the kind of long-term dedication of part of the valley's overall water supply which the Department of Water and Power resisted most. As the largest of the proposed projects, the Fish Slough plan was particularly troubling to the department in this respect. The prospect of evaporative losses, however, would require the state officials to secure the approval of all the downstream owners of water rights before any progress could be made on their plans.[71] Thus the stage was set for a replay of Mulholland's original confrontation over the Fish Slough reservoir project in the early 1920s. The denouement was precisely the same. The state's detailed studies revealed that Mulholland's initial suspicions had been correct. The rock foundation for the dam site at Fish Slough was too badly fractured to be sealed, and the eastern rim of the reservoir was unstable. In addition, the reservoir would lie astride a fault line in one of the two most active earthquake zones in California, thereby posing an unacceptable risk to anyone downstream. The project was abandoncd.[72]

Following the rejection of the Fish Slough reservoir project, the state's water rights filings remained in trust, but the plans for their use were for the most part set aside. Aubrey Lyon succeeded in obtaining $50,000 from the California Wildlife Conservation Board for the implementation of his plan. But further progress on his project was halted by the city's refusal to provide the lands needed for his ponds. The construction of the Pleasant Valley Dam at the foot of the Owens River Gorge, however, helped mitigate the effect on the downstream fisheries of the city's diversions by preventing extreme fluctuations in the flow of water out of the power plants. At Lyon's insistence, the city included a spawning channel for the trout in this new project. The department further agreed to limit its releases from the Mono Tunnel to a maximum of four hundred cubic feet per second. And in 1970, Los Angeles joined in forming an interagency committee composed of representatives from the city, Inyo and Mono counties, and the state and federal forestry and wildlife agencies which has been entrusted with overseeing the development of programs and policies for the enhancement of the area's fish and wildlife resources.[73]

Recreational development was not the only area in which Inyo County sought to establish a greater measure of control over its own economic growth. Equally important was another controversy which raged throughout this period over the issue of taxation. Since the adoption of the constitutional amendment of 1914 authorizing the assessment of the city's lands in the Owens Valley, Los Angeles had become the largest individual taxpayer in Inyo County. In 1955, the county began splitting its assessment rolls in order to levy a separate assessment on the city's water rights, thereby more than doubling the city's tax debt on the lands affected. Although the power to tax water rights was an established principle of California law by this time, the state Board of Equalization found that the methods employed by the county assessor had been improper, and the state supreme court upheld this decision.[74] But once the necessary adjustments had been made in its assessment procedures, the county after 1958 persisted in levying a separate tax on the city's right to export water, contending generally that a portion of the value of the exported commodity should be returned to its place of origin.

Los Angeles invariably protested its new assessments each year to the Board of Equalization. The time consumed in hearings before the board and the annual uncertainty over the rate which state officials would actually approve became disruptive for the ongoing programs of the county departments.[75] And the board further complicated matters by ruling that the county's right to fix these assessments applied only at the actual point at which the waters were diverted into the aqueduct. This meant that the greater part of the revenues derived from the new assessments were concentrated in a single school district. The problem might have been resolved by consolidating all the county's school districts, but that approach was never seriously considered by Inyo's officials. Clearly, a compromise was needed.

Under the 1914 constitutional amendment, both Los Angeles' lands and its water rights were taxable if they had been taxed at the time they were acquired. Accordingly, 44,673 acres of the 246,876 owned by the city were exempt from taxation because they had not been subject to property taxes when they were acquired by purchase or exchange from various public agencies such as the federal Forest Service and the Bureau of Indian Affairs.[76] Under the terms of the amendment, moreover, improvements added to the land after its acquisition were also not taxable unless they replaced or substituted for improvements that had previously been taxed. But the heart of the problem involved the fixing of a value for the city's water rights. Should the value of the water right, for example, be determined on the basis of what the water would be worth in Inyo or Mono county, or on the basis of its value in Los Angeles? The city argued, of course, that the water had no value without the means of transporting it.[77]

The resolution of this problem was of vital importance to many people outside Inyo and Los Angeles. The East Bay Municipal Utility District, for example, maintained its principal reservoirs in the mountain counties of Amador and Calaveras. The city of San Francisco similarly held extensive water rights in rural Tuolumne County. And the question of the value of improvements had a special significance for San Francisco, which had built its airport on reclaimed swamp lands in neighboring San Mateo County with a sure and certain confidence that this new facility would continue to be taxed as if it were a swamp.[78]

The prolonged negotiations over a settlement between Inyo and Los Angeles were marked by charges of bad faith on both sides. The effort was made all the more difficult by the fact that any formula for future assessments agreed upon by the two sides would have to meet the tests of constitutionality imposed by the Board of Equalization. Eventually, rumors began to circulate that the city was planning to line up San Francisco and the East Bay Municipal Utility District in support of an outright repeal of the constitutional amendment of 1914.[79] Out of this threat blossomed the formula for compromise. A new constitutional amendment was drawn up establishing the basis for assessment on the tax rolls of a selected year, but allowing the assessment to rise in future years in accordance with the per capita increase in property values that obtained throughout the state. Since assessed valuation in California as a whole was growing much faster than property values in the Owens Valley, the proposal on its face looked like a good bet for Inyo. But by tying future increases to the per capita increase in statewide property values, the county was in fact gambling that land values throughout the state would increase at a much faster rate than the growth in population. To sweeten the deal, the base year for Inyo and Mono was fixed as 1966 because the allocation of water rights values by the Board of Equalization that year had been especially favorable to the two counties. And Los Angeles further acceded to the insertion of special provisions assuring that the city's new power plants in the gorge would be included under the act's provisions. On these terms, the compromise was accepted by all concerned and the Board of Equalization gave its blessing to the arrangement.[80]

Although most of the proposed amendment's complex provisions dealt with the problems between Los Angeles and Inyo, no mention of this controversy was made in the ballot pamphlet presented to the voters when the issue came up in the general election of 1968. The amendment had been carried in the state legislature by San Francisco's Senator George Moscone, and the arguments pro and con that appeared in the ballot pamphlet were drafted entirely by legislators from San Francisco and San Mateo who were concerned with the amendment's effect on the airport.[81] Although the Commonwealth Club of San Francisco opposed the proposal and the California Taxpayers Association chose to remain neutral, the amendment won the support of the *Sacramento Bee*, the *San Francisco Chronicle*, the State Chamber of Commerce, and the Property Owners Association of California.[82] The *Los Angeles Times* pronounced the formula "a fair and reasonable way to resolve the yearly assessment fights" and urged its passage.[83] But on election day, Los Angeles' voters rejected the proposed constitutional amendment, as did the voters in forty-one of California's fifty-eight counties, including San Mateo and every one of the rural counties that would be affected by its provisions except Inyo. Only the vote in San Francisco saved the compromise; the measure was approved there by 75,335 votes, barely enough to boost it to success by a margin of 54,815 votes out of more than 6,000,000 ballots cast statewide.[84]

The negotiated settlement of the tax controversy confirmed the uneasy alliance that had formed between the city and the valley in the quarter-century since the end of World War II. So long as Los Angeles did not seek to alter or expand its land and water holdings, the city's interest in preserving the quality and quantity of the water supply entering the aqueduct was accepted as a central element of and an unavoidable constraint upon any plans the individual communities of the valley might make for their future. And there were many in the valley who regarded these constraints as beneficial. The report prepared for the Izaak Walton League in 1971, for example, criticized specific aspects of Los Angeles' programs for fish and wildlife enhancement but ended by proposing a policy for the future of the valley which differed in no significant way from that which the city was already pursuing. This report, moreover, applauded the city's role in suppressing growth and development in the region, noting with ridiculous hyperbole that the Owens Valley as a result was the only area of California that had not been changed by the postwar boom in population.[85] In a similar vein, the chairman of the Eastern Sierra Nevada Task Force of the Sierra Club told a visiting reporter, "We recognize that Los Angeles is probably the savior of the valley."[86]

These remarks reveal the danger in confusing effects with motivation. By the logic of this Sierra Club spokesman, so might Genghis Khan be admired today as an early advocate of open space preservation for his work in obliterating the cities of Central Asia. The conservationists' accolades for Los Angeles ignored the essential fact that the city's interest was not in the preservation of the environment in any general sense but in the protection of its water resources. And as events in the 1970s would reveal, the Department of Water and Power was ready to risk injury to the valley environment for the sake of the further development of that resource.

The Second Aqueduct

Although the city had resolutely followed through on nearly all the programs and policies Mulholland had initiated, one aspect of his legacy remained unfulfilled. And that was perhaps the most important of all. Mulholland had seen the operation of his aqueduct as a process dependent ultimately upon the management of the Owens Valley groundwater basin for storage in wet years and as a supplemental source of supply in periods of drought. This vision had informed his original tolerance toward the development of valley agriculture, and it had later inspired his war with the valley at a time when he believed the city's need demanded complete control of the valley's most productive pumping fields.

In the years immediately following his victory in the valley and fall from power, the Department of Water and Power continued to sink new wells and intensify its pumping rates in accordance with his design. In just four years, from the beginning of the 1929 water year through 1932, Los Angeles extracted an estimated 336,000 acre-feet from the groundwater reservoirs around Bishop and Independence. And by 1931, the city's wells in the valley were producing fully 30 percent of the total aqueduct supply.[87] The department's bond issue of 1930, which provided funds to complete the acquisition of the valley, was endorsed by the *Los Angeles Times* in part on the grounds that: "Unchallenged control of these underground water resources requires the ownership by the city of all lands and water rights of every nature within the confines of the valley."[88] So compelling had been Mulholland's arguments for reliance upon this groundwater supply that some city officials actually opposed the plan for tapping the Colorado on the basis that it would be more economical for the city to draw whatever additional water it needed by pumping the Owens Valley to a depth of 500 feet.[89]

After 1932, however, the department all but stopped pumping in the valley. With precipitation levels returning to normal, and the Mono and Colorado projects already under way, the additional water which pumping could provide scarcely seemed worth the expense of defending against the litigation which the further lowering of the valley's groundwater table inevitably produced. Groundwater extractions in the thirty years from 1933 to 1963 consequently dropped to an annual average of only ten cubic feet per second.[90] By 1935, the natural artesian wells first observed by the United States Geological Survey in 1906 were flowing freely once again.[91] And on August 26, 1940, Los Angeles voluntarily gave up the right to continue pumping water for export from a 98-square-mile area southwest of Bishop.

This remarkable action seemed at the time to offer a means of

achieving speedy settlement of the extensive litigation that had
been prompted by the operation of the city's wells on lands formerly owned by the Hillside Water Company. A group of downstream well owners had taken up a suit originally filed by the
company in order to protect those water rights first adjudicated
as a result of the ranchers' seizure of the Southern Sierras Power
Company reservoir in 1921. The Inyo superior court granted the
ranchers' request for an injunction, but the state supreme court
overturned this judgment, determining instead that the ranchers
were entitled to damages. Rather than go to the trouble of calcu-
lating the value of these claims, the Department of Water and
Power simply stipulated its acceptance of the original court-
ordered prohibition on further pumping for export.[92]

In 1946, Los Angeles for the first time achieved full utilization of the total capacity of its aqueduct to the Owens Valley.
Since the department by this time had access to a supply from the
Colorado which it could not use and rights to approximately
three times as much water from the Mono Basin as the aqueduct
was capable of carrying, further development of the Owens Valley groundwater reservoirs appeared superfluous.[93] Feasibility
studies for the construction of the second aqueduct that would be
needed to make use of the Mono water were dismissed that year
as uneconomical.[94] Critics of the department's policies continued
to call for more extensive use of the valley's groundwater storage
capacity. But the department's efforts in this regard were limited
to the periodic spreading of small amounts of excess water. By
1948, Los Angeles maintained only 110 wells in the valley with a
combined pumping capacity of three hundred cubic feet per second. And even these facilities, the department asserted, would
not be needed except in the unlikely event of a drought lasting
more than thirteen years.[95]

This indifference toward the development of the Owens Valley groundwater basin was a natural reflection of the altered
circumstances in which the city found itself after World War II.
Los Angeles was at last nearing the limit of its growth. And in the
absence of any new area for expansion like the San Fernando
Valley, there could be no expectation that the city would ever be
able to use all the water it had secured. By 1955, the city's rate of

population growth had dropped to half that of the South Coast metropolitan region as a whole. Neighboring communities were meanwhile doubling and tripling in size on the Colorado water Los Angeles did not use.[96] These conditions created an inevitable tension between the city's interests and those of its fellow members on the board of the Metropolitan Water District. By the mid-1950s Los Angeles had paid 62 percent of the taxes supporting the district's operations for less than 9 percent of the water the district delivered.[97] And although the department did its best to mask these costs in its annual reports, an independent management study conducted in 1948 by the Board of Water and Power Commissioners estimated that the actual costs of water delivery to the people of Los Angeles were 50 percent higher than the department reported because of the city's subsidy of the Metropolitan Water District. The department blithely responded to this criticism with the observation that an interested taxpayer could find these costs by consulting the separate reports prepared by the district itself.[98]

The inherent conflict between the city's water independence and the district's growing need for additional supplies came to a head in the late 1950s when the state Department of Water Resources sought to secure the district's participation in the proposed development of the State Water Project. The state statute creating the district prohibited Los Angeles from exercising more than 50 percent of the votes on the district board regardless of how much money the city contributed to the district's support. But even with only half the votes, Los Angeles dominated district policy through a unit rule that required each city to cast its votes on the board as a block. The city's delegation to the district board was therefore able to lead the district in forceful opposition to any participation in the state project.[99]

Whereas the Metropolitan Water District's campaign against the State Water Project was fought on a broad range of issues, the conflict within the board focused ultimately on the system for funding the additional supplies offered by the state. Since the new water from Northern California would be even more expensive than the water the district drew from the Colorado, Los Angeles had no desire to find itself in the position once again of having to pay the major part of the costs of developing a resource it could not use. Without the State Water Project, the department reported, the cost of the original aqueduct to the Colorado would be paid off by 1965 and the price of district deliveries would thereafter drop off sharply. The department therefore proposed that the financing of the Colorado project should be separated from the financing of the State Water Project by shifting the tax burden for future water imports from the district property owners to the actual water consumers. In this way, Los Angeles would have paid very little for the development of the State Water Project. But even the city's own delegates to the district board recognized that this proposal would have bankrupted the district and crippled the State Water Project. With their position within the board becoming increasingly isolated, Los Angeles' delegation abruptly switched to support of the new project in the closing days of the campaign for passage of the bonds to implement the state's plan in 1960.[100]

The conflict within the board over the State Water Project revealed new limitations on Los Angeles' ability to assure that its interests would prevail in the policies of the district it had created. And because votes on the district board are distributed in accordance with the assessed valuation of each of its member agencies, the city could look forward only to a further diminution of its influence as the other communities of the South Coast continued to outstrip its rate of economic growth. The conflict arose, moreover, in the midst of a succession of dry years which had forced the department to restrict irrigation in the Owens Valley and renew its pumping operations there. Even with the aqueduct running at capacity, the city in 1959 was drawing 16 percent of its water supply from the Metropolitan Water District.[101] And although this was still less than a fifth of the total amount of water the city was entitled to receive from the district, the approval of the State Water Project assured that any supplemental supplies the department might require from the district to meet similar temporary shortages in the future would be more, rather than less expensive.

In addition, Arizona's longstanding suit to secure a greater portion of the Colorado's flows for itself was by this time pending before the United States Supreme Court. The possibility that

Arizona might succeed, thereby reducing the district's diversions from the Colorado, created a further risk that the more costly supplies from the state would constitute an even greater proportion of any water the district had available in the future.[102] For all these reasons, it suddenly appeared advisable for the city to reestablish its independence from the district by examining once again the prospects for a more intensive development of its own water resources.

In 1959, detailed studies were ordered for the construction of the second aqueduct Thomas Means had recommended nearly forty years before. When the preliminary results of these investigations suggested that such a project would be feasible, the department began comparing the costs of this new development with the expenses associated with obtaining additional supplies from the Metropolitan Water District, saltwater conversion, or the reclamation of waste water. Satisfied that more intensive development of the Mono Basin and increased pumping in the Owens Valley offered the best prospect for obtaining upward of two hundred cubic feet per second of additional, high-quality water at the lowest price, the Board of Water and Power Commissioners in July 1963 authorized engineering to begin on the so-called second barrel of Mulholland's aqueduct to the Owens Valley.[103]

Los Angeles' problems with the Metropolitan Water District would probably not of themselves have constituted a sufficient basis for undertaking what was expected to be a $91-million project. But there were additional reasons for the department to make haste. The state was growing impatient with the city's failure to make use of its extensive water rights in the Mono Basin. A routine application by the department for an extension of time for the use of these rights brought a stern warning from the state Water Rights Board in 1959. If Los Angeles did not demonstrate its intention to make full use of these rights promptly, the board advised, the city could lose them altogether. Submission of the preliminary plans for the second aqueduct in June 1960 satisfied the board's demand for diligence, and the extension the city had requested was granted.[104] But Los Angeles by this time was facing additional pressure from the legislature.

The state Department of Water Resources had reported in

1956 that Los Angeles was exporting only 320,000 of the 590,000 acre-feet of water annually available in the Owens Valley. This revelation prompted the legislature in 1959 to direct the Department of Water Resources to prepare a detailed investigation of how the water Los Angeles left behind could be more efficiently applied to the economic development of the valley.[105] Far from quieting these concerns, the announcement of the city's plans to build a second aqueduct encouraged the legislature to redouble its efforts. Noting that Los Angeles' intention to export "practically the entire water supply of this area" had made the residents of Inyo and Mono counties "gravely apprehensive," the legislature ordered still more studies along these lines in 1964 and 1966.[106]

Residents of the valley initially insisted that the state should reserve to their use all the water beyond the 320,000 acre-feet which Los Angeles was already taking. The director of the Department of Water Resources, however, argued that such an action would be "premature" in the absence of any detailed plans or demonstrated ability on the part of the valley residents to raise the necessary capital to make use of this water. The state therefore limited its filings on the valley's behalf to those sites which seemed to offer the best potential for recreational development.[107] After 1960, the state's efforts focused increasingly on aid for the valley's newfound enthusiasm for tourism. And in this context, the prospects for development of the valley's groundwater basin came to assume nearly as much importance as the surface flows Los Angeles was not using.

Valley residents had long complained that the city's spreading of excess water to comply with the Natural Soda Products case decree was turning potentially irrigable land north of Big Pine into swamps. To alleviate the problem, they sought permission to pump the city's lands, arguing that the water thus derived could be used to support additional agricultural development. Los Angeles, however, had refused these requests out of a concern that, if its groundwater pumping rights were once used for this purpose, the ranchers might insist on continuing the practice.[108]

Aubrey Lyon introduced a further refinement to this appeal

in connection with his efforts to establish a chain of warm-water fisheries in the valley. Lyon proposed that the water for his fisheries could be drawn from the lands outside Bishop which the city had agreed never to pump for export. As Lyon pointed out in 1961:

> There is no enjoinment for pumping for use on the land. Therefore, if leases could be executed to the [federal] Fish and Wildlife Service and they should pump for development of the project, the actual consumptive use would be less than half of the amount pumped and would flow by gravity into the [city's] water-gathering facilities lower in the basin. In this manner the city would be gaining water which otherwise they may not touch, and actually at no expense to them.[109]

The state agreed that development of the groundwater basin offered the least costly method of achieving its recreational objectives in the valley.[110] And although the elaborate plans for recreational and fish and wildlife development were eventually sidetracked, the kernel of Lyon's idea would re-emerge years later as an essential element in Los Angeles' plans for the operation of the second aqueduct.

The reports prepared by the Department of Water Resources in the early 1960s signaled the state's readiness to intervene in the valley's development if Los Angeles did not hasten its own plans for the second aqueduct. But in terms of illuminating any problems created by the city's use of the valley's water resources or measuring the potential effect of the second aqueduct on the valley's development, the reports were singularly ineffectual. The problem in large part lay with the legislature. The principal sponsor of the bills ordering the preparation of these reports was Inyo's new state senator, William Symons, Jr., whose father had played so central a role in bringing on the conflict of the 1920s. When directing the Department of Water Resources to conduct a new study, Symons relied on the parliamentary device of a resolution passed only by his colleagues in the senate. Such resolutions are nonbinding to the extent that they do not carry the force of law; but more important, they provided no funding for the work they asked to have done. And since the deadlines

Symons specified for his reports were usually quite short, the Department of Water Resources conducted little research of its own but relied instead upon whatever data the Department of Water and Power provided. After complaining of the legislature's failure to provide financial support for the first two studies, the state water resources director proposed in 1965 that $200,000 be appropriated for a serious two-year investigation.[111] When this suggestion was ignored, the last of Symons' three reports was simply turned over to Los Angeles to prepare.[112]

As compilations of already available information, the reports were certainly no less than accurate. But the limitations imposed on their preparation just as certainly restricted the state's ability to recommend any solution to the valley's problems or even to perceive what problems might exist. Thus, the last report, prepared by the Department of Water and Power, simply passed over the key quesiton of how much water the valley might require for its future development with this sweeping observation: "There is no indication that these needs are not being fully met or will not continue to be fully met in the future."[113] And though the state Water Rights Board in a separate investigation noted that the development of the second aqueduct would almost certainly "influence the amount of local lands which have been previously irrigated . . . and possibly reduce the amount of lands which may have been subirrigated in the past," the board similarly concluded that in the absence of any data other than Los Angeles' it could not evaluate the potential effect of these changes.[114]

If the impact of the second aqueduct upon life in the valley evaded prediction in Sacramento, it was apparent that the principal effect of the state's efforts had been to encourage Los Angeles to make haste with its new project. The first bonds for the second aqueduct were issued in October 1963, and construction began the following August. Thanks to the charter revision of 1947, the Department of Water and Power did not have to appeal for taxpayer support of its endeavor. But the department also chose to make a further departure from tradition. Rather than raising funds for the new aqueduct in one lump sum, as Mulholland had always done, the department decided to issue new bonds only as revenues were needed. The financing of the second aqueduct, moreover, was rolled into the overall capital requirements of the city's total water program. This kind of step-by-step financing when used by federal water agencies had produced inevitable construction delays and cost overruns, and the system worked no better for Los Angeles.

The department described the consequences of this decision in its final report on the second aqueduct:

> As the construction of the aqueduct progressed, some rather drastic changes in the national economy invalidated some of the basic assumptions on which the financial studies had been made. Accelerated inflation caused greater increases in the cost of operating and maintaining the Water System than had been forecast, and interest rates on borrowed money rose to levels unprecedented in recent years . . . [As a result] the largest borrowings for Second Aqueduct construction were made at the peak of high interest rates. The resulting higher debt service, together with the escalating inflation, required earlier and larger increases in water rates than had been forecast. The unanticipated delays experienced in design and construction which resulted in a later completion date, also contributed to the changes in rate planning.

The project was completed within its assigned budget. But because of the higher costs of debt service, the department was forced to boost its rates by nearly 63 percent, instead of the 26-percent increase originally projected to pay for the second aqueduct.[115]

The finished project was approximately half the size of the original aqueduct. Operating together, the aqueducts were expected to increase the volume of the city's exports to an annual average of 666 cubic feet per second. In its initial studies, the department had considered building the second aqueduct with capacities ranging from 150 to 250 cubic feet per second; but it settled on a long-term average of 210 as a compromise which would enable the city to exercise most of its rights in the Owens and Mono basins while still leaving some water for maintenance of the lands it leased in the area. Additional exports from the Mono Basin, however, were expected to provide only 50 of the

210 cubic feet per second needed to keep the new aqueduct full. The balance, more than three-fourths of the total capacity of the project, would be made up by pumping in the Owens Valley and by reductions in the amount of water spread or applied to irrigation within the Owens River watershed.[116] How these increased efficiencies would be achieved consequently became the crucial question, not only for the operation of the second aqueduct but also for the future of the Owens Valley.

In light of the uproar that followed, the most remarkable thing about the second aqueduct may be that it did not stir more opposition in the Owens Valley during the initial stages of planning and development. One reason for this is that no one in the city or the valley could foresee what the ultimate impact of the project upon the valley would be. This was the very point on which the state reports were least informative, and their shortcomings thus assumed a critical importance. The boards of supervisors in Inyo and Mono counties did retain independent consultants in 1964 to assess the probable effects of the second aqueduct; but their report for the most part simply resifted the information already available in the state studies, without raising any new specifics that might cause alarm.[117] In addition, the department's financing plans were not all that changed while the second aqueduct was under construction. As with the first aqueduct, many of the most important aspects of its operation were decided after the project was under way. The cloak of obscurity with which Mulholland had successfully draped the first aqueduct during all the critical decisions on its authorization reappeared to serve as well again.

Groundwater pumping, for example, was an essential part of the department's plans for the operation of the second aqueduct from the very beginning, as a way of both meeting local needs and reducing water losses due to evapotranspiration by lowering the water table in marshy areas of the valley where native grasses and other water-dependent plants flourished. But as construction progressed and the projections of local demand for water were refined, the size of the department's proposed pumping program increased drastically.

When the city first announced its intention to build the second aqueduct in 1963, it estimated that its groundwater pumping program in the valley could be held to a long-term average of 89 cubic feet per second. In 1966, the Department of Water and Power raised this estimate to 100 cubic feet per second. By the time the project was completed in 1970, the figure had increased again to 140 cubic feet per second. And in 1972, Los Angeles announced that its average demand on the valley's groundwater basin would be 180 cubic feet per second—even though the city that year was in fact pumping at a rate of 200 cubic feet per second.[118] From the perspective of the valley residents, this sudden revelation of so massive a rate of groundwater extraction conjured fears of a process of devastation that could end in transforming much of the area from scrub rangeland into a northern extension of the Mojave Desert. "Instead of fighting for a ranch," one longtime valley resident observed, "we're now fighting for the survival of the plant and animal communities."[119]

Another reason the department's plans for the second aqueduct did not stir earlier opposition can be found in the twenty years of comparative calm which the department had succeeded in bringing to its relations with the Owens Valley from 1950 to 1970. While the fabric of comity was certainly strained at points, examples of successful cooperation abounded. Those who had lived all their lives in the valley made up a steadily decreasing component of the overall population, and even they were separated by two generations from the violent confrontations of a half-century before. The memory of the early conflict had consequently been obscured as the published record of those events became more distorted. And the identification of the Department of Water and Power as the valley's savior by the Sierra Club's local spokesman defined the basis for a greater measure of confidence in a future of mutual benefits than had existed at any time since the second decade of the twentieth century. If the city and the valley had experienced no serious conflicts since 1950, it was because there was little on which they disagreed. Decades of pacific coexistence had produced a sense of mutual objectives and a shared vision of the valley's future. When Los Angeles in 1971 produced an outline of its objectives for the long-term management of city-owned land and water resources in Inyo and

Mono counties, for example, it fixed recreation as the mainspring of the local economy and enunciated a policy of resistance to any significant future increases in population in either county. And Inyo, for its part, found nothing objectionable in this.[120]

Far from threatening to disrupt amicable relations with the valley, the advent of the second aqueduct was seen by the city's water planners as the beginning of a new era of even greater and more specific cooperation with the valley's interests. For throughout all the changes that had been made in the department's plans for financing and managing the second aqueduct, 666 cubic feet per second had remained fixed as an unalterable constant for the combined operation of the first and second aqueducts. Barring the construction of yet a third aqueduct, this set an absolute upper limit on the city's exports from the Owens and Mono watersheds, which meant in turn that the department for the first time would be able to contemplate making the kind of long-term commitments for water use within the valley that the city had regarded as anathema since the end of World War II. Los Angeles was not, of course, prepared simply to assign to the valley residents all its water rights above this limit of 666 second-feet. But at least the opening of the second aqueduct offered the prospect that access to the water the city left behind would henceforth be negotiable.

Valley agriculture was again the first to sample the nature of these new opportunities. In order to achieve the efficiencies required to keep the second aqueduct full, the department proposed to cut back the amount of valley land which it provided with irrigation water to approximately 15,000 acres. Although this was only half the area the city had irrigated since 1945, the department promised to supply these lands on a more continuing basis than had been its earlier practice. This offer was attractive to the valley's cattle ranchers because in the past they had never known from one year to the next how much water they would actually receive. And, at the time the city was preparing its detailed plans for the second aqueduct, the ranchers were recovering from a succession of three dry years in which the irrigated area of the valley had been reduced to only 4,880 acres. The special consultants which Inyo and Mono counties retained to review the department's plans in 1964 concurred with the city's assurances that by concentrating more reliable water deliveries on the better quality lands in the valley, overall production would not be reduced. And the city followed through on its promise to support the improvement of local agricultural practices by initiating a series of studies in cooperation with the University of California aimed at helping the ranchers make the most efficient use of the water available through the installation of sprinklers and other water-saving devices.[121] With this model of successful cooperation behind them, the city's water officials in 1971 looked forward to providing similar assistance in the form of increased water deliveries to support recreational and fish and wildlife enhancement projects throughout the valley.[122]

From the point of view of the valley, however, there was an all-important catch in the city's offers of assistance. The city made it clear that any water applied to new uses within the valley would be drawn for the most part from increased pumping of the valley's groundwater reservoirs. Aubrey Lyon's idea of substituting groundwater for local uses and thereby enhancing the flows south to Los Angeles had become a key article of faith for the operation of the second aqueduct. The department admitted that the drastic increases in its proposed pumping program were due in part to its own failure to achieve the efficiencies expected in its diversions to the new aqueduct, resulting most noticeably from the city's decision not to line the canal to Tinemaha as originally planned. But it contended, nonetheless, that by far the greater part of the water obtained from the increases in the pumping program would be applied to local uses that had not been considered when construction of the second aqueduct began.[123]

The dilemma this policy posed for the valley was acute. The city was clearly prepared to share its water rights more fully, but only by exercising them more intensively. Any improvement in the valley's condition that might result from the new applications of water would be accomplished at the expense of the valley's groundwater reservoirs. For those most concerned with the long-term effects of increased pumping on the valley's environment, the problem recalled a syndrome identified with the nation's involvement in Vietnam: in effect, the city seemed to be taking the position that it could save the valley only by destroying it. "Those bastards 'bout picked the valley to bones by now, so now they're goin' after the marrow," remarked one longtime valley resident with a pungency Willie Arthur Chalfant himself might have envied.[124]

At the time the city began building the second aqueduct in the fall of 1964, Inyo County proposed the adoption of a formal agreement with Los Angeles to assure that operation of the new project would not interfere with development of the recreational projects the county considered most promising. In addition, Inyo called for an expansion of the department's plans for irrigated agriculture in order to provide 20,000 acres with a firm supply of water; an absolute limit on groundwater pumping to 50,000 acre-feet per year; and a restoration of any federal lands which were currently withdrawn on the city's behalf but not actually needed for the operation of the city's water program. As work on the project progressed and local fears regarding its potential effects grew, the county's position stiffened, with the result that by the fall of 1971, Inyo was demanding a plan for the operation of the second aqueduct that would not only guarantee preservation of the valley's environment but would also provide for its progressive enhancement through the steady expansion of irrigated agriculture and a positive program to induce the spread of native vegetation. To bolster this appeal, the county called on the state Secretary for Resources Norman B. "Ike" Livermore to intercede in the valley's negotiations with Los Angeles.[125]

At first, the prospects for settlement appeared promising. Los Angeles by this time had agreed to expand the area it would serve with irrigation water to 18,840 acres. And the department was well embarked upon the development of a comprehensive statement of its long-term objectives for management of the valley's land and water resources when Livermore convened his first meeting on June 11, 1971. The department's efforts to solicit opinions on the contents of this plan from other interest groups in the valley, moreover, drew a positively sunny response from Bishop's Mayor Betty Denton in which she expressed no disagreement with the city's current policies and applauded the department's willingness to "dream of a distant future."[126]

But a preliminary briefing on its plan that the department submitted at a meeting in Sacramento on November 10 prompted concern. The county was essentially asking for the same clear statement of Los Angeles' intentions that Sylvester Smith, Mary Austin, and the Watterson brothers had, one by one, demanded in vain throughout all the major confrontations of the past. Now that the city was at last prepared to make such a statement, the county was not satisfied with its contents. Los Angeles affirmed its commitment to supply water for irrigation, recreation, and fish and wildlife enhancement in the valley, and it further promised not to interfere with the area's natural stream courses. Rather than set an annual limit on groundwater extractions, it proposed to limit its pumping to the "safe yield" of the basin so that no more water would be removed on a long-term basis than was naturally flowing into these underground reservoirs. But the city's proposal also asserted the department's "primary responsibility . . . to preserve the integrity of the City's water rights and insure a full supply to the First and Second Aqueducts." On this basis, the city rejected any proposal to "arbitrarily restrict or cut back the aqueduct flow or groundwater production." And, on the vital question of building a third aqueduct sometime in the future, the city seemed to hedge its bets, noting simply that the environmental impact of that project "could most likely be of a magnitude to make such a proposal impractical for social and political reasons."[127]

Following the November meeting, further progress on a negotiated settlement slowed while the county representatives went back to consult with their constituents and the city set about expanding the scope of its plan to incorporate the interests of the various federal agencies involved in Inyo and Mono counties. To address this new range of concerns, the department proposed splitting its treatment of water and land use issues and delaying the development of an overall plan to the middle of 1973. Livermore was worried by the decision to bifurcate and slow the preparation of an overall plan. Though he appreciated the city's desire to solicit wider "input," he urged the department's representatives to recognize the need for "interface" between its statement of land and water use objectives.[128]

Livermore's expressions of anxiety were unavailing. As the

months passed, the city and county representatives shifted from a stance of wary accommodation to one of open defiance. Los Angeles announced the latest increases in its pumping program. And on August 30, 1972, the Inyo supervisors formally rejected the department's preliminary briefing, demanding instead an annual limit on groundwater pumping that would be backed up by monthly monitoring of the city's wells, the establishment of guarantees for the minimum and maximum flows in the Owens River in order to prevent erosion, and an outright prohibition on construction of a third aqueduct. In addition, the county renewed its appeal for a program of active enhancement of the valley's environment. And perhaps most troubling of all from the city's perspective, Inyo flatly rejected Los Angeles' most basic contention that it already possessed sufficient water rights to keep the first and second aqueducts full. As an alternative to the city's program, the Inyo supervisors revived the compromise first suggested by Congressman Smith in 1906, proposing that the needs of the valley should take precedence in the implementation of any long-term management plan and that Los Angeles' rights should extend only to water left over after those needs had been met.[129] Three months later, the breach was made complete. On November 15, 1972, Inyo County filed suit under the California Environmental Quality Act of 1970 contending that the city should be required to assess the environmental effects of its pumping program before any further extractions from the valley's groundwater basin were permitted.

The Battle Renewed

The filing of Inyo's suit was the first shot fired in what has become the second war of the Owens Valley. Unlike the conflict of the 1920s, this battle has been fought more with legal briefs than with guns and dynamite. But its potential impact, not only upon relations between the city and the valley but also upon the independence of Los Angeles' water programs and the entire system of water law in California, may ultimately prove to be even greater than the contest Mulholland fought to his bitter victory.

Los Angeles initially responded to the county's action with disbelief that the operation of its project could be bound by the strictures of a law which had not even been imagined when work began on the second aqueduct, and which still had not taken effect by the time the new system was placed in service.[130] But the city had not reckoned with the attention this new conflict with the Owens Valley would prompt in the Third District Court of Appeal in Sacramento. During the early phases of the county's litigation, the superior court indicated its sympathy with the city's argument and refused to grant Inyo's request for an immediate injunction on the pumping program. But when Inyo filed a routine appeal of this denial of an injunction, the court of appeal took the extraordinary action of recasting the county's petition as a petition for mandamus, and on that basis the appeals court assumed original jurisdiction in the case for itself. The following June, the court of appeal ruled that although construction of the second aqueduct did not fall under the provisions of the environmental quality act, its operation and especially the department's greatly expanded pumping program did. The city was therefore ordered to prepare an environmental impact report on this ongoing program.[131]

State law requires that an environmental impact report must consider the alternatives to the action or project under study. In the draft report the city released on August 29, 1974, however, all three of the alternatives discussed would have involved some lowering of the valley's groundwater table and the consequent degradation of the landscape in the areas affected to "semidesert scrubland." And though the department addressed the possibility of taking no action whatsoever, it warned that this would result in the elimination of all water deliveries to its agricultural lessees.[132]

Inyo once again sought an injunction to force the withdrawal of what it argued was an inadequate response to the court's demand for an environmental assessment. The city responded by making good its threat against the valley's cattle ranchers. On Friday, September 20, 1974, the Department of Water and Power mailed notices that it was cutting off all water deliveries to its agricultural and recreational lessees on the following Monday, September 23. To fulfill this order, the *Los Angeles Times* reported, city workers had to dynamite irrigation valves which had been rusted open since completion of the original aqueduct sixty years before. In a public statement, the city engineer responsible for aqueduct operations denied that this was intended as a punitive measure and described it instead as "educational."[133]

Within a week, the superior court ordered Los Angeles to restore its water deliveries in the valley. The Department of Water and Power voluntarily withdrew its draft report, which had barely been out a month, and promised to prepare a more systematic study that would include consideration of a reduction in the city's exports from the valley.

While the city and county were wrangling over the problem of how to prepare a proper assessment of the environmental effects of the department's pumping program, the pumping continued. Neither the superior court nor the district court of appeal had granted Inyo's request to stop the wells. When the court of appeal ordered Los Angeles to prepare an environmental impact report, however, it did restrict the pumping program to 89 cubic feet per second—the rate at the time the environmental quality act had taken effect. Three months later, Los Angeles was able to persuade the superior court to raise this limit to 221 cubic feet per second. Five days after publication of the department's draft report, the court of appeal again assumed jurisdiction and once more ordered an immediate return to the pumping rate it had previously fixed at 89 cubic feet per second. Inyo agreed to permit the city to extract a greater quantity of water from the valley's groundwater basin that winter, once the city had withdrawn its draft report and promised to include participation by Inyo's citizens and elected officials in preparing its new study. But by May 1975, Los Angeles had again succeeded in obtaining a higher pumping rate of 178 cubic feet per second from the superior court.

It was evident by this time that the department had become entangled in a new field of environmental law which was then evolving rapidly in the courts. And although the city's water officials might not have been able to predict the full extent of their obligations under the new statute as the court would define them, there could be no doubt that the operation of the second aqueduct would come under a greater intensity of scrutiny than they had ever encountered before. As the incident of the water shutoff revealed, they were not responding well to this unexpected pressure. In the preparation of its revised and expanded report, the department maintained that since the court had required an assessment of the environmental effects of groundwater pumping but not of the second aqueduct, the city's only obligation was to examine that portion of its groundwater pumping program intended to serve local needs within the valley that had not been anticipated when the second aqueduct was begun in 1963. Any pumping of water for export would therefore not be considered. When Inyo's representatives objected to this interpretation of the court order, the department responded that its position was supported by the California attorney general. The sole effect of this assertion was that it prompted the attorney general's office to issue a vigorous denunciation of the city's "grudging, miserly reading" of the court's mandate.[134]

The new report was consequently mired in controversy even before it appeared. The Inyo County Grand Jury in 1976 damned it as a "subterfuge." Local residents who attended the department's public meetings complained that their concerns were not being considered. Officials of the Naval Weapons Center at nearby China Lake expressed a fear to the local air pollution control district that increased dust storms resulting from the loss of vegetation in the valley would injure human health and force the eventual closure of their facility. In response, city officials argued that there was no medical evidence proving that more dust would pose an identifiable risk to the breathing of valley residents. And the department in its environmental impact report confidently predicted that any plants that died as a result of the lowering of the valley's groundwater table would soon be replaced by other species. "The DWP has not been too honest about this," protested a local botanist who had originally been retained by the city as one of its consultants for the report. "The likelihood is that when the alkali scrubs die, those sections of the valley will become barren."[135]

At the time this report was being prepared, it was unclear whether the identification of an environmental risk created any obligation upon the city to avoid it. The department took the position that the report was only an informational document, and that its duties under the environmental quality act would be fulfilled simply by preparing the report and having it certified by the Board of Water and Power Commissioners. The department therefore published its new three-volume study in May 1976, and the commissioners announced their intention to certify it within a month. Appeals from Inyo's representatives to the mayor and city attorney of Los Angeles for delay and more careful consideration were ignored. On July 15, the water and power commissioners certified the environmental impact report and authorized the department to commence full pumping operations. Six days later, the court of appeal opened oral argument on Inyo's contention that the law required not just an environmental impact report but an adequate report.

On August 17, Los Angeles lost again when the court announced that it would review the adequacy of the department's report. In the meantime, the city's pumping program would be cut back to an average of 149 cubic feet per second. Even as the court acted, however, it was apparent that California was entering the preliminary stages of the worst drought in its history. When the customarily rainy winter months brought no relief, mandatory rationing went into effect in cities throughout the northern half of the state. At the beginning of 1977, deliveries from the State Water Project to the Metropolitan Water District were cut off so that agriculture in the Central Valley could continue to flourish. And in Los Angeles, where the drought was much less severe, the prospect suddenly loomed that the city might at last have to start drawing water from the Colorado supply it had paid hundreds of millions of dollars to secure.

Rather than pay higher prices for lower quality water from the Colorado, the department petitioned the court of appeal in February 1977, for permission to begin pumping in the Owens Valley at a rate of 315 cubic feet per second for the duration of the drought. Once again the city attempted to enlist the valley cattlemen in support of this appeal for relief by warning them that their irrigation supplies would be cut off if the county did not relent in its opposition. But these threats ran directly counter to the court's order the previous August, which had directed Los

Angeles to continue making its customary deliveries in the valley despite the reduction in pumping.[136] In a preliminary memorandum of March 24, 1977, the court indicated that it would be disinclined to grant the department's request for increased pumping in the absence of any effort by the city to implement an effective water conservation program during the drought. The irrigation season began on April 1 with no indication whether the department would in fact deliver water to the valley ranchers. Finally, on April 15, faced with a new appeal by the county and the risk of a contempt order from the court, the department announced that it would supply irrigation water at half the normal rate. On April 25, however, the court of appeal ordered the city to increase its deliveries to three-fourths the normal rate.

The burden of the extended litigation was by this time beginning to tell upon Los Angeles. Not only had its independence from the Metropolitan Water District not been increased, the city was now more dependent than ever upon the district's Colorado supplies as a result of the controversy the second aqueduct had stirred. The department had invested three years in the preparation of an environmental impact report which appeared to be in danger of total rejection by the court of appeal. City officials had meanwhile taken to warring among themselves. The chairperson of the water and power commission, along with various members of the staff of the mayor's office and the Department of Water and Power, were privately blaming the city's long succession of defeats in the court of appeal on a lack of diligence by the city attorney in pursuing their case.[137] The *Los Angeles Times* began calling upon the city to accept a longstanding offer from the state Department of Water Resources to intervene in the conflict and prepare an independent evaluation of the environmental effects of the department's pumping program.[138] And as a result of the court's March memorandum concerning water conservation, Los Angeles for the first time in its history was faced with the threat of interference, not only with its water resources in the Owens Valley, but also in the management of its own water system.

The court's call for an effective water conservation program was a particularly bitter blow because, even without the drought, the efficiencies the department had achieved in its operation of the municipal water system gave Los Angeles one of the lowest per capita rates of water consumption in the South Coast.[139] Despite the fact that the city had paid more for less water than any other member of the Metropolitan Water District, none of them faced the prospect of mandatory rationing. And most galling of all, the towns of the Owens Valley, according to figures published by the Department of Water and Power but hotly contested by valley officials, maintained water consumption rates which were in some instances eight times greater than those of Los Angeles.[140]

Nevertheless, in an effort to demonstrate its good faith and win the favor of the court of appeal, the Los Angeles City Council on May 12 unanimously approved an ordinance instituting mandatory water rationing. For the Sunday edition before the ordinance was to take effect, the *Times* retained Remi Nadeau to prepare the lead article of a special section devoted to water conservation. Nadeau's hortatory histories of the Department of Water and Power had done much to quiet criticism of the city's treatment of the valley since the 1950s. And he now likened the prospect of a reduction in water use in Los Angeles to Arnold Toynbee's theories of the collapse of human civilization: "It is true that nearly 40 percent of Los Angeles' water goes for 'outside uses' such as lawns, gardens, swimming pools, and public parks . . . but such amenities are at the heart of Los Angeles' way of life. Indeed, such deprivation would constitute . . . a cultural decline in the Toynbeean sense."[141] The very next morning, the court of appeal threw out Los Angeles' environmental impact report, denouncing the department's "egregious" and "wishful" misreading of its mandate.[142]

The *Times* was outraged and urged the city to file an immediate appeal with the state supreme court.[143] But the rejection of the environmental impact report had not affected the department's request for an increase in its pumping rate, and the department by this time had secured the necessary permission to retain special legal counsel, as Inyo County had done the year before. On June 29, only two days after the court's ruling, Los Angeles renewed its petition for a pumping rate of 315 cubic feet per second. San Diego and the Metropolitan Water District joined in this appeal with briefs describing the hardships that would be visited upon the district's other customers if Los Angeles were compelled to exercise still more of its entitlement to water from the Colorado.[144] On July 1, the mandatory water rationing program went into effect. Two weeks later, the Department of Water and Power announced, mirabile dictu, that the conservation program had effectively reduced the city's water use by 15 percent.[145] This was apparently all the court needed to hear. After one last round of oral argument, the court of appeal on July 22 authorized a doubling of the city's pumping rate to 315 cubic feet per second until March of the following year. The *Times*, which had given little space to news reports of the department's successive defeats, ran the announcement of this victory as a front-page banner headline. City water officials, who only a week before had been warning of increased water charges to pay for the more expensive supplies from the Colorado, jubilantly predicted a 10-percent reduction in charges to city water users as a result of the court's decision.[146]

In a sense, the county's suit had always been pointed toward the state supreme court. Fully a third of the brief it had filed against the pumping program in 1976 was devoted to an extended appeal to apply the principles of the County of Origin statute as a reasonable basis for settlement of the valley's claim. So radical a change in the efficacy of the city's water rights would almost inevitably have wound up in the supreme court's docket on appeal by one side or the other in the litigation. And indeed, there were many who believed this was the best course for the valley's representatives to pursue. "The case is certain to be appealed to the environment-minded state Supreme Court, where observers believe Inyo County stands a good chance of winning," enthused *New West* magazine in early 1977. "The end of the most bitter war in the state's history is now in sight."[147]

But when the case at last was brought before the supreme court, it was Los Angeles that filed the action and Inyo that opposed it. Flushed with its initial victory in securing a temporary increase in the pumping rate, the city now sought to overturn all the previous actions of the Third District Court of Appeal. In the absence of an adequate environmental impact report from the city, however, Inyo's attorneys feared they would not be able to make a sufficient showing of the alternatives available to Los

Angeles if its pumping program were permanently restricted. And without such a showing, in turn, the county might have had a hard time demonstrating that the city's demands on the valley's water supply were in fact unreasonable. Rather than risk losing everything it had achieved in five years of expensive litigation, Inyo chose to set aside the larger questions posed by its suit and concentrate, for the time being at least, on the procedural problems involved in obtaining a precise and comprehensive assessment of the environmental effects of the city's project.

On October 6, the supreme court rejected Los Angeles' appeal without comment. The valley's special legal counsel gamely described this action as the county's "greatest judicial victory of 1977."[148] And in an article prepared for the *Los Angeles Times* two weeks later, the Inyo district attorney made it clear that, instead of a fundamental shift in the legal principles governing the relationship of the city and the valley, the county was now prepared to negotiate a compromise in the form of a long-term management plan for the operation of the second aqueduct. "Neither party should press its theoretical position too far," he wrote. "Rather we should be working to determine the exact amount of groundwater pumping that is best for the Owens Valley while still providing maximum benefit to water users in Los Angeles."[149]

The county's legal representatives later explained that the decision to avoid the supreme court was based in part on concern that the process of judicial review would delay an ultimate settlement of the controversy for months or possibly years.[150] But in the three years since the high court refused to intervene, a formula for compromise has continued to elude the parties to the dispute. In May 1978, Inyo and the Department of Water and Power entered into an agreement with the Department of Water Resources for a joint study of the valley's environment in the hope that this effort might in turn establish the basis for a long-term management plan. But as the study progressed, the contending parties continued to wrangle over definitions, with the result that the state fell far behind the schedule for its contribution to the first phase of this project. And there is no assurance that the city and the county will agree to go on to a second phase.[151]

In the meantime, Los Angeles' third attempt at an acceptable environmental impact report has not met with much more favor than did its predecessors. The draft version published in August 1978 was vigorously denounced by the country's scientific consultants, and six of the state agencies that reviewed it have similarly found fault with the city's latest effort. But the dispute over the adequacy of the city's environmental assessment had by this time become only a subsidiary element in a much larger debate in which more fundamental questions involving the city's independence of action are at stake. Neither side, consequently, can afford to give much ground on the issue of the report itself. Acceptance of Inyo's demands for a wider-ranging report, for example, would pose the danger for Los Angeles that a still greater part of the city's water programs could be brought under court review. And indeed, California's secretary for resources has joined the county in calling for yet another study that would embrace all the water-collecting activities of the Department of Water and Power. Inyo, alternatively, must continue to insist on a still more refined scientific analysis for fear that adoption of Los Angeles' environmental impact report might bring an abrupt end to the court-ordered limitations on the city's pumping program.[152]

There are grave risks for the county in continued stalemate as well. The cost of sustaining the legal and scientific consultants required for its litigation has created a severe strain on the county's limited finances. But an effort to force Los Angeles to pay more than $85,000 of the county's attorney fees was turned back by the Third District Court of Appeal in 1978. And in rejecting Inyo's contention that the city had acted in bad faith by preparing an inadequate environmental impact report, the court based its decision in part on the very point that the county's opposition was impelled not so much by the report's limitations as by its own interest in prolonging the injunctive restrictions on the city's pumping program.[153] "Does this represent a victory for either side?" Inyo's District Attorney L. H. "Buck" Gibbons pondered at the end of 1978. "I think that victory, if we ever achieve it, will come when the city and county recognize our obligations and work together to solve our mutual problems."[154]

This elaborate end game, however, is being played out in an

atmosphere of mutual hostility that is deeper now than at any time since the 1920s. The renewal of conflict has brought the establishment of a new valley newspaper, the *Inyo County News-Letter*, which has taken up reporting on the valley's tribulations in the vigorous tradition of Chalfant and Glasscock. Acts of defiance and intimidation have been committed by both sides. In the spring of 1976, for example, the department delayed filling a recreational lake which is used heavily by valley residents during the summer. Late one night in May, the gates controlling flows into the lake were cut open with blowtorches.[155] That fall, part of the aqueduct itself was blown up; and a huge arrow with a stick of dynamite attached was fired into the William Mulholland Memorial Fountain in Los Angeles.[156] In the months that followed, vandalism against city-owned equipment and facilities in the Owens Valley increased, and valley residents took to hissing whenever an official Department of Water and Power vehicle passed by, with the result that many department officials by the late 1970s were traveling in unmarked cars.[157]

As the pattern of amicable relations that had formed since 1950 began to disintegrate, issues once considered settled began to arise again. Local agitation for restrictions on the Tule Elk herds and for increases in taxes the city pays on its valley lands, for example, has been renewed. And when the department began inserting new clauses in its leases for commercial properties emphasizing the point that no lessee has a right to renewal after his lease runs out, the town merchants began pressing for a more liberal leasing policy and a restoration of the city's sales program.

In some instances, the city and the valley have still been able to find the grounds for accommodation. The department responded to the demands of the town merchants, for example, by offering the possibility of 15- or 20-year leases, regardless of the provisions of the city charter, if the merchants would agree in turn to modifications in the state statute requiring lessees to receive a right of first refusal when their properties were put up for sale. The amendments the department at first proposed, however, would have voided not only the restriction on sales but also the so-called Brown Act's prohibition on excessive rental charges without offering any assurance that leases longer than five years would ever be granted. A compromise was eventually achieved in 1979 through the adoption of an amendment to the Brown Act which simply permits a lessee to waive his right to first refusal. In exchange for taking his chances in a public auction of the property, the department proposed to offer such a lessee the opportunity of obtaining a longer term on his lease. And with this agreement in place, the department's sales of town properties have been renewed.[158]

But in other areas of dispute, negotiation and compromise have been replaced by the thrust and counterthrust of unyielding adversaries. The passage of the Jarvis-Gann tax-cutting initiative in 1978 cut so deeply into the county's revenues as to upset the assumptions on which Inyo's acceptance of the constitutional amendment of 1968 had been based. The county responded by reverting to a split roll of assessments, boosting the taxes on the city's lands by $540,000 while levying no corresponding increase on the other local property owners. Los Angeles retaliated by passing these increased taxes along to its lessees through a 24-percent increase in the rents charged on the city's agricultural leases. This move has in turn prompted the county supervisors to press for the immediate adoption of a rent control ordinance for Inyo.[159]

Two new issues have become the focus for even more widespread public concern. In the early 1970s, Los Angeles began installing water meters on many of its commercial properties in the valley. In the summer and fall of 1978, however, the city announced it was investing a quarter of a million dollars for the installation of water meters throughout the Owens Valley. City officials regard the meters as water-saving devices, and from their point of view, it seemed only just that the residents of the valley should be forced to practice the same diligence at conservation that Inyo insisted should be inflicted upon Los Angeles during the drought of 1976-77. But the number of homes affected is so small that even the department's own reports estimate that the water saved by metering will amount to only three-tenths of 1 percent of the aqueduct's supply. Nevertheless, department spokesmen confidently have predicted that the metering program would save the city upward of $40,000 a year by 1982.

Since the city charges valley residents the same prices for their own water that residential users in Los Angeles pay 250 miles away, the metering program has increased the water bills for some parts of Inyo by 2,000 percent. Inyo immediately appealed for a review of this rate structure by the Public Utilities Commission—an apparently hopeless gesture because the commission under its constitutional mandate has never exercised authority over the rates charged by municipal utilities on the theory that such agencies are controlled by their electorates. Inyo County, of course, presented a special case in that its residents have no vote in the municipality whose utility was perpetrating the program they opposed. But the Public Utilities Commission nevertheless declared itself powerless to intervene. When the county took its case to the state supreme court, however, the court came to the startling conclusion that whereas the commission had been correct in determining that the constitution gave it no specific authority to upset the city's rate structure, there was nothing to prevent the legislature from assigning it this authority. The judiciary thus passed the problem on to the legislative branch, and Inyo County has subsequently set about trying to raise support there for a bill that would make just such an unprecedented expansion of the commission's jurisdiction.[160]

The county has also begun laying the groundwork for an equally unprecedented assertion of its own authority. Frustrated after nearly ten years of trying to achieve a permanent restriction on the city's groundwater pumping, the board of supervisors drafted an ordinance arrogating to a commission of its own creation the power to regulate groundwater extractions within the Owens Valley basin. When the supervisors placed this proposal on the November 1980 ballot for countywide approval, Los Angeles immediately brought legal action to prevent a vote from being taken, alleging that the form of submission was technically invalid and that the county should be required to prepare an environmental impact report of its own on the proposed ordinance before the measure could take effect. But the city did not prevail, and on November 4, 1980, the citizens of Inyo endorsed the new ordinance by a margin of more than three to one. The measure is certain to be taken next to the courts, where Los Angeles is likely to find numerous powerful allies rallying to support its efforts to overturn this new county law. For if the ordinance is allowed to stand, it would establish a precedent for local action which might ultimately upset more than a century of customs and practices in the exercise of water rights throughout California.[161]

The conflicts over the city's water rate schedule and the county's groundwater pumping ordinance have momentous implications for a host of interests far removed from the Owens Valley. And the specter of Mulholland's war has been revived to stalk the city in other ways as well. In Sacramento, for example, debates in the late 1970s over the proposed construction of the Peripheral Canal to increase deliveries from the State Water Project were studded with repeated references to Southern California's water imperialism and the rape of the Owens Valley. And in the San Joaquin Valley, Los Angeles' plans to build the nation's largest nuclear power plant were overwhelmingly rejected in 1976 by the voters of Kern County, where the plant would have been located. "They raped the Owens Valley and bled Inyo County dry. Now it's Kern County's turn?" thundered the *Bakersfield Californian* in an editorial just before the votes were cast. "Mountains make safe neighbors . . . Our water is for agriculture. Los Angeles shall not drill one well . . . Let LADWP go where sea water abounds. Stick it up in El Segundo!"[162]

A new threat to the operation of the second aqueduct has also arisen in Mono County, where the city's increased diversions have substantially reduced the level of Mono Lake. The lake is a saline remnant of a vast inland sea that covered an estimated 316 square miles of the Mono Basin and neighboring Aurora Valley more than thirteen thousand years ago. Since the retreat of the glaciers, the lake has dwindled in size to approximately 85 square miles, and its level has subsequently fluctuated continuously by as much as a hundred feet. Because the modern lake lacks any natural outlet, its waters have become concentrated with carbonates, sulphates, and chlorides. Detailed analyses conducted by the United States Geological Survey at the turn of the century, however, revealed that it was not as rich a source of natural soda deposits as Owens Lake, to the south. And given Mono's harsh climate and remote location, the federal surveyors concluded, "It is doubtful whether this lake can be developed commercially."[163]

Early explorers dubbed Mono Lake the Dead Sea of the West. But its ancient waters in fact support myriads of infusoria, flies, and brine shrimp. The abundance of these tiny creatures has made the lake an attractive breeding area and stopover for thousands of gulls, grebes, phalaropes, snowy plovers, avocets, and other migratory shorebirds. Until quite recently, Negit Island in Mono Lake supported the second largest rookery for California gulls in the world. But the level of the lake began to decline steadily at the rate of one foot per year when the Mono extension went into operation in 1941. Since the advent of the second aqueduct, the rate of decline has increased to 1.6 feet per year. It is not known whether the brine shrimp endemic to Mono Lake can survive the increasing salinity that will come with further reductions in the lake's volume. But as the lake level declines, the rookery itself became endangered by the formation of land bridges to the mainland which give predators access to the gulls' nests.[164]

The resistance of the Owens Valley to the operation of the second aqueduct sprang from the unexpected increase in ground-water pumping that the Department of Water and Power discovered would be needed to operate its new project. In the case of Mono Lake, however, there was never any question that construction of the second aqueduct would result in a substantial reduction of the lake level. Thomas Means' original plans for the second aqueduct assumed that the diversions from the Mono Basin would be substantially greater than they are today. The various state reports prepared during the early 1960s on the water supply of the Owens and Mono basins predicted that the department's diversions into the second aqueduct would reduce the flows into Mono Lake by 40 percent. And the department itself estimates that the lake will continue to decline over the next fifty to one hundred years until it stabilizes at approximately one-third of its size before the diversions began.[165]

When the Mono extension and the second aqueduct were first conceived in the 1920s, there was no reason to expect that there would be any more resistance to the reduction of Mono Lake than there had been to the elimination of Owens Lake. The department's efforts to reduce opposition were therefore limited to the negotiation of agreements and the payment of damages to those persons owning littoral rights along the lake's shoreline. In 1974, when the city sought and received a permanent license from the State Water Resources Control Board authorizing the diversion of up to 167,000 acre-feet annually from the creeks feeding the lake, only the Sierra Club's Toiyabe chapter in Nevada and the eastern Sierra expressed any formal concern about the effect these diversions would have on the lake. And the only alternatives the club's representative could propose involved either a further reduction of water use by the residents of the Owens Valley or a greater reliance upon the augmented supplies of the State Water Project once the proposed Peripheral Canal was built. Since the construction of the Peripheral Canal posed serious environmental questions of its own, while the proposal for drying up Inyo County was not likely to gain favor with the people there, the club soon dropped this position and reverted to calling for an extension of the boundaries of Yosemite National Park to include Mono Lake.[166]

But as Inyo County's litigation gained success, and concerns for the environmental effects of the second aqueduct spread, a campaign to save Mono Lake blossomed in its own right. Apart from the fact that both are aimed at limiting the operation of the second aqueduct, the efforts in Inyo and Mono counties could hardly be more dissimilar. The residents of the Owens Valley went to court because they thought their own lands were threatened. The campaign to save Mono Lake, in contrast, drew its original support from an Audubon Society chapter in far-off Santa Monica, which had a greater concern for the future of the lake than local county officials initially exhibited. Inyo's litigation is practically a model of the complexity of modern environmentalism. It is a conflict waged between government agencies, sustained by public funds, attended by battalions of consultants and expert witnesses, and aimed ultimately at achieving an enforceable regulatory compromise. The campaign to save Mono Lake, at least in its formative stages, was almost a throwback to the loose-leaf appeals of the early environmental movement. Underfunded, loosely organized, it was an effort sustained principally by the dedication of a small band of bird-watchers and graduate students who were activated by nothing more complex than their deep affection for a place few Californians will ever see. But because the effort in Mono taps that love of wild places that has always been the basic wellspring of conservationist sentiment, the campaign soon overshadowed the conflict in Inyo County in terms of popular attention and support.

By the late 1970s, bills were being introduced in the state legislature to halt Los Angeles' exports from the Mono Basin. Editorials and opinion columns began to appear in newspapers around Northern California condemning the city's "drive to slake its insatiable thirst." Other environmental groups such as Friends of the Earth and the Natural Resources Defense Council soon joined the Sierra Club in rallying to the cause. Suits were filed and petitions drafted charging a violation of the public trust and urging the Department of the Interior to exercise its authority to protect the public lands of Mono County. And at the end of 1978, the Resources Agency of California assembled a special task force to draw up a plan for the preservation of the natural resources of the Mono Basin.[167]

In its formative stages, the campaign to save Mono Lake seemed to be fighting little more than a holding action intended to slow the rate of the city's water exports until a more detailed plan for the preservation of the lake could be worked out.[168] The Department of Water and Power refused these appeals, however, and the mayor of Los Angeles professed himself powerless to intervene.[169] When a land bridge to Negit Island first formed in the fall of 1978, the lake's defenders threw their support behind an effort by the California National Guard to blast a temporary channel between the rookery and the mainland. State and federal taxes paid for this elaborate exercise, and Los Angeles contributed a boat. But when the charges were detonated, the birds took off and the soil and rock that made up the bridge settled back into pretty much their original configuration. A second attempt in April 1979 was no more successful. By the summer of 1979, all the adult breeding gulls on Negit Island had left the scene of battle. Many of the birds have since resettled on other islands in the lake, but only 12,500 gulls nested there in 1979 as compared to 46,700 in 1978. Nevertheless, a fence has been erected to keep predators off the Negit Island breeding grounds which the birds no longer use.[170]

With the publication of the state task force report at the end of 1979, the campaign's objectives gained new definition. After reviewing nineteen possible alternatives, the task force fastened upon a plan calling for an immediate reduction in the city's exports from Mono Basin from a hundred thousand to fifteen thousand acre-feet of water a year. To make up for this loss of approximately 17 percent of Los Angeles' current water supply, the committee proposed that the city should step up its production of reclaimed wastewater and perpetuate the water conservation efforts it had initiated during the drought. Recognizing that the city might not be able to implement these recommendations immediately, the task force suggested that the state and federal governments should help to bear the cost of additional supplies from the State Water Project to cover the city's losses in the first five years.[171]

Although the Department of Water and Power participated in the formation of the state task force, it did not, needless to say, endorse these conclusions. With more than a little justice, department officals felt they were being ill treated by the state and federal agency representatives who held five of the seven voting positions on the task force. The department, after all, had spent $100 million to build the second aqueduct under a threat that the state would otherwise condemn its water rights in the Mono Basin. And now it was being condemned by the state for exercising those same rights to operate its new project.

The suggestion that the city should give up the water it had spent so much to secure met with no more cordial reception in the other official quarters of Los Angeles. The city council voted unanimously to oppose any attempt to implement the recommendations of the task force report. This position was endorsed as well by the California Farm Bureau Federation and the Kern County Water Agency, which recognized that a successful effort to compel the city to forego the exercise of its rights in the Mono Basin would not only reduce the amount of water available for Central Valley agriculture from the State Water Project, but would also establish yet another precedent with dangerous portent for the entire system of water rights in California.[172]

Despite its shortcomings, the task force report has at least succeeded in helping reduce the argument to its essential elements. For unlike all the battles of the past, the controversy over the second aqueduct has little to do with any question of the city's need for water. The years when Los Angeles required a superabundance of water to serve an ever-expanding population have passed; the city's population growth has in fact stabilized since 1970. The second aqueduct was developed simply as a management device to enable the department to make use of the water rights it had already acquired and to assure that it would be able to continue providing its customers with the highest quality water available at the lowest possible price. And despite the intense opposition that the operation of the project has engendered in Inyo and Mono counties, the second aqueduct has succeeded in achieving these objectives. By the mid-1970s, deliveries from the Metropolitan Water District, which cost Los Angeles nearly twice as much as the water from its own aqueducts, had dwindled to less than 3 percent of the city's overall supply.[173]

The city therefore regards the prospect of continued resistance to the second aqueduct as fundamentally a problem of economics. Any reduction in the project's flows means not only less water but also less power generated within the municipal system. These losses can only be made up by purchases from other sources. The *Los Angeles Times* has generally cooperated with the department line, portraying the opposition of the Owens Valley as the reflection of little more than a misguided concern for plants over the needs of the people of Los Angeles. And as soon as it became apparent what direction the state task force would take, the department was quick to begin mailing out thousands of brochures warning that a cessation of its diversions from Mono Lake would increase the bills of the city's rate-payers by a billion dollars over the next twenty-five or thirty years.[174]

The state task force itself estimates that implementation of its recommendations would cost $250 million, but contends that 80 percent of these costs could be recovered in the form of reduced energy use if the people of Los Angeles would cut back 15 percent of the water they pass through their water heaters.[175] The Department of Water and Power does not, however, share the state's beamish confidence in the efficacy of water conservation and in the accuracy of these projections. Department officials argue that the actual cost of the state plan would run closer to $2 billion and that it would be unfair to expect the city to absorb these costs unless the state accepts the burden of providing Los Angeles with water and power to replace the supplies it is asking the city to forego. In addition, the department has portrayed the state program as a demand for uniform reductions in water usage by all the city's customers, which would fall hardest on the inner city poor, who already use far less water than suburban home-owners and who can least afford the increased rates the department is certain would follow.[176] This appeal has been successful in prompting endorsements of the department's position from organizations representing low-income families throughout Los Angeles.[177] And though the department does not deny that continued operation of the second aqueduct will have significant environmental effects, it refuses to concede either the immediacy or the irreversibility of these problems.[178] In the meantime, the pumps are still running in the Owens Valley and the city's exports from the Mono Basin continue unabated.

Nevertheless, as the city celebrates the two-hundredth anniversary of its founding in 1981, it faces a host of new threats to its water supply that are as severe as any in its history. The ability of the Department of Water and Power to continue to meet the needs of Los Angeles is not in jeopardy. What is at stake instead is the freedom the city has enjoyed to draw upon the supplies at its disposal in whatever manner it considers most efficient from the point of view of its citizens. The supreme court's decision in the dispute over water rates in the Owens Valley, and Inyo's continuing demands for a wider consideration of alternatives to the city's pumping program in connection with its environmental suit create the possibility for outside interference with the management of the city's water program on an order never before attempted. In addition, Inyo's suggestion that the principles of the County of Origin statute should be applied to work a fundamental shift in the relationship between the city and the valley remains to be addressed by any court. The adoption and successful enforcement of Inyo's new groundwater pumping ordinance however, would go a long way toward achieving just such a change in the county's ability to deal forcefully with the Department of Water and Power. As the Inyo district attorney has observed, "It is not just the water. This ordinance will allow us to control our destiny. We will be making the decisions that will affect the future; they will not be made 300 miles away in Los Angeles."[179]

Of all these challenges to the department's authority, none is perhaps more threatening than the controversy over Mono Lake because it is the least refined, the least tractable, and the least likely to admit any possibility of compromise. The state task force report has clearly failed to define a mutually acceptable resolution to this conflict; but it is difficult to imagine any way that the concerns of the defenders of Mono Lake can be served without a substantial reduction in the city's exports from the Mono Basin. There is danger in this prospect for Inyo County as well. Its interests, after all, are not the same as Mono's, and any success in reducing Los Angeles' diversions from the lake is certain to increase the determination of the Department of Water and Power to stand firm in the Owens Valley. But for the successors of William Mulholland, the real stuff of nightmares must consist in the thought that a significant part of the work of three-quarters of a century might be undone for the sake of some tiny shrimp and a flock of birds.

Conclusion

It is a truism that Los Angeles today would not exist without the panoply of reservoirs and cross-country conduits that make up the modern water system of California. What is perhaps not so self-evident, however, is that the reverse may also be true. The early and overwhelming success of Los Angeles' aqueduct to the Owens Valley provided a forceful demonstration of the efficacy of public water development. And in inspiring officials at the state level to press for the construction of still larger delivery systems to benefit California as a whole, the example of the city's aqueduct established a tradition for water development in California that is altogether different from the other areas of the West which developed under the aegis of the federal Bureau of Reclamation. Los Angeles' approach to water development was muscular, competitive, self-reliant; and these same virtues were reflected as well in the later construction of the Colorado Aqueduct and California's State Water Project. In contrast to the bureau's programs, which depend upon massive subsidies, these projects sprang from local initiatives and were designed to be self-funding. Even the Central Valley project, which gave the bureau its first major inroad into California, was initially conceived as a state project and would, no doubt, have been developed as such if the intervention of the Great Depression had not temporarily stripped the state of its ability to fund the undertaking.

San Francisco, of course, also paid for the Hetch Hetchy project by itself. But Los Angeles' example was the more influential because it was the more immediately successful. San Francisco's new system was not even completed until after the Central Valley and Colorado projects had been begun. San Francisco's project has commanded more scholarly attention than Los Angeles' aqueduct because the conflict over the Hetch Hetchy Valley so clearly revealed the division within the American conservation movement over the principles represented by Gifford Pinchot and John Muir. But the construction of the Hetch Hetchy project also revealed the folly of attempting to build a water delivery system on any basis other than absolute control of the water rights involved. Los Angeles' officials understood this intuitively, so they were able to press forward with the development of their aqueduct while San Francisco wasted ten years in a futile attempt to secure a federal permit for its project. In addition, the delays and unexpected expenditures San Francisco encountered in the course of building its project demonstrated the diseconomices associated with constructing a project with consecutive appropriations. Los Angeles, in contrast, succeeded in part because it chose to pay its own way by committing all the funds needed for the aqueduct at the very beginning.

Los Angeles' water system is small in comparison to the state and federal projects that operate in California today. But by consistently building ahead of demand and fighting to maintain the independence of its sources of supply, the city has been able to secure far more water than its citizens will ever be able to consume. As a result, it has continued to exercise a measure of influence over the course of water development within California that is considerably greater than the proportionate size of its municipal water system. Los Angeles' water delivery systems today extend over hundreds of miles of the Southwest, and its power is drawn from projects scattered across six states. And through its control of the largest block of votes within the Metropolitan Water District, Los Angeles is able to affect decisions which will shape the future not only of California but of the entire West.

It is not sufficient, however, to assess the aqueduct simply as a water project for Los Angeles. If its success was an inspiring example of the potential benefits of public water development, the price it exacted in the devastation of the Owens Valley served as an equally forceful warning of the need to develop some means of balancing competing demands for California's limited water resources. These two aspects of the project are inextricably intertwined. And in the context of the city's relations with the valley, those virtues of self-reliance, a competitive spirit, and a commitment to paying one's own way came to be seen in other parts of the state as examples of the arrogance of independence, avarice, and the flaunting of superior financial power. The sectional rivalries that spring to life in Northern California whenever a new project is proposed to increase water exports to the south are consequently as much a part of the aqueduct's heritage for California as the constitutional and statutory provisions that were adopted to protect other regions of the state from suffering the experience of the Owens Valley.

Any emphasis on Los Angeles' self-reliance must be qualified, of course, by acknowledgment of the extraordinary part the federal government played in protecting the city's project during its formative stages. Probably no character in this narrative has appeared so villainous as J. B. Lippincott. He alone consistently broke faith with his public trust and then lied to cover his actions. In comparison to Lippincott's accomplishments, Fred Eaton's endless scheming appears almost comically ineffectual. Lippincott was certainly not the bland and inconsequential figure Nadeau describes, nor was he the maligned victim of a bad press that other historians have attempted to make of him. For his was the crucial and indispensable role in pressing the project upon an initially reluctant Mulholland and then arguing for destruction of the valley's agriculture long before the city recognized the necessity. If any one of the far more distinguished engineers and hydrologists then working in Northern California, the Central Valley, and the other western states had been appointed to the post Lippincott held with the Reclamation Service, it is inconceivable that the federal government would have acted as it did in the Owens Valley.

Any judgment of Lippincott, however, must be tempered with the observation that he was, in fact, correct. Los Angeles could not have developed without the water supply of the Owens Valley. As bitterly as they condemned his actions in private, Lippincott's superiors in Washington protected him. Their actions were not motivated simply by a desire to save the Reclamation Service from embarrassment. More important, they recognized that the success of Los Angeles' aqueduct would help to prove the very principles of systematic water development which they were working to establish. Their decision represented a choice between competing public interests, and the valley was consequently sacrificed to the ethic of growth the Reclamation Service had been created to serve. Without their intervention, however, first in suspending the economic growth of the Owens Valley and later in the Mono Basin, the aqueduct would never have been possible.

The same critical importance cannot be ascribed to the San Fernando land syndicate. It seems foolish to contend, as some Southern California historians have done, that the syndicate never existed or that delivery of the aqueduct water to its lands was simply a "happy coincidence."[1] But whereas the syndicate's interest was considerably more than coincidental, it was somewhat less than corrupting. To say that the financial leaders of Los Angeles in the early part of this century exercised great influence over the conduct of municipal affairs, and that some consequently benefited from the exercise of this influence, is simply to state a characteristic which was obvious in many aspects of the city's administration during this era. For all the profits it derived from the project, the syndicate did not pervert the aqueduct's purpose. There was never any doubt that the aqueduct would deliver more water than the city could initially consume and that the wisest application of the surplus would be for agriculture at the headwaters of the city's natural source of supply in the San Fernando Valley. The syndicate's involvement certainly helped unify the business community's support of the aqueduct. But these political advantages were more than counterbalanced by the difficulties the syndicate's participation created for Mulholland in securing approval of the project from Washington.

In any event, the people of Los Angeles were not misled where the syndicate was concerned. The facts of its existence and of the profits it would reap from the aqueduct had been revealed by the time the votes were cast on the first bond issue for the project. But this revelation did nothing to dissuade the taxpayers from endorsing a proposal that promised prosperity for all. There is no question that the aqueduct was conceived and promoted as an extension of the ambitions of the local business community.

The principles of the marketplace, in fact, permeated every aspect of its early operation. But Los Angeles' shift to public ownership of its water supply was only possible because government at the turn of the century was seen as the handmaiden of free enterprise. And the assumption that government has a legitimate role in promoting economic development through public works was no more debated then than it is today.

The tragedy of Mulholland is that the magnitude of his achievements has been obscured by the mistakes made in his last years in office. The collapse of the Saint Francis Dam destroyed the image of infallibility he had so carefully nurtured. His hysterical rush to create the Metropolitan Water District left the city saddled with a massive debt for a water supply it has never been able to use. And his destruction of the Owens Valley economy undermined the cause of public water development he had championed. It would be tempting to suggest of Mulholland that any wrongs he did to the Owens Valley were learned from Lippincott. But this is incorrect. Lippincott simply foresaw the ultimate consequences of the aqueduct before Mulholland did. The conflict of the 1920s was fixed and certain the instant President Roosevelt determined that the greater good would be served by a greater Los Angeles. Mulholland's mistakes in the early 1920s merely hastened an inevitable confrontation. His fall was consequently as much an expression of his character as were his many triumphs.

If Mulholland does not truly fit the mold of the heroic masterbuilder that historians of Los Angeles have attempted to cast for him, one also looks in vain in these events for the stalwart defenders of agrarian virtue that the partisans of the Owens Valley have portrayed. To the extent that the controversy over the aqueduct involved an attempt by private interests to undermine an ideal of public service, it was the businessmen and ranchers of Inyo and not the members of the San Fernando land syndicate who were fighting that battle. In Los Angeles, there was no such conflict because the public and the private interests were perceived as identical by nearly all but the local power companies. But the fact that the residents of the valley who led the opposition to Los Angeles in the early part of this century were fighting to maintain the sources of their livelihood does not, however, diminish the validity of their complaint. They failed in part because the special qualities of their case became submerged in the much broader campaign that defenders of the free enterprise system were waging at the time against government involvement in public resource development throughout the West. Mary Austin's comments with regard to those who plot without knowledge and the incurable desire of men to be played upon have some application to their actions. But no matter how futile or ill-conceived the ranchers' resistance may have been, the extent of their folly in no way corresponds to the loss the valley has sustained as a result of their defeat.

If the development of the aqueduct and the city's subsequent treatment of the Owens Valley are to be judged as bad in some sense, it is necessary to specify on what score. There is no question that the city's water officials have consistently exaggerated the need for the projects they propose, and that the local newspapers have just as consistently abetted this deception. But the only cost the taxpayers of Los Angeles have paid for their victimization has been sustained economic growth and abundant water at low prices. With respect to the Owens Valley, the city's land and water management policies certainly compare favorably with those of any state or federal agency exercising jurisdiction over a similar expanse of property. Current residents of Los Angeles may regret the congestion, the smog, and the loss of many of the region's principal natural assets that have come with the economic growth water development made possible. But these afflictions are the consequence of failures for which the Department of Water and Power cannot be blamed. Within its own sphere of authority, the department has effectively preserved and, for the city's purposes, enhanced the productivity of the valley's water resources. And in this sense, its policies are in the best traditions of the movement for scientific conservation espoused by Gifford Pinchot.

Even when tested by the tenets of the preservationist wing of American conservation, which places greater emphasis on the protection of natural and esthetic values, the department's policies do not fare badly—at least, not until the announcement of the expanded pumping program for the second aqueduct. By default more than by intent, the department has preserved the Owens Valley with its fragile deserts and spectacular scenic beauty more or less intact. The valley, in fact, has not simply been frozen in time in a way no other part of California can claim. Rather, by removing wherever it could all traces of human development that had been set upon the land prior to 1930, the department has effectively reversed the valley in time, forcing it back to the conditions that existed at the beginning of this century. Under other circumstances, this process might be applauded from a preservationist point of view as being in some vague sense an environmental good. Alternatively, allowing the valley to develop economically into some recreational version of Fresno would presumably have been in the same vague sense environmentally bad. Where, then, does the evil of Los Angeles' actions lie?

The problem with judgments of this kind is that they derive from standards which are themselves external to the situation at hand, blind to specific conditions, and therefore ultimately meaningless. The environmental issues at stake in the current controversy are simply the terms in which an older and more basic conflict is being waged today. In an earlier phase of this conflict the issues were economic, and the controversy consequently focused on questions involving how the valley might have developed in the absence of Los Angeles. But the problem of the Owens Valley is not simply an economic or environmental matter. It is instead a problem of people and the institutions they construct. What is important about the valley's development is that its people have had very little to do with shaping it. Many of the most vital decisions affecting the future of their lives on the land are made in Los Angeles, where their interests are not represented. The residents of the Owens Valley have thus been effectively disenfranchised. And in a system of representative government, that is wrong.

From this essential evil flow all the problems the valley has encountered. For if there is any lesson to be drawn from the long history of relations between Los Angeles and the Owens Valley, it is that the policies of the Department of Water and Power are neither benevolent nor malicious; they are merely practical. The department's interest is focused exclusively upon the protection of the water resource it has acquired for the city's welfare. Everything that the residents of the valley build, the work they perform, and the dreams they fashion for their children are at best irrelevant to that interest. This attitude has not changed in the half-century since Mulholland's fall, and the current controversy over the second aqueduct is its natural consequence.

Given the department's institutional setting and its isolation from public control, however, the relationship between the city and the valley could scarcely have taken any other form. Mulholland's successors are not monsters any more than he was. They are public servants with a primary responsibility to deliver water and power to the citizens of Los Angeles at the lowest possible price. From this narrow perspective, they would not be serving their public trust if they elected to forego a portion of the city's water rights for the sake of an abstract theory of fairness.

Los Angeles' relations with the Owens Valley may, as the department's critics have suggested, present an extreme example of the dangers of single-purpose planning or of the need for greater regulatory control over the exercise of water rights in a state where the competition for scarce water supplies is particularly intense. But the Department of Water and Power is by no means an agency out of control. Rather, it is an agency in large part without control, and as such it is functioning precisely as its creators intended. The influence which the voters of Los Angeles exercise over the activities of the department, after all, is only marginally greater than that of the residents of the Owens Valley. Even if a constituency existed within the city's electorate for some substantial change in the department's treatment of the valley, it is difficult to imagine how it would go about effectuating its will. Not since the peak of the furor over the operations of the Water and Power Machine in the 1930s has it appeared even remotely possible that a mayor of Los Angeles could be turned out of office because of his appointments to the Board of Water and Power Commissioners. And in view of the department's unswerving devotion to the city's best interests, there is little reason for the people of Los Angeles to contemplate changing the structure of its governance. The evil which grows from entrusting a politically nonresponsible agency with so sensitive an area of municipal policy as the city's relations with the Owens Valley is consequently self-perpetuating precisely because it is so efficient.

The department's insulation from public control, though vitally important to any understanding of the controversy over the aqueduct, is hardly unique. In fact, one of the reasons why this controversy deserves so many hundreds of pages of study is that it presents in such high relief a wide range of problems that exist generally in the management of water throughout California. When Mulholland set about creating the Metropolitan Water District, for example, he took care to provide it with the same measure of protection from political interference by assuring that its directors would also never have to appeal for popular support to keep their seats. As a result, this most influential of all local water agencies in California operates today without any direct control by the citizens it represents. By the same token, Mulholland did not invent the politics of panic as a way of promoting his water projects, but he did refine the tactical skills involved to a high art. And his success in this regard has become such a model for emulation that few water projects in California are ever put forward without the accompaniment of a full chorus of dire predictions of the dreadful consequences that will follow if construction is not authorized immediately. Even in other areas of the state, where members of public water boards are directly elected, the campaigns for these offices are seldom hotly contested, nor are they the object of much widespread popular attention. Ignorance and indifference accomplish the same degree of insulation that in Los Angeles is provided by charter. And these conditions, of course, make the practice of the politics of panic all the easier.

Los Angeles may present a special case in this regard in view of the particularly active role that the media in general and the *Los Angeles Times* in particular have played in defending the city's water programs from criticism or close examination. But if the *Times* is the last place to look for objective analysis of water problems, there are few newspapers in California that do a distinctly better job. For one thing, water development is so tightly linked to the prospects for economic growth in all areas of the state that there is little to encourage a local newspaper to dwell at length upon the shortcomings of a proposed project that promises greater prosperity to the region it serves. Perhaps more important, water policy does not seem to lend itself to journalistic endeavor. The projects take years and sometimes decades to evolve. And the issues involved are often so complex that they cannot be mastered without a detailed familiarity with several exacting disciplines ranging from hydrology to law to engineering. In consequence, water remains, although the most vital, probably the least popularly understood of all natural resources.

These difficulties are reflected as well in the disagreements that have helped prolong the controversy over Los Angeles' aqueduct. The individual disputes, for example, have frequently been conducted between engineers representing the city and average citizens who happen to hold public office in the valley. The difference in expertise creates an imbalance that encourages misunderstanding. As a result, their debates are often contrapuntal and the positions taken by the opposing sides sometimes purposefully oblique. The city and the valley can look at the same thing separately and see it in reverse; thus Mulholland and the Watterson brothers argued with perfect sincerity over who was truly the destroyer and who the protector of the Owens Valley. Similarly, in today's conflict, the city's representatives persist in describing the pumping program as beneficial and the second aqueduct as a boon to the valley because of the opportunities they create to serve a whole new range of the valley's needs. Inyo's residents, in contrast, see in the same program an engine of irreversible devastation.

The city enjoys an advantage as well in the longevity of its purpose. As a result of its insulation from outside interference, the Department of Water and Power has been able to pursue its objectives and sustain its basic policies with a consistency which is certainly rare among public agencies. In some instances, department officials today are addressing problems defined decades earlier. What is most remarkable about Mulholland's leadership in creating the modern metropolis of Los Angeles is not that he so completely dominated the city's water programs in his own time but that he continues to do so even now, nearly half a century after his death. The fact that his successors have not deviated in any significant way from the precepts and policies he laid down for the operation of the aqueduct is more a testament to the scope of his vision than a comment on their inability to conceive of any alternatives. But the consequence for the Owens Valley has been that the modern leaders of the resistance to Los Angeles are in many ways fighting over the same issues that agitated their ancestors. The current controversy, for example, is not simply a dispute over a water management plan that has been forming for the past ten years. Rather, it is an extension of the same demand for a formal division of the valley's waters that the residents of Inyo have sought ever since Mulholland announced his plans for the first aqueduct.

Under certain circumstances, the durability and consistency of the department's policies can cause it problems. This is most clearly the case with respect to its conflict with the state over the second aqueduct. Whereas the federal government actively assisted Los Angeles in developing its water supply until the government chose to withdraw from the resulting controversy altogether after 1950, the state has failed to define any consistent or practical policy toward the conflict between the city and the valley. The state first created the conditions which helped compel Los Angeles to construct the second aqueduct, for example; yet a new generation of bureaucrats under a different administration in Sacramento seems just as determined to prevent the city from fully operating the new project. And certainly the recommendations of the interagency task force on Mono Lake offer no more reasonable a basis for settlement than did the demands raised in the legislature during the 1920s to restore the Owens Valley to its condition prior to construction of the aqueduct. In general, state officials have tended to exhibit sympathy toward the valley's appeals for assistance, but only so long as the effort does not prove too expensive or threaten an open and impolitic breach with Los Angeles. Otherwise, the state has been content to look away, treating the conflict as if it were a private dispute between a landlord and his tenants.

The valley has, of course, always been weakened in its dealings with the state by its lack of any common sense of purpose and its inability to define precisely what form of relief it most desires. Los Angeles' often clumsy response to the valley's concerns over the second aqueduct, however, appears to have united the valley residents in a way they never were during the 1920s. Even Mono County, which has rarely displayed any taste for fighting with the city, has been drawn into the current fray. The opportunities Mulholland found for dividing his opponents and dealing with them in piecemeal fashion have been lost. To some extent, the department's efforts alternately to bully and cajole the valley ranchers into siding with the city in the current dispute may reflect an attempt to repeat Mulholland's success in this regard. But the city's repeated threats to cut off water deliveries to its agricultural lessees if the pumping program is reduced have not deterred Inyo County from proceeding with its suit. And the overwhelming support for the county's new groundwater ordinance suggests that the modern residents of the valley are unlikely to allow their concerns for the long-term effects of the second aqueduct to be held hostage for the sake of protecting the remnants of the region's agricultural heritage.

There is a more fundamental difference as well between the battle Mulholland fought and the controversy of today. The ranchers who banded together in the 1920s to seize the Alabama Gates and bomb the aqueduct had no plan or program for the long-term preservation of the valley. They were fighting instead to extract the highest price they could for their homes and businesses. It was a conflict waged for immediate gain, and consideration for the valley's future had little part in it. The valley's litigation over the second aqueduct, in contrast, constitutes a declaration of sorts that the people of Inyo are committed to maintaining the valley and their own place within it. Even if the court ultimately gives Inyo judgment, it cannot, of course, give the residents of the valley their future. That is something they must fashion for themselves. But the existence of this new resolve, signified by the filing of the suit, possesses a significance which may eventually prove greater than anything the county will win or lose in court.

Throughout this century, the ongoing conflict between Los Angeles and the Owens Valley has exercised a sustained influence on the evolution of legal principles governing the relationship between public agencies and the management of water in California and, to a lesser extent, the West. Passage of the constitutional amendments of 1914, 1928, and 1968, as well as the numerous statutes adopted at the state and federal levels to address specific aspects of the controversy, have accomplished basic alterations in the authority of the federal reclamation service, the taxing power of local agencies, and the relations among all water users in California. The first war of the Owens Valley arose at a time when the need to establish some way of balancing competing demands for the state's limited water resources had assumed the dimensions of a crisis. The second war of the Owens Valley has broken out at another critical juncture in the state's history. Having used water as a means of overcoming other natural obstacles to economic development—as Los Angeles has done to establish a great city in the midst of a semi-arid plain—water officials throughout California are now beginning to confront the limits of the water resource itself. As a result, greater emphasis for the future is being placed upon the discovery of new ways to accomplish greater efficiencies in the management of existing water supplies, rather than upon the construction of new development projects. These activities, however, pose just as grave a threat as did the constitutional amendment of 1928 to the traditional exercise of water rights which, in many areas of the state, constitute a significant obstacle to the implementation of more efficient management strategies. The problem of balancing rights and needs in relation to a scarce resource is, of course, central to the current conflict in the Owens Valley. And the likelihood is therefore great that the controversy between the city and the valley will once again have a profound effect upon the way these problems are addressed elsewhere.

For the short term, none of the topics in contention in the valley today possesses so great a potential for statewide impact as Inyo's new groundwater ordinance. The rapid depletion of the state's major groundwater reservoirs as a result of overpumping by agricultural corporations in the Central Valley has already emerged as one of the most critical issues for the future of California's agricultural productivity. But efforts at the state level to establish, for the first time, a system of standards regulating the extraction of groundwater supplies have been smothered in the legislature. And a related attempt to link the construction of the proposed Peripheral Canal to the adoption of even the most minimal constraints on pumping has similarly been blocked by agribusiness interests who contend that these problems can be more effectively resolved at the local level, where any standards which are ultimately adopted can be more finely tuned to the special needs of the industry. But it has been in Inyo County and not the Central Valley that an affirmative attempt has been mounted to regulate groundwater pumping by a local agency. And if the courts eventually determine that Inyo's action poses an unacceptable interference with the city's water rights, this decision can only increase the pressure for adoption of a state-wide program to prevent agribusiness from destroying the basis of its own long-term prosperity.

The adoption of the groundwater ordinance strikes at the heart of an important weakness in the city's power: although Los Angeles pays taxes in Inyo County, it cannot vote there. This assertion of local authority and electoral independence may, therefore, help to redress the imbalance that has characterized the valley's relations with the city until now. But in its appeal to the court for a more fundamental shift in this relationship through a retroactive application of the strictures of the County of Origin statute, Inyo has raised a host of questions with even more ominous implications for the future, not only of Los Angeles but all of California. On the face of it, the claim that the city's right to export water from the Owens and Mono basins should be restricted in order to preserve local economic and environmental values would appear to be consistent with both the purposes of the County of Origin statute and the principles incorporated into the vast array of environmental laws adopted in the past thirty years. But the state constitution directs that water should be developed for its highest beneficial uses. In compliance with this mandate, the export of water to serve an urban populace would seem to supersede its use to preserve a remote saline lake like Mono or to maintain native vegetation in the Owens Valley. And if this is so, the constitution may invalidate all the environmental and governmental restrictions imposed on the development of water in California since 1928.

There are great risks to the city, however, in pressing such a claim. To do so, it would presumably be required to demonstrate not only that its use of the valley's water is reasonable, but also that its need for the water is real. It was to avoid having to demonstrate in court a need that did not exist—and not because of some altruistic impulse to deal fairly with the residents of the Owens Valley—that Los Angeles first sent Fred Eaton to begin buying up valley lands which the city might otherwise have secured through condemnation. And now that Los Angeles has access to far more water than it can ever consume, the problem of demonstrating a need would be all the greater. If, on the other hand, Los Angeles were ever compelled to begin exercising its rights to the supplies from the Colorado which it has paid so much to secure, it would set off a massive disruption of deliveries to all the other customers of the Metropolitan Water District who have grown prosperous on the water Los Angeles does not use. And with that, the apocalypse Mary Austin imagined in the desert might at last be upon the South Coast and all Mulholland's works.

It is quite possible that neither side will carry its position to these extremes. Indeed, both sides may eventually determine that their better course lies in hammering out an agreement among themselves, rather than in allowing a settlement to be imposed from outside by the legislature or the courts. But the magnitude of the questions involved in the current litigation, and the impact any resolution of them would have upon the state as a whole, make it clear that the dispute in the Owens Valley is no more peripheral to the life of California today than it ever was. What happens between the city and the valley can touch every inhabitant of the state. As successful as Mulholland and his successors have been in providing an abundant water supply for the South Coast, the region remains extremely vulnerable to any disruption in the operation of the artificial delivery systems upon which its vitality depends. And in a nation which has become so tightly bound together as a result of the development of the modern water system, we all share a part of that vulnerability.

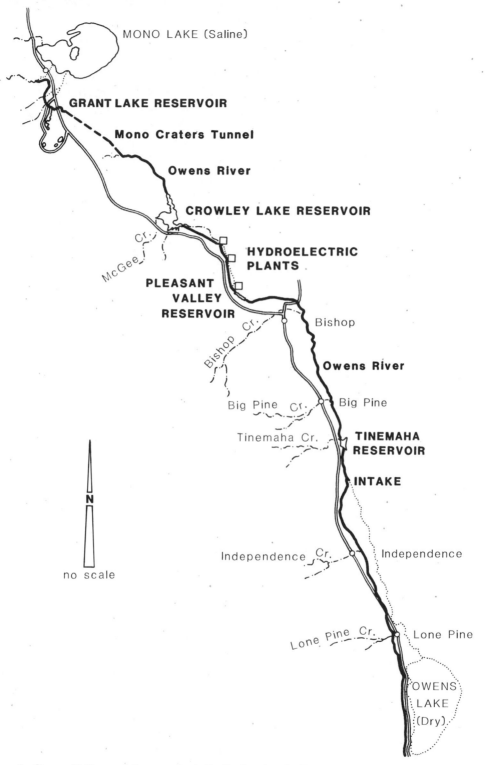

MONO LAKE (Saline)

GRANT LAKE RESERVOIR

Mono Craters Tunnel

Owens River

CROWLEY LAKE RESERVOIR

McGee Cr.

HYDROELECTRIC PLANTS

PLEASANT VALLEY RESERVOIR

Bishop Cr.

Bishop

Owens River

Big Pine Cr.

Big Pine

Tinemaha Cr.

TINEMAHA RESERVOIR

INTAKE

N

no scale

Independence Cr.

Independence

Lone Pine Cr.

Lone Pine

OWENS LAKE (Dry)

1. Owens Valley and the aqueduct. Credit: Los Angeles Department of Water and Power.

2. THE CITY WATER BUILT.

Los Angeles City
Annexations

1781–1913
1914–1923
1924–1977

1. Big Tujunga Canyon
2. San Fernando Valley
3. Pasadena
4. Hollywood
5. Narrows of Los Angeles River
6. Buena Vista Reservoir
7. Santa Monica
8. San Pedro
9. Long Beach

Indicates Area of
Original Grant 1781

Credit: Los Angeles Department of Water and Power.

Los Angeles River

Original Grant
1781

N

3. Water supply systems of Southern California. Credit: Los Angeles Department of Water and Power.

Notes

CHAPTER ONE
Organizing for Development

1. Warren Thompson, *Growth and Changes in California's Population* (1955), pp. 11-17.
   A more detailed version of this introductory essay appears in William L. Kahrl, ed., *The California Water Atlas* (1979), pp. 28-29.
2. Thompson, *Growth and Changes*, table II-2, p. 10; see also pp. 258, 260, 333, and table II-4, p. 13.
3. Nelson M. Blake, *Water for the Cities* (1956), p. 267. The other three were Buffalo, New Orleans, and Providence.
4. Harris Newmark, *Sixty Years in Southern California, 1853-1913* (1926), p. 322.
5. William A. Spaulding, *History and Reminiscences of Los Angeles* (1931), p. 167.
6. Charles A. Moody, "Los Angeles and the Owens River," *Out West* (October 1905).
7. City of Los Angeles, Archives, vol. VI, p. 680. See also J. M. Guinn, *A History of California and an Extended History of Los Angeles and Environs* (1915), vol. I, pp. 393-94.
8. City of Los Angeles, Archives, vol. VI, pp. 668-69.
9. Ibid., pp. 684-85.
10. Boyle Workman, *The City That Grew* (1935), pp. 87-88; Guinn, *History of ... Los Angeles and Environs*, pp. 392-93; Vincent Ostrom, *Water and Politics: A Study of Water Policies and Administration in the Development of Los Angeles* (1953), pp. 43-44.
11. The only major system that did not fall into the grasp of the Los Angeles City Water Company was that of the West Los Angeles Water Company. See Ostrom, *Water and Politics*, p. 44, and J. J. Warner, *An Illustrated History of Los Angeles County California* (1889), p. 266.

12. Guinn, *History of... Los Angeles and Environs*, pp. 393-94.

13. Although it was a widely used unit for the measurement of water flow during this period, a miner's inch (or "inch") varied in exact value with location and custom. As used by Southern California hydrographers at the turn of the century, an inch was equivalent to one-fiftieth of a cubic foot per second.

14. Ostrom, *Water and Politics*, p. 45.

15. United States Department of Agriculture, Office of Experiment Stations, *Report of Irrigation Investigations in California*, by Elwood Mead, Bulletin 100 (1901), p. 337. (Hereinafter cited as Mead, *Irrigation Investigations*.) See also *Los Angeles City Water Company* v. *City of Los Angeles*, 55 Cal. 176.

16. Ostrom, *Water and Politics*, p. 45.

17. California Legislature, *Statutes of 1873-74* (Sacramento, 1874), p. 633.

18. *Anastacio Feliz* b. *City of Los Angeles*, 58 Cal. 73, 79.

19. J.M. Guinn, *Historical and Biographical Record of Los Angeles and Vicinity* (1901), pp. 811-12.

20. Ibid., pp. 247-48; Warner, *Illustrated History*, pp. 462-63.

21. For summary treatments of the battle over the harbor at San Pedro and the extent of the Southern Pacific monopoly on western transportation, see Walton Bean, *California: An Interpretive History* (1968), pp. 206, 214, 222, 300-301, 305; also Ralph J. Roske, *Everyman's Eden* (1968), p. 451. For greater detail, see Spencer Crump, *Ride the Big Red Cars* (1970), pp. 11-16, 25-26, 74-91.

22. Robert M. Fogelson, *The Fragmented Metropolis: Los Angeles 1850-1930* (1967), p. 229.

23. Ibid., p. 95; Ostrom, *Water and Politics*, p. 46.

24. City of Los Angeles, Bureau of Engineering, *Plans for City Waterworks: Full Report by City Engineer Dockweiler for the Council* (March 30, 1897).

25. Workman, *City That Grew*, p. 72.

26. *City of Los Angeles* v. *Pomeroy*, 124 Cal. 597, 63.

27. Spaulding, *History and... Reminiscences*, p. 321.

28. City of Los Angeles, "Charter as Adopted January 1889 and Amended January 1903," art. XVIII, pp. 58-60.

29. Ibid., art. XXII, sec. 219, p. 57.

30. Quoted in John Russell McCarthy, "Water: The Story of Bill Mulholland," *Los Angeles Saturday Night*, February 12, 1938.

31. Robert William Matson, *William Mulholland: A Forgotten Forefather* (1967), p. 5.

32. H. A. Van Norman, "Memoir of William Mulholland," *Transactions of the American Society of Civil Engineers* (1936), pp. 1604-8.

33. Quoted in Richard Prosser, "William Mulholland: Maker of Los Angeles," *Western Construction News* (April 25, 1926), pp. 43-44.

34. I have been unable to find any trace of this autobiographical sketch. Mulholland, however, made it available to Elisabeth Mathieu Spriggs, and she quotes from it extensively in her thesis, "The History of the Domestic Water Supply of Los Angeles," January 1, 1931. The passage quoted here appears on page 67.

35. Ibid., p. 69.

36. Thomas Brooks, *Notes on Los Angeles Water Supply* (1938), n.p.

37. Quoted in Prosser, "William Mulholland."

38. See, e.g., Brooks, *Notes*; Van Norman, "Memoir"; Prosser, "William Mulholland"; W. W. Hurlbut, "The Man and the Engineer," *Western Construction News* (April 25, 1926), p. 44; Meyer Lissner, "Bill Mulholland," *American Magazine* (April 1912), pp. 674-76; and Joseph B. Lippincott, "Mulholland's Memory," *Civil Engineering* (March 1939), p. 199.

39. Quoted in McCarthy, "Water," December 18, 1937.

40. Lissner, "Bill Mulholland."

41. Burt A. Heinly, "Aladdin of the Aqueduct," *Sunset* (April 1912), pp. 465-67.

42. Joseph B. Lippincott, "William Mulholland: Engineer, Pioneer, Raconteur," *Civil Engineering* (March 1941), pp. 161-64.

43. Spriggs, "History of the Domestic Water Supply," pp. 57-58.

44. Quoted in *Constructive Californians* (Los Angeles, 1926), p. 132.

45. Mead, *Irrigation Investigations*, p. 344. See also Donald J. Pisani, "Water Law Reform in California, 1900-1913," *Agricultural History* (April 1980), pp. 295-317.

46. Ibid., pp. 33-35.

47. Ibid., p. 344.

48. City of Los Angeles, Department of Public Works, *First Annual Report of the Chief Engineer of the Los Angeles Aqueduct to the Board of Public Works* (March 15, 1907), p. 4. (Hereinafter cited as Los Angeles, *First Report of Chief Engineer.*)

49. Moody, "Los Angeles and the Owens River."

50. Brooks, *Notes.*

51. United States Department of the Interior, United States Geological Survey, *Underflow Tests in the Drainage Basin of the Los Angeles River*, by Homer Hamlin (1905), p. 40.

52. Moody, "Los Angeles and the Owens River"; Guinn, *History of . . . Los Angeles and Environs*, p. 398.

53. Heinly, "Aladdin."
54. Moody, "Los Angeles and the Owens River."
55. Los Angeles, *First Report of Chief Engineer*, p. 4.

CHAPTER TWO
Competing Public Interests

1. William E. Smythe, *The Conquest of Arid America* (1900), p. 140.
2. Ibid., p. 147.
3. United States Department of Agriculture, Office of Experiment Stations, *Report of Irrigation Investigations in California*, by Elwood Mead, Bulletin 100 (1901), p. 17. (Hereinafter cited as Mead, *Irrigation Investigations*.)
4. Ibid., p. 346. The statement quoted here is by Edward Boggs.
5. *Lux v. Haggin*, 69 Cal. 255. See also Walton Bean, *California: An Interpretive History* (1968), pp. 225-26, 279, and Ralph J. Roske, *Everyman's Eden* (1968), p. 409.
6. See Samuel P. Hays, *Conservation and the Gospel of Efficiency* (1959), pp. 21-68; Harold H. Dunham, *Government Handout* (1941); and Paul W. Gates, "Public Land Disposal in California," *Agricultural History* (January 1975).
7. See Charles P. Korr, "William Hammond Hall: The Failure of Attempts at State Water Planning in California, 1878-1888," *Historical Society of Southern California Quarterly* (December 1963), and William L. Kahrl, ed., *The California Water Atlas* (1979), p. 23.
8. Smythe, *Conquest*, p. 140; Bean, *California*, pp. 276-77; Kahrl, *California Water Atlas*, pp. 21-24. See also Oscar Osburn Winther, "The Colony System of Southern California," *Agricultural History* (July 1953).
9. Mead, *Irrigation Investigations*, pp. 18, 24, 32, 36, 40.
10. Ibid., p. 32.
11. Smythe, *Conquest*, p. 131.
12. Ibid., p. 145.
13. John Muir, "In the Heart of the California Alps," *Scribner's* (July 1880). See also Darryl R. Goehring, "Bishop California: A Recreational Satellite" (thesis, 1966); Don Goldman, "Owens Valley and Its Water" (thesis, December 1960); Paul Bateman, "Geology," in Genny Schumacher Smith, ed., *Deepest Valley* (Los Altos, Calif., 1978); and California Department of Natural Resources, Division of Mines, *Salt in California*, by W. E. Ver Planck (1957).

14. Julian H. Steward, "Ethnography of the Owens Valley Paiute," *University of California Publications in American Archaeology and Ethnology*, 33 (1933), pp. 247-50; Goehring, "Bishop," p. 36; Harry Erlich and P. N. McGauhey, "Economic Evaluation of Water," University of California Water Resources Center, *Jurisdictional Considerations in Water Resources Management*, Contribution no. 42, pt. 2, p. 45n; correspondence from "Quis," *Los Angeles Star*, August 27, 1859.

15. Philip J. Wilke and Harry W. Lawton, eds., *The Expedition of Captain J. W. Davidson from Fort Tejon to the Owens Valley in 1859* (1976), pp. 25-27.

16. *Inyo County California, Anno Domini 1912*, prepared by the *Inyo Register* (1912); Willie Arthur Chalfant, *The Story of Inyo* (1922), p. 302; Peggy and Clarence Streeter, eds., *Saga of Inyo County* (1977), p. 21.

17. Chalfant, *Story of Inyo*, 1st ed., pp. 295-98; Mary DeDecker, "The Eastern Sierra: From the Days of Gold to the Time of Recreation," *T 'n' T* (March-April 1967).

18. Ruth E. Baugh, "Land Use Changes in the Bishop Area of Owens Valley, California," *Economic Geography* (January 1937); United States Census Office, *Twelfth Census of Agriculture*, vol. VI, pt. 2: "Crops and Irrigation" (Washington, D.C., 1902), p. 94.

19. Quoted in Streeter, *Saga of Inyo*, pp. 212-13.

20. Ibid., p. 9.

21. Wilke and Lawton, *Expedition*, p. 24.

22. Streeter, *Saga of Inyo*, p. 10.

23. See, e.g., City of Los Angeles, Department of Public Service, *Owens Valley and the Los Angeles Aqueduct* (January 1925); City of Los Angeles, Department of Water and Power, *The Water Trail* by Don J. Kinsey (1928), p. 7; article on behalf of the Los Angeles Department of Water and Power in Streeter, *Saga of Inyo*, pp. 41-43; and Louis H. Winnard, "The Rape That's Not," *Los Angeles Times*, October 26, 1976 (also in *Intake* [December 1976]).

24. Report of Thomas H. Means to Joseph B. Lippincott, September 14, 1904, in National Archives, Records of the Bureau of Reclamation, Record Group 115, Owens Valley Project File no. 527 (hereinafter cited as NA BUREC RG 115 OV 527).

25. United States *Census of Agriculture, 1900*, vol. V, pt. 1: "Farms, Livestock and Animal Products," pp. 62, 268; vol. VI, pt. 2, pp. 826, 828.

26. United States *Census of Agriculture, 1900*, vol. VI, pt. 2, p. 231.

27. Means, Report, September 14, 1904, NA BUREC RG 115 OV 527.

28. United States *Census of Agriculture, 1900*, vol. VI, pt. 2, pp. 155,

624. See also Erlich and McGauhey, *Jurisdictional Considerations*, fig. OR-9, p. 93, and table OR-5, p. 94.

29. Dorothy C. Cragen, "A Brief History of Inyo County," *Eastern California Museum Handbook* (Independence, Calif., 1961), pp. 10-11.

30. Chalfant, *Story of Inyo*, 1st ed., pp. 239, 302.

31. Frances Corey Krautter, *The Story of Keeler* (1959).

32. Baugh, "Land Use Changes," p. 32.

33. Remi Nadeau, *The Water Seekers* (1950), p. 128.

34. C. Lorin Ray, ed., *Mementos of Bishop, California, 1861-1961: 100 Years of Real Living* (1961), p. 15; *Inyo County California*, p. 15; Streeter, *Saga of Inyo*, pp. 32, 101-4.

35. Krautter, *Story of Keeler*.

36. *Los Angeles Times*, October 10, 1901.

37. Newell to Lippincott, April 29, 1903, NA BUREC RG 115 OV 527.

38. "Record of an Interview with J. C. Clausen by Mr. Chapell," November 30 [no year], O. W. Larson Papers, box 1, Water Filings, California Historical Society Library.

39. Mary Austin, *Land of Little Rain*, special ed. with photography by Ansel Adams (New York, 1950), p. 1.

40. Chalfant, *Story of Inyo*, 1st ed., pp. 312-14; *Skidoo News*, April 25, 1908.

41. "Record of an Interview with J. C. Clausen," Larson Papers.

42. There were initially two forms of withdrawal: the first form, intended to be used for lands needed for actual works, prohibited the filing of any type of entry; the second form, intended to cover irrigable areas, prohibited entry under all but the Homestead Act. Of the initial series of withdrawals made for the Owens Valley project in 1903 and 1904, all but 71,000 acres were of the second form. See A. W. Dent, Memorandum for the Secretary, May 11, 1928, in National Archives, Department of the Interior, Office of the Secretary, Central Classified File, Record Group 48, File 8-3, pt. 1, "Orland/Owens River." (Hereinafter cited as NA INT RG 48 8-3.) See also Memorandum for Mr. Bissell, [no day], 1928, same location; sec. 3 of the Act of June 17, 1902 (32 Stat. L. 388); and the Administrative Decisions of the Secretary of the Interior of February 11, 1903 (32 L.D. 6), June 28, 1904 (33 L.D. 360), July 12, 1904 (33 L.D. 104), and February 18, 1905 (33 L.D. 415).

43. Lippincott to Newell, July 6, 1903, and Newell to Lippincott, July 20, 1903, NA BUREC RG 115 OV 527.

44. Lippincott to Newell, August 6, 1903, ibid.

45. See Lippincott to Newell, September 24, 1903; Newell to Lippin-

cott, October 2, 1903; and Newell to Lippincott, December 11, 1903, ibid.

46. Holgate to Lippincott, December 5, 1903, National Archives, Reclamation Service, General File 1902-1919, Record Group 115, File 63-B "Correspondence re Right of Way Applications in Owens River Valley." (Hereinafter cited as NA BUREC RG 115 63-B.)

47. Holgate to Newell, December 7, 1903, NA BUREC RG 115 63-B.

48. Holgate to Lippincott, December 5, 1903, ibid.

49. See Holgate to Lippincott, December 1, 1903; Davis to Holgate, March 2, 1904; and Holgate to Newell, December 7, 1903, ibid.

50. Holgate to Lippincott, December 5, 1903, ibid.

51. United States Department of the Interior, United States Geological Survey, *Second Annual Report of the Reclamation Service, 1902-03* (Washington, 1904), pp. 54-55, 93-96. (Hereinafter cited as Reclamation Service, *Second Annual Report.*)

52. Joseph B. Lippincott, "The Reclamation Service in California," *Forestry and Irrigation* (April, 1904).

53. Lippincott to Newell, April 30, 1904, NA BUREC RG 115 OV 527. See also Lippincott to Hydrographer, USGS, September 1, 1904, ibid.

54. Lippincott to Newell, July 6, 1903, ibid.

55. Kenneth Q. Volk and Edgar Alan Rowe, "Memoir of Joseph B. Lippincott," *Transactions of the American Society of Civil Engineers* (1943), pp. 1543-50; Lippincott to Newell, June 30, 1905, and Walcott to Secretary of the Interior, December 1, 1893, in National Personnel Records Center, Civilian Personnel Records, Status of Employees, File 23 Alphabetical, Joseph Barlow Lippincott. (Hereinafter cited as NPRC Lippincott Personnel File.)

56. See Testimony of J. B. Lippincott, City of Los Angeles, Aqueduct Investigation Board, *Report . . . to the City Council of Los Angeles* (August 31, 1912), p. 53. See also United States Geological Survey, Water Supply and Irrigation Papers nos. 59 and 60, *Development and Application of Water near San Bernardino, Colton, and Riverside, California* (Washington, D.C., 1902) and no. 81, *California Hydrography* (Washington, D.C., 1903), both by Lippincott.

57. Walcott to Secretary of the Interior, May 24, 1899, NPRC Lippincott Personnel File.

58. Newell to Walcott, June 24, 1903, in Bissell Memorandum, NA INT RG 48 8-3; Lippincott to Newell, July 25, 1904, Library of Congress, Newell Papers; Lippincott to Newell, June 30, 1905, and Walcott to Hitchcock, November 6, 1905, NPRC Lippincott Personnel File.

59. Vincent Ostrom, *Water and Politics: A Study of Water Policies and*

Administration in the Development of Los Angeles (1953), pp. 46, 53; J. B. Lippincott, "Mulholland's Memory," *Civil Engineering* (March 1939).

60. See A. E. Chandler to Newell, November 22, 1905, NA BUREC RG 115 63-B; and Newell to E. A. Hitchcock, December 9, 1905, NPRC Lippincott Personnel File.

61. Testimony of Mulholland, City of Los Angeles, Aqueduct Investigation Board, *Report*, p. 42.

62. Davis to Hitchcock, September 12, 1905, NA BUREC RG 115 63-B.

63. City of Los Angeles, Department of Public Works, *First Annual Report of the Chief Engineer of the Los Angeles Aqueduct to the Board of Public Works* (March 15, 1907), p. 17. (Hereinafter cited as Los Angeles, *First Report of Chief Engineer*.) *Los Angeles Times*, August 5, 1905; *Los Angeles Express*, August 4, 1905.

64. See S. W. Austin, "The Owens River Reclamation Project," in Transcript of Owens Valley Project Hearing Board, NA BUREC RG 115 63-B; also in Perkins to Hitchcock, July 25, 1905, in National Archives, Department of the Interior, Lands and Railroads Division, Record Group 48, Reclamation Projects box 37 (hereinafter cited as NA L&RR RG 48 37). See also Testimony of Lippincott, City of Los Angeles, Aqueduct Investigation Board, *Report*, p. 53, and the letter from Eaton quoted in the same report, p. 7. In the subsequent investigations of Eaton's relationship with Lippincott, Eaton denied being in the valley in the spring of 1904, but Lippincott confirmed Austin's account. See Eaton to O'Fallon, September 29, 1905, in NPRC Lippincott Personnel File, and Lippincott to W. H. Sanders, July 27, 1905, NA BUREC RG 115 63-B.

65. See Sworn Statement of James W. Sherwin, September 30, 1905, submitted as part of the report of S. F. O'Fallon to Thomas Ryan, October 5, 1905, NPRC Lippincott Personnel File. See also Lippincott to Clausen, July 23, 1904, Larson Papers.

66. "Record of an Interview with J. C. Clausen," Larson Papers.

67. Testimony of E. T. Earl, City of Los Angeles, Aqueduct Investigation Board, *Report*, p. 46.

68. *Los Angeles Examiner*, August 5, 1905.

69. See, e.g., Testimony of Lippincott, City of Los Angeles, Aqueduct Investigation Board, *Report*, p. 53; also Mulholland to O'Fallon, October 3, 1905, NPRC Lippincott Personnel File.

70. Lippincott to Newell, September 17, 1904, NPRC Lippincott Personnel File.

71. "Record of an Interview with J. C. Clausen," Larson Papers.

72. Means, Report, September 14, 1904, NA BUREC RG 115 OV 527.
73. Report of J. C. Clausen; Means, Report, ibid.
74. J. S. Cotton, "Agricultural Conditions of Inyo County, California" (1905), in Inyo Free Library.
75. *Inyo Independent*, August 8, 1870.
76. Chalfant, *Story of Inyo*, 1st ed., p. 338.
77. Report of J. C. Clausen, p. 23, NA BUREC RG 115 OV 527.
78. United States *Census of Agriculture, 1900*, vol. VI, pt. 2, p. 826.
79. Report of J. C. Clausen, pp. 47-48, NA BUREC RG 115 OV 527. See also United States Geological Survey, Water Supply and Irrigation Paper no. 181, *The Geology and Water Resources of the Owens Valley, California*, by Willis T. Lee (Washington, D.C., 1906).
80. Means, Report, September 14, 1904, NA BUREC RG 115 OV 527.
81. Report of J. C. Clausen, pp. 28-29, 66-68, ibid.
82. "Record of an Interview with J. C. Clausen," Larson Papers.
83. Report of J. C. Clausen, NA BUREC RG 115 OV 527.
84. Petition, "People of the Owens Valley" to Hitchcock, November [no day], 1904, ibid.
85. Lippincott to Newell, September 5, 1905, NPRC Lippincott Personnel File; Testimony of Lippincott, City of Los Angeles, Aqueduct Investigation Board, *Report*, p. 53; Lippincott to Newell, October 4, 1905, NA BUREC RG 115 63-B.
86. Eaton to W. B. Mathews, March 25, 1905, City of Los Angeles, Aqueduct Investigation Board, *Report*, p. 8.
87. Newell to George Watterson, December 6, 1904, NA BUREC RG 115 OV 527-A.
88. Davis to Hitchcock, September 12, 1905, NA BUREC RG 115 63-B.
89. United States Department of the Interior, United States Geological Survey, *Third Annual Report of the Reclamation Service, 1903-04* (Washington, D.C., 1905), pp. 50-54, 64-65, 200 (hereinafter cited as Reclamation Service, *Third Annual Report*). F. H. Newell, "The Reclamation Service," *Popular Science Monthly* (December 1904).
90. Reclamation Service, *Third Annual Report*, pp. 29, 32.
91. Reclamation Service, *Second Annual Report*, pp. 53-54; Lippincott, "Reclamation Service in California."
92. Newell, Circular Letter, November 1, 1904, NPRC Lippincott Personnel File.
93. Report of J. C. Clausen, pp. 70-72, NA BUREC RG 115 OV 527; Chalfant, *Story of Inyo*, 2nd ed., pp. 340-41.

94. Newell, Circular Letter, November 1, 1904, NPRC Lippincott Personnel File.

95. Reclamation Service, *Third Annual Report*, pp. 50-52.

96. See Reclamation Service, *Second Annual Report*, pp. 53-54, for the problems on the Kings River.

97. Lippincott to Newell, May 26, 1905, and Lippincott to Davis, August 8, 1905, NPRC Lippincott Personnel File.

98. Lippincott to Hydrographer, USGS, September 1, 1904, NA BU-REC RG 115 OV 527; Reclamation Service, *Third Annual Report*, p. 65.

99. Lippincott to Newell, February 10, 1905, and Newell to Lippincott, February 17, 1905, NA BUREC RG 115 63-B.

100. See Lippincott to Newell, May 26, 1905, June 30, 1905, and September 6, 1905, NPRC Lippincott Personnel File.

101. Testimony of Mulholland, City of Los Angeles, Aqueduct Investigation Board, *Report*, p. 43.

102. Minutes of the Regular Meeting of the Board of Commissioners of the Water Department, March 6, 1905, NPRC Lippincott Personnel File. See also the record of appointments and salaries in the same location. Chalfant was clearly wrong when he claimed in the first edition of his *Story of Inyo* (p. 324) that Lippincott and an aide (presumably Parker) were paid $1,000 for three months of work on this report. Nordskog, however, claimed that Lippincott was paid a total of $4,511.93 for services rendered to Los Angeles in April, June, September, and November, 1905, and in January, 1906. See Andrae Nordskog, "Communication to the California Legislature Relating to the Owens Valley Water Situation," *Journal of the California Assembly*, April 27, 1931, p. 14.

103. The paper as a whole was reprinted in *Out West* (July 1905). See also the postscript to the letter of S. W. Austin and Richard Fysh to W. A. Richards, July 12, 1905, NA BUREC RG 115 63-B.

104. *Report of S. F. O'Fallon*, pp. 20, 51, NPRC Lippincott Personnel File.

105. Minutes of the Regular Meeting of the Board of Commissioners of the Water Department, May 22, 1905, ibid.

106. Lippincott to Newell, May 26, 1905, ibid.

107. United States Department of the Interior, United States Geological Survey, Water Supply and Irrigation Paper no. 146, *Proceedings of the Second Conference of Engineers of the Reclamation Service* (Washington, D.C., 1905), p. 235.

108. Newell to Lippincott, May 17, 1905, NPRC Lippincott Personnel File.

109. Lippincott to Newell, May 26, 1905, ibid.

110. Newell to Lippincott, June 3, 1905, ibid.

111. Lippincott to Newell, June 8, 1905, ibid.

112. Lippincott to Newell, June 30, 1905, ibid.

113. Lippincott to Eaton, March 3, 1905, ibid.; Lippincott to Davis, March 10, 1905; Davis to Lippincott, March 18, 1905; Lippincott to Davis, March 20, 1905—NA BUREC RG 115 63-B.

114. See Sworn Statements of Richard Fysh, September 19, 1905, and S. W. Austin, September 22, 1905, also *Report of S. F. O'Fallon*, pp. 28-30—NPRC Lippincott Personnel File.

115. Eaton to Mathews, March 23, 1905, in City of Los Angeles, Aqueduct Investigation Board, *Report*, p. 8.

116. Holgate to Newell, December 7, 1903, NA BUREC RG 115 63-B.

117. *Report of S. F. O'Fallon*, p. 29, NPRC Lippincott Personnel File.

118. Bissell Memorandum, NA INT RG 48 8-3.

119. *Los Angeles Express*, August 4, 1905.

120. See Lippincott to Davis, March 10, 1905, NA BUREC RG 115 63-B.

121. Eaton to Lippincott, March 16, 1905; Lippincott to Clausen, March 20, 1905; Clausen to Lippincott, March 24, 1905; Lippincott to Newell, May 29, 1905—NPRC Lippincott Personnel File.

122. Eaton to Mathews, March 25, 1905, in City of Los Angeles, Aqueduct Investigation Board, *Report*, p. 154.

123. City of Los Angeles, Department of Public Service, *Complete Report on Construction of the Los Angeles Aqueduct* (Los Angeles, 1916), p. 48.

124. Testimony of J. M. Elliott, City of Los Angeles, Aqueduct Investigation Board, *Report*, p. 35.

125. Boyle Workman, *The City that Grew* (1935), p. 304.

126. *Los Angeles Express*, August 4, 1905. See also *Los Angeles Examiner*, July 29, 1905.

127. Report of Ingle Carpenter, City of Los Angeles, Aqueduct Investigation Board, *Report*, p. 10. See also Minutes of the Board of Commissioners of the Water Department for May 22, May 29, and June 5, 1905, NPRC Lippincott Personnel File.

128. *Los Angeles Express*, August 4, 1905; *Los Angeles Examiner*, July 20, 1905; City of Los Angeles, Aqueduct Investigation Board, *Report*, p. 7; Los Angeles, *First Report of Chief Engineer*, pp. 45-46, 78-86; City of Los Angeles, Department of Public Service, *Complete Report on Aqueduct*, p. 48; A. E. Chandler to Newell, November 22, 1905, NA BUREC RG 115 63-B.

129. Testimony of Elliott, City of Los Angeles, Aqueduct Investigation Board, *Report*, p. 38.

130. Austin, "Owens River Reclamation Project," NA BUREC RG 115 63-B. Eaton confirmed these statements in his letter to O'Fallon, September 29, 1905, NPRC Lippincott Personnel File.

131. Joseph B. Lippincott, "Mountain Stream Characteristics of Southern California," *Out West* (July 1905), and "General Outlook for Reclamation Work in California," *Forestry and Irrigation* (August 1905).

132. "Record of an Interview with J.C. Clausen," Larson Papers.

133. Testimony of Elliott, City of Los Angeles, Aqueduct Investigation Board, *Report*, p. 38; Statement of E.M. Nordyke in State of California, State Engineer W.F. McClure, *Letter of Transmittal and Report of State Engineer Concerning the Owens Valley-Los Angeles Controversy to Governor Friend Wm. Richardson* (Sacramento, 1925), p. 44.

134. Newell to Lippincott, May 24, 1905, NA BUREC RG 115 63-B.

135. Lippincott to Clausen, June 7, 1905, NA BUREC RG 115 OV 527.

136. Newell to Davis, June 6, 1905, in Bissell Memorandum, NA INT RG 48 8-3.

137. Davis to Lippincott, June 13, 1905, NA BUREC RG 115 OV 527; Davis to Newell, June 10 and June 22, 1905, in Bissell Memorandum, NA INT RG 48 8-3; United States Department of the Interior, United States Geological Survey, Water Supply and Irrigation Paper no. 139, *Development of Underground Waters in the Western Coastal Plain Region of Southern California*, by Walter C. Mendenhall (Washington, D.C., 1905). See also, by the same author, "Report on Underground Waters in the Vicinity of Los Angeles," which appears as app. A to Los Angeles, *First Report of Chief Engineer*. Mendenhall's endorsement of the aqueduct is quoted by Mulholland on pp. 12-14 of that report.

138. Davis to Newell, June 21 and June 22, 1905, in Bissell Memorandum, NA INT RG 48 8-3.

139. Newell to Davis, June 11, 1905, ibid.

140. Davis to D.C. Henny, June 13, 1905, ibid.

141. Henny to Davis, June 20, 1905, ibid. See also Henny to Hydrographer, USGS, June 20, 1905, NA BUREC RG 115 63-B.

142. Davis to Hitchcock, September 12, 1905, ibid. See also Walcott to Hitchcock, November 6, 1905, NPRC Lippincott Personnel File.

143. Newell to Davis, June 21, 1905, NA BUREC RG 115 63-B.

144. Newell to Lippincott, June 3, 1905, NPRC Lippincott Personnel File.

145. James P. Vroman, Secretary to the Board of Water Commissioners, to Newell, June 5, 1905, Exhibit 4 in Transcript of Owens Valley Project Board Hearing, NA BUREC RG 115 63-B.
146. See *Report of S. F. O'Fallon*, pp. 9-11, and Lippincott to Newell, September 7, 1905, NPRC Lippincott Personnel File.
147. Davis to Newell, June 22, 1905, in Bissell Memorandum, NA INT RG 48 8-3.
148. *Report of S. F. O'Fallon*, pp. 11-13, 52, NPRC Lippincott Personnel File.
149. Ibid., pp. 33-35.
150. Austin and Fysh to Richards, July 12, 1905, NA BUREC RG 115 63-B.
151. Ibid.
152. See G. C. Perkins to Hitchcock, July 25, 1905, NA L&RR RG 48 37.
153. See Davis to Newell, July 28, 1905, NA BUREC RG 115 63-B.
154. Telegram, Lippincott to Eaton, July 27, 1905, NPRC Lippincott Personnel File.
155. Lippincott to Eaton, July 27, 1905, ibid.
156. Statement of Richard Fysh, September 19, 1905, in *Report of S. F. O'Fallon*, ibid.
157. See Eaton to Lippincott, July 29, 1905, ibid.; *Inyo Independent*, August 4, 1905.
158. See Lippincott to Clausen, July 19, 1905, Larson Papers.
159. Transcript, Owens Valley Project Board Hearing, pp. 1-5, NA BUREC RG 115 63-B.
160. Lippincott to Sanders, July 27, 1905, Exhibit 5, ibid.
161. Ibid., pp. 5-19.
162. Ibid., pp. 20-21.
163. Ibid., pp. 22-28.
164. *Los Angeles Times*, July 29, 1905.
165. Ibid.

CHAPTER THREE

The Politics of Appropriation

1. *Los Angeles Express*, August 4, 1905.
2. *Los Angeles Examiner*, July 30, 1905; *Los Angeles Times*, July 30, 1905.

3. Julia Norton McCorkle, "A History of Los Angeles Journalism" *Historical Society of Southern California* (1916), pp. 29, 50-51.

4. Minutes of the Regular Meeting of the Board of Commissioners, Water Department of the City of Los Angeles, July 31, 1905, in National Personnel Records Center, Civilian Personnel Records, Status of Employees, File 23 Alphabetical, Joseph Barlow Lippincott. (Hereinafter cited as NPRC Lippincott Personnel File.)

5. *Los Angeles Examiner*, August 2 and August 20, 1905.

6. *Los Angeles Times*, July 31, 1905.

7. Testimony of Henry Loewenthal in City of Los Angeles, Aqueduct Investigation Board, *Report . . . to the City Council of Los Angeles* (August 31, 1912), p. 95.

8. See, e.g., *Los Angeles Examiner*, August 16 and August 18, 1905.

9. *Los Angeles Times*, August 17-21, 1905.

10. *Los Angeles Express*, August 4, 1905.

11. Testimony of William Mulholland, City of Los Angeles, Aqueduct Investigation Board, *Report*, p. 44. See also Anthony Cifarelli, "The Owens River Aqueduct and the *Los Angeles Times*: A Study in Early Twentieth Century Business Ethics and Journalism" (thesis, 1969), p. 26.

12. *Los Angeles Examiner*, August 17, 1905.

13. Ibid., August 28, 1905.

14. Erwin Cooper, *Aqueduct Empire: A Guide to Water in California, Its Turbulent History, and Its Management Today* (1968), p. 60; United States Department of Agriculture, Weather Bureau, *Climatic Summary of the United States*, sec. 18: "Southern California and Owens Valley" (1930), pp. 3-5, 17, 18.

15. Remi Nadeau, *The Water Seekers* (1950) pp. 20-21.

16. Rainfall in August 1904 totaled 0.17 inches as compared with the average rainfall for August in the period 1891-1930 of 0.03 inches. The next greatest August rainfall in this forty-year period occurred in 1901: 0.09 inches. There was no August rainfall at all in thirty-one of the forty years included in the United States Weather Bureau's *Climatic Summary*, sec. 18, pp. 3-5, 17, 18.

17. Long-term averages for precipitation can and usually do vary between reporting agencies. Walter Mendenhall in his reports for the United States Geological Survey fixed a long-term average of 15.60 inches of precipitation for Los Angeles in the twenty-nine-year period between the water years 1877-78 and 1904-05. His recorded level of precipitation for the 1904-05 water year of 19.52 inches was 25 percent above this average. See City of Los Angeles, Department of Public Works, *First Annual Report of the Chief Engineer of the Los Angeles Aqueduct to the Board of Public*

Works (March 15, 1907), pp. 69-71. (Hereinafter cited as Los Angeles, *First Report of Chief Engineer*.) The United States Weather Bureau's *Climatic Summary* recorded an overall level of precipitation of 19.19 inches in calendar year 1905, 28 percent above its long-term average of 14.95 inches.

18. See Robert Gottlieb and Irene Wolt, *Thinking Big: The Story of the Los Angeles Times, Its Publishers, and Their Influence on Southern California* (1977), pp. 127-28.
19. *Los Angeles Times*, July 31, 1905.
20. Cifarelli, "Owens River Aqueduct," p. 40.
21. See City of Los Angeles, Board of Water Commissioners, *Fourth Annual Report* (Los Angeles, 1905), p. 4. See also *Los Angeles Examiner*, July 31, 1905.
22. Cifarelli, "Owens River Aqueduct," p. 132.
23. John Russell McCarthy, "Water: The Story of Bill Mulholland," *Los Angeles Saturday Night*, December 11, 1937.
24. *Los Angeles Herald*, September 3, 1905.
25. Report of S.F. O'Fallon, October 5, 1905, p. 52, NPRC, Lippincott Personnel File.
26. *Los Angeles Examiner*, July 31, 1905. Mulholland at first claimed that the city's residents attained an average daily per capita consumption level of 190 gallons only on the hottest days. He later asserted that this peak rate of consumption was constant for all the months of May through October; see Los Angeles, *First Report of Chief Engineer*, pp. 6-8.
27. Los Angeles, *First Report of Chief Engineer*, pp. 6-8.
28. See City of Los Angeles, Department of Public Service, *Complete Report on Construction of the Los Angeles Aqueduct* (Los Angeles, 1916), p. 35. See also Thomas H. Means, "Additional Water Supply for the City of Los Angeles in Owens Valley and Mono Basin" (San Francisco, January 1924) in Water Resources Center Archives, University of California, Berkeley, Means Papers.
29. Using figures supplied by the Los Angeles Board of Water Commissioners, Thomas Means in 1924 reported that the flow of the Los Angeles River measured at the Narrows was forty-three cubic feet per second in water year 1904-05 and forty-four cubic feet per second in 1905-06; see Means, "Additional Water for Los Angeles," p. 4. In 1928, however, the Department of Water and Power reported that the continuous flow of the river in calendar year 1905 was fifty-one cubic feet per second; see City of Los Angeles, Department of Water and Power, *Data on Available Water Supply and Future Requirements of the City of Los Angeles and the Metropolitan Area* (October 1928), p. 44.

30. See State of California, Department of Water Resources, *Interim Report on Inyo-Mono Area Water Resources Investigation* (1965), p. 11; City of Los Angeles, Board of Public Service Commissioners, *Report on Available Water Supply of City of Los Angeles and Metropolitan Area,* by Louis C. Hill, J.B. Lippincott, and A.L. Sonderegger (1924), p. 50; Thomas Means, *Report on Mono Basin Water Supply for Southern California* (San Francisco, October (1923), p. 26; and William L. Kahrl, ed., *The California Water Atlas* (1979), p. 72.

31. The table below compares the streamflow records the city provided to its consultant Thomas Means in 1924 with those it published in its *Data on Available Water Supply* in 1928. See note 29 above.

Means		DWP	
Water year	cfs.	Water year	cfs.
1901-02	48	1902	48
1902-03	44	1903	48
1903-04	43	1904	50
1904-05	43	1905	51
1905-06	44	1906	54

32. Mulholland's comment appears in his "History of Water Supply Development for the Metropolitan Area of Los Angeles," *Hydraulic Engineering* (July 1928). See also City of Los Angeles, Department of Public Service, *Complete Report on Construction,* p. 10. The successive increases in population estimates appear in the following publications of the Department of Water and Power: *The Water Trail,* by Don J. Kinsey (1928); *The Water Miracle* (1936); and *William Mulholland: Father of the Los Angeles Municipal Water System* (1939).

33. United States Department of the Interior, United States Geological Survey, Water Supply and Irrigation Paper no. 81, *California Hydrography,* by J.B. Lippincott (1903), p. 23.

34. United States Department of the Interior, United States Geological Surveys, Water Supply and Irrigation Paper no. 138, *Development of Underground Waters in the Central Coastal Plain Region of Southern California,* by Walter C. Mendenhall (1905), p. 26.

35. Los Angeles, *First Report of Chief Engineer,* p. 73.

36. United States Department of the Interior, United States Geological Survey, Water Supply and Irrigation Paper no. 139, *Development of Underground Waters in the Western Coastal Plain Region of Southern California,* by Walter C. Mendenhall (1905), pp. 16-17.

37. City of Los Angeles, *Data on Available Water Supply*, p. 64; City of Los Angeles, Board of Public Service Commissioners, *Report on Available Water Supply*, p. 78.

38. City of Los Angeles, *Data on Available Water Supply*, p. 63; Los Angeles, *First Report of Chief Engineer*, pp. 6-8.

39. City of Los Angeles, *Data on Available Water Supply*, p. 44, reports the flow of the Los Angeles River increasing 6.25 percent from 48 cubic feet per second continuous flow in 1902 to 51 cubic feet per second in 1905. The overall average per capita consumption measured in gallons per day, however, is shown here to have declined 33.9 percent in the same period, from 242 to 160.

40. Ibid.

41. Los Angeles, *First Report of Chief Engineer*, p. 4.

42. See *Los Angeles Examiner*, August 20, 1905, and Thomas Brooks, *Notes on Los Angeles Water Supply* (1938).

43. *Los Angeles Examiner*, August 2, 1905. See also *Los Angeles Times*, July 31, 1905, regarding plans for canal and irrigation systems in the San Fernando-Burbank area.

44. See Testimony of J.M. Elliott, City of Los Angeles, Aqueduct Investigation Board, *Report*, p. 35.

45. See *Report of S. F. O'Fallon*, pp. 16-17, NPRC Lippincott Personnel File.

46. Report of Walter C. Mendenhall in Los Angeles, *First Report of Chief Engineer*, p. 14, app. A.

47. *Los Angeles Express*, August 4, 1905.

48. *Los Angeles Times*, September 7, 1905.

49. Los Angeles, *First Report of Chief Engineer*, pp. 16-17.

50. Charles A. Moody, "Los Angeles and the Owens River" *Out West* (October 1905).

51. *Los Angeles Examiner*, August 2, 1905.

52. Ibid., July 30, 1905.

53. Testimony of William Mulholland, City of Los Angeles, Aqueduct Investigation Board, *Report*, p. 42.

54. Ibid., p. 51.

55. Los Angeles, *First Report of Chief Engineer*, app. B, p. 88.

56. City of Los Angeles, *Complete Report on Construction*, p. 48. On October 15, 1906, the city revised its contract with Eaton to pay him a direct 5-percent commission on all the land sales he arranged.

57. *Los Angeles Times*, August 5, 1905. See also Minutes of the Regular Meeting of the Board of Commissioners of the Water Department, June 12, 1905, NPRC Lippincott Personnel File.

58. *Los Angeles Examiner*, August 15, 1905.

59. Ibid., August 16, 1905.

60. For further detail see Spencer Crump, *Henry Huntington and the Pacific Electric* (1970), pp. 11-16, and *Ride the Big Red Cars* (1970), pp. 36-38, 42-54, 58-74.

61. Gottlieb and Wolt, *Thinking Big*, p. 145.

62. Crump, *Ride the Big Red Cars*, pp. 109-115.

63. McCarthy, "Water," *Los Angeles Saturday Night*, November 13, 1937.

64. Vincent Ostrom, *Water and Politics: A Study of Water Policies and Administration in the Development of Los Angeles* (1953), p. 54.

65. *Los Angeles Times*, July 29, 1905.

66. Ibid., July 30 and August 10, 1905.

67. Gottlieb and Wolt, *Thinking Big*, pp. 24, 28.

68. *Los Angeles Examiner*, August 5, 1905.

69. *Los Angeles Times*, August 25, 1905.

70. Gottlieb and Wolt, *Thinking Big*, pp. 66-67.

71. Testimony of Henry Loewenthal, City of Los Angeles, Aqueduct Investigation Board, *Report*, p. 95.

72. *Los Angeles Times*, August 26, 1905. See also Testimony of E. T. Earl, City of Los Angeles, Aqueduct Investigation Board, *Report*, pp. 89-91.

73. *Los Angeles Examiner*, August 24 and August 28, 1905.

74. Ibid., August 24 and August 25, 1905.

75. Testimony of Elliott, City of Los Angeles, Aqueduct Investigation Board, *Report*, p. 35.

76. Crump, *Ride the Big Red Cars*, pp. 36-38.

77. Ibid., pp. 75-76.

78. Hank Johnston, *The Railroad that Lighted Southern California* (1965), p. 10.

79. Elmo Richardson, *The Politics of Conservation: Crusades and Controversies, 1897-1913* (1962), p. 15; Walton Bean, *California: An Interpretive History* (1968), p. 345.

80. Los Angeles, *First Report of Chief Engineer*, pp. 47-48.

81. United States Department of the Interior, United States Geological Survey, *Fourth Annual Report of the Reclamation Service* (Washington, D.C., 1906), p. 44.

82. See Crump, *Ride the Big Red Cars*, pp. 74-91. On March 19, 1906, Sherman sold the Los Angeles Pacific Railroad to Huntington's competitor, the Southern Pacific, only days after Huntington helped him secure a $12.5-million loan.

83. See, e.g., Bean, *California*, pp. 300-301.
84. See, e.g., Gottlieb and Wolt, *Thinking Big*, pp. 29-30.
85. Testimony of Earl, City of Los Angeles, Aqueduct Investigation Board, *Report*, p. 90.
86. *Los Angeles Times*, May 6, 1903.
87. Ibid., August 26, 1905.
88. *Los Angeles Examiner*, September 2, 1905.
89. *Los Angeles Examiner*, August 16, 1905; *Los Angeles Times*, August 22, 1905.
90. W.A. Swanberg, *Citizen Hearst* (1961), pp. 221-22.
91. Testimony of Loewenthal, City of Los Angeles, Aqueduct Investigation Board, *Report*, p. 95.
92. *Los Angeles Examiner*, September 3, 1905. The report of the Chamber of Commerce committee is quoted on pp. 19-20 of Los Angeles, *First Report of Chief Engineer*.
93. *Los Angeles Times*, September 3, 1905.
94. Ibid., September 6, 1905.
95. There were 27,740 ballots cast on December 4, 1904, and 23,736 cast on June 2, 1905, as compared to 11,500 cast in the aqueduct bond election of September 7, 1905. See Cifarelli, "Owens River Aqueduct," p. 76; and Gottlieb and Wolt, *Thinking Big*, p. 134.
96. *Los Angeles Times*, July 29, 1905; *Inyo Register*, August 3, 1905.
97. J.M. Guinn, *A History of California and an Extended History of Los Angeles and Environs* (1915), pp. 301-4.
98. Gottlieb and Wolt, *Thinking Big*, pp. 25-26.
99. See Charles F. Lummis, "The Struggle for Water" and "The Perils of Water Monopoly," *Land of Sunshine* (October and November 1901).
100. Mary Austin, *Earth Horizon* (1932), p. 290.
101. Carl Van Doren, Introduction, in Mary Austin, *Land of Little Rain*, special ed. with photography by Ansel Adams (New York, 1950), pp. xii-xv.
102. Austin, *Earth Horizon*, pp. 227, 241.
103. Ibid., p. 274. See also Helen MacKnight Doyle, *Mary Austin: Woman of Genius* (1939), pp. 28, 127.
104. C. Lorin Ray, ed., *Inyo, 1866-1966* (1966), pp. 60-61.
105. Doyle, *Mary Austin*, pp. 251-52.
106. Ibid., pp. 205-7.
107. Austin, *Earth Horizon*, pp. 235, 274.
108. Mary Austin to "Messrs. Houghton, Mifflin and Co.," November 5, 1902, reprinted in Doyle, *Mary Austin*, p. 201.

109. Austin, *Earth Horizon*, p. 243.

110. Doyle, *Mary Austin*, p. 38.

111. Ibid., p. 218.

112. *San Francisco Chronicle*, September 3, 1905.

113. S. W. Austin to President Theodore Roosevelt, August 4, 1905, National Archives, Reclamation Service, General File 1902-1919, Record Group 115, File 63-B, "Correspondence re Right of Way Applications in Owens River Valley." (Hereinafter cited as NA BUREC RG 115 63-B.)

114. See Petition to the Secretary of the Interior, August 9, 1905, in National Archives, Department of the Interior, Lands and Railroads Division, Reclamation Projects, Record Group 48, Box Number 37. (Hereinafter cited as NA L&RR RG 48 37.) See also Austin to Roosevelt, August 23, 1905, NA BUREC RG 115 63-B.

115. *Los Angeles Times*, July 29, 1905.

116. J. B. Lippincott to A. P. Davis, July 29, 1905, NA BUREC RG 115 63-B.

117. Personnel Committee to F. H. Newell, July 12, 1905, in Memorandum for Mr. Bissell, [no day], 1928, National Archives, Department of the Interior, Office of the Secretary, Central Classified File 1907-1936, Record Group 48, File 8-3 "Orland, Owens River." (Hereinafter cited as NA INT RG 48 8-3.)

118. D. C. Henny to Davis, August 2, 1905, NA BUREC RG 115 63-B. See also Henny to Davis, July 31, 1905, ibid.

119. Henny to Davis, "Personal," August 2, 1905, ibid.

120. See Davis to Newell, July 28, 1905, ibid.

121. Lippincott to Davis, July 29, 1905, ibid.

122. Davis to Newell, July 29, 1905, ibid.

123. Newell to Davis, August 14, 1905, ibid.

124. See, e.g., George Watterson to Newell, August 6, 1905; Davis to Watterson, August 7, 1905; Davis to E. A. Hitchcock, August 14, 1905; Senator George Nixon (Nevada) to Walcott, August 9, 1905; Davis to Hitchcock, August 11, 1905; and Davis to Henny, August 14, 1905—NA BUREC RG 115 63-B. See also Lesta V. Parker to Roosevelt, August 15, 1905, NA L&RR RG 48 37, and Thomas Ryan to Walcott, August 29, 1905, in National Archives, Records of the Bureau of Reclamation, Record Group 115, Owens Valley Project File no. 527 (hereinafter cited as NA BUREC RG 115 OV 527).

125. See Newell's note to Davis of August 6, 1905, on Lippincott to Newell, June 13, 1905, NPRC Lippincott Personnel File.

126. Davis to Henny, August 14, 1905, NA BUREC RG 115 63-B.

127. See Newell's note on Lippincott to Newell, June 30, 1905, NPRC Lippincott Personnel File.

128. *Report of S. F. O'Fallon*, pp. 33-35, 41, ibid.

129. See Lippincott to Walcott, September 1, 1905, NA BUREC RG 115 63-B.

130. P. R. Lehmann to Davis, August 2, 1905, ibid.

131. George Y. Wisner to Newell, August 19, 1905, in Bissell Memorandum, NA INT RG 48 8-3.

132. See Samuel P. Hays, *Conservation and the Gospel of Efficiency* (1959), pp. 242-45, 22-23; also Lawrence B. Lee, "100 Years of Reclamation Historiography," *Pacific Historical Review* (November 1978), pp. 515-21.

133. See Richardson, *Politics of Conservation*, pp. 27, 61-62; Hays, *Conservation and the Gospel of Efficiency*, pp. 13, 21-22.

134. United States Department of the Interior, United States Geological Survey, *Third Annual Report of the Reclamation Service* (Washington, D.C., 1905), pp. 53-54.

135. Wisner to Newell, August 19, 1905, Bissell Memorandum, NA INT RG 48 8-3; Henny to Davis, August 2, 1905, NA BUREC RG 115 63-B.

136. Henny to Davis, August 2, 1905, NA BUREC RG 115 63-B.

137. See Richardson, *Politics of Conservation*, pp. 22-23; Lee, "Reclamation Historiography," pp. 527, 538; Hays, *Conservation and the Gospel of Efficiency*, pp. 199-218, 242-45.

138. Thomas Ryan, Acting Secretary of the Interior, to Austin, August 30, 1905, NA L&RR RG 48 37.

139. Davis to Hitchcock, August 11, August 14, and September 12, 1905, NA BUREC RG 115 63-B.

140. Davis to Newell, August 24, 1905, ibid.

141. See Lippincott's Charge Sheet for August 6, 1905, NA BUREC RG 115 OV 527.

142. Davis to Newell, August 24, 1905, NA BUREC RG 115 63-B.

143. Davis to Hitchcock, August 31, 1905, ibid.

144. Telegram, Ryan to O'Fallon, August 31, 1905, ibid.

145. Ryan to O'Fallon, August 31, 1905, NPRC Lippincott Personnel File.

146. Ryan to Austin, August 30, 1905, NA L&RR RG 48 37.

147. Austin to Ryan, September 7, 1905, ibid. See also William Lorrimer to Hitchcock, September 11, 1905, ibid.

148. Lippincott to Newell, September 8, 1905, NPRC Lippincott Personnel File.

149. Lippincott to Hitchcock, September 12, 1905, NA BUREC RG 115 63-B. See also Lippincott to Newell, September 22, 1905, ibid.

150. Lippincott to Newell, September 19, 1905, NPRC Lippincott Personnel File.

151. See Newell to Lippincott, September 26, 1905, ibid.

152. Lippincott to Newell, September 28, 1905, NA BUREC RG 115 63-B. See also Newell to Lippincott, September 18, 1905, NPRC Lippincott Personnel File.

153. See Davis to Hitchcock, September 12, 1905, NA BUREC RG 115 63-B.

154. Newell to W. B. Mathews, September 12, 1905, ibid.

155. See, e.g., Hitchcock to Newell, November 1, 1905, and Newell to Hitchcock, November 6, 1905, ibid. The various files of the Reclamation Service and the Secretary of the Interior contain more than a dozen such exchanges.

156. Newell to Lippincott, September 26, 1905, NPRC Lippincott Personnel File.

157. Newell to Lippincott, November 3, 1905, NA BUREC RG 115 63-B.

158. Newell to Lippincott, November 8, 1905, ibid.

159. Newell to Sanders and Henny, November 8, 1905, and Henny to Newell, November 17, 1905, ibid.

160. Resolution, Donald W. Campbell to Lippincott, September 9, 1905, NPRC Lippincott Personnel File.

161. Lippincott to Newell, September 12, 1905, ibid.

162. See J. O. Koepfli to Hitchcock, October 6, 1905, ibid.

163. See Mulholland to O'Fallon, October 3, 1905, and Jon S. Fay to O'Fallon, October 4, 1905, ibid.

164. Regarding Flint, see Lippincott to Newell, September 28, 1905, ibid.

165. Richardson, *Politics of Conservation*, p. 43.

166. George C. Pardee to Hitchcock, September 15, 1905, and Hitchcock to Newell, September 28, 1905, NA L&RR RG 48 37.

167. See Austin to Pardee, September 24, 1905; Pardee to Newell, September 30, 1905; and Newell to Pardee, October 7, 1905—NA BUREC RG 115 63-B. See also Abraham Hoffman, "Origins of a Controversy: The United States Reclamation Service and the Owens Valley-Los Angeles Water Dispute," *Arizona and the West* (Winter 1977).

168. *Report of S. F. O'Fallon*, pp. 47-49, NPRC Lippincott Personnel File. See also Lippincott to Newell, September 5, 1905, ibid.

169. *Report of S.F. O'Fallon*, pp. 30, 31, 42, 50, 53-54, NPRC Lippincott Personnel File.

170. Ibid., pp. 54-55.

171. Ibid., pp. 56-57.

172. Davis to Lippincott, January 26, 1906, Bissell Memorandum, NA INT RG 48 8-3.

173. Los Angeles Chamber of Commerce to Walcott, February 2, 1906, ibid.

174. Pardee to Hitchcock, February 2, 1906, NA L&RR RG 48 37.

175. Walcott to Hitchcock, February 28, 1906, ibid.

176. Hitchcock to Walcott, March 1, 1906, ibid.

177. Walcott to Hitchcock, February 28, 1906, ibid.

178. J.S. Cotton, "Agricultural Conditions of Inyo County, California" Manuscript (1905), in Inyo Free Library.

179. Davis to Henny, August 14, 1905, NA BUREC RG 115 63-B.

180. Davis to Hitchcock, September 12, 1905, ibid.

181. F.H. Newell, "The Reclamation Service and the Owens Valley," *Out West* (October 1905), and "Work of the Reclamation Service in California," *Forestry and Irrigation* (August 1905).

182. See A.E. Chandler to Newell, November 10, November 15, and November 16, 1905, NA BUREC RG 115 63-B.

183. Mrs. A. Mattick to Roosevelt, September 11, 1905, NPRC Lippincott Personnel File.

184. Resolution of Board of Supervisors of the County of Inyo, October 5, 1905, and letter of transmittal, William Dehy to Hitchcock, October 7, 1905, ibid.

185. See Davis to Hitchcock, September 18, 1905, and Hitchcock to Newell, October 20, 1905, NA BUREC RG 115 63-B. See also Hitchcock to Walcott and Hitchcock to E.H. Sterling, both October 20, 1905, NPRC Lippincott Personnel File.

186. See Davis to Hitchcock, September 18, 1905; Ryan to Walcott, September 20, 1905; Newell to Owen McAleer (Mayor of Los Angeles), September 21, 1905; and McAleer to Newell, September 28, 1905—NA BUREC RG 115 63-B.

187. See Flint to Hitchcock, September 28, 1905, and Hitchcock to Flint, October 11, 1905, NPRC Lippincott Personnel File.

188. See United States, Congress, House, Subcommittee on Public Lands of the House Committee on Public Lands, *Hearings on H.R. 83, H.R. 727, H.R. 728, H.R. 1833, and H.R. 6697, May 19, 20, 21, 1947, and June 4, 5, 7, 14, 15, 1948*, 80th Congress, 2d session (1948).

189. McAleer to Newell, November 2, 1905, NA BUREC RG 115 63-B.
190. Resolution of the City Council of Los Angeles, December 11, 1905, NPRC Lippincott Personnel File.
191. See Editor's Introduction to Newell, "Reclamation Service and the Owens Valley."
192. Lippincott to Newell, October 4, 1905, NA BUREC RG 115 63-B.
193. See, e.g., C. E. Grunsky to Walcott, September 16, 1905, National Archives, Record Group 200, Papers of E. A. Hitchcock, Reclamation 1901-1906. (Hereinafter cited as NA 200 Hitchcock.)
194. Acting Director of Geological Survey to Hitchcock, September 1, 1905, NA BUREC RG 115 OV 527.
195. *Report of S. F. O'Fallon*, p. 40, NPRC Lippincott Personnel File.
196. William E. Smythe, "The Social Significance of the Owens River Project," *Out West* (October 1905).
197. See *Los Angeles Express*, August 4, 1905.
198. Louis H. Schwaebe, Los Angeles City Auditor, to Hitchcock, January 27, 1906, NA L&RR RG 48 37.
199. See, e.g., Los Angeles, *First Report of Chief Engineer*, pp. 16-17.
200. *Report of S. F. O'Fallon*, pp. 40-44, NPRC Lippincott Personnel File.
201. Austin to Roosevelt, August 23, 1905, NA BUREC RG 115 63-B.
202. Austin to Pardee, September 24, 1905, ibid.
203. Acting Director of the Geological Survey to Hitchcock, September 1, 1905, NA BUREC RG 115 OV 527.
204. Grunsky to Walcott, September 16, 1905, NA 200 Hitchcock.
205. Grunsky to Hitchcock, January 4, 1906, NA BUREC RG 115 63-B.
206. Henny to Newell, August 2, 1905, ibid.
207. *Report of S. F. O'Fallon*, p. 45, NPRC Lippincott Personnel File.
208. Chandler to Newell, November 22, 1905, NA BUREC RG 115 63-B.
209. See Newell to Hitchcock, December 2 and December 9, 1905, ibid.
210. *Report of S. F. O'Fallon*, p. 45, NPRC Lippincott Personnel File.
211. Sec. 4, P.L. 394, *U.S. Statutes at Large* 801 (June 30, 1906). See also United States, Congress, House, Committee on Public Lands, 66th Congress, *Hearings . . . on H.R. 406 . . . ,* October 31-November 4, 1919 (1919).
212. See S. C. Smith to Roosevelt, June 25, 1906, NA BUREC RG 115 63-B.
213. For Walcott's doubts, see Walcott to William Loeb (personal secretary to President Roosevelt), June 27, 1906, ibid.

214. See Los Angeles, *First Report of Chief Engineer*, p. 25; Guinn, *History of California*, pp. 307-9.

215. *Los Angeles Times*, June 23, 1906.

216. Ibid., June 24, 1906.

217. Henry F. Pringle, *Theodore Roosevelt* (1931), p. 302.

218. John Morton Blum, *The Republican Roosevelt* (1966), pp. 106-113.

219. Hays, *Conservation and the Gospel of Efficiency*, pp. 1-3.

220. Roosevelt to Hitchcock, June 25, 1906, repr. in Elting E. Morrison, ed., *The Letters of Theodore Roosevelt* (Cambridge, Mass., 1952), vol. V, pp. 315-16.

221. Ibid.

222. Hays, *Conservation and the Gospel of Efficiency*, pp. 72-73.

223. Richardson, *Politics of Conservation*, pp. 22-23.

224. See Willie Arthur Chalfant, *The Story of Inyo*, 2d ed. (1933), p. 355. See also *Los Angeles Times*, June 27 and June 28, 1906.

225. See sec. 6, P.L. 394, *U.S. Statutes at Large* 801 (June 30, 1906).

226. *Los Angeles Times*, June 29, 1906.

227. Roosevelt to Hitchcock, June 25, 1906, see note 220 above.

228. Roosevelt to Smith, June 26, 1906, NA BUREC RG 115 63-B.

229. *Los Angeles Times*, June 28, 1906.

230. Sec. 4, P.L. 394, *U.S. Statutes at Large* 801 (June 30, 1906). See also United States Department of the Interior, United States Geological Survey, *Fifth, Sixth,* and *Seventh Annual Reports* of the Reclamation Service, pp. 47, 30-31, and 65, respectively, for accounting of expenditures.

231. Testimony of Lippincott, City of Los Angeles, Aqueduct Investigation Board, *Report*, p. 54.

232. "The Theft in Water," *Inyo Magazine* (October 1908).

233. Lippincott to Newell, April 10, 1912, NA BUREC RG 115 63-B.

234. See chap. 3559, 34 *Stat.* 519 (June 27, 1906).

235. See Richardson, *Politics of Conservation*, pp. 61-62, 113; Hays, *Conservation and the Gospel of Efficiency*, pp. 246-48; Lee, "100 Years of Reclamation Historiography," pp. 519-21.

236. See Michael C. Robinson, *Water for the West* (Chicago, 1979), pp. 42-44; Arthur P. Davis, George W. Goethals, and William Mulholland, "Water Supply Problem of the East Bay Municipal Utility District," in East Bay Municipal Utility District, *Additional Water Supply of East Bay Municipal Utility District: A Report to the Board of Directors by Arthur Powell Davis* (October 1, 1924).

237. W. P. Yancy (secretary, Owens Valley Water Protective Association) to Hitchcock, October 28, 1905, NPRC Lippincott Personnel File.

238. See Austin to Hitchcock, October 24, 1905, ibid.

239. *Los Angeles Examiner*, October 16, 1905.

240. *San Francisco Chronicle*, October 21, 1905.

241. Lippincott to Newell, November 2, 1905, NA BUREC RG 115 63-B. See also Kahrl, ed., *California Water Atlas*, p. 39.

242. Chandler to Newell, November 10, 1905, NA BUREC RG 115 63-B. See also Walcott to Hitchcock, November 9, 1905, and Hitchcock to Commissioner of the General Land Office, November 10, 1905, NPRC Lippincott Personnel File.

243. *San Francisco Chronicle*, October 21, 1905.

244. Austin, *Earth Horizon*, pp. 349-50.

245. Doyle, *Mary Austin*, pp. 299-300.

246. Austin, *Earth Horizon*, pp. 307-8.

CHAPTER FOUR

Forging the Link

1. Lewis H. Schwaebe, Los Angeles City Auditor, to E. A. Hitchcock, January 27, 1906, in National Archives, Department of the Interior, Lands and Railroads Division, Record Group 48, Reclamation Projects, box 37. (Hereinafter cited as NA L&RR RG 48 37.) See also City of Los Angeles, Department of Public Service, *Complete Report on Construction of the Los Angeles Aqueduct* (1916), pp. 266-67.

2. Burt A. Heinly, "Aladdin of the Aqueduct," *Sunset* (April 1912).

3. See Report of Charles H. Lee, app. D in City of Los Angeles, Department of Public Works, *First Annual Report of the Chief Engineer of the Los Angeles Aqueduct to the Board of Public Works* (March 15, 1907). (Hereinafter cited as Los Angeles, *First Report of Chief Engineer*.)

4. Mulholland's estimate appears in Charles A. Moody, "Los Angeles and the Owens River," *Out West* (October 1905). For the alternative estimates, see the *Los Angeles Examiner*, August 2 and August 20, 1905; also the "File Memorandum regarding Owens Valley Project," January 5, 1906, in National Archives, Records of the Bureau of Reclamation, Record Group 115, Owens Valley Project File no. 527-A (hereinafter cited as NA BUREC RG 115 OV 527-A).

5. Los Angeles, *First Report of Chief Engineer*, p. 59.

6. See Testimony of Henry Loewenthal in City of Los Angeles, Aqueduct Investigation Board, *Report . . . to the City Council of Los Angeles* (August 31, 1912), p. 95.

7. See "Report of the Board of Consulting Engineers on the Project of the Los Angeles Aqueduct from Owens River to San Fernando Valley," by John R. Freeman, Frederic P. Stearns, and James D. Schuyler (Los Angeles, December 22, 1906), app. E in Los Angeles, *First Report of Chief Engineer*, pp. 123-24.

8. Regarding the Palmdale purchases, see City of Los Angeles, Aqueduct Investigation Board, *Report*, p. 3.

9. See J. B. Lippincott, "Distribution of the Water of the Los Angeles Aqueduct," pp. 1-2 (manuscript [ca. 1912] in Water Resources Center Archives, Lippincott Papers, File 69-2.

10. "Report of the Board of Consulting Engineers," Los Angeles, *First Report of Chief Engineer*, p. 117.

11. See "Report on Proposed Los Angeles Aqueduct Railway," by W. S. Post, app. H in Los Angeles, *First Report of Chief Engineer*, p. 143.

12. Los Angeles, *First Report of Chief Engineer*, pp. 54-55.

13. Ibid., pp. 47-48; Willie Arthur Chalfant, *The Story of Inyo*, 2d ed. (1933), pp. 360-61; Burt A. Heinly, "Carrying Water through a Desert," *National Geographic* (July 1910). See also right-of-way applications by the Los Angeles and Owens Valley Railroad Co. and the Nevada and California Railroad Co. in National Archives, Reclamation Service, General File 1902-1919, Record Group 115, File 63-B. (Hereinafter cited as NA BUREC RG 115 63-B.)

14. See Nelson VanValen, "A Neglected Aspect of the Owens River Aqueduct Story: The Inception of the Los Angeles Municipal Electrical System," *Southern California Quarterly* (Spring 1977); "Report of the Board of Consulting Engineers," Los Angeles, *First Report of Chief Engineer*, p. 132.

15. See Samuel P. Hays, *Conservation and the Gospel of Efficiency* (1959), pp. 114-16. See also Ellis L. Armstrong, ed., *History of Public Works in the United States, 1776-1976* (1976), pp. 343-48.

16. Vincent Ostrom, *Water and Politics: A Study of Water Politics and Administration in the Development of Los Angeles* (1953), p. 49.

17. Heinly, "Carrying Water."

18. For a brief summary of this conflict, see William L. Kahrl, ed., *The California Water Atlas* (1979), pp. 29-31.

19. See VanValen, "Neglected Aspect of the Owens River Aqueduct Story."

20. See *Los Angeles Examiner*, August 15 and August 17, 1905.

21. See Robert M. Fogelson, *The Fragmented Metropolis: Los Angeles, 1850-1930* (1967), pp. 230-33, and *Los Angeles Times*, March 11, 1907.

22. Los Angeles, *First Report of Chief Engineer*, pp. 56-58.

23. VanValen, "Neglected Aspect of the Owens River Aqueduct Story." Ostrom, *Water and Politics*, pp. 83-84.

24. "Report of the Board of Consulting Engineers," Los Angeles, *First Report of Chief Engineer*, pp. 119-20.

25. See, e.g., *Los Angeles Times*, May 20, May 21, and May 24, 1907.

26. *Los Angeles Times*, July 23, 1935.

27. Ibid., May 24, 1907.

28. See *Los Angeles Evening News*, May 26, 1907.

29. *Los Angeles Herald*, June 4, 1907.

30. *Los Angeles Times*, May 26, 1907. See also the *Times*, May 29, 1907, and *Los Angeles Evening News*, April 10 and April 11, 1907.

31. *Los Angeles Times*, May 23, 1907.

32. *Los Angeles Examiner*, June 11, 1907.

33. *Los Angeles Times*, June 12, 1907.

34. Ibid., June 13, 1907.

35. *Los Angeles Examiner*, June 13, 1907.

36. Testimony of William Mulholland in United States, Congress, House, Committee on Irrigation and Reclamation, *Hearings . . . [on] H. R. 2903, by Mr. Swing.* 68th Cong., 1st sess., pt. 1 (1924), pp. 108-9.

37. W. S. B., "The Record of the Owens River Project," *Out West*, 30 (April 1909).

38. Richard Prosser, "William Mulholland: Maker of Los Angeles," *Western Construction News* (April 25, 1926).

39. Heinly, "Carrying Water."

40. John Russell McCarthy, "Water: The Story of Bill Mulholland," *Los Angeles Saturday Night*, January 15, 1938.

41. *Los Angeles Times*, September 12, 1909.

42. Interview with Rose Mulholland by Robert William Matson, cited in Matson, *William Mulholland: A Forgotten Forefather* (1976), p. 28.

43. W. S. B., "Record of the Owens River Project."

44. Los Angeles City Council, *Report on the Los Angeles Aqueduct*, by Edward Johnson and Edward S. Cobb (July 15, 1912), p. 13.

45. *Los Angeles Herald*, February 26, 1911.

46. City of Los Angeles, Department of Water and Power, *The Romance of Water and Power*, by Don J. Kinsey (1926), p. 12.

47. Ostrom, *Water and Politics*, p. 94.

48. Ibid.; also Heinly, "Carrying Water."

49. "Report of the Board of Consulting Engineers," Los Angeles, *First Report of Chief Engineer*, p. 129.

50. Frederick C. Cross, "My Days on the Jawbone," *Westways* (May 1968).

51. Gertrude Pentland, "Los Angeles Aqueduct with Special Reference to the Labor Problem" (thesis, May 25, 1916), pp. 6-7.

52. Dick Nelson, "Men and Mules," *Intake* (October 1971).

53. Pentland, "Los Angeles Aqueduct . . . Labor Problem," p. 19.

54. Cross, "My Days on the Jawbone."

55. Heinly, "Carrying Water"; Janet Beneda, "The Los Angeles Aqueduct: The Men Who Constructed It" (thesis, May 1974), pp. 18-20, 29-32.

56. *Los Angeles Times*, July 2, 1911.

57. Beneda, "Los Angeles Aqueduct," pp. 8, 25; Pentland, "Los Angeles Aqueduct . . . Labor Problem," p. 20.

58. Pentland, "Los Angeles Aqueduct . . . Labor Problem," p. 20.

59. City of Los Angeles, Aqueduct Investigation Board, *Report*, p. 20.

60. Allen Kelley, *Historical Sketch of the Los Angeles Aqueduct* (Los Angeles, 1913), p. 27.

61. Beneda, "Los Angeles Aqueduct," pp. 21-23.

62. W. S. B., "Record of the Owens River Project."

63. Pentland, "Los Angeles Aqueduct . . . Labor Problem," p. 14.

64. "Report of the Board of Consulting Engineers," Los Angeles, *First Report of Chief Engineer*, p. 129.

65. Kelley, *Historical Sketch*, p. 25.

66. Beneda, "Los Angeles Aqueduct," pp. 16-17.

67. Heinly, "Carrying Water."

68. Kelley, *Historical Sketch*, p. 25.

69. Beneda, "Los Angeles Aqueduct," pp. 27-29.

70. Heinly, "Carrying Water."

71. Roscoe E. Shrader, "A Ditch in the Desert," *Scribner's* (May 1912).

72. See Report of J. K. Connor, City of Los Angeles, Aqueduct Investigation Board, *Report*, p. 15; Los Angeles City Council, *Report on Los Angeles Aqueduct*, pp. 12-13; Pentland, "Los Angeles Aqueduct . . . Labor Problems," p. 11.

73. See Los Angeles City Council, *Report on Los Angeles Aqueduct*, pp. 8-11; F. C. Finkle, "Los Angeles Aqueduct Mistakes," *Journal*

of Electricity, Power and Gas, (January 9, 1915); Gervaise Purcell, W. H. Sanders, F. C. Finkle, Chester B. Loomis, *Report of Municipally Manufactured Cements, Los Angeles Aqueduct* (1912).

74. W. S. B., "Record of the Owens River Project;" City of Los Angeles, Department of Public Service, *Complete Report on Construction*, pp. 266-67; McCarthy, "Water," *Los Angeles Saturday Night,* January 15, 1938.

75. Report of Benjamin F. McLouth, City of Los Angeles, Aqueduct Investigation Board, *Report*, p. 10.

76. See City of Los Angeles, Department of Public Service, *Complete Report on Construction*, p. 268.

77. Boyle Workman, *The City That Grew* (1935), pp. 296-97.

78. Report of McLouth, City of Los Angeles, Aqueduct Investigation Board, *Report*, p. 11.

79. W. S. B., "Record of the Owens River Project."

80. According to the syndicate's schedule, there should have been $15,039,000 in unsold bonds on February 1, 1911, when it had the option of taking up another $4,896,000 for sale. By Mulholland's accounting (p. 68, City of Los Angeles, Department of Public Services, *Complete Report on Construction*) however, there was in fact only $5,748,000 in bonds outstanding and unsold on this date.

81. Heinly, "Aladdin."

82. *Los Angeles Times*, May 27, 1910. See also "Shall Los Angeles Lease or Distribute Aqueduct Power?" *Pacific Outlook* (February 4, 1911).

83. City of Los Angeles, Department of Public Service, *Complete Report on Construction*, p. 268.

84. VanValen, "Neglected Aspect of the Owens River Aqueduct Story."

85. Ostrom, *Water and Politics*, pp. 50, 54-55.

86. Heinly, "Aladdin"; see also "Shall Los Angeles Lease or Distribute."

87. "Shall Los Angeles Lease or Distribute"; City of Los Angeles, Department of Public Service, *Complete Report on Construction*, p. 268.

88. City of Los Angeles, Department of Public Service, *Complete Report on Construction*, pp. 268-69.

89. Beneda, "Los Angeles Aqueduct," pp. 29-32.

90. Pentland, "Los Angeles Aqueduct . . . Labor Problem," p. 26.

91. Ibid., pp. 22-24.

92. Beneda, "Los Angeles Aqueduct," pp. 34-35.

93. For general background on this strike, see Walton Bean, *California: An Interpretive History* (1968), pp. 290-91.

94. Merchants and Manufacturers Association, *Fiftieth Annual Report: The Story of Fifty Years "For Better Employment Relations"* (Los Angeles, 1946), pp. 22-25.

95. Ralph J. Roske, *Everyman's Eden* (1968), p. 495.

96. George E. Mowry, *The California Progressives* (1951), pp. 48-50.

97. Quoted in William G. Bonelli, *Billion Dollar Blackjack: The Story of Corruption and the Los Angeles Times* (1954), pp. 78-80.

98. See Frederick Palmer on the Merchants and Manufacturers Association in *Hampton's Magazine*, 6 (January 1911). See also Louis and Richard Perry, *History of the Los Angeles Labor Movement, 1911-1941* (1963), pp. 5, 17, 21.

99. See Mowry, *California Progressives*, pp. 39-46.

100. Martin J. Schiesl, "Progressive Reform in Los Angeles under Mayor Alexander, 1909-1913," *California Historical Quarterly* (Spring 1975).

101. Meyer Lissner, "Expressions of Prominent Citizens on the Election Results," *Pacific Outlook* (December 11, 1909). See also George Alexander, "What I Am Going to Do," *Pacific Outlook* (April 3, 1909).

102. See Mowry, *California Progressives*, pp. 39-46; Schiesl, "Progressive Reform"; and Robert Gottlieb and Irene Wolt, *Thinking Big: The Story of the Los Angeles Times, Its Publishers, and Their Influence on Southern California* (1977), pp. 74-77.

103. Mowry, *California Progressives*, pp. 49-55.

104. Harriman's campaign platform appears in Alexander Irvine, *Revolution in Los Angeles* (1911), p. 84. The Socialists' case against the aqueduct is "refuted" point by point in the *Los Angeles Herald*, November 28, 1911.

105. See Gottlieb and Wolt, *Thinking Big*, pp. 106-7.

106. *Los Angeles Times*, November 1, 1911.

107. *Los Angeles Herald*, November 4, 1911.

108. See, e.g., *Los Angeles Herald*, November 8, November 9, November 20, and November 21, 1911.

109. *Los Angeles Herald*, November 9, 1911.

110. The history of the trial has been told often and well from a wide range of perspectives. How Darrow's negotiations were intertwined with the course of Harriman's campaign is brought out in detail in Irving Stone, *Clarence Darrow for the Defense* (1943), pp. 248-343. For additional detail, see Gottlieb and Wolt, *Thinking Big*, pp. 555-57.

111. Lincoln Steffens, *The Autobiography of Lincoln Steffens* (1931), p. 666.
112. Ibid., p. 672.
113. Ibid., p. 683.
114. See Gottlieb and Wolt, *Thinking Big*, pp. 98-99.
115. Clarence Darrow, *The Story of My Life* (1932), p. 184.
116. Steffens, *Autobiography*, p. 689.
117. *Los Angeles Times*, December 6, 1911.
118. Gottlieb and Wolt, *Thinking Big*, pp. 106-8.

CHAPTER FIVE

Years of Excess

1. See Vincent Ostrom, *Water and Politics: A Study of Water Policies and Administration in the Development of Los Angeles* (1953), pp. 148-49.
2. Robert M. Fogelson, *The Fragmented Metropolis: Los Angeles, 1850-1930* (1967), p. 223.
3. See Winston W. Crouch and Beatrice Dinerman, *Southern California Metropolis* (1964), pp. 154-58.
4. See Burt A. Heinly, "Carrying Water through a Desert," *National Geographic* (July 1910).
5. See John Russell McCarthy, "Water: The Story of Bill Mulholland," *Los Angeles Saturday Night*, January 29 and February 12, 1938.
6. Reynold E. Blight, "Municipal Government 50 Years from Now," *California Outlook* (October 21, 1911).
7. J.B. Lippincott, "Distribution of the Water of the Los Angeles Aqueduct," manuscript in File 69-2 of the Lippincott Papers, Water Resources Center Archives, University of California, Berkeley.
8. Testimony of William Mulholland in City of Los Angeles, Aqueduct Investigation Board, *Report . . . to the City Council of Los Angeles* (August 31, 1912), p. 48.
9. City of Los Angeles, Department of Public Service, *Report upon the Distribution of the Surplus Waters of the Los Angeles Aqueduct*, by John Henry Quinton, W.H. Code, and Homer Hamlin (Los Angeles, 1911), pp. 4-5, 15-18.
10. Ibid., pp. 4-5, 11, 19.
11. W.T. Spilman, *The Conspiracy: An Exposure of the Owens River Water and San Fernando Land Frauds* (1912).

12. See Gordon Miller, "Los Angeles and the Owens River Aqueduct" (dissertation, 1977), p. 231 n. 15.

13. See Spilman, *Conspiracy*, pp. 60-62. The story of Mulholland draining the city's reservoirs through the sewers, which becomes a central plot device in the film *Chinatown*, apparently originated with a story that appeared in the *Los Angeles Examiner* on September 1, 1905, where it was reported in conjunction with Mulholland's claim of impending drought that the city was losing an estimated twenty-four thousand gallons of water a day from leaks in the municipal high service reservoirs. The city's water and sewer systems in this period did not interconnect. See also *Los Angeles Times*, September 2, 1905, for editorial denials of the *Examiner's* report.

14. Spilman, *Conspiracy*, pp. 41-42.

15. See Spencer Crump, *Henry Huntington and the Pacific Electric* (1970), pp. 11-16, and *Ride the Big Red Cars* (1970), pp. 42-54. See also Walton Bean, *California: An Interpretive History* (1968), p. 282.

16. Robert Gottlieb and Irene Wolt, *Thinking Big: The Story of the Los Angeles Times, Its Publishers, and Their Influence on Southern California* (1977), pp. 120-23.

17. Ibid. pp. 66-67.

18. Ibid., p. 123.

19. "Effectively Transplanted New Englander," *Saturday Evening Post* (June 5, 1926).

20. Gottlieb and Wolt, *Thinking Big*, p. 152.

21. Frank M. Keffer, *History of San Fernando Valley* (1934), pp. 73-74. See also *Los Angeles Tribune*, December 1, 1911.

22. See W.W. Robinson, *The Story of San Fernando Valley* (1961), pp. 37-38; also Crump, *Ride the Big Red Cars*, pp. 109-22. Regarding Tejon Ranch, see Gottlieb and Wolt, *Thinking Big*, p. 148.

23. Testimony of E.T. Earl, City of Los Angeles, Aqueduct Investigation Board, *Report*, p. 91.

24. Keffer, *History of San Fernando*, p. 80.

25. Robinson, *Story of San Fernando*, p. 38.

26. See Gottlieb and Wolt, *Thinking Big*, p. 79.

27. Irving Stone, *Clarence Darrow for the Defense* (1943), p. 267.

28. See City of Los Angeles, Aqueduct Investigation Board, *Report*, p. 29.

29. *Los Angeles Times*, July 17, 1912.

30. McCarthy, "Water," *Los Angeles Saturday Night*, February 12, 1938.

31. Testimony of William Mulholland, City of Los Angeles, Aqueduct Investigation Board, *Report*, p. 48.
32. *Los Angeles Times*, June 6, 1907.
33. Testimony of Mulholland, City of Los Angeles, Aqueduct Investigation Board, *Report*, p. 41.
34. Ibid., p. 51.
35. United States Department of the Interior, United States Geological Survey, Water Supply Paper no. 237, *The Quality of the Surface Waters of California*, by Walton Van Winkle and Frederick M. Eaton, (1910), p. 120.
36. See Gervaise Purcell, W. H. Sanders, F. C. Finkle, and Chester B. Loomis, *Report of Municipally Manufactured Cements, Los Angeles Aqueduct* (1912), pp. 9, 36-37.
37. McCarthy, "Water," *Los Angeles Saturday Night*, February 12, 1938. Although most of the faulty cement was replaced soon after the aqueduct's completion, some segments of the sidewalls were still collapsing as late as 1950. See, e.g., *Los Angeles Times*, January 9, 1950.
38. Testimony of J. B. Lippincott, City of Los Angeles, Aqueduct Investigation Board, *Report*, p. 56.
39. City of Los Angeles, City Council, *Report on the Los Angeles Aqueduct*, by Edward Johnson and Edward S. Cobb (July 15, 1912), pp. 5-6.
40. See Gottlieb and Wolt, *Thinking Big*, pp. 29-30.
41. See Testimony of E. T. Earl, City of Los Angeles, Aqueduct Investigation Board, *Report*, p. 91; and, in the same volume, "Conclusions," p. 4. Earl's argument makes sense only if one first ignores the fact that irrigation of the San Fernando Valley was acknowledged as one of the primary purposes of the aqueduct and then assumes that distribution systems for some reason could not have been built to accomplish this purpose. Curiously, Earl's argument is repeated uncritically as one of the central theses of Miller's "Los Angeles and the Owens River Aqueduct."
42. See Los Angeles City Council, *Report on Los Angeles Aqueduct*, pp. 5-6.
43. See City of Los Angeles, Aqueduct Investigation Board, *Report*, p. 4.
44. Ibid., p. 32.
45. Ibid., p. 4.
46. Ibid., p. 31.
47. Caldwell's letter of September 20, 1912, and Alexander's reply of October 11, 1912, are reprinted in City of Los Angeles, Aqueduct

Investigation Board, *Report*, p. 29. Regarding the loan, see *Los Angeles Times*, January 7, 1913.

48. Mulholland's letter to F. G. Henderson is reprinted in *Los Angeles Times*, April 13, 1913.

49. See William Mulholland, J. B. Lippincott, and H. J. Quinton, *Report of the Consulting Board on Gibraltar Dam* (Santa Barbara, 1914), in the Lippincott Papers, Water Resources Center Archives, University of California, Berkeley.

50. Testimony of Mulholland, City of Los Angeles, Aqueduct Investigation Board, *Report*, p. 43.

51. See, e.g., *Los Angeles Times*, November 3, 1912.

52. J. B. Lippincott, "The Dual Usage of Water for Domestic and Irrigation Purposes," *Journal of the American Water Works Association* (September 1936).

53. *Los Angeles Record*, September 12, 1912. See also H. D. Barrows, "Water for Domestic Purposes vs. Water for Irrigation," *Publications of the Historical Society of Southern California*, (1912).

54. *Los Angeles Times*, April 15, 1913.

55. Lippincott, "Distribution."

56. Carey McWilliams, *Southern California Country: An Island on the Land* (1946), p. 277.

57. See, e.g., *Los Angeles Times*, November 5, 1912.

58. *Los Angeles Times*, April 16, 1913.

59. See Mulholland letter in *Los Angeles Times*, April 13, 1913.

60. See *Los Angeles Times*, April 15, 1913.

61. See, e.g., *Los Angeles Tribune*, July 13, 1913.

62. See Ostrom, *Water and Politics*, pp. 154-56; and Gottlieb and Wolt, *Thinking Big*, pp. 139-40.

63. *Los Angeles Times*, November 5, 1913. See also J. M. Guinn, *A History of California and an Extended History of Los Angeles and Environs* (1915), p. 309.

64. Franklin K. Lane to Woodrow Wilson, June 3, 1913, in National Archives, Department of the Interior, Office of the Secretary, Central Classified File 1907-1936, Record Group 48, File 2-11. (Hereinafter cited as NA INT RG 48 2-11.)

65. Dick Nelson, "Men and Mules," *Intake* (October 1971), p. 5.

66. See Janet Beneda, "The Los Angeles Aqueduct: The Men Who Constructed It" (thesis, May 1974), pp. 10-12.

67. See Kenneth Q. Volk and Edgar Alan Rowe, "Memoir of Joseph B. Lippincott," *Transactions of the American Society of Civil Engineers* (1943).

68. City of Los Angeles, Department of Public Service, *Complete Report on Construction of the Los Angeles Aqueduct* (1916), p. 29. See also McCarthy, "Water," *Los Angeles Saturday Night*, February 26, 1938.

69. See, e.g., F. C. Finkle, "Los Angeles Aqueduct Mistakes," *Journal of Electricity, Power and Gas* (January 9, 1915), and "Los Angeles' $40,000,000 White Elephant," *Irrigation Age* (May 1915).

70. Ethel Leonard, *Report of Sanitary Investigation of the Tributaries and Mountain Streams Emptying into Owens River . . .* (1914), pp. 3-7, 12-14, 19-24.

71. Ibid., p. 2.

72. *Los Angeles Examiner*, August 16, 1914.

73. See City of Los Angeles, Department of Public Service, *Complete Report on Construction*, pp. 291-99.

74. See City of Los Angeles, Board of Public Service Commissioners, *Report upon the Sanitary Quality of the Owens River Water Supply*, by Charles Gilman Hyde (1915). See also E. H. Miller and Luther M. Powers, *Reports on the Sanitary Investigation of Owens River and the Los Angeles Aqueduct* (Los Angeles, 1914).

75. See J. D. Galloway, "Report on the Proposed Storage Reservoir at Fish Slough and the Supply Ditch from the Owens River near Bishop, Inyo County, California" (San Francisco, January 1906), and W. A. Chalfant to E. A. Hitchcock, February 3, 1906, both in National Archives, Records of the Bureau of Reclamation, Record Group 115, Owens Valley Project File no. 527-A. (Hereinafter cited as NA BUREC RG 115 OV 527-A.)

76. See the Report of J. C. Clausen, November 1904, in National Archives, Records of the Bureau of Reclamation, Record Group 115, Owens Valley Project File no. 527. (Hereinafter cited as NA BUREC RG 115 OV 527.) See also Chalfant to Hitchcock, February 9, 1906, NA BUREC RG 115 OV 527-A.

77. J. B. Lippincott to F. H. Newell, February 15, 1906, in National Archives, Reclamation Service, General File 1902-1919, Record Group 115, File 63-B. (Hereinafter cited as NA BUREC RG 115 63-B.)

78. Ibid.

79. Lippincott to Newell, February 20, 1906, ibid.

80. F. H. Newell to L. H. Taylor, February 28, 1906, ibid.

81. Taylor to Newell, July 9, 1906, ibid.

82. A. P. Davis to Hitchcock, July 19, 1906, ibid. See also Hitchcock to C. D. Walcott, January 16, 1907, and Walcott to Hitchcock, January 25, 1907, ibid.

83. See F. G. Newlands to Hitchcock, July 8, 1906, and S. C. Smith to Hitchcock, September 19, 1906, and January 2, 1907, in National Archives, Department of the Interior, Lands and Railroads Division, Record Group 48, Reclamation Projects, box 37. (Hereinafter cited as NA L&RR RG 48 37.) See also Chalfant to Hitchcock, December 1, 1906, NA BUREC RG 115 63-B. As the author of the Reclamation Act of 1902, Newlands might seem an unlikely ally in the valley's opposition to the Reclamation Service. But he was at all times attentive to complaints about the administration of the service. And because of the valley's physical isolation from the rest of California and its strong economic ties to the nearby mining fields in Nevada, it was not uncommon in this period for valley residents to appeal to Nevada officials rather than to their own elected representatives.

84. See Jno. Fay, President of the Los Angeles Board of Water Commissioners, to Newell, July 27, 1906, NA BUREC RG 115 63-B.

85. See F. P. Flint to Walcott, September 21, 1906, and Walcott to Flint, October 3, 1906, NA BUREC RG 115 OV 527-A.

86. Newell to Taylor, December 24, 1906, NA BUREC RG 115 63-B. See also Taylor to Newell, August 7, 1906, ibid.

87. Taylor to Newell, June 17, 1907, ibid.

88. Newell to the Commissioner of the General Land Office, July 16, 1906, ibid.

89. Walcott to Hitchcock, December 24, 1906, NA L&RR RG 48 37.

90. Lippincott to Walcott, March 2, 1907, and Walcott and Pinchot to T. Roosevelt, March 8, 1907, NA BUREC RG 115 63-B.

91. Newell to Walcott, March 6, 1907, ibid.

92. Ibid.

93. Newell to J. R. Garfield, April 30, 1907, ibid.

94. See Morris Bein to the Commissioner of the General Land Office, July 12, 1907, ibid. See also A. C. Harper, Mayor of Los Angeles, to Garfield, May 29, 1907; Garfield to Harper, June 3, 1907; Lippincott to Newell, June 10, 1907; Bein to Lippincott, June 28, 1907; and Bein to Garfield, July 2, 1907—ibid.

95. See Thayer and Rankin, Attorneys for the City of Los Angeles, to Walcott, Janaury 5, 1907; and Walcott and Pinchot to T. Roosevelt, March 8, 1907—ibid. See also George W. Woodruff, Acting Secretary of the Interior, to the Commissioner of the General Land Office, July 12, 1907, NA BUREC RG 115 OV 527. See also Garfield to Harper, November 29, 1907, NA INT RG 48 2-11.

96. W. A. Chalfant, *The Story of Inyo*, 2nd ed. (1933), p. 329. (Hereinafter cited as Chalfant 2d.)

97. See Davis, Memo for the Secretary of Interior, March 26, 1909, NA INT RG 48 2-11.

98. See Commissioner of the General Land Office to the Register and Receiver of Independence, May 5, 1911, ibid.

99. See Fred Dennett to Franklin Pierce, First Assistant Secretary of the Interior, September 28, 1908, ibid.

100. See Commissioner of the General Land Office to the Register and Receiver of Independence, May 5, 1911, ibid.

101. See Recommendation of the Acting Secretary of the Department of Agriculture, May 8, 1907, in National Archives, Department of the Interior, Office of the Secretary, Record Group 48, General Land Office, Inyo National Forest, File 2-5. (Hereinafter cited as NA INT RG 48 2-5.)

102. City of Los Angeles, Department of Public Service, *Complete Report on Construction*, p. 68.

103. Chalfant 2d, p. 367.

104. D. H. Anderson, "Oppressive Use of Power," *Irrigation Age* (January 1909).

105. Chalfant 2d, p. 368.

106. L. M. Holt, "How the Reclamation Service is Robbing the Settler," *Overland Monthly* (November 1907).

107. Anonymous, "An Indictment and Demand," handbill addressed to the Fifteenth Irrigation Congress, NA BUREC RG 115 63-B.

108. *San Francisco Call*, September 4, 1907.

109. See Samuel P. Hays, *Conservation and the Gospel of Efficiency* (1959), pp. 22-24.

110. See Elmo R. Richardson, *The Politics of Conservation: Crusade and Controversies, 1897-1913* (1962), pp. 5, 33-34. See also Hays *Conservation and the Gospel of Efficiency*, pp. 1-2, 127, 133-35, 142-43.

111. See D. H. Anderson, "Are Government Officials Playing Fair? Some Facts about the Owens River Valley Condition"; "Oppressive Use of Power"; and "Why Was the Owens River Project Abandoned?" *Irrigation Age* (December 1908 through February 1909).

112. See, e.g., "Indictment and Demand," NA BUREC RG 115 63-B.

113. Chalfant 2d, pp. 363-64.

114. See, e.g., Flint to R. Ballinger, February 19, 1910, NA INT RG 48 2-5.

115. The order was issued March 2, 1909. See Ballinger to W. H. Taft, May 25, 1909, NA INT RG 48 2-11.

116. See Hays, *Conservation and the Gospel of Efficiency*, pp. 150-54, 161-63, and 246-48.

117. Regarding Owens Valley petitions, see Pierce to James Wilson, Secretary of Agriculture, September 8, 1909, NA INT RG 48 2-5.

118. *Owens Valley Herald*, January 14, 1910.

119. See Alexander Vogelsang, Acting Secretary of the Interior, to W. Wilson, March 14, 1919; Executive Proclamation 1518, April 8, 1919—ibid. See also (ibid.) President Warren G. Harding's Executive Proclamation 1659, May 7, 1923, transferring certain lands from the Sequoia National Forest to the Inyo National Forest.

120. G. Yoell Parkhurst, *Inyo County, California* (1911).

121. *Inyo County, California, Anno Domini 1912* prepared by the *Inyo Register* (1912), p. 3.

122. Parkhurst, *Inyo County*.

123. See W. A. Chalfant, "Charley's Butte," *Irrigation Age*, (December 1908).

124. City of Los Angeles, Department of Water and Power, *The Water Trail*, by Don J. Kinsey (1928), p. 12.

125. Testimony of Mulholland, City of Los Angeles, Aqueduct Investigation Board, *Report*, p. 41.

126. City of Los Angeles, Department of Public Service, *Complete Report on Construction*, pp. 72, 274.

127. Leonard, *Report of Sanitary Investigation*, pp. 14-15.

128. *Inyo Register*, November 6, 1913.

129. See Smith to Ballinger, October 8, 1909; Alfred A. Hubbard, President of the Los Angeles Board of Public Works, to Ballinger, December 8, 1909; Ballinger to the Commissioner of the General Land Office, March 30, 1910; Commissioner of the General Land Office to the Register and Receiver of Independence, May 5, 1911 —NA INT RG 48 2-11. See also Testimony of Mulholland, City of Los Angeles, Aqueduct Investigation Board, *Report*, p. 44; *Inyo County California*, p. 38; and John Glanville Dixon, "The Valley of Broken Hearts," in Peggy and Clarence Streeter, eds., *Saga of Inyo County* (1977).

130. See Commissioner of the General Land Office to the Register and Receiver of Independence, May 5, 1911, and Samuel Adams, First Assistant Secretary of Interior to W. B. Matthews, August 7, 1912, NA INT RG 48 2-11.

131. See J. A. Alexander, *The Life of George Chaffey* (1928), pp. 358-59. See also William L. Kahrl, ed., *The California Water Atlas* (1979), pp. 24, 39.

132. See two letters, one "Private" Lippincott to Newell, January 11, 1906, and letter from Mulholland to Lippincott, January 9, 1906, NA BUREC RG 115 63-B.

133. Lippincott to Newell, January 19, 1906, ibid.

134. Lippincott to Newell, April 14, 1906, ibid.

135. See Thayer and Rankin to Walcott, January 5, 1907, ibid.

136. See John M. Gorman, *I Remember Manzanar* (1967); Owens Valley Improvement Company, *Fortunes in Apples in Owens Valley* [ca. 1911].

137. See telegram, Mulholland and Lippincott to Newell, January 16, 1912; Newell to Mulholland, January 17, 1912-NA BUREC RG 115 63-B.

138. See Alexander, *Life of George Chaffey*, pp. 359-60.

139. Adna R. Chaffee to Newell, February 10, 1912, NA BUREC RG 115 63-B.

140. *Inyo County California*, p. 12.

141. This determination was made in 1907. See *Los Angeles Times*, May 25, 1907. The assurance has been codified in secs. 3(b) and 11, art. XIII of the Constitution of California.

142. City of Los Angeles, Department of Public Service, *Complete Report on Construction*, p. 72.

143. See McCarthy, "Water," *Los Angeles Saturday Night*, January 15, 1938; and Testimony of Mulholland, City of Los Angeles, Aqueduct Investigation Board, *Report*, p. 42.

144. State of California, California Development Board, *Agricultural and Industrial Survey of Inyo County, California* (1917), p. 5.

145. Ruth E. Baugh, "Land Use Changes in the Bishop Area of Owens Valley California," *Economic Geography* (January 1937).

146. United States, *Census of Agriculture 1920*, vol. 7: *Irrigation and Drainage* (Washington, 1922), pp. 358-59; California Development Board, *Survey of Inyo County*, pp. 7, 27-30; City of Los Angeles, *Complete Report on Aqueduct*, p. 274; Parkhurst, *Inyo County*.

147. California Development Board, *Agricultural and Industrial Survey of Inyo County*, pp. 56-58, 64-70, 74-92.

148. *Big Pine Citizen*, August 28, 1915.

149. *Inyo County California*, p. 39. See also Parkhurst, *Inyo County*.

150. California Development Board, *Agricultural and Industrial Survey of Inyo County*, pp. 121-22, 134-36, 137-41, 148, 153-55; Park-County California*, p. 20; H. D. Ruth and Associates, *1990 General Plan for Development: Inyo County, California* (August 5, 1968), p. 83.

151. California Development Board, *Agricultural and Industrial Survey of Inyo County*, pp. 121-22, 134-36, 137-41, 148, 153-55; Parkhurst, *Inyo County*; Clarabelle E. Hawkins, *Story of Laws, California* (1975); *Deep Springs*, pamphlet (Deep Springs, California, December 1957). See also Deep Springs College Board of Trustees, *Constitution of Deep Springs and the Deed of Trust* (1950).

152. See Harry Erlich and P. N. McGauhey, *Economic Evaluation of Water*, pt. 2: "Jurisdictional Considerations in Water Resources Management" (1964), table OR-2, p. 76, and table R-3, pp. 77. United States, *Census of Agriculture, 1910*, vol. 6: *Reports by States* (Washington, D.C., 1912), pp. 148-49, 160-61, 178. United States, *Census of Agriculture, 1920*, pp. 344-45, 350-51, and 358-59. Graydon Oliver, "Prosperous Condition of Owens Valley District Revealed by Many Vital Statistics," *Modern Irrigation* (August 1927). For comparative purposes with regard to the use of statistics by the city in its public reports, see City of Los Angeles, Department of Public Service *Complete Report on Construction*, p. 273, and City of Los Angeles, Department of Water and Power, *Water Trail*, p. 15.

153. *Los Angeles Times*, July 31, 1915.

154. City of Los Angeles, Bureau of Engineering, *Annexation and Detachment Map* (1978).

155. See Keffer, *History of San Fernando*, p. 86; Robinson, *Story of San Fernando*, p. 40; Gottlieb and Wolt, *Thinking Big*, p. 140; Ostrom, *Water and Politics*, pp. 156-58.

156. See Gottlieb and Wolt, *Thinking Big*, p. 138, and materials relating to the annexation of Pasadena and the formation of San Fernando Irrigation District 3 in the J. B. Lippincott Papers, Water Resources Center Archives, University of California, Berkeley.

157. Thomas Means, *Report on Mono Basin Water as Supply for Southern California* (San Francisco, October 1923), File no. 11, Means Papers, Water Resources Center Archives, University of California, Berkeley. See also Ostrom, *Water and Politics*, p. 161.

158. C. W. Geiger, "Using Los Angeles Aqueduct Water for Irrigation Purposes," *Municipal and County Engineering* (July 1918).

159. City of Los Angeles, Board of Public Service Commissioners, *Seventeenth Annual Report . . . for the Fiscal Year Ending June 30, 1918* (Los Angeles, 1918), pp. 6, 39. Mean daily consumption for all uses in the city was 88.3 cubic feet per second in 1913 and 175.0 in 1918; see City of Los Angeles, Board of Public Service Commissioners, *Report on Available Water Supply of the City of Los Angeles and Metropolitan Area*, by Louis C. Hill, J. B. Lippincott, and A. L. Sonderegger (Los Angeles, 1924), p. 193.

160. Geiger, "Using Los Angeles Aqueduct Water."

161. City of Los Angeles, Department of Public Service, "Report on Irrigation from Owens River Sources and Crops Produced Therefrom during the Season of 1919" *Public Service*, vol. 4, no. 1 (January 1920).

162. City of Los Angeles, Department of Public Service, *Complete Report on Construction*, p. 10.

163. Ostrom, *Water and Politics*, p. 161.

164. City of Los Angeles, Board of Public Service Commissioners, *Available Water Supply*, p. 193.

CHAPTER SIX

The Politics of Exploitation

1. Burt A. Heinly, "Aladdin of the Aqueduct," *Sunset* (April 1912).

2. Meyer Lissner, "Bill Mulholland," *American Magazine* (April 1912).

3. See William L. Kahrl, ed., *The California Water Atlas* (1979), pp. 31-33.

4. See esp. City of Los Angeles, Department of Water and Power, *The Romance of Water and Power*, by Don J. Kinsey (1928), p. 21.

5. Lissner, "Bill Mulholland."

6. See H. A. Van Norman, "Memoir of William Mulholland," *Transactions of the American Society of Civil Engineers* (1936); William Mulholland, Arthur P. Davis, and George W. Goethals, "Water Supply Problem of the East Bay Municipal Utility District," in Arthur Powell Davis, *Additional Water Supply of East Bay Municipal Utility District* (Oakland, October 1, 1924); Erwin Cooper, *Aqueduct Empire: A Guide to Water in California, Its Turbulent History, and Its Management Today* (1968), pp. 50-52; Kahrl, *California Water Atlas*, p. 47; and William Mulholland and Joseph B. Lippincott, "The Fundamental Conditions of San Fernando Valley . . ." in Spring Valley Water Company, *The Future Water Supply of San Francisco* (October 31, 1912), pp. 187-92.

7. United States, Congress, House, Committee on Irrigation and Reclamation, *Hearings . . . [on] H.R. 2903, by Mr. Swing*. 68th Cong., 1st sess., pt. 1 (1924), p. 95; Van Norman, "Memoir."

8. See George E. Mowry, *The California Progressives* (1951), pp. 205-9; *Los Angeles Times*, June 12, 1978; and J. M. Guinn, *A History of California and an Extended History of Los Angeles and Environs* (1915), vol. II: *Biographical*, p. 435.

9. Heinly, "Aladdin."

10. City of Los Angeles, City Council, *Report on the Los Angeles Aqueduct*, by Edward Johnson and Edward S. Cobb (July 15, 1912), p. 17; Elisabeth Mathieu Spriggs, "The History of the Domestic Water Supply of Los Angeles" (thesis, January 1, 1931), p. 74.

11. Boyle Workman, *The City That Grew* (1935), pp. 341-42.

12. Joseph B. Lippincott, "William Mulholland: Engineer, Pioneer, Raconteur," *Civil Engineering* (February and March 1941).

13. Spriggs, "History of the Domestic Water Supply," p. 68.

14. See City of Los Angeles, Board of Public Service Commissioners, *Reply . . . to the Proposal and Accompanying Documents Dated November 29, 1924, Submitted by W. W. Watterson to Los Angeles Clearing House Association* (January 6, 1925), pp. 22-28; Vincent Ostrom, *Water and Politics: A Study of Water Policies and Administration in the Development of Los Angeles* (1953), pp. 118-19; *Bishop Creek Ditch Co. et al. v. City of Los Angeles*, Inyo County Superior Court, no. 1410; and *Henry A. Hart et al. v. City of Los Angeles*, Los Angeles Superior Court, no. B 2566. W. A. Chalfant, *Story of Inyo*, 2d ed. (1933), pp. 373-74 (hereinafter cited as Chalfant 2d), claimed that the agreement of 1913 also would have permitted an expansion of irrigation into Long Valley and would have prohibited Los Angeles from interfering with the groundwater supply of the Owens Valley. These claims are not supported by other accounts of the agreement. According to Chalfant, however, the failure of this agreement was not a complete loss for the valley; as a condition for their acceptance of the agreement, the valley's representatives did extract a promise that the city would support legislation which was passed in 1914 specifying Los Angeles' responsibility to pay property taxes on its holdings in the Owens Valley.

15. For further detail regarding the conflict over municipal power in Los Angeles, see Ostrom, *Water and Politics*, pp. 58-61, 83-84, 95-96; Robert M. Fogelson, *The Fragmented Metropolis: Los Angeles, 1850-1930* (1967), pp. 230-36; City of Los Angeles, Department of Water and Power, "Romance of Water and Power;" Nelson VanValen, "A Neglected Aspect of the Owens River Aqueduct Story: The Inception of the Los Angeles Municipal Electrical System," *Southern California Quarterly* (Spring 1977); and "Shall Los Angeles Lease or Distribute Aqueduct Power?" *Pacific Outlook* (February 4, 1911).

16. See City of Los Angeles, Department of Public Service, *Complete Report on Construction of the Los Angeles Aqueduct* (1916), pp. 236, 247. In later reports the department revised these figures

upward; see, e.g., Samuel B. Morris, "Owens Gorge Project," a paper prepared for the Power Division of the American Society of Civil Engineers, February 6, 1955, available in the Department of Water and Power library. Morris reports 100,000 kilowatts obtainable from the river and a "like amount" from the gorge (NB: 1 horsepower equals 746 watts).

17. See Morris, "Owens Gorge Project," and T. Eugene Barrows, "History of the Owens Valley Power Plants," in Peggy and Clarence Streeter, eds., *Saga of Inyo County* (1977), pp. 68-69.

18. United States, Congress, House, Committee on Public Lands, *Water Supply of Los Angeles: Hearings on H. R. 406* . . . October 31-November 4, 1919. 66th Cong., 1st sess., pp. 19, 21, 46-47.

19. United States Department of the Interior, United States Geological Survey, *Review of Waterpower Withdrawals, Mono Lake and Owens Lake Basins, California*, by Kenneth W. Sax (May 1964).

20. United States, Congress, *Water Supply of Los Angeles: Hearings on H.R. 406*, p. 80. See also Harry Erlich and P.N. McGauhey, *Economic Evaluation of Water*, pt. 2: "Jurisdictional Considerations in Water Resources Management," Water Resources Center Contribution no. 42 (June 1964), pp. 50-51.

21. United States, Congress, *Water Supply of Los Angeles: Hearings on H.R. 406*, pp. 129, 132. See also *Mohave Press*, March 21, 1919.

22. See Commissioner of General Land Office to Register of Independence, January 3, 1912, and Deposition of William Rowan, February 9, 1912, in O.W. Larson Papers, box 2, Rowan File, California Historical Society library.

23. G.A. Dixon to H.S. Beckman, September 24, 1919, Larson Papers, box 2, Miscellaneous.

24. See form letter, D.A. Chappelle to Owens Valley ditch owners, December 15, 1913, Larson Papers, box 1, folder 1.

25. Dixon to Beckman, September 24, 1919, Larson Papers, box 2, Miscellaneous.

26. Dixon to Commissioner of Indian Affairs, "Supplemental," February 15, 1919, Larson Papers, box 1, folder 2.

27. Ibid. See also City of Los Angeles, Board of Public Service Commissioners, *Report on Available Water Supply of City of Los Angeles and Metropolitan Area*, by Louis C. Hill, J.B. Lippincott, and A.L. Sonderegger (August 1924), p. 94; Consaul and Heltman to Commissioner of the General Land Office, February 11, 1919, Larson Papers, box 1, folder 3; and Commissioner of the General Land Office to the Department of the Interior, March 6, 1919, Larson Papers, box 1, folder 2.

28. Commissioner of the General Land Office to Register of Independence, January 3, 1912, Larson Papers, box 2, Rowan File.

29. W. W. Watterson to A. P. Davis, January 24, 1919, and Davis to Watterson, February 5, 1919, National Archives, Records of the Bureau of Reclamation, Record Group 115, Project File 1902-1919, Owens Valley Project File no. 527-A. (Hereinafter cited as NA BUREC RG 115 OV 527-A.)

30. Davis to W. B. Mathews, January 27, 1919, ibid.

31. Dixon to Elwood Mead, undated, Larson Papers, box 1, folder 2.

32. See, e.g., Dixon to Mead, n.d., and Dixon to Congressmen W. B. Kettner and J. E. Raker, n.d., ibid.

33. See United States, Congress, *Water Supply of Los Angeles: Hearings on H.R. 406*, pp. 1-5, 43, 60-61. See also *S. 4023*, 65th Congress.

34. See multiple telegrams of January 28 and 29, 1919, Larson Papers, box 1, folder 2.

35. George Watterson and G. Dixon to Owens Valley Associated Ditches, April 25, 1919, Larson Papers, box 1, folder 1.

36. Charles F. Outland, *Man-Made Disaster: The Story of Saint Francis Dam* (1977), p. 21.

37. United States, Congress, *Water Supply of Los Angeles, Hearings on H.R. 406*, pp. 31, 46-47.

38. Ibid., pp. 34-36.

39. Ibid., pp. 23-24, 61.

40. H. S. Beckman and Henry Shaw to Owens Valley Associated Ditches, February 5, 1919, Larson Papers, box 1, folder 2.

41. Beckman to Dixon, May 21, 1919, ibid.

42. See Memorandum for Mr. Bein, November 8, 1911, National Archives, Records of the Bureau of Reclamation, Record Group 115, Owens Valley Project file no. 527. (Hereinafter cited as NA BUREC RG 115 OV 527.)

43. See Dixon to Commissioner of Indian Affairs, February 15, 1919, Larson Papers, box 1, folder 2. See also form letter, Chappelle to Owens Valley ditch owners, December 15, 1913, Larson Papers, box 1, folder 1.

44. See Thomas H. Means, *Report on Water Requirements of Bishop Creek Lands* (San Francisco, September 1919), pp. 1-4, and Willie Arthur Chalfant, *Story of Inyo* (1922), p. 317 (hereinafter cited as Chalfant 1st).

45. Beckman to Dixon, May 21, 1919, Larson Papers, box 1, folder 2. See also Articles of Agreement for the ditch companies, September 22, 1900, Larson Papers, box 1, folder 1.

46. See Articles of Incorporation, Owens Valley Associated Ditches, July 12, 1919; Dixon to Beckman, May 26, 1919; Resolution of the Owens River Canal Company, July 7, 1919; and Petition of the Owens River Canal Company to the Secretary of the Interior, July 7, 1919—Larson Papers, box 1, folder 2. See also Minutes of the Owens Valley Associated Ditches, Larson Papers, box 2.

47. See Dixon to A. B. West, August 25, 1919, West to Dixon, August 14 and September 2, 1919, and Dixon to Beckman, October 3, 1919—Larson Papers, box 1, folder 1. See also Dixon to Beckman, September 24, 1919, Larson Papers, box 2, Miscellaneous.

48. See Consaul and Heltman to Dixon, February 11, 1919, Larson Papers, box 1, folder 1. Also Consaul and Heltman to Dixon, October 30, 1919; Dixon to Commissioner of Indian Affairs, March 7, 1919; and Commissioner of Indian Affairs to Commissioner of General Land Office, March 14, 1919—Larson Papers, box 1, folder 3. Further, Dixon to Commissioner of Indian Affairs, February 15, 1919, and Consaul and Heltman to Dixon, September 23, 1919, Larson Papers, box 1, folder 2.

49. Consaul to Dixon, October 23, 1919, also Dixon to Consaul, October 29, 1919—Larson Papers, box 1, folder 1.

50. Consaul to Dixon, October 30 and November 6, 1919, ibid.

51. See Agreement between Owens River Canal Company and Hillside Water Company, November 27, 1919; Dixon to West, November 12, 1919; and West to Dixon, November 17, 1919—ibid.

52. See Dixon to Beckman, October 3, 1919, ibid.

53. Dixon to A. P. Davis, November 17, 1919, ibid.

54. Dixon to Beckman, October 1, 1919, Larson Papers, box 2, Miscellaneous.

55. Consaul and Heltman to O. W. Larson, April 20, 1922, ibid. See also Consaul and Heltman to Larson, December 27, 1920, and March 25, 1922, and Larson to Consaul and Heltman, April 10, 1922, ibid.

56. Dixon to Beckman, October 1, 1919, ibid.

57. Beckman to Dixon, October 7, 1919, ibid.

58. See Report of J. C. Clausen, November, 1904, pp. 69-71, NA BUREC RG 115 OV 527.

59. See Report of Charles H. Lee, app. D in City of Los Angeles, Department of Public Works, *First Annual Report of the Chief Engineer of the Los Angeles Aqueduct to the Board of Public Works* (March 15, 1907), p. 112. (Hereinafter cited as Los Angeles, *First Report of the Chief Engineer.*) See also p. 35 in the main body of that report; and City of Los Angeles, Department of Public

Service, *Complete Report on Construction of the Los Angeles Aqueduct* (1916), pp. 25, 273.

60. Testimony of J. M. Elliott in City of Los Angeles, Aqueduct Investigation Board, *Report ... to the City Council of Los Angeles* (August 31, 1912), p. 35.

61. See "Report of the Board of Consulting Engineers on the Project of the Los Angeles Aqueduct from Owens River to San Fernando Valley," by John R. Freeman, Frederick P. Stearns, and James D. Schuyler (December 22, 1906), app. E in Los Angeles, *First Report of the Chief Engineer*, p. 125.

62. Testimony of Mulholland, City of Los Angeles, Aqueduct Investigation Board, *Report*, p. 41. See also p. 43 of that report; and Walcott and Pinchot to Roosevelt, March 8, 1907, in National Archives, Reclamation Service, General File 1902-1919, Record Group 115, File 63-B, "Correspondence re Right of Way Applications in Owens River Valley." (Hereinafter cited as NA BUREC RG 115 63-B.)

63. 41 *Stats.* 983. See also "Report of Consaul and Heltman re H.R. 406," Larson Papers, box 2, Miscellaneous.

64. See United States Reclamation Service, "Preliminary Report on Owens Valley Project, California," by Harold Conkling (Washington, D.C., September 1920). See also City of Los Angeles, Department of Water and Power, *Water Supply Management in Inyo and Mono Counties* (September 1966), p. 9; Thomas H. Means, *Report on Mono Basin Water as Supply for Southern California* (San Francisco, October 1923), pp. 3-4; and State of California, Department of Public Works, *Report on Development of Water Resources in Mono Basin Based on Investigations Made for the Division of Engineering and Irrigation*, by S.T. Harding (1922): "Supplemental," app. N pp. 51-52. Chalfant in 1922 understood that the Long Valley proposal was intended solely for power development; see Chalfant 1st, p. 328.

65. See Minutes of the Owens Valley Associated Ditches, August 12, 1920, and April 21, 1921, Larson Papers, box 2.

66. See "Open Letter to W. A. Chalfant" from George Watterson and William Symons, January 11, 1924, Larson Papers, box 1, Miscellaneous; *Inyo Register*, December 6, 1924; United States Reclamation Service, *Report on Owens Valley Project, California*, by Harold Conkling (Washington, DC., September 1921), p. 35; Minutes of the Owens Valley Associated Ditches, September 28, 1921, Larson Papers, box 2; City of Los Angeles, Board of Public Service Commissioners, *Reply to ... Watterson*, pp. 104-14; and J.C. Clausen to Associated Ditch Companies, Inc., October 3, 1921, Larson Papers, box 2, Miscellaneous.

67. J.C. Clausen to Associated Ditch Companies, Inc., October 3, 1921, and March 17, 1922, Larson Papers, box 2, Miscellaneous; *Inyo Register*, January 17, 1924.

68. See United States Reclamation Service, *Report on Owens Valley Project*, pp. 31-32, also pp. 3-4 of synopsis.

69. Testimony of Mulholland, City of Los Angeles, Aqueduct Investigation Board, *Report*, p. 41.

70. Ibid., p. 51.

71. Ibid., pp. 9, 50, 57-58.

72. Municipal League of Los Angeles, "The Owens Valley 'Revolt,'" *Bulletin of the Municipal League of Los Angeles*, vol. 1, no. 12) (July 15, 1924); Chalfant 2d, pp. 382-83.

73. Watterson and Symons, "Open Letter," January 11, 1924, Larson Papers, box 2, Miscellaneous.

74. Owens Valley Associated Ditches, Inc., to Los Angeles Board of Public Service Commissioners, October 21, 1921, Larson Papers, box 2, Miscellaneous.

75. Beckman to Larson, November 22, 1921, ibid.

76. Watterson and Symons, "Open Letter," January 11, 1924, ibid.

77. See Minutes of the Owens Valley Associated Ditches, November 12, 1921, and March 4, 1922, Larson Papers, box 2.

78. See *Mono Power Company* v. *City of Los Angeles*, 284 Fed. 784,792 (1922). See also Ostrom, *Water and Politics*, pp. 119-21; Chalfant 2d, pp. 376-78; and *Inyo Register*, November 28 and December 6, 1924.

79. See, e.g., Remi Nadeau, *The Water Seekers* (1950), p. 108.

80. See *Inyo Register*, January 7, 1924; and Chalfant 2d, p. 357.

81. Thomas H. Means, *Correspondence re Natural Soda Products* v. *City of Los Angeles*, Means Papers, file no. 18, Water Resources Center Archives, University of California, Berkeley, Means' notes for testimony, November 6, 1941.

82. See Carey McWilliams, *Southern California Country: An Island on the Land* (New York, 1946), pp. 189-91.

83. Mulholland and Lippincott, "Fundamental Conditions," p. 192.

84. Testimony of Mulholland, City of Los Angeles, Aqueduct Investigation Board, *Report*, pp. 43, 51.

85. See Charles A. Moody, "Los Angeles and the Owens River," *Out West* (October 1905).

86. City of Los Angeles, Aqueduct Investigation Board, *Report*, p. 25.

87. Testimony of E.T. Earl, ibid., p. 92.

88. United States Department of the Interior, United States Geological

Survey, *The Geology and Water Resources of Owens Valley, California*, by Willis T. Lee, Water Supply Paper no. 181 (1906), pp. 13-15.

89. See United States Department of the Interior, United States Geological Survey, *An Intensive Study of the Water Resources of a Part of the Owens Valley California*, by Charles H. Lee, Water Supply Paper no. 294 (1912).

90. Charles H. Lee, "Well Development in Owens Valley Equalizes Supply of Los Angeles Aqueduct," *Western Construction News* (October 25, 1926).

91. *Los Angeles Times*, September 12, 1909.

92. Lee, "Well Development." J. E. Phillips, "Underground Water Development in Owens Valley," in University of Southern California School of Government, Water Supply and Sanitary Engineering Section, *Papers, 1930* (1930), pp. 105-6. See also C. W. Geiger, "Using Los Angeles Aqueduct Water for Irrigation Purposes," *Municipal and County Engineering* (July 1918).

93. See *City of Los Angeles* v. *Thomas D. Buffington et al.*, 156 Cal. 603 (1909). See also City of Los Angeles, Bureau of Water Works and Supply, *Water Supply and Distribution Problems in Los Angeles*, by Verne G. Saunders (December 6, 1937), p. 3.

94. See Ellis L. Armstrong, ed., *History of Public Works in the United States, 1776-1976* (1976), pp. 295-97; Cooper, *Aqueduct Empire: A Guide to Water in California, Its Turbulent History, and Its Management Today* (1968), pp. 129-30, 365-66; Kenneth Q. Volk and Edgar Alan Rowe, "Memoir of Joseph B. Lippincott," in *Transactions of the American Society of Civil Engineers* (1943); and City of Los Angeles, Department of Water and Power, *Data on Available Water Supply and Future Requirements of the City of Los Angeles and the Metropolitan Area* (October 1928), p. 29.

95. Means, *Report on Mono Basin Water*, pp. 26-29.

96. City of Los Angeles, Department of Water and Power, *Data on Available Water Supply*, p. 63. See also City of Los Angeles, City Council, *Report of the Special Sewage Disposal Commission*, by George W. Fuller, George C. Whipple, and William Mulholland (April 16 and August 10, 1921), Part 1, p. 4.

97. See Thomas H. Means, *Additional Water Supply for the City of Los Angeles in Owens Valley and Mono Basin* (San Francisco, January 1924).

98. Means, *Report on Water Requirements of Bishop Creek Lands*, pp. 12-18.

99. State of California, California Conservation Commission, *Annual Report, 1912* (Sacramento, 1913), p. 238.

100. Means, *Report on Water Requirements of Bishop Creek Lands*, pp. 19-20.

101. Ibid., pp. 17-18.

102. State of California, California Development Board, *Agricultural and Industrial Survey of Inyo County, California* (1917), pp. 7-9, 16-21.

103. California Conservation Commission, *Annual Report, 1912*, p. 238; Means, *Report on Water Requirements of Bishop Creek Lands*, p. 12; and United States Department of Agriculture, Bureau of Chemistry and Soils, *Soil Survey of the Bishop Area California*, by E. B. Watson and R. Early Storie (1928), pp. 91-93.

104. State of California, California Development Board, *Agricultural and Industrial Survey*, pp. 5, 7.

105. Means, *Report on Water Requirements of Bishop Creek Lands*, pp. 11-12, 14.

106. See A. P. Davis to W. B. Mathews, January 27, 1919, and Davis to W. W. Watterson, February 5, 1919, NA BUREC RG 115 OV 527-A.

107. Means, *Report on Water Requirements of Bishop Creek Lands*, pp. 4-7, 17-19.

108. United States, Congress, *Hearings . . . [on] H.R. 2903*, p. 115. See also City of Los Angeles, Department of Water and Power, *Water Supply Management in Inyo and Mono*, pp. 20-21.

109. United States, Congress, *Hearings . . . [on] H.R. 2903*, pp. 113, 115.

110. Quoted in Ralph J. Roske, *Everyman's Eden* (1968), pp. 484, 486.

111. City of Los Angeles, Board of Public Service Commissioners, *Report on Available Water Supply*, pp. 28-30. See also Means, *Report on Mono Basin Water*, p. 26.

112. United States, Congress, *Hearings . . . [on] H.R. 2903*, p. 112.

113. City of Los Angeles, Board of Public Service Commissioners, *Report on Available Water Supply*, p. 98.

114. City of Los Angeles, Department of Water and Power, *Water Supply Management in Inyo and Mono*, p. 6.

115. See Means, *Report on Mono Basin Water*, p. 30, and *Additional Water Supply*, pp. 9, 12; State of California, Water Resources Board, *Los Angeles County Land and Water Use Survey, 1955* (1956), table 4, p. 22.

116. See City of Los Angeles, Board of Public Service Commissioners, *Report on Available Water Supply*, pp. 3-4, 38; United States Department of Agriculture, Weather Bureau, *Climatic Summary of the United States*, sec. 18, "Southern California and Owens Valley" (1930), pp. 3-5, 17-18.

117. Thomas Means, *Report on Recent Purchases of Water in Owens*

Valley California by the City of Los Angeles (San Francisco, November 1923), p. 5; City of Los Angeles, Department of Water and Power, *Data on Available Water Supply*, pp. 4-8.

118. City of Los Angeles, City Council, *Report of the Special Sewage Disposal Commission*, p. 4.

119. Ibid.

120. Ibid. See also D.W. Longyer and E.A. Partridge to Dixon and Beckman, April 17, 1920, National Archives, Department of the Interior, Office of the Secretary, Central Classified File, 1907-1936, Record Group 48, File 2-10. (Hereinafter cited as NA INT RG 48 2-10.)

121. See State of California, Department of Water Resources, *Feasibility of Reclamation of Water from Wastes in the Los Angeles Metropolitan Area* (December 1961), pp. 22-23. See also State of California, Legislature, Assembly, "Communication to the California Legislature Relating to the Owens Valley Water Situation," by Andrae Nordskog, *Assembly Journal* (April 27, 1931), p. 25.

122. Means, Notes for Testimony, *Correspondence re Natural Soda Products.*

123. See Means, *Additional Water Supply*, p. 11; and City of Los Angeles, Board of Public Service Commissioners, *Report on Available Water Supply*, pp. 1-2. Means's was the gloomier prediction: that the city's population would rise to 2.5 million by 1940, whereas the city's report assumed a population of 1.72 million by that date. Mulholland's estimates in 1921 projected a population of 1.95 million in 1940. For the period after 1940, Mulholland's estimates turned hysterical, although he confidently described them as conservative. By 1950, he guessed, the city would contain an incredible total of 3.3 million people; the city's report fixed the 1950 population at only 2.18 million. See City of Los Angeles, City Council, *Report of the Special Sewage Disposal Commission*, p. 10. In fact, Los Angeles' population in 1940 was only 1.5 million; by 1950 it had risen to 1.97 million.

124. City of Los Angeles, Board of Public Service Commissioners, *Twenty-First Annual Report for the Fiscal Year Ending June 30, 1922* (Los Angeles, 1922), p. 11.

125. See Means, *Report on Mono Basin Water*, pp. 30-31.

126. See Outland, *Man-Made Disaster*, pp. 29-30.

127. For details of the controversy over development of the Colorado River, see Norris Hundley, *Water and the West: The Colorado River Compact and the Politics of Water in the American West* (1975), esp., for the points covered in this paragraph, pp. 55-59, 93-95, 113-15, 120-37.

128. Ibid., pp. 13-16, 116-19.

129. See Ostrom, *Water and Politics*, pp. 168-70, and Burt I. Twilegar, "Mulholland's Pipe Dream," *Westways* (January 1949).

130. United States, Congress, *Hearings . . . [on] H.R. 2903*, pp. 97, 100.

131. Ibid., pp. 106-7, 109.

132. In 1921 the vote count was 51,271 (65 percent) for the aqueduct bonds and 27,723 against; a two-thirds majority was needed for passage. In 1922, the tally was 78,007 (70 percent) for and 32,699 against. See Ostrom, *Water and Politics*, pp. 58-62.

133. See Robert Gottlieb and Irene Wolt, *Thinking Big: The Story of the Los Angeles Times, Its Publishers, and Their Influence on Southern California* (1977), pp. 166-68, 173-74.

134. See Hundley, *Water and the West*, pp. 34-35, 90-91, and Gottlieb and Wolt, *Thinking Big*, pp. 181-83.

135. Hundley, *Water and the West*, pp. 33-34.

136. See Walton Bean, *California: An Interpretive History* (1968), p. 394.

137. See Fogelson, *Fragmented Metropolis*, pp. 218-20, 240-41.

138. William Mulholland, "Water from the Colorado River," *Community Builder* (March 1928); City of Los Angeles, Department of Water and Power, *Data on Available Water Supply*, pp. 3-4.

139. Mulholland, "Water from the Colorado."

140. Mulholland, in "Water from the Colorado," uses an eight-year deadline; his department's *Data on Available Water Supply*, published at the same time as his article, specifies ten or twelve years.

141. See Hundley, *Water and the West*, pp. 251-53.

142. City of Los Angeles, Department of Water and Power, *Data on Available Water Supply*, p. 32.

143. State of California, Department of Public Works, Division of Engineering and Irrigation, *Water Resources of Southern California*, by Paul Baily (1927).

144. W.C. Yeatman, *Population Growth of Los Angeles and Its Relation to Water Demand* (August 10, 1932), p. 1.

145. Rockwell D. Hunt, *California and Californians* (1926), vol. III, pp. 389-90.

146. Means's expertise was respected as well by the Owens Valley ranchers, and his various reports on water supply conditions in the area are cited frequently in Chalfant's *Story of Inyo* and in the state engineer's report to Governor Richardson.

147. See Means, *Report on Water Requirements of Bishop Creek Lands*, pp. 19-20, 26-27.

148. Means, *Report on Mono Basin Water*, pp. 31-32.

149. See Means, *Report on Recent Purchases of Water*, pp. 6-9, and *Additional Water Supply*, p. 24. Mulholland's estimate of his losses appears in United States, Congress, *Hearings . . . [on] H.R. 2903*, p. 115.

150. See Means, *Report on Mono Basin Water*, p. 39, and *Additional Water Supply*, pp. 30-31.

151. Means, *Additional Water Supply*, p. 21.

152. Means, *Report on Mono Basin Water*, p. 8, and *Additional Water Supply*, p. 24.

153. *Owens Valley Herald*, November 3, 1926.

154. *Owens Valley Herald*, December 10, 1912.

155. Mary Austin, *The Flock* (1906), p. 13.

156. See Dell Yandell to C. L. Newmiller, February 13, 1932, Mary W. Gorman Papers, Independence, Calif.

157. Ibid.; C. Lorin Ray, ed., *Mementos of Bishop, California, 1861-1961: 100 Years of Real Living* (1961), p. 18; Streeter, *Saga of Inyo*, p. 32; *Owens Valley Herald*, November 3, 1926.

158. See Frances Corey Krautter, *The Story of Keeler* (1959); *Engineering News-Record*, vol. 143, no. 12 (September 22, 1949); and, in the Gorman Papers, Yandell to Newmiller, February 13, 1932, and Charles C. Cole to Newmiller, January 15, 1929.

159. See United States Naval Weapons Center, *A Land Use History of Coso Hot Springs, Inyo County, California*, by the Iroquois Research Institute et al. (January 1979), pp. 141-47.

160. See Cole to Newmiller, January 15, 1929, Gorman Papers. See also R. Coke Wood, "Owens Valley As I Knew It," *Pacific Historian* (Summer 1972).

161. See Ray, *Mementos of Bishop*, p. 15, and Chalfant 1st, p. 318.

162. Articles of Agreement of the Owens Valley Associated Ditches, September 22, 1900, Larson Papers, box 1, folder 1.

163. The November 1904 petition is in NA BUREC RG 115 OV 527. The later petition is in the National Archives, Department of the Interior, Lands and Railroads Division, Record Group 48, Reclamation Projects, box 37. (Hereinafter cited as NA L&RR RG 48 37.)

164. See Los Angeles, *First Report of the Chief Engineer*, p. 133.

165. See W. W. Watterson to A. P. Davis, January 24, 1919, and Davis to Watterson, February 5, 1919, NA BUREC RG 115 OV 527-A.

166. See Dixon to Beckman, October 1, 1919, Larson Papers, box 2, Miscellaneous.

167. *Inyo Register*, March 19, 1925. See also Municipal League of Los Angeles, "Owens Valley Revolt."

168. See Report of Thomas Means to J. B. Lippincott, September 14, 1904, NA BUREC RG 115 OV 527.

169. See Streeter, *Saga of Inyo*, p. 21, and C. Lorin Ray, ed., *Inyo, 1866-1966* (1966), p. 47.

170. Watterson and Symons, "Open Letter," January 11, 1924, Larson Papers, box 2, Miscellaneous.

171. Owens Valley Irrigation District, *Engineer's Report on the Owens Valley Irrigation District* (March 20, 1923), pp. 1-4.

172. Ibid., pp. 4-6, 13, 25. City of Los Angeles, Board of Public Service Commissioners, *Report on Available Water Supply*, p. 94. Means, *Report on Mono Basin Water*, pp. 35-36.

173. Owens Valley Irrigation District, *Engineer's Report*, pp. 12, 17-18, 25.

174. See State of California, State Engineer W. F. McClure, *Letter of Transmittal and Report of the State Engineer Concerning the Owens Valley-Los Angeles Controversy* (Sacramento, 1925), pp. 7-8 (hereinafter cited as McClure, *Owens Valley Controversy*), and affidavits therein of White Smith, December 2, 1924, and W. W. Yandell, November 29, 1924, pp. 41-43. (NB: Yandell was an employee of the Watterson banks; White Smith was the irrigation district's attorney and an uncle by marriage of Wilfred and Mark Watterson.)

175. See "Statement of the Farmers Ditch Company," September 1924, in McClure, *Owens Valley Controversy*, p. 32. Chalfant 2d, p. 385, has it that Hall boasted of cutting off the district's left arm.

176. See *Owens Valley Herald*, April 4, 1923, and "Statement of the Farmers Ditch Company," in McClure, *Owens Valley Controversy*, pp. 31-34.

177. *Owens Valley Herald*, March 21, 1923.

178. See "Sworn Statement of Karl Keough," December 1, 1924, in McClure, *Owens Valley Controversy*, p. 39.

179. See appendix to Thomas Means, *Purchases of Water in Owens Valley by the City of Los Angeles* (San Francisco, 1925). (Hereinafter cited as Means, *Purchases in Owens Valley*.)

180. See "Statement of Farmers Ditch Company," in McClure, *Owens Valley Controversy*, p. 36, and City of Los Angeles, Board of Public Service Commissioners, *Reply to . . . Watterson*, pp. 30-31.

181. See *Inyo Register*, January 3, 1924.

182. Owens Valley Irrigation District, *Engineer's Report*, p. 25.

183. McClure, *Owens Valley Controversy*, pp. 7-8.

184. See *Owens Valley Herald*, August 8, 1923; McClure, *Owens Valley Controversy*, pp. 64-68; Chalfant 2d, pp. 386-87; and Means, *Report on Recent Purchase of Water*, p. 1.

185. *Owens Valley Herald,* August 29, 1923. See also *Sacramento Union,* March 30, 1927.
186. See City of Los Angeles, Board of Public Service Commissioners, *Reply to ... Watterson,* pp. 36-37; "Statement of Farmers Ditch Company," in McClure, *Owens Valley Controversy,* pp. 33-35; "Deposition of Fred Naphan," December 1, 1924, also in McClure, *Owens Valley Controversy,* pp. 44-45; and Chalfant 2d, pp. 384-85.
187. *Inyo Register,* January 3, 1924.
188. Watterson and Symons, "Open Letter," January 11, 1924, Larson Papers, box 2, Miscellaneous.
189. *Inyo Register,* January 10, 1924.
190. Chalfant 2d, p. 386. Hall resettled in Glendale.
191. See Los Angeles, *First Report of the Chief Engineer,* pp. 45-46.
192. See Means, *Purchases in Owens Valley,* pp. 11, 12, 17.
193. See Chalfant 1st, p. 319; Chalfant 2d, p. 337; City of Los Angeles, Department of Public Service, *Owens Valley and the Los Angeles Aqueduct* (1925); and Means, *Purchases in Owens Valley,* p. 16, and *Report on Water Requirements of Bishop Creek Lands,* pp. 12-13.
194. Chalfant 1st, pp. 329-30.
195. McClure, *Owens Valley Controversy,* pp. 11-13, 26-28; Chalfant 2d, pp. 387-88; Means, *Report on Recent Purchases of Water,* p. 1.
196. Chalfant 2d, p. 388.
197. *Los Angeles Times,* May 28, 1924.
198. See, e.g., City of Los Angeles, Department of Public Service, *Owens Valley and the Aqueduct,* and City of Los Angeles, Department of Water and Power, *The Water Trail,* by Don J. Kinsey (1928), p. 24 (hereinafter cited as Kinsey, *Water Trail*).
199. See Means, *Additional Water Supply,* p. 24, and *Purchases of Water by Los Angeles,* p. 1.
200. *Los Angeles Times,* May 28, 1924. Ostrom, in *Water and Politics,* pp. 128-29, argues rather disingenuously that Mulholland was so "unimpeachably honest" that he was incapable of dealing with the Wattersons or anyone else whose integrity he doubted.
201. See Lee, "Well Development"; Phillips, "Underground Water Development"; City of Los Angeles, Department of Water and Power, *Water Supply Management in Inyo and Mono,* p. 25; Chalfant 2d, p. 382; and State of California, Legislature, Senate, "Report of the Special Investigating Committee on Water Situation in Inyo and Mono Counties," in *Journal of the Senate* (May 7, 1931), p. 2448.
202. Aqueduct deliveries in the water year ending September 30, 1924, were 149,900 acre-feet; they were 127,800 in the next year. This is down from 186,300 acre-feet in the 1923 water year and 204,600

acre-feet in the year before that. See State of California, Water Resources Board, *Los Angeles County Land and Water Use*, table 4, p. 22.

203. This estimate, as of June 30, 1924, includes all aqueduct expenditures for power plants and land and water rights purchases in the Owens Valley. See City of Los Angeles, Board of Public Service Commissioners, *Report on Available Water Supply*, p. 97.

204. See Means, *Purchases in Owens Valley*, pp. 15, 17; *Report on Mono Basin Water*, p. 1; and *Report on Purchases of Water*, pp. 11-12.

205. See *San Francisco Call*, April 21-May 3, 1924.

206. See *Los Angeles Times*, May 22 and 23, 1924.

207. See, e.g., *Los Angeles Record*, June 24, 1924.

208. See McClure, *Owens Valley Controversy*, pp. 20-23.

209. *Inyo Register*, November 28, 1924.

210. Municipal League of Los Angeles, "Owens Valley Revolt."

211. McClure, *Owens Valley Controversy*, pp. 15-16.

212. See City of Los Angeles, Board of Public Service Commissioners, *Reply to ... Watterson*, p. 43; *Inyo Register*, December 4, 1924; and Chalfant 2d, p. 389.

213. See Ostrom, *Water and Politics*, p. 62.

214. Municipal League of Los Angeles, "Owens Valley Revolt."

215. City of Los Angeles, Board of Public Service Commissioners, *Report on Available Water Supply*, pp. 1-2.

216. Ibid., pp. 10-13, 141-45.

217. Municipal League of Los Angeles, "Owens Valley Revolt."

218. "Owens Valley Problems," *Intake* (November 1924). See also Ostrom, *Water and Politics*, p. 122.

219. City of Los Angeles, Department of Water and Power, *Special Committee Report on Conditions in Owens Valley*, by Clarence A. Dykstra, James Brader, and J. F. Neal (1928).

220. See Ostrom, *Water and Politics*, pp. 129-30.

221. McClure, *Owens Valley Controversy*, p. 10; Genny Schumacher Smith, *Deepest Valley*, rev. ed. (Los Altos, Calif., 1978), p. 33.

222. See exchange of telegrams, Collins to Richardson, November 16 and 17, 1924, and Richardson to Collins, November 17 and 19, 1924, repr. in City of Los Angeles, Board of Public Service Commissioners, *Reply to ... Watterson*, pp. 52-53.

223. See *Los Angeles Examiner*, November 21, 1924; *Exeter Sun*, November 27, 1924; *Los Angeles Times*, November 18, 1924; and "California's Little Civil War," *Literary Digest* (December 6, 1924).

See also Marian L. Ryan, "Los Angeles Newspapers Fight the Water War, 1924-1927," *Southern California Quarterly* (June 1968).

224. Telegram, W.W. Watterson to M.Q. Watterson, November 20, 1924, repr. in McClure, *Owens Valley Controversy*, p. 7.
225. McClure, *Owens Valley Controversy*, pp. 15-16.
226. *Los Angeles Examiner*, November 21, 1924.
227. *Fresno Republican*, December 5, 1924.
228. McClure, *Owens Valley Controversy*, p. 17.
229. See "Better Prospects for Settlement of Owens Valley Dispute," *Engineering News-Record* (May 7, 1925).
230. See Hundley, *Water and the West*, pp. 143, 206-10.
231. McClure, *Owens Valley Controversy*, Letter of Transmittal to Governor Richardson, January 9, 1925.
232. See Roske, *Everyman's Eden*, pp. 498-99, and Bean, *California*, p. 364.
233. See chap. 109 (Senate Bill 757—Inman), *Statutes of 1925*, California.
234. See City of Los Angeles, Department of Water and Power, *Facts Concerning the Owens Valley Reparations Claims* (n.d.).
235. City of Los Angeles, Board of Public Service Commissioners, *Reply to . . . Watterson*, pp. 1 and 91. See also Kinsey, *Water Trail*, pp. 32-33.
236. See, e.g., City of Los Angeles, Department of Public Service, *Owens Valley and the Aqueduct*; Kinsey, *Water Trail*, p. 25; and City of Los Angeles, Board of Public Service Commissioners, *Owens Valley and the Los Angeles Water Supply, Including a Statement of Facts Omitted by the State Engineer in His Report to Governor Richardson* (February 1925), pp. 6-7.
237. See City of Los Angeles, Board of Public Service Commissioners, *Owens Valley and Los Angeles*, pp. 8-10; Graydon Oliver, "Prosperous Condition of Owens Valley District Revealed by Many Vital Statistics," *Modern Irrigation* (August 1927).
238. See City of Los Angeles, Board of Water and Power Commissioners, *The Dynamite Holdup* (n.d.); Oliver, "Prosperous Condition of Owens Valley"; and City of Los Angeles, Board of Public Service Commissioners, *Reply to . . . Watterson*, pp. 7-9, 46-47. See also City of Los Angeles, Board of Public Service Commissioners, *Owens Valley and Los Angeles*, p. 13; City of Los Angeles, Department of Public Service, *Owens Valley and the Aqueduct*; and "The Owens Valley Controversy" (by a Special Correspondent), *The Outlook* (July 13, 1927).

239. City of Los Angeles, Board of Public Service Commissioners, *Owens Valley and Los Angeles*, p. 21; "Owens Valley Controversy," *Outlook*.

240. City of Los Angeles, Board of Water and Power Commissioners, *Dynamite Holdup*; Kinsey, *Water Trail*, p. 24; "Owens Valley Controversy," *Outlook*. See also "The Los Angeles Aqueduct Seizure: What Really Happened," *Fire and Water Engineering* (December 17, 1924).

241. Kinsey, *Water Trail*, pp. 20-21.

242. City of Los Angeles, Department of Public Service, *Owens Valley and the Aqueduct*.

243. City of Los Angeles, Board of Public Service Commissioners, *Reply to ... Watterson*, pp. 26-28.

244. See Report of J.C. Clausen, p. 51, NA BUREC RG 115 OV 527.

245. Freeman, Stearns, and Schuyler, "Report of Board of Consulting Engineers," in Los Angeles, *First Report of the Chief Engineer*, p. 125.

246. Testimony of Mulholland, City of Los Angeles, Aqueduct Investigation Board, *Report*, p. 42.

247. City of Los Angeles, Department of Public Service, *Complete Report on Construction*, pp. 25, 75.

248. See United States Reclamation Service, *Report on Owens Valley Project*, and Means, *Report on Mono Basin Water*.

249. United States Department of the Interior, United States Geological Survey, *Geology and Water Resources of Owens Valley*, pp. 16, 25.

250. City of Los Angeles, Board of Public Service Commissioners, *Report on Available Water Supply*, pp. 148-49.

251. See Kinsey, *Water Trail*, p. 21, and Municipal League of Los Angeles, "Owens Valley Revolt."

252. See State of California, Water Resources Board, *Reconnaissance Investigation of the Water Resources of Mono and Owens Basins* (August 1960), pp. 44, 64-67.

253. See, e.g., City of Los Angeles, Board of Water and Power Commissioners, *Report of the Board of Consulting Engineers on the Storage and Distribution of Water*, by Louis C. Hill, R.E. McDonnell, and Robert T. Hill (October 1928).

254. See Thomas H. Means, *Value of Water Rights in Owens River Valley Based upon City of Los Angeles Land Purchases from 1923 to 1926* (San Francisco, July 1928), Means Papers, Water Resources Center Archives, University of California, Berkeley. See also Means, *Purchases in Owens Valley*, pp. 1-2.

255. See Kinsey, *Water Trail*, p. 27.

256. *Santa Barbara Press*, November 27, 1924. See also Robert Glass Cleland, *California in Our Time, 1900-1940* (New York, 1947), pp. 187-94.

257. *Sacramento Union*, April 5, 1927.

258. See Kahrl, *California Water Atlas*, p. 27. See also Wells A. Hutchins, *The California Law of Water Rights* (1956), and *Amelia Herminghaus* v. *Southern California Edison Company*, 200 Cal. 81 (1926).

259. See *Sacramento Union*, March 30, 31, and April 3, 1927.

260. Assembly Concurrent Resolution 34 (Williams) *Assembly Bills, California, 1927* (Sacramento, 1927).

261. See *Sacramento Union*, April 21, 1927.

262. California Legislature, *Assembly Journal*, April 22, 1927.

263. Telegram, Owens Valley Property Owners Protective Association to George E. Cryer, May 13, 1927, Andrae B. Nordskog Papers, Water Resources Center Archives, University of California, Berkeley.

264. See, e.g., *Los Angeles Times*, May 29, 1927; *Sacramento Union*, April 17, 1927; and Chalfant 2d, pp. 394, 396.

265. See *Los Angeles Times*, June 24, 1927, and Workman, *City That Grew*, pp. 329-30.

266. *Los Angeles Times*, July 2 and 16, 1927; City of Los Angeles, Department of Water and Power, *Facts Concerning . . . Reparations*, p. 1.

267. See *Sacramento Union*, April 1, 1927, and *Los Angeles Times*, August 13, 1927.

268. See Roske, *Everyman's Eden*, pp. 498-99, and Bean, *California*, p. 364.

269. See A. B. Whieldon to Jerome Watterson, December 2, 1930, Gorman Papers, and *Los Angeles Times*, August 13, 1927.

270. *Sacramento Union*, April 1, 1927.

271. See Chalfant 2d, pp. 397-98, and *Los Angeles Times*, November 8 and 9, 1927. See also Yandell to Newmiller, February 13, 1932, Gorman Papers.

272. *Los Angeles Times*, August 5, 6, 11, 12, and 14 and November 2 and 10, 1927; *Inyo Register*, August 18, 1927; Yandell to Newmiller, February 13, 1932, Gorman Papers.

273. *Los Angeles Times*, November 2, 9, 11, and 15, 1927; Chalfant 2d, pp. 397-98. Regarding the sign at Bishop, see Wood, "Owens Valley As I Knew It."

274. See Workman, *City That Grew*, pp. 329-30, and Kinsey, *Water Trail*, p. 39. Those charged were A.K. Betker, Frank Spaulding,

Walter Young, William L. Smith, Percy Sexton, Fred Napham, and Maj. C. Percy Watson, who was charged in both 1927 and 1928.

275. See Charles A. Meyer to James B. Holshan, June(?) 1930, Gorman Papers.

276. Albert A. Rosenshine to Jerome Watterson, January 6, 1930, ibid.

277. T.C. Knoles to C.L. Newmiller, April 3, 1931, ibid. Regarding Knole's involvement with the Owens Valley, see Reginald R. Stuart and Grace D. Stuart, *Tully Knoles of Pacific* (1956) p. 48.

278. See Streeter, *Saga of Inyo*, p. 32, and open letters on behalf of George Watterson from Jess Hession, March 2, 1934, and from Will C. Wood, January 9, 1934, Larson Papers, box 1, Miscellaneous.

279. *Los Angeles Times*, November 12, 1927.

280. Kinsey, *Water Trail*, p. 39.

281. See City of Los Angeles, Department of Water and Power, *Water Supply Management in Inyo and Mono*, pp. 20-21.

282. See Outland, *Man-Made Disaster*, pp. 28-42.

283. See City of Los Angeles, Bureau of the Los Angeles Aqueduct, *Sixth Annual Report to the Board of Public Works* (1911).

284. It is no accident that the Saint Francis Dam disaster has never achieved the prominence in California history of the San Francisco earthquake, despite the fact that the death tolls in both incidents were roughly equivalent. In preparing his history of the dam's collapse, Outland discovered that much of the official testimony offered by city officials was perjured and that many of the most important records of the event have been destroyed or otherwise withdrawn from public inspection. As a result, it is impossible to determine exactly how many people were killed, although Outland advises that any death count over 450 or under 400 is unrealistic. See Outland, *Man-Made Disaster*, pp. 95-200 and 254-57.

285. Quoted in ibid., pp. 212-20. Outland is curiously ambivalent on the question of sabotage. His own theory of the dam's collapse does not rule out the possibility of sabotage, and he qualifies his explanation by stating that it would apply only if the sabotage theory is discounted. See also Pierson M. Hall, "Review of the First Edition of *Man-Made Disaster*," *California Historical Society Quarterly*, vol. 45, no. 1 (March 1965).

286. Outland, *Man-Made Disaster*, p. 118.

287. Ibid., p. 237.

288. See Ostrom, *Water and Politics*, pp. 125-27; Chalfant 2d, pp. 399-400; State of California, Legislature, "Report of the Senate Special

Investigating Committee," pp. 2448-50; and Means, *Value of Water Rights.*

289. Ruth E. Baugh, "Land Use Changes in the Bishop Area of Owens Valley California," *Economic Geography* (January 1937). See also Dorothy C. Cragen, *A Brief History of the Schools of Inyo County* (December 1954).

290. Marie Louise Parcher and Will C. Parcher, *Dry Ditches* (1934), pp. 13, 19. The quotation from Chalfant appears in his introduction to the Parcher volume.

291. Ehud Yonay, "How Green Was My Valley," *New West* (March 28, 1977).

292. See, e.g., State of California, Legislature, Assembly, "Communication," by Nordskog, p. 27.

293. *Western Construction News*, vol. 10, no. 8 (August 1935).

294. *Sacramento Union*, April 3, 1927.

295. See, e.g., Van Norman, "Memoir of William Mulholland"; Joseph B. Lippincott, "Mulholland's Memory," *Civil Engineering* (March 1939), and "William Mulholland: Engineer, Pioneer, Raconteur;" City of Los Angeles, Department of Water and Power, *William Mulholland: Father of the Los Angeles Municipal Water System* (October 1939); *Los Angeles Times*, July 22, 1937, and August 2, 1940; *Constructive Californians* (1926); and "The Los Angeles Aqueduct Seizure," *Fire and Water Engineering.*

296. See, e.g., Spriggs, "History of the Domestic Water Supply"; *Engineering News-Record*, vol. 115, no. 4 (July 25, 1935), and vol. 101, no. 1 (November 22, 1928); and "Mulholland: Man of Broad Vision" *Southern California Business* (September 1929).

297. *Los Angeles Times*, July 23, 1935.

298. Van Norman, "Memoir of William Mulholland."

299. Poem, "Builder of the Los Angeles Aqueduct," by "W. E. C.," dated July 23, 1935, at Los Angeles Department of Water and Power.

CHAPTER SEVEN
Legacy

1. See City of Los Angeles, Department of Water and Power, *The Water and Power Building* (1969).

2. Ibid.

3. See Clarence Streeter and Peggy Streeter, eds., *Saga of Inyo County* (1977), p. 21.

4. Morrow Mayo, *Los Angeles* (1933), pp. 245-46.

5. State of California, Legislature, Assembly, "Communication to the California Legislature Relating to the Owens Valley Water Situation," by Andrae Nordskog, in *Assembly Journal*, April 27, 1931. See also *Gridiron*, February 24, April 21, and May 19, 1931; "Minutes of the Southwest Water League" meeting of October 16, 1931, and "Submission to the Los Angeles County Grand Jury," March 27, 1935, Nordskog Papers, Water Resources Center Archives, University of California, Berkeley. Willie Arthur Chalfant acknowledges his debt to Nordskog on page 338 of his *Story of Inyo*, 2d ed. (1933). (Hereinafter cited as Chalfant 2d.) In an article based on heavily edited excerpts of letters purportedly stolen from the records of the Inyo banks which were then in the custody of state authorities, the Municipal League of Los Angeles charged that Nordskog had received some financial support from the Watterson brothers. See "Out of Their Own Mouths," *Municipal League of Los Angeles Bulletin*, October 31, 1927.

6. Will Rogers, Dispatch for August 25, 1932.

7. Quoted in Robert Gottlieb and Irene Wolt, *Thinking Big: The Story of the Los Angeles Times, Its Publishers, and Their Influence on Southern California* (1977), p. 142.

8. Also released under the title *Frontier Horizon*.

9. Quoted in Frances Gragg and George Palmer Putnam, *Golden Valley: A Novel of California* (1950), pp. 126, 145.

10. Peter B. Kyne, *The Long Chance* (1914), pp. 12, 115, 201-3.

11. Mary Austin, *The Ford* (1917), pp. 365, 368.

12. Ibid., pp. 71, 287-89.

13. Ibid., p. 409.

14. For other fictional works which use the controversy as an incidental element or background to other action, see Victoria Wolf, *Fabulous City* (1957), Cedric Belfrage, *Promised Land* (1938), and the 1974 film *Chinatown*. See also Harry Carr, *Los Angeles: City of Dreams* (1935), and Abraham Hoffman, "Fact and Fiction in the Owens Valley Water Controversy," *Los Angeles Westerners Corral, Brand Book No. 15* (1978). In addition, a nuclear power plant which the Department of Water and Power has proposed to build in the San Joaquin Valley appears as the last rallying point for human civilization in the apocalyptic novel *Lucifer's Hammer*, by Larry Niven and Jerry Pournelle (1977).

15. See *Los Angeles Record*, August 4, 1925, and May 8, 1929.

16. *Los Angeles Times*, July 2, 1929.

17. See Robert M. Fogelson, *The Fragmented Metropolis: Los Ange-*

les, 1850-1930 (1967), pp. 242-44; Gottlieb and Wolt, *Thinking Big*, pp. 200-201; Vincent Ostrom, *Water and Politics: A Study of Water Policies and Administration in the Development of Los Angeles* (1953), pp. 80-85; and *W. W. Mines* v. *R. F. Del Vaile*, 201 Cal. 273 (1927).

18. *Los Angeles Herald*, January 13, 1931.

19. See Ostrom, *Water and Politics*, pp. 68-85, 89-90, 100-10.

20. *Los Angeles Times*, February 28, 1929.

21. Chalfant 2d, p. 400; Ostrom, *Water and Politics*, p. 127.

22. John C. Porter to Los Angeles Water and Power Commission, June 11, 1930, reprinted in City of Los Angeles, Office of the Mayor, *Statement on Owens Valley and Mono Basin Land Purchases*, by Mayor John C. Porter (June 24, 1930).

23. *Los Angeles Times*, January 14, 1931.

24. *Los Angeles Record*, May 25, 1931.

25. Hubert Work to A.B. Nordskog, April 7, 1928, in National Archives, Department of the Interior, Office of the Secretary, Central Classified File 1907-1936, Record Group 48, File 8-3, pt. 1, "Orland/Owens River." (Hereinafter cited as NA INT RG 48 8-3.) In the same collection, see also the letters from Nordskog to Lawrence C. Phipps, May 1, 1928, and the memoranda prepared by P.W. Dent for Hubert Work, May 11, 1928, and for "Mr. Bissell," April 2, 1928. See also "Submission to the Los Angeles County Grand Jury," Nordskog Papers.

26. State of California, Legislature, Assembly, "Communication to the California Legislature." See also *Gridiron*, April 21, 1931.

27. State of California, Legislature, "Senate Report of the Special Investigating Committee on Water Situation in Inyo and Mono Counties," *Journal of the Senate* (May 7, 1931).

28. See chap. 720, State of California, *Statutes of 1931* (Senate Bill 141—Crittenden).

29. See City of Los Angeles, Department of Water and Power, *Water Supply Management in Inyo and Mono Counties* (September 1966), p. 9.

30. See State of California, Department of Public Works, Division of Engineering and Irrigation, *Supplemental Report and Notes on Mono Basin Investigation*, by S.T. Harding, app. N (October 17, 1922), pp. 51-52. (Hereinafter cited as Harding, *Supplemental Report*.)

31. See United States Department of the Interior, Reclamation Service, *Owens Valley Project Preliminary Report*, by Harold Con-

kling (September 1920), pp. 1-8. (Hereinafter cited as Conkling, *Preliminary Report on Owens Valley Project.*)

32. Ibid., p. 10. United States Department of the Interior, Reclamation Service, *Report on Owens Valley Project California*, by Harold Conkling (September 1921), p. 6. (Hereinafter cited as Conkling, *Report on Owens Valley Project—1921.*)

33. See State of California, Department of Public Works, Division of Engineering and Irrigation, *Report on Development of Water Resources in Mono Basin . . .* by S. T. Harding (December 1922), pp. 2-12. (Hereinafter cited as Harding, *Report on Mono Basin.*) See also Harding, *Supplemental Report*, app. A.

34. Conkling, *Report on Owens Valley Project—1921*, p. 6. Harding, *Report on Mono Basin*, pp. 13-15, 17-18.

35. Conkling, *Preliminary Report on Owens Valley Project*, p. 9. Conkling reported that 40,000 of the 73,000 irrigable acres in the Bishop area were then under irrigation, whereas only 6,000 of the 64,000 irrigable acres around Independence were similarly served. Los Angeles at this time owned 22,600 acres in the Bishop region and 72,400 acres in Independence. See also Conkling, *Report on Owens Valley Project—1921*, p. 8.

36. Conkling, *Preliminary Report on Owens Valley Project*, pp. 30-31.

37. Conkling, *Report on Owens Valley Project—1921*, p. 6 of synopsis and pp. 26-29 of body of report.

38. Ibid., pp. 7-8 of synopsis and 25 and 44 of report.

39. Ibid., pp. 4 and 6 of synopsis and 15-16, 18, and 41-42 of report.

40. Conkling, *Preliminary Report on Owens Valley Project*, p. 3.

41. See Harding, *Report on Mono Basin*, pp. 1-2, and *Supplemental Report*, app. N, p. 51.

42. Harding, *Supplemental Report*, app. N, pp. 52-53.

43. Harding, *Report on Mono Basin*, p. 24, and *Supplemental Report*, app. G, p. 22. The city's protests involved applications filed by E. G. Ryan, the Pacific Power Corporation, and the California-Nevada Canal, Water, and Power Company.

44. A. P. Davis, Memorandum for the Secretary of the Interior, March 26, 1920; Department of the Interior, Board of Appeals, to Davis, March 31, 1920, with Davis' response noted at bottom—all in NA INT RG 48 8-3.

45. Harding, *Supplemental Report*, app. N, pp. 54-55.

46. Consaul and Heltman to Secretary of the Interior, May 1, 1920, NA INT RG 48 8-3.

47. The state engineer, W. F. McClure, formally protested the withdrawals on September 6, 1922. See Harding, *Supplemental Report*,

app. N, p. 55, and orders of modification dated May 3 and August 30, 1920, and November 22, 1922, in NA INT RG 48 8-3.

48. E.C. Finney to M.Y.S. Kirkwood, Chairman, Mono County Board of Supervisors, January 26, 1924, NA INT RG 48 8-3.

49. Finney to Los Angeles Board of Public Service Commissioners, January 26, 1924, ibid.

50. W.B. Mathews to F.E. Weymouth, July 10, 1924, quoted in F.E. Weymouth to Elwood Mead, September 23, 1924, ibid.

51. See Mead to Finney, October 18, 1924; Finney to Pat Parker, December 26, 1924; and Weymouth to the Secretary of the Interior, May 15, 1923—ibid. Regarding Weymouth's later career, see "William Mulholland," *Western Construction News and Highways Builder* (August 1933).

52. Thomas R. White to President Herbert Hoover, May 2, 1930, in National Archives, Department of the Interior, Office of the Secretary, Central Classified File 1907-1936, Record Group 48, General Land Office, File 2-173, "Water Supply Los Angeles, California, 1929-1934." (Hereinafter cited as NA INT RG 48 2-173.)

53. Mead to Hubert Work, May 15, 1928, NA INT RG 48 8-3.

54. See Work to Mead, May 17, 1928, ibid.

55. See City of Los Angeles, Board of Water and Power Commissioners, *Report of the Board of Consulting Engineers on the Storage and Distribution of Water*, by Louis C. Hill, R.E. McDonnell, and Robert T. Hill (October 1928), pp. 2, 12-13, 20; City of Los Angeles, Department of Water and Power, *Data on Available Water Supply and Future Requirements of the City of Los Angeles and the Metropolitan Area* (October 1928), pp. 6-11; and State of California, Department of Public Works, Division of Engineering and Irrigation, *Water Resources of Southern California*, bull. 12 (Sacramento, 1927).

56. Jas. P. Vroman, Secretary, Board of Water and Power Commissioners, to R.L. Wilbur, March 20, 1931, NA INT RG 48 2-173. Regarding Bishop opposition, see, e.g., in the same location, Joseph M. Dixon, Acting Secretary of the Interior, to O.S. Braught, June 22, 1929. The withdrawals were made by Executive Orders 5117 of May 16, 1929; 5229 of November 25, 1929; 5319 of April 7, 1930; 5380 of June 24, 1930; 5401 of July 23, 1930; 5472 of October 27, 1930; and 5512 of December 11, 1930.

57. United States, Congress, House, Committee on Irrigation and Reclamation, *Hearings ... [on] H.R. 2903, by Mr. Swing*. 68th Cong., 1st sess., pt. 1 (1924), p. 114.

58. The vote was 147,799 (63 percent) for and 86,893 against.

59. *Los Angeles Times*, February 28, 1929.

60. See ibid., March 16, 1930.
61. "Victory," *Intake*, June, 1930. See also Ostrom, *Water and Politics*, p. 83.
62. See United States, Congress, House, Committee on Public Lands, *Hearings on H.R. 83, H.R. 727, H.R. 728, H.R. 1883, and H.R. 6697...* (1948), p. 79 (hereinafter cited as *Mono Hearings, 1948*); *Los Angeles Times*, March 16, 1930, and October 21, 1933; Thomas Means, *Report on the Value of Property of the Hillside Water Company, Inyo County, California* (San Francisco, September 14, 1928). See also John H. Edwards, Assistant Secretary of the Interior, to the United States Attorney General, December 19, 1930, December 12, 1931, and November 30, 1932, and T.A. Waters, Assistant Secretary of the Interior, to the Attorney General, May 7, 1934—in National Archives, Department of the Interior, Office of the Secretary, Central Classified File 1907-1936, Record Group 48, File 2-10 "General." (Hereinafter cited as NA INT RG 48 2-10.)
63. See City of Los Angeles, Bureau of Water Works and Supply, *Water Supply and Distribution Problems in Los Angeles*, by Verne G. Saunders (December 6, 1937), p. 8; H.A. Van Norman, "The Limitations of Civil Service," *Journal of the American Water Works Association* (September 1941); United States Department of the Interior, United States Geological Survey, *Review of Waterpower Withdrawals: Mono Lake and Owens Lake Basins, California*, by Kenneth W. Sax (May 1964), p. 4; and the foreword by David Gaines to David W. Winkler, ed. *An Ecological Study of Mono Lake, California* (1977).
64. See Thomas Means, *Report on Mono Basin Water as Supply for Southern California* (San Francisco, October 1923), and *Additional Water Supply for the City of Los Angeles in Owens Valley and Mono Basin* (San Francisco, January 1924); City of Los Angeles, Department of Water and Power, *Water Supply Management*, pp. 8-9; and *Los Angeles Times*, March 16, 1930.
65. Department of the Interior, Board of Appeals, to Davis, March 31, 1920, NA INT RG 48 8-3.
66. See the request for withdrawals issued in connection with the executive orders cited in note 56 above in NA INT RG 48 2-173.
67. Jacob N. Wasserman, Chief Counsel to the General Land Office, to a Mr. Wolfsohn, Assistant Commissioner, November 5, 1945, in National Archives, Department of the Interior, Office of the Secretary, Central Classified File 1937-1953, Record Group 48, File 2-173, pt. 3, "General Land Office, Water Supply, Los Angeles, California." (Hereinafter cited as NA INT RG 48 2-173 New.)
68. United States, Congress, House, *Congressional Record*, January 21, 1931, p. 2855; also, *Mono Hearings, 1948*, pp. 86-87.

69. See Act of March 4, 1931, 46 *Stat.* 1530-1548; C. C. Moore, Commissioner of the General Land Office, to J. H. Favorite, Chief of San Francisco Field Division, April 18, 1931, NA INT RG 48 2-173; *Los Angeles Express*, March 2, 1931; and United States, Department of the Interior, Circular 1247, April 18, 1931.

70. Executive Order 5631, May 26, 1931.

71. See R. L. Wilbur to Joe Crail, February 2, 1931, and to Harry L. Englebright, May 31, 1932, NA INT RG 48 2-173.

72. See Wasserman to Wolfsohn, November 4, 1945, NA INT RG 48 2-173 New; Act of June 23, 1936, 49 *Stat.* 1892; and Executive Order 6206, July 16, 1933.

73. Ibid. See also *Los Angeles Times*, October 4, 1970.

74. City of Los Angeles, Bureau of Water Works and Supply, *The Problem of Boron in the Los Angeles Water Supply*, by R. F. Goudey (July 1936), pp. 6-8, and, by the same author, *The Boron Problem As Related to the Los Angeles Water Supply* (January 1937), pp. 17-18. (Hereinafter cited as *Boron Problem, 1936*, and *Boron Problem, 1937*.)

75. Thomas Means to W. P. Rowe, Deputy Attorney General for California, February 8, 1940, in *Correspondence Regarding Natural Soda Products Company* v. *City of Los Angeles*, Means Papers, Water Resources Center Archives, University of California, Berkeley.

76. United States Department of Agriculture, Bureau of Plant Industry, *Boron in the Los Angeles (Owens River) Aqueduct*, by L. V. Wilcox (December 3, 1946), pp. 1, 7.

77. *Boron Problem, 1936*, p. 3, and *Boron Problem, 1937*, pp. 4-7.

78. *Boron Problem, 1936*, pp. 1, 3-5, 10; *Boron Problem, 1937*, pp. 4-7.

79. See Joseph B. Lippincott, "The Dual Usage of Water for Domestic and Irrigation Purposes," *Journal of the American Water Works Association* (September 1936).

80. State of California, Office of the State Engineer, *Letter of Transmittal and Report of the State Engineer Concerning the Owens Valley-Los Angeles Controversy to Governor Friend William Richardson*, by W. F. McClure (1925), p. 11.

81. See City of Los Angeles, Bureau of Municipal Research, *Consolidated Water for Los Angeles County* (1933).

82. W. C. Yeatman, *Population Growth of Los Angeles and Its Relation to Water Demand* (August 10, 1932), pp. 7-10, 15. The population of the city of Los Angeles was in fact 2,473,261 in 1960 and 2,809,596 in 1970.

83. William L. Kahrl, ed., *The California Water Atlas* (1979), pp. 36, 42. Erwin Cooper, *Aqueduct Empire: A Guide to Water in Cali-*

fornia, Its Turbulent History, and Its Management Today (1968), pp. 89-99. See also United States, Department of the Interior, Office of Water Resources Research, *The Market Structure of the Southern California Water Industry*, prepared by the Copley International Corporation (June 1974), table D-1, pp. 182-83.

84. Chalfant 2d, p. 404. See also Ruth E. Baugh, "Land Use Changes in the Bishop Area of Owens Valley California," *Economic Geography* (January 1937).

85. *Los Angeles Times*, January 30, 1927.

86. Clarence A. Dykstra, "Owens Valley: A Problem in Regional Planning," *Community Builder* (February 1928).

87. Ibid.

88. Ibid.

89. City of Los Angeles, Department of Water and Power, *A Resume of the Activities in Connection with the Fixing of Values . . .* by A. J. Ford (1932), p. 19. See also City of Los Angeles, Department of Water and Power, *Statement Regarding Condition of the Indians in Owens Valley California*, by A. J. Ford (Los Angeles, October 1, 1932), p. 15. (Hereinafter cited as *Statement re Indians*).

90. See Chalfant 2d, p. 402.

91. Dykstra, "Owens Valley."

92. Chalfant 2d, p. 402.

93. Ibid. See also Ostrom, *Water and Politics*, pp. 134-36, and City of Los Angeles, Department of Water and Power, *33rd Annual Report for the Fiscal Year Ending June 30, 1934* (Los Angeles, 1934), p. 128.

94. R. L. Wilbur to Guy C. Earl, May 28, 1929, in National Archives, Department of the Interior, Office of the Secretary, Central Classified File 1907-1936, Record Group 48, File 5-1, "Indian Office, California Indians, Exchange of Lands." (Hereinafter cited as NA INT RG 48 4-1 Cal. Ind.)

95. Samuel Adams to President William Howard Taft, March 11, 1912, in National Archives, Department of the Interior, Office of the Secretary, Central Classified File 1907-1936, Record Group 48, File 5-1, "Indian Office, Bishop, General or Land Purchase or Withdrawals and Restorations." (Hereinafter cited as NA INT RG 48 5-1 Bishop.)

96. See Executive Orders 1529, May 9, 1912; 1603, September 7, 1912; 2264, October 28, 1915; and 2375, April 29, 1916—together with associated correspondence—ibid.

97. Adams to Taft, March 11, 1912, and Commissioner of Indian Affairs to Secretary of the Interior, March 4, 1932, ibid.

98. E. B. Merritt to Secretary of the Interior, June 4, 1919, ibid.
99. John H. Edwards to Mrs. Louis J. Gillespie, March 31, 1925, ibid.
100. Wilbur to Earl, May 28, 1929, NA INT RG 48 5-1 Cal. Ind.
101. Ibid. See also Act of March 3, 1925, 43 *Stat.* 1101; and three letters from Charles H. Burke, the commissioner of Indian Affairs, to Hubert Work (June 24, 1922, and September 8, 1926) and to Ray Parrett (March 27, 1926), NA INT RG 48 5-1 Bishop.
102. Louis C. Cramton, Memorandum for the Secretary of the Interior, June 14, 1932, NA INT RG 48 2-173.
103. See Merritt to Secretary of the Interior, June 4, 1919, NA INT RG 48 5-1 Bishop.
104. Cramton, Memorandum, June 14, 1932, NA INT RG 48 2-173.
105. *Statement re Indians*, pp. 15-16.
106. City of Los Angeles, Department of Water and Power, *33rd Annual Report*, p. 128.
107. See City of Los Angeles, Department of Water and Power, *Report on the Condition of the Indians in Owens Valley California*, by A. J. Ford, E. A. Porter, and C. D. Carll (June 30, 1932). (Hereinafter cited as *Report on Indians*.) See also City of Los Angeles, Department of Water and Power, *31st Annual Report for the Fiscal Year Ending June 30, 1932* (Los Angeles, 1932), p. 99.
108. See City of Los Angeles, Department of Water and Power, *Final Report on the Owens Valley Indian Situation Including a Suggested Plan for Adjustment of Same*, by E. A. Porter (January 9, 1936), p. 15.
109. *Report on Indians*, pp. 17-18, 22.
110. See Willie Arthur Chalfant, *The Story of Inyo* (1922), pp. 152-54; also, *Statement re Indians*, pp. 11-15.
111. *Report on Indians*, pp. 16-17.
112. Ibid., pp. 13-14.
113. See United States Bureau of Indian Affairs, Sacramento Land Operations Office, *Multiple Purpose Water Resources Investigations, Owens Valley Region Indian Reservations, California*, prepared for the tribal councils of Bridgeport, Benton, Bishop, Big Pine, Fort Independence, and Lone Pine by VTN (Sacramento, June, 1976), Special Investigation II: "The Owens Valley Land Exchange." See also City of Los Angeles, Department of Water and Power, *Final Report on the Owens Valley Indian Situation*, and the extensive correspondence relating to the land exchange between the Department of Water and Power, the Department of the Interior, and the Bureau of Indian Affairs, 1937 to 1939, in National Archives, Department of the Interior, Office of the Secre-

tary, Central Classified File 1937-1953, Record Group 48, File 5-1, "Indian Office, California Indians, Exchange of Lands."

114. City of Los Angeles, Department of Water and Power, *Final Report on the Owens Valley Indian Situation*, p. 15.

115. Dale R. McCullough, *The Tule Elk: Its History, Behavior, and Ecology* (1969), pp. 25-29; Committee for the Preservation of the Tule Elk, *Owens Valley: Home of the Tule Elk* (n.d.); State of California, Department of Fish and Game, "Tule Elk," *Outdoor California* (March 1963).

116. Gerhard Bakker, *History of the California Tule Elk* (1962); State of California, Department of Fish and Game, *Owens Valley Tule Elk Habitat Mangement Plan* (October 15, 1976), p. 3; *Los Angeles Times*, November 23, 1969.

117. McCullough, *Tule Elk*, pp. 159-61; State of California, Department of Fish and Game, *Owens Valley Tule Elk*, pp. 20-23; Anthony A. Amaral, "Struggle in the Owens Valley," *American Forests* (August 1964); *Los Angeles Herald-Examiner*, April 1, 1976.

118. See Jessie A. Garrett and Ronald C. Larson, eds., *Camp and Community: Manzanar and the Owens Valley* (1977), pp. 21, 37-38.

119. John J. Crowley, "Inyo: The County of Contrasts," *The Tidings* (August 8, 1924). See also *Inyo Independent*, March 22, 1940.

120. Very Reverend Monsignor John J. Crowley to Daniel O'Brien, April 24, 1931, Mary W. Gorman Papers, Independence, Calif.

121. "Mass of the Fisher Folk," *Westways* (April 1940).

122. Garrett and Larson, *Camp and Community*, pp. 21, 103-5.

123. Irving Stone, "Desert Padre," *Saturday Evening Post* (May 20, 1944).

124. Ibid.

125. Genny Schumacher Smith, *Deepest Valley*, rev. ed. (Los Altos, Calif., 1978), p. 160; United States Department of Agriculture, Forest Service, Inyo National Forest, *Habitat Management Plan for Native Golden Trout Waters* (1965), pp. 2, 25; *Bristlecone View*, May 3, 1967.

126. See Stone, "Desert Padre," and "Mass of the Fisher Folk," *Westways*.

127. Ostrom, *Water and Politics*, pp. 127, 135-36; Stone, "Desert Padre."

128. See Ostrom, *Water and Politics*, pp. 73-76, 136. See also *Intake*, vol. 18, no. 10 (October 1941).

129. *Inyo Independent*, March 22, 1940. See also Stone, "Desert Padre."

130. *Inyo Register*, October 23, 1941.

131. Thomas Means, *Review of Appraisals: Manzanar Relocation Center* (San Francisco, July 31, 1944), pp. 1-3.

132. Garrett and Larson, *Camp and Community*, pp. 18, 26, 33. Both Austin's *Ford* and Gragg's and Putnam's *Golden Valley* feature Chinese cooks.

133. See United States Department of the Interior, War Relocation Authority: *WRA: A Story of Human Conservation* (n.d.), p. 8, and *Impounded People: Japanese Americans in the Relocation Centers* (1946), p. 18. The hostility toward the Japanese was specifically racial. When efforts were made in San Francisco to remove other Americans of hostile alien extraction, for example, a great storm of protest was raised to prevent any discomfiture to the mother of the baseball star Joe Dimaggio. See *Impounded People*, pp. 13-15.

134. *Inyo Independent*, February 13, 1942.

135. Ibid., March 6, 1942.

136. Streeter, *Saga of Inyo*, pp. 21, 25.

137. *Inyo Independent*, March 6, 1942.

138. Garrett and Larson, *Camp and Community*, pp. 4-7, 38, 159.

139. See, e.g., in the Inyo County Free Library an unsigned manuscript dated December 3, 1943, of notes taken on an address by Ralph Merritt. See also Garrett and Larson, *Camp and Community*, p. 53.

140. Letter quoted in United States Department of the Interior, War Relocation Authority, *WRA*, p. 100. See also *Denver Post*, May 23, 1943.

141. United States Department of the Interior, War Relocation Authority, *WRA*, pp. 77-78, 113-16; manuscript of notes on Merritt, Inyo County Library (1943).

142. See United States Department of the Interior, War Relocation Authority, *WRA*, pp. 46-51; Allan R. Bosworth, *America's Concentration Camps* (1967), pp. 158-62; *Inyo Register*, December 11, 1942; Garrett and Larson, *Camp and Community*, p. 88; and Dorothy Swaine Thomas and Richard S. Nishimoto, *The Spoilage* (1946), pp. 49-52, 363-70.

143. Bosworth, *America's Concentration Camps*, p. 144.

144. Thomas and Nishimoto, *Spoilage*, p. 368; Ansel Adams, *Born Free and Equal* (1944), p. 25. See also James D. Houston and Jeanne Wakatsuki Houston, *Farewell to Manzanar* (1973).

145. Manuscript of notes on Merritt, Inyo County Library (1943); Houston, *Farewell to Manzanar*, p. 81; United States Department of the Interior, War Relocation Authority, *Semi-Annual Report, January 1-June 30, 1944* (1944).

146. Means, *Review of Appraisals*, pp. 11-17.
147. United States Department of the Interior, War Relocation Author-
     ity, *WRA*, p. 197, and *Impounded People*, p. 192; American Coun-
     cil on Public Affairs, *The Displaced Japanese-Americans* (1944),
     pp. 15-16.
148. United States Department of the Interior, War Relocation Author-
     ity, *Impounded People*, p. 200; Garrett and Larson, *Camp and
     Community*, pp. 37-38, 110, 211.

CHAPTER EIGHT
The Ties That Bind

1. United States, Congress, *Congressional Record*, 60th Cong., 2d
   sess., December 8, 1908, vol. 43, p. 22.
2. The provisions of the County of Origin law, expanded to apply to
   whole watersheds, were made an integral part of the state act
   authorizing the construction of the Central Valley project. See
   William L. Kahrl, ed., *The California Water Atlas* (1979), pp. 36,
   69; and Erwin Cooper, *Aqueduct Empire: A Guide to Water in
   California, Its Turbulent History, and Its Management Today*
   (1968), pp. 414-15.
3. *Natural Soda Products Company* v. *City of Los Angeles*, 23 Cal. 2d
   (1943). See also State of California, Water Resources Board, *Reconnaissance Investigation of Water Resources of Mono and
   Owens Basins* (August 1960), p. 40.
4. See Stanley Pedder to Thomas Means, April 26, 1939, in *Correspondence re Natural Soda Products Company v. City of Los
   Angeles*, Means Papers, Water Resources Center Archives, University of California, Berkeley. See also United States, Congress,
   House, Committee on Public Lands, *Hearings on H.R. 83, H.R.
   727, H.R. 728, H.R. 1833, and H.R. 6697 . . .* (1948), pp. 47, 59.
   (Hereinafter cited as *Mono Hearings, 1948*.) See also State of
   California, Water Rights Board, *Memorandum Report of the Water Supply of the Mono and Owens Basins . . .*, by John H. Gant
   and David W. Sabiston (December 1963), p. 3.
5. *Natural Soda Products Company* v. *City of Los Angeles*. See also
   City of Los Angeles, Department of Water and Power, *Water and
   Power Problem of California Municipalities*, by Samuel B. Morris
   (December 1945).
6. See *Engineering News-Record*, vol. 143, no. 12 (September 22,
   1949), and Vincent Ostrom, *Water and Politics: A Study of Water*

Politics and Administration in the Development of Los Angeles (1953), pp. 140-41.

7. See Pedder to State Senator Jesse M. Mayo, May 4, 1939, in *Correspondence re Natural Soda Products*, Means Papers.

8. State of California, chap. 1344, *Statutes of 1945* (Senate Bill 1272— Brown).

9. Under current court-ordered restrictions, Los Angeles may, in fact, waste even larger amounts of water into Owens Lake than were involved in the Natural Soda Products case, but only after it has taken all reasonable steps to prevent such wastage. See *People* v. *City of Los Angeles*, 34 Cal. 2d (1950), and *Morrison and Weatherly* v. *City of Los Angeles*, San Bernardino County Superior Court, no. 152656.

10. City of Los Angeles, Board of Water and Power Commissioners, Resolution no. 179, September 29, 1938.

11. Ostrom, *Water and Politics*, pp. 136-37.

12. See State of California, chap. 1343, *Statutes of 1945*, and chap. 894, *Statutes of 1947*; Memorandum, Ray L. Chesebro, City Attorney, to Samuel B. Morris, General Manager and Chief Engineer, Los Angeles Department of Water and Power, March 23, 1945, at the Department of Water and Power; and Darryl Richard Goehring, "Bishop California: A Recreational Satellite" (thesis, 1966), p. 252. Regarding Los Angeles' confidence in the supremacy of its charter, see especially *Wehrle* v. *Los Angeles Board of Water and Power Commissioners*, 211 Cal. 70 (1930).

13. City of Los Angeles, Department of Water and Power, *Post-War Problems and the Prospects of the Los Angeles Metropolitan Area* (May 25, 1945), p. 13, *Owens Gorge Project* (February 1955), pp. 8-10, and *The Water Problem* (September 16, 1948)—all by Samuel B. Morris. See also Memorandum for the Acting Secretary of the Interior by Mr. Wolfsohn, February 25, 1946, and Memorandum for the Secretary of the Interior by Fred R. Johnson, May 15, 1946, both in National Archives, Department of the Interior, Office of the Secretary, Central Classified File 1937-1953, Record Group 48, File 2-173, pt. 3, "General Land Office, Water Supply, Los Angeles, California." (Hereinafter cited as NA INT RG 48 2-173 New.)

14. State of California, Legislature, Senate, Committee on Local Governmental Agencies, *Report Concerning Application of City of Los Angeles for Purchase of Federal Lands in Mono County* (October 19, 1945), pp. 4, 6. See also minority report by Senator Tenney attached thereto; also *Mono Hearings*.

15. Wolfsohn memorandum, February 25, 1946, NA INT RG 48 2-173 New. State of California, Legislature, Senate, *Report Concerning . . . Purchase of Federal Lands*, p. 7.

16. *Mono Hearings*, p. 131.
17. State of California, Legislature, Senate, *Report Concerning... Purchase of Federal Lands*, pp. 8-10.
18. Ibid., p. 11.
19. See State of California, Legislature, Senate, Resolution 81, May 12, 1947; William E. Warne, Assistant Secretary of the Interior to J. Stuart Watson, Executive Office, California State Lands Commission, July 2, 1947, NA INT RG 48 2-173 New.
20. *Los Angeles Daily News*, May 21, 1947.
21. *Los Angeles Times*, June 13, 1947.
22. See City of Los Angeles, Department of Water and Power, *Post-War Problems*, p. 16.
23. *Mono Hearings*, p. 40.
24. See, e.g., *Sacramento Bee*, June 24, 1979. Tenney was the only member of Brown's committee who refused to sign the report on the city's relations with Inyo and Mono counties.
25. *Los Angeles Daily News*, May 14, 1947.
26. See State of California, Legislature, Senate, *Report Concerning ... Purchase of Federal Lands*, Minority Report by Tenney.
27. See *Mono Hearings*, p. 321, and United States, Congress, H.R. 6697 (Poulson), 80th Cong., 2d sess. (1948). Conflicting accounts of the actual terms of the compromise appear in Ostrom, *Water and Politics*, pp. 139-40, and in the *Los Angeles Daily News*, March 21, 1949. In 1949 the city did obtain congressional approval of a right-of-way for its transmission lines, but this bill affected other lands than those involved in the controversy over the Poulson legislation. Mono, Inyo, and Kern counties, all of which had lands included in the right-of-way, raised no objection to this bill. See H.R. 5764 and S. 2332, 81st Cong., 1st sess., 63 *Stat.* 663, October 10, 1949, and the report thereon by Oscar L. Chapman, Acting Secretary of the Interior, in a letter to J. H. Peterson, Chairman of the House Committee on Public Lands, August 5, 1949, reprinted in the committee's report on H.R. 5764. Subsequent attempts by the city to revive the Poulson bill in various amended forms have gone nowhere. See S. 3191, 91st Cong., 2d sess. (1970); H.R. 14069 and S. 3332, 93d Cong., 2d sess. (1974); H.R. 6856, 95th Cong., 1st sess. (1977); and H.R. 13521, 95th Cong., 2d sess. (1978). Regarding Owens Valley resistance to these attempts, see *Los Angeles Times*, October 4, 1970, and Committee to Preserve the Ecology of Inyo-Mono, *Our Views on the Proposed Inyo-Mono Land Exchange Bill* (1970). The Mono County Board of Supervisors, however, has consistently supported these efforts to repeal the 1936 act.
28. *Los Angeles Times*, November 5, 1945.

29. See Ostrom, *Water and Politics*, pp. 75-78.
30. City of Los Angeles, Department of Water and Power, Special Educational Committee: *Report on Charter Amendment No. 2 Establishing a Water and Power Revenue Bond Plan and Charter Amendment No. 4 Amending the Vacation Ordinance, General Election May 27, 1947* (Los Angeles, August 15, 1947), and *Comments at Kickoff Meeting April 14, 1947* (Los Angeles).
31. Out of 347,251 votes cast, 186,155 voted for the amendment and 89,388 against.
32. Clayton Allen, Special Educational Committee Chairman, to Water and Power Employees Association, May 28, 1947, in City of Los Angeles, Department of Water and Power, *Report on Charter Amendment No. 2*.
33. Ostrom, *Water and Politics*, p. 246.
34. Ibid., p. 78.
35. *Mono Hearings*, p. 20.
36. State of California, Legislature, Senate, Committee on Local Governmental Agencies, *Hearings, February 16, 1945* (1945), vol. 4, p. 494.
37. State of California, Water Resources Board, *Reconnaissance Investigation*, p. 27. The remaining 1 percent included Indian lands, lands belonging to the city of Bishop and to Inyo County, and land the status of which was "uncertain" at the time of the survey. Such uncertainties are not uncommon, for Los Angeles has sometimes been reluctant to provide specific figures on its land ownership in the valley; see, e.g., State of California, Board of Equalization, *Property Tax Assessment in Inyo County* (1950). In Inyo County as a whole, federal ownership accounts for approximately 91 percent of the total area, ownership by Los Angeles for 4 percent, and private ownership for 2 percent. See, e.g., State of California, Board of Equalization, *Assessment Practices Survey, Inyo County, 1972-73* (April 1973), and County of Inyo, Office of the Assessor, *Inyo County Facts* (Independence, Calif., 1972).
38. Joseph T. Radd to City of Los Angeles, Board of Water and Power Commissioners, November 2, 1965, quoted in City of Los Angeles, Department of Water and Power, *Water Supply Management in Inyo and Mono Counties* (September 1966), pp. 39-41.
39. Ibid., p. 38.
40. Harry Erlich and P. N. McGauhey, *Economic Evaluation of Water*, pt. 2: "Jurisdictional Considerations in Water Resources Management" (1964), p. 98. See also H. D. Ruth and Associates, *1990 General Plan for Development, Inyo County, California* (adopted August 5, 1968), p. 22.

41. City of Los Angeles, Department of Water and Power, *Water Supply Management*, p. 50.

42. See, e.g., an unsigned article for the Department of Water and Power: "The Owens Valley Controversy in Perspective," in Peggy Streeter and Clarence Streeter, eds., *Saga of Inyo County* (1977), pp. 41-43.

43. State of California, Department of Water Resources, *Southern Lahontan Area of California: Land and Water Use Survey, 1961* (August 1965), pp. 27, 30-33; State of California, Water Resources Board, *Reconnaissance Investigation*, pp. 29-32; Goehring, "Bishop," pp. 193, 196-98; Ruth, *1990 General Plan*, pp. 79-81; P. Dean Smith, *Agriculture in Inyo and Mono Counties* (1968); United States Department of the Interior, Bureau of Indian Affairs, *Multiple Purpose Water Resources Investigations: Owens Valley Region Indian Reservations, California*, by VTN (June 1976), p. 18.

44. Erlich and McGauhey, *Economic Evaluation of Water*, pp. 91, 97-98; Ruth, *1990 General Plan*, p. 84; United States Department of the Interior, United States Geological Survey, *Review of Waterpower Withdrawals: Mono Lake and Owens Lake Basins, California*, by Kenneth W. Sax (1964), p. 2.

45. Goehring, "Bishop," p. 183; United States Department of the Interior, United States Geological Survey, *Waterpower Withdrawals*, p. 2; Erlich and McGauhey, *Economic Evaluation of Water*, p. 91; Ruth, *1990 General Plan*, pp. 84, 96.

46. See State of California, Department of Water Resources, *Southern Lahontan Survey*, p. 11.

48. Izaak Walton League of America, California Division, *Owens Valley Mono Basin Report*, by Charles H. Stoddard (October 15, 1971), p. ii of Foreword and p. 1 of body of report.

48. Goehring, "Bishop," p. 71.

49. Ruth, *1990 General Plan*, p. 3.

50. Ibid., p. 96. See also City of Los Angeles, Department of Water and Power, *Water Supply Management*, p. 44.

51. See City of Los Angeles, Department of Water and Power, *Report by C. P. Garman, Assistant Chief Electrical Engineer to the Board of Water and Power Commissioners* (December 11, 1944); Ruth, *1990 General Plan*, p. 96; Erlich and McGauhey, *Economic Evaluation of Water*, p. 91.

52. Testimony of William L. Berry, Chief of the Division of Resources Planning for the California Department of Water Resources, before the State Senate Fact-Finding Committee on Commerce and Economic Development, Bishop, Calif., May 16, 1958, quoted in Erlich and McGauhey, *Economic Evaluation of Water*, p. 103.

53. State of California, Department of Water Resources, *Fish Slough*

Dam and Reservoir Feasibility Investigation (October 1964), pp. 19, 61-63.

54. Erlich and McGauhey, *Economic Evaluation of Water*, p. 91. See also Goehring, "Bishop," p. 97.

55. See, e.g., Goehring, "Bishop," and Don Goldman, "Owens Valley and Its Water" (thesis, December 1960).

56. See Goehring, "Bishop," pp. 143, 144, 154, 199; Ruth, *1990 General Plan*, pp. 79-80; and United States Department of the Interior, Bureau of Indian Affairs, *Multiple Purpose Water Resources Investigations*, p. 18.

57. In 1960, persons under fifteen years of age constituted 31 percent of California's total population; in Inyo County, however, this component of the population amounted to only 29.8 percent, and by 1965 it had been reduced to 27.2 percent. Persons over forty-five, in contrast, represented 28.3 percent of the statewide population in 1960 but 34.9 percent of the Inyo population in 1960 and 36.4 percent by 1965. See Ruth, *1990 General Plan*, table "Percentage Distribution of Total Population by Age." By 1980, persons under eighteen years of age were estimated to constitute 29.6 percent of California's population but 28.1 percent of Inyo's. For that year, persons fifty-five and older constituted 19.0 percent of the state's population but 25.1 percent of Inyo's. See County Supervisors Association of California, *California County Fact Book, 1977-78* (1977).

58. Ibid., pp. 78-79. By 1976 the median income for California was $10,469; for Inyo it was $9,842 and for Mono, $6,809. State of California, Department of Finance, *California Statistical Abstract* (Sacramento, 1978), p. 42.

59. These various projections are summarized in Ruth, *1990 General Plan*, table "Inyo County Population Estimates and Projections, 1967-1990."

60. Ibid., p. 10.

61. Goehring, "Bishop," pp. 67, 71. See also City of Los Angeles, Department of Water and Power, *Recreation and Other Public Uses of the City of Los Angeles Lands in the Owens Valley-Mono Basin Area* (January 1967).

62. Erlich and McGauhey, *Economic Evaluation of Water*, p. 107.

63. State of California, Department of Water Resources, *Fish Slough Dam*, p. 17.

64. Erlich and McGauhey, *Economic Evaluation of Water*, pp. 108-10; State of California, Department of Water Resources, *Interim Report on Inyo-Mono Area Water Resources Investigation* (January 1965), p. 4.

65. United States Department of the Interior, United States Geological

Survey, *Erosion and Sediment Transport in the Owens River near Bishop*, by Rhea P. Williams (1975), p. 41.

66. Ibid., p. 2; Erlich and McGauhey, *Economic Evaluation of Water*, p. 107.

67. State of California, Department of Water Resources, *Fish Slough Dam*, pp. 19, 27.

68. See Interview with Aubrey Lyon by Ellis Delameter, November 20, 1976, Oral History Department, California State University, Fullerton, pp. I-26-27; Erlich and McGauhey, *Economic Evaluation of Water*, pp. 104-5.

69. State of California, Water Resources Board, *Reconnaissance Investigation*, pp. 67-70.

70. Ibid., pp. 85-86; State of California, Department of Water Resources, *Interim Report on Inyo-Mono*, pp. 18-19.

71. State of California, Water Resources Board, *Reconnaissance Investigation*, pp. 70-75.

72. State of California, Department of Water Resources, *Fish Slough Dam*, pp. 61-63.

73. Erlich and McGauhey, *Economic Evaluation of Water*, pp. 104-5; Delameter, Interview with Lyon, pp. I-26-27; City of Los Angeles, Department of Water and Power, *Water Supply Management*, pp. 12-18.

74. See *City of Los Angeles* v. *County of Inyo*, 167 Cal. App. 2d 736 (1959).

75. James S. Marevalas, Inyo County Assessor, to Inyo County Grand Jury, August 30, 1974, Office of the Assessor, County of Inyo, Independence, California.

76. The specific acreage figures are those reported by Marevalas to the Inyo County Grand Jury, August 30, 1974.

77. League of Women Voters of California, *Taxation of Property of Local Governments: Analysis of Proposition 2, Legislative Constitutional Amendment, General Election of 1968* (1968).

78. Ibid.

79. State of California, Office of Planning and Research, "Taxation of Municipally Owned Property Outside Their Boundaries," by Georgann Eberhardt (December 1976), with note attached concerning a meeting with Ray Welch, formerly of the California Board of Equalization staff, December 27, 1976.

80. State of California, Office of Planning and Research, "Taxation of Municipally Owned Property"; Marevalas to the Inyo County Grand Jury, August 30, 1974.

81. See State of California, Legislative Counsel and Secretary of State,

Proposed Amendments to Constitution, Propositions, and Proposed Laws Together with Arguments, General Election, Tuesday, November 5, 1968 (Sacramento, 1968): "Proposition Two," pp. 6-8.

82. See, e.g., *Cal-Tax News*, vol. 9 no. 9 (September 1968); and *Commonwealth*, vol. 62, no. 40 (September 30, 1968).

83. *Los Angeles Times*, October 11, 1968.

84. State of California, Secretary of State, *Statement of Vote, 1968 General Election* (Sacramento, 1969), p. 27.

85. Izaak Walton League of America, California Division, *Owens Valley Mono Basin*, pp. 1, 41. See also Genny Schumacher Smith, *Deepest Valley*, rev. ed. (Los Altos, Calif., 1978), pp. 198-99.

86. Judith Morgan and Neil Morgan, "California's Parched Oasis," *National Geographic* (January 1976).

87. State of California, Water Resources Board, *Reconnaissance Investigation*, p. 49; Charles H. Lee, "Well Development in Owens Valley Equalizes Supply of Los Angeles Aqueduct," *Western Construction News* (October 25, 1926); J. E. Phillips, "Underground Water Development in Owens Valley," University of Southern California School of Government, Water Supply and Sanitary Engineering Section, *Papers, 1930* (1930); Means to Pedder, April 18, 1939, *Correspondence re Natural Soda Products*, Means Papers.

88. *Los Angeles Times*, March 16, 1930.

89. See City of Los Angeles, Bureau of Municipal Research, *Consolidated Water for Los Angeles County* (1933).

90. City of Los Angeles, Department of Water and Power, *The Second Los Angeles Aqueduct* (1971), p. 2.

91. See Ruth E. Baugh, "Land Use Changes in the Bishop Area of Owens Valley California," *Economic Geography* (January 1937); and United States Department of the Interior, United States Geological Survey, *The Geology and Water Resources of Owens Valley, California*, by Willis T. Lee (1906).

92. See *Hillside Water Company* v. *City of Los Angeles*, 10 Cal. 2d 677 (1938), and the so-called Chandler Decree, issued August 26, 1940, in *Hillside Water Company* v. *City of Los Angeles*, Inyo County Superior Court, no. 2073. See also State of California, Water Resources Board, Reconnaissance Investigation, p. 54; and Thomas Means, *Report on Value of Property of Hillside Water Company, Inyo County, California* (San Francisco, September 14, 1928), Means Papers.

93. City of Los Angeles, Department of Water and Power, *Water Supply Management*, pp. 24-25; State of California, Water Re-

sources Board, *Reconnaissance Investigation*, p. 57; State of California, Water Rights Board, *Memorandum Report*, p. 3.

94. See City of Los Angeles, Department of Water and Power: *Second Los Angeles Aqueduct*, pp. 2-3, and Memorandum, H. L. Jacques to Burton Grant, May 21, 1946.

95. City of Los Angeles, Department of Water and Power, *Owens Gorge*, pp. 8-9. See also Ford, Bacon and Davis Inc., *Report on the Department of Water and Power, Los Angeles, California* (Los Angeles, 1948), and City of Los Angeles, Department of Water and Power, *Comments of the General Manager and Chief Engineer of the Department of Water and Power on the Ford, Bacon, and Davis Report of November 26, 1948* (Los Angeles, October 4, 1949), p. 59.

96. State of California, Water Resources Board, *Los Angeles County Land and Water Use Survey, 1955* (June 1956), pp. 14, 52.

97. United States Department of the Interior, Office of Water Resources Research, *The Market Structure of the Southern California Water Industry*, prepared by the Copley International Corporation (June 1974), p. 185.

98. See City of Los Angeles, Department of Water and Power, *Comments . . . on the Ford, Bacon, and Davis Report*, pp. 28-29.

99. See City of Los Angeles, Board of Water and Power Commissioners: *Statement before the Sub-Committee on Economic and Financial Policies for State Water Projects* by William S. Peterson (September 17, 1958), and *Statement of the Board of Water and Power Commissioners before the Senate Fact-Finding Committee on Water* (Los Angeles, October 8, 1959).

100. See City of Los Angeles, Board of Water and Power Commissioners, *Why the Metropolitan Water District Act Must be Amended* (Los Angeles, February 1961). See also Cooper, *Aqueduct Empire*, pp. 271-88. The dual system of rates Los Angeles advocated was eventually adopted in a much amended form four years later. But the system the district adopted was permissive rather than mandatory, and it has never been implemented.

101. *Los Angeles Times*, January 26, 1960.

102. Later publications by the Department of Water and Power place particular stress upon the Arizona v. California case as a reason for construction of the second aqueduct, suggesting thereby, perhaps unintentionally, that the second aqueduct might never have been built if California had won the case. See, e.g., City of Los Angeles, Department of Water and Power, *Second Los Angeles Aqueduct*, pp. xix, 5; and Paul H. Lane, "Water to the City," in Smith, *Deepest Valley*, p. 220. Detailed planning for the second

aqueduct, however, began fully four years before the Supreme Court's ruling and at a time when Los Angeles' representatives on the Metropolitan Water District board were arguing against participation in the State Water Project on the grounds that the availability of a new water supply for the South Coast might weaken the state's position in the dispute with Arizona.

103. See City of Los Angeles, Department of Water and Power: *Second Los Angeles Aqueduct*, pp. 2-5, and *Preliminary Report on the Feasibility of Developing Additional Water Supply . . .* (April 1960), *Proposed Second Barrel, Los Angeles Aqueduct, Haiwee Reservoir to San Fernando Valley* (May 1959), and *Report on the Proposed Second Barrel of the Los Angeles Aqueduct* (June 1962).

104. City of Los Angeles, Department of Water and Power, *Second Los Angeles Aqueduct*, p. 2. In later publications, the department has claimed that the loss of a portion of this filing would have increased the city's dependence on the State Water Project; see, e.g., Lane, "Water to the City," in Smith, *Deepest Valley*, p. 220. Since the city was not exercising these rights and so would not lose any water as a result of their reassignment, the logic of the department's argument is elusive.

105. State of California, Legislature, Senate, Resolution no. 182, June 19, 1959. See also State of California, Water Resources Board, *Reconnaissance Investigation*, pp. 1-3.

106. See State of California, Legislature, Senate, Resolution no. 59, adopted May 13, 1964, and Senate, Resolution no. 184, adopted June 23, 1966.

107. State of California, Water Resources Board, *Reconnaissance Investigation*, pp. 85-86. See also Erlich and McGauhey, *Economic Evaluation of Water*, p. 84. The Inyo County General Plan in 1968 even suggested reflooding Owens Lake as a way of applying the surplus waters of the valley; see Ruth, *1980 General Plan*, pp. 25-26.

108. See Erlich and McGauhey, *Economic Evaluation of Water*, pp. 99-100.

109. Letter from Aubrey Lyon, June 24, 1961, quoted in ibid., p. 105. See also Delameter, Interview with Lyon, pp. I-30-31, 35.

110. State of California, Water Resources Board, *Reconnaissance Investigation*, pp. 85-86.

111. See letter of transmittal by William E. Warne in State of California, Department of Water Resources, *Interim Report on Inyo-Mono.*

112. The Department of Water Resources did conduct a brief, unfunded, noncommital, but nevertheless formal review of the city's study; see State of California, Department of Water Resources,

Review of a Report by the City of Los Angeles on Water Supply Management in Inyo and Mono Counties, California (Sacramento, 1966).

113. City of Los Angeles, Department of Water and Power, *Water Supply Management*, pp. 43-44.

114. State of California, Water Rights Board, *Memorandum Report*, p. 10.

115. City of Los Angeles, Department of Water and Power, *Second Los Angeles Aqueduct*, p. 16.

116. Ibid., p. 2; State of California, Water Rights Board, *Memorandum Report*, pp. 6-8; City of Los Angeles, Department of Water and Power, *Water Supply Management*, pp. 28-31, and Memorandum, Jacques to Burton, May 21, 1946.

117. See Howard Stoddard and Henry Karrer, *A Report on the Plans of the City of Los Angeles to Construct the Second Barrel ...* (August 4, 1964), passim, and pp. 3-5 for a summary of conclusions and recommendations.

118. Antonio Rossmann, "Water for the Valley," in Smith, *Deepest Valley*, p. 203; City of Los Angeles, Department of Water and Power, *Water Supply Management*, pp. 30-31.

119. National Science Foundation, *Effects of Groundwater Pumping on the Environment of Owens Valley and the Users of Owens Valley Water*, Deborah J. Wilson, ed. (Washington, D.C., 1978), p. 7; City of Los Angeles, Department of Water and Power, *Water Supply Management*, p. 54; State of California, Water Rights Board, *Memorandum Report*, pp. 7-9.

120. See City of Los Angeles, Department of Water and Power, *Preliminary Briefing on Management Plan for City of Los Angeles Water Resources and Lands in Inyo and Mono Counties* (November 10, 1971) p. 3. See also Walter W. Rollins, Chairman, Inyo County Board of Supervisors, to Robert V. Phillips, General Manager, Los Angeles Department of Water and Power (August 30, 1972).

121. State of California, Department of Water Resources, *Southern Lahontan Survey*, p. 26; City of Los Angeles, Department of Water and Power, *Water Supply Management*, pp. 45-54, and *Draft Environmental Impact Report on Increased Pumping of the Owens Valley Groundwater Basin* (August 1978), pp. 3-4 through 3-5; Goldman, "Owens Valley and Its Water," pp. 135-36; Stoddard and Karrer, *Report on the Plan*, p. 4.

122. City of Los Angeles, Department of Water and Power, *Preliminary Briefing*, p. 1.

123. *Ibid.* See also, e.g., Lane, "Water to the City," in Smith, *Deepest Valley*, pp. 220, 223; also City of Los Angeles, Department of

Water and Power, *Water Resources Management Plan, Owens Valley Groundwater Basin: Review Copy* (October 1972).

124. *Los Angeles Times*, December 1, 1976.

125. See Jack B. Hopkins, Chairman, Inyo County Board of Supervisors, to Los Angeles Board of Water and Power Commissioners, October 27, 1964; County of Inyo, Board of Supervisors, Resolution no. 67-84, September 18, 1967, and *Statement of Objectives to Develop a Comprehensive Water Management and Protection Plan for the Owens River Basin* (June 7, 1971); and Herbert London, Chairman, Inyo County Board of Supervisors, to R. V. Phillips, September 7, 1971.

126. Betty S. Denton to R. V. Phillips, September 21, 1971; see also "Desires and Needs of City of Bishop in Regard to Water Management and Land Use Plan for City of Los Angeles Lands in Inyo County," attached thereto. See, too, letters between Norman B. Livermore and John W. Luhring, President, Los Angeles Board of Water and Power Commissioners, July 23 and August 19, 1971.

127. City of Los Angeles, Department of Water and Power, *Preliminary Briefing*, pp. 1, 2.

128. See R. V. Phillips to N. B. Livermore, April 6, 1927, and Livermore to Phillips, May 16, 1972.

129. W. W. Rollins to R. V. Phillips, August 30, 1972. Stoddard and Karrer, in *Report on the Plan*, also questioned whether Los Angeles possessed all the rights necessary to operate the second aqueduct.

130. The second aqueduct went into operation June 26, 1970, although its last components were not completed until December 1970. The California Environmental Quality Act, chap. 1433, *Statutes of 1970*, was enacted in November to take effect the following January.

131. *County of Inyo* v. *Yorty*, 32 Cal. App. 3d 795 (1973).

132. See City of Los Angeles, Department of Water and Power, *Draft Environmental Impact Report on Increased Pumping of the Owens Valley Groundwater Basin* (August 29, 1974).

133. *Los Angeles Times*, December 1, 1974. Los Angeles' officials today deny that any dynamiting was necessary to shut off valves which are normally opened and closed at each irrigation season.

134. See amicus curiae brief for the State of California, Evelle J. Younger, Attorney General, in the Court of Appeal, Third Appellate District, *County of Inyo* v. *City of Los Angeles*, December 31, 1976. Although the attorney general attempted to intervene on the county's behalf at this point, the brief was not accepted by the court because it was presented after the deadline for submissions.

135. *Los Angeles Times*, August 30, 1976; *Inyo Daily Independent*,

October 5, 1976; County of Inyo, Grand Jury, *Grand Jury Report for 1976-77* (1977).

136. See Rossmann, "Water for the Valley," in Smith, *Deepest Valley*, Ehud Yonay, "How Green Was My Valley," *New West* (March 28, 1977).

137. See *Los Angeles Times*, June 16, 1977.

138. *Los Angeles Times*, June 15, 1977.

139. According to the state Department of Water Resources, Division of Planning, Water Use and Economics Unit, per capita water consumption in the city of Los Angeles averaged 179 gallons per day in the period 1971-1975. By comparison, the state estimated that consumption rates during this period averaged 179 gallons per day in San Diego, 235 in Riverside, 219 in Anaheim, and 161 in Long Beach. The Los Angeles Department of Water and Power in 1977 reported a figure for domestic use alone of 95 gallons per capita per day. See Kahrl, *California Water Atlas*, p. 80, and *Los Angeles Times*, June 15, 1977.

140. Ibid. See also County of Inyo, *Grand Jury Report*.

141. *Los Angeles Times*, June 26, 1977.

142. *County of Inyo* v. *City of Los Angeles*, 71 Cal. App. 3d 185 (1977).

143. *Los Angeles Times*, June 29, 1977.

144. The Kern County Water Agency also filed an amicus brief on the city's behalf. San Diego was actively considering adopting a water conservation program of its own until Los Angeles won the higher pumping rate it sought; see *San Diego Union*, July 28, 1977.

145. *Los Angeles Times*, July 14, 1977.

146. See *Los Angeles Times*, July 14 and 23, 1977. For contrast in the *Times*'s coverage of the court's rejection of the environmental impact report, see its edition of June 28, 1977.

147. Yonay, "How Green Was My Valley."

148. Rossmann, "Water for the Valley," in Smith, *Deepest Valley,* p. 215. See also Iris S. Malsman, "Is There a 'Project'? The Unsolved Riddle of CEQA in the Owens Valley," *San Fernando Valley Law Review* (Spring 1978).

149. L. H. "Buck" Gibbons (Inyo District Attorney), "Water: Los Angeles and Inyo *Can* Get Along," *Los Angeles Times*, October 18, 1977.

150. See, e.g., Rossmann, "Water for the Valley," in Smith, *Deepest Valley*, pp. 215-16.

151. See State of California, Department of Water Resources, *Owens Valley Groundwater Investigation, Phase I, Southern District Re-*

port (September 1980), and "Cooperative Agreement between the County of Inyo , the City of Los Angeles, and Its Department of Water and Power, and the State of California, Department of Water Resources, concerning the Owens Valley Ground Water Investigation," executed May 4, 1978.

152. See *Los Angeles Times*, December 17, 1978, and City of Los Angeles, Department of Water and Power, *Draft Environmental Impact Report* (1978).

153. *County of Inyo* v. *City of Los Angeles*, 78 Cal. App. 3d 82 (1978).

154. *Los Angeles Times*, December 8, 1978.

155. See *Los Angeles Times*, August 30, 1976, and Delameter, Interview with Lyon, p. I-40.

156. See *Los Angeles Times*, September 16 and 17, 1976.

157. See, e.g., Peter Steinhart, "The City and the Inland Sea," *Audubon* (September 1980).

158. See City of Los Angeles, Department of Water and Power, "Proposed Section 50307," distributed by James Wickser, Northern District Engineer, Aqueduct Division, to members of the Bishop Chamber of Commerce in the summer of 1977; chap. 271, *Statutes of 1979*; *Los Angeles Times*, August 30, 1976; and James F. Wickser to James Lackey, President, Bishop Chamber of Commerce, March 27, 1979.

159. See *Los Angeles Times*, November 1, 1980.

160. *County of Inyo* v. *Public Utilities Commission*, 26 Cal. 3d 154 (1980). See also *Inyo County* v. *Public Utilities Commission*, S.P. 23990 (1979), and Assembly Bill 2549 (Wyman), introduced in 1980.

161. See County of Inyo, Board of Supervisors, *An Ordinance to Regulate the Extraction of Groundwater within the Owens Valley Groundwater Basin* (1980), and *City of Los Angeles* v. *County of Inyo*, 4 Civil 25014 (Cal. App. September 25, 1980).

162. *Bakersfield Californian*, August 1, 1976. See also City of Los Angeles, Department of Water and Power, *Proposed Nuclear Power Plant in Tulare County* (October 20, 1971).

163. United States Department of the Interior, United States Geological Survey: *Eighth Annual Report, 1886-87* (Washington, D.C., 1887), pt. 1: "Quaternary History of Mono Valley California" by Israel C. Russell, pp. 287-89, 298-99, and *The Quality of the Surface Waters of California*, by Walton Van Winckle and Frederick M. Eaton (1910), pp. 123-24. See also K.R. Lajoie, "Quaternary Stratigraphy and Geologic History of Mono Basin," in David W. Winkler, ed., *An Ecological Study of Mono Lake, California* (June 1977), p. 189.

164. State of California, Department of Water Resources, *Report to Interagency Task Force on Mono Lake* (December 1979), pp. 6, 16-17, 21.

165. Ibid., pp. 6, 9; State of California, Water Resources Board, *Reconnaissance Investigation*, pp. 38-40, 57; State of California, Department of Water Resources, *Interim Report on Inyo-Mono*, p. 10; Thomas Means, *Report on Mono Basin Water as Supply for Southern California* (San Francisco, October 1923), p. 4, Means Papers; City of Los Angeles, Department of Water and Power, *Water Rights and Operations in the Mono Basin* (Los Angeles, 1974) pp. 4, 12.

166. See City of Los Angeles, Department of Water and Power, *Water Rights and Operations in Mono*, pp. 5-6, 12-13, and, as app. Ia thereto, Roger Mitchell, Chairman Toiyabe Chapter, Sierra Club, to Robert V. Phillips, Department of Water and Power, July 16, 1973. See also *Sierra Club Yodeler*, February, 1979.

167. See, e.g., *Sacramento Bee*, November 19, 1978; *San Francisco Chronicle*, February 11, 1979; State of California, Department of Water Resources, *Report of Interagency Task Force*, p. 41; and State of California, Legislature, chap. 670, *Statutes of 1979* (Assembly Bill 367—Waters).

168. David Gaines, Chairperson, Mono Lake Committee of the Santa Monica Bay Audubon Society, to Sara C. Stivelman, President, Los Angeles Board of Water and Power Commissioners, January 19, 1979, available from the committee.

169. See form letter mailed in response to inquiries concerning Mono Lake by the office of Los Angeles' Mayor Tom Bradley in the spring and summer of 1979. The copy in my possession is addressed to Ms. Edith Gaines and is dated February 15, 1979. The operative sentence reads: "While I share your concern in this important matter, my office has no direct jurisdiction."

170. State of California, Department of Water Resources, *Report of Interagency Task Force*, pp. 17-18.

171. Ibid., pp. 2-3, 45-52. See also Steinhart, "The City and the Inland Sea." The state interagency task force also called for the enactment of legislation requiring all California cities to adopt rate structures that encourage conservation, and a five-year study of environmental problems in Mono Basin. Under the task force plan, Los Angeles would be permitted annually to export more than fifteen thousand acre-feet of water in future years, so long as the lake was maintained at a minimum level defined by the task force. The task force noted that special legislation would be needed to protect the water rights which the city would be prohibited from exercising immediately under this plan. The task force further assumed that

adoption of its recommended plan would also result in the termination of all pending environmental suits against Los Angeles in connection with Mono Lake. It is not clear how many of these diverse elements would have to fail before the task force considered its plan inoperable.

172. See Duane L. Georgeson, Engineer, Los Angeles Aqueduct, to Jack J. Coe, Chairman, Interagency Task Force on Mono Lake, December 18, 1979, in State of California, Department of Water Resources, *Report of Interagency Task Force*, app. A.

173. City of Los Angeles, Office of the Mayor, *Mayor's Blue Ribbon Committee on Department of Water and Power Rate Structure: Water Rate Structure Report* (October 1977), pp. 6, 22-23; City of Los Angeles, Department of Water and Power, *Draft Environmental Impact Report* (1978), pp. 2-2, 2-5.

174. City of Los Angeles, Department of Water and Power, *Mono Lake Billion Dollar Threat to California's Water Supply* (1979). See also, e.g., *Los Angeles Times*, December 17, 1978.

175. State of California, Department of Water Resources, *Report of Interagency Task Force*, pp. 47-50.

176. Steinhart, "The City and the Inland Sea."

177. Georgeson to Coe, December 18, 1979, in State of California, Department of Water Resources, *Report of Interagency Task Force*, app. A.

178. Steinhart, "The City and the Inland Sea."

179. *Los Angeles Times*, November 1, 1980.

Conclusion

1. Warren A. Beck and David A. Williams, *California: A History of the Golden State* (New York, 1971) pp. 308-9.

Bibliography

I. Unpublished Materials

A. NATIONAL ARCHIVES

Department of the Interior, Lands and Railroads Division. Record Group 48. Reclamation Projects, boxes 37, 38.

Department of the Interior, Office of the Secretary. Record Group 48. Central Classified File 1907-1936:

FILE 2-5. General Land Office, Inyo National Forest.

FILE 2-10. General.

FILE 2-11. General Land Office, Rights of Way, Miscellaneous, Los Angeles.

FILE 2-143. General Land Office, U.S. Land Office, Independence.

FILE 2-173. General Land Office, Water Supply, Los Angeles.

FILE 5-1. Indian Office, California Indians, Exchange of Lands.

FILE 5-1. Indian Office, Bishop, General or Land Purchase or Withdrawals and Restorations.

FILE 8-3. Pt. 1, Orland, Owens River.

Department of the Interior, Office of the Secretary. Record Group 48. Central Classified File 1937-1953:

FILE 2-173. Pt. 3, General Land Office, Water Supply, Los Angeles.

FILE 5-1. Indian Office, California Indians, Exchange of Lands.

Department of the Interior, Reclamation Service. Record Group 115. General File 1902-1919:

FILE 63-B. Correspondence re Right of Way Applications in Owens River Valley.

Department of the Interior, Reclamation Service. Record Group 115. Project File 1902-1919:

FILE 527. Owens Valley Project, Preliminary Reports on General Plans.

FILE 527-A. Owens Valley Project, Miscellaneous.

Department of the Interior. Papers of E. A. Hitchcock. Record Group 200. Reclamation 1901-1906.

B. MANUSCRIPT COLLECTIONS

Mary W. Gorman Papers. Private Collection. Independence, Calif.

Franklin Hichborn Papers. University of California, Los Angeles. Public Affairs Library.

Walter Leroy Huber Papers. University of California, Berkeley. Water Resources Center Archives.

O. W. Larson Papers. California Historical Society Library. San Francisco.

J. B. Lippincott Papers. University of California, Berkeley. Water Resources Center Archives.

J. B. Lippincott Personnel File. National Personnel Records Center, St. Louis.

Thomas Means Papers. University of California, Berkeley. Water Resources Center Archives.

Andrae B. Nordskog Papers. University of California, Berkeley. Water Resources Center Archives.

George Pardee Papers. University of California, Berkeley. Bancroft Library.

Moses H. Sherman Papers. Sherman Foundation. Corona Del Mar, Calif.

C. DISSERTATIONS, THESES, AND MISCELLANEOUS DOCUMENTS

Beneda, Janet, "The Los Angeles Aqueduct: The Men Who Constructed It." Thesis, institution unidentified, May 1974. Currently in Los Angeles Department of Water and Power Library.

Bettinger, Robert L. "The Surface Archaeology of Owens Valley, Eastern California: Prehistoric Man-Land Relationships in the Great Basin." Ph.D. dissertation, University of California, Riverside, 1975.

Cifarelli, Anthony. "The Owens River Aqueduct and the *Los Angeles Times*: A Study in Early Twentieth Century Business Ethics and Journalism." Master's thesis, University of California, Los Angeles, 1969.

Cotton, J. S. "Agricultural Conditions of Inyo County, California." Manuscript. Inyo Free Library, Independence, Calif. 1905.

Delameter, Ellis. "Interview with Aubrey Lyon, November 20, 1976." Transcript. Oral History Department, California State University, Fullerton.

Estes, Paul. "Recreational Uses of the High Sierras." Thesis, University of California, Los Angeles, 1953.

Flandreau, John H. "The Los Angeles Aqueduct: A Study of Its Significance in the History of the City of Los Angeles." Thesis, Occidental College, 1947.

Goehring, Darryl Richard. "Bishop California: A Recreational Satellite." Master's thesis, University of Nebraska, 1966.

Goldman, Don. "Owens Valley and Its Water." Master's thesis, University of California, Los Angeles, December 1960.

Jones, William K. "The History of the Los Angeles Aqueduct." Thesis, University of Oklahoma, 1967.

Kirk, W. H. "Property of the Inyo Development Company." Map prepared at Keeler, California. University of California, Berkeley. Water Resources Center Archives. 1911.

Lajoie, K. R. "Quaternary Stratigraphy and Geologic History of Mono Basin, Eastern California." Dissertation, University of California, Berkeley, 1968.

McCarthy, W. R., and Clausen, J. C. "Report on the Owens Valley Irrigation District, Inyo County, California." March 20, 1923.

Mason, D. T. "Limnology of Mono Lake, California." Dissertation, University of California, Davis, 1965.

Miller, Gordon. "Los Angeles and the Owens River Aqueduct." Ph.D. dissertation, Claremont Graduate School, Claremont, Calif., 1977.

Pentland, Gertrude. "Los Angeles Aqueduct with Special Reference to the Labor Problem." Thesis prepared as "Report to Department of Economics," institution unidentified, May 25, 1916. Currently in Los Angeles Department of Water and Power Library.

Phillips, William Emerson. "Regional Development of the Owens Valley, California: An Economic Base Study of Natural Resources." Dissertation, University of California, Berkeley, n.d.

Rice, Richard Brewer. "The Manzanar War Relocation Center." Thesis, University of California, Berkeley, October 29, 1947.

Spriggs, Elisabeth Mathieu. "The History of the Domestic Water Supply of Los Angeles." Master's thesis, University of Southern California, Los Angeles, January 1, 1931.

Thomas, Eleanor Pyle. "The History and Settlement of the Owens River Valley Region." Thesis, University of Southern California, Los Angeles, 1934.

VanValen, Nelson S. "Power Politics: The Struggle for Municipal Ownership of Electric Utilities in Los Angeles, 1905-1937." Dissertation, Claremont Graduate School, Claremont, Calif., 1963.

II. Government Documents

NOTE: Not included here are statutes, resolutions, constitutional and charter provisions, proposed legislation, annual reports of public agencies, and publications of the United States Census Bureau, specifically cited in the text. Contemporary correspondence used in Chapter 8 can be obtained from the agencies involved. Except as specifically noted, all documents listed below were published at the respective seats of government.

A. UNITED STATES

Department of Agriculture, Bureau of Chemistry and Soils. *Soil Survey of the Bishop Area California*, by E. B. Watson and R. Earl Storie. No. 3, ser. 1924, 1928. 1928.

Department of Agriculture, Bureau of Plant Industry. *Boron in the Los Angeles (Owens River) Aqueduct*, by L. V. Wilcox. Research Report no. 78, Rubidoux Laboratory. Riverside, Calif. December 3, 1940.

Department of Agriculture, Forest Service. *Fishery Habitat Management Plan for the Golden Trout*. Prepared with California Department of Fish and Game, Region V. 1965.

————. *Habitat Management Plan for Native Golden Trout Waters.* 1965.

————. *Water for Millions*, by Wallace I. Hutchinson. San Francisco, 1954.

Department of Agriculture, Office of Experiment Stations. *Report of Irrigation Investigations in California*, by Elwood Mead, Expert in Charge, assisted by William E. Smythe, Marsden Manson, J. M. Wilson, Charles D. Marx, Frank Soule, C. E. Grunsky, Edward Boggs, and James D. Schuyler. Bulletin no. 100. 1901.

Department of Agriculture, Weather Bureau. *Climatic Summary of the United States*, sec. 18: "Southern California and Owens Valley." 1930.

Congress, House, Committee on Public Lands, *Water Supply of Los Angeles: Hearings . . . on H.R. 406 Granting Rights of Way over Certain Lands for the Water Supply of Los Angeles California*, 66th Cong., 1st sess., October 31-November 4, 1919.

Congress, House, Committee on Irrigation and Reclamation, *Hearings . . . on Protection and Development of Lower Colorado River Basin: H.R. 2903, by Mr. Swing*, 68th Cong., 1st sess., 1924.

Congress, Senate, Committee on Public Lands and Surveys, *Report ... on H.R. 11969*, 71st Cong., 3rd sess., February 17, 1931.

Congress, House, Committee on Public Lands, *Hearings on H.R. 83, H.R. 727, H.R. 728, H.R. 1833, and H.R. 6697, May 19, 20, 21, 1947, and June 4, 5, 7, 14, 15, 1948.* 80th Cong., 2nd sess., 1948.

Department of the Interior, Bureau of Indian Affairs. *Multiple Purpose Water Resources Investigations: Owens Valley Region Indian Reservations, California*, by VTN. June, 1976.

Department of the Interior, Office of Water Resources Research. *The Market Structure of the Southern California Water Industry*, prepared by the Copley International Corporation, R. Paul Weddell, Project Director. La Jolla, Calif. June 1974.

Department of the Interior, Reclamation Service. *Owens Valley Project Preliminary Report*, by Harold Conkling. September 1920.

_____. *Report on Owens Valley Project California*, by Harold Conkling. September 1921.

Department of the Interior, United States Geological Survey. *California Hydrography*, by J. B. Lippincott. Water Supply Paper no. 81. 1903.

_____. *Composition of the River and Lake Waters of the United States*, by Frank Wigglesworth Clarke. Professional Paper no. 135. 1924.

_____. *Development and Application of Water near San Bernardino, Colton, and Riverside, California*, by J. B. Lippincott. Water Supply and Irrigation Papers nos. 59 and 60. 1902.

_____. *Development of Underground Waters in the Central Coastal Plain Region of Southern California*, by Walter C. Mendenhall. Water Supply and Irrigation Paper no. 138. 1905.

_____. *Development of Underground Waters in the Eastern Coastal Plain Region of Southern California*, by Walter C. Mendenhall. Water Supply and Irrigation Paper no. 137. 1905.

_____. *Development of Underground Waters in the Western Coastal Plain Region of Southern California*, by Walter C. Mendenhall. Water Supply and Irrigation Paper no. 139. 1905.

_____. *Erosion and Sediment Transport in the Owens River near Bishop*, by Rhea P. Williams. Water Resources Investigation no. 49-75. Menlo Park, Calif., 1975.

_____. *Geology and Tungsten Mineralization of the Bishop District, California*, by P. C. Bateman. Professional Paper no. 470. 1965.

_____. *The Geology and Water Resources of Owens Valley, California*, by Willis T. Lee. Water Supply Paper no. 181. 1906.

_____. *Hydrology and Mineralogy of Deep Springs Lake, Inyo County, California*, by Blair F. Jones. Professional Paper no. 502-A. 1965.

————. *An Intensive Study of the Water Resources of a Part of the Owens Valley California*, by Charles H. Lee. Water Supply Paper no. 294. 1912.

————. *The Quality of the Surface Waters of California*, by Walton Van Winkle and Frederick M. Eaton. Water Supply Paper no. 237. 1910.

————. "Quaternary History of Mono Valley California," by Israel C. Russell, in *Eighth Annual Report, 1886-1887, Part One*. 1887.

————. *Review of Waterpower Withdrawals: Mono Lake and Owens Lake Basins, California*, by Kenneth W. Sax. May 1964.

————. *Surface Water Supply of California*, by W. B. Clapp. Water Supply Paper no. 213. 1907.

————. *Underflow Tests in the Drainage Basin of the Los Angeles River*, by Homer Hamlin. Water Supply and Irrigation Paper no. 112. 1905.

Department of the Interior, War Relocation Authority. *Community Analysis Reports from Granada, Minidoka, and Manzanar Relocation Centers*. Community Analysis Report no. 17. April 23, 1946.

————. *Impounded People: Japanese Americans in the Relocation Centers*. 1946.

————. *Semi-Annual Report, January 1-June 30, 1944*. 1944.

————. *WRA: A Story of Human Conservation*. N.d.

National Science Foundation. *Effects of Groundwater Pumping on the Environment of Owens Valley and the Users of Owens Valley Water*, Deborah J. Wilson, ed. 1978.

Naval Weapons Center. *A Land Use History of Coso Hot Springs, Inyo County, California*, by the Iroquois Research Institute, Cecil R. Brooks, William M. Clements, Jo Ann Kantner, and Genevieve Y. Poirier. China Lake, Calif. January 1979.

————. *Remote Sensing Survey of the Coso Geothermal Area, Inyo County, California*, by James B. Koenig, et al. China Lake, Calif. February 1972.

Outdoor Recreation Resources Review Commission. *The Future of Outdoor Recreation in Metropolitan Regions of the United States*: vol. III, *The Impact of Growth of the Los Angeles Metropolitan Region on the Demand for Outdoor Recreation Facilities in Southern California, 1976 and 2000*. 1962.

B. STATE OF CALIFORNIA

Board of Equalization, *Assessment Practices Survey, Inyo County, 1972-73*. April 1973.

————. *Property Tax Assessment in Inyo County*. 1950.

Council of Defense, Committee on Transportation, Housing, Works, and Facilities. *Reports on Municipal Water Supply Systems, Report No. 2: Los Angeles Region.* July 1942.

California Development Board. *Agricultural and Industrial Survey of Inyo County, California.* June-July 1917.

Office of the State Engineer. *Letter of Transmittal and Report of State Engineer Concerning the Owens Valley-Los Angeles Controversy to Governor Friend William Richardson,* by W. F. McClure. 1925.

Department of Fish and Game. "Tule Elk," *Outdoor California,* vol. 24, no. 3 (March 1963).

_____. *Owens Valley Tule Elk Habitat Management Plan,* rev. ed. Prepared with Inyo National Forest, Los Angeles Department of Water and Power, and Bureau of Land Management. October 15, 1976.

Legislature, Assembly, "Communication to the California Legislature Relating to the Owens Valley Water Situation," by Andrae Nordskog, *Assembly Journal,* April 27, 1931.

Legislature, Assembly, Interim Committee on Conservation, Planning, and Public Works. *Transcript of Proceedings: Subcommittee on Impact of Public Land Ownership on the Local Tax Base, Hearings of August 30, 1957 and May 23, 1958 in Bishop, California.* 1958.

Legislature, Senate, Committee on Local Governmental Agencies, *Report Concerning Application of City of Los Angeles for Purchase of Federal Lands in Mono County,* October 19, 1945.

Legislature, Senate, Committee on Local Governmental Agencies, *Hearings, February 16, 1945.* 1945.

Legislature, Senate, *Report of the Special Investigating Committee on Water Situation in Inyo and Mono Counties,* in *Journal of the Senate,* May 7, 1931.

Department of Natural Resources, Division of Mines. *Economic Geology of the Darwin Quadrangle, Inyo County, California,* by Wayne E. Hall and E. M. Mackevett. San Francisco, October 1958.

_____. "Mines and Mineral Resources of Inyo County," by L. A. Norman, Jr., and Richard M. Stewart, *California Journal of Mines and Geology,* vol. 47, no. 1 (January 1951).

_____. *Salt in California,* by W. E. Ver Planck. Bulletin no. 175. 1957.

Office of Planning and Research. "Taxation of Municipally Owned Property Outside Their Boundaries," by Georgann Eberhardt. December 1976.

Public Outdoor Recreation Plan Committee. *California Public Outdoor Recreation Plan, Part II.* November 1960.

Department of Public Works, Division of Engineering and Irrigation.

Consumption of Water Table, San Gabriel Valley, Also Hydrograph for Rainfall at Los Angeles. 1929.

————. *Report on Development of Water Resources in Mono Basin Based on Investigations Made for the Division of Engineering and Irrigation,* by S.T. Harding. December 1922.

————. *Supplemental Report and Notes on Mono Basin Investigation,* by S.T. Harding. October 17, 1922.

————. *Water Resources of Southern California.* Bulletin no. 12. 1927.

Department of Public Works, Division of Water Resources. *Groundwater Levels and Precipitation Records in Los Angeles, San Gabriel, and Santa Ana River Basins and Antelope Valley and Water Supply Summary for Southern Portion of California.* Bulletin no. 39-W. June, 1956.

————. *Office Report on the Diversion of Mono Basin Water into the Owens River Basin for the Generation of Power.* July 1927.

————. *Report to Senate Committee on Local Governmental Agencies on Water Supply and Use of Water in Mono-Inyo Basin, California, Pursuant to Committee Resolution Adopted November 25, 1947.* March 1948.

————. *Reports of Consulting Board on Safety of the Mulholland Dam, Hollywood.* June 1930.

————. *South Coastal Basin: A Symposium.* Bulletin no. 32. 1930.

————. *South Coastal Basin Investigation: Geology and Ground Water Storage Capacity of Valley Fill.* Bulletin no. 45. 1934.

————. *South Coastal Basin Investigation: Overdraft on Ground Water Basins.* Bulletin no. 53. 1947.

————. *South Coastal Basin Investigation: Value and Cost of Water for Irrigation in Coastal Plain of Southern California.* Bulletin no. 43. 1933.

Department of Public Works, Division of Water Rights. *Fluctuation of Water Plane at Certain Wells with Long-Time Records,* by Harold Conkling. Bulletin no. 5. September 30, 1926.

California Railroad Commission. *Los Angeles Aqueduct: General Construction and Auxiliary Costs,* compiled by O.E. Clemens. February 1, 1915.

Saint Francis Dam commission. *Report of the Commission Appointed by Governor C.C. Young to Investigate Causes Leading to Failure of the Saint Francis Dam near Saugus California.* 1928.

California Water Commission. *Investigation of Applications to Appropriate Water in the Owens River Valley and Vicinity.* September 21, 1915.

Department of Water Resources. *The California State Water Project: 1976 Activities and Future Management Plans*. Bulletin no. 132-77. November 1977.

——. *California Water*. Bulletin no. 201-77. February 1978.

——. *Crustal Strain and Fault Movement Investigation*. Bulletin no. 116-2. January 1964.

——. *Feasibility of Reclamation of Water from Wastes in the Los Angeles Metropolitan Area*. Bulletin no. 80. December 1961.

——. *Fish Slough Dam and Reservoir Feasibility Investigation*. Bulletin no. 126. October 1964.

——. *Hydrologic Data: 1975. Volume 5: Southern California*. Bulletin no. 130-75. March 1977.

——. *Interim Report on Inyo-Mono Area Water Resources Investigation*. January 1965.

——. *Owens Valley Groundwater Investigation, Phase I, Southern District Report*. September 1980.

——. *Report of Interagency Task force on Mono Lake*. December 1979.

——. *Southern Lahontan Area of California: Land and Water Use Survey, 1961*. Bulletin no. 121. August 1965.

Water Resources Board. *Los Angeles County Land and Water Use Survey, 1955*. Bulletin 24. June 1956.

——. *Reconnaissance Investigation of the Water Resources of Mono and Owens Basins*. August 1960.

Water Rights Board. *Memorandum Report of the Water Supply of the Mono and Owens Basins with Relationship to the Proposed Second Barrel of the Los Angeles Aqueduct*, by John H. Gant and David W. Sabiston. December 1963.

C. CITY OF LOS ANGELES

Aqueduct Investigation Board. *Report of the Aqueduct Investigation Board to the City Council of Los Angeles*. August 31, 1912.

Board of Public Service Commissioners. *Owens Valley and the Los Angeles Water Supply, Including a Statement of Facts Omitted by the State Engineer in His Report to Governor Richardson*. February 1925.

——. *Reply of the Board of Public Service Commissioners to the Proposal and Accompanying Documents Dated November 29, 1924, Submitted by W. W. Watterson to the Los Angeles Clearing House Association*. January 6, 1925.

————. *Report on Available Water Supply of City of Los Angeles and Metropolitan Area*, by Louis C. Hill, J.B. Lippincott, and A.L. Sonderegger. August 1924.

————. *Report upon the Sanitary Quality of the Owens River Water Supply*, by Charles Gilman Hyde. 1915.

Board of Public Works. *Report of the Board of Consulting Engineers on the Project of the Los Angeles Aqueduct from Owens River to San Fernando Valley*, by John R. Freeman, Frederic P. Stearns, and James D. Schuyler. December 22, 1906.

Board of Water Commissioners. *Report upon the Distribution of the Surplus Waters of the Los Angeles Aqueduct*, by John Henry Quinton, W.H. Code, and Homer Hamlin. 1911.

Board of Water and Power Commissioners. *Comments of the General Manager and Chief Engineer, Department of Water and Power, on the Ford, Bacon and Davis Report of November 16, 1948*. October 4, 1949.

————. *The Dynamite Holdup*. N.d.

————. *Report of the Board of Consulting Engineers on the Storage and Distribution of Water*, by Louis C. Hill, R.E. McDonnell, and Robert T. Hill. October 1928.

————. *Report on the Department of Water and Power*, by Ford, Bacon and Davis. November 26, 1948.

————. *Statement of Board before Senate Fact-Finding Committee on Water*, by William S. Peterson. October 8, 1959.

————. *Statement of Water and Power Requirements of the City of Los Angeles and the Metropolitan Water District*. Also published as *Metropolitan Water District Report No. 163*. July 5, 1929.

————. *Survey of Business and Properties of Department of Water and Power of the City of Los Angeles California*, by EBASCO Services, Inc. August 15, 1957.

————. *Why the MWD Act Must Be Amended*. February 1961.

Bureau of Budget and Efficiency. *Financial Relationship between the Department of Water and Power and the Government of the City of Los Angeles*. May 1941.

Bureau of Engineering. *Annexation and Detachment Map*. February 1978.

————. *Plans for City Waterworks: Full Report by City Engineer Dockweiler for the Council*. March 30, 1897.

Bureau of Municipal Research. *California Population Forecast, 1935 to 1960*, by Warren S. Thompson, P.K. Whelpton, and W.C. Yeatman. 1935.

_____. *Consolidated Water for Los Angeles County*. 1933.

Bureau of Water Works and Supply. *The Boron Problem As Related to the Los Angeles Water Supply*, by R. F. Goudey. January 1937.

_____. *The Problem of Boron in the Los Angeles Water Supply*, by R. F. Goudey. July 1936.

_____. *The Water Miracle*. 1936.

_____. *Water Supply and Distribution Problems in Los Angeles*, by Verne G. Saunders. December 6, 1937.

City Chemist. *Report on the Sanitary Investigation of Owens River and the Los Angeles Aqueduct*, by E. H. Miller and Luther M. Powers. 1914.

City Council. *Report of the Committee to Investigate and Report the Cause of the Failure of the Saint Francis Dam*. March 1928.

_____. *Report on the Los Angeles Aqueduct*, by Edward Johnson and Edward S. Cobb. July 15, 1912.

_____. *Report of the Special Sewage Disposal Commission*, by George W. Fuller, George C. Whipple, and William Mulholland. Pts. 1 and 2, April 16, 1921. Pt. 3, August 10, 1921.

Commission of Engineers. *Report . . . to Assist the Board of Arbitrators in Appraising the Value of the Improvements Made to City Water Works of Los Angeles by Los Angeles City Water Company, July 1868 to July 1898*. December 6, 1898.

Compromise Committee. *Final Report on Agreement of Sale Between Los Angeles City Water Company and City of Los Angeles*. July 19, 1901.

Department of Public Service. *Complete Report on Construction of the Los Angeles Aqueduct*. 1916.

_____. *Owens Valley and the Los Angeles Aqueduct*. January 1925.

_____. *Report on Irrigation from Owens River Sources and Crops Produced Therefrom during the Season of 1919*. Reprinted in *Public Service*, vol. 4, no. 1 (January 1920).

Department of Public Works. *First Annual Report of the Chief Engineer of the Los Angeles Aqueduct to the Board of Public Works*. March 15, 1907.

Department of Water and Power. *City of Los Angeles 1850-1950: Growth of the Water and Power Systems under American Law*. 1950.

_____. *Data on Available Water Supply and Future Requirements of the City of Los Angeles and the Metropolitan Area*. October 1928.

_____. *Draft Environmental Impact Report on Increased Pumping of the Owens Valley Groundwater Basin*. August 29, 1974.

————. *Draft Environmental Impact Report on Increased Pumping of the Owens Valley Groundwater Basin.* August 1978.

————. *Facts Concerning the Owens Valley Reparations Claims.* N.d.

————. *The Feather River Project.* November 1, 1951.

————. *The Feather River Project,* by Samuel B. Morris. December 4, 1952.

————. *The Feather River Project,* by Samuel B. Morris. June 10, 1954.

————. *The Feather River Project and California Water Plan,* by Samuel B. Morris. September 19, 1956.

————. *Final Report on the Owens Valley Indian Situation Including a Suggested Plan for Adjustment of Same,* by E. A. Porter. January 9, 1936.

————. *Financing and Repayment of the Feather River Project.* December 14, 1956.

————. *From Pueblo to Metropolis: Water and Power in the Story of Los Angeles.* 1968.

————. *Future Water Supply.* 1976.

————. *Land and Water Right Purchases, Fiscal Years 1933-34 to 1936-37.* 1937.

————. *Little Journeys into Water and Power Land.* 1929.

————. *Los Angeles and the Feather River,* by William S. Peterson. 1958.

————. *Los Angeles Water and Power Bureau Pay Their Own Way.* 1928.

————. *Los Angeles Water Rights in the Mono Basin and the Impact of the Department's Operations on Mono Lake,* by P. H. Lane, D. L. Georgeson, C. L. Anderson, R. A. McCoy, and M. Abalos. 1974.

————. *Los Angeles' Interest in the Feather River Project,* by Samuel B. Morris. January 4, 1952.

————. *Mono Lake and the Billion Dollar Threat to California's Water Supply.* 1979.

————. *Owens Gorge Project,* by Samuel B. Morris. February 1955.

————. *The Owens Valley Dispute,* by Don J. Kinsey. N.d.

————. *Owens Valley Vacation Land Is Calling You.* 1928.

————. *Post-War Problems and the Prospects of the Los Angeles Metropolitan Area,* by Samuel B. Morris. May 25, 1945.

————. *Preliminary Briefing on Management Plan for City of Los Angeles Water Resources and Lands in Inyo and Mono Counties.* November 10, 1971.

————. *Preliminary Report on the Feasibility of Developing Additional Water Supply in the Mono-Owens Valley Area and Transporting It to Upper Van Norman Lake.* April 1960.

_____. *Proposed Charter Amendment Establishing Revenue Bond Plan for Department of Water and Power*. April 1, 1947.

_____. *The Proposed Los Angeles-Colorado River Aqueduct*, by H. A. Van Norman. July, 1927.

_____. *Proposed Nuclear Power Plant in Tulare County*. October 20, 1971.

_____. *Proposed Second Barrel, Los Angeles Aqueduct*. May 1963.

_____. *Proposed Second Barrel, Los Angeles Aqueduct, Haiwee Reservoir to San Fernando Valley*. May 1959.

_____. *Recreation and Other Public Uses of the City of Los Angeles Lands in the Owens Valley-Mono Basin Area*. January 1967.

_____. *Report by C. P. Garman, Assistant Chief Electrical Engineer to the Board of Water and Power Commissioners*. December 11, 1944.

_____. *Report on the Condition of the Indians in Owens Valley California*, by A. J. Ford, E. A. Porter, and C. D. Carll. June 30, 1932.

_____. *Report Covering a Plan for the Future Economic Development of City of Los Angeles Lands Located in the Owens River Drainage Area and the Utilization of Available Excess Water Therein*, by J. E. Phillips and T. R. Silvius. May 20, 1938.

_____. *Report on the Feasibility of Wastewater Reclamation by the City of Los Angeles*. October 10, 1968.

_____. *Report on the Proposed Second Barrel of the Los Angeles Aqueduct*. June 1962.

_____. *Report of Special Education Committee on Charter Amendment No. 2 Establishing a Water and Power Revenue Bond Plan and Charter Amendment No. 4 Amending the Vacation Ordinance, General Election May 27, 1947*. August 15, 1947.

_____. *A Resume of the Activities in Connection with the Fixing of Values and Proposed Purchase of Privately Owned Property within the Towns of Laws, Bishop, Big Pine, Independence, and Lone Pine in Owens River Valley by the City of Los Angeles*, by A. J. Ford. 1932.

_____. *River of Destiny—The Story of the Colorado River*, by Don J. Kinsey. 1928.

_____. *The Romance of Water and Power*, by Don J. Kinsey. 1926.

_____. *San Joaquin Nuclear Project: Draft Environmental Impact Report*. April 22, 1975.

_____. *The Second Los Angeles Aqueduct*. 1971.

_____. *The Snake-Colorado Project: A Plan to Transport Surplus Columbia River Basin Water to the Arid Pacific Southwest*. October 1963.

_____. *Special Committee Report on Conditions in Owens Valley*, by Clarence A. Dykstra, James Brader, and J. F. Neal. 1928.

_____. *Statement before Sub-Committee on Economic and Financial Policies for State Water Projects*, by William S. Peterson. Bakersfield, September 17, 1958.

_____. *Status of Owens Valley Town Property Purchase Program As of June 30, 1933*, by Right of Way and Land Division. 1933.

_____. *Ultimate Water Supply and Irrigable Areas of the Lower Colorado Basin*, by J. B. Lippincott. June 1926.

_____. *Water Development, Conservation, and Recreational Use of Natural Resources*. 1964.

_____. *The Water and Power Building*. 1969.

_____. *Water and Power Points of Interest Along the Los Angeles-Owens River Aqueduct System*. February 1968.

_____. *Water and Power Problem of California Municipalities*, by Samuel B. Morris. December 1945.

_____. *The Water Problem*, by Samuel B. Morris. September 16, 1948.

_____. *Water Question*. 1929.

_____. *Water Resources Management Plan, Owens Valley Groundwater Basin: Review Copy*. October 1972.

_____. *Water Supply Management in Inyo and Mono Counties*. September 1966.

_____. *The Water Trail*, by Don J. Kinsey. 1928.

_____. *Water Wheels of Progress*. 1935.

_____. *William Mulholland: Father of the Los Angeles Municipal Water System*. October 1939.

_____. *Yours!* 1929.

Office of the Mayor. *Mayor's Blue Ribbon Committee on Department of Water and Power Rate Structure: Water Rate Structure Report*. October 1977.

_____. *Statement on Owens Valley and Mono Basin Land Purchases*, by Mayor John C. Porter. June 24, 1930.

D. COURT CASES

Bishop Creek Ditch Company et al. v. *City of Los Angeles*, Inyo County Superior Court, no. 1410.

City of Los Angeles v. *Pomeroy*, 124 Cal. 597, 63 (1899).

City of Los Angeles v. *County of Inyo*, 167 Cal. App. 2d 736 (1959).

City of Los Angeles v. *County of Inyo*, 4 Civil 25014 (Cal. App. September 25, 1980).

City of Los Angeles v. *Thomas D. Buffington et al.*, 156 Cal. 603 (1909).

County of Inyo v. *City of Los Angeles*, 71 Cal. App. 3d 185 (1977).

County of Inyo v. *City of Los Angeles*, 78 Cal. App. 3d 82 (1978).

County of Inyo v. *Public Utilities Commission*, 26 Cal. 3d 154 (1980).

County of Inyo v. *Yorty*, 32 Cal. App. 3d 795 (1973).

Anastacio Feliz v. *City of Los Angeles*, 58 Cal. 73, 79.

Henry A. Hart et al. v. *City of Los Angeles*, Los Angeles County Superior Court, no. B 2566.

Amelia Herminghaus v. *Southern California Edison Company*, 200 Cal. 81 (1926).

Hillside Water Company v. *City of Los Angeles*, 10 Cal. 2d 677 (1938).

Hillside Water Company v. *City of Los Angeles*, Inyo County Superior Court, no. 2073.

Los Angeles City Water Company v. *City of Los Angeles*, 55 Cal. 176.

Lux v. *Haggin*, 69 Cal. 255.

W. W. Mines v. *R. F. Del Valle*, 201 Cal. 273 (1927).

Mono Power Company v. *City of Los Angeles*, 284 Fed. 784, 792 (1922).

Morrison and Weatherly v. *City of Los Angeles*, San Bernardino County Superior Court, no. 152656.

Natural Soda Products Company v. *City of Los Angeles*, 23 Cal. 2d (1943).

People v. *City of Los Angeles*, 34 Cal. 2d (1950).

Wehrle v. *Los Angeles Board of Water and Power Commissioners*, 221 Cal. 70 (1930).

E. MISCELLANEOUS

County of Inyo. *Handbook of County Facts.* 1972.

————. *Inyo the Peerless.* Bishop, Calif. [ca. 1913].

County of Inyo, Board of Supervisors. *Changes in the Owens Valley Shallow Groundwater Levels from 1970 to 1978*, by Philip B. Williams. San Francisco, June 1978.

————. *Inyo County and the Famous Owens River Valley.* [Circa 1910.]

————. *Statement of Objectives to Develop a Comprehensive Water Management and Protection Plan for the Owens River Basin.* June 7, 1971.

County of Inyo, Grand Jury. *Grand Jury Report for 1976-77.* 1977.

County of Los Angeles, County Coroner. *Verdict of the Coroner's Jury in the Saint Francis Dam Disaster.* April 1928.

County of Los Angeles, County Engineer. *Water Supplies for Los Angeles County*, by Stephen J. Koonce and A. E. Brueington. February 1977.

Metropolitan Water District. *The Great Aqueduct: The Story of the Planning and Building of the Colorado River Aqueduct.* 1941.
————. *Owens Valley: Fact and Fable of a Water War.* 1977.
Owens Valley Irrigation District. *Data and Digest of Reports to Accompany Proposal for Settlement with Owens Valley Submitted to the Los Angeles Clearing House Association.* Bishop, Calif., November 29, 1924.
————. *Engineer's Report on the Owens Valley Irrigation District.* Bishop, Calif., March 20, 1923.

III. Periodicals

A. NEWSPAPERS

Bakersfield Californian
Big Pine Citizen
Bristlecone View
Cal-Tax News
The Commonwealth
Denver Post
Engineering News-Record
Exeter Sun
Fresno Republican
Gridiron
Intake
Inyo Independent

Inyo Register
Los Angeles Daily News
Los Angeles Examiner
Los Angeles Express
Los Angeles Herald
Los Angeles Herald-Examiner
Los Angeles Record
Los Angeles Star
Los Angeles Times
Los Angeles Tribune
Mohave Press

Owens Valley Herald
Sacramento Bee
Sacramento Union
San Diego Union
San Francisco Call
San Francisco Chronicle
Santa Barbara Press
Sierra Club Yodeler
Skidoo News
Western Construction News

B. SIGNED ARTICLES

Ahrens, Robert E. "Rivers of Steel that Flow to Los Angeles." *Travel,* 91 (October 1933).
Alexander, George. "What I Am Going To Do." *Pacific Outlook*, vol. 6, no. 7 (April 3, 1909).
Amaral, Anthony A. "Struggle in the Owens Valley." *American Forests,* vol. 80, no. 8 (August 1964).
Anderson, D. H. "Are Government Officials Playing Fair? Some Facts About the Owens River Valley Condition." *Irrigation Age,* vol. 24, no. 2 (December 1908).

———. "Oppressive Use of Power." *Irrigation Age*, vol. 24, no. 3 (January 1909).

———. "Why Was the Owens River Project Abandoned?" *Irrigation Age*, vol. 24, no. 4 (February 1909).

Barrows, H. D. "Water for Domestic Purposes vs. Water for Irrigation." *Publications of the Historical Society of Southern California*, vol. 8, pt. 3. Los Angeles, 1912.

Baugh, Ruth E. "Land Use Changes in the Bishop Area of Owens Valley California." *Economic Geography*, vol. 13, no. 1 (January 1937).

Blight, Reynold E. "Municipal Government 50 Years from Now." *California Outlook*, vol. 11, nos. 11-12 (October 21, 1911).

Bowen, H. C. "Water Conservation in California." *Institution of Water Engineers Journal*, 18 (January 31, 1964).

Brooks, Benjamin. "The Power Planners." *Scribners*, vol. 51, no. 8 (May 1912).

Chalfant, W. A. "Charley's Butte." *Irrigation Age*, vol. 24, no. 2 (December 1908).

Conable, Polly. "Mount Whitney Hatchery Closing Hinted." *Bristlecone View*, May 3, 1967.

Cross, Frederick C. "My Days on the Jawbone." *Westways*, vol. 110, no. 5 (May 1968).

Crowley, John J. "Inyo: The County of Contrasts." *The Tidings*, August 8, 1924.

Davis, Arthur, P.; Goethals, George W.; and Mulholland, William. "Water Supply Problem of the East Bay Municipal Utility District." In East Bay Municipal Utility District, *Additional Water Supply of East Bay Municipal Utility District: A Report to the Board of Directors by Arthur Powell Davis*. Oakland, October 1, 1924.

DeDecker, Mary, "The Eastern Sierra: From the Days of Gold to the Time of Recreation." *T'n'T* (Title Insurance and Trust Company), March-April 1967.

Dykstra, Clarence A. "Owens Valley: A Problem in Regional Planning." *Community Builder*, vol. 1, no. 3 (February 1928).

Finkle, F. C. "Los Angeles Aqueduct Mistakes." *Journal of Electricity, Power and Gas*, vol. 34, no. 2 (January 9, 1915).

———. "Los Angeles' $40,000,000 White Elephant." *Irrigation Age*, vol. 30, no. 7 (May 1915).

Gates, Paul W. "Public Land Disposal in California." *Agricultural History*, vol. 49, no. 1 (January 1975).

Geiger, C. W. "Using Los Angeles Aqueduct Water for Irrigation Purposes." *Municipal and County Engineering*, vol. 55, no. 1 (July 1918).

Guinn, J. W. "Some Early History of Owens River Valley." *Annual Publications of the Historical Society of Southern California*, vol. 10, pt. 3. Los Angeles, 1917.

Hayden, Frederick. "Los Angeles Aqueduct." *Building and Engineering News*, August 15, 1915.

Heinly, Burt A. "Aladdin of the Aqueduct." *Sunset*, vol. 28, no. 4 (April 1912).

———. "An Aqueduct Two Hundred and Forty Miles Long." *Scientific American*, vol. 145, no. 21 (May 12, 1912).

———. "Carrying Water through a Desert." *National Geographic*, vol. 21, no. 1 (July 1910).

———. "The Los Angeles Aqueduct." *Municipal Engineering*, vol. 37, no. 5 (November 1909).

———. "Restoring the Los Angeles Siphon." *Municipal Journal*, 36 (May 7, 1941).

Hoffman, Abraham. "Fact and Fiction in the Owens Valley Water Controversy." In Los Angeles Westerners Corral, *Brand Book No. 15*. Los Angeles, 1978.

———. "Joseph B. Lippincott and the Owens Valley Controversy: Time for Revision." *Southern California Quarterly*, vol. 54, no. 3 (Fall 1972).

———. "Origins of a Controversy: The United States Reclamation Service and the Owens Valley-Los Angeles Water Dispute." *Arizona and the West*, 19 (Winter 1977).

Holt, L. M. "How the Reclamation Service Is Robbing the Settler." *Overland Monthly*, vol. 50, ser. 2 (November 1907).

Hurlbut, W. W. "The Man and the Engineer." *Western Construction News*, vol. 1, no. 8 (April 25, 1926).

Jacques, H. L. "Mono Crater Tunnel Construction Problem." *Journal of the American Water Works Association*, vol. 32, no. 1 (January 1940).

Kahrl, William L. "The Politics of California Water: Owens Valley and the Los Angeles Aqueduct." *California Historical Quarterly*, vol. 55, nos. 1 and 2 (Spring and Summer 1976).

Kelly, Allen. "The Story of the Owens River." *West Coast Magazine*, vol. 2, no. 3 (June 1907).

Korr, Charles P. "William Hammond Hall: The Failure of Attempts at State Water Planning in California, 1878-1888." *Historical Society of Southern California Quarterly*, 45 (December 1963).

Lee, Charles H. "The Determination of Safe Yield of Underground Reservoirs of the Closed Basin Type." *Transactions of the American Society of Civil Engineers*, 78 (1915).

———. "Well Development in Owens Valley Equalizes Supply of Los

Angeles Aqueduct." *Western Construction News*, 1 (October 25, 1926).

Lee, Lawrence B. "100 Years of Reclamation Historiography." *Pacific Historical Review*, vol. 47, no. 4 (November 1978).

Lingenfelter, Richard E. "The Desert Steamers." *Journal of the West*, vol. 1, no. 2 (October 1962).

Lippincott, Joseph B. "The Dual Usage of Water for Domestic and Irrigation Purposes." *Journal of the American Water Works Association*, vol. 28, no. 9 (September 1936).

_____. "General Outlook for Reclamation Work in California." *Forestry and Irrigation*, vol. 11, no. 8 (August 1905).

_____. "Mulholland's Memory." *Civil Engineering*, vol. 9, no. 3 (March 1939).

_____. "The Reclamation Service in California." *Forestry and Irrigation*, vol. 10, no. 4 (April 1904).

_____. "William Mulholland: Engineer, Pioneer, Raconteur." *Civil Engineering*, vol. 11, nos. 2 and 3 (February and March 1941).

_____. "The Yuma Project." *Out West*, vol. 20, no. 12 (June 1904).

Lissner, Meyer. "Bill Mulholland." *American Magazine*, vol. 73, no. 6 (April 1912).

_____. "Expressions of Prominent Citizens on the Election Results." *Pacific Outlook*, vol. 7, no. 24 (December 11, 1909).

Lummis, Charles F. "The Perils of Water Monopoly." *Land of Sunshine*, 15 (November 1901).

_____. "The Struggle for Water." *Land of Sunshine*, 15 (October 1901).

McCarthy, John Russell. "Water: The Story of Bill Mulholland." *Los Angeles Saturday Night*, October 30, 1937, through March 26, 1938.

McCorkle, Julia Norton. "A History of Los Angeles Journalism." *Historical Society of Southern California, 1915-16*, vol. 10. Los Angeles, 1916.

Malsman, Iris S. "Is There a 'Project'? The Unsolved Riddle of CEQA in the Owens Valley." *San Fernando Valley Law Review*, vol. 6, no. 2 (Spring 1978).

Moody, Charles A. "Los Angeles and the Owens River." *Out West*, vol. 23, no. 4 (October 1905).

Morgan, Judith, and Morgan, Neil. "California's Parched Oasis." *National Geographic*, vol. 149, no. 1 (January 1976).

Muir, John. "In the Heart of the California Alps." *Scribners*, vol. 19, no. 10 (July 1880).

Mulholland, William. "A Brief Historical Sketch of the Growth of the Los Angeles City Water Department." *Public Service*, vol. 4, no. 6 (June 1920).

————. "Earthquakes in their Relation to the Los Angeles Aqueduct." *Bulletin of the Seismological Society of America*, vol. 8, no. 1 (March 1918).

————. "History of Water Supply Development for the Metropolitan Area of Los Angeles." *Hydraulic Engineering*, vol. 4, no. 7 (July 1928).

————. "Projected Los Angeles to Colorado River Aqueduct." *Municipal and County Engineering*, vol. 63, no. 10 (April 1927).

————. "Proposed Aqueduct from the Colorado River." *Journal of the American Water Works Association*, vol. 30, no. 10 (April 1927).

————. "Water from the Colorado River." *Community Builder*, 1 (March 1928).

————. "Water Supply of Los Angeles." *Journal of the American Water Works Association*, vol. 20, no. 4 (October 1928).

Mulholland, William, and Lippincott, Joseph B. "The Fundamental Conditions of San Fernando Valley from which Los Angeles Receives Its Entire Water Supply Are Parallel to Those in the Livermore Valley"; "Report on the Development of Ground Waters of the Livermore Valley"; "Report on the Productivity of Livermore Valley"; "Review of Certain Conclusions Presented by Mr. John R. Freeman." All in Spring Valley Water Company, *The Future Water Supply of San Francisco*. San Francisco, October 31, 1912.

Murbarger, Nell. "The Ghost Towns of Inyo." In Los Angeles Westerners Corral, *The California Deserts: Brand Book No. 11*. Los Angeles, 1964.

Nadeau, Remi. "Water War." *American Heritage*, 13 (December 1961).

Nelson, Dick. "Men and Mules." *Intake*, vol. 40, no. 10 (October 1971).

Newell, F. H. "The Reclamation Service." *Popular Science Monthly*, vol. 66, no. 2 (December 1904).

————. "The Reclamation Service and the Owens Valley." *Out West*, vol. 23, no. 4 (October 1905).

————. "Work of the Reclamation Service in California." *Forestry and Irrigation*, vol. 11, no. 8 (August 1905).

Oliver, Graydon. "Prosperous Condition of Owens Valley District Revealed by Many Vital Statistics." *Modern Irrigation*, vol. 3, no. 8 (August 1927).

Osborne, Henry A. "The Completion of the Los Angeles Aqueduct." *Scientific American*, vol. 109, no. 19 (November 8, 1913).

Outland, Charles F. "Historical Water Diversion Proposals." *Ventura County Historical Society Quarterly*, vol. 5, no. 4 (August 1960).

Phillips, J. E. "Underground Water Development in Owens Valley." In

University of Southern California School of Government, Water Supply and Sanitary Engineering Section, *Papers, 1930*. Los Angeles, 1930.

Pisani, Donald J. "Water Law Reform in California, 1900-1913." *Agricultural History*, vol. 54, no. 2 (April 1980).

Pitt, Leonard. "Los Angeles in Owens River Valley: Was It Rape or Enlightened Self-Interest?" In *California Controversies*. Glenview, Illinois, 1968.

Prosser, Richard. "William Mulholland: Maker of Los Angeles." *Western Construction News*, vol. 1, no. 8 (April 25, 1926).

Randau, John A. "Bringing River to the People." *Westways*, May 1968.

Reichard, G. A. "Aqueduct of the Los Angeles, California, Municipal Water System." *National Engineer*, September 1913.

Reinking, R. F.; Mathews, L. A.; St. Amand, P. "Dust Storms Due to the Desication of Owens Lake." In *International Conference on Environmental Sensing and Assessment*. Las Vegas, September 14-19, 1975.

Romer, Margaret. "The Story of Los Angeles." *Journal of the West*, January 1964.

Ryan, Marian L. "Los Angeles Newspapers Fight the Water War, 1924-1927." *Southern California Quarterly*, vol. 50, no. 2 (June 1968).

Schiesl, Martin J. "Progressive Reform in Los Angeles under Mayor Alexander, 1909-1913." *California Historical Quarterly*, vol. 104, no. 1 (Spring 1975).

Shrader, Roscoe E. "A Ditch in the Desert." *Scribners*, vol. 51, no. 5 (May 1912).

Smythe, William E. "The Social Significance of the Owens River Project." *Out West*, vol. 23, no. 4 (October 1905).

Stallcup, R., and Greenberg, R. "Middle Pacific Coast Region Report." *American Birds*, 28 (1974).

Steinhart, Peter. "The City and the Inland Sea." *Audubon*, vol. 82, no. 5 (September 1980).

Stewart, William R. "A Desert City's Far Reach for Water." *The World's Work*, vol. 15, no. 1 (November 1907).

Stone, C. H., and Eaton, F. M. "A New Analysis of the Water of Owens Lake." *Journal of the American Chemical Society*, vol. 28, no. 10 (September 1906).

Stone, Irving. "Desert Padre." *Saturday Evening Post*, vol. 216, no. 47 (May 20, 1944).

Treganza, Adan E. "Horticulture with Irrigation among the Great Basin Paiute: An Example of Stimulus Diffusion and Cultural Survival." In *Papers of the Third Great Basin Archaeological Conference, Anthropological Papers 26*, University of Utah. Salt Lake City, 1956.

Trowbridge, Arthur C. "The Terrestrial Deposits of Owens Valley, California." *Journal of Geology*, vol. 19, no. 6 (November-December 1911).

Twilegar, Burt I. "Mulholland's Pipe Dream." *Westways*, vol. 41, no. 1 (January 1949).

Van Norman, H. A. "The Limitations of Civil Service." *Journal of the American Water Works Association*, vol. 33, no. 9 (September 1941).

_____. "Memoir of William Mulholland." *Transactions of the American Society of Civil Engineers*, vol. 62, no. 8 (1936).

_____. "Why Los Angeles Voted $38,800,000 for Water and How It Will Be Spent." *Western City*, 6 (June 1930).

VanValen, Nelson. "A Neglected Aspect of the Owens River Aqueduct Story: The Inception of the Los Angeles Municipal Electrical System." *Southern California Quarterly*, vol. 59, no. 1 (Spring 1977).

Volk, Kenneth Q., and Rowe, Edgar Alan. "Memoir of Joseph B. Lippincott." *Transactions of the American Society of Civil Engineers*, 108 (1943).

White, Manger. "Thirsty Cities." *Saturday Evening Post*, vol. 201, no. 46 (May 18, 1929).

Wilson, Robert R., and Mayeda, Henry S. "The First and Second Los Angeles Aqueducts." In Association of Engineering Geologists, Los Angeles Section, *Engineering Geology in Southern California*. Los Angeles, 1966.

Winther, Oscar Osburn. "The Colony System of Southern California." *Agricultural History*, vol. 27, no. 3 (July 1953).

_____. "Los Angeles: Its Aquatic Life Lines." *Journal of Geography*, 49 (February 1950).

Wollaber, A. B. "Owens Valley and Los Angeles Aqueduct." *Monthly Weather Review*, 38 (January 1910).

Wood, R. Coke. "Owens Valley As I Knew It." *Pacific Historian*, vol. 16, nos. 1-4 (Summer 1972).

Wyckoff, W. W. "Mono Craters Tunnelling Has Involved Struggle with Water and Gas Flows." *Western Construction News*, 13 (December 1938).

Yonay, Ehud. "How Green Was My Valley." *New West*, vol. 2, no. 7 (March 28, 1977).

C. UNSIGNED ARTICLES

"Better Prospects for Settlement of Owens Valley Dispute." *Engineering News-Record*, vol. 94, no. 19 (May 7, 1925).

"California's Little Civil War." *Literary Digest*, vol. 83, no. 10 (December 6, 1924).

"Effectively Transplanted New Englander." *Saturday Evening Post*, vol. 198, no. 49 (June 5, 1926).

"The Great Aqueduct and What It Means to Los Angeles." *Los Angeles Financier*, October 3-7, 1910.

"How It All Began: William Mulholland and the Owens River Aqueduct." *Pacific Business*, vol. 64, no. 2 (March-April 1975).

"The Los Angeles Aqueduct Seizure: What Really Happened." *Fire and Water Engineering*, December 17, 1924.

"Mass of the Fisher Folk." *Westways*, vol. 32, no. 4 (April 1940).

"A Modern Tale of Two Cities." *The Arena*, vol. 38, no. 212 (July 1907).

"Mulholland: Man of Broad Vision." *Southern California Business*, vol. 8, no. 8 (September 1929).

"Mulholland Retires after 50-Year Service at Los Angeles." *Engineering News-Record*, vol. 101, no. 1 (November 22, 1928).

"Nine Miles of Siphons." *Literary Digest*, vol. 46, no. 9 (March 1, 1913).

"The Owens Valley Controversy" (by a Special Correspondent). *The Outlook*, July 13, 1927.

"Out of Their Own Mouths." *Municipal League of Los Angeles Bulletin*, October 31, 1927.

"The Owens Valley Revolt." *Municipal League of Los Angeles Bulletin*, vol. 1, no. 12 (July 15, 1924).

"The Record of the Owens River Project" (by W. S. B.). *Out West*, vol. 30, no. 10 (April 1909).

"Shall Los Angeles Lease or Distribute Aqueduct Power?" *Pacific Outlook*, vol. 10, no. 6 (February 4, 1911).

"State Wins Nominal Judgment Against Los Angeles in Owens River Valley Case." *Engineering News-Record*, vol. 143, no. 12 (September 22, 1949).

"The Theft in Water." *Inyo Magazine*, October 1908.

"Two Prominent Engineers Die." *Western Construction News*, vol. 10, no. 8 (August 1935).

"Unit Costs and Methods of Construction of Los Angeles Aqueduct." *Western Engineering*, November 1916.

"William Mulholland." *Western Construction News and Highways Builder*, vol. 8, no. 14 (August 1933).

"William Mulholland, Los Angeles Water Supply Engineer, Dies." *Engineering News-Record*, vol. 115, no. 4 (July 25, 1935).

IV. Books, Pamphlets and Nongovernment Reports

Adams, Ansel. *Born Free and Equal.* New York, 1944.

Alexander, J. A. *The Life of George Chaffey.* London, 1928.

American Council on Public Affairs. *The Displaced Japanese-Americans.* Washington, D.C., 1944.

Armstrong, Ellis L., ed. *History of Public Works in the United States, 1776-1976.* Chicago, 1976.

Associated Student Body of Manzanar High School. *Valediction 1945.* Manzanar, Calif., 1945.

Austin, Mary. *Earth Horizon.* New York, 1932.

———. *The Flock.* Boston, 1906.

———. *The Ford.* Boston, 1917.

———. *Land of Little Rain.* Boston, 1903.

Bain, Joe Staten; Caves, Richard E.; and Margolis, Julius. *Northern California's Water Industry.* Baltimore, 1966.

Bakker, Gerhard. *History of the California Tule Elk*, rev. ed. Los Angeles, 1962.

Bean, Walton. *California: An Interpretive History.* New York, 1968.

Belfrage, Cedric. *Promised Land.* London, 1938.

Bemis, George W., and Basche, Nancy. *Los Angeles County as an Agency of Municipal Government.* Los Angeles, 1946.

Bird, Frederick Lucien, and Ryan, Frances M. *Public Ownership on Trial.* New York, 1930.

Blake, Nelson M. *Water for the Cities.* Syracuse, N.Y., 1956.

Blum, John Morton. *The Republican Roosevelt.* New York, 1966.

Bogart, Ernest L. *The Water Problem of Southern California.* Claremont Library Series no. 2. Urbana, Ill., 1934.

Bonelli, William G. *Billion Dollar Blackjack: The Story of Corruption and the Los Angeles Times.* Beverly Hills, Calif., 1954.

Bosworth, Allan R. *America's Concentration Camps.* New York, 1967.

Brooks, Thomas. *Notes on Los Angeles Water Supply.* Los Angeles, 1938.

Cain, E. M. *The Story of Early Mono County.* N.p., 1961.

Calvert, M. A. *The Mechanical Engineer in America, 1830-1910: Professional Cultures in Conflict.* Baltimore, 1967.

Carr, Harry. *Los Angeles: City of Dreams*. New York, 1935.

Caughey, John. *Los Angeles: Biography of a City*. Berkeley, 1976.

Chalfant, Willie Arthur. *The Story of Inyo*. 1922. 2d ed. 1933.

Cleland, Robert Glass. *California in Our Time, 1900-1940*. New York, 1947.

Coleman, Charles M. *PG&E of California*. New York, 1952.

Committee for the Preservation of the Tule Elk. *Owens Valley: Home of the Tule Elk*. Los Angeles, n.d.

Committee to Preserve the Ecology of Inyo-Mono. *Our Views on the Proposed Inyo-Mono Land Exchange Bill*. Lone Pine, Calif., 1970.

Conrat, Richard, and Conrat, Maisie. *Executive Order 9066*. San Francisco, 1972.

Constructive Californians. Los Angeles: Saturday Night Publishing Company, 1926.

Cooper, Erwin. *Aqueduct Empire: A Guide to Water in California, Its Turbulent History, and Its Management Today*. Glendale, Calif., 1968.

County Supervisors Association of California. *California County Fact Book, 1977-78*. Sacramento, 1977.

Cragen, D.C. *The Boys in the Sky Blue Pants*. Independence, Calif., 1975.

_____. *A Brief History of the Schools of Inyo County and a Statistical and Financial Report Covering 16 Years*. Independence, Calif., December 1954.

Crouch, Winston W., and Dinerman, Beatrice. *Southern California Metropolis*. Berkeley, 1964.

Crump, Spencer. *Henry Huntington and the Pacific Electric*. Los Angeles, 1970.

_____. *Ride the Big Red Cars*. Cosa Mesa, Calif., 1970.

Darrow, Clarence. *The Story of My Life*. New York, 1932.

Deep Springs College Board of Trustees. *Constitution of Deep Springs and the Deed of Trust*. Deep Springs, Calif., 1950.

DeRoos, Robert William. *The Thirsty Land: Story of the Central Valley*. Palo Alto, Calif., 1948.

Doyle, Helen MacKnight. *Mary Austin: Woman of Genius*. New York, 1939.

Dunham, Harold H. *Government Handout*. New York, 1941.

Eastern California Museum Association. *Eastern California Museum Handbook*. Independence, Calif., 1961.

Economic Research Associates. *California Tourism Industry: Trends and Investment Opportunities*. Los Angeles, 1967.

Erlich, Harry, and McGauhey, P. N. *Economic Evaluation of Water*. Water Resources Center Contribution no. 42. Berkeley, June 1964.

Farnsworth, R. W. C. *A Southern California Paradise*. Pasadena, Calif., 1883.

Farquhar, Francis P. *History of the Sierra Nevada*. Berkeley, 1965.

Fogelson, Robert M. *The Fragmented Metropolis: Los Angeles, 1850-1930*. Cambridge, Mass., 1967.

Garrett, Jessie A., and Larson, Ronald C., eds. *Camp and Community: Manzanar and the Owens Valley*. Fullerton, Calif., 1977.

Golze, Alfred R. *Reclamation in the United States*. New York, 1952.

Gorman, John M. *I Remember Manzanar*. Bishop, Calif., 1967.

Gottlieb, Robert, and Wolt, Irene. *Thinking Big: The Story of the Los Angeles Times, Its Publishers, and Their Influence on Southern California*. New York, 1977.

Gragg, Frances, and Putnam, George Palmer. *Golden Valley: A Novel of California*. New York, 1950.

Guinn, J. M. *Historical and Biographical Record of Los Angeles and Vicinity*. Chicago, 1901.

──────. *A History of California and an Extended History of Los Angeles and Environs*. 3 vols. Los Angeles, 1915.

Hahn, Wise, and Associates. *General Plan: City of Bishop*. San Carlos, Calif., 1963.

Harding, Sidney Twichell. *Water in California*. Palo Alto, Calif., 1960.

Hart, Alan S. *The Story of District IX Bishop*. 1952.

Hawkins, Clarabelle E. *Story of Laws, California*. Bishop, Calif., 1975.

Hays, Samuel P. *Conservation and the Gospel of Efficiency*. Cambridge, Mass., 1959.

Hirschleifer, Jack; De Haven, James C.; and Milliman, Jerome W. *Water Supply: Economics, Technology, and Policy*. Chicago, 1960.

Hodge, Carle. *Aridity and Man: The Challenge of the Arid Lands in the United States*. Washington, D.C., 1963.

Hollon, W. Eugene. *The Great American Desert: Then and Now*. New York, 1966.

Houston, Jeanne Wakatsuki, and Houston, James D. *Farewell to Manzanar*. Boston, 1973.

Huffman, Roy E. *Irrigation Development and Public Water Policy*. New York, 1953.

Hundley, Norris. *Water and the West: The Colorado River Compact and the Politics of Water in the American West*. Berkeley, 1975.

Hunt, Rockwell D. *California and Californians*. 3 vols. Chicago, 1926.

Hutchins, Wells A. *The California Law of Water Rights*. Sacramento, 1956.

An Illustrated History of Los Angeles County. Chicago: Lewis, 1889.

Inyo County, California, Anno Domini 1912. Prepared by the *Inyo County Register.* Bishop, Calif., 1912.

Irvine, Alexander. *Revolution in Los Angeles.* Los Angeles, 1911.

Izaak Walton League of America, California Division. *Owens Valley Mono Basin Report,* by Howard Stoddard. October 15, 1971.

Johnston, Hank. *The Railroad that Lighted Southern California.* Los Angeles, 1965.

Jones, G. M. *Preliminary Cost Estimate of Pumping Plants and 1500 cfs Conduit from Sacramento-San Joaquin Delta to Dry Canyon Reservoir on Los Angeles Aqueduct.* N.p., November 7, 1930.

Kahrl, William L., ed. *The California Water Atlas.* Sacramento, 1979.

Keffer, Frank M. *History of San Fernando Valley.* Glendale, Calif., 1934.

Knoph, Adolph. *Geologic Reconnaissance of the Inyo Range and the Eastern Slope of the Sierra Nevada.* Washington, D.C., 1918.

Knowles, Ralph. *Owens Valley Study: A Natural Ecological Framework for Settlement.* Los Angeles, 1969.

Krautter, Frances Corey. *The Story of Keeler.* Acoma Acres, Calif., 1959.

Kyne, Peter B. *The Long Chance.* New York, 1914.

Layton, Edwin T. *The Revolt of the Engineers: Social Responsibility and the American Engineering Profession.* Cleveland, 1971.

League of Women Voters of California. *Taxation of Property of Local Governments: Analysis of Proposition 2, Legislative Constitutional Amendment, General Election of 1968.* San Francisco, 1968.

Leonard, Ethel. *Report of Sanitary Investigation of the Tributaries and Mountain Streams Emptying into Owens River from the Upper End of Long Valley via Owens River Gorge, Following the Course of Owens River and Los Angeles Aqueduct to Fairmount Reservoir.* Los Angeles, 1914.

Los Angeles Chamber of Commerce. *Mono Basin Project Will Greatly Add to Los Angeles Water Supplies.* Los Angeles [ca. 1930].

———. *Water and Power Problems of the Los Angeles Metropolitan Area.* Los Angeles, 1931.

Los Angeles Chamber of Commerce (J. B. Lippincott and J. S. Nickerson, signators). *Report of Sub-Committee to the Reclamation and Power Development Committee of the Los Angeles Chamber of Commerce.* Los Angeles, September 29, 1923.

Los Angeles Chamber of Commerce (Water and Power Committee). *Report on Water Demand and Supplies for Southern California Coastal Area.* Los Angeles, June 1968.

McCullough, Dale R. *The Tule Elk: Its History, Behavior, and Ecology*. University of California Publications in Zoology, vol. 68. Berkeley, 1969.

McGroarty, John Steven. *Los Angeles: From the Mountains to the Sea*. Chicago, 1921.

McWilliams, Carey. *Southern California Country: An Island on the Land*. New York, 1946.

Marcosson, Isaac F. *A Littleknown Master of Millions: The Story of Henry E. Huntington, Constructive Capitalist*. Boston, 1914.

Marquis, James, and James, Bessie R. *Biography of a Bank*. New York, 1954.

Matson, Robert William. *William Mulholland: A Forgotten Fore-father*. Pacific Center for Western Studies, Monograph no. 6. Stockton, Calif., 1976.

Mayo, Morrow. *Los Angeles*. New York, 1933.

Mono County. Reno: McIntosh, 1908.

Mowry, George E. *The California Progressives*. Berkeley, 1951.

————. *The Era of Theodore Roosevelt*. New York, 1958.

Nadeau, Remi. *Los Angeles*. New York, 1960.

————. *The Water Seekers*. Garden City, N.Y., 1950.

National Corporation Service, Inc. *Prospectus: Proposed Water Development, Lewis Ranch, Inyo County*. Los Angeles, 1933.

Newmark, Harris. *Sixty Years in Southern California, 1853-1913*. New York, 1926.

Niven, Larry, and Pournelle, Jerry. *Lucifer's Hammer*. New York, 1977.

Ostrom, Vincent. *Water and Politics: A Study of Water Policies and Administration in the Development of Los Angeles*. Los Angeles, 1953.

Outland, Charles F. *Man-Made Disaster: The Story of Saint Francis Dam*. Rev. ed. Glendale, Calif., 1977.

Owens Valley Improvement Company. *Fortunes in Apples in Owens Valley*. Bishop, Calif. [ca. 1911].

Parcher, Marie Louise, and Parcher, Will C. *Dry Ditches*. Bishop, Calif., 1934.

Parkhurst, G. Yoell. *Inyo County, California*. San Francisco, 1911.

Peffer, E. Louise. *The Closing of the Public Domain: Disposal and Reservation Policies, 1900-1950*. Palo Alto, Calif., 1951.

Perry, Louis, and Perry, Richard. *History of the Los Angeles Labor Movement, 1911-1941*. Berkeley, 1963.

Pringle, Henry F. *Theodore Roosevelt*. New York, 1931.

Purcell, Gervaise; Sanders, W. H.; Finkle, F. C.; and Loomis, Chester B. *Report of Municipally Manufactured Cements, Los Angeles Aqueduct*. Philadelphia, 1912.

Putnam, George Palmer. *Up In Our Country*. New York, 1950.

Putnam, William C. *Origins of Rock Creek and Owens River Gorges of Mono County California*. University of California Publications in Geological Sciences, vol. 34, no. 5. Berkeley, 1960.

Rand, Christopher. *Los Angeles: The Ultimate City*. New York, 1967.

Ray, C. Lorin, ed. *Inyo, 1866-1966*. Bishop, Calif., 1966.

––––––. *Mementos of Bishop, California, 1861-1961: 100 Years of Real Living*. Bishop, Calif., 1961.

Richardson, Elmo. *The Politics of Conservation: Crusades and Controversies, 1897-1913*. University of California Publications in History, vol. 70. Berkeley, 1962.

Robinson, W.W. *Land in California*. Berkeley, 1948.

––––––. *Ranchos Become Cities*. Pasadena, Calif., 1939.

––––––. *The Story of San Fernando Valley*. Los Angeles, 1961.

––––––. *What They Say About the Angels*. Pasadena, Calif., 1942.

Rodman, Willoughby. *History of the Bench and Bar of Southern California*. Los Angeles, 1909.

Rogers, Harold E., and Nichols, Alan H. *Water for California*. San Francisco, 1967.

Roske, Ralph J. *Everyman's Eden*. New York, 1968.

Ruth, H.D., and Associates. *1990 General Plan for Development: Inyo County, California*. Adopted August 5, 1968. Berkeley.

Schad, Robert O. *Henry Edwards Huntington: The Founder and the Library*. San Marino, Calif., 1931.

Smith, P. Dean. *Agriculture in Inyo and Mono Counties*. Bishop, Calif., 1968.

Smythe, William E. *The Conquest of Arid America*. New York, 1900.

Socha, Max K. *Construction of the Second Los Angeles Aqueduct*. San Diego, October 29, 1964.

Spaulding, William A. *History and Reminiscences of Los Angeles*. Los Angeles, 1931.

Spilman, W.T. *The Conspiracy: An Exposure of the Owens River Water and San Fernando Land Frauds*. Los Angeles, 1912.

Steffens, Lincoln. *The Autobiography of Lincoln Steffens*. New York, 1931.

Steward, Julian H. *Ethnography of the Owens Valley Paiute*. University of California Publications in American Archaeology and Ethnology, vol. 33. Berkeley, 1933.

––––––. *Myths of the Owens Valley Paiute*. University of California Publications in American Archaeology and Ethnology, vol. 34. Berkeley, 1936.

Stoddard, Howard, and Karrer, Henry. *A Report on the Plan of the City of Los Angeles to Construct the Second Barrel of the Los Angeles Aqueduct and Increase Diversions from the Mono and Owens Basins.* Los Banos, Calif., August 4, 1964.

Stone, Irving. *Clarence Darrow for the Defense.* Garden City, N.Y., 1943.

Streeter, Peggy, and Streeter, Clarence, eds. *Saga of Inyo County.* Covina, Calif., 1977.

Stuart, Reginald R. and Grace D. *Tully Knoles of Pacific.* Stockton, Calif., 1956.

Swanberg, W. A. *Citizen Hearst.* New York, 1961.

Thomas, Dorothy Swaine, and Nishimoto, Richard S. *The Spoilage.* Berkeley, 1946.

Thompson, Carl D. *Confessions of the Power Trust.* New York, 1932.

————. *Public Ownership: A Survey of Public Enterprises, Municipal, State, and Federal in the United States and Elsewhere.* New York, 1925.

Thompson, Warren. *Growth and Changes in California's Population.* Los Angeles, 1955.

Warner, J. J. *An Illustrated History of Los Angeles County, California.* Chicago, 1889.

Watkins, Louise Ward. *Henry Edwards Huntington: A Character Sketch of a Great Man.* Gardena, Calif., 1928.

White, Magner. *Our Great Water Problem.* Los Angeles, 1957.

Wiebe, Robert H. *Businessmen and Reform: A Study of the Progressive Movement.* Cambridge, Mass., 1962.

Wilke, Philip J., and Lawton, Harry W., eds. *The Expedition of Captain J. W. Davidson from Fort Tejon to the Owens Valley in 1859.* Socorro, N.M., 1976.

Winkler, David W., ed. *An Ecological Study of Mono Lake, California.* University of California, Institute of Ecology Publication no. 12. Davis, Calif., June, 1977.

Wolf, Victoria. *Fabulous City.* London, 1957.

Workman, Boyle. *The City That Grew.* Los Angeles, 1935.

Yeatman, W. C. *Population Growth of Los Angeles and Its Relation to Water Demand.* Los Angeles, August 10, 1932.

Index

Designer: Wolfgang Lederer
Compositors: Sue Somit and Sallie Wells
Text: Compset 500 Times Roman
Display: Compset 500 Hanover
Printer: Vail-Ballou Press
Binder: Vail-Ballou Press